GENERAL CHEMISTRY

GENERAL CHEMISTRY

Understanding Moles, Bonds, and Equilibria

VOLUME I

STUDENT SOLUTION MANUAL

Richard Langley

cognella®
SAN DIEGO

Bassim Hamadeh, CEO and Publisher
Amy Smith, Senior Project Editor
Alia Bales, Production Editor
Emely Villavicencio, Senior Graphic Designer
Stephanie Kohl, Licensing Coordinator
Kim Scott/Bumpy Design, Interior Designer
Natalie Piccotti, Director of Marketing
Kassie Graves, Vice President of Editorial
Jamie Giganti, Director of Academic Publishing

Cover image Copyright © 2017 iStockphoto LP/ktsimage
Design Image: Copyright © 2018 Depositphotos/Pro500.

Printed in the United States of America.

cognella® | ACADEMIC PUBLISHING
3970 Sorrento Valley Blvd., Ste. 500, San Diego, CA 92121

Table of Contents

CHAPTER 1

The Tools of Chemistry

S uccessful completion of these problems requires the following ten items.

1. It is important to know the SI base units, presented below and in **Table 1.1** of the textbook.

TABLE 1.1 The Seven SI Base Units

Quantity	SI Base Unit	Abbreviation
Length	Meter	m
Mass	Kilogram	kg
Time	Second	s
Temperature	Kelvin	K
Amount of a substance	Mole	mol
Electric current	Ampere	A
Luminous intensity	Candela	cd

2. Learn the more important prefixes, such as centi = 0.01. These will appear throughout this textbook and in your class. The most commonly used prefixes are listed in the following table. (Table 1.2 in the textbook shows many more of the SI prefixes.)

The Most Common SI Prefixes

Prefix	Abbreviation	Numerical Value	
mega	M	10^6	1 000 000
kilo	k	10^3	1 000
deci	d	10^{-1}	0.1
centi	c	10^{-2}	0.01
milli	m	10^{-3}	0.001
micro	μ	10^{-6}	0.000 001
nano	n	10^{-9}	0.000 000 001
pico	p	10^{-12}	0.000 000 000 001

Your instructor will tell you if you need to know any additional prefixes for this class.

3. Most of the SI-to-SI conversions in this chapter involve the prefixes in the above table. In later chapters, you may need to relate the conversions using the SI base units.

4. Your instructor will tell you which English-to-SI conversions, if any, you need to know.

5. Know how to determine the number of significant figures in a number. Also, know the rules for adjusting the significant figures during a calculation.

6. In general, SI–to–SI conversions and English-to-English conversions are exact numbers, while most English-to-SI conversions are not exact numbers and will require you to pay attention to the rules for significant figures.

7. The Unit Conversion Method requires you to pay close attention to the units. For this reason, it is very important to always write down your units. It is nearly impossible to get a wrong answer if you carefully follow the units.

8. It is possible to apply the Unit Conversion Method to many types of problems in addition to unit conversions.

9. Nearly every chemistry calculation has a two-part answer. One part is a number, which must have the correct number of significant figures. The other part is a unit, which must be appropriate to the question and must agree with the units used in the calculation.

10. When you're solving a problem in this textbook, the "Connections" section should include whatever you think you will need to solve the problem. Your section may or may not match the Connections information given in the following solutions. Initially, the key is for you to include some connections, no matter what they are. With practice, you will be able to develop a useful Connections section.

Example Problems From the Text

Example Problem 1.1
Provide the name and abbreviation for the SI unit that is equal to (a) 10^{-3} meters, (b) 10^6 seconds, (c) 10^{-6} grams, (d) 10^3 moles, (e) 10^{-9} candelas.

Information
Five values that can be converted to an equivalent SI unit:

(a) 10^{-3} meter = ? (The "?" indicates that this is the value sought.)

(b) 10^6 second = ?

(c) 10^{-6} gram = ?

(d) 10^3 mole = ?

(e) 10^{-9} candela = ?

Connections
The SI prefixes in table 1.2 (or in the inside back cover) provide the connections between the given value and the unit required as an answer.

Solution
In each case, the solution involves a simple substitution of a letter(s) for a number. According to table 1.2, 10^{-3} = milli (m), 10^6 = mega (M), 10^{-6} = micro (μ), 10^3 = kilo (k), 10^{-9} = nano (n). Adding these prefixes to the given units results in the following answers: (a) millimeter (mm), (b) megasecond (Ms), (c) microgram (μg), (d) kilomole (kmol), (e) nanocandela (ncd).

Reality Check
Each answer contains the name and abbreviation for the converted unit. A positive exponent indicates a value larger than the original, and a negative exponent indicates a value smaller than the original.

Follow-Up Problem 1.1a
Provide the SI name and abbreviation for the unit that is equal to (a) 10^{-2} grams, (b) 10^{-1} meters, (c) 10^3 amperes, (d) 10^{-12} moles, (e) 10^{-2} seconds.

Information
Five values that can be converted to an equivalent SI unit:

(a) 10^{-2} grams = ?

(b) 10^{-1} meters = ?

(c) 10^3 amperes = ?

(d) 10^{-12} moles = ?

(e) 10^{-2} seconds = ?

Connections
The SI prefixes in table 1.2 (or in the inside back cover) provide the connections between the given value and the unit required as an answer.

Solution
According to table 1.2, 10^{-2} = centi (c), 10^{-1} = deci (d), 10^{-12} = pico (p), and 10^3 = kilo (k). Adding these prefixes to the given units results in the following answers: (a) centigram (cm), (b) decimeter (dm), (c) kiloampere (kA), (d) picomole (pmol), (e) centisecond (cs).

Reality Check
Each answer contains the name and abbreviation for the converted unit. A positive exponent indicates a value larger than the original, and a negative exponent indicates a value smaller than the original.

Follow-Up Problem 1.1b
Replace the SI prefix with the corresponding power-of-ten (exponential) value for each of the following units: (a) kilogram, (b) millimeter, (c) picosecond, (d) μmole, (e) nanoKelvin

Information

Five values that can be converted to a corresponding power-of-ten (exponential) value:

(a) kilogram = ?

(b) millimeter = ?

(c) picosecond = ?

(d) μmole = ?

(e) nanoKelvin = ?

Connections

The SI prefixes in table 1.2 (or on the inside back cover of this textbook) provide the connections between the given value and the unit required as an answer.

Solution

According to table 1.2, 10^3 = kilo (k), 10^{-3} = milli (m), 10^{-12} = pico (p), 10^{-6} = micro (μ), 10^{-9} = nano (n). Replacing the prefixes with their numerical values results in the following answers: **(a)** 10^3 grams, **(b)** 10^{-3} meters, **(c)** 10^{-12} seconds, **(d)** 10^{-6} moles, **(e)** 10^{-9} Kelvin

Reality Check

Each answer contains the name and abbreviation for the converted unit. A positive exponent indicates a value larger than the original, and a negative exponent indicates a value smaller than the original.

Example Problem 1.2

Determine the number of significant figures in each of the following numbers: **(a)** 473.2, **(b)** 378.052, **(c)** 0.032, **(d)** 1.6750×10^4, **(e)** 100

Information

Collect the information from the problem:

(a) 473.2 = ? sig figs

(b) 378.052 = ? sig figs

(c) 0.032 = ? sig figs

(d) 1.6750×10^4 = ? sig figs

(e) 100 = ? sig figs

Connections

The significant figure rules connect the given information to the number of significant figures.

Solution

For each of the given values, go through the rules for determining significant figures: All the nonzero values are significant, as are all embedded zeros (zeroes between nonzero digits); no zeros to the left of the first nonzero digit are significant; zeros on the right are significant only if there is a decimal point. For example, the number 473.2 contains no zeros, so according to rule 1, all of its digits are significant. **(a)** All four numbers are significant; **(b)** all six numbers are significant; **(c)** only the last two numbers are significant; **(d)** the first five numbers are significant; **(e)** the 1 is significant, but the zeros are assumed not to be significant.

Reality Check

All answers appear reasonable. No answer has more significant figures than the number of digits originally present.

Follow-Up Problem 1.2a

Determine the number of significant figures in each of the following numbers: (a) 27.45, (b) 22.0875, (c) 0.0014875, (d) 1.000×10^3, (e) 220

Information

Collect the information from the problem:

(a) 27.45 = ? sig figs

(b) 22.0875 = ? sig figs

(c) 0.0014875 = ? sig figs

(d) 1.000×10^3 = ? sig figs

(e) 220 = ? sig figs

Connections

The significant figure rules connect the given information to the number of significant figures.

Solution

For each of the given values, go through the rules for determining significant figures: All the nonzero values are significant, as are all embedded zeros (zeroes between nonzero digits); no zeros to the left of the first nonzero digit are significant; zeros on the right are only significant if there is a decimal point. For example, 27.45 contains no zeros, so according to rule 1, all its digits are significant.

(a) All four numbers are significant; (b) all six numbers are significant; (c) only the last five numbers are significant; (d) the all four numbers are significant (not the power of ten); (e) all but the zero are significant, so there are two significant figures.

Reality Check

All answers appear reasonable. No answer has more significant figures than the number of digits originally present.

Follow-Up Problem 1.2b

Arrange the following reported values in order of decreasing number of significant figures:

(a) 317 m, (b) 0.000087 ft, (c) 32000.0 mi, (d) 1000 yd, (e) 2.455×10^{-6} in

Information

Collect the information from the problem:

(a) 317 m, (b) 0.000087 ft, (c) 32,000.0 mi, (d) 1,000 yd, (e) 2.455×10^{-6} in

Connections

The significant figure rules connect the given information to the number of significant figures.

Solution

For each of the given values, go through the rules for determining significant figures: All the nonzero values are significant, as are all embedded zeros (zeroes between non-zero digits); no zeros to the left of the first nonzero digit are significant; zeros on the right are significant only if there is a decimal point. The units do not alter the number of significant figures present. For example, 317 contains no zeros, so according to rule 1, all of its digits are significant.

(a) All three numbers are significant; **(b)** none of the zeroes is significant, so there are only two significant figures; **(c)** since there is a decimal point present, all the zeroes are significant giving a total of six significant figures; **(d)** there is no decimal point, so only the 1 is significant; **(e)** there are four significant figures. The number of significant figures in each part is **(a)** 3, **(b)** 2, **(c)** 6, **(d)** 1, **(e)** 4; placing these in decreasing order gives **(c)**, **(e)**, **(a)**, **(b)**, **(d)**.

Reality Check
All answers appear reasonable. No answer has more significant figures than the number of digits originally present.

Example Problem 1.3
Perform each of the following mathematical operations assuming the numbers are measured values, and report the answer to the proper number of significant figures: **(a)** 8.475 cm + 3.72 cm + 2.487 cm, **(b)** 3.25 in – 0.25 in, **(c)** 4.99 ft × 3.22 ft × 1 ft, **(d)** 18.25 mi / 3.5 h, **(e)** (18.1 m × 2.544 m) / 3.1 m

Information
Collect the information from the problem:

(a) 8.475 cm + 3.72 cm + 2.487 cm = ?

(b) 3.25 in – 0.25 in = ?

(c) 4.99 ft × 3.22 ft × 1 ft = ?

(d) 18.25 mi / 3.5 h = ?

(e) (18.1 m × 2.544 m) / 3.1 m = ?

Determine all answers to the proper number of significant figures.

Connections
To solve this problem, you must apply the rules for determining the number of significant figures in the results of each kind of arithmetical operation.

Solution
First, perform each of the mathematical operations without regard to significant figures or units:

(a) 8.475 cm + 3.72 cm + 2.487 cm = 14.682 cm

(b) 3.25 in – 0.25 in = 3 in

(c) 4.99 ft × 3.22 ft × 1 ft = 16.0678 ft^3

(d) 18.25 mi / 3.5 h = 5.214285714 mi/h

(e) (18.1 m × 2.544 m) / 3.1 m = 14.85367742 m

Now apply the rules concerning the number of significant figures allowed in the answers, rounding when necessary:

(a) This is an example of addition. The least number of digits past the decimal point in the given measured values is two; thus, the answer should have only two digits to the right of the decimal point: **14.68 cm.**

(b) The operation performed here is subtraction. The least number of digits past the decimal point is two; thus, the answer should have two digits past the decimal point: **3.00 in.**

(c) This is a multiplication problem. The answer should have the same number of significant figures as the least number of significant figures (one) in the calculation. This means that only the first digit is significant, so the answer is **20 ft^3**.

(d) This is a division example. The answer should have the same number of significant figures as the number with the least number of significant figures used in the calculation (two). Therefore, the answer is **5.2 mi/h**.

(e) This example requires both multiplication and division. The answer should have the same number of significant figures as the least number (two) in the calculation, and is therefore **15 m**.

Reality Check

None of the answers has significantly more or fewer digits than the least precise number in the calculation.

Follow-Up Problem 1.3a

Perform each of the following mathematical operations, assuming the values to be measurements, and report the answer to the correct number of significant figures: **(a)** 3.225 mi + 13.72 mi + 71 mi, **(b)** 183.25 ft − 0.25 ft − 180.0 ft, **(c)** 3.227 cm × 5.822 cm × 1.0 cm, **(d)** 177.5 m / 35.5 s, **(e)** (22.14 lb + 0.53462 lb) / 17.1 lb

Information

Collect the information from the problem:

(a) 3.225 mi + 13.72 mi + 71 mi = ?

(b) 183.25 ft − 0.25 ft − 180.0 ft = ?

(c) 3.227 cm × 5.822 cm × 1.0 cm = ?

(d) 177.5 m / 35.5 s = ?

(e) (22.14 lb + 0.53462 lb) / 17.1 lb = ?

Connections

To solve this problem, you must apply the rules for determining the number of significant figures in the results of each kind of arithmetical operation.

Solution

First, perform each of the mathematical operations without regard to significant figures or units:

(a) 3.225 mi + 13.72 mi + 71 mi = 87.945 mi

(b) 183.25 ft − 0.25 ft − 180.0 ft = 3 ft

(c) 3.227 cm × 5.822 cm × 1.0 cm = 18.78759 cm^3

(d) 177.5 m / 35.5 s = 5 m/s

(e) (22.14 lb + 0.53462 lb) / 17.1 lb = 1.326

(a) This is an example of addition. The least number of digits past the decimal point in the given measured values is none; thus, the answer should have no digits to the right of the decimal point (this will require rounding): **88 mi.**

(b) The operation to be performed here is subtraction. The least number of digits past the decimal point is one; thus, the answer should have one digit past the decimal point: **3.0 ft.**

(c) This is a multiplication problem. The answer should have the same number of significant figures as the least number of significant figures (two) in the calculation. So, after rounding, the answer is **19 cm³**.

(d) This is a division example. The answer should have the same number of significant figures as the number with the least number of significant figures used in the calculation (three). Therefore, the answer is **5.00 m/s.**

(e) This example requires both addition and division. The addition calculation in parentheses will give an answer with two decimal places, which means that the answer should have four significant figures. The division involves a four-significant figure number divided by a three-significant figure number. The answer will have the same number of significant figures as the least number (two) in the calculation; after rounding, the answer is **1.33 m.**

Reality Check

None of the answers has significantly more or fewer digits than the least precise number in the calculation.

Follow-Up Problem 1.3b

Calculate the answer to each of the following operations, assuming the values to be measurements: **(a)** $144.875 + 3.22 - 8.5$, **(b)** $(3.20 \times 16.10) + 8.48$, **(c)** $1.45 \times 10^{-3} + 0.00145$, **(d)** $(8.45 \times 10^3 + 1678) / 14.22$, **(e)** $7.45 - 9.90 \times 10^{-9}$

Information

Collect the information from the problem:

(a) $144.875 + 3.22 - 8.5 = \underline{?}$

(b) $(3.20 \times 16.10) + 8.48 = \underline{?}$

(c) $1.45 \times 10^{-3} + 0.00145 = \underline{?}$

(d) $(8.45 \times 10^3 + 1678) / 14.22 = \underline{?}$

(e) $7.45 - 9.90 \times 10^{-9} = \underline{?}$

Connections

To solve this problem, you must apply the rules for determining the number of significant figures in the results of each kind of arithmetical operation.

Solution

First, perform each of the mathematical operations without regard to significant figures or units:

(a) $144.875 + 3.22 - 8.5 = 139.595$

(b) $(3.20 \times 16.10) + 8.48 = 60.$

(c) $1.45 \times 10^{-3} + 0.00145 = 0.0029$

(d) $(8.45 \times 10^3 + 1678) / 14.22 = 712.2362869$

(e) $7.45 - 9.90 \times 10^{-9} = 7.4499999901$

(a) This is an example of addition combined with subtraction. The least number of digits past the decimal point in the given measured values is one; thus, the answer should have only one digit to the right of the decimal point: **139.6** (after rounding).

(b) This example combines multiplication and addition. You should deal with the calculation given in the parentheses first. The multiplication operation inside the parentheses involves a three-significant figure number times a four-significant figure number and will give a three-significant figure answer (51.52), which means the answer will have one digit after the decimal place. Adding a one-decimal place value to a two-decimal place number will give a one-decimal place answer: **60.0** (adding an extra 0).

(c) This is an addition problem. The answer should have the same number of digits as the least number after the decimal point. To facilitate recognizing the correct number of decimal places, it helps to convert the number in scientific notation to a decimal number (1.45×10^{-3} = 0.00145). Both numbers in the problem have five digits after the decimal point; therefore, the answer should also have five digits after the decimal point, or **0.00290** (add an additional 0).

(d) This is an addition example combined with a division example. You should deal with the calculation given in the parentheses first. The addition gives 10128; however, the last digit is not significant because of the limitation imposed by 8.45×10^3. The division involves a four-significant figure number divided by a four-significant figure number to give a four-significant figure answer. This means that the answer is **712.2**.

(e) The operation performed here is subtraction. The least number of digits past the decimal point is two; thus, the answer should have two digits past the decimal point: **7.45** (after rounding).

Reality Check

None of the answers has significantly more or fewer digits than the least precise number in the calculation.

Example Problem 1.4

Use unity factors to make the following conversions: **(a)** 14 inches to centimeters, **(b)** 14 centimeters to inches

Information

Collect the information from the problem:

(a) 14 in = ? cm

(b) 14 cm = ? in

The units to be interconverted are inches and centimeters.

Connections

Table 1.3 contains the relationship between inches and centimeters (1 inch = 2.54 centimeters).

Solution

The two parts of this problem are shown in parallel below to illustrate similarities in the steps used to solve them.

Start the problem by listing the given value (number and unit) and the desired value (showing the desired unit):

(a) 14 in = ? cm

(b) 14 cm = ? in

In part **(a)**, we want an answer that contains the unit "cm" rather than the unit "in." In this case, we set up our unity factor so that "in" will cancel out: we rearrange the relationship 1 in = 2.54 cm so that the inches are on the bottom of the fraction (i.e., in the denominator).

In part, **(b)** we want an answer containing the unit "in" and we need to eliminate the unit "cm." We can do this by rearranging the relationship 1 in = 2.54 cm to place centimeters on the bottom, which will then cancel the centimeters in the given value.

Multiplying the given value by the correct unity factor gives

(a)   **(b)**

$$14 \text{ in} \left(\frac{2.54 \text{ cm}}{1 \text{ in}} \right) = \text{? cm} \qquad\qquad 14 \text{ cm} \left(\frac{1 \text{ in}}{2.54 \text{ cm}} \right) = \text{? in}$$

Canceling the units and performing the mathematical operations gives

(a)	**(b)**	
35.56 cm	5.5118 in	not the final answers

You will see these values on your calculator's display, but they are not the final answers, because we have yet to consider the number of significant figures. The inch-to-centimeter relationship is an exact number and, as such, has no effect on the significant figures in the answer. However, 14 in and 14 cm are measurements. In both cases, these values have only two significant figures. Therefore, the final answers should be **(a) 36 cm** and **(b) 5.5 in.**

Reality Check

Both answers have the desired unit, and they have the same number of significant figures as the original data that was to be converted. In addition, for part **(a)** we know that 14 inches would contain between two and three times that number of centimeters (since 2.54 cm = 1 in), so the answer should be somewhere between 2 × 14 = 28 cm and 3 × 14 = 42 cm. The answer we obtained, 36 cm, falls within that range. Using similar logic, we know that in part **(b)**, the number of inches would be between one-half and one-third of 14, somewhere between 7 and 4.6. The calculated answer, 5.5, falls within that range and is therefore reasonable.

Follow-Up Problem 1.4a

Use unity factors to make the following conversions: **(a)** 271.0 in to centimeters, **(b)** 0.13 cm to inches.

Information

Collect the information from the problem:

(a)   271.0 inches = ? centimeters

(b)   0.13 centimeters = ? inches

Connections

Table 1.3 contains the relationship between inches and centimeters (1 in = 2.54 cm).

Solution

The two parts of this problem are shown in parallel below to illustrate similarities in the steps used to solve them.

Start the problem by listing the given value (number and unit) and the desired value (showing the desired unit):

(a)	**(b)**
271.0 in = ? cm	0.13 cm = ? in

In part **(a)**, we want an answer that contains the unit "cm" rather than the unit "in." In this case, we set up our unity factor so that "in" will cancel out: we rearrange the relationship 1 in = 2.54 cm so that the inches are on the bottom (denominator) of the fraction.

In part **(b)**, we want an answer containing the unit "in" and we need to eliminate the unit "cm." We achieve this by rearranging the relationship 1 in = 2.54 cm to place centimeters on the bottom (denominator), which will then cancel the centimeters in the given value.

Multiplying the given value by the correct unity factor gives

(a)   **(b)**

$$271.0 \text{ in} \left(\frac{2.54 \text{ cm}}{1 \text{ in}} \right) = ? \text{ cm} \qquad\qquad 0.13 \text{ cm} \left(\frac{1 \text{ in}}{2.54 \text{ cm}} \right) = ? \text{ in}$$

Canceling the units and performing the mathematical operations gives

(a)	**(b)**	
688.34 cm	0.0511811 in	not the final answers

You will see these values on your calculator's display, but they are not the final answers, because we have yet to consider the number of significant figures. The inch-to-centimeter relationship is an exact number, and as such, has no effect on the significant figures in the answer. However, 271.0 in and 0.13 cm are measurements. The first value has four significant figures and the second has two significant figures. Therefore, the final answers should be **(a) 688.3 cm** and **(b) 0.051 in**.

Reality Check

Both answers have the desired unit, and they have the same number of significant figures as the original data that was to be converted.

Follow-Up Problem 1.4b

(a) How many inches are in 33,285 cm? **(b)** How many centimeters are in 14,440 in?

Information

Collect the information from the problem:

(a) 33,285 cm = ? in

(b) 14,440 in = ? cm

Connections

Table 1.3 contains the relationship between inches and centimeters (1 in = 2.54 cm).

Solution

The two parts of this problem are shown in parallel below to illustrate similarities in the steps used to solve them.

Start the problem by listing the given value (number and unit) and the desired value (showing the desired unit):

(a)   **(b)**

33,285 cm = ? in   14,440 in = ? cm

In part **(a)**, we want an answer that contains the unit "in" rather than the unit "cm." In this case, we set up our unity factor so that "cm" will cancel out: we rearrange the relationship 1 in = 2.54 cm so that the centimeters are on the bottom (denominator) of the fraction.

In part **(b)**, we want an answer containing the unit "cm" and we need to eliminate the unit "in." We achieve this by rearranging the relationship 1 in = 2.54 cm to place the inches on the bottom, which will then cancel the inches in the given value.

Multiplying the given value by the correct unity factor gives

(a) $\qquad\qquad\qquad\qquad\qquad$ **(b)**

$$33285 \text{ cm} \left(\frac{1 \text{ in}}{2.54 \text{ cm}} \right) = \text{? in} \qquad\qquad 14440 \text{ in} \left(\frac{2.54 \text{ cm}}{1 \text{ in}} \right) = \text{? cm}$$

Canceling the units and performing the mathematical operations gives

(a)	**(b)**	
13104.33 in	36677.6 cm	not the final answers

You will see these values on your calculator's display, but they are not the final answers because we have yet to consider the number of significant figures. The inch-to-centimeter relationship is an exact number, and as such it has no effect on the significant figures in the answer. However, 33,285 cm and 14,440 in are measurements. The first value has five significant figures and the second has four significant figures (the trailing 0 is not significant). Therefore, the final answers should be **(a) 13,104 in** and **(b) 36,680 cm**.

Reality Check

Both answers have the desired unit, and they have the same number of significant figures as the original data that was to be converted.

Example Problem 1.5

Using 2.54 cm = 1 in to construct your only SI-to-English conversion factor, convert 3.25 mi to meters.

Information

We must use 2.54 cm = 1 in to solve 3.25 mi = ? m.

Connections

Various English–English length conversions, (displayed on the inside back cover of this textbook) are needed to solve this problem. The definition of one of the metric prefixes in table 1.2 (specifically, c = 0.01) is also necessary, since we have been given information in centimeters and are asked for an answer in meters.

Solution

The problem states that the only SI-to-English conversion factor we may use in our solution is 2.54 cm = 1 in, which eliminates the use of conversions such as 1,609 m = 1 mi. We can begin constructing a path from miles to inches by using a relationship between miles and any other English length unit. For example, 5,280 ft = 1 mi:

$$(3.25 \text{ mi}) \left(\frac{5,280 \text{ ft}}{1 \text{ mi}} \right) = 17,160 \text{ ft}$$

We can then use a conversion factor relating feet to some other unit. In this case, we will use 1 ft = 12 in:

$$(17,160 \text{ ft}) \left(\frac{12 \text{ in}}{1 \text{ ft}} \right) = 205,920 \text{ in}$$

At this point, we can use the SI-to-English conversion given in the problem:

$$(205,920 \text{ in}) \left(\frac{2.54 \text{ cm}}{1 \text{ in}} \right) = 523,036.8 \text{ cm}$$

Finally, we can use the definition given in table 1.2 for the metric prefix *centi* (centi = c = 0.01) to construct a conversion factor for changing the magnitude of the metric unit of length:

$$(523{,}036.8 \text{ cm})\left(\frac{0.01}{c}\right) = 5{,}230.368 \text{ m} \qquad \text{not the final answer}$$

Applying the rules for significant figures to this answer gives a final answer of 5.23×10^3 m.

We can significantly simplify this long problem by combining the steps. To do this, we place all the unity factors in a row without pausing to calculate any intermediate answers. Before even working the problem, you can check to see that the units cancel as desired.

$$(3.25 \text{ mi})\left(\frac{5{,}280 \text{ ft}}{1 \text{ mi}}\right)\left(\frac{12 \text{ in}}{1 \text{ ft}}\right)\left(\frac{2.54 \text{ cm}}{1 \text{ in}}\right)\left(\frac{0.01}{c}\right) = 5{,}230.368 \text{ m}$$
$$= \mathbf{5.23 \times 10^3 \text{ m}}$$

Notice that the conversions in the parentheses are the same in both the long and the condensed versions of this problem.

Reality Check

The unit in the answer (m) is the requested unit. From table 1.3, we see that 1 mi = 1.6 km, or 1 mi = 1.6×10^3 m. This indicates that a measurement in miles converts to measurements in a magnitude of 10^3 m, which is consistent with our calculated answer.

Follow-Up Problem 1.5a

Using 2.54 cm = 1 in as your only SI-to-English conversion, convert 17.25 mi to meters.

Information

We must use 2.54 cm = 1 in to solve 17.25 mi = ? m.

Connections

Various English–English length conversions, displayed on the inside back cover of this textbook, are needed to solve this problem. The definition of one of the metric prefixes in table 1.2 (specifically, c = 0.01) is also needed, since we have been given information in centimeters and are asked for an answer in meters.

Solution

The problem states that the only SI-to-English conversion factor we may use in our solution is 2.54 cm = 1 in, which eliminates the use of conversions such as 1609 m = 1 mi. We can begin constructing a path from miles to inches by using a relationship between miles and any other English length unit. For example, 5,280 ft = 1 mi:

$$(17.25 \text{ mi})\left(\frac{5{,}280 \text{ ft}}{1 \text{ mi}}\right) = 91{,}080 \text{ ft}$$

We can then use a conversion factor relating feet to some other unit. In this case, we will use 1 ft = 12 in:

$$(91{,}080 \text{ ft})\left(\frac{12 \text{ in}}{1 \text{ ft}}\right) = 1{,}092{,}960 \text{ in}$$

At this point, we can use the SI-to-English conversion we were given in the problem:

$$(1{,}092{,}960 \text{ in})\left(\frac{2.54 \text{ cm}}{1 \text{ in}}\right) = 2{,}776{,}118.4 \text{ cm}$$

Finally, we can use the definition given in table 1.2 for the metric prefix *centi* (centi = c = 0.01) to construct a conversion factor for changing the magnitude of the metric unit of length:

$$(2{,}776{,}118.4 \text{ cm})\left(\frac{0.01}{c}\right) = 27{,}761.184 \text{ m} \qquad \text{not the final answer}$$

Applying the rules for significant figures to this answer gives a final answer of 2.776×10^4 m.

We can significantly simplify this long problem by combining the steps. To do this, we place all the unity factors in a row without pausing to calculate any intermediate answers. Before even working the problem, you can check to see that the units cancel as desired.

$$(17.25 \text{ mi})\left(\frac{5280 \text{ ft}}{1 \text{ mi}}\right)\left(\frac{12 \text{ in}}{1 \text{ ft}}\right)\left(\frac{2.54 \text{ cm}}{1 \text{ in}}\right)\left(\frac{0.01}{c}\right) = 27{,}761.184 \text{ m} = \mathbf{2.776 \times 10^4 \text{ m}}$$

Notice that the conversions in the parentheses are the same in both the long and the condensed version of this problem.

Reality Check

The unit in the answer (m) is the requested unit. From table 1.3, we see that 1 mi = 1.6 km, or 1 mi = 1.6×10^3 m. This plus an additional power of ten from the distance (17.25) indicates that a measurement in miles converts to measurements in a magnitude of 10^4 m, which is consistent with our calculated answer.

Follow-Up Problem 1.5b

Using 1 kg = 2.205 lb as your only SI-to-English conversion, convert 4.37 tons to grams.

Information

We must use 1 kg = 2.205 lb in to solve 4.37 tons = ? g.

Connections

Various English–English length conversions, displayed on the inside back cover of this textbook, are necessary to solve this problem. The definition of one of the metric prefixes in table 1.2 (specifically, k = 1,000) is also necessary, since we have been given information in kilograms and are asked for an answer in grams.

Solution

The problem states that the only SI-to-English conversion factor we may use in our solution is 1 kg = 2.205 lb, which eliminates the use of other SI-to-English conversions. We can begin constructing a path from miles to inches by using a relationship between miles and any other English length unit. For example, 2,000 lb = 1 ton:

$$(4.37 \text{ tons})\left(\frac{2{,}000 \text{ lbs}}{1 \text{ ton}}\right) = 8{,}740 \text{ lb}$$

At this point, the SI-to-English conversion we are given in the problem may be used:

$$(8{,}740 \text{ lb})\left(\frac{1 \text{ kg}}{2.205 \text{ lbs}}\right) = 3{,}963.7188 \text{ kg}$$

Finally, we can use the definition given in table 1.2 for the metric prefix *kilo* (kilo = k = 1,000) to construct a conversion factor for changing the magnitude of the metric unit of mass:

$$(3{,}963.7188 \text{ kg})\left(\frac{1{,}000}{k}\right) = 3{,}963{,}718.821 \text{ g} \qquad \text{not the final answer}$$

Applying the rules for significant figures to this answer gives a final answer of 3.96×10^6 g.

We can significantly simplify this long problem by combining the steps. To do this, we place all the unity factors in a row without pausing to calculate any intermediate answers. Before even working the problem, you can check to see that the units cancel as desired.

$$(4.37 \text{ tons})\left(\frac{2{,}000 \text{ lbs}}{1 \text{ ton}}\right)\left(\frac{1 \text{ kg}}{2.205 \text{ lbs}}\right)\left(\frac{1{,}000}{k}\right) = 3{,}963{,}718.821 \text{ g} = \mathbf{3.96 \times 10^6 \text{ g}}$$

Notice that the conversions in the parentheses are the same in both the long and the condensed versions of this problem.

Reality Check

The unit in the answer (g) is the requested unit, and the significant figures are correct.

Example Problem 1.6

Copper is used as an electrical conductor. A particular copper cable weighs 1.5 lb/m. How many kilograms of copper are present in 125 km of copper cable?

Information

Cable mass = (1.5 lb/m)
125 km cable = ? kg

Connections

Table 1.3 contains equivalences that may enable us to construct a useful unity factor for the conversion.

Solution

This is a unit conversion problem, so we can begin with any piece of the given information. Table 1.3 tells us that 1 lb = 453.59 g. If we begin setting up our calculation with 1.0 lb/m, then the unity factor 453.59 g/lb will cancel the pound unit:

$$\left(\frac{1.5 \text{ lb}}{m}\right)\left(\frac{453.59 \text{ g}}{1 \text{ lb}}\right) = 680.385 \text{ g/m}$$

(It is not necessary to calculate this intermediate answer.) Now we need a unity factor that will cancel the unit meter (m). Inserting the other value from the problem (125 km) accomplishes this:

$$\left(\frac{1.5 \text{ lb}}{m}\right)\left(\frac{453.59 \text{ g}}{1 \text{ lb}}\right)(125 \text{ km}) = 85048.1 = 8.5 \times 10^4 \text{ kg}$$

Notice that the cancellation of meters leaves the k from km, which combines with the uncancelled g to give kg.

Alternatively, we could have used the definition k = 1,000 both to construct a unity factor for converting grams to kilograms and to construct another unity factor (this time the reciprocal, $10^3/k$) to convert kilometers to meters:

$$\text{Cable mass} = \left(\frac{1.5 \text{ lb}}{m}\right)\left(\frac{453.59 \text{ g}}{1 \text{ lb}}\right)\left(\frac{k}{10^3}\right)(125 \text{ km})\left(\frac{10^3}{k}\right) = 85{,}048.1 = \mathbf{8.5 \times 10^4 \text{ kg}}$$

Reality Check

The units are correct, and so is the number of significant figures. Copper is a relatively dense metal, so a cable 125 km in length should be massive.

Follow-Up Problem 1.6a

A certain copper cable weighs 32 oz/m. How many kilometers of cable can be made from 5.21×10^5 kg of copper?

Information

The first step is to collect and label the information given in the problem:

Weight of copper per meter = 32 oz/m
5.21×10^5 kg copper = ? km cable

Connections

Table 1.3 contains equivalences that may enable us to construct a useful unity factor for the conversion.

Solution

This is a unit conversion problem, so we can begin with any piece of the given information. Table 1.3 tells us that 28.35 g = 1 oz. Since we are seeking a length (km), we should invert the weight conversion to m/32 oz. We can now use the unity factor 1 oz/28.35 g to cancel the pound unit:

$$\left(\frac{1\ m}{32\ oz}\right)\left(\frac{1\ oz}{28.35\ g}\right) = 0.00110229\ m/g$$

(It is not necessary to calculate this intermediate answer.) Inserting the other value from the problem (125 km) accomplishes this:

$$\left(\frac{0.00110229\ m}{g}\right)(5.21 \times 10^5\ kg) = 574.2945 = 5.7 \times 10^2\ km$$

Alternatively, we could have used the definition k = 1,000 both to construct a unity factor for converting grams to kilograms and to construct another unity factor (this time the reciprocal, $10^3/k$) to convert kilometers to meters.

$$\text{Cable mass} = \left(\frac{1\ m}{32\ oz}\right)\left(\frac{1\ oz}{28.35\ g}\right)\left(\frac{k}{10^3}\right)(5.21 \times 10^5\ kg)\left(\frac{10^3}{k}\right) = 574.2945 = \mathbf{5.7 \times 10^2\ km}$$

Reality Check

The units are correct, and so is the number of significant figures.

Follow-Up Problem 1.6b

How many kilograms of copper are needed to produce 175 mi of copper cable weighing 1.5 lb/m? (1.6093 km = 1 mi)

Information

The first step is to collect and label the information given in the problem:

Weight of copper per meter = 1.5 lb/m
175 mi cable = ? kg copper
1.6093 km = 1 mi

Connections

Table 1.3 contains equivalences that may enable us to construct a useful unity factor for the conversion.

Solution

This is a unit conversion problem, so we can begin with any piece of the given information. Table 1.3 tells us that 1 kg = 2.2046 lb. We can now use the unity factor 2.2046 lb/kg to cancel the pound unit:

$$\left(\frac{1.5\ lb}{1\ m}\right)\left(\frac{1\ kg}{2.2046\ lbs}\right) = 0.6803955\ kg/m$$

(It is not necessary to calculate this intermediate answer.) The next step uses the conversion given in the problem (1.6093 km = 1 mi) and the conversion kilo = k = 1,000:

$$\left(\frac{0.6803955\ kg}{m}\right)\left(\frac{1.6093\ km}{1\ mi}\right)\left(\frac{10^3}{k}\right) = 1,094.96\ kg/mi$$

Finally, using the 175 mi from the problem, we can determine the mass of copper needed:

$$(175\ mi)\left(\frac{1094.96\ kg}{mi}\right) = 191618 = 1.9 \times 10^5\ kg$$

Alternatively, we could set this up as one calculation:

$$Cable\ mass = \left(\frac{1.5\ lb}{1\ m}\right)\left(\frac{1\ kg}{2.2046\ lbs}\right)\left(\frac{1.6093\ km}{1\ mi}\right)\left(\frac{10^3}{k}\right)(175\ mi) = 191{,}618 = \mathbf{1.9 \times 10^5\ kg}$$

Reality Check

The units are correct, and so is the number of significant figures.

Example Problem 1.7

A sample of copper metal weighs 2.75 ounces. The volume of the sample is 3.086×10^{-4} ft^3. **(a)** Determine the density of the copper metal in ounces per cubic foot. **(b)** Express the density of the copper metal in grams per cubic centimeter.

Information

Collect the information from the problem:

(a) Mass = 2.75 oz

(b) Density from part (a) = ? g/cm^3

Volume = 3.086×10^{-4} ft^3

Density = ?

Connections

(a) Only the definition of *density* is needed. **(b)** We will be converting ounces to grams and cubic feet to cubic centimeters, requiring information from table 1.2 (1,000 = k) and table 1.3 (1 kg = 2.2046 lb and 2.54 cm = 1 in), along with two English-to-English conversions (1 lb = 16 oz and 1 ft = 12 in).

Solution

(a) Since we have the mass and the volume of the copper sample in the units required for the first part of the problem, we simply insert these values into the definition of density (mass/volume):

$$Density = Mass/Volume$$

$$Density \ of \ copper = \frac{(2.75 \ oz)}{(3.086 \times 10^{-4} \ ft^3)}$$

$$= 8.9112 \times 10^3 \ (calculator \ display)$$

$$= 8.91 \times 10^3 \ oz/ft^3 \ (correct \ significant \ figures)$$

(b) In this part, we are asked to express the same density in different units. The easiest approach is to begin with the answer to part (a) and apply appropriate unity factors to convert ounces to grams and cubic feet to cubic centimeters. We can do these conversions in any order. Here, we will do the ounce-to-gram conversion first:

$$Density = \left(\frac{8.9112 \times 10^3 \ oz}{ft^3}\right)\left(\frac{1 \ lb}{16 \ oz}\right)\left(\frac{1 \ kg}{2.2046 \ lbs}\right)\left(\frac{1000}{k}\right) = 2.5263 \times 10^5 \ g/ft^3$$

The first factor converts the given number of ounces to pounds. The next, using information from table 1.3, converts pounds to kilograms. The final unity factor uses the definition of *kilo* from table 1.2 to eliminate the prefix. Note that the value used for the initial density in this calculation is the *unrounded* value from part (a). We have used this unrounded value because we do not want to introduce an error by using a rounded value from an intermediate calculation.

Next, we need to convert the cubic feet to cubic centimeters. To illustrate an important mathematical consideration in this part of the conversion, let's isolate it temporarily from the rest of the problem. The conversions of cubic feet to cubic centimeter are

$$\left(\frac{1}{ft^3}\right)\left(\frac{1 \ ft}{12 \ in}\right)^3\left(\frac{1 \ in}{2.54 \ cm}\right)^3 = \left(\frac{1}{ft^3}\right)\left(\frac{1 \ ft^3}{1728 \ in^3}\right)\left(\frac{1 \ in^3}{16.38706 \ cm^3}\right) = 3.53147 \times 10^{-5} \ cm^3$$

The first step converts cubic feet to cubic inches. Note that we must cube the number 12. In the second step, we use the inch-to-centimeter relationship found in table 1.3. Again, we must remember to cube the number 2.54.

Inserting both conversion steps into the density relationship gives

$$Density = \left(\frac{8.9112 \times 10^3 \ oz}{ft^3}\right)\left(\frac{1 \ lb}{16 \ oz}\right)\left(\frac{1 \ kg}{2.2046 \ lbs}\right)\left(\frac{1,000}{k}\right)\left(\frac{1 \ ft}{12 \ in}\right)^3\left(\frac{1 \ in}{2.54 \ cm}\right)^3$$

$$= 8.92157 = \mathbf{8.92 \ g/cm^3}$$

(Remember to cube the numbers along with the units in the last two conversion factors.)

Combining all the conversions into one setup reduces the total amount of work and circumvents the errors that might occur from intermediate rounding.

Reality Check

Both answers have the correct units. In part **(a)**, we divided the mass by a very small number (10^{-4}), and we should expect a large number as the result (in the range of 10^3). In part **(b)**, we divided the large answer from part (a) by a series of terms in the denominators of the unity factors. The repeated divisions should be expected to reduce the numerical value.

Follow-Up Problem 1.7a

A sample of iron metal weighs 1.92 oz. The volume of the sample is 2.414×10^{-4} ft^3. **(a)** Determine the density of the iron metal. **(b)** Express the density of the iron metal in grams per cubic centimeter.

Information

The first step is to collect and label the information given in the problem:

Mass of iron = 1.92 oz

Volume of iron = 2.414×10^{-4} ft^3

(a) Density of iron = ?

(b) Density of iron = ? g/cm^3

Connections

(a) Only the definition of *density* is needed. **(b)** We will be converting ounces to grams and cubic feet to cubic centimeters, requiring information from table 1.2 (1,000 = k) and table 1.3 (1 kg = 2.2046 lb and 2.54 cm = 1 in), along with two English-to-English conversions (1 lb = 16 oz and 1 ft = 12 in).

Solution

(a) Since we have the mass and volume of the iron sample in the units required for the first part of the problem, we simply insert these values into the definition of *density* (mass/volume):

$$\text{Density} = \frac{\text{Mass}}{\text{Volume}}$$

$$\text{Density of iron} = \frac{(1.92 \text{ oz})}{(2.414 \times 10^{-4} \text{ ft}^3)}$$
$$= 7.9536 \times 10^3 \text{ (calculator display)}$$
$$= 7.95 \times 10^3 \text{ oz/ft}^3 \text{ (correct significant figures)}$$

(b) In this part, we are asked to express the same density in different units. The easiest approach is to begin with the answer to part (a) and apply appropriate unity factors to convert ounces to grams and cubic feet to cubic centimeters. We can do these conversions in any order. Here, we will do the ounce-to-gram conversion first:

$$\text{Density} = \left(\frac{7.9536 \times 10^3 \text{ oz}}{\text{ft}^3}\right)\left(\frac{1 \text{ lb}}{16 \text{ oz}}\right)\left(\frac{1 \text{ kg}}{2.2046 \text{ lbs}}\right)\left(\frac{1000}{\text{k}}\right) = 2.25568 \times 10^5 \text{ g/ft}^3$$

The first factor converts the given number of ounces to pounds. The next, using information from table 1.3, converts pounds to kilograms. The final unity factor uses the definition of *kilo* from table 1.2 to eliminate the prefix. Note that the value used for the initial density in this calculation is the *unrounded* value from part (a). We have used this unrounded value because we do not want to introduce error by using a rounded value from an intermediate calculation.

Next, we need to convert the cubic feet to cubic centimeters. To illustrate an important mathematical consideration in this part of the conversion, let's isolate it temporarily from the rest of the problem. The cubic feet to cubic centimeter conversions are as follows:

$$\left(\frac{1}{\text{ft}^3}\right)\left(\frac{1 \text{ ft}}{12 \text{ in}}\right)^3\left(\frac{1 \text{ in}}{2.54 \text{ cm}}\right)^3 = \left(\frac{1}{\text{ft}^3}\right)\left(\frac{1 \text{ ft}^3}{1{,}728 \text{ in}^3}\right)\left(\frac{1 \text{ in}^3}{16.38706 \text{ cm}^3}\right) = 3.53147 \times 10^{-5} \text{ cm}^3$$

The first step converts cubic feet to cubic inches. Note that we must cube the number 12. In the second step, we use the inch-to-centimeter relationship found in table 1.3. Again, we must remember to cube the number 2.54.

Inserting both conversion steps into the density relationship gives this:

$$\text{Density} = \left(\frac{7.9536 \times 10^3 \text{ oz}}{\text{ft}^3} \right) \left(\frac{1 \text{ lb}}{16 \text{ oz}} \right) \left(\frac{1 \text{ kg}}{2.2046 \text{ lbs}} \right) \left(\frac{1000}{k} \right) \left(\frac{1 \text{ ft}}{12 \text{ in}} \right)^3 \left(\frac{1 \text{ in}}{2.54 \text{ cm}} \right)^3$$

$$= 7.96586 = \textbf{7.96 g/cm}^3$$

(Do not forget to cube the numbers along with the units in the last two conversion factors.)

Combining all the conversions into one set-up reduces the total amount of work and circumvents the errors that might occur from intermediate rounding.

Reality Check

Both answers have the correct units. In part (**a**), we divided the mass by a very small number (10^{-4}) and we should expect a large number as the result (in the range of 10^3). In part (**b**), we divided the large answer from part (a) by a series of terms in the denominators of the unity factors. The repeated divisions should be expected to reduce the numerical value.

Follow-Up Problem 1.7b

A sample of lithium metal weighs 3.62×10^{-4} tons. The volume of the sample is 8.04×10^{-4} yd^3. (**a**) Determine the density of lithium metal. (**b**) Express the density of lithium metal in grams per cubic centimeter.

Information

The first step is to collect and label the information given in the problem:

Weight of lithium metal = 3.62×10^{-4} tons

Volume of sample = 8.04×10^{-4} yd^3

(**a**) Density of lithium = ?

(**b**) Density of lithium = ? g/cm^3

Connections

(**a**) Only the definition of density is needed. (**b**) We will be converting tons to grams and cubic yards to cubic centimeters, requiring information from tables 1.2 (1,000 = k) and table 1.3 (1 kg = 2.2046 lb and 2.54 cm = 1 in), along with two English-to-English conversions (1 ton = 2,000 lb, and 1 yd = 36 in).

Solution

(**a**) Since we have the mass and volume of the iron sample in the units required for the first part of the problem, we simply insert these values into the definition of *density* (mass/volume):

$$\text{Density} = \frac{\text{Mass}}{\text{Volume}}$$

$$\text{Density of iron} = \frac{\left(3.62 \times 10^{-4} \text{ tons} \right)}{\left(8.04 \times 10^{-4} \text{ yd}^3 \right)}$$

$$= 0.450248756 \text{ (calculator display)}$$

$$= \textbf{0.450 tons/yd}^3 \text{ (correct significant figures)}$$

(b) In this part, we are asked to express the same density in different units. The easiest approach is to begin with the answer to part (a) and apply appropriate unity factors to convert ounces to grams, and cubic feet to cubic centimeters. We can do these conversions in any order. Here, we will do the ounce-to-gram conversion first:

$$\text{Density} = \left(\frac{0.450248756 \text{ tons}}{\text{yd}^3}\right)\left(\frac{2{,}000 \text{ lbs}}{1 \text{ ton}}\right)\left(\frac{1 \text{ kg}}{2.2046 \text{ lbs}}\right)\left(\frac{1{,}000}{\text{k}}\right) = 4.0846299 \times 10^5 \text{ g/yd}^3$$

The first factor converts the given number of ounces to pounds. The next, using information from table 1.3, converts pounds to kilograms. The final unity factor uses the definition of *kilo* from table 1.2 to eliminate the prefix. Note that the value used for the initial density in this calculation is the *unrounded* value from part (a). We have used this unrounded value because we do not want to introduce an error by using a rounded value from an intermediate calculation.

Next, we will need to convert the cubic yards to cubic centimeters. To illustrate an important mathematical consideration in this part of the conversion, let's isolate it temporarily from the rest of the problem. The cubic yard to cubic centimeter conversions are as follows:

$$\left(\frac{1}{\text{yd}^3}\right)\left(\frac{1 \text{ yd}}{36 \text{ in}}\right)^3\left(\frac{1 \text{ in}}{2.54 \text{ cm}}\right)^3 = \left(\frac{1}{\text{yd}^3}\right)\left(\frac{1 \text{ yd}^3}{46{,}656 \text{ in}^3}\right)\left(\frac{1 \text{ in}^3}{16.38706 \text{ cm}^3}\right) = 1.3079509 \times 10^{-6} \text{ cm}^3$$

The first step converts cubic yards to cubic inches. Note that we must cube the number 36. In the second step, we use the inch-to-centimeter relationship found in table 1.3. Again, we must remember to cube the number 2.54.

Inserting both these conversion steps into the density relationship gives

$$\text{Density} = \left(\frac{0.450248756 \text{ tons}}{\text{yd}^3}\right)\left(\frac{2{,}000 \text{ lbs}}{1 \text{ ton}}\right)\left(\frac{1 \text{ kg}}{2.2046 \text{ lbs}}\right)\left(\frac{1{,}000}{\text{k}}\right)\left(\frac{1 \text{ yd}}{36 \text{ in}}\right)^3\left(\frac{1 \text{ in}}{2.54 \text{ cm}}\right)^3 = 0.53429$$

$$= \mathbf{0.534 \text{ g/cm}^3}$$

(Remember to cube the numbers along with the units in the last two conversion factors.)

Combining all the conversions into one setup reduces the total amount of work and circumvents the errors that might occur from intermediate rounding.

Reality Check
Both answers have the correct units. In part (a) the 10^{-4} factors cancel, leaving a simple division. In part (b), we divided the answer from part (a) by a series of terms in the denominators of the unity factors. The repeated divisions should be expected to reduce the numerical value.

Example Problem 1.8
How many grams of aluminum are in a cube of aluminum measuring 2.0 in on an edge? The density of aluminum is 2.70 g/cm³.

Information
Collect the information from the problem:

Length of aluminum cube = 2.0 in
Density of aluminum = 2.70 g/cm³
Mass of aluminum cube = ? g

Connections
Table 1.3 contains the required inch-to-centimeters conversion (2.54 cm = 1 in).

Solution

Knowing one dimension of the cube allows us to state its volume in cubic inches, which we can convert to cubic centimeters. We can then use this volume along with aluminum's density (given in grams per cubic centimeter) to calculate the number of grams present:

$$\text{Volume of cube} = (2.0 \text{ in})^3 \left(\frac{2.54 \text{ cm}}{1 \text{ in}} \right)^3 = 131.096512 \text{ cm}^3 \text{ (unrounded)}$$

Multiplying the cube's volume by the density of aluminum gives the number of grams of aluminum present:

$$\text{Mass} = (131.096512 \text{ cm}^3) \left(\frac{2.70 \text{ g}}{\text{cm}^3} \right) = 353.96058$$

$$= 3.5 \times 10^2 \text{ g aluminum (rounded to the correct number of significant figures)}$$

Combining all the factors into one step would have simplified the calculation:

$$\text{Mass} = (2.0 \text{ in})^3 \left(\frac{2.54 \text{ cm}}{1 \text{ in}} \right)^3 \left(\frac{2.70 \text{ g}}{\text{cm}^3} \right) = \mathbf{3.5 \times 10^2 \text{ g aluminum}}$$

Reality Check

The answer has the requested unit. The calculation requires cubing two terms and multiplying by another. This should result in a value larger than any of the original ones. The value of 350 g is a little over half a pound (454.6 g = 1 lb), which seems a reasonable value for a cube of metal that size.

Follow-Up Problem 1.8a

A rectangular piece of copper metal measures 2.0 in × 3.0 in × 0.5 in. If the density of copper is 8.92 g/cm^3, what is the mass of this piece of copper?

Information

Collect the information from the problem:

Dimensions of the copper metal = 2.0 in × 3.0 in × 0.5 in
Density of copper = 8.92 g/cm^3
Mass of copper = ?

Connections

Table 1.3 contains the required inch-to-centimeters conversion (2.54 cm = 1 in).

Solution

We need to state the copper's volume in cubic inches, which we can convert to cubic centimeters. We can then use this volume along with copper's density (given in grams per cubic centimeter) to calculate the number of grams present.

$$\text{Volume of cube} = (2.0 \text{ in} \times 3.0 \text{ in} \times 0.5 \text{ in}) \left(\frac{2.54 \text{ cm}}{1 \text{ in}} \right)^3 = 49.16119 \text{ cm}^3 \text{ (unrounded)}$$

Multiplying the cube's volume by the density of copper gives the number of grams of copper present:

$$\text{Mass} = (49.16119 \text{ cm}^3) \left(\frac{8.92 \text{ g}}{\text{cm}^3} \right) = 438.5178$$

$$= 4 \times 10^2 \text{ g copper (rounded to the correct number of significant figures)}$$

Combining all the factors into one step would have simplified the calculation:

$$\text{Mass} = (2.0 \text{ in} \times 3.0 \text{ in} \times 0.5 \text{ in}) \left(\frac{2.54 \text{ cm}}{1 \text{ in}} \right)^3 \left(\frac{8.92 \text{ g}}{\text{cm}^3} \right) = \mathbf{4 \times 10^2 \text{ g copper}}$$

Reality Check

The answer has the requested unit. The calculation requires cubing two terms and multiplying by another. This should result in a value larger than any of the original ones. The value of 350 g is a little over half a pound (454.6 g = 1 lb), which seems a reasonable value for a cube of metal that size.

Follow-Up Problem 1.8b

A person fills an ice cube tray with water to a depth of 1.00 in. If the tray has 16 compartments, each measuring 1.55 in by 1.05 in, how many grams of water does the tray hold? The density of water is 1.00 g/cm^3.

Information

Collect the information from the problem:

    Depth of water = 1.00 in
    Dimensions of each compartment = 1.55 in × 1.05 in
    Number of compartments = 16
    Density of water = 1.00 g/cm^3
    Mass of water = ? grams

Connections

Table 1.3 contains the required inch-to-centimeters conversion (2.54 cm = 1 in).

Solution

We need to state the volume in cubic inches, which we can convert to cubic centimeters. In addition, we must multiply the volume of each compartment by the number of compartments (16). We can then use this volume along with water's density (given in grams per cubic centimeter) to calculate the number of grams present:

$$\text{Volume of cube} = 16 \left[(1.00 \text{ in} \times 1.55 \text{ in} \times 1.05 \text{ in}) \left(\frac{2.54 \text{ cm}}{1 \text{ in}} \right)^3 \right] = 426.719 \text{ cm}^3 \text{ (unrounded)}$$

Multiplying the cube's volume by the density of water gives the number of grams of water present:

$$\text{Mass} = (426.719 \text{ cm}^3) \left(\frac{1.00 \text{ g}}{\text{cm}^3} \right) = 426.719$$

$$= 4.27 \times 10^2 \text{ g water (rounded to the correct number of significant figures)}$$

Combining all the factors into one step would have simplified the calculation:

$$\text{Mass} = 16 \left[(1.00 \text{ in} \times 1.55 \text{ in} \times 1.05 \text{ in}) \left(\frac{2.54 \text{ cm}}{1 \text{ in}} \right)^3 \right] \left(\frac{1.00 \text{ g}}{\text{cm}^3} \right) = \mathbf{4.27 \times 10^2 \text{ g water}}$$

Reality Check

The answer has the requested unit. The calculation requires cubing two terms and multiplying by another. This should result in a value larger than any of the original ones. The value of 350 g is a little over half a pound (454.6 g = 1 lb), which seems a reasonable value for a cube of metal that size.

Example Problem 1.9

The density of ebony is 1.20 g/cm³. Determine the volume in milliliters of a piece of ebony wood weighing 275 g.

Information

Density of ebony = 1.20 g/cm³
Mass of ebony sample = 275 g
Volume of ebony sample = ? mL

Connections

Table 1.3 gives the relation connecting milliliters to cubic centimeters (1 mL = 1 cm³).

Solution

Begin with the given mass (grams) and rearrange the density term so that the mass unit of grams will cancel. Next, using the relationship 1 mL = 1 cm³ (table 1.3), convert the volume to milliliters:

$$\text{Volume} = (275 \text{ g})\left(\frac{\text{cm}^3}{1.20 \text{ g}}\right)\left(\frac{1 \text{ mL}}{1 \text{ cm}^3}\right) = 229.167 = \textbf{229 mL}$$

Reality Check

The answer has the correct unit. Division of the original value by a number slightly greater than 1 should give an answer slightly smaller, numerically, than the original value. The volume we calculated seems reasonable with respect to the given mass.

Follow-Up Problem 1.9a

Determine the volume in milliliters of a piece of magnesium metal weighing 175.25 g. The density of magnesium is 1.74 g/cm³.

Information

The first step is to collect and label the information given in the problem:

Mass of magnesium = 175.25 g
Density of magnesium = 1.74 g/cm³
Volume of magnesium = ? mL

Connections

Table 1.3 gives the relation connecting milliliters to cubic centimeters (1 mL = 1 cm³).

Solution

Begin with the given mass (grams) and rearrange the density term so that the mass unit of grams will cancel. Next, using the relationship 1 mL = 1 cm³ (table 1.3), convert the volume to milliliters:

$$\text{Volume} = (175.25 \text{ g})\left(\frac{\text{cm}^3}{1.74 \text{ g}}\right)\left(\frac{1 \text{ mL}}{1 \text{ cm}^3}\right) = 100.718 = \textbf{101 mL}$$

Reality Check

The answer has the correct unit. Division of the original value by a number about 100 times larger should give an answer around 100. The volume we calculated seems reasonable with respect to the given mass.

Follow-Up Problem 1.9b

Gold has a density of 19.3 g/cm³. A chemistry student drops a piece of gold weighing 52.35 g into a graduated cylinder containing water initially at the 15.8-mL mark. The gold causes the water level to rise. What will be the final volume reading in the graduated cylinder?

Information

The first step is to collect and label the information given in the problem:

Density of gold = 19.3 g/cm³
Mass of gold = 52.35 g
Initial volume of water = 15.8-mL
Final volume of water = ? mL

Connections

Table 1.3 gives the relation connecting milliliters to cubic centimeters (1 mL = 1 cm³).

Solution

Begin with the given mass (grams) and rearrange the density term so that the mass unit of grams will cancel. Next, using the relationship 1 mL = 1 cm³ (table 1.3), convert the volume to milliliters:

$$\text{Volume} = (52.35 \text{ g})\left(\frac{\text{cm}^3}{19.3 \text{ g}}\right)\left(\frac{1 \text{ mL}}{1 \text{ cm}^3}\right) = 2.7124 = 2.71 \text{ mL}$$

The final volume will be equal to the initial volume of water plus the volume of the gold:

$$\text{Final Volume} = 15.8 \text{ mL} + 2.71 \text{ mL} = 18.51 = \textbf{18.5 mL}$$

Reality Check

The answer has the correct unit. Division of the original value by a number about 100 times larger should give an answer around 100. The volume we calculated seems reasonable with respect to the given mass.

Practice Problem 1.10

Modern automobile airbags inflate by generating nitrogen through the decomposition of a nitrogen-containing compound called sodium azide (much the way Ramsay obtained nitrogen from various compounds to compare with nitrogen from the air). In one experiment, an airbag with a volume of 20.0 ft³ was filled with 1.548 lb of nitrogen gas. Determine the density of the nitrogen gas in grams per liter.

Information

Volume of nitrogen sample = 20.0 ft³
Mass of nitrogen sample = 1.548 lb
Density of nitrogen sample = ? g/L

Connections

We will use the definition of *density*; the English-English conversion of feet to inches; the relationships between pounds and grams, inches and centimeters, and milliliters and cubic centimeters from table 1.3; and the definition of the prefix *milli* from table 1.2.

Solution

Express the given amount and volume of the gas as a density followed by unity factors to convert to the desired units:

$$\text{Density of nitrogen} = \left(\frac{1.548 \text{ lbs}}{20.0 \text{ ft}^3}\right)\left(\frac{453.59 \text{ g}}{1 \text{ lb}}\right)\left(\frac{1 \text{ ft}}{12 \text{ in}}\right)^3\left(\frac{1 \text{ in}}{2.54 \text{ cm}}\right)^3\left(\frac{1 \text{ cm}^3}{1 \text{ mL}}\right)\left(\frac{m}{10^{-3}}\right) = 1.23982$$

$$= \textbf{1.24 g/L}$$

Reality Check

The answer has the correct units. Gases are low in weight, so the density should be low.

Practice Problem 1.11

Assuming that the density of a urine sample is the same as its specific gravity (1.025), calculate the mass of 2.00 gal of urine.

Information

Specific gravity of urine sample = 1.025 = density of sample
Volume of sample = 1.00 gal
Mass of sample = ?

Connections

The relation between quarts and gallons (4 qt = 1 gal) is necessary, as well as other conversions supplied in tables 1.2 and 1.3.

Solution

We can assume the density of the urine sample to be 1.025 g/mL. There is no indication of the desired mass unit in the problem, and so any unit should be acceptable. The simplest unit to use would be grams, since this is the mass unit appearing in the assumed density. Converting from milliliters to liters to quarts gives the following

$$\left(\frac{1.025 \text{ g}}{\text{mL}}\right)\left(\frac{m}{10^{-3}}\right)\left(\frac{1 \text{ L}}{1.0567 \text{ qt}}\right)\left(\frac{4 \text{ qt}}{1 \text{ gal}}\right)(2.00 \text{ gal}) = 7760.008 = \textbf{7760 g}$$

Reality Check

The answer has units of mass. This number of grams is about 17 lb, or about 8.5 lb/gal. You have probably held a gallon container of milk and can judge that the answer seems consistent with its weight.

Practice Problem 1.12

Later chapters introduce various units for measuring heat energy; two examples are calories and joules (1 cal = 4.184 J). In an MRE heater, 24.305 g of magnesium produces 351 kJ of heat. A typical heater has a mass of 38.8 g. If 80.0% of the mass of the heater is magnesium, how many kilocalories of energy will be released?

Information

24.305 g Mg = 351 kJ (Mg is the chemical symbol for magnesium)
Mass of a typical heater = 38.8 g
Amount of heater consisting of magnesium = 80.0%
1 cal = 4.184 J
Amount of energy released = ? kcal

Connections

No additional relationships are necessary.

Solution

If 80.0% of the mass of the heater is magnesium, then there are 80.0 g of Mg in every 100 g of heater:

$$(38.8 \text{ g heater substance})\left(\frac{80.0 \text{ g Mg}}{100 \text{ g heater}}\right)$$

We insert a unity factor to calculate the kilojoules of energy produced by the magnesium:

$$(38.8 \text{ g heater substance})\left(\frac{80.0 \text{ g Mg}}{100 \text{ g heater}}\right)\left(\frac{351 \text{ kJ}}{24.305 \text{ g Mg}}\right)$$

We insert another unity factor to convert that amount to kilocalories:

$$(38.8 \text{ g heater substance})\left(\frac{80.0 \text{ g Mg}}{100 \text{ g heater}}\right)\left(\frac{351 \text{ kJ}}{24.305 \text{ g Mg}}\right)\left(\frac{1 \text{ cal}}{4.184 \text{ J}}\right) = 107.138 \text{ kcal}$$
$$= \textbf{107 kcal}$$

Reality Check

The answer has the desired unit, kilocalories. The mass of magnesium in the MRE is about 30 g, and since we know that 24 g of magnesium produces about 350 kJ of heat, we can estimate that 30 g should produce about 400 kJ, which divided by 4 (4 kJ is approximately 1 kcal) should give approximately 100 kcal. The answer of 107 kcal is therefore reasonable.

END-OF-CHAPTER PROBLEMS

1.1 Getting Started

1.2 Make a list of all the physical properties of water that you might observe when you're examining water in a glass.

Solution

Many, including color (or lack of), size, and shape.

1.4 Which properties of a baseball will be the same on Earth as on Mars?

Solution

Mass (not weight), size, shape, color

1.5 Define the terms *mass* and *weight*. Which of these terms is constant for an object?

Solution

The **mass** of a substance is a measure of the quantity of matter present. The **weight** of an object is a measure of the gravitational attraction of a body on the mass of an object. The mass of an object is constant, and the weight may vary.

1.8 What is the state of matter under normal conditions for each of the following? **(a)** gasoline, **(b)** copper, **(c)** nitrogen, **(d)** sucrose (cane sugar), **(e)** helium

Solution

(a) gasoline is a liquid, **(b)** copper is a solid, **(c)** nitrogen is a gas, **(d)** sucrose (cane sugar) is a solid, **(e)** helium is a gas

1.10 Describe each of the following as representing a chemical change or a physical change: **(a)** charcoal being burned, **(b)** wood being cut, **(c)** iron rusting, **(d)** water changing to ice, **(e)** table salt dissolving in water

Solution

(a) Chemical change, (b) physical change, (c) chemical change, (d) physical change, (e) physical change

1.15 Classify each of the following as either an extensive property or an intensive property: **(a)** volume, **(b)** temperature, **(c)** boiling point, **(d)** density, **(e)** mass.

Solution

(a) extensive, (b) intensive, (c) intensive, (d) intensive, (e) extensive

1.2 The Scientific Method and Serendipity

1.17 What is the difference between a hypothesis, a theory, and a law?

Solution

A **hypothesis** is a tentative explanation consistent with the observations and capable of being tested by experimentation. A **theory**, sometimes called a **model,** is a generally accepted, testable explanation of observations. A **law** is a mathematical or verbal summary of well-established relationships that have been derived because of experiments.

1.21 A 5.0 g piece of aluminum wire was placed in a beaker containing 25.0 g of dilute sulfuric acid. The metal reacted with the acid to release hydrogen gas, which escaped into the atmosphere. After the reaction was complete, 28.9 g of material remained in the beaker. How many grams of hydrogen gas escaped?

Solution

Conservation of mass: $5.0 \text{ g} + 25.0 \text{ g} = 28.9 \text{ g} + x \text{ g}$
$$x = \textbf{1.1 g}$$

1.3 Elements, Compounds, and Mixtures

1.23 Define a *pure substance* and a *mixture*. Give an example of each.

Solution

A **pure substance** is one that cannot be separated into simpler substances by physical means. Table salt is an example of a pure substance. **A mixture** is a physical combination of pure substances. Table salt dissolved in water is an example of a mixture.

1.27 Using the periodic table on the inside front cover of this textbook, list the symbol for each of the following elements: **(a)** hydrogen, **(b)** lithium, **(c)** aluminum, **(d)** xenon, **(e)** samarium, **(f)** iron, **(g)** copper, **(h)** sodium, **(i)** mercury **(j)** lead

Solution

(a) hydrogen	**H**	**(e)** samarium	**Sm**	**(h)**	sodium	**Na**
(b) lithium	**Li**	**(f)** iron	**Fe**	**(i)**	mercury	**Hg**
(c) aluminum	**Al**	**(g)** copper	**Cu**	**(j)**	lead	**Pb**
(d) xenon	**Xe**					

1.30 Use the tables on the inside front cover of this textbook to, first, classify each of the following elements as a metal, a metalloid, or a nonmetal and second, give the element's symbol: **(a)** rubidium, **(b)** rhenium, **(c)** iodine, **(d)** hydrogen, **(e)** silicon.

Solution

(a) rubidium	**metal**	**Rb**
(b) rhenium	**metal**	**Re**
(c) iodine	**nonmetal**	**I**
(d) hydrogen	**nonmetal**	**H**
(e) silicon	**metalloid**	**Si**

1.4 Units of Measure

1.35 You perform a calculation to determine the volume of a box. You enter 12. × 12.0 × 12 into your calculator, and you report 1,728 as the answer. It is very likely that your instructor will count the answer wrong. Why?

Solution

The value 12 limits the answer to two significant figures; therefore, the answer (with rounding) is 1,700, two significant figures.

1.36 Identify the SI units that would be appropriate for measuring the following quantities: **(a)** the temperature of a glass of water, **(b)** the volume of a bottle of a soft drink, **(c)** the surface area of a football field, **(d)** the distance from Earth to the moon, **(e)** the speed of a bullet

Solution

(a) Kelvin, (b) cubic meters (or cubic centimeters), **(c) square meters, (d) megameters, (e) meters per second**

1.39 Express each of the following units as a power of ten: **(a)** c, **(b)** m, **(c)** μ, **(d)** d, **(e)** k, **(f)** a, **(g)** G, **(h)** n, **(i)** M, **(j)** p

Solution

(a) $c = 10^{-2}$, **(b)** $m = 10^{-3}$, **(c)** $\mu = 10^{-6}$, **(d)** $d = 10^{-1}$, **(e)** $k = 10^{3}$, **(f)** $a = 10^{-18}$, **(g)** $G = 10^{9}$, **(h)** $n = 10^{-9}$, **(i)** $M = 10^{6}$, **(j)** $p = 10^{-12}$

1.5 Reporting and Using Measurements

1.44 Define *accuracy* and *precision*. Give an example of a situation in which accuracy is high, but precision is low. Give an example of a situation in which accuracy is low but precision is high. Hint: You may use a "bull's-eye" target to illustrate both situations.

Solution

Accuracy is how well the measurement agrees with the accepted or true value. **Precision** is how well a set of measurements agree with each other. A scatter of darts all at about the same distance from the center would have low precision; however, if the average of their positions is near the center, the accuracy might be high. A cluster of darts on the side of a target represents high precision; however, if the cluster is not near the center, the accuracy is low.

1.46 How many significant figures are in Mega = 1 000 000?

Solution
This is an exact value; therefore, there are an infinite number of significant figures.

1.49 Does an increase in the number of significant figures indicate an increase in precision, or does it indicate an increase in accuracy?

Solution
An increase in the number of significant figures indicates an increase in precision, not accuracy.

1.54 How would you distinguish between a measured value and an exact value?

Solution
Measured values are inexact numbers that have uncertainty associated with them. **Exact numbers** are numbers that have no uncertainty associated with them.

1.56 How many significant figures are present in each of the following measurements? (a) 3,842 kg, (b) 4.27×10^2 s, (c) 9.004735 ft, (d) 0.000427 g, (e) 34,000 mi

Solution
(a) **4**, (b) **3**, (c) **7**, (d) **3**, (e) **2** (but ambiguous)

1.58 Round the following numbers to two significant figures: (a) 11.3, (b) –122, (c) 10.00, (d) 2,000, (e) 5.280×10^3

Solution
(a) **11**, (b) **–120**, (c) **10.**, (d) $\mathbf{2.0 \times 10^3}$, (e) $\mathbf{5.3 \times 10^3}$

1.61 Perform the following operations, and round the answers to the appropriate number of significant figures: (a) 1.3827 g + 1.46 g, (b) 412.32°C – 12.32°C, (c) 3.52 ft × 5312 ft, (d) 0.3235 g / 22.5 cm³, (e) 3.726 in + 5.427 in + 2.0 in

Information
(a) 1.3827 g + 1.46 g, (b) 412.32°C – 12.32°C, (c) 3.52 ft × 5312 ft, (d) 0.3235 g / 22.5 cm³, (e) 3.726 in + 5.427 in + 2.0 in

Connections
Basic mathematical operations and the rules for significant figures.

Solution
(a) 1.3827 g + 1.46 g = 2.8427 = **2.84 g**

(b) 412.32°C – 12.32°C = **400.00°C**

(c) 3.52 ft × 5312 ft = 18698 = $\mathbf{1.87 \times 10^4}$ **ft²** (or 18,700 ft²)

(d) 0.3235 g / 22.5 cm³ = 0.014377778 = **0.0144 g/cm³**

(e) 3.726 in + 5.427 in + 2.0 in = 11.15 = **11.2 in**

Reality Check
The numbers seem reasonable, the units are correct, and the significant figures are correct.

1.6 Unit Conversion and Problem Solving

1.66 What are the two conversion factors that can come from 1 mi = 5,280 ft?

Solution

$$\frac{1\ mi}{5,280\ ft} \quad and \quad \frac{5,280\ ft}{1\ mi}$$

1.68 When a person picks up a 1 lb piece of steel and says it is heavier than a 1 lb bag of feathers, what does she really mean?

Solution

The steel is denser than the feathers are.

1.71 Perform the following conversions: **(a)** 526 m to kilometers **(b)** 3.42 μs to seconds, **(c)** 954 ng to grams, **(d)** 0.024 m³ to cubic centimeters, **(e)** 7351 kg/m³ to grams per cubic centimeter

Information

(a) 526 m to kilometers, **(b)** 3.42 μs to seconds, **(c)** 954 ng to grams, **(d)** 0.024 m³ to cubic centimeters, **(e)** 7351 kg/m³ to grams per cubic centimeter.

Connections

The basic SI prefixes and the rules for significant figures.

Solution

(a) $(526\ \text{m})\left(\dfrac{\text{k}}{1,000}\right) = \textbf{0.526 km}$

(b) $(3.42\ \mu\text{s})\left(\dfrac{10^{-6}}{\mu}\right) = \textbf{3.42} \times \textbf{10}^{-6}\ \textbf{s}$

(c) $(954\ \text{ng})\left(\dfrac{10^{-9}}{\text{n}}\right) = \textbf{9.54} \times \textbf{10}^{-7}\ \textbf{g}$

(d) $(0.024\ \text{m}^3)\left(\dfrac{\text{c}}{0.01}\right)^3 = \textbf{2.4} \times \textbf{10}^4\ \textbf{cm}^3$

(e) $\left(\dfrac{7,351\ \text{kg}}{\text{m}^3}\right)\left(\dfrac{10^3}{\text{k}}\right)\left(\dfrac{0.01}{\text{c}}\right)^3 = \textbf{7.351 g/cm}^3$

Reality Check

The numbers seem reasonable, the units are correct, and the significant figures are correct.

1.74 Carry out the following conversions: **(a)** 1.00 ft³ to cubic inches, **(b)** 45.3 ft² to square meters, **(c)** 1,760 lb/m³ to kilograms per cubic meter, **(d)** 745 mL to cubic meters, **(e)** 186,000 mi/hr to meters per second

Information

(a) 1.00 ft³ to cubic inches, **(b)** 45.3 ft² to square meters, **(c)** 1760 lb/m³ to kilograms per cubic meter, **(d)** 745 mL to cubic meters, **(e)** 186,000 mi/h to meters per second

Connections

The basic SI prefixes (0.01 = c), some English conversions (12 in = 1 ft, 1 h = 3,600 s), various English-to-SI conversions (2.54 cm = 1 in, 1 kg = 2.205 lb, and 1609 m = 1 mi), 1 cm³ = 1 mL, and the rules for significant figures.

Solution

In all cases, alternate conversions are possible. In parts (c) and (e), there are two conversion series happening. One conversion series concerns the numerator and the other conversion series concerns the denominator.

(a) $(1.00 \text{ ft}^3)\left(\dfrac{12 \text{ in}}{1 \text{ ft}}\right)^3 = 1{,}728 = \mathbf{1.73 \times 10^3 \text{ in}^3}$

(b) $(45.3 \text{ ft}^2)\left(\dfrac{12 \text{ in}}{1 \text{ ft}}\right)^2\left(\dfrac{2.54 \text{ cm}}{1 \text{ in}}\right)^2\left(\dfrac{0.01}{c}\right)^2 = 4.2085 = \mathbf{4.21 \text{ m}^2}$

(c) $\left(\dfrac{1{,}760 \text{ lbs}}{\text{m}^3}\right)\left(\dfrac{1 \text{ kg}}{2.205 \text{ lbs}}\right) = 798.1859 = \mathbf{798 \text{ kg/m}^3}$

(d) $(745 \text{ mL})\left(\dfrac{1 \text{ cm}^3}{1 \text{ mL}}\right)\left(\dfrac{0.01}{c}\right)^3 = \mathbf{7.45 \times 10^{-4} \text{ m}^3}$

(e) $\left(\dfrac{186{,}000 \text{ mi}}{\text{h}}\right)\left(\dfrac{1609 \text{ m}}{1 \text{ mi}}\right)\left(\dfrac{1 \text{ h}}{3{,}600 \text{ s}}\right) = 8.31317 \times 10^4 = \mathbf{8.31 \times 10^4 \text{ m/s}}$

Reality Check

The numbers seem reasonable, the units are correct, and the significant figures are correct.

1.77 Highly toxic hydrogen cyanide (HCN) has many industrial uses. As little as 1.0×10^{-5} g/L is cause for concern. Calculate the number of grams of HCN at 1.0×10^{-5} g/L in a room measuring 25 ft × 22 ft × 8.0 ft.

Information

? grams of HCN at 1.0×10^{-5} g/L
a room measuring 25 ft × 22 ft × 8.0 ft

Connections

SI prefixes (c = 0.01 and d = 0.1), 1 L = 1 dm³, 12 in = 1 ft, 2.54 cm = 1 in, and the rules for significant figures.

Solution

This is an extended unit conversion problem.

$$\left(\dfrac{1.0 \times 10^{-5} \text{ g}}{\text{L}}\right)(25 \times 22 \times 8.0)\text{ft}^3\left(\dfrac{12 \text{ in}}{1 \text{ ft}}\right)^3\left(\dfrac{2.54 \text{ cm}}{1 \text{ in}}\right)^3\left(\dfrac{0.01}{c}\right)^3\left(\dfrac{d}{0.1}\right)^3\left(\dfrac{L}{\text{dm}^3}\right) = 1.2459 = \mathbf{1.2 \text{ g}}$$

Reality Check

The answer seems reasonable, the units are correct, and the significant figures are correct.

1.81 Antifreeze contains the compound ethylene glycol. This compound not only lowers the freezing point of water but also increases the boiling point of water. The density of ethylene glycol is 9.35 lb/gal, and the density of water is 62.5 lb/ft³.

(a) Is the density of water greater than the density of ethylene glycol? **(b)** Convert the density of ethylene glycol and water to grams per milliliter. **(c)** Assuming that the density of a mixture of water and ethylene glycol is simply the weighted average of the amounts of the two liquids mixed, what is the density in grams per cubic centimeter of a mixture containing 1.00 gal of ethylene glycol in 3.00 gal of water? (Hint: To determine the weighted average density, multiply each individual density by the fraction of the final solution that is that particular substance.)

Information

density of ethylene glycol = 9.35 lb/gal, and density of water = 62.5 lb/ft^3

(a) Which density is higher?

(b) Convert the density of ethylene glycol = ? g/mL and water = g/mL.

(c) density = ? grams/cm^3 for a mixture of 1.00 gal of ethylene glycol in 3.00 gal of water? (Hint: To determine the weighted average density, multiply each individual density by the fraction of the final solution that is that particular substance.)

Connections

Various SI prefixes (c = 0.01, d = 0.1, and m = 0.001), English-to-English conversions (1 gal = 4 qt and 12 in = 1 ft), English-to-SI conversions (1 in = 2.54 cm, 1 L = 1.057 qt, and 453.59 g = 1 lb), SI-to-SI relationships (1 dm^3 = 1 L and 1 cm^3 = 1 mL), and the rules for significant figures.

Solution

(a) To compare the densities, it is necessary to convert them to the same units. Either density may be converted to the other. So, if the choice is to convert to lb/gal.

$$\left(\frac{62.5\ \text{lb}}{\text{ft}^3}\right)\left(\frac{1\ \text{ft}}{12\ \text{in}}\right)^3\left(\frac{1\ \text{in}}{2.54\ \text{cm}}\right)^3\left(\frac{c}{0.01}\right)^3\left(\frac{0.1}{d}\right)^3\left(\frac{1\ \text{dm}^3}{1\ \text{L}}\right)\left(\frac{1\ \text{L}}{1.057\ \text{qt}}\right)\left(\frac{4\ \text{qt}}{1\ \text{gal}}\right) = 8.35257 = 8.35\ \text{lb/gal}$$

The density of water is lower than the density of ethylene glycol.

(b) $\left(\dfrac{9.35\ \text{lb}}{\text{gal}}\right)\left(\dfrac{453.59\ \text{g}}{1\ \text{lb}}\right)\left(\dfrac{1\ \text{gal}}{4\ \text{qt}}\right)\left(\dfrac{1.057\ \text{qt}}{1\ \text{L}}\right)\left(\dfrac{0.001}{\text{m}}\right) = 1.1207 = \mathbf{1.12\ g/mL}$

$\left(\dfrac{8.35257\ \text{lb}}{\text{gal}}\right)\left(\dfrac{453.59\ \text{g}}{1\ \text{lb}}\right)\left(\dfrac{1\ \text{gal}}{4\ \text{qt}}\right)\left(\dfrac{1.057\ \text{qt}}{1\ \text{L}}\right)\left(\dfrac{0.001}{\text{m}}\right) = 1.0011 = \mathbf{1.00\ g/mL}$

(c) It is possible to solve this problem by determining the average density in lb/gal and then converting to the desired units, or by converting each of the densities to the desired units and then taking the average. The first approach involves only one conversion, so it should be faster.

$$\left[\frac{(9.35 + 3(8.35))\ \text{lb}}{4\ \text{gal}}\right]\left(\frac{453.59\ \text{g}}{1\ \text{lb}}\right)\left(\frac{1\ \text{gal}}{4\ \text{qt}}\right)\left(\frac{1.057\ \text{qt}}{1\ \text{L}}\right)\left(\frac{0.001}{\text{m}}\right)\left(\frac{\text{mL}}{1\ \text{cm}^3}\right) = 1.0308 = \mathbf{1.03\ g/cm^3}$$

Reality Check

The numbers seem reasonable, the units are correct, and the significant figures are correct.

1.84 In the United States, rainfall is typically measured in inches. If 0.75 in of rain is measured, how many liters of rain fall on an acre of land? (1 square mile = 640 acres)

Information

? L of rain on an acre of land from 0.75 in of rain (1 square mile = 640 acres)

Connections

The values given in the problem, an SI prefix (m = 0.001), an SI relationship (1 mL = 1 cm^3), an SI-to-English conversion (2.54 cm = 1 in), two English-to-English conversions (5280 ft = 1 mi and 12 in = 1 ft), and the rules for significant figures.

Solution

To find the volume, it is necessary to multiply the depth of water by the area. The remainder of the problem is unit conversions. There are alternate conversions available.

$$(0.75 \text{ in})(\text{acre})\left(\frac{1 \text{ mi}^2}{640 \text{ acre}}\right)\left(\frac{5280 \text{ ft}}{1 \text{ mi}}\right)^2\left(\frac{12 \text{ in}}{1 \text{ ft}}\right)^2\left(\frac{2.54 \text{ cm}}{1 \text{ in}}\right)^3\left(\frac{1 \text{ mL}}{1 \text{ cm}^3}\right)\left(\frac{0.001}{\text{m}}\right) = 77092.6 = \mathbf{7.7 \times 10^4 \text{ L}}$$

Reality Check

The answer seems reasonable, the units are correct, and the significant figures are correct.

1.7 Applications and Extensions

1.87 Louis Pasteur made many significant discoveries, one of which was pasteurization. This process consists of heating a substance, such as milk, to kill the bacteria responsible for spoilage. Pasteurization of milk requires a temperature of 145°F. Determine the pasteurization temperature for milk in degrees Celsius and in kelvins.

Information

145°F, ? °C, ? K

Connections

°C = (5/9) (°F – 32°), K = °C + 273.15, and the rules for significant figures.

Solution

°C = (5/9) (°F – 32°) = (5/9) (145°F – 32°) = 62.77778 = **62.8°C**

K = °C + 273.15 = 62.77778 + 273.15 = 335.92778 = **335.9 K**

Reality Check

The numbers seem reasonable, the units are correct, and the significant figures are correct.

1.91 A sample of urine from a diabetic patient has a specific gravity of 1.020 (see section 1.7). Determine the mass in kilograms of 1.00 pint of this urine.

Information

Specific gravity = 1.020, and 1.00 pint = ? kg

Connections

The two SI prefixes (k = 1,000 and m = 10^{-3}), an English-to-SI conversion (1 L = 1.057 qt), an English-to-English conversion (1 qt = 2 pt), and the rules for significant figures.

Solution

The specific gravity is numerically equivalent to a density in terms of g/mL. This relationship simplifies the problem.

$$\left(\frac{1.020 \text{ g}}{\text{mL}}\right)\left(\frac{k}{1,000}\right)\left(\frac{m}{10^{-3}}\right)\left(\frac{1 \text{ L}}{1.0567 \text{ qt}}\right)\left(\frac{1 \text{ qt}}{2 \text{ pt}}\right)(1.00 \text{ pt}) = 0.4826 = \mathbf{0.483 \text{ kg}}$$

Reality Check

The answer seems reasonable, the units are correct, and the significant figures are correct.

1.93 Dissolving ammonium nitrate in water (see box 1.2, Hot Packs, Cold Packs, and MREs) is a convenient way to lower the water's temperature. The amount of heat absorbed by ammonium nitrate is 76.75 cal/g. How many kilojoules of heat will be absorbed when 1.750 oz of ammonium nitrate completely dissolves in water? (1 cal = 4.184 J)

Information
Heat absorbed by ammonium nitrate = 76.75 cal/g

? kilojoules of heat will be absorbed by 1.750 oz of ammonium nitrate (1 cal = 4.184 J)

Connections
In addition to the values given in the problem and the rules for significant figures, one English-to-SI conversion (28.35 g = 1 oz), and one SI prefix (k = 1,000) are needed.

Solution
This is an extended unit conversion problem.

$$\text{Heat} = (1.750 \text{ oz})\left(\frac{28.35 \text{ g}}{\text{oz}}\right)\left(\frac{76.75 \text{ cal}}{\text{g}}\right)\left(\frac{4.184 \text{ J}}{1 \text{ cal}}\right)\left(\frac{\text{k}}{1,000}\right) = 15.931 = \mathbf{15.93 \text{ kJ}}$$

Reality Check
The answer seems reasonable, the units are correct, and the significant figures are correct.

Putting It All Together
1.95 Round the following mass values to two significant figures, and round the length values to three significant figures: **(a)** 11.345 kg, **(b)** 122.22 km, **(c)** 10.7500 cm, **(d)** 6,000 g, **(e)** 5.280×10^3 μm

Solution
(a) Mass   **11 kg**, **(b)** Length   **122 km**, **(c)** Length   **10.8 cm**, **(d)** Mass   **6.0 × 10³ g**, **(e)** Length   **5.28 × 10³ μm**

1.97 In 1994, the United States produced 89.20 billion pounds of sulfuric acid. The density of this sulfuric acid was 1.84 g/mL.

(a) Determine the kilograms of sulfuric acid produced.

(b) Determine the gallons of sulfuric acid produced in 1994, considering that 1 L = 1.057 qt.

(c) Determine the cubic millimeters of sulfuric acid produced.

Information
89.20 billion pounds of sulfuric acid produced. Density of sulfuric acid = 1.84 g/mL.

(a) ? kilograms of sulfuric acid, **(b)** ? gallons of sulfuric acid, 1 L = 1.057 qt, **(c)** ? mm³ sulfuric acid

Connections
The following relationships must be used: SI prefixes (k = 1,000, m = 0.001, and c = 0.01), English-to-SI conversions (1 kg = 2.2046 lb and 1 L = 1.057 qt), English-English conversion (1 gal = 4 qt), and an SI-to-SI relationship (1 cm³ = 1 mL). In addition, the rules for significant figures must be applied.

Solution

(a) $(89.20 \times 10^9 \text{ lb}) \left(\dfrac{1 \text{ kg}}{2.2046 \text{ lb}} \right) = 4.04608 \times 10^{10} = \mathbf{4.046 \times 10^{10} \text{ kg}}$

(b) $(4.046 \times 10^{10} \text{ kg}) \left(\dfrac{1{,}000}{\text{k}} \right) \left(\dfrac{\text{mL}}{1.84 \text{ g}} \right) \left(\dfrac{0.001}{\text{m}} \right) \left(\dfrac{1.057 \text{ qt}}{\text{L}} \right) \left(\dfrac{1 \text{ gal}}{4 \text{ qt}} \right) = 5.8106 \times 10^9$

$$= \mathbf{5.81 \times 10^9 \text{ gal}}$$

(c) $(4.046 \times 10^{10} \text{ kg}) \left(\dfrac{1{,}000}{\text{k}} \right) \left(\dfrac{\text{mL}}{1.84 \text{ g}} \right) \left(\dfrac{1 \text{ cm}^3}{1 \text{ mL}} \right) \left(\dfrac{0.01}{\text{c}} \right)^3 \left(\dfrac{\text{m}}{0.001} \right)^3 = 2.1989 \times 10^{16}$

$$= \mathbf{2.20 \times 10^{16} \text{ mm}^3}$$

Reality Check

The numbers seem reasonable, the units are correct, and the significant figures are correct.

1.99 Many of the units in the English system are no longer in common use. Some examples are the palms (0.1666667 cubits), the rood (40 square perches), and the tun (4 hogsheads). **(a)** A cubit is 1.5 ft. How many centimeters are in 10.5 palms? **(b)** A square perch is 30.25 yd². How many square millimeters are in 3.25 roods? **(c)** A hogshead is 63 gal. How many cubic centimeters are in 4.2 tuns?

Information

Palms = 0.1666667 cubits, rood = 40 perches², tun = 4 hogsheads

(a) cubit = 1.5 ft   ? cm = 10.5 palms

(b) perch² = 30.25 yd²   ? mm² = 3.25 roods

(c) hogshead = 63 gal   ? cm³ = 4.2 tuns

Connections

The relationships given in the problem must be supplemented by a variety of other conversions. The additional conversions include SI-to-English (2.54 cm = 1 in and 1 L = 1.057 qt), SI-to-SI (1 dm³ = 1 L), English-to-English (1 ft = 12 in, 1 yd = 36 in, and 1 gal = 4 qt), and SI prefixes (c = 0.01, m = 0.001, and d = 0.1). In addition, the rules for significant figures must be applied.

Solution

(a) $(10.5 \text{ palms}) \left(\dfrac{0.16666667 \text{ cubits}}{1 \text{ palm}} \right) \left(\dfrac{1.5 \text{ ft}}{1 \text{ cubit}} \right) \left(\dfrac{12 \text{ in}}{1 \text{ ft}} \right) \left(\dfrac{2.54 \text{ cm}}{1 \text{ in}} \right) = 80.010 = \mathbf{80.0 \text{ cm}}$

(b) $(3.25 \text{ roods}) \left(\dfrac{40 \text{ perch}^2}{1 \text{ rood}} \right) \left(\dfrac{30.25 \text{ yd}^2}{1 \text{ perch}^2} \right) \left(\dfrac{36 \text{ in}}{\text{yd}} \right)^2 \left(\dfrac{2.54 \text{ cm}}{1 \text{ in}} \right)^2 \left(\dfrac{0.01}{\text{c}} \right)^2 \left(\dfrac{\text{m}}{0.001} \right)^2 = 3.288 \times 10^9$

$$= \mathbf{3.29 \times 10^9 \text{ mm}^2}$$

(c) $(4.2 \text{ tuns}) \left(\dfrac{4 \text{ hogshead}}{\text{tun}} \right) \left(\dfrac{63 \text{ gal}}{1 \text{ hogshead}} \right) \left(\dfrac{4 \text{ qt}}{\text{gal}} \right) \left(\dfrac{1 \text{ L}}{1.057 \text{ qt}} \right) \left(\dfrac{1 \text{ dm}^3}{1 \text{ L}} \right) \left(\dfrac{0.1}{\text{d}} \right)^3 \left(\dfrac{\text{c}}{0.01} \right)^3 = 4.005 \times 10^6$

$$= \mathbf{4.0 \times 10^6 \text{ cm}^3}$$

Reality Check

The numbers seem reasonable, the units are correct, and the significant figures are correct.

1.102 You have an irregular-shaped sample of an unknown metal. The sample weighs 15.68 g. To determine the volume of the sample, you carefully place it in a graduated cylinder that already contains 5.5 mL of water. The volume of the water plus metal in the graduated cylinder is 7.0 mL. Determine the density of the metal.

Information
Sample = 15.68 g. Initial volume of water = 5.5 mL. Volume of water + metal = 7.0 mL. Density of the metal = ?

Connections
The definition of *density* and the rules for significant figures.

Solution

$$\text{Density} = \frac{mass}{volume} = \frac{15.68 \text{ g}}{(7.0 - 5.5) \text{ mL}} = 10.453 = \mathbf{10. \text{ g/mL}}$$

Reality Check
The answer seems reasonable, the units are correct, and the significant figures are correct.

1.104 Calculate the thickness, in micrometers, of a piece of gold foil, given the following information: width = 3.27 in, length = 0.51 in, mass = 1.66×10^{-3} g, density = 19.3 g/cm^3

Information
Thickness = ? μm, width = 3.27 in, length = 0.51 in, mass = 1.66×10^{-3} g, density = 19.3 g/cm^3.

Connections
In addition to the information given in the problem, it is necessary to know one SI-to-English conversion (2.54 cm = 1 in) and two SI prefixes (c = 0.01 and μ = 10^{-6}). Also, the rules regarding significant figures must be applied.

Solution
This is an extended unit conversion problem. The first step converts the mass to a volume ($l \times w \times h$); therefore, dividing by the area ($l \times w$) leaves the height (h = thickness).

$$(1.66 \times 10^{-3} \text{ g})\left(\frac{cm^3}{19.3 \text{ g}}\right)\left(\frac{1}{(3.27 \times 0.51)in^2}\right)\left(\frac{1 \text{ in}}{2.54 \text{ cm}}\right)^2\left(\frac{0.01}{c}\right)\left(\frac{\mu}{10^{-6}}\right) = 0.07994 = \mathbf{0.080 \ \mu m}$$

Reality Check
The answer seems reasonable, the units are correct, and the significant figures are correct.

CHAPTER 2

Atoms

S uccessful completion of these problems requires the following nine (9) items.

1. The basic components of an atom are the proton, the neutron, and the electrons. Neutrons are slightly heavier than protons, and both neutrons and protons are significantly heavier than are electrons.

2. Protons are in the atomic nucleus, and the number of protons present is the **atomic number**. All atoms of an element have the same atomic number.

3. Neutrons are also in the atomic nucleus, and the number of protons plus the number of neutrons is the **mass number**. Variations in the number of neutrons lead to isotopes, which have different mass numbers.

4. The **atomic mass** is the weighted average of the masses of the isotopes.

5. The sum of the atomic masses of the elements gives the **molecular mass** or the **formula mass**.

6. The **periodic table** lists information on the elements in an organized manner. This table will be of use in this chapter, and in every other chapter and every other chemistry course.

7. Chemical changes (chemical reactions) may be described by chemical equations.

8. The naming of compounds is *chemical nomenclature*, which is important to all aspects of chemistry. The Nomenclature Resource covers all the nomenclature in this textbook.

9. Atoms and compounds are always neutral (for example, Na, Cl_2, and NaCl), while separated ions always have charges (for example, Na^+ and Cl^-).

Example Problems From the Text

Example Problem 2.1

A chemist performed an analysis on a series of three chlorine–oxygen compounds. She found them to contain the following amounts of chlorine and oxygen:

Compound	Mass of chlorine (g)	Mass of oxygen (g)
1	2.352	0.5307
2	2.593	1.755
3	2.752	4.347

(a) Calculate the grams of chlorine per gram of oxygen in each compound. **(b)** Divide each of the answers from part (a) by the smallest value. How do these results support the law of multiple proportions?

Information

(a) The table lists the mass of chlorine and the mass of oxygen in each compound. From this list we can calculate the grams of chlorine per gram of oxygen.

Connections

The law of multiple proportions indicates that there should be a certain kind of relationship between the grams of chlorine per gram of oxygen.

Solution

(a) Set up the appropriate ratios as grams of chlorine/grams of oxygen and divide to get the amount of chlorine per gram of oxygen:

Compound	Ratio
1	$\left(\dfrac{2.352 \text{ g Cl}}{0.5307 \text{ g O}}\right) = 4.43188 = 4.432 \text{ g Cl/g O}$
2	$\left(\dfrac{2.593 \text{ g Cl}}{1.755 \text{ g O}}\right) = 1.47749 = 1.477 \text{ g Cl/g O}$
3	$\left(\dfrac{2.752 \text{ g Cl}}{4.347 \text{ g O}}\right) = 0.633080 = 0.6331 \text{ g Cl/g O}$

(b) Use the ratios calculated in part (a) to determine if the law of multiple proportions relates to these substances. While there are various ways to do this, the easiest is to divide all the results by the smallest ratio. (Note: Use the unrounded ratios to avoid introducing errors by intermittent rounding. This does not alter the fact that the final answers will have only four significant figures.)

Compound	Ratio
1	$\left(\dfrac{4.43188}{0.633080}\right) = 7.0005 = \mathbf{7.000}$
2	$\left(\dfrac{1.47749}{0.633080}\right) = 2.33381 = \mathbf{2.334}$
3	$\left(\dfrac{0.633080}{0.633080}\right) = \mathbf{1.000}$

To eliminate the decimal fraction in compound 2 and make the relationship between the values easier to see, multiply each of the values by 3. The ratios are now 21:7:3. These whole-number relationships illustrate the law of multiple proportions.

Reality Check

The law of multiple proportions indicates that there should be a simple relation between the amounts of combining elements, and the results supports this.

Follow-Up Problem 2.1a

A scientist analyzed two different chlorine–oxygen compounds and found that they contained the following amounts of chlorine and oxygen:

Compound	Mass of chlorine (g)	Mass of oxygen (g)
1	2.840	2.563
2	2.115	2.386

(a) Calculate the grams of chlorine per gram of oxygen in each compound. (b) Divide each of the answers from part (a) by the smallest value. How do these results support the law of multiple proportions?

Information

(a) The table lists the mass of chlorine and the mass of oxygen in each compound. From this list we can calculate the grams of chlorine per gram of oxygen. (b) Divide each of the answers from part (a) by the smallest value. How do these results support the law of multiple proportions?

Connections

The law of multiple proportions indicates that there should be a certain kind of relationship between the grams of chlorine per gram of oxygen.

Solution

(a) Set up the appropriate ratios as grams of chlorine/grams of oxygen and divide to get the amount of chlorine per gram of oxygen:

Compound	Ratio
1	$\left(\dfrac{2.840 \text{ g Cl}}{2.563 \text{ g O}}\right) = 1.108076 = 1.108 \text{ g Cl/g O}$
2	$\left(\dfrac{2.115 \text{ g Cl}}{2.386 \text{ g O}}\right) = 0.886421 = 0.8864 \text{ g Cl/g O}$

(b) Use the ratios calculated in part (a) to determine if the law of multiple proportions relates these substances. While there are various ways of doing this, the easiest is to divide the results by the smaller ratio. (Note: Use the unrounded ratios to avoid introducing errors by intermittent rounding. This does not alter the fact that the final answers will only have four significant figures.

Compound	Ratio
1	$\left(\dfrac{1.108076}{0.886421}\right) = 1.250056 = \mathbf{1.250}$
2	$\left(\dfrac{0.886421}{0.886421}\right) = \mathbf{1.000}$

To eliminate the decimal fraction in compound 1 and make the relationship between the values easier to see, multiply each of the values by 4. The ratios are now 5:4. These whole-number relationships illustrate the law of multiple proportions.

Reality Check
The law of multiple proportions indicates that there should be a simple relation between the amounts of combining elements, and the results support this.

Follow-Up Problem 2.1b
Carbon forms two compounds when it reacts with oxygen. In one compound, there are 1.332 g of oxygen for every gram of carbon, and in the other compound, there are 2.664 g of oxygen for every gram of carbon. Show how these compounds are consistent with the law of multiple proportions.

Information
Carbon forms two compounds with oxygen. In one compound, there are 1.332 g of oxygen for every gram of carbon, and in the other compound, there are 2.664 g of oxygen for every gram of carbon.

Connections
The law of multiple proportions indicates that there should be a certain kind of relationship between the grams of chlorine per gram of oxygen.

Solution
Set up the appropriate ratios as grams of oxygen/grams of carbon and divide to get the amount of oxygen per gram of carbon:

Compound	Ratio
1	$\left(\dfrac{1.332 \text{ g O}}{\text{g C}}\right) = 1.332$ g O/g C
2	$\left(\dfrac{2.664 \text{ g O}}{\text{g C}}\right) = 2.664$ g O/g C

(b) Use the ratios calculated in part (a) to determine if the law of multiple proportions relates these substances. While there are various ways of doing this, the easiest is to divide the results by the smaller ratio.

Compound	Ratio
1	$\left(\dfrac{1.332}{1.332}\right) = \textbf{1.000}$
2	$\left(\dfrac{2.664}{1.332}\right) = \textbf{2.000}$

These whole-number relationships illustrate the law of multiple proportions.

Reality Check
The law of multiple proportions indicates that there should be a simple relation between the amounts of combining elements, and the results support this.

Example Problem 2.2
Determine the numbers of protons, electrons, and neutrons in $^{81}_{36}\text{Kr}$, $^{142}_{57}\text{La}$, and $^{15}_{6}\text{C}$.

Information

We have the full isotopic symbols of three elements.

Connections

From the subscripts and superscripts on the isotopic symbols, we can find the numbers of protons and neutrons. Since the chemical species are neutral, the number of electrons must equal the number of protons. (Note that the mass number is not the same as the atomic mass; therefore, the mass numbers do not need to match the atomic masses reported on the periodic table.)

Solution

The subscript (atomic number) indicates the number of protons, and for neutral atoms (not ions) this is also the number of electrons. The superscript (mass number, A) minus the subscript (atomic number, Z) gives the number of neutrons (A–Z).

Isotope	Protons	Electrons	Neutrons
$^{81}_{36}\text{Kr}$	36	36	45
$^{142}_{57}\text{La}$	57	57	85
$^{15}_{6}\text{C}$	6	6	9

Reality Check

Locate each of the chemical symbols on the periodic table. The atomic number provided on the table must match the number of protons found. For atoms, such as the examples in this problem, Protons = Electrons. The number of protons plus the number of neutrons should add up to the mass number (superscript in the symbol).

Follow-Up Problem 2.2a

Determine the number of protons, electrons, and neutrons in $^{41}_{19}\text{K}$, $^{162}_{66}\text{Dy}$, and $^{10}_{5}\text{B}$.

Information

We have the full isotopic symbols of three elements.

Connections

From the subscripts and superscripts on the isotopic symbols, we can find the numbers of protons and neutrons. Since the chemical species are neutral, the number of electrons must equal the number of protons. (Note that the mass number is not the same as the atomic mass; therefore, the mass numbers do not need to match the atomic masses reported on the periodic table.)

Solution

The subscript (atomic number) indicates the number of protons, and for neutral atoms (not ions) this is also the number of electrons. The superscript (mass number, A) minus the subscript (atomic number, Z) gives the number of neutrons (A–Z).

Isotope	Protons	Electrons	Neutrons
$^{41}_{19}\text{K}$	19	19	22
$^{162}_{66}\text{Dy}$	66	66	96
$^{10}_{5}\text{B}$	5	5	5

Reality Check

Locate each of the chemical symbols on the periodic table. The atomic number provided on the table must match the number of protons found. For atoms, such as the examples in this problem, Protons = Electrons. The number of protons plus the number of neutrons should add up to the mass number (superscript in the symbol).

Follow-Up Problem 2.2b

Determine the number of protons, electrons, and neutrons in $^{223}_{87}\text{Fr}$, ^{56}Fe, and fluorine-18.

Information

We have the full isotopic symbols of three elements; however, one is in a different form.

Connections

From the subscripts and superscripts on the isotopic symbols, we can find the numbers of protons and neutrons. Since the chemical species are neutral, the number of electrons must equal the number of protons. (Note, the mass number is not the same as the atomic mass; therefore, the mass numbers do not need to match the atomic masses reported on the periodic table.)

Solution

The subscript (atomic number) indicates the number of protons, and for neutral atoms (not ions), this is also the number of electrons. It is necessary to look on the periodic table to find the atomic numbers of Fe and fluorine. The superscript (mass number, A) minus the subscript (atomic number, Z) gives the number of neutrons ($A–Z$).

Isotope	Protons	Electrons	Neutrons
$^{223}_{87}\text{Fr}$	87	87	136
^{56}Fe	26	26	30
Fluorine-18	9	9	9

Reality Check

Locate each of the chemical symbols on the periodic table. The atomic number provided on the table must match the number of protons found. For atoms, such as the examples in this problem, Protons = Electrons. The number of protons plus the number of neutrons should add up to the mass number (superscript in the symbol).

Example Problem 2.3

Determine the number of protons, electrons, and neutrons in $^{40}_{19}\text{K}^+$, $^{87}_{39}\text{Y}^{3+}$ and $^{30}_{15}\text{P}^{3-}$.

Information

We have the isotopic symbols that include a subscript on the left and two superscripts.

Connections

From the isotopic symbol, we can find the relationship between the number of protons and the number of neutrons. Using the magnitude and type of charge (the superscripts to the right), we can determine the number of electrons present. For anions, each negative charge represents the gain of an electron, and for cations, each positive charge represents the loss of an electron.

Solution

The subscript indicates the number of protons. An atom has the same number of electrons as protons; however, this is not true for ions. A positive charge indicates the number of electrons removed from the neutral atom, and a negative charge indicates the number of electrons added. The mass number (superscript preceding the element symbol) minus the atomic number (subscript) gives the number of neutrons.

Isotope	Protons	Electrons	Neutrons
$^{40}_{19}K^+$	19	$19 - 1 = 18$	$40 - 19 = 21$
$^{87}_{39}Y^{3+}$	39	$39 - 3 = 36$	$87 - 39 = 48$
$^{30}_{15}P^{3-}$	15	$15 + 3 = 18$	$30 - 15 = 15$

Reality Check

Locate each of the chemical symbols on the periodic table. The atomic number presented there should match the number of protons in our answer. For ions, such as the examples in this problem, Protons – Electrons = Charge. The number of protons plus the number of neutrons should add up to the mass number (superscript in the symbol).

Follow-Up Problem 2.3a

Determine the number of protons, electrons, and neutrons in $^{41}_{20}Ca^{2+}$, $^{128}_{52}Te^{2-}$, and $^{35}_{17}Cl^-$.

Information

We have the isotopic symbols that include a subscript on the left and two superscripts.

Connections

From the isotopic symbol, we can find the relationship between the number of protons and neutrons. Using the magnitude and type of charge (the superscripts to the right), we can determine the number of electrons present. For anions, each negative charge represents the gain of an electron, and for cations, each positive charge represents the loss of an electron.

Solution

The subscript indicates the number of protons. An atom has the same number of electrons as protons; however, this is not true for ions. A positive charge indicates the number of electrons removed from the neutral atom, and a negative charge indicates the number of electrons added. The mass number (superscript preceding the element symbol) minus the atomic number (subscript) gives the number of neutrons.

Isotope	Protons	Electrons	Neutrons
$^{41}_{20}Ca^{2+}$	20	18	21
$^{128}_{52}Te^{2-}$	52	54	76
$^{35}_{17}Cl^-$	17	18	18

Reality Check

Locate each of the chemical symbols on the periodic table. The atomic number presented there should match the number of protons in our answer. For ions, such as the examples in this problem, Protons – Electrons = Charge. The number of protons plus the number of neutrons should add up to the mass number (superscript in the symbol).

Follow-Up Problem 2.3b

Determine the number of protons, electrons, and neutrons in $^{51}_{24}Cr^{6+}$, $^{56}Fe^{3+}$, and $^{200}_{78}Pt^{4+}$.

Information

We have the isotopic symbols that include a subscript on the left and two superscripts.

Connections

From the isotopic symbol, we can find the relationship between the number of protons and neutrons. Using the magnitude and type of charge (the superscripts to the right), we can determine the number of electrons present. For anions, each negative charge represents the gain of an electron, and for cations, each positive charge represents the loss of an electron. It is necessary to look on the periodic table to find the atomic number of Fe.

Solution

The subscript indicates the number of protons. An atom has the same number of electrons as protons; however, this is not true for ions. A positive charge indicates the number of electrons removed from the neutral atom, and a negative charge indicates the number of electrons added. The mass number (superscript preceding the element symbol) minus the atomic number (subscript) gives the number of neutrons.

Isotope	Protons	Electrons	Neutrons
$^{51}_{24}\text{Cr}^{6+}$	24	18	27
$^{56}_{26}\text{Fe}^{3+}$	26	23	30
$^{200}_{78}\text{Pt}^{4+}$	78	74	122

Reality Check

Locate each of the chemical symbols on the periodic table. The atomic number presented there should match the number of protons in our answer. For ions, such as the examples in this problem, Protons – Electrons = Charge. The number of protons plus the number of neutrons should add up to the mass number (superscript in the symbol).

Example Problem 2.4

Fill in the blanks in the following table:

	$^{25}_{12}\text{Mg}^{2+}$	$^{15}_{7}\text{N}^{3-}$			
Protons			45	13	53
Neutrons				14	
Electrons				10	
Charge			2+		1–
Mass Number			102		127

Information

Clues are present in the table above and in the periodic table.

Connections

From the isotopic symbol, we can find the numbers of protons and neutrons, and vice versa.

Solution

The subscript in the symbol indicates the number of protons, and the number of protons identifies the element. We can then incorporate this information (shown below in bold) into the above table:

	$^{25}_{12}\text{Mg}^{2+}$	$^{15}_{7}\text{N}^{3-}$	$^{102}_{45}\text{Rh}^{2+}$	$^{27}_{13}\text{Al}^{3+}$	$^{127}_{53}\text{I}^{-}$
Protons	**12**	**7**	**45**	**13**	**53**

The mass number (left superscript) minus the atomic number (subscript) gives the number of neutrons. Incorporating this information, gives the following:

	$^{25}_{12}Mg^{2+}$	$^{15}_{7}N^{3-}$	$^{102}_{45}Rh^{2+}$	$^{27}_{13}Al^{3+}$	$^{127}_{53}I^{-}$
Protons	12	7	45	13	53
Neutrons	13	8	57	14	74

If these were atoms instead of ions, the number of electrons would equal the number of protons. For positive ions, remove a number of electrons equal to the charge. For negative ions, add a number of electrons equal to the charge. This allows us to make the following additions to the table:

	$^{25}_{12}Mg^{2+}$	$^{15}_{7}N^{3-}$	$^{102}_{45}Rh^{2+}$	$^{27}_{13}Al^{3+}$	$^{127}_{53}I^{-}$
Protons	12	7	45	13	53
Neutrons	13	8	57	14	74
Electrons	10	10	43	10	54
Charge	2+	3−	2+	3+	1−

The left superscript, or the sum of the protons plus the neutrons, is the mass number:

	$^{25}_{12}Mg^{2+}$	$^{15}_{7}N^{3-}$	$^{102}_{45}Rh^{2+}$	$^{27}_{13}Al^{3+}$	$^{127}_{53}I^{-}$
Protons	12	7	45	13	53
Neutrons	13	8	57	14	74
Electrons	10	10	43	10	54
Charge	2+	3−	2+	3+	1−
Mass Number	25	15	102	27	127

Reality Check
Locate each of the chemical symbols on the periodic table. The given atomic number should match the number of protons found. For ions, such as the examples in this problem, Protons − Electrons = Charge. The number of protons plus the number of neutrons should add up to the mass number (superscript in the symbol).

Follow-Up Problem 2.4a
Fill in the blanks in the following table:

	$^{88}_{38}Sr^{2+}$	$^{74}_{33}As^{3-}$			
Protons			21	14	35
Neutrons				14	
Electrons				10	
Charge				3+	1−
Mass Number			45		81

Information
Clues are present in the table above and in the periodic table.

Connections
From the isotopic symbol, we can find the numbers of protons and neutrons, and vice versa.

Solution

The subscript in the symbol indicates the number of protons, and the number of protons identifies the element. We can then incorporate this information into the above table:

	$_{38}^{88}Sr^{2+}$	$_{33}^{74}As^{3-}$	$_{21}^{45}Sc^{3+}$	$_{14}^{28}Si^{4+}$	$_{35}^{81}Br^{-}$
Protons	38	33	21	14	35
Neutrons	50	41	24	14	46
Electrons	36	36	18	10	36
Charge	2+	3–	3+	4+	1–
Mass Number	88	74	45	28	81

Reality Check

Locate each of the chemical symbols on the periodic table. The given atomic number should match the number of protons found. For ions, such as the examples in this problem, Protons – Electrons = Charge. The number of protons plus the number of neutrons should add up to the mass number (superscript in the symbol).

Follow-Up Problem 2.4b

Fill in the blanks in the following table:

	$_{63}^{152}Eu^{2+}$	$_{11}^{23}Na^{-}$			
Protons			6	50	16
Neutrons					17
Electrons				48	
Charge			4+		2–
Mass Number			13	118	

Information

Clues are present in the table above and in the periodic table.

Connections

From the isotopic symbol, we can find the numbers of protons and neutrons, and vice versa.

Solution

	$_{63}^{152}Eu^{2+}$	$_{11}^{23}Na^{-}$	$_{6}^{13}C^{4+}$	$_{50}^{118}Sn^{2+}$	$_{16}^{33}S^{2-}$
Protons	63	11	6	50	16
Neutrons	89	12	7	68	17
Electrons	61	12	2	48	18
Charge	2+	1–	4+	2+	2–
Mass Number	152	23	13	118	33

Reality Check

Locate each of the chemical symbols on the periodic table. The given atomic number should match the number of protons found. For ions, such as the examples in this problem, Protons – Electrons = Charge. The number of protons plus the number of neutrons should add up to the mass number (superscript in the symbol).

Example Problem 2.5

There are two naturally occurring isotopes of the element boron, B. The masses and the percent abundances of each of the isotopes are listed below.

Isotope	Mass (amu)	Abundance (%)
Boron-10	10.0129371	19.9
Boron-11	11.0093055	80.1

Determine the atomic mass of boron from these data.

Information

The masses of the isotopes and the abundance of each isotope are given. We need to find the atomic mass (weighted average). (It is very important to keep the mass paired with the correct abundance.)

Connections

The weighted average mass is the sum of the individual contribution of each isotope.

Solution

Determine the contribution of each isotope to the weighted atomic mass by multiplying the mass of each isotope by its abundance. The significant figures for each calculation are underlined. Based on the significant figure rules for addition and subtraction, the final answer should have two digits past the decimal point:

$$^{10}\text{B} \qquad (10.0129371 \text{ amu})\left(\frac{19.9\%}{100\%}\right) = 1.992574 \text{ amu}$$

$$^{11}\text{B} \qquad (11.0093055 \text{ amu})\left(\frac{80.1\%}{100\%}\right) = 8.818454 \text{ amu}$$

$$\text{Total} = 10.811028 \text{ amu}$$
$$= \mathbf{10.81 \text{ amu}}$$

Reality Check

Examination of the periodic table shows that all atomic masses are between 1 and 300. This answer falls in that range. The value provided for boron (B) on the periodic table should be near this calculated value (variations in data obtained from different sources lead to slight differences in calculated values).

Follow-Up Problem 2.5a

There are five naturally occurring isotopes of the element titanium, Ti. The masses and the percent abundances of each of the isotopes are listed below:

Isotope	Mass (amu)	Abundance (%)
Titanium-46	45.952630	8.25
Titanium-47	46.951764	7.44
Titanium-48	47.947947	73.72
Titanium-49	48.947871	5.41
Titanium-50	49.944792	5.18

Determine the atomic mass of titanium from this data.

Information

The masses of the isotopes and the abundance of each isotope are given. We need to find the atomic mass (weighted average). (It is very important to keep the mass paired with the correct abundance.)

Connections

The weighted average mass is the sum of the individual contribution of each isotope.

Solution

Determine the contribution of each isotope to the weighted atomic mass by multiplying the mass of each isotope by its abundance. The significant figures for each calculation are underlined. Based on the significant figure rules for addition and subtraction, the final answer should have two digits past the decimal point.

^{46}Ti $\quad (45.952630 \text{ amu})\left(\dfrac{8.25\%}{100\%}\right) = \underline{3.79}092 \text{ amu}$

^{47}Ti $\quad (46.951764 \text{ amu})\left(\dfrac{7.44\%}{100\%}\right) = \underline{3.49}321 \text{ amu}$

^{48}Ti $\quad (47.947947 \text{ amu})\left(\dfrac{73.72\%}{100\%}\right) = \underline{35.34}723 \text{ amu}$

^{49}Ti $\quad (48.947871 \text{ amu})\left(\dfrac{5.41\%}{100\%}\right) = \underline{2.64}808 \text{ amu}$

^{50}Ti $\quad (49.944792 \text{ amu})\left(\dfrac{5.18\%}{100\%}\right) = \underline{2.58}714 \text{ amu}$

$$\text{Total} = \underline{47.86}658 \text{ amu}$$
$$= \textbf{47.87 amu}$$

Reality Check

Examination of the periodic table shows that all atomic masses are between 1 and 300. This answer falls in that range. The value provided for titanium (Ti) on the periodic table should be near this calculated value (variations in data obtained from different sources lead to slight differences in calculated values).

Follow-Up Problem 2.5b

Chromium occurs in nature as a mixture of four isotopes. The masses and abundances of these isotopes are ^{50}Cr: 49.946050 amu, 4.345%; ^{52}Cr: 51.940512 amu, 83.789%; ^{53}Cr: 52.940653 amu, 9.501%; and ^{54}Cr: 53.938885 amu, 2.365%. Determine the atomic mass of chromium from these data.

Information

The masses of the isotopes and the abundance of each isotope are given. We need to find the atomic mass (weighted average). (It is very important to keep the mass paired with the correct abundance.)

Connections

The weighted average mass is the sum of the individual contribution of each isotope.

Solution

Determine the contribution of each isotope to the weighted atomic mass by multiplying the mass of each isotope by its abundance. The significant figures for each calculation are underlined. Based on the significant figure rules for addition and subtraction, the final answer should have three digits past the decimal point.

$$^{50}Cr \quad (49.946050 \text{ amu})\left(\frac{4.345\%}{100\%}\right) = \underline{2.170}1559 \text{ amu}$$

$$^{52}Cr \quad (51.940512 \text{ amu})\left(\frac{83.789\%}{100\%}\right) = \underline{43.520}436 \text{ amu}$$

$$^{53}Cr \quad (52.940653 \text{ amu})\left(\frac{9.501\%}{100\%}\right) = \underline{5.029}8914 \text{ amu}$$

$$^{54}Cr \quad (53.938885 \text{ amu})\left(\frac{2.365\%}{100\%}\right) = \underline{1.275}6546 \text{ amu}$$

$$\text{Total} = \underline{51.996}1379 \text{ amu}$$
$$= \textbf{51.996 amu}$$

Reality Check

Examination of the periodic table shows that all atomic masses are between 1 and 300. This answer falls in that range. The value provided for chromium (Cr) on the periodic table should be near this calculated value (variations in data obtained from different sources lead to slight differences in calculated values).

Example Problem 2.6

The atomic mass of thallium, Tl, is 204.3833 amu. Natural thallium consists of two isotopes: thallium-203 and thallium-205. The mass of a thallium-203 atom is 202.972329 amu, and the mass of a thallium-205 atom is 204.974412 amu. Determine the percent abundance of each isotope.

Information

We have the mass of each isotope and the atomic mass of thallium from which to calculate the percent of thallium-203 and the percent of thallium-205.

Connections

The total percent abundance must be 100%, and the contributions from each isotope must add up to the atomic mass.

Solution

Let x % = percentage of thallium-203 and y % = percentage of thallium-205.
We need two important relationships:

1. $x \% + y \% = 100\%$ (The total of all isotopes must be exactly 100%.)
2. $(202.972329 \text{ amu})\left(\dfrac{x \%}{100\%}\right) + (204.974412 \text{ amu})\left(\dfrac{y \%}{100\%}\right) = 204.3833 \text{ amu}$

Simplifying by factoring out the 100% gives the following:

1. $x + y = 1$ (This 1 is an exact number.)
2. $(202.972329 \text{ amu}) (x) + (204.974412 \text{ amu}) (y) = 204.3833 \text{ amu}$

Solving equation (1) for x gives $x = 1 - y$.

Then substitute for x in equation (2):
$(202.972329 \text{ amu}) (1 - y) + (204.974412 \text{ amu}) (y) = 204.3833 \text{ amu}$
Multiplying gives
$202.972329 \text{ amu} - (202.972329 \text{ amu}) y + (204.974412 \text{ amu}) (y) = 204.3833 \text{ amu}$

Rearranging gives

$$[(204.974412 - 202.972329) \text{ amu}] \, y = (204.3833 - 202.972329) \text{ amu}$$

Then,

$$y = [(204.3833 - 202.972329) \text{ amu}] \, / \, [(204.974412 - 202.972329) \text{ amu}]$$

$$= \left(\frac{1.410971 \text{ amu}}{2.2002083 \text{ amu}} \right) = 0.704751501$$

$$= 0.70475$$

From earlier,

$$x = 1 - y = 1 - 0.704751501 = 0.295248498 = 0.29525$$

These two answers are decimal answers. To convert the answers to percentage answers, multiply the decimal values by 100%:

$$x = (0.29525)(100\%) = \textbf{29.525\%} \; ^{203}\textbf{Tl}$$
$$y = (0.70475)(100\%) = \textbf{70.475\%} \; ^{205}\textbf{Tl}$$

Reality Check

The values do total 100%. The contribution from thallium-205 is greater than that of thallium-203, so the atomic mass should be closer to the mass of thallium-205 than to thallium-203.

Follow-Up Problem 2.6a

The atomic mass of iridium, Ir, is 192.217 amu. Natural iridium consists of two isotopes: iridium-191 and iridium-193. The mass of an iridium-191 atom is 190.960591 amu, and the mass of an iridium-193 atom is 192.962923 amu. Determine the percent abundance of each isotope.

Information

We have the mass of each isotope and the atomic mass of iridium from which to calculate the percent iridium-191 and percent iridium-193.

Connections

The total percent abundance must be 100%, and the contributions from each isotope must add up to the atomic mass.

Solution

Let x % = percentage of iridium-191 and y % = percentage of iridium-193.
We need two important relationships:

1. $x \% + y \% = 100\%$ (The total of all isotopes must be exactly 100%.)
2. $(190.960591 \text{ amu}) \left(\dfrac{x\%}{100\%} \right) + (192.962923 \text{ amu}) \left(\dfrac{y\%}{100\%} \right) = 192.217 \text{ amu}$

Simplifying by factoring out the 100% gives

1. $x + y = 1$ (This 1 is an exact number.)
2. $(190.960591 \text{ amu}) \, (x) + (192.962923 \text{ amu}) \, (y) = 192.217 \text{ amu}$

Solving equation (1) for x gives $x = 1 - y$.
Then substitute for x in (2):

$$(190.960591 \text{ amu}) \, (1 - y) + (192.962923 \text{ amu}) \, (y) = 192.217 \text{ amu}$$

Multiplying gives

$$190.960591 \text{ amu} - (190.960591 \text{ amu}) \, y + (192.962923 \text{ amu}) \, (y) = 192.217 \text{ amu}$$

Rearranging gives

$$[(192.962923 - 190.960591) \text{ amu}] \, y = (192.217 - 190.960591) \text{ amu}$$

Then,

$$y = [(192.217 - 190.960591)\ \text{amu}] / [(192.962923 - 190.960591)\ \text{amu}]$$

$$= \left(\frac{1.256409\ \text{amu}}{2.002332\ \text{amu}}\right) = 0.627472867 = 0.6275$$

From earlier,

$$x = 1 - y = 1 - 0.627472867 = 0.372527133 = 0.3725$$

These two answers are decimal answers. To convert the answers to percentage answers, multiply the decimal values by 100%:

$$x = (0.3725)\ (100\%) = \textbf{37.25\% }^{191}\textbf{Ir}$$
$$y = (0.6275)\ (100\%) = \textbf{62.75\% }^{193}\textbf{Ir}$$

Reality Check

The values do total 100%. The contribution from iridium-193 is greater than that of iridium-191, so the atomic mass should be closer to the mass of iridium-193 than to iridium-191.

Follow-Up Problem 2.6b

Natural rhenium consists of ^{185}Re and ^{187}Re only. The atomic mass of rhenium is 186.207 amu, and the masses of the isotopes are 184.952955 amu and 186.955751 amu, respectively. Determine the percent abundance of each isotope.

Information

We have the mass of each isotope and the atomic mass of rhenium from which to calculate the percent of rhenium-185 and the percent of rhenium-187.

Connections

The total percent abundance must be 100%, and the contributions from each isotope must add up to the atomic mass.

Solution

Let x % = percentage of rhenium-185 and y % = percentage of rhenium-187.
We need two important relationships:

1. x % + y % = 100%   (The total of all isotopes must be exactly 100%.)
2. $(184.952955\ \text{amu})\left(\dfrac{x\ \%}{100\%}\right) + (186.955751\ \text{amu})\left(\dfrac{y\ \%}{100\%}\right) = 186.207\ \text{amu}$

Simplifying by factoring out the 100% gives

1. $x + y = 1$ (This 1 is an exact number.)
2. $(184.952955\ \text{amu})\ (x) + (186.955751\ \text{amu})\ (y) = 186.207\ \text{amu}$

Solving equation (1) for x gives $x = 1 - y$.
Then substitute for x in (2):

$$(184.952955\ \text{amu})\ (1 - y) + (186.955751\ \text{amu})\ (y) = 186.207\ \text{amu}$$

Multiplying gives

$$184.952955\ \text{amu} - (184.952955\ \text{amu})\ y + (186.955751\ \text{amu})\ (y) = 186.207\ \text{amu}$$

Rearranging gives

$$[(186.955751 - 184.952955)\ \text{amu}]\ y = (186.2073 - 184.952955)\ \text{amu}$$

Then,

$$y = [(186.207 - 184.952955)\ \text{amu}] / [(186.955751 - 184.952955)\ \text{amu}]$$

$$= \left(\frac{1.254045\ \text{amu}}{2.002796\ \text{amu}}\right) = 0.6261471 = 0.6261$$

From earlier,

$$x = 1 - y = 1 - 0.6261471 = 0.37385285 = 0.3739$$

These two answers are decimal answers. To convert the answers to percentage answers, multiply the decimal values by 100%:

$$x = (0.3739)(100\%) = \textbf{37.39\%} \ ^{185}\textbf{Re}$$
$$y = (0.6261)(100\%) = \textbf{62.61\%} \ ^{187}\textbf{Re}$$

Reality Check
The values do total 100%. The contribution from rhenium-187 is greater than that of rhenium-185, so the atomic mass should be closer to the mass of rhenium-187 than to rhenium-185.

Example Problem 2.7
Determine the formula mass for each of the following substances: (a) carbon monoxide, CO; (b) aluminum bromide, $AlBr_3$; (c) sucrose (cane sugar), $C_{12}H_{22}O_{11}$

Information
We are given the formula of each substance, and we need to determine its formula mass. We can get the atomic mass for each of the elements in the formulas from the periodic table: C = 12.0107 amu; O = 15.9994 amu; Al = 26.981538 amu; Br = 79.904 amu; H = 1.00794 amu

Connections
The chemical formulas connect the atomic masses to the formula masses.

Solution
For each compound, multiply the atomic mass of each component element by the number of atoms of that type (subscript) in the compound. Then add together all the results for the compound. Finally, round the total to the proper number of significant figures.

(a) C + O = 12.0107 amu + 15.9994 amu = **28.0101 amu**

(b) Al + 3 Br = 26.981538 amu + 3 (79.904 amu) = 266.693538 = **266.694 amu**

(c) 12 C + 22 H + 11 O = 12 (12.0107 amu) + 22 (1.00794 amu) + 11 (15.9994 amu) = 342.29648 = **342.2965 amu**

Reality Check
All formula masses must be greater than or equal to the mass of hydrogen. In general, unless very large molecules are under consideration, the masses will be less than 500 amu.

Follow-Up Problem 2.7a
Determine the formula mass for each of the following substances: (a) nitrogen oxide, NO; (b) calcium bromide, $CaBr_2$; (c) glycerin, $C_3H_8O_3$

Information
We are given the formula of each substance, and we need to determine its formula mass. We can get the atomic mass for each of the elements in the formulas from the periodic table: N = 14.007 amu; C = 12.0107 amu; O = 15.9994 amu; Ca = 40.078 amu; Br = 79.904 amu; H = 1.00794 amu

Connections
The chemical formulas connect the atomic masses to the formula masses.

Solution

(a) $N + O = 14.007$ amu $+ 15.9994$ amu $= 30.0064 = $ **30.006 amu**

(b) $Ca + 2 Br = 40.078$ amu $+ 2 (79.904$ amu$) = $ **199.886 amu**

(c) $3 C + 8 H + 3 O = 3 (12.0107$ amu$) + 8 (1.00794$ amu$) + 3 (15.9994$ amu$) = 92.09382 = $ **92.0938 amu**

Reality Check

All formula masses must be greater than or equal to the mass of hydrogen. In general, unless very large molecules are under consideration, the masses will be less than 500 amu.

Follow-Up Problem 2.7b

Determine the formula mass for each of the following substances: **(a)** dinitrogen pentoxide, N_2O_5; **(b)** aluminum sulfate, $Al_2(SO_4)_3$; **(c)** trinitrotoluene (TNT), $C_7H_5N_3O_6$

Information

We are given the formula of each substance, and we need to determine its formula mass. We can get the atomic mass for each of the elements in the formulas from the periodic table: $N = 14.007$ amu; $C = 12.0107$ amu; $O = 15.9994$ amu; $Al = 26.981538$ amu; $S = 32.065$ amu; $H = 1.00794$ amu

Connections

The chemical formulas connect the atomic masses to the formula masses.

Solution

(a) $2 N + 5 O = 2(14.007$ amu$) + 5(15.9994$ amu$) = 108.0110 = $ **108.011 amu**

(b) $2 Al + 3 S + 12 O = 2 (26.981538$ amu$) + 3 (32.065$ amu$) + 12 (15.9994$ amu$) = 342.150876 = $ **342.151 amu**

(c) $7 C + 5 H + 3 N + 6 O = 7 (12.0107$ amu$) + 5 (1.00794$ amu$) + 3 (14.007$ amu$) + 6 (15.9994$ amu$) = 227.1296 = $ **227.130 amu**

Reality Check

All formula masses must be greater than or equal to the mass of hydrogen. In general, unless very large molecules are under consideration, the masses will be less than 500 amu.

Example Problem 2.8

Convert each of the following formulas to an empirical formula: **(a)** dinitrogen tetroxide, N_2O_4; **(b)** dinitrogen pentoxide, N_2O_5; **(c)** glucose, or blood sugar, $C_6H_{12}O_6$

Information

The chemical formulas are given; we need to determine the empirical formulas.

Connections

For many compounds, the chemical formula is a multiple of the empirical formula.

Solution

Examine the subscripts to see if there is any common whole-number factor. In part **(a)**, the subscript values are both even, so we can divide by two. Part **(b)** has no factor, so only division by one is possible. In part **(c)**, the largest divisor is six; this gives **(a)** NO_2, **(b)** N_2O_5, **(c)** CH_2O.

Reality Check
Any further reduction of the formulas would result in non-integer subscripts.

Follow-Up Problem 2.8a
Convert each of the following molecular formulas to an empirical formula: (a) tetraphosphorus decaoxide, P_4O_{10}; (b) disulfur decafluoride, S_2F_{10}; (c) dichlorine heptoxide, Cl_2O_7

Information
The chemical formulas are given; we need to determine the empirical formulas.

Connections
For many compounds, the chemical formula is a multiple of the empirical formula.

Solution
Examine the subscripts to see if there is any common whole-number factor. In part (a), the subscript values are both even, so we can divide by two. In part (b), the subscript values are both even, so we can divide by two. In part (c), there is no common factor. This gives (a) P_2O_5, (b) SF_5, (c) Cl_2O_7.

Reality Check
Any further reduction of the formulas would result in non-integer subscripts.

Follow-Up Problem 2.8b
Convert each of the following molecular formulas to an empirical formula: (a) acetylene, C_2H_2; (b) cyclobutadiene, C_4H_4; (c) benzene, C_6H_6

Information
The chemical formulas are given; we need to determine the empirical formulas.

Connections
For many compounds, the chemical formula is a multiple of the empirical formula.

Solution
Examine the subscripts to see if there is any common whole-number factor. In part (a), the subscript values are both two, so we can divide by two. In part (b), the subscript values are both four, so we can divide by four. In part (c), the subscript values are both six, so we can divide by six. This gives (a) CH, (b) CH, (c) CH.

Reality Check
Any further reduction of the formulas would result in non-integer subscripts.

Example Problem 2.9
Using **tables 2.2, 2.3,** and **2.4** or the Nomenclature Resource, combine the following ions to produce a compound; then name each compound: (a) Na^+ and Br^-, (b) Mg^{2+} and SO_4^{2-}, (c) NH_4^+ and NO_3^-, (d) O^{2-} and Al^{3+}, (e) Ca^{2+} and $C_2H_3O_2^-$

Information
We have pairs of ion formulas, showing the elements they consist of and their charges. We need to find the chemical formula and name.

Connections

The total charge for any compound must be 0 (zero).

Solution

The cation (positive ion) always goes first in both the name and the chemical formula. To name the compounds, locate the names of the ions on the appropriate table or in the Nomenclature Resource. We drop the word *ion* from those names when we combine them to name an ionic compound.

(a) Na^+ and Br^-: The charges are equal but opposite, so combining one of each ion will give a total charge of 0. The positive ion goes first in the formula: NaBr. Because Na^+ is the sodium ion and Br^- is the bromide ion, combining the names and removing the word *ion* gives **sodium bromide**.

(b) Mg^{2+} and SO_4^{2-}: The charges are equal but opposite, so combining one of each ion will give a total charge of 0. The positive ion goes first in the formula: $MgSO_4$. Because Mg^{2+} is the magnesium ion and SO_4^{2-} is the sulfate ion, combining the names gives **magnesium sulfate.**

(c) NH_4^+ and NO_3^-: The charges are equal but opposite, so combining one of each ion will give a total charge of 0. The positive ion goes first in the formula: NH_4NO_3. Because NH_4^+ is the ammonium ion and NO_3^- is the nitrate ion, combining the names gives **ammonium nitrate**.

(d) O^{2-} and Al^{3+}: The charges are not equal. It will take two Al^{3+} ions (total charge = +6) to balance three O^{2-} ions (total charge = –6) to add to 0. The Al will have a subscript of 2, and the O will have a subscript of 3. The positive ion goes first in the formula: Al_2O_3. Because O^{2-} is the oxide ion and Al^{3+} is the aluminum ion, combining the names (cation first) gives **aluminum oxide.**

(e) Ca^{2+} and $C_2H_3O_2^-$: The charges are not equal. It will take one Ca^{2+} ion (total charge = +2) to balance two $C_2H_3O_2^-$ ions (total charge = –2) and add to 0. The Ca will have an understood subscript of 1, and the $C_2H_3O_2^-$ will have a subscript of 2. The fact that there are multiple $C_2H_3O_2^-$ ions will require us to place this ion in parentheses. The positive ion goes first in the formula: $Ca(C_2H_3O_2)_2$. Because Ca^{2+} is the calcium ion and $C_2H_3O_2^-$ is the acetate ion, combining the names gives **calcium acetate**.

Reality Check

In all cases, the total charge is 0. All the names are simple combinations of the individual components with the word *ion* removed.

Follow-Up Problem 2.9a

Using either **tables 2.2**, **2.3**, and **2.4** or the Nomenclature Resource, combine the following ions to produce a compound; then name each compound: (a) Li^+ and F^-, (b) Ca^{2+} and CO_3^{2-}, (c) SO_3^{2-} and NH_4^+, (d) Ba^{2+} and PO_4^{3-}, (e) Al^{3+} and $C_2H_3O_2^-$

Information

We have pairs of ion formulas, showing the elements they consist of and their charges. We need to find the chemical formula and name.

Connections

The total charge for any compound must be 0.

Solution

The cation (positive ion) always goes first in both the name and the chemical formula. To name the compounds, locate the names of the ions on the appropriate table or in the Nomenclature Resource. We drop the word *ion* from those names when we combine them to name an ionic compound.

(a) Li$^+$ and F$^-$: The charges are equal but opposite, so combining one of each ion will give a total charge of 0. The positive ion goes first in the formula: LiF. Because Li$^+$ is the lithium ion and F$^-$ is the fluoride ion, combining the names gives **lithium fluoride.**

(b) Ca^{2+} and CO$_3^{2-}$: The charges are equal but opposite, so combining one of each ion will give a total charge of 0. The positive ion goes first in the formula: CaCO$_3$. Because Ca^{2+} is the calcium ion and CO$_3^{2-}$ is the carbonate ion, combining the names gives **calcium carbonate.**

(c) SO$_3^{2-}$ and NH$_4^+$: The charges are not equal. It will take two NH$_4^+$ ion (total charge = +2) to balance one SO$_3^{2-}$ ions (total charge = –2) and add to 0. The NH$_4^+$ will have a subscript of 2 (which requires a set of parentheses), and the SO$_3^{2-}$ will have an understood subscript of 1. The positive ion goes first in the formula: (NH$_4$)$_2$SO$_3$. Because NH$_4^+$ is the ammonium ion and SO$_3^{2-}$ is the sulfate ion, combining the names gives **ammonium sulfite**.

(d) Ba^{2+} and PO$_4^{3-}$: The charges are not equal. It will take three Ba^{2+} ions (total charge = +6) to balance two PO$_4^{3-}$ ions (total charge = –6) to add to 0. The PO$_4^{3-}$ will have a subscript of 2 (which requires a set of parentheses), and the Ba^{2+} will have a subscript of 3. The positive ion goes first in the formula: Ba$_3$(PO$_4$)$_2$. Because Ba^{2+} is the barium ion and PO$_4^{3-}$ is the phosphate ion, combining the names (cation first) gives **barium phosphate.**

(e) Al^{3+} and C$_2$H$_3$O$_2^-$: The charges are not equal. It will take one Al^{3+} ion (total charge = +3) to balance three C$_2$H$_3$O$_2^-$ ions (total charge = –3) and add to 0. The Al^{3+} will have an understood subscript of 1, and the C$_2$H$_3$O$_2^-$ will have a subscript of 3. The fact that there are multiple C$_2$H$_3$O$_2^-$ ions will require us to place this ion in parentheses. The positive ion goes first in the formula: Al(C$_2$H$_3$O$_2$)$_3$. Because Al^{3+} is the aluminum ion and C$_2$H$_3$O$_2^-$ is the acetate ion, combining the names gives **aluminum acetate**.

Reality Check

In all cases, the total charge is 0. All the names are simple combinations of the individual components with the word *ion* removed.

Follow-Up Problem 2.9b

Using either **tables 2.2, 2.3,** and **2.4** or the Nomenclature Resource, give the formulas for each of the following compounds: **(a)** potassium oxide, **(b)** strontium sulfate, **(c)** aluminum nitrite, **(d)** ammonium phosphate, **(e)** sodium oxalate

Information

We have the names of five compounds. We need to determine the formulas and charges of the ions in the compound. We need to find the chemical formula and name.

Connections

The total charge for any compound must be 0.

Solution

(a) Potassium oxide: The potassium ion is K$^+$ and the oxide ion is O^{2-}. The charges are not equal. It will take two K$^+$ ion (total charge = +2) to balance one O^{2-} ion (total charge = –2) and add to 0. The K$^+$ will have a subscript of 2, and the O^{2-} will have an understood subscript of 1. The positive ion goes first in the formula: **K$_2$O**.

(b) Strontium sulfate: The strontium ion is Sr^{2+} and the sulfate ion is SO$_4^{2-}$. The charges are equal but opposite, so combining one of each ion will give a total charge of 0. The positive ion goes first in the formula: **SrSO$_4$**.

(c) Aluminum nitrite: The aluminum ion is Al^{3+} and the nitrite ion is NO_2^-. The charges are not equal. It will take one Al^{3+} ion (total charge = +3) to balance three NO_2^- ions (total charge = –3) and add to 0. The Al^{3+} will have an understood subscript of 1, and the NO_2^- will have a subscript of 3 (which will require a set of parentheses). The positive ion goes first in the formula: $\mathbf{Al(NO_2)_3}$.

(d) Ammonium phosphate: The ammonium ion is NH_4^+ and the phosphate ion is PO_4^{3-}. The charges are not equal. It will take three NH_4^+ ions (total charge = +3) to balance one PO_4^{3-} ion (total charge = –3) and add to 0. The NH_4^+ will have a subscript of 3 (which requires a set of parentheses), and the PO_4^{3-} will not need a subscript. The positive ion goes first in the formula: $\mathbf{(NH_4)_3PO_4}$.

(e) Sodium oxalate: The sodium ion is Na^+ and the oxalate ion is $C_2O_4^{2-}$. The charges are not equal. It will take two Na^+ ion (total charge = +2) to balance one $C_2O_4^{2-}$ ion (total charge = –2) and add to 0. The Na^+ will have a subscript of 2, and the $C_2O_4^{2-}$ will have an understood subscript of 1. The positive ion goes first in the formula: $\mathbf{Na_2C_2O_4}$.

Reality Check

In all cases, the total charge is 0. All the names are simple combinations of the individual components with the word *ion* removed.

Example Problem 2.10

Decide whether the following compounds are ionic or covalent: (a) NaCl, (b) CH_4, (c) BF_3, (d) FeS, (e) PbO

Information

The compound formulas are given; we need to classify them as ionic or covalent.

Connections

The positions of the elements on the periodic table indicate whether they are metals, nonmetals, or metalloids, which in turn will tell us whether the compounds are ionic or covalent.

Solution

From its location on the periodic table, classify each of the above elements as a metal, a nonmetal, or a metalloid. This gives the following:

(a)	Na metal	Cl nonmetal
(b)	C nonmetal	H nonmetal
(c)	B metalloid	F nonmetal
(d)	Fe metal	S nonmetal
(e)	Pb metal	O nonmetal

The ionic compounds are those containing a metal and a nonmetal. (The presence of a polyatomic ion would also make the compound ionic.) Compounds containing only nonmetals, metalloids, or both are usually covalent. (However, the presence of a polyatomic ion makes the compound ionic.) The ionic compounds are (a), (d), and (e). The covalent compounds are (b) and (c).

Reality Check

The position of the metalloids on the periodic table serves as a dividing line. Ionic compounds contain an element from each side of this dividing line, with the usual exception of hydrogen.

Follow-Up Problem 2.10a

Decide whether the following compounds are ionic or covalent: (a) CCl_4, (b) NH_3, (c) SiF_4, (d) $MnSO_4$, (e) $(NH_4)_2SO_4$

Information

The compound formulas are given; we need to classify them as ionic or as covalent.

Connections

The positions of the elements on the periodic table tell whether they are metals, nonmetals, or metalloids, which in turn will tell us whether the compounds are ionic or covalent.

Solution

From its location on the periodic table, classify each element as a metal, a nonmetal, or a metalloid. This gives the following:

(a)	C nonmetal	Cl nonmetal
(b)	N nonmetal	H nonmetal
(c)	Si metalloid	F nonmetal
(d)	Mn metal	$SO_4{}^{2-}$ polyatomic ion
(e)	$NH_4{}^+$ polyatomic ion	$SO_4{}^{2-}$ polyatomic ion

The ionic compounds are those containing a metal and a nonmetal. (The presence of a polyatomic ion would also make the compound ionic.) Compounds containing only nonmetals, metalloids, or both are usually covalent. (However, the presence of a polyatomic ion makes the compound ionic.) The ionic compounds are (d) and (e). The covalent compounds are (a), (b), and (c).

Reality Check

The position of the metalloids on the periodic table serves as a dividing line. Ionic compounds contain an element from each side of this dividing line, with the usual exception of hydrogen.

Follow-Up Problem 2.10b

Decide whether the following compounds are ionic or covalent: (a) H_2O, (b) NH_4NO_3, (c) SiO_2, (d) $Ce_2(SO_4)_3$, (e) $C_6H_{12}O_6$

Information

The compound formulas are given; we need to classify them as ionic or covalent.

Connections

The positions of the elements on the periodic table tell whether they are metals, nonmetals, or metalloids, which in turn will tell us whether the compounds are ionic or covalent.

Solution

From its location on the periodic table, classify each element as a metal, a nonmetal, or a metalloid. This gives the following:

(a)	H nonmetal	O nonmetal	
(b)	$NH_4{}^+$ polyatomic ion	$NO_3{}^-$ polyatomic ion	
(c)	Si metalloid	O nonmetal	
(d)	Ce metal	$SO_4{}^{2-}$ polyatomic ion	
(e)	C nonmetal	H nonmetal	O nonmetal

The ionic compounds are those containing a metal and a nonmetal. (The presence of a polyatomic ion would also make the compound ionic.) Compounds containing only nonmetals or only metalloids or containing both are usually covalent. (However, the presence of a polyatomic ion makes the compound ionic.) The ionic compounds are (b) and (d). The covalent compounds are (a), (c), and (e).

Reality Check

The position of the metalloids on the periodic table serves as a dividing line. Ionic compounds contain an element from each side of this dividing line, with the usual exception of hydrogen.

Example Problem 2.11

Decide whether the following compounds are inorganic or organic: **(a)** CH_2O, **(b)** $NaNO_3$, **(c)** $CaCO_3$, **(d)** CH_4, **(e)** $C_6H_{12}O_6$

Information

The compound formulas are present, identifying the component elements. We need to classify the compounds as inorganic or organic.

Connections

Organic compounds must contain carbon, and they should be covalent. If the compound is not organic, it must be inorganic.

Solution

Compound (b) contains no carbon, so it cannot possibly be organic. All the remaining compounds contain carbon; thus, they are possibly organic. However, compound (c) has a metal present. That means it is ionically bonded, not covalent, so it is not organic. The remaining compounds—(a), (d), and (e)—are organic.

Reality Check

Each of the compounds meets the definition of the category to which we assigned it.

Follow-Up Problem 2.11a

Decide whether the following compounds are inorganic or organic: **(a)** CH_3NH_2, **(b)** $NaHCO_3$, **(c)** CaC_2, **(d)** C_4H_{10}, **(e)** K_2CO_3

Information

The compound formulas are present, identifying the component elements. We need to classify the compounds as inorganic or organic.

Connections

Organic compounds must contain carbon, and they should be covalent. If the compound is not organic, it must be inorganic.

Solution

All the compounds contain carbon; therefore, they are possibly organic. However, compounds (b), (c), and (e) have a metal present. That means they are ionically bonded, not covalent, so they are not organic. The remaining compounds, (a) and (d), are organic.

Reality Check

Each of the compounds meets the definition of the category to which we assigned it.

Follow-Up Problem 2.11b

Decide whether the following compounds are inorganic or organic: **(a)** CH_3OH, **(b)** $HC_2H_3O_2$, **(c)** $(NH_4)_2CO_3$, **(d)** NH_2CH_2COOH, **(e)** CuC_2H

Information

The compound formulas are present, identifying the component elements. We need to classify the compounds as inorganic or organic.

Connections

Organic compounds must contain carbon, and they should be covalent. If the compound is not organic, it must be inorganic.

Solution

All the compounds contain carbon; therefore, they are possibly organic. However, compounds (c) and (e) have a metal or a polyatomic ion present. That means they are ionically bonded, not covalent, so they are not organic. The remaining compounds—(a), (b), and (d)—are organic.

Reality Check

Each of the compounds meets the definition of the category to which we assigned it.

Example Problem 2.12

Examine the following balanced chemical equations:

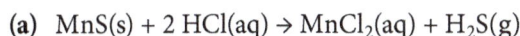

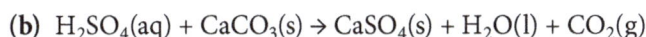

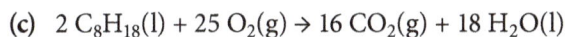

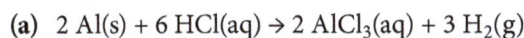

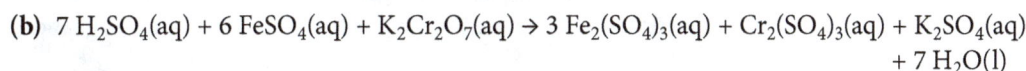

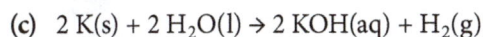

(a) $MnS(s) + 2\ HCl(aq) \rightarrow MnCl_2(aq) + H_2S(g)$

(b) $H_2SO_4(aq) + CaCO_3(s) \rightarrow CaSO_4(s) + H_2O(l) + CO_2(g)$

(c) $2\ C_8H_{18}(l) + 25\ O_2(g) \rightarrow 16\ CO_2(g) + 18\ H_2O(l)$

In each reaction, identify the reactants and products. Then explain the abbreviations in parentheses.

Information

We have the balanced equations. We need to identify the reactants and products in each, and then explain the abbreviations in parentheses.

Connections

Balanced chemical equations show the reactant and product compounds with their state of matter, indicated by (s), (aq), (g), and (l).

Solution

The reactants are the substances to the left of the arrows, and the products are the substances to the right of the arrows.

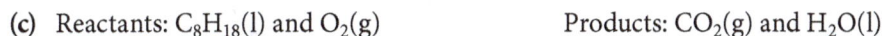

(a) Reactants: $MnS(s)$ and $HCl(aq)$ Products: $MnCl_2(aq)$ and $H_2S(g)$

(b) Reactants: $H_2SO_4(aq)$ and $CaCO_3(s)$ Products: $CaSO_4(s)$, $H_2O(l)$, and $CO_2(g)$

(c) Reactants: $C_8H_{18}(l)$ and $O_2(g)$ Products: $CO_2(g)$ and $H_2O(l)$

Recall that (s) = solid, (l) = liquid, (g) = aqueous, and (aq) = aqueous solution (dissolved in water).

Reality Check

The answers are consistent with the definitions.

Follow-Up Problem 2.12a

Examine the following balanced chemical equations:

(a) $2\ Al(s) + 6\ HCl(aq) \rightarrow 2\ AlCl_3(aq) + 3\ H_2(g)$

(b) $7\ H_2SO_4(aq) + 6\ FeSO_4(aq) + K_2Cr_2O_7(aq) \rightarrow 3\ Fe_2(SO_4)_3(aq) + Cr_2(SO_4)_3(aq) + K_2SO_4(aq)$
$$+ 7\ H_2O(l)$$

(c) $2\ K(s) + 2\ H_2O(l) \rightarrow 2\ KOH(aq) + H_2(g)$

In each reaction, identify the reactants and products. Then explain all the abbreviations in parentheses.

Information

We have the balanced equations. We need to identify the reactants and products in each, and then explain the abbreviations in parentheses.

Connections

Balanced chemical equations show the reactant and product compounds with their state of matter, indicated by (s), (aq), (g), and (l).

Solution

The reactants are the substances to the left of the arrows, and the products are the substances to the right of the arrows.

(a) Reactants: $Al(s)$ and $6\ HCl(aq)$
Products: $AlCl_3(aq)$ and $3\ H_2(g)$

(b) Reactants: $H_2SO_4(aq)$, $FeSO_4(aq)$, and $K_2Cr_2O_7(aq)$
Products: $Fe_2(SO_4)_3(aq)$, $Cr_2(SO_4)_3(aq)$, $K_2SO_4(aq)$, and $7\ H_2O(l)$

(c) Reactants: $K(s)$ and $H_2O(l)$
Products: $KOH(aq)$ and $H_2(g)$

Recall that (s) = solid, (l) = liquid, (g) = aqueous, and (aq) = aqueous solution (dissolved in water).

Reality Check

The answers are consistent with the definitions.

Follow-Up Problem 2.12b

In a homogeneous reaction, all the reactants and products are in the same phase (physical state), whereas in a heterogeneous reaction there are two or more different states of matter (phases) present. Classify each of the following reactions below as homogeneous or heterogeneous.

(a) $NH_3(aq) + HCl(aq) \rightarrow NH_4Cl(aq)$

(b) $Mg(s) + H_2SO_4(aq) \rightarrow MgSO_4(aq) + H_2(g)$

(c) $Ba(OH)_2(s) + (NH_4)_2SO_4(s) \rightarrow BaSO_4(s) + 2\ NH_3(g) + 2\ H_2O(l)$

Information

We have the balanced equations, and we need to identify whether the reactions are homogeneous or heterogeneous.

Connections

Homogeneous reactions have all reactants and products in the same phase (solid, liquid, gas, or in aqueous solution). Heterogeneous reactions involve two or more different phases.

Solution

(a) homogeneous because all the phases are (aq); **(b)** heterogeneous because all the phases are not the same (s, aq, and g); **(c)** heterogeneous because all the phases are not the same (s, g, and l)

Reality Check

The answers are consistent with the definitions.

Example Problem 2.13

This chemical equation is balanced:

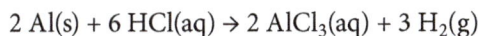

$$2\ Al(s) + 6\ HCl(aq) \rightarrow 2\ AlCl_3(aq) + 3\ H_2(g)$$

If the following numbers of aluminum (Al) atoms were used in the reaction, what amounts of each of the other substances would keep the equation balanced: **(a)** 2 Al atoms, **(b)** 1 dozen Al atoms, **(c)** 1,000 Al atoms

Information

We have the balanced equation and different numbers of Al atoms to be used in a balanced reaction. We need to find the numbers of HCl, $AlCl_3$, and H_2 that balance the reaction for each number of Al atoms.

Connections

The balanced chemical equation supplies all the necessary ratios.

Solution

The balanced chemical equation gives the following ratios between Al and the other substances:

$\left(\dfrac{6\ HCl}{2\ Al}\right), \left(\dfrac{2\ AlCl_3}{2\ Al}\right)$, and $\left(\dfrac{3\ H_2}{2\ Al}\right)$. These ratios lead to the following solutions:

(a) $(2\ Al)\left(\dfrac{6\ HCl}{2\ Al}\right) = \mathbf{6\ HCl}$

  $(2\ Al)\left(\dfrac{2\ AlCl_3}{2\ Al}\right) = \mathbf{2\ AlCl_3}$

  $(2\ Al)\left(\dfrac{3\ H_2}{2\ Al}\right) = \mathbf{3\ H_2}$

(b) $(1\ dozen\ Al)\left(\dfrac{12\ Al}{1\ dozen\ Al}\right)\left(\dfrac{6\ HCl}{2\ Al}\right) = \mathbf{36\ HCl}$

  $(1\ dozen\ Al)\left(\dfrac{12\ Al}{1\ dozen\ Al}\right)\left(\dfrac{2\ AlCl_3}{2\ Al}\right) = \mathbf{12\ AlCl_3}$

  $(1\ dozen\ Al)\left(\dfrac{12\ Al}{1\ dozen\ Al}\right)\left(\dfrac{3\ H_2}{2\ Al}\right) = \mathbf{18\ H_2}$

(c) $(1{,}000\ Al)\left(\dfrac{6\ HCl}{2\ Al}\right) = \mathbf{3{,}000\ HCl}$

  $(1{,}000\ Al)\left(\dfrac{2\ AlCl_3}{2\ Al}\right) = \mathbf{1{,}000\ AlCl_3}$

  $(1{,}000\ Al)\left(\dfrac{3\ H_2}{2\ Al}\right) = \mathbf{1{,}500\ H_2}$

Reality Check

The amounts of the other substances should be comparable in magnitude to the amount of aluminum.

Follow-Up Problem 2.13a

This chemical equation is balanced:

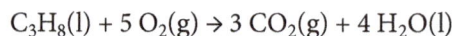

$$C_3H_8(l) + 5\ O_2(g) \rightarrow 3\ CO_2(g) + 4\ H_2O(l)$$

Given that the following numbers of C_3H_8 molecules were used in the reaction, what amounts of each of the other substances would keep the equation balanced: **(a)** 2 C_3H_8 molecules, **(b)** 1 dozen C_3H_8 molecules, **(c)** 1,000 C_3H_8 molecules

Information

We have the balanced equation and different numbers of C_3H_8 molecules to be used in a balanced reaction. We need to find the numbers of O_2, CO_2, and H_2O that balance the reaction for each number of **(a)** 2 C_3H_8 molecules, **(b)** 1 dozen C_3H_8 molecules, and **(c)** 1,000 C_3H_8 molecules.

Connections

The balanced chemical equation supplies all the necessary ratios.

Solution

The balanced chemical equation gives the following ratios between C_3H_8 and the other substances:

$\left(\dfrac{5\ O_2}{C_3H_8}\right), \left(\dfrac{3\ CO_2}{C_3H_8}\right)$, and $\left(\dfrac{4\ H_2O}{C_3H_8}\right)$. These ratios lead to the following solutions:

(a) $(2\ C_3H_8)\left(\dfrac{5\ O_2}{C_3H_8}\right) = \textbf{10 } \mathbf{O_2}$

$(2\ C_3H_8)\left(\dfrac{3\ CO_2}{C_3H_8}\right) = \textbf{6 } \mathbf{CO_2}$

$(2\ C_3H_8)\left(\dfrac{4\ H_2O}{C_3H_8}\right) = \textbf{8 } \mathbf{H_2O}$

(b) $(1\ \text{dozen}\ C_3H_8)\left(\dfrac{12\ C_3H_8}{1\ \text{dozen}\ C_3H_8}\right)\left(\dfrac{5\ O_2}{C_3H_8}\right) = \textbf{60 } \mathbf{O_2}$

$(1\ \text{dozen}\ C_3H_8)\left(\dfrac{12\ C_3H_8}{1\ \text{dozen}\ C_3H_8}\right)\left(\dfrac{3\ CO_2}{C_3H_8}\right) = \textbf{36 } \mathbf{CO_2}$

$(1\ \text{dozen}\ C_3H_8)\left(\dfrac{12\ C_3H_8}{1\ \text{dozen}\ C_3H_8}\right)\left(\dfrac{4\ H_2O}{C_3H_8}\right) = \textbf{48 } \mathbf{H_2O}$

(c) $(1{,}000\ C_3H_8)\left(\dfrac{5\ O_2}{C_3H_8}\right) = \textbf{5,000 } \mathbf{O_2}$

$(1{,}000\ C_3H_8)\left(\dfrac{3\ CO_2}{C_3H_8}\right) = \textbf{3,000 } \mathbf{CO_2}$

$(1{,}000\ C_3H_8)\left(\dfrac{4\ H_2O}{C_3H_8}\right) = \textbf{4,000 } \mathbf{H_2O}$

Reality Check

The amounts of the other substances should be comparable in magnitude to the amount of C_3H_8.

Follow-Up Problem 2.13b

Write a balanced chemical equation showing two molecules of hydrogen gas, H_2, reacting with one molecule of oxygen gas (O_2) to form two molecules of liquid water.

Information

We need to derive a balanced chemical equation for the reaction described.

Connections

We need to derive a balanced chemical equation based on the ratios given.

Solution

The balanced chemical equation is $2\ H_2(g) + O_2(g) \rightarrow 2\ H_2O(l)$.

Reality Check

This equation uses the quantities given in the problem and, like all balanced equations, obeys the law of conservation of mass.

Practice Exercise

Using the modern periodic table, locate each of the elements in the short version of Döbereiner's table, shown below and discussed earlier in this section. To which columns in the modern periodic table do these elements belong?

Li	Ca	S	Cl
Na	Sr	Se	Br
K	Ba	Te	I

Information

Collect the necessary information from Döbereiner's table and the modern periodic table.

Connections

The purpose of both tables is to classify the elements in chemically meaningful ways.

Solution

Locating the elements shows that the elements in Döbereiner's first column (Li, Na, and K) are alkali metals in group IA (1). The elements in Döbereiner's second column (Ca, Sr, and Ba) are alkaline earth metals in group IIA (2). The elements of his third column (S, Se, and Te) are in group VIA (16), and those in his last column (Cl, Br, and I) are halogens in group VIIA (17).

Reality Check

These answers are consistent with the idea that in both tables the elements that are grouped together have similar chemical properties.

Practice Problem 2.14

Hydrogen was proposed as a possible choice for the element on which to base atomic masses. It is possible to convert the current atomic masses to a different elemental basis by multiplying each (current) atomic mass by a ratio of the newly proposed standard's ideal atomic mass to the newly proposed standard's current, carbon-12–based mass. For hydrogen, the ratio would be (1.0000/1.0079). Determine the hydrogen-based atomic masses for the following elements. Also determine the differences between the masses on the two scales.

(a) H, (b) C, (c) O, (d) Fe, (e) U

Information

The atomic masses given on the periodic table, and the ratio 1.0000/1.0079

Connections

The ratio comparing the mass of each of the elements to that of carbon (1.0000/1.0079) is a unit conversion.

Solution

(a) H: $1.0079 \text{ amu} \left(\dfrac{1.0000}{1.0079} \right) = \textbf{1.0000 amu}$

$(1.0079 - 1.0000) \text{ amu} = \textbf{0.0079 amu}$

(b) C: $12.011 \text{ amu} \left(\dfrac{1.0000}{1.0079} \right) = \textbf{11.917 amu}$

$(12.011 - 11.917) \text{ amu} = \textbf{0.094 amu}$

(c) O: $15.999 \text{ amu} \left(\dfrac{1.0000}{1.0079} \right) = \textbf{15.874 amu}$

$(15.999 - 15.874) \text{ amu} = \textbf{0.125 amu}$

(d) Fe: $55.845 \text{ amu} \left(\dfrac{1.0000}{1.0079} \right) = \textbf{55.407 amu}$

$(55.845 - 55.407) \text{ amu} = \textbf{0.438 amu}$

(e) U: $238.02891 \text{ amu} \left(\dfrac{1.0000}{1.0079} \right) = \textbf{236.16}$

$(238.02891 - 236.16) \text{ amu} = \textbf{1.869 amu}$

Reality Check

The positive differences should be small and should increase with the atomic mass.

Follow-Up Problem 2.14a

Oxygen was the element originally used as the basis for atomic masses. It is possible to convert the current atomic masses to a different elemental basis by multiplying each one by the ratio of the new standard element's ideal atomic mass to the new standard element's previous, carbon-12–based mass. For changing to an oxygen basis, the ratio would be 16.0000/15.9994. Determine the atomic masses for the following elements on an oxygen-based table. Also, determine the differences between the masses on the two scales.

(a) H, (b) C, (c) O, (d) Fe, (e) U

Information

The atomic masses given on the periodic table, and the ratio 16.0000/15.9994

Connections

The ratio comparing the mass of each of the elements to that of oxygen (16.0000/15.9994) is a unit conversion.

Solution

(a) H: 1.0079 amu $\left(\dfrac{16.0000}{15.9994}\right)$ = **1.0079 amu**

(1.0079 – 1.0079) amu = **0.0000 amu**

(b) C: 12.011 amu $\left(\dfrac{16.0000}{15.9994}\right)$ = **12.011 amu**

(12.011 – 12.011) amu = **0.000 amu**

(c) O: 15.999 amu $\left(\dfrac{16.0000}{15.9994}\right)$ = **15.999 amu**

(15.999 – 15.999) amu = **0.000 amu**

(d) Fe: 55.845 amu $\left(\dfrac{16.0000}{15.9994}\right)$ = **55.847 amu**

(55.845 – 55.847) amu = **–0.002 amu**

(e) U: 238.02891 amu $\left(\dfrac{16.0000}{15.9994}\right)$ = **238.03784**

(238.02891 – 238.03784) amu = **–0.00893 amu**

Reality Check
The differences should be small and should increase with the atomic mass.

Follow-Up Problem 2.14b
It is possible to choose any isotope as the basis of atomic masses. It is possible to convert the current atomic masses to a different elemental basis by multiplying each current atomic mass by a ratio of the new standard's ideal atomic mass to the new standard element's previous, carbon-12–based mass. If cesium-133 were used, the ratio would be 133.00000/132.90545. Determine the atomic masses for the following elements on a cesium-based table. Also, determine the differences between the masses on the two scales.

(a) H, (b) C, (c) O, (d) Fe, (e) U

Information
The atomic masses given on the periodic table, and the ratio 133.00000/132.90545

Connections
The ratio comparing the mass of each of the elements to that of fluorine (133.00000/132.90545) is a unit conversion.

Solution

(a) H: 1.0079 amu $\left(\dfrac{133.00000}{132.90545}\right)$ = **1.0086 amu**

(1.0079 – 1.0086) amu = **–0.0007 amu**

(b) C: 12.011 amu $\left(\dfrac{133.00000}{132.90545}\right)$ = **12.020 amu**

(12.011 – 12.020) amu = **–0.009 amu**

(c) O: 15.999 amu $\left(\dfrac{133.00000}{132.90545}\right)$ = **16.010 amu**

(15.999 – 16.010) amu = **–0.011 amu**

(d) Fe: 55.845 amu $\left(\dfrac{133.00000}{132.90545}\right)$ = **55.885 amu**

(55.845 – 55.885) amu = **–0.040 amu**

(e) U: 238.02891 amu $\left(\dfrac{133.00000}{132.90545}\right)$ = **238.19825**

(238.02891 – 238.19825) amu = **–0.16934 amu**

Reality Check

The differences should be small and should increase with the atomic mass.

END-OF-CHAPTER PROBLEMS

2.1 The Modern Concept of the Atom

2.1 What is an atom?

Solution

An atom is the smallest particle of an element.

2.3 List the basic postulates of Dalton's atomic theory. Which of these postulates have required modification since Dalton's time?

Solution

1. Atoms, small indivisible particles, are the components of all matter.
2. Atoms of the same element are identical.
3. Atoms of different elements are different.
4. Atoms of one element cannot be changed into atoms of a different element.
5. Atoms are neither created nor destroyed.
6. Atoms combine in specific ratios to form compounds.

Postulates 2, 4, 5, and 6 each needed modification.

2.6 **(a)** What was the first subatomic particle to be discovered? **(b)** Which was the last of the basic subatomic particles to be discovered?

Solution

(a) Electron (b) Neutron

2.8 A sample of carbon dioxide from a burning piece of charcoal contains 27% carbon and 73% oxygen. A different sample of carbon dioxide also contains 27% carbon and 73% oxygen. The percentages are the same for all samples analyzed. Explain these observations with respect to atomic theory.

Solution

This illustrates the law of constant composition.

2.12 Glucose (blood sugar) combines with oxygen in your body to produce carbon dioxide, water, and energy. A sample of glucose weighing 18.0 g combines with 19.2 g of oxygen to produce 26.4 g of carbon dioxide. How many grams of water formed?

Information

The given masses, and the question of what mass of water is formed

Connections

The law of conservation of mass

Solution

18.0 g + 19.2 g = 26.4 g + ? g H_2O
Grams H_2O = 18.0 g + 19.2 g − 26.4 g = **10.8 g**

2.2 Properties of Protons, Neutrons, and Electrons

2.14 (a) Which subatomic particle(s) is/are in the nucleus of an atom? (b) Which subatomic particle(s) is/are outside the nucleus of an atom?

Solution

(a) The protons and neutrons are inside the nucleus of an atom. (b) The electrons are outside the nucleus of an atom.

2.16 Why is it preferable to use the number of protons instead of the number of electrons to identify the atomic number of an atom?

Solution

It is relatively easy to change the number of electrons present; however, it is difficult to change the number of protons.

2.18 Two forms of oxygen occur in nature: (1) the oxygen gas we breathe and (2) ozone gas in the upper atmosphere and in certain types of air pollution. Are the two types of oxygen isotopes or are they allotropes? Explain.

Solution

An allotrope is one of two or more pure forms of an element that exist in the same physical state. The two forms of oxygen are allotropes, as they are different forms of the same element in the same physical state.

2.19 (a) Why does removing electrons produce an ion with a positive charge (a cation)?
(b) Why does adding electrons produce an ion with a negative charge (an anion)?

Solution

(a) An atom is neutral because there are equal numbers of positive charges (protons) and negative charges (electrons). Removing electrons will leave an ion with fewer electrons than protons. The excess protons result in an overall positive charge. (b) Similarly, the addition of electrons to an atom leads to an excess of electrons over protons. The excess electrons result in an overall negative charge.

2.21 A xenon atom has a radius of about 2.2 Å. (a) What is the radius of a xenon atom in picometers? (b) How many xenon atoms would it take to produce a line 1.0 inch long?

Information

(a) The radius of one xenon atom (2.2 Å), and the question of what is the radius in picometers; (b) the question of how many xenon atoms are necessary to produce a 1.0-inch line

Connections

(a) A conversion for angstroms to an SI unit and various SI prefixes (if necessary) to get to picometers. (b) It is possible to start with the answer to (a) and add an SI-to-English conversion; it is also necessary to convert the radius to a diameter.

Solution

(a) This problem requires two unit conversions. The relationship between angstroms (Å) and meters is given on the inside back cover of this textbook (1 Å = 10^{-10} m) and from **table 1.2**: $p = 10^{-12}$.

$$\text{Radius} = (2.2\ \text{Å})\left(\frac{10^{-10}\ \text{m}}{1\ \text{Å}}\right)\left(\frac{p}{10^{-12}}\right) = 220 = \mathbf{2.2 \times 10^2\ pm}$$

(b) This problem requires several unit conversions and the fact that the diameter is twice the radius. The unit conversions that you use will depend upon the ones that you know. The following is one of the many possible ways of correctly solving this problem (the other solutions use different unit conversions). Note: You are looking for atoms; therefore, the unit "atom" must appear in the calculation.

$$(1.0\ \text{in})\left(\frac{2.54\ \text{cm}}{1\ \text{in}}\right)\left(\frac{0.01}{c}\right)\left(\frac{p}{10^{-12}}\right)\left(\frac{1\ \text{atom}}{2 \times 2.2 \times 10^2\ \text{pm}}\right) = 5.7727 \times 10^7 = \mathbf{5.8 \times 10^7\ atoms}$$

2.24 Determine the number of protons, electrons, and neutrons in each of the following atoms: (a) $^{10}_{5}$B, (b) $^{40}_{18}$Ar, (c) $^{56}_{26}$Fe, (d) $^{105}_{47}$Ag, (e) $^{239}_{94}$Pu

Solution

	Protons	Electrons	Neutrons
(a)	5	5	5
(b)	18	18	22
(c)	26	26	30
(d)	47	47	58
(e)	94	94	145

2.26 Determine the number of protons, electrons, and neutrons in each of the following isotopes used in medicine: (a) chromium-51, (b) strontium-85, (c) gadolinium-153, (d) cobalt-60, (e) cobalt-57

Solution

	Protons	Electrons	Neutrons
(a)	24	24	27
(b)	37	37	48
(c)	65	65	88
(d)	27	27	33
(e)	27	27	30

2.32 Complete the following table describing the atoms of five atoms or ions:

Symbol	$^{81}_{35}Br$	$^{55}_{26}Fe^{3+}$			
Protons			36	82	52
Electrons					54
Neutrons			50		76
Net charge			0	2+	
Mass Number				207	

Solution

Symbol	$^{81}_{35}Br$	$^{55}_{26}Fe^{3+}$	$^{86}_{36}Kr$	$^{207}_{82}Pb^{2+}$	$^{128}_{52}Te^{2-}$
Protons	**35**	**26**	36	82	52
Electrons	**35**	**23**	**36**	**80**	54
Neutrons	**46**	**29**	50	**125**	76
Net charge	**0**	**3+**	**0**	2+	**2–**
Mass Number	**81**	**55**	**86**	207	**128**

2.3 Atomic and Molecular Masses

2.34 Dalton stated that all atoms of an element are identical. Of the following properties, which are identical for all the atoms of an element—mass number, atomic mass, atomic number?

Solution

Only the atomic number is identical for all atoms of an element.

2.36 Is it possible for the molecular formula and the empirical formula to be the same? Explain why or why not.

Solution

If it is not possible to simplify the molecular formula, then the molecular and empirical formulas will be the same. An example of this situation is water. It is not possible to reduce H_2O further.

2.38 Silicon, Si, is the second most abundant element in the Earth's crust. This element has three naturally occurring isotopes. Their masses and abundances are as follows: silicon-28 (27.9769265 amu), 92.23%; silicon-29 (28.9764947 amu), 4.67%; and silicon-30 (29.9737702 amu), 3.10%. Determine the atomic mass of natural silicon.

Information

The masses and abundances of the three silicon isotopes (silicon-28 = 27.9769265 amu and 92.23%; silicon-29 = 28.9764947 amu and 4.67%; and silicon-30 = 29.9737702 amu and 3.10%); the question of what is the atomic mass of silicon

Connections

The knowledge that the atomic mass is the weighted average of the masses of the isotopes

Solution

Significant figures are underlined.

$$\left(\frac{92.23\%}{100\%}\right)(27.9769265 \text{ amu}) = \underline{25.80}311931 \text{ amu}$$

$$\left(\frac{4.67\%}{100\%}\right)(28.9764947 \text{ amu}) = \underline{1.35}3202302 \text{ amu}$$

$$\left(\frac{3.10\%}{100\%}\right)(29.9737702 \text{ amu}) = \underline{0.929}186876 \text{ amu}$$

$$\text{Total} = \underline{28.08}550849$$

$$= \mathbf{28.08 \ amu}$$

Reality Check

This is the value reported on the periodic table.

2.40 The noble gas krypton, Kr, consists of six natural isotopes. The masses and percent abundance for each of these isotopes are given in the following table:

Isotope	Mass (amu)	Abundance (%)
Krypton-78	77.9204	0.35
Krypton-80	79.9164	2.25
Krypton-82	81.9135	11.6
Krypton-83	82.9141	11.5
Krypton-84	83.9115	57.0
Krypton-86	85.9106	17.3

Determine the atomic mass of krypton from these data.

Information

The information on the atomic masses and the abundances of the isotopes given in the table, and the question of what is the atomic mass of krypton

Connections

The knowledge that the atomic mass is the weighted average of the masses of the isotopes

Solution

Significant figures are underlined.

$$\left(\frac{0.35\%}{100\%}\right)(77.9204 \text{ amu}) = \underline{0.27}27214 \text{ amu}$$

$$\left(\frac{2.25\%}{100\%}\right)(79.9164 \text{ amu}) = \underline{1.79}8119 \text{ amu}$$

$$\left(\frac{11.6\%}{100\%}\right)(81.9135 \text{ amu}) = \underline{9.50}1966 \text{ amu}$$

$$\left(\frac{11.5\%}{100\%}\right)(82.9141 \text{ amu}) = \underline{9.53}51215 \text{ amu}$$

$$\left(\frac{57.0\%}{100\%}\right)(83.9115 \text{ amu}) = \underline{47.8}29555 \text{ amu}$$

$$\left(\frac{17.3\%}{100\%}\right)(85.9106 \text{ amu}) = \underline{14.8}625338 \text{ amu}$$

$$\text{Total} = \underline{83.8}000167$$

$$= \textbf{82.8 amu}$$

Reality Check

This is the value reported on the periodic table.

2.42 The lanthanide element europium, Eu, consists of two natural isotopes. The lighter isotope is ^{151}Eu, with a mass of 150.919846 amu, and the heavier isotope is ^{153}Eu, with a mass of 152.921226 amu. The atomic mass of europium is 151.964 amu. **(a)** Determine the composition of each isotope in terms of protons, neutrons, and electrons. **(b)** Calculate the percent abundance of each of the two isotopes.

Information

The atomic mass of europium (151.964 amu) and data on the two isotopes (^{151}Eu = 150.919846 amu and ^{153}Eu = 152.921226 amu); **(a)** the question about the number of protons, electrons, and neutrons in each isotope; **(b)** the question about the abundances of each isotope

Connections

(a) the relationships between the components of an atom and the identity of the isotope; **(b)** the knowledge that the atomic mass is the weighted average of the masses of the isotopes and that the sum of the percent abundances must be exactly 100%

Solution

(a)

	Protons	Electrons	Neutrons
Europium-151	63	63	88
Europium-153	63	63	90

(b) Let x % = percentage of Europium-151 and y % = percentage of Europium-153.

We need two important relationships:

1. $x\% + y\% = 100\%$ (The total of all isotopes must be exactly 100%.)

2. $(150.919846 \text{ amu})\left(\frac{x\%}{100\%}\right) + (152.921226 \text{ amu})\left(\frac{y\%}{100\%}\right) = 151.964 \text{ amu}$

Simplifying by factoring out the 100% gives

1. $x + y = 1$ (This 1 is an exact number.)
2. $(150.919846 \text{ amu})(x) + (152.921226 \text{ amu})(y) = 151.964 \text{ amu}$

Solving equation (1) for x gives

$$x = 1 - y$$

Then substitute for x in (2):

$(150.919846 \text{ amu})(1 - y) + (152.921226 \text{ amu})(y) = 151.964 \text{ amu}$

Multiplying gives

$$150.919846 \text{ amu} - (150.919846 \text{ amu}) \, y + (152.921226 \text{ amu}) \, (y) = 151.964 \text{ amu}$$

Rearranging:

$$[(152.921226 - 150.919846) \text{ amu}] \, y = 151.964 - 150.919846) \text{ amu}$$

Then:

$$y = [(151.964 - 150.919846) \text{ amu}] \, / \, [(152.921226 - 150.919846) \text{ amu}] = \left(\frac{1.044154 \text{ amu}}{2.00138 \text{ amu}} \right)$$

$$= 0.521717015 = 0.5217$$

From earlier:

$$x = 1 - y = 1 - 0.521717015 = 0.478282985 = 0.4783$$

These two answers are decimal answers. To convert the answers to percentage answers, multiply the decimal values by 100%:

$$x = (0.5217) \, (100\%) = \mathbf{52.17\%} \; {}^{151}\mathbf{Eu}$$
$$y = (0.4783) \, (100\%) = \mathbf{47.83\%} \; {}^{153}\mathbf{Eu}$$

The total must be 100%.

2.44 Calculate the formula mass for each of the following to three decimal places: (a) O_3, (b) Fe_3O_4, (c) CCl_4, (d) $(NH_4)_2SO_4$, (e) $C_6H_{12}O_6$

Information
The formulas of five substances—(a) O_3, (b) Fe_3O_4, (c) CCl_4, (d) $(NH_4)_2SO_4$, (e) $C_6H_{12}O_6$—and the question of what are their formula masses

Connections
The atomic masses of the elements from the periodic table, or a list of atomic masses

Solution
(a) 3×15.999 amu = **47.997 amu**

(b) 3×55.453 amu $+ 4 \times 15.999$ amu = **231.531 amu**

(c) 12.011 amu $+ 4 \times 35.453$ amu **153.823 amu**

(d) 2×14.007 amu $+ 8 \times 1.008$ amu $+ 32.065 + 4 \times 15.999$ amu = **132.139 amu**

(e) 6×12.011 amu $+ 12 \times 1.008$ amu $+ 6 \times 15.999$ amu = **180.156 amu**

2.46 Convert the following empirical formulas to molecular formulas. The approximate molecular masses for each substance are in parentheses. (a) NO_2 (90 amu), (b) CH_2O (180 amu), (c) CH_2O (120 amu), (d) $MnSO_4$ (151 amu), (e) P_2O_5 (284 amu)

Information
The empirical formulas and molecular masses of five substances—(a) NO_2 (90 amu), (b) CH_2O (180 amu), (c) CH_2O (120 amu), (d) $MnSO_4$ (151 amu), (e) P_2O_5 (284 amu)—and the question of what are their molecular formulas

Connections
The atomic masses of the elements from the periodic table or a list of atomic masses, and that the sum of the atomic masses must equal the formula masses

Solution
(a) The approximate formula mass of NO_2 is 46 amu, which must be multiplied by 2 to equal the reported molecular mass (92 amu) so the molecular formula is N_2O_4

(b) The approximate formula mass of CH_2O is 30 amu, which must be multiplied by 6 to equal the reported molecular mass (180 amu) so the molecular formula is $C_6H_{12}O_6$

(c) The approximate formula mass of CH_2O is 30 amu, which must be multiplied by approximate formula mass of CH_2O is 30 amu, which must be multiplied by 4 to equal the reported molecular mass (120 amu) so the molecular formula is $C_4H_8O_4$

(d) The approximate formula mass of $MnSO_4$ is 151 amu, which means the empirical and molecular formulas are the same, or $MnSO_4$.

(e) The approximate formula mass of P_2O_5 is 142 amu, which must be multiplied by 2 to equal the reported molecular mass (284 amu) so the molecular formula is P_4O_{10}.

2.49 (a) What is the molecular formula for the compound shown in the following picture? (b) Is this likely to be an ionic compound or a covalent compound?

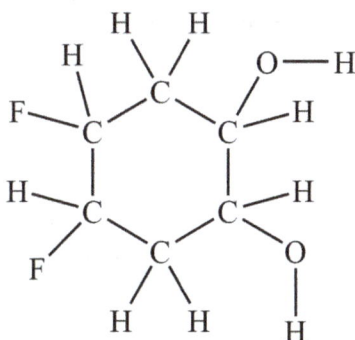

Solution
(a) $C_6H_{10}O_2F_2$. (b) All the elements are nonmetals; therefore, this is likely to be a covalent compound.

2.4 The Periodic Table
2.53 (a) How many of the elements are nonmetals? (b) How many of the elements are metalloids? (c) How many of the elements are metals?

Solution
(a) 19, (b) 5, (c) 90

2.55 Locate each of the following elements on the periodic table. Give the symbol for the element, and classify it as a metal, a metalloid (semimetal), or a nonmetal: (a) titanium, (b) tellurium, (c) tantalum, (d) fluorine, (e) bromine

Solution
(a) titanium: **Ti, metal**; (b) tellurium: **Te, metalloid**; (c) tantalum: **Ta, metal**; (d) fluorine: **F, nonmetal**; (e) bromine: **Br, nonmetal**

2.58 From the list provided here, choose the best match for each of the descriptions that follow—S, Fr, Ge, At, Yb, Sr, Po, Bh, Tl, H, and Ne. Use each element only once.

(a) Which element is a metalloid? **(b)** Which element is a transition metal? **(c)** Which element is an alkaline earth metal? **(d)** Which element is most like aluminum? **(e)** Which element is a noble gas? **(f)** Which element is an alkali metal? **(g)** Which element is a halogen? **(h)** Which is the heaviest member of the oxygen family?

Solution

Locate each element on the periodic table. **(a) Ge, (b) Bh, (c) Sr, (d) Tl, (e) Ne, (f) Fr, (g) At, (h) Po**

2.5 How Does Chemical Change Occur?

2.59 The most reactive of all the metals are the alkali metals, and the most reactive of all the nonmetals are the halogens. What type(s) of ions do you expect reactions of elements in these two groups to form?

Solution

Alkali metals, since they are metals, should form cations. The halogens, since they are nonmetals should form anions.

2.62 Based on the position of the elements on the periodic table, which of the following ions would you expect to be unlikely to form? **(a)** Ca^{3+}, **(b)** O^{2-}, **(c)** Cl^{+}, **(d)** Ba^{+}, **(e)** N^{3-}

Solution

(a) No, should be Ca^{2+}

(b) OK

(c) No, should be Cl^{-}

(d) No, should be Ba^{2+}

(e) OK

2.64 Predict the formula of the compound formed when the following ions combine: **(a)** Sr^{2+} and S^{2-}, **(b)** Fe^{3+} and O^{2-}, **(c)** NH_4^{+} and NO_3^{-}, **(d)** Al^{3+} and NO_2^{-}, **(e)** Ca^{2+} and PO_4^{3-}

Solution

The total charge must be zero.

(a) Sr^{2+} and S^{2-}: **SrS**

(b) Fe^{3+} and O^{2-}: **Fe_2O_3**

(c) NH_4^{+} and NO_3^{-}: **NH_4NO_3**

(d) Al^{3+} and NO_2^{-}: **$Al(NO_2)_3$**

(e) Ca^{2+} and PO_4^{3-}: **$Ca_3(PO_4)_2$**

2.66 Predict the formula of the compound formed by each of the following pairs of elements, assuming each element forms an ion with the charge predicted from its position on the periodic table: **(a)** K and Br, **(b)** Ba and Se, **(c)** Mg and N, **(d)** Ca and I, **(e)** Al and Cl

Solution

The position of the element on the periodic table indicates the charge on the ion formed and the total charge must be zero.

(a) K^+ and Br^- give **KBr**.

(b) Ba^{2+} and Se^{2-} give **BaSe**.

(c) Mg^{2+} and N^{3-} give **Mg_3N_2**.

(d) Ca^{2+} and I^- give **CaI_2**.

(e) Al^{3+} and Cl^- give **$AlCl_3$**.

2.68 Classify each of the following as an ionic compound or as a molecular compound:
(a) NaCl, **(b)** $C_6H_{12}O_6$, **(c)** CO_2, **(d)** YF_3, **(e)** $RaCl_2$

Solution

(a) NaCl—**ionic**, **(b)** $C_6H_{12}O_6$—**molecular**, **(c)** CO_2—**molecular**, **(d)** YF_3—**ionic**, **(e)** $RaCl_2$—**ionic**

2.71 Which of the following compounds are organic: **(a)** CH_2O, **(b)** $(NH_4)HCO_3$, **(c)** CS_2, **(d)** C_2H_5OH, **(e)** CaC_2

Solution

The organic compounds are CH_2O, CS_2, and C_2H_5OH.

2.6 Chemical Reactions and Equations

2.74 Define the terms *reactant* and *product*.

Solution

A **reactant** is a starting substance in a chemical reaction. A **product** is a substance formed in a chemical reaction.

2.77 List the reactants and products in the following equation and tell what the terms in parentheses mean.

$$Hg(l) + 2 H_2SO_4(aq) \rightarrow HgSO_4(s) + SO_2(g) + 2 H_2O(l)$$

Solution

Reactants: $Hg(l)$ and $H_2SO_4(aq)$

Products: $HgSO_4(s)$, $SO_2(g)$, and $H_2O(l)$

(l) = **liquid**, (aq) = **aqueous solution**, (s) = **solid**, and (g) = **gas**

2.80 A student balances the equation $H_2(g) + Cl_2(g) \rightarrow HCl(g)$ as

$$H(g) + Cl(g) \rightarrow HCl(g)$$

Explain why the final "balanced" equation is wrong.

Solution

It is not acceptable to alter the chemical formulas when balancing an equation.

2.82 **(a)** What is the scientific basis (or law) exhibited by a balanced chemical equation?
(b) How do the meanings of "8 S" and "S_8" differ?

Solution

(a) The law of conservation of matter/mass. **(b)** "S_8" represents a group, not eight individual S atoms.

2.84 How do the compounds NO, NO_2, and N_2O_3 illustrate the law of multiple proportions?

Solution

In these compounds, the number of nitrogen atoms is either the same or simply doubled ($\times$ 2). The number of oxygen atoms is either one or a simple multiple ($\times$ 2 or $\times$ 3).

2.7 Applications

2.86 Describe Moseley's contribution to the periodic table.

Solution

Moseley's contribution was the determination of the atomic numbers of the elements. Now the elements are arranged in the periodic table in order of increasing atomic number.

2.88 What element was used before carbon-12 as the basis for atomic weights? Why was it necessary to change to another element?

Solution

Oxygen was used previously; however, there were two different interpretations of how to use oxygen giving two different mass scales.

2.93 BAL was developed to treat poisoning due to arsenic in the poison gas Lewisite. Later it was used to treat other types of poisoning. Which of the following elements would be most likely to respond to treatment by BAL: **(a)** Pb, **(b)** Be, **(c)** Tl, **(d)** Cd, **(e)** Ba

Solution

BAL binds to the chalcophile elements. The chalcophile elements listed are (a) **Pb**, (c) **Tl**, and (d) **Cd**.

Putting It All Together

2.95 Name each of the following compounds: **(a)** CO, **(b)** BCl_3, **(c)** I_2O, **(d)** P_4O_{10}, **(e)** SiF_4, **(f)** KrF_2, **(g)** BrF_5, **(h)** $TeCl_4$, **(i)** SeO_3, **(j)** Br_2O_5

Solution

(a) CO	**carbon monoxide**	
(b) BCl_3	**boron trichloride**	
(c) I_2O	**diiodine oxide**	
(d) P_4O_{10}	**tetraphosphorus decoxide**	
(e) SiF_4	**silicon tetrafluoride**	
(f) KrF_2	**krypton difluoride**	
(g) BrF_5	**bromine pentafluoride**	
(h) $TeCl_4$	**tellurium tetrachloride**	
(i) SeO_3	**selenium trioxide**	
(j) Br_2O_5	**dibromine pentoxide**	

2.97 Give the formula of each of the following compounds: **(a)** silicon dioxide, **(b)** diphosphorus trioxide, **(c)** dinitrogen tetroxide, **(d)** sulfur tetrabromide, **(e)** carbon dioxide, **(f)** xenon difluoride, **(g)** phosphorus trichloride, **(h)** disulfur decafluoride, **(i)** boron trifluoride, **(j)** diboron tetroxide

Solution

(a) silicon dioxide	SiO_2
(b) diphosphorus trioxide	P_2O_3
(c) dinitrogen tetroxide	N_2O_4
(d) sulfur tetrabromide	SBr_4
(e) carbon dioxide	CO_2
(f) xenon difluoride	XeF_2
(g) phosphorus trichloride	PCl_3
(h) disulfur decafluoride	S_2F_{10}
(i) boron trifluoride	BF_3
(j) diboron tetroxide	B_2O_4

2.102 What information is needed to convert an empirical formula to a molecular formula and then to a structural formula?

Solution

There needs to be information about the number of atoms present in the molecule to convert an empirical formula to a molecular formula. Then there must be information on the arrangement of the atoms to create a structural formula.

2.104 The atomic mass of antimony, Sb, is 121.760 amu. Natural antimony consists of two isotopes: antimony-121 and antimony-123. The mass of an antimony-121 atom is 120.9038 amu, and the mass of an antimony-123 atom is 122.9041 amu. **(a)** Determine the percent abundance of each isotope. **(b)** A sample of antimony from another planet contained 24.35% antimony-121 and 75.65% antimony. What was the atomic mass of the antimony from this other planet?

Information

The atomic mass of antimony (121.760 amu); the masses of two antimony isotopes (antimony-121 = 120.9038 amu and antimony-123 = 122.9041 amu); **(a)** the question about the abundances of the two isotopes; **(b)** the abundances of the two antimony isotopes on another planet (24.35% antimony-121 and 75.65% antimony), and the question of what is the atomic mass of antimony on this other planet

Connections

That the atomic mass is the weighted average of the masses of the isotopes, and that the sum of the percent abundances must be exactly 100%

Solution

(a) Let x % = percentage of antimony-121 and y % = percentage of antimony-123.

We need two important relationships:

1. $x\% + y\% = 100\%$ (The total of all isotopes must be exactly 100%.)

2. $(120.9038 \text{ amu})\left(\dfrac{x\%}{100\%}\right) + (122.9041 \text{ amu})\left(\dfrac{y\%}{100\%}\right) = 121.760 \text{ amu}$

Simplifying by factoring out the 100% gives

1. $x + y = 1$ (This 1 is an exact number.)
2. $(120.9038 \text{ amu}) (x) + (122.9041 \text{ amu}) (y) = 121.760 \text{ amu}$

Solving equation (1) for x gives

$$x = 1 - y$$

Then substitute for x in equation (2):

$$(120.9038 \text{ amu}) (1 - y) + (\text{ amu}) (y) = 121.760 \text{ amu}$$

Multiplying gives

$$120.9038 \text{ amu} - (120.9038 \text{ amu}) y + (\text{ amu}) (y) = 121.760 \text{ amu}$$

Rearranging:

$$[(122.9041 - 120.9038) \text{ amu}] y = (121.760 - 120.9038) \text{ amu}$$

Then:

$$y = [(121.760 - 120.9038) \text{ amu}] / [(122.9041 - 120.9038) \text{ amu}] = \left(\frac{0.8562 \text{ amu}}{2.0003 \text{ amu}} \right) = 0.428036 = 0.428$$

From earlier:

$$x = 1 - y = 1 - 0.428036 = 0.571964 = 0.572$$

These two answers are decimal answers. To convert the answers to percentage answers, multiply the decimal values by 100%:

$$x = (0.572) (100\%) = \mathbf{57.2\% \ ^{121}Sb}$$
$$y = (0.428) (100\%) = \mathbf{42.8\% \ ^{123}Sb}$$

(b) Significant figures are underlined:

$$\left(\frac{24.35\%}{100\%} \right) (120.9038 \text{ amu}) = \underline{29.44}0075311931 \text{ amu}$$

$$\left(\frac{75.65\%}{100\%} \right) (122.9041 \text{ amu}) = \underline{92.97}698165 \text{ amu}$$

$$\text{Total} = 122.417027$$

$$= \mathbf{122.42 \ amu}$$

CHAPTER 3

Stoichiometry—Mass and Moles

The successful completion of these problems requires the following eight (8) items.

1. This chapter introduces moles. Moles are one of the most important concepts in this textbook. Expect moles to appear throughout the remainder of this textbook. This means that you <u>need</u> to understand moles and mole relationships.

2. While Avogadro's number is a very useful concept. You will find that it is only necessary in a very few chemistry problems. You will only use Avogadro's <u>number</u> if you are given the number of particles or are asked to find the number of particles. For example, if you want to know the <u>number</u> of hydrogen atoms in 10 grams of water or if there are 1.0×10^{15} sodium atoms (<u>number</u> of atoms), how many moles of sodium atoms are present. In all other cases, <u>avoid</u> using Avogadro's number.

3. Chemical equations are very important when dealing with moles. However, if the equation is not balanced, it is of little use. Make sure you are only using balanced chemical equations.

4. The first step in most of the calculations in this chapter is to convert whatever you are given to <u>moles</u>. Remember, moles are the key.

5. The molecular mass (formula mass) may be expressed as amu/molecule or grams/mole. When grams/mole are used, this form of the molecular mass is known as the *molar mass*, which will continue to appear in other chapters.

6. The molar mass not only allows you to find moles from grams, but also to find to find grams from moles. One or both uses will appear in most problems.

7. A mole ratio allows you to convert from one substance to another.
8. You will note that certain steps (calculations) in many occur over and over again. Examples include the conversion of mass to moles and the use of a mole ratio. It will help you to learn not only these steps but the circumstances where they are necessary.

Example Problems From the Text

Example Problem 3.1

Decomposition reactions break a substance down into two or more different substances. When solid potassium chlorate, $KClO_3$, is heated, it undergoes a decomposition reaction to produce solid potassium chloride, KCl, and gaseous oxygen, O_2. Write a balanced chemical equation for the decomposition of potassium chlorate. (Note: Adding manganese(IV) oxide to the potassium chlorate facilitates this reaction.)

Solution

The first step in balancing an equation is to write down the chemical formulas of the reactants and products on either side of an arrow. In this case, the formulas are

$$KClO_3(s) \rightarrow KCl(s) + O_2(g)$$

Under no conditions are any of these formulas to be changed. The symbols in parentheses (the states of matter) have no bearing in balancing the equation. Rewriting the unbalanced equation with blanks in front of each formula may help:

$$\underline{\quad} KClO_3(s) \rightarrow \underline{\quad} KCl(s) + \underline{\quad} O_2(g)$$

This has now become a fill-in-the-blank problem. Balancing the equation requires only placing the correct numbers into the blanks.

Balancing may begin with any of the blanks (any element). If we enter a "1" in the first blank, we get

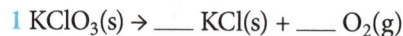

$$1\ KClO_3(s) \rightarrow \underline{\quad} KCl(s) + \underline{\quad} O_2(g)$$

(This "1" is not necessary in a finalized balanced equation. Its purpose here is to serve as a reminder that the first blank is "full." In complicated equations, this type of reminder may keep you from making the mistake of altering a "filled" blank.)

The "1" tells you that there are now one K, one Cl, and three O's on the reactant side. You can now pick any one of these elements to balance first. We will pick potassium, K. To balance the one K on the left, we need one K on the right. To get one K on the right. we will need a "1" in front of the KCl.

$$1\ KClO_3(s) \rightarrow 1\ KCl(s) + \underline{\quad} O_2(g)$$

This "1" not only balances the K, but also balances the Cl. This leaves only the oxygen, O, to balance.

The three O's on the left require three O's on the right. However, on the right, O's occur in pairs. One way to get three O's from pairs is to use a coefficient of "3/2." (The temporary use of a fraction is acceptable. It does not matter what values are in the blanks during the balancing process. Only the final equation needs whole numbers.) The fractional coefficients give

$$1\ KClO_3(s) \rightarrow 1\ KCl(s) + 3/2\ O_2(g)$$

All the atoms are now balanced, but the presence of a fraction requires a solution. The simplest way to eliminate this fraction is to multiply the entire equation by the denominator of the fraction. In this case, the multiplier is "2":

$$2 \times [1\ KClO_3(s) \rightarrow 1\ KCl(s) + 3/2\ O_2(g)]$$

The equation now becomes

$$2\ KClO_3(s) \rightarrow 2\ KCl(s) + 3\ O_2(g)$$

If any of the coefficients were a "1," it could be eliminated now. The final step in balancing any equation is checking to see if everything on the reactant side balances everything on the product side. In this case, the reactant side has 2 K, 2 Cl, and 6 O, and the product side has 2 K, 2 Cl, and 6 O. Since the numbers are the same and the coefficients are in the lowest whole-number ratio, the equation is balanced.

If, for any reason, one of the numbers does not match, quickly check over your work. If you do not see where your error is, it is usually best to start over instead of trying to fix a mistake that is not obvious. It may help to start with a different blank.

Follow-Up Problem 3.1a
The reverse of a decomposition reaction is a formation reaction. In a formation reaction, one or more reactants combine to produce a single product. Solid iron metal, Fe, combines with oxygen gas, O_2, to produce solid Fe_3O_4. Balance the chemical equation for this reaction.

Solution
It is acceptable to begin with either the iron, Fe, or the oxygen, O. (Note that oxygen begins as O_2 molecules, which is the form of oxygen in the atmosphere.) Beginning with Fe means there will need 3 Fe and 1 Fe_3O_4. To finish balancing, there needs to be 2 O_2:

$$3\ Fe(s) + 2\ O_2(g) \rightarrow Fe_3O_4(s)$$

The equation is balanced with 3 Fe on each side and 4 O on each side.

Follow-Up Problem 3.1b
Respiration involves the combination of glucose, $C_6H_{12}O_6$, in your body with oxygen, O_2, to produce carbon dioxide, CO_2, water, H_2O, and energy. Water is a liquid, and all the other substances are in aqueous solution. Write a balanced equation for this reaction.

Solution
It is possible to begin with either carbon, C, or hydrogen, H; however, since oxygen occurs everywhere in the problem, it is probably best to leave it until last.

Beginning with C requires 1 $C_6H_{12}O_6$ and 6 CO_2. Moving on to H with 1 $C_6H_{12}O_6$, there needs to be 6 H_2O to give 12 hydrogen atoms on each side. At this point, there are 18 O on the left side and the $C_6H_{12}O_6$ contains 6 O, which means the O_2 must make up for the 12 O deficiency. This means 6 O_2.

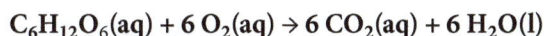

$$C_6H_{12}O_6(aq) + 6\ O_2(aq) \rightarrow 6\ CO_2(aq) + 6\ H_2O(l)$$

The equation is balanced with 6 C, 12 H, and 18 O on each side.

Example Problem 3.2
Bases, such as calcium hydroxide, $Ca(OH)_2$, react with acids, like phosphoric acid, H_3PO_4, to produce a salt, in this case calcium phosphate, $Ca_3(PO_4)_2$, and water, H_2O. Write a balanced chemical equation for the combination of aqueous solution of the acid and base to produce solid calcium phosphate and liquid water.

Solution

First, write the formulas of the reactants and products of this reaction with a blank in front of each formula:

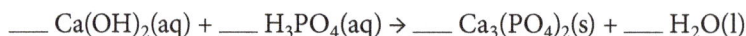

$$\underline{\quad} Ca(OH)_2(aq) + \underline{\quad} H_3PO_4(aq) \rightarrow \underline{\quad} Ca_3(PO_4)_2(s) + \underline{\quad} H_2O(l)$$

We may begin with any of the four blanks. Let's pick the most complicated formula, the $Ca_3(PO_4)_2$, and place a "1" in its blank. This gives

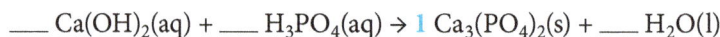

$$\underline{\quad} Ca(OH)_2(aq) + \underline{\quad} H_3PO_4(aq) \rightarrow 1\ Ca_3(PO_4)_2(s) + \underline{\quad} H_2O(l)$$

We can try to balance any of the elements in this formula. However, oxygen, or any element appearing in more than one compound in the equation, is not a good choice. We will balance Ca first. The "1" coefficient indicates that there are three Ca's on the product side. To get three Ca's on the reactant side, we need a "3" in the blank in front of $Ca(OH)_2$. We now have

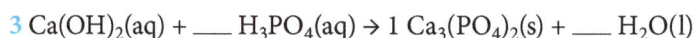

$$3\ Ca(OH)_2(aq) + \underline{\quad} H_3PO_4(aq) \rightarrow 1\ Ca_3(PO_4)_2(s) + \underline{\quad} H_2O(l)$$

Now we need to pick another element and repeat the process. Still working with the "1" coefficient, we can now choose phosphorus, P. There are two P's on the right (two phosphate ions, PO_4^{3-}, each containing one P), so we need two P's on the left. This requires a "2" in the blank before the H_3PO_4. The equation becomes

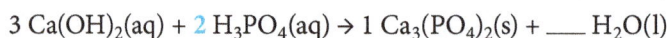

$$3\ Ca(OH)_2(aq) + 2\ H_3PO_4(aq) \rightarrow 1\ Ca_3(PO_4)_2(s) + \underline{\quad} H_2O(l)$$

There is one blank remaining, and we may fill this blank by counting hydrogen, H, or oxygen, O. We will use oxygen. (You should try this step on your own using hydrogen.) There are a total of fourteen O's on the reactant side and eight O's on the product side. There is a deficiency of six O's on the product side. Placing a "6" in the water blank takes care of the oxygen deficiency and gives this:

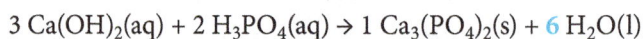

$$3\ Ca(OH)_2(aq) + 2\ H_3PO_4(aq) \rightarrow 1\ Ca_3(PO_4)_2(s) + 6\ H_2O(l)$$

We can now delete the "1" coefficient and check the equation for balance:

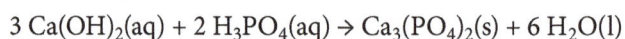

$$3\ Ca(OH)_2(aq) + 2\ H_3PO_4(aq) \rightarrow Ca_3(PO_4)_2(s) + 6\ H_2O(l)$$

Reactant side: 3 Ca, 2 P, 14 O, and 12 H
Product side: 3 Ca, 2 P, 14 O, and 12 H

The coefficients are in the lowest whole-number ratio, 3:2:1:6.

Alternatively, since the polyatomic phosphate ion, PO_4^{3-}, appears on both sides of the equation, you could balance the phosphate ions as a unit. In this case, the balancing would proceed as follows:

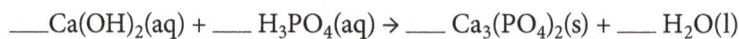

$$\underline{\quad} Ca(OH)_2(aq) + \underline{\quad} H_3PO_4(aq) \rightarrow \underline{\quad} Ca_3(PO_4)_2(s) + \underline{\quad} H_2O(l)$$

As we previously saw, we place a "1" in front of the calcium phosphate:

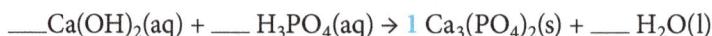

$$\underline{\quad} Ca(OH)_2(aq) + \underline{\quad} H_3PO_4(aq) \rightarrow 1\ Ca_3(PO_4)_2(s) + \underline{\quad} H_2O(l)$$

We can use a "3" to balance the calcium atoms:

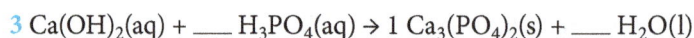

$$3\ Ca(OH)_2(aq) + \underline{\quad} H_3PO_4(aq) \rightarrow 1\ Ca_3(PO_4)_2(s) + \underline{\quad} H_2O(l)$$

Now, instead of looking at the phosphorus atom, we will look at the phosphate ion. There are two phosphate ions on the product side, so we need two phosphate ions on the reactant side. To accomplish this, there needs to be a "2" in front of the phosphoric acid:

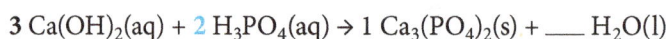

$$3\ Ca(OH)_2(aq) + 2\ H_3PO_4(aq) \rightarrow 1\ Ca_3(PO_4)_2(s) + \underline{\quad} H_2O(l)$$

This takes care of some of the oxygen atoms, but there are still six oxygen atoms unaccounted for (in the calcium hydroxide). These oxygen atoms require six additional oxygen atoms, which a "6" in front of the water will accomplish:

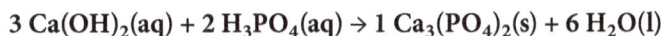

$$3\ Ca(OH)_2(aq) + 2\ H_3PO_4(aq) \rightarrow 1\ Ca_3(PO_4)_2(s) + 6\ H_2O(l)$$

This gives the same balanced equation we saw previously. (Of course, we still need to check the result to make sure the final answer is, in fact, a balanced equation.)

Follow-Up Problem 3.2a

Liquid ethanol, C_2H_5OH, will burn in oxygen gas, O_2, to produce carbon dioxide gas, CO_2, and water vapor, H_2O. Write a balanced chemical equation for this reaction.

Solution

It is acceptable to begin with C or H but not O (since O appears in four places). Beginning with 1 C_2H_5OH leads to 2 CO_2 and then to 3 H_2O. The coefficients on the product side indicate the need for 7 O atoms. To get the same number of O atoms on the reactant side, it is necessary to use the 1 O in C_2H_5OH, plus placing a 3 in front of the O_2 to give a total of 7 on each side.

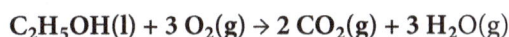

$$C_2H_5OH(l) + 3\ O_2(g) \rightarrow 2\ CO_2(g) + 3\ H_2O(g)$$

The equation is balanced with 2 C, 6 H, and 7 O atoms on each side.

Follow-Up Problem 3.2b

Solid copper(II) nitrate, $Cu(NO_3)_2$, will decompose when heated to produce solid copper(II) oxide, CuO, gaseous nitrogen dioxide, NO_2, and oxygen gas, O_2. Write a balanced equation for this reaction.

Solution

Since there is only one reactant, it will be easiest to begin with it. Starting with 1 $Cu(NO_3)_2$ will require 1 Cu, 2 N, and 6 O on the reactant side. This leads to 1 CuO (balancing the Cu and accounting for 1 O), and 2 NO_2 (balancing the N and accounting for 4 O). This leaves 1 O to account for, which can be done as 1/2 O_2:

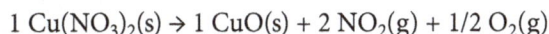

$$1\ Cu(NO_3)_2(s) \rightarrow 1\ CuO(s) + 2\ NO_2(g) + 1/2\ O_2(g)$$

This balances all the atoms; however, the final answer needs to have no fractions; therefore, it is necessary to multiply all the coefficients by 2 to clear all the fractions:

$$2\ Cu(NO_3)_2(s) \rightarrow 2\ CuO(s) + 4\ NO_2(g) + O_2(g)$$

Checking shows 2 Cu, 4 N and 12 O on each side.

Example Problem 3.3

One property of organic compounds is that they will undergo combustion (burning) reactions. This is why many organic compounds are fuels. When an organic compound burns, it combines with gaseous oxygen, O_2, to produce carbon dioxide, CO_2 gas, and water, H_2O. The presence of other elements in the organic compound may yield other products. Variations in the amount of oxygen present may also lead to other products. Write a balanced chemical equation for the reaction of liquid octane, C_8H_{18}, with oxygen gas, O_2, to produce gaseous carbon dioxide, CO_2, and water, H_2O, vapor. Octane is a component of gasoline.

▶ In combustion reactions, if sufficient oxygen is present, the principle products are carbon dioxide, CO_2 gas, and water. However, if there is limited oxygen present, the principle products are carbon monoxide, CO gas (or elemental carbon if the oxygen is severely limited), and water.

Solution

Begin by writing the formulas of the reactants and products of this reaction with a blank in front of each formula:

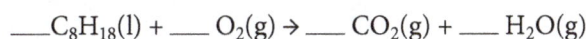

$$\underline{\quad}C_8H_{18}(l) + \underline{\quad}O_2(g) \rightarrow \underline{\quad}CO_2(g) + \underline{\quad}H_2O(g)$$

As usual, we can begin with any of the blanks, but because of the multiple appearances of oxygen, it is probably best not to begin with oxygen. We will place a 1 in the blank in front of the octane to give this:

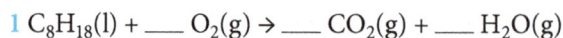

$$1\ C_8H_{18}(l) + \_\_\_ O_2(g) \rightarrow \_\_\_ CO_2(g) + \_\_\_ H_2O(g)$$

Starting here, we can balance either the carbon or the hydrogen. If we pick the carbon, we will need an 8 in front of the carbon dioxide:

$$1\ C_8H_{18}(l) + \_\_\_ O_2(g) \rightarrow 8\ CO_2(g) + \_\_\_ H_2O(g)$$

Following through with the octane "1," we can now balance the hydrogen. The 18 hydrogen atoms in the octane require a 9 in front of the water to give an equal number of hydrogen atoms on the product side:

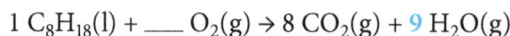

$$1\ C_8H_{18}(l) + \_\_\_ O_2(g) \rightarrow 8\ CO_2(g) + 9\ H_2O(g)$$

> Remember that the coefficients in the final balanced equation cannot be fractions; they must be whole numbers.

This leaves only the oxygen to balance. There are 25 O's total on the product side. To get 25 O's on the reactant side, since the oxygen atoms occur in pairs, will require a coefficient of 25/2:

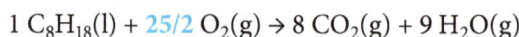

$$1\ C_8H_{18}(l) + 25/2\ O_2(g) \rightarrow 8\ CO_2(g) + 9\ H_2O(g)$$

We now need to multiply the entire equation by two to clear the fraction:

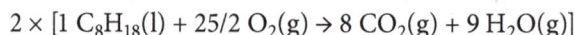

$$2 \times [1\ C_8H_{18}(l) + 25/2\ O_2(g) \rightarrow 8\ CO_2(g) + 9\ H_2O(g)]$$

This gives

$$2\ C_8H_{18}(l) + 25\ O_2(g) \rightarrow 16\ CO_2(g) + 18\ H_2O(g)$$

Finally, check the reaction for balance:

Reactant side: 16 C, 36 H, and 50 O
Product side: 16 C, 36 H, and 50 O

The coefficients are in the lowest whole-numbe)r ratio, 2:25:16:18.

Follow-Up Problem 3.3a

The liquid hydrocarbon hexane, C_6H_{14}, burns in oxygen gas, O_2, producing gaseous carbon dioxide, CO_2, and liquid water, H_2O. Write a balanced chemical equation for this reaction.

Solution

Begin by writing the formulas of the reactants and products of this reaction with a blank in front of each formula:

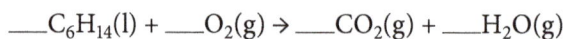

$$\_\_\_C_6H_{14}(l) + \_\_\_O_2(g) \rightarrow \_\_\_CO_2(g) + \_\_\_H_2O(g)$$

Beginning with 1 C_6H_{14} leads to 6 CO_2 and then, since 14 H atoms are necessary, 7 H_2O. The 6 CO_2 and 7 H_2O give 19 O atoms on the product side, which requires 19 O atoms of the reactant side. To get 19 O requires 19/2 O_2, which balances all atoms. However, balancing is not complete because of the fraction:

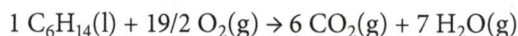

$$1\ C_6H_{14}(l) + 19/2\ O_2(g) \rightarrow 6\ CO_2(g) + 7\ H_2O(g)$$

To clear the fraction, it is necessary to multiply all coefficients by 2:

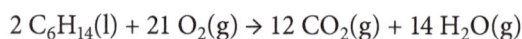

$$2\ C_6H_{14}(l) + 21\ O_2(g) \rightarrow 12\ CO_2(g) + 14\ H_2O(g)$$

This gives a balanced chemical equation, with 12 C, 28 H, and 42 O on each side.

Follow-Up Problem 3.3b

The detonation of many explosives is similar to combustion reactions. In addition, detonations are often decomposition reactions. Explosives contain their own oxygen, and they do not need an external source of oxygen. Write a balanced chemical equation for the detonation of liquid nitroglycerine, $C_3H_5N_3O_9$, to produce the following gases: carbon dioxide, CO_2, water, H_2O, nitrogen, N_2, and oxygen, O_2.

Solution

First, write the formulas of the reactants and products of this reaction with a blank in front of each formula:

$$\_\_C_3H_5N_3O_9(l) \rightarrow \_\_CO_2(g) + \_\_H_2O(g) + \_\_N_2(g) + \_\_O_2(g)$$

Beginning with 1 $C_3H_5N_3O_9$ leads to 3 CO_2 and then, since 5 H atoms are necessary, 5/2 H_2O. In addition, since 3 N atoms are needed, we must have 3/2 N_2. Instead of waiting, clear the fraction now by multiplying the coefficients present by 2:

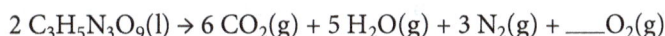

$$2\ C_3H_5N_3O_9(l) \rightarrow 6\ CO_2(g) + 5\ H_2O(g) + 3\ N_2(g) + \_\_O_2(g)$$

The 2 $C_3H_5N_3O_9$ gives 18 O atoms on the reactant side, which requires 18 O atoms of the product side. There are already 17 O atoms on the product side (6 CO_2 and 5 H_2O); the remaining O atoms means 1/2 O_2, which balances all atoms. However, balancing is not complete because of the fraction:

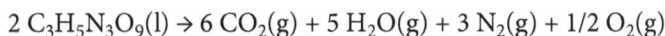

$$2\ C_3H_5N_3O_9(l) \rightarrow 6\ CO_2(g) + 5\ H_2O(g) + 3\ N_2(g) + 1/2\ O_2(g)$$

To clear the fraction, multiply all coefficients by 2:

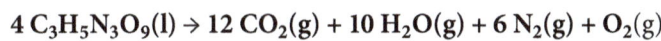

$$\mathbf{4\ C_3H_5N_3O_9(l) \rightarrow 12\ CO_2(g) + 10\ H_2O(g) + 6\ N_2(g) + O_2(g)}$$

This gives a balanced chemical equation, with 12 C, 20 H, 12 N, and 36 O on each side.

Example Problem 3.4

A teaspoon of water contains 4.0 grams of water. How many moles of water are in a teaspoon of water?

Information

The mass of water present in a teaspoon, and the question of how many moles are present

Connections

Moles are the key. The molar mass of water determined from values on the periodic table

Solution

To relate grams of a substance to the moles of that substance, or vice versa, we need the molar mass of the substance. Using the atomic weights from the periodic table, and the formula for water, we get

$$H_2O = 2\ H + O = 2(1.008\ g/mole) + (15.999\ g/mole) = 18.015\ g/mole$$

Combining the mass of the water in the teaspoon with the molar mass gives the moles of water:

$$\text{Moles}\ H_2O = \left(4.0\ g\ H_2O\right)\left(\frac{1\ mol\ H_2O}{18.015\ g\ H_2O}\right) = 0.2220 = \mathbf{0.22\ mole\ H_2O}$$

Reality Check

The 4.0 grams are about one-quarter of a mole, and 0.22 mole is about one-quarter. The significant figures are correct.

Follow-Up Problem 3.4a

There are about 355 grams of water in a typical 12-oz soft drink can. How many moles of water are in 355 grams of water?

Information

The mass of water present in a typical 12-oz soft drink can (355 g), and the question of how many moles are present

Connections

Moles are the key. The molar mass of water determined from values on the periodic table

Solution

Determine the molar mass of water:

$$H_2O = 2\,H + O = 2(1.008 \text{ g/mole}) + (15.999 \text{ g/mole}) = 18.015 \text{ g/mole}$$

Combining the mass of the water in the soft drink can with the molar mass gives the moles of water:

$$\text{Moles } H_2O = \left(355 \text{ g } H_2O\right)\left(\frac{1 \text{ mol } H_2O}{18.015 \text{ g } H_2O}\right) = 19.7058 = \textbf{19.7 mole } H_2O$$

Reality Check

The mass of water is about 360 grams and the molar mass of water is about 18 g/mole, which means that there should be about $360/18 \approx 20$ moles.

Follow-Up Problem 3.4b

The density of methanol, CH_3OH, is 0.7914 g/mL. How many moles of methanol are in 40.0 mL?

Information

The density of methanol, CH_3OH, is 0.7914 g/mL, and the question of how many moles of methanol are in 40.0 mL

Connections

Moles are the key. The molar mass of methanol determined from values on the periodic table; the definition of *density* (Density = Mass/Volume)

Solution

Determine the molar mass of methanol:

$$
\begin{aligned}
CH_3OH &= C + 4\,H + O \\
&= (12.011 \text{ g/mole}) + 4(1.008 \text{ g/mole}) + (15.999 \text{ g/mole}) \\
&= 32.042 \text{ g/mole}
\end{aligned}
$$

Combining the volume and density of methanol with the molar mass gives the moles of methanol:

$$\text{Moles } CH_3OH = \left(40.0 \text{ mL } CH_3OH\right)\left(\frac{0.7914 \text{ g } CH_3OH}{\text{mL } CH_3OH}\right)\left(\frac{1 \text{ mol } CH_3OH}{32.042 \text{ g } CH_3OH}\right)$$

$$= 0.987953 = \textbf{0.988 mole } CH_3OH$$

Example Problem 3.5

A teaspoon of water contains 4.0 grams of water. How many molecules of water are in a teaspoon of water?

Information

The mass of water present in a teaspoon, and the question of how many molecules are present

Connections

Moles are the key. The molar mass of water determined from values on the periodic table and Avogadro's number

Solution

Moles are the key. You must go through moles to relate mass and molecules. To get moles, we need the molar mass of water. From the atomic weights on the periodic table, and from the formula for water, we get

$$H_2O = 2\,H + O = 2(1.008 \text{ g/mole}) + (15.999 \text{ g/mole}) = 18.015 \text{ g/mole}$$

To relate moles to the number of molecules, we need Avogadro's number. The mass to moles relationship is

$$\text{Moles } H_2O = \left(4.0 \text{ g } H_2O\right)\left(\frac{1 \text{ mol } H_2O}{18.015 \text{ g } H_2O}\right) = 0.2220 \text{ mole } H_2O \qquad \text{(unrounded)}$$

The moles-to-molecules relationship is

$$\text{Molecules } H_2O = \left(0.2220 \text{ mol } H_2O\right)\left(\frac{6.022 \times 10^{23} \text{ molecules } H_2O}{1 \text{ mol } H_2O}\right)$$

$$= 1.3371 \times 10^{23}$$
$$= 1.3 \times 10^{23} \text{ molecules of water}$$

(Notice that we used the unrounded intermediate value for the number of moles to avoid unintentional rounding that might change the final value.)

We may shorten the problem by combining the above two steps:

$$\text{Molecules } H_2O = \left(4.0 \text{ g } H_2O\right)\frac{1 \text{ mol } H_2O}{18.015 \text{ g } H_2O}\left(\frac{6.022 \times 10^{23} \text{ molecules } H_2O}{1 \text{ mol } H_2O}\right)$$

$$= 1.3371 \times 10^{23}$$
$$= \mathbf{1.3 \times 10^{23} \text{ molecules of water}} \text{ (rounded to the correct number}$$
$$\text{of significant figures)}$$

Reality Check

The mass of water is less than one-fourth the molar mass of water; therefore, the molecules of water should be less than one-fourth Avogadro's number ($< 1.5 \times 10^{23}$ molecules of water).

Follow-Up Problem 3.5a

A quart of water weighs 946 grams. How many molecules of water are in a quart of water?

Information

Moles are the key. The mass of water present in a quart (946 g); the question of how many molecules are present

Connections

The molar mass of water determined from values on the periodic table and Avogadro's number

Solution

Determine the molar mass of water:

$$H_2O = 2\,H + O = 2(1.008 \text{ g/mole}) + (15.999 \text{ g/mole}) = 18.015 \text{ g/mole}$$

We can now determine the molecules of water present:

$$\text{Molecules } H_2O = \left(946 \text{ g } H_2O\right)\left(\frac{1 \text{ mol } H_2O}{18.015 \text{ g } H_2O}\right)\left(\frac{6.022 \times 10^{23} \text{ molecules } H_2O}{1 \text{ mol } H_2O}\right)$$

$$= 3.16226 \times 10^{25}$$
$$= \mathbf{3.16 \times 10^{25} \text{ molecules of water}}$$

Reality Check

The mass is about 1,000 grams and the molar mass of water is about 20 g/mole so the number of molecules should be about 1,000/20 = 50 times Avogadro's number.

Follow-Up Problem 3.5b

Pure 2-propanol (isopropyl alcohol) diluted with water produces rubbing alcohol. The density of 2-propanol, C_3H_8O, is 0.7809 g/mL. How many molecules of 2-propanol are in 125 mL?

Information

The density of 2-propanol, C_3H_8O (0.7809 g/mL); a 125 mL-sample of 2-propanol; the question of how many molecules are present

Connections

Moles are the key. The molar mass of 2-propanol determined from values on the periodic table; Avogadro's number; the definition of *density* (Density = Mass/Volume)

Solution

Determine the molar mass of C_3H_8O:

$$C_3H_8O = 3\,C + 8\,H + O = 3\,(12.011 \text{ g/mole}) + 8(1.008 \text{ g/mole}) + (15.999 \text{ g/mole})$$
$$= 60.096 \text{ g/mole}$$

We can now determine the molecules of C_3H_8O present:

Molecules C_3H_8O

$$= \left(125 \text{ mL } C_3H_8O\right)\left(\frac{0.7809 \text{ g } C_3H_8O}{mL \text{ } C_3H_8O}\right)\left(\frac{1 \text{ mol } C_3H_8O}{60.096 \text{ g } C_3H_8O}\right)\left(\frac{6.022 \times 10^{23} \text{ molecules } C_3H_8O}{1 \text{ mol } C_3H_8O}\right)$$

$$= 9.78139 \times 10^{23} = \mathbf{9.78 \times 10^{23} \text{ molecules of } C_3H_8O}$$

Example Problem 3.6

Upon analysis, a chemist found that a sample of a reddish-brown gas, produced by the reaction of copper metal with nitric acid, contained 4.00 grams of nitrogen and 9.14 grams of oxygen. Determine the empirical formula of this reddish-brown gas. This reaction is shown in **figure 3.5**.

Information

The composition of a gas sample (4.00 grams of nitrogen and 9.14 grams of oxygen), and the question "what is the empirical formula?"

Connections

Moles are the key. The molar mass of nitrogen and oxygen from values on the periodic table

Solution

To determine the empirical formula of a compound, we must first determine the number of moles of each component. In this case, we need the moles of nitrogen and moles of oxygen. We calculate these two values by using the masses in the problem, and the atomic weights from the periodic table. The following setups show how to determine these two values:

$$\text{N: } (4.00 \text{ g N}) \left(\frac{1 \text{ mol N}}{14.007 \text{ g N}} \right) = 0.28557 \text{ mole N}$$

$$\text{O: } (9.14 \text{ g O}) \left(\frac{1 \text{ mol O}}{15.999 \text{ g O}} \right) = 0.57129 \text{ mole O}$$

(Note: These intermediate values are <u>not</u> rounded to the proper number of significant figures.)

These values give us the number of moles of each element. However, we want the empirical formula (simplest whole-number ratio). One method to convert these values to whole numbers is to divide each value by the smaller number of moles. This leads to the following calculations:

$$\text{N: } \left(\frac{0.28557 \text{ mol N}}{0.28557 \text{ mol N}} \right) = 1.00$$

$$\text{O: } \left(\frac{0.57129 \text{ mol O}}{0.28557 \text{ mol N}} \right) = 2.00 \text{ mole O/mole N}$$

Thus, the N to O ratio is 1 N to 2 O, or **NO$_2$**.

▶ Numbers like 1.99 and 2.03 usually round to 2.

Reality Check

The empirical formula obtained does have the simplest whole-number ratio.

Follow-Up Problem 3.6a

Preparation of xenon compounds began in the early 1960s. The first was a binary compound containing xenon and fluorine. (A binary compound contains only two elements.) Analysis of a sample of this colorless compound found 6.334 grams of xenon, Xe, and 3.666 grams of fluorine, F. Determine the empirical formula of this compound.

Information

The composition of a compound sample (6.334 grams of xenon, Xe, and 3.666 grams of fluorine, F); the question of what is the empirical formula

Connections

Moles are the key. The molar mass of xenon and fluorine from values on the periodic table

Solution

First, determine the moles of Xe and F, and then divide by the smaller value:

$$\text{Xe: } (6.334 \text{ g Xe}) \left(\frac{1 \text{ mol Xe}}{131.293 \text{ g Xe}} \right) = \left(\frac{0.0482432 \text{ mole Xe}}{0.0482432} \right) = 1.000$$

$$\text{F: } (3.666 \text{ g F}) \left(\frac{1 \text{ mol F}}{18.998 \text{ g F}} \right) = \left(\frac{0.1929768 \text{ mole F}}{0.0482432} \right) = 4.001$$

Therefore, the empirical formula is **XeF$_4$**.

Reality Check

The empirical formula obtained does have the simplest whole-number ratio.

▸ When we indicate that a substance is "in excess" in a reaction, all the other reactant(s) will be totally consumed and some of the excess reactant will be left over. In this case, all the bismuth will react and some of the fluorine will remain.

Follow-Up Problem 3.6b

Heating a 3.0000-gram sample of the element bismuth, Bi, in an excess of fluorine, F_2, gave 4.3636 grams of a bismuth fluorine compound. Determine the empirical formula of this compound.

Information

The partial composition of a compound sample (3.0000 grams of bismuth and 4.3636 grams of compound), and the question (what is the empirical formula)

Connections

Moles are the key. The molar mass of bismuth and fluorine from values on the periodic table

Solution

First, we need to determine the mass of fluorine in the compound. To do this, subtract the mass of bismuth from the mass of the compound:

$$\text{Mass F} = 4.3636 \text{ g (Bi + F)} - 3.0000 \text{ g Bi} = 1.3636 \text{ g F}$$

Now, determine the moles of Bi and F, and then divide by the smaller value:

$$\text{Bi: } (3.0000 \text{ g Bi})\left(\frac{1 \text{ mol Bi}}{208.980 \text{ g Bi}}\right) = \left(\frac{0.0143554 \text{ mole Bi}}{0.0143554}\right) = 1.000$$

$$\text{F: } (1.3636 \text{ g F})\left(\frac{1 \text{ mol F}}{18.998 \text{ g F}}\right) = \left(\frac{0.07177597 \text{ mole F}}{0.0143554}\right) = 4.9999$$

Therefore, the empirical formula is **BiF_5**.

Reality Check

The empirical formula obtained does have the simplest whole-number ratio.

Example Problem 3.7

Analysis of a sample of an unknown odoriferous liquid found it to contain 48.6% carbon, 8.3% hydrogen, and 43.2% oxygen. Determine the empirical formula of this compound.

Information

The percent composition of a compound (48.6% carbon, 8.3% hydrogen, and 43.2% oxygen), and the question of what is the empirical formula

Connections

Moles are the key. The molar mass of carbon, hydrogen, and oxygen from values on the periodic table

Solution

As with all empirical formula determinations, we first need to find the moles of each element. Beginning this task with percentages is only slightly different from beginning with grams. To get to moles, just choose any mass of material, and apply the percentages to this mass so you can find the mass of each element. The simplest mass to choose is exactly 100 grams. Choosing this mass makes the mass determinations easier because the percentages become the mass, in grams, of each element. (Other masses will work, but the calculations are more involved and longer.) Using exactly 100 grams gives the following masses of the three elements: 48.6 g carbon, 8.3 g hydrogen, and 43.2 g oxygen. (Note: If exactly 15 grams of material were used the masses would be 7.29 g carbon, 1.23 g hydrogen, and 6.48 g oxygen. (You should use these values to confirm that you will get the same answer.) Now, calculate the moles of each of the elements:

$$\text{C: } (48.6 \text{ g C})\left(\frac{1 \text{ mol C}}{12.011 \text{ g C}}\right) = 4.04629 \text{ mole C}$$

$$H: (8.3 \text{ g H})\left(\frac{1 \text{ mol H}}{1.008 \text{ g H}}\right) = 8.2341 \text{ mole H}$$

$$O: (43.2 \text{ g O})\left(\frac{1 \text{ mol O}}{15.999 \text{ g O}}\right) = 2.70017 \text{ mole O}$$

(Note: These intermediate values are not rounded to the proper number of significant figures.)

To get the simplest ratio, divide each of the moles by the smallest value:

$$C: \left(\frac{4.04629 \text{ mol C}}{2.70017 \text{ mol O}}\right) = 1.499 \text{ mole C/mole O}$$

$$H: \left(\frac{8.2341 \text{ mol H}}{2.70017 \text{ mol O}}\right) = 3.050 \text{ mole H/mole O}$$

$$O: \left(\frac{2.70017 \text{ mol O}}{2.70017 \text{ mol O}}\right) = 1.00$$

The empirical formula numbers need to be whole numbers. Values such as 3.050 (for hydrogen) will round to a whole number. (In general, a value within 0.1 of a whole number rounds to the whole number.) The carbon value is too far from a whole number to simply round to an integer. It is necessary to convert values, such as 1.499, to an integer value by multiplying by the smallest whole number to get close to an integer. The smallest value to do this, in this case, is 2. If we multiply one of the values by 2, then all values need the same multiplier. This step changes 1.5 C, 3.0 H, and 1.0 O to 3.0 C, 6.0 H, and 2.0 O. Thus, the empirical formula is $C_3H_6O_2$.

Reality Check
The empirical formula obtained does have the simplest whole-number ratio.

Follow-Up Problem 3.7a
Analysis of a white solid yielded the following data: 40.9% N, 7.36% H, and 51.8% Cl. Determine the empirical formula of this compound.

Information
The percent composition of a compound (40.9% N, 7.36% H, and 51.8% Cl), and the question of what is the empirical formula.

Connections
Moles are the key. The molar mass of nitrogen, hydrogen, and chlorine from values on the periodic table

Solution
Assume there are 100 grams of solid; therefore, the percentages of each of the elements are numerically equal to the mass of that element in grams.

Next, determine the moles of N, H, and Cl, and then divide by the smallest value:

$$N: (40.9 \text{ g N})\left(\frac{1 \text{ mol N}}{14.0067 \text{ g N}}\right) = \left(\frac{2.92003 \text{ mole N}}{1.461089}\right) = 2.00$$

$$H: (7.36 \text{ g H})\left(\frac{1 \text{ mol H}}{1.0079 \text{ g H}}\right) = \left(\frac{7.30231 \text{ mole H}}{1.461089}\right) = 5.00$$

$$Cl: (51.8 \text{ g Cl})\left(\frac{1 \text{ mol Cl}}{35.453 \text{ g Cl}}\right) = \left(\frac{1.461089 \text{ mole Cl}}{1.461089}\right) = 1.00$$

Therefore, the empirical formula is N_2H_5Cl.

Reality Check
The empirical formula obtained does have the simplest whole-number ratio.

Follow-Up Problem 3.7b
Analysis of a white acidic solid gave 15.2% Na, 1.00% H, and 30.8% P, with the remainder being oxygen. Determine the empirical formula of this solid.

Information
The percent composition of a compound (15.2% Na, 1.00% H, and 30.8% P, with the remainder being oxygen), and the question of what is the empirical formula).

Connections
Moles are the key. The molar mass of sodium, hydrogen, phosphorus, and oxygen from values on the periodic table

Solution
Assume there are 100 grams of solid; therefore, the percentages of each of the elements are numerically equal to the mass of that element in grams. To determine the percent (grams) of oxygen, subtract the given percentages from 100%:

$$100.0\% - 15.2\% - 1.00\% - 30.8\% = 53.0\%$$

Next, determine the moles of Na, H, and P, and then divide by the smallest value:

$$\text{Na:} (15.2 \text{ g N})\left(\frac{1 \text{ mol Na}}{22.9898 \text{ g Na}}\right) = \left(\frac{0.66116 \text{ mole Na}}{0.99216}\right) = 0.666$$

$$\text{H:} (1.00 \text{ g H})\left(\frac{1 \text{ mol H}}{1.0079 \text{ g H}}\right) = \left(\frac{0.99216 \text{ mole H}}{1.461089}\right) = 1.00$$

$$\text{P:} (30.8 \text{ g Cl})\left(\frac{1 \text{ mol P}}{30.9738 \text{ g P}}\right) = \left(\frac{0.9943888 \text{ mole P}}{0.99216}\right) = 1.00$$

$$\text{O:} (53.0 \text{ g Cl})\left(\frac{1 \text{ mol O}}{15.999 \text{ g O}}\right) = \left(\frac{3.312707 \text{ mole O}}{0.99216}\right) = 3.34$$

The Na and O values are not close enough to a whole number to simply round off the values. We need to multiply all values by a number to get all values near a whole number. The smallest multiplier that will work is 3.

Na: $3 \times 0.666 = 2.00$
H: $3 \times 1.00 = 3.00$
P: $= 3 \times 1.00 = 3.00$
O: $3 \times 3.34 = 10.0$

Therefore, the empirical formula is **$Na_2H_3P_3O_{10}$**.

Reality Check
The empirical formula obtained does have the simplest whole-number ratio.

Example Problem 3.8
Chlorophyll-a is a magnesium-containing molecule in green plants. Removing the magnesium from a sample of chlorophyll-a gave 10.000 grams of solid material. Burning this solid in excess oxygen produced 27.85 grams of carbon dioxide, CO_2, 7.46 grams of water, H_2O, and 0.645 grams

of nitrogen, N_2, gas. The magnesium deficient sample contained C, H, N, and O. Determine the empirical formula of this sample.

Information

A 10.000-gram sample that was burned in excess oxygen to give 27.85 grams of carbon dioxide, CO_2; 7.46 grams of water, H_2O; and 0.645 grams of nitrogen, N_2, gas. What is the empirical formula of a compound containing C, H, N, and O?

Connections

Moles are the key. The molar mass of carbon, hydrogen, nitrogen, and oxygen from values on the periodic table

Solution

As with all empirical formula determinations, first you need to determine the moles of each element or polyatomic ion in the formula. Substances like carbon dioxide will not work directly, because we need the moles of carbon, not the moles of carbon dioxide. We need to determine the moles of C, H, and N atoms from the masses given:

$$C: (27.85 \text{ g CO}_2)\left(\frac{1 \text{ mol CO}_2}{44.009 \text{ g CO}_2}\right)\left(\frac{1 \text{ mol C}}{1 \text{ mol CO}_2}\right) = 0.632825 \text{ mole C}$$

$$H: (7.46 \text{ g H}_2O)\left(\frac{1 \text{ mol H}_2O}{18.015 \text{ g H}_2O}\right)\left(\frac{2 \text{ mol H}}{1 \text{ mol H}_2O}\right) = 0.828199 \text{ mole H}$$

$$N: (0.645 \text{ g N}_2)\left(\frac{1 \text{ mol N}_2}{28.028 \text{ g N}_2}\right)\left(\frac{2 \text{ mol N}}{1 \text{ mol N}_2}\right) = 0.046025 \text{ mole N}$$

Notice that, in each case, we convert to moles of the element and not the compound formed. (Note: We do not round these intermediate values to the proper number of significant figures.)

We cannot determine oxygen by this procedure, because we added an unknown quantity of this element when we burned the sample in excess oxygen. The oxygen calculation will utilize the one remaining piece of information presented in the problem—the mass of the sample. The 10.000 grams will be the sum of the masses of the elements present. We can determine the mass of three elements (C, H, and N) from their moles, and subtract these from the total mass of the sample; the difference will be the mass of oxygen in the original sample. The masses of carbon and hydrogen are determined as follows:

$$C: (0.632825 \text{ mol C})\left(\frac{12.011 \text{ g C}}{1 \text{ mol C}}\right) = 7.5939 \text{ g C}$$

$$H: (0.828199 \text{ mol H})\left(\frac{1.008 \text{ g H}}{1 \text{ mol H}}\right) = 0.8348246 \text{ g H}$$

The mass of nitrogen could be determined in a similar manner. However, the nitrogen was originally isolated as the element, not as part of a compound. According to the law of conservation of matter/mass, the nitrogen should weigh the same no matter what state it is in. (You can check this for yourself by performing a calculation like the above using the moles of nitrogen. The mass of the oxygen may now be determined:

Mass of sample (C, H, N, O) – (mass C + mass H + mass N) = mass O
10.000-g sample (C, H, N, O) – (7.5939 g C + 0.8348246 g H + 0.645 g N) = 0.92628 g O

We can now convert the mass of oxygen to moles:

$$O: (0.92628 \text{ g O})\left(\frac{1 \text{ mol O}}{15.999 \text{ g O}}\right) = 0.057896 \text{ mole O}$$

Next, we must divide the moles of each element by the smallest value:

$$C: \left(\frac{0.632825 \text{ mol C}}{0.046025 \text{ mol N}}\right) = 13.75 \text{ mol C/mol N}$$

$$H: \left(\frac{0.828199 \text{ mol H}}{0.046025 \text{ mol N}}\right) = 18.0 \text{ mol H/mol N}$$

$$N: \left(\frac{0.046025 \text{ mol N}}{0.046025 \text{ mol N}}\right) = 1.00$$

$$O: \left(\frac{0.057896 \text{ mol O}}{0.046025 \text{ mol N}}\right) = 1.26 \text{ mol O/mol N}$$

The carbon and oxygen values are not close enough to round to whole numbers. The smallest multiplier to get both the carbon and the oxygen close to a whole number is four. Multiplying all the ratios above by four gives:

$13.75 \times 4 = 55 \text{ C}$
$18.0 \times 4 = 72 \text{ H}$
$1.00 \times 4 = 4 \text{ N}$
$1.26 \times 4 = 5.04 = 5 \text{ O}$

Thus, the empirical formula is **$C_{55}H_{72}N_4O_5$**.

Reality Check
The empirical formula obtained does have the simplest whole-number ratio.

Follow-Up Problem 3.8a
The combustion of a 15.000-gram sample of the drug morphine produced 39.33 grams of carbon dioxide, CO_2; 9.00 grams of water, H_2O; and 0.7363 grams of nitrogen, N_2. The morphine sample contained C, H, N, and O. Determine the empirical formula of this sample.

Information
A 15.000-gram sample that was burned in excess oxygen to give 39.33 grams of carbon dioxide, CO_2; 9.00 grams of water, H_2O; and 0.7363 grams of nitrogen, N_2. What is the empirical formula of a compound containing C, H, N, and O.

Connections
Moles are the key. The molar mass of carbon, hydrogen, nitrogen, and oxygen from values on the periodic table

Solution
As with all empirical formula determinations, first we need to determine the moles of each element or polyatomic ion in the formula:

$$C: (39.33 \text{ g CO}_2)\left(\frac{1 \text{ mol CO}_2}{44.009 \text{ g CO}_2}\right)\left(\frac{1 \text{ mol C}}{1 \text{ mol CO}_2}\right) = 0.8936808 \text{ mole C}$$

$$H: (9.00 \text{ g H}_2O)\left(\frac{1 \text{ mol H}_2O}{18.015 \text{ g H}_2O}\right)\left(\frac{2 \text{ mol H}}{1 \text{ mol H}_2O}\right) = 0.999167 \text{ mole H}$$

$$N: (0.7363 \text{ g N}_2)\left(\frac{1 \text{ mol N}_2}{28.028 \text{ g N}_2}\right)\left(\frac{2 \text{ mol N}}{1 \text{ mol N}_2}\right) = 0.0525403 \text{ mole N}$$

We cannot determine oxygen by this procedure, because we added an unknown quantity of this element when we burned the sample in excess oxygen. The oxygen calculation will utilize the one remaining piece of information presented in the problem: the mass of the sample. The 15.000 grams will be the sum of the masses of the elements present. We can determine the mass of three elements (C, H, and N) from their moles, and subtract these from the total mass of the sample; the difference will be the mass of oxygen in the original sample. The masses of carbon and hydrogen are determined as follows:

$$C: (0.8936808 \text{ mol C})\left(\frac{12.011 \text{ g C}}{1 \text{ mol C}}\right) = 10.7340 \text{ g C}$$

$$H: (0.999167 \text{ mol H})\left(\frac{1.008 \text{ g H}}{1 \text{ mol H}}\right) = 1.00716 \text{ g H}$$

The mass of nitrogen could be determined in a similar manner. However, the nitrogen was originally isolated as the element not as part of a compound.

The mass of the oxygen may now be determined:

Mass of sample (C, H, N, O) – (mass C + mass H + mass N) = mass O

15.000-g sample (C, H, N, O) – (10.7340 g C + 1.00716 g H + 0.7363 g N) = 2.52254 g O

We can now convert the mass of oxygen to moles:

$$O: (2.52254 \text{ g O})\left(\frac{1 \text{ mol O}}{15.999 \text{ g O}}\right) = 0.1576686 \text{ mole O}$$

Next, we must divide the moles of each element by the smallest value:

$$C: \left(\frac{0.8936808 \text{ mol C}}{0.0525403 \text{ mol N}}\right) = 17.01 \text{ mol C/mol N}$$

$$H: \left(\frac{0.999167 \text{ mol H}}{0.0525403 \text{ mol N}}\right) = 19.0 \text{ mol H/mol N}$$

$$N: \left(\frac{0.0525403 \text{ mol N}}{0.0525403 \text{ mol N}}\right) = 1.000$$

$$O: \left(\frac{0.1576686 \text{ mol O}}{0.0525403 \text{ mol N}}\right) = 3.00 \text{ mol O/mol N}$$

Thus, the empirical formula is: $\mathbf{C_{17}H_{19}NO_3}$.

Reality Check
The empirical formula obtained does have the simplest whole-number ratio.

Follow-Up Problem 3.8b
The combustion of a 20.000-gram sample of the amino acid cysteine produced 21.79 grams of carbon dioxide, CO_2; 10.41 grams of water, H_2O; 10.6 grams of sulfur dioxide, SO_2; and 2.31 grams of nitrogen, N_2. The cysteine sample contained C, H, N, S, and O. Determine the empirical formula of this sample.

Information
A 20.000-gram sample that was burned in excess oxygen to give 21.79 grams of carbon dioxide, CO_2; 10.41 grams of water, H_2O; 10.6 grams of sulfur dioxide, SO_2; and 2.31 grams of nitrogen, N_2. What is the empirical formula of a compound containing C, H, N, S, and O.

Connections

Moles are the key. The molar mass of carbon, hydrogen, nitrogen, sulfur, and oxygen from values on the periodic table

Solution

As with all empirical formula determinations, first you need to determine the moles of each element or polyatomic ion in the formula:

$$\text{C:} \left(21.79 \text{ g CO}_2\right)\left(\frac{1 \text{ mol CO}_2}{44.009 \text{ g CO}_2}\right)\left(\frac{1 \text{ mol C}}{1 \text{ mol CO}_2}\right) = 0.495126 \text{ mole C}$$

$$\text{H:} \left(10.41 \text{ g H}_2\text{O}\right)\left(\frac{1 \text{ mol H}_2\text{O}}{18.015 \text{ g H}_2\text{O}}\right)\left(\frac{2 \text{ mol H}}{1 \text{ mol H}_2\text{O}}\right) = 1.15570 \text{ mole H}$$

$$\text{S:} \left(10.6 \text{ g SO}_2\right)\left(\frac{1 \text{ mol SO}_2}{64.063 \text{ g SO}_2}\right)\left(\frac{1 \text{ mol S}}{1 \text{ mol SO}_2}\right) = 0.165462 \text{ mole S}$$

$$\text{N:} \left(2.31 \text{ g N}_2\right)\left(\frac{1 \text{ mol N}_2}{28.028 \text{ g N}_2}\right)\left(\frac{2 \text{ mol N}}{1 \text{ mol N}_2}\right) = 0.164835 \text{ mole N}$$

We cannot determine oxygen by this procedure, because we added an unknown quantity of this element when we burned the sample in excess oxygen. The oxygen calculation will utilize the one remaining piece of information presented in the problem: the mass of the sample. The 20.000 grams will be the sum of the masses of the elements present. We can determine the mass of four elements (C, H, S, and N) from their moles, and subtract these from the total mass of the sample; the difference will be the mass of oxygen in the original sample. The masses of carbon and hydrogen are determined as follows:

$$\text{C:} (0.495126 \text{ mol C})\left(\frac{12.011 \text{ g C}}{1 \text{ mol C}}\right) = 5.946958 \text{ g C}$$

$$\text{H:} (1.15570 \text{ mol H})\left(\frac{1.008 \text{ g H}}{1 \text{ mol H}}\right) = 1.1649 \text{ g H}$$

$$\text{S:} (0.165462 \text{ mol S})\left(\frac{32.065 \text{ g S}}{1 \text{ mol S}}\right) = 5.30504 \text{ g S}$$

The mass of nitrogen could be determined in a similar manner. However, the nitrogen was originally isolated as the element not as part of a compound.

The mass of the oxygen may now be determined:

Mass of sample (C, H, N, S, O) – (mass C + mass H + mass S + mass N) = mass O
20.000 g sample (C, H, N, S, O) – (5.946958 g C + 1.1649 g H + 5.30504 g S + 2.31 g N) = 5.2731 g O

We can now convert the mass of oxygen to moles:

$$\text{O:} (5.2731 \text{ g O})\left(\frac{1 \text{ mol O}}{15.999 \text{ g O}}\right) = 0.329589 \text{ mole O}$$

Next, we must divide the moles of each element by the smallest value:

$$\text{C:} \left(\frac{0.4951268 \text{ mol C}}{0.164835 \text{ mol N}}\right) = 3.004 \text{ mol C/mol N}$$

$$\text{H:} \left(\frac{1.15570 \text{ mol H}}{0.164835 \text{ mol N}}\right) = 7.011 \text{ mol H/mol N}$$

$$N: \left(\frac{0.164835 \text{ mol N}}{0.164835 \text{ mol N}} \right) = 1.000$$

$$S: \left(\frac{0.165462 \text{ mol S}}{0.164835 \text{ mol N}} \right) = 1.004 \text{ mol S/mol N}$$

$$O: \left(\frac{0.329589 \text{ mol O}}{0.164835 \text{ mol N}} \right) = 2.00 \text{ mol O/mol N}$$

Thus, the empirical formula is: $C_3H_7NSO_2$.

Reality Check
The empirical formula obtained does have the simplest whole-number ratio.

Example Problem 3.9
A 1.778-gram sample of an unknown solid was burned in oxygen, and 2.842 g of CO_2, 0.2609 g of H_2O, and 0.4056 g of N_2 were produced. The molar mass of the unknown was about 740 g/mole. The compound contained C, H, N, and O. Determine the molecular formula of this compound.

Information
A 1.778-gram sample that was burned in excess oxygen to give 2.842 g of CO_2, 0.2609 g of H_2O, and 0.4056 g of N_2; the questions of what is the molecular formula of the compound containing C, H, N, and O and what is the molar mass of the unknown $\approx$ 740 g/mole

Connections
Moles are the key. The molar mass of carbon, hydrogen, nitrogen, and oxygen from values on the periodic table

Solution
It will be necessary to determine the empirical formula before we can determine the molecular formula. We will need to determine the moles of each of the four elements. The determination of the moles of oxygen will be different from the others, because the sample "was burned in oxygen." Burning the sample in oxygen added an unknown quantity of oxygen to the sample. We will need to determine the moles of oxygen from the grams of oxygen. The grams of oxygen in the sample are the grams of the original sample minus the masses of carbon, hydrogen, and nitrogen. Therefore, as our first step towards the solution, we will need to determine the moles and masses of all elements other than oxygen.

We determine the moles and mass of carbon and hydrogen as follows:

$$(2.842 \text{ g CO}_2) \left(\frac{1 \text{ mol CO}_2}{44.009 \text{ g CO}_2} \right) \left(\frac{1 \text{ mol C}}{1 \text{ mol CO}_2} \right) = 0.06458 \text{ mole C}$$

$$(0.06458 \text{ mol C}) \left(\frac{12.011 \text{ g C}}{1 \text{ mol C}} \right) = 0.7756 \text{ g C}$$

$$(0.2609 \text{ g H}_2\text{O}) \left(\frac{1 \text{ mol H}_2\text{O}}{18.015 \text{ g H}_2\text{O}} \right) \left(\frac{2 \text{ mol H}}{1 \text{ mol H}_2\text{O}} \right) = 0.02896 \text{ mole H}$$

$$(0.02896 \text{ mol H}) \left(\frac{1.008 \text{ g H}}{1 \text{ mol H}} \right) = 0.02920 \text{ g H}$$

Nitrogen is slightly different. After combustion, the nitrogen was present in a state in which it is not in combination with another element, and so the mass of nitrogen originally in the sample is the same as the mass of nitrogen remaining. We still need to determine the moles of nitrogen, N, not moles of N_2:

$$(0.4056 \text{ g N}_2)\left(\frac{1 \text{ mol N}_2}{28.028 \text{ g N}_2}\right)\left(\frac{2 \text{ mol N}}{1 \text{ mol N}_2}\right) = 0.02896 \text{ mole N}$$

Once we have the masses of carbon, hydrogen, and nitrogen, we can determine the mass and moles of oxygen:

Mass O = mass of sample – (mass of carbon + mass of hydrogen + mass of nitrogen)
Mass O = 1.778 g sample – 0.7756 g C – 0.02920 g H – 0.4056 g N = 0.5676 g

This allows us to calculate the moles of oxygen:

$$(0.5676 \text{ g O})\left(\frac{1 \text{ mol O}}{15.999 \text{ g O}}\right) = 0.03548 \text{ mole O}$$

Hydrogen and nitrogen have the same number of moles, and it is the smallest number of moles present; thus, we may divide the moles by either of these. Using nitrogen gives

$$\left(\frac{0.06458 \text{ mol C}}{0.02896 \text{ mol N}}\right) = 2.230 \text{ mol C/mol N}$$

$$\left(\frac{0.02896 \text{ mol H}}{0.02896 \text{ mol N}}\right) = 1.000 \text{ mol H/mol N}$$

$$\left(\frac{0.02896 \text{ mol N}}{0.02896 \text{ mol N}}\right) = 1.000$$

$$\left(\frac{0.03548 \text{ mol O}}{0.02896 \text{ mol N}}\right) = 1.225 \text{ mol O/mol N}$$

The carbon and oxygen values are not close enough to round to whole numbers. The smallest multiplier to get both the carbon and the oxygen to near a whole number is four. Multiplying all the ratios above by four gives

2.230 × 4 = 8.820 C ≈ 9
1.000 × 4 = 4.000 H = 4
1.000 × 4 = 4.000 N = 4
1.225 × 4 = 4.900 O ≈ 5

▸ If the calculations had been done using only two significant figures, the final multiplication would have been by five instead of four. This would give the empirical formula $C_{11}H_5N_5O_6$, which is incorrect.

This gives the empirical formula $C_9H_4N_4O_5$.

Once we have determined the empirical formula, we can use the molar mass of the compound (about 740 g/mole) to determine the molecular formula.

We need to compare the molar mass of the empirical formula to the observed molar mass of the compound. The molar mass of $C_9H_4N_4O_5$ is 248 g/mol. This value is about one-third the observed molar mass; therefore, the empirical formula is one-third of the molecular formula. This means that to find the molecular formula, we must multiply the empirical formula by three. So, in this case, Molecular formula = Empirical formula × 3 = $(C_9H_4N_4O_5)$ × 3 = $C_{27}H_{12}N_{12}O_{15}$. As a check, we can determine the molar mass of this formula (744 g/mole), and if the value is close to the observed value, the result is reasonable.

As an alternative, in any case where the relationship between the molar masses is not obvious, the following procedure will determine the multiplier:

$$\text{Multiplier} = \left(\frac{\text{Molecular mass}}{\text{Empirical mass}}\right)$$

In this case:

$$\text{Multiplier} = \frac{\left(740\ {}^{g}\!/_{mol}\right)}{\left(248\ {}^{g}\!/_{mol}\right)} = 2.98$$

Rounding this result to the nearest whole number gives the multiplier needed to convert the empirical formula to a molecular formula, as Molecular formula = Empirical formula × 3 = $(C_9H_4N_4O_5) \times 3 = C_{27}H_{12}N_{12}O_{15}$.

▸ If the multiplier, determined by this method, is not close to a whole number, then there is an error.

Reality Check

The empirical formula obtained does have the simplest whole-number ratio and the molecular formula is a simple multiple of the empirical formula.

Follow-Up Problem 3.9a

Burning a 1.0972-g sample of an unknown solid in oxygen produced 2.5956 g of CO_2, 0.5312 g of H_2O, and a solid residue. The solid residue was iron(III) oxide, Fe_2O_3, and it weighed 0.4709 grams. The molar mass of the unknown was about 185 g/mole. The compound contained C, H, and Fe. Determine the molecular formula of this compound.

Information

Burning a 1.0972-g sample of an unknown solid in oxygen produced 2.5956 g of CO_2, 0.5312 g of H_2O, and a solid residue. The solid residue was iron(III) oxide, Fe_2O_3, and it weighed 0.4709 grams. The molar mass of the unknown was about 185 g/mole. The compound contained C, H, and Fe. Determine the molecular formula of this compound.

Connections

Moles are the key. The molar mass of carbon, hydrogen, and iron from values on the periodic table

Solution

As with all empirical formula determinations, first we need to determine the moles of each element or polyatomic ion in the formula:

$$\text{C: } (2.5956\ \text{g}\ CO_2)\left(\frac{1\ \text{mol}\ CO_2}{44.009\ \text{g}\ CO_2}\right)\left(\frac{1\ \text{mol}\ C}{1\ \text{mol}\ CO_2}\right) = 0.0589788\ \text{mole C}$$

$$\text{H: } (0.5312\ \text{g}\ H_2O)\left(\frac{1\ \text{mol}\ H_2O}{18.015\ \text{g}\ H_2O}\right)\left(\frac{2\ \text{mol}\ H}{1\ \text{mol}\ H_2O}\right) = 0.058973\ \text{mole H}$$

$$\text{Fe: } (0.4709\ \text{g}\ Fe_2O_3)\left(\frac{1\ \text{mol}\ Fe_2O_3}{159.687\ \text{g}\ Fe_2O_3}\right)\left(\frac{2\ \text{mol}\ Fe}{1\ \text{mol}\ Fe_2O_3}\right) = 0.005897788\ \text{mole Fe}$$

Next, we must divide the moles of each element by the smallest value:

$$\text{C: } \left(\frac{0.0589788\ \text{mol C}}{0.005897788\ \text{mol Fe}}\right) = 9.999\ \text{mol C/mol Fe} \approx 10$$

$$\text{H: } \left(\frac{0.058973\ \text{mol H}}{0.005897788\ \text{mol Fe}}\right) = 9.999\ \text{mol H/mol Fe} \approx 10$$

$$\text{Fe: } \left(\frac{0.164835\ \text{mol Fe}}{0.005897788\ \text{mol Fe}}\right) = 1.000$$

Thus, the empirical formula is $C_{10}H_{10}Fe$.

Once we have determined the empirical formula, we can use the molar mass of the compound (about 185 g/mole) to determine the molecular formula.

We need to compare the molar mass of the empirical formula to the observed molar mass of the compound. The molar mass of $C_{10}H_{10}Fe$ is 186 g/mol. This value is close to 185 g/mol; therefore, the empirical and molecular formulas are the same, with both being **$C_{10}H_{10}Fe$**.

Reality Check

The empirical formula obtained does have the simplest whole-number ratio.

Follow-Up Problem 3.9b

Burning a 1.7825-g sample of an unknown, thought to be cysteine, in oxygen produced 1.9587 g of CO_2, 0.8018 g of H_2O, 0.9504 g of SO_2, and 0.2079 g of N_2. The molar mass of the unknown was about 240 g/mole. The compound contained C, H, N, S, and O. Determine the molecular formula of this compound.

Information

A 1.7825-gram sample that was burned in excess oxygen to give 1.9587 g of CO_2, 0.8018 g of H_2O, 0.9504 g of SO_2, and 0.2079 g of N_2; the questions of what is the molecular formula of a compound containing C, H, N, S, and O and what is the molar mass of the unknown $\approx$ 185 g/mole

Connections

Moles are the key. The molar mass of carbon, hydrogen, nitrogen, sulfur, and oxygen from values on the periodic table

Solution

As with all empirical formula determinations, first we need to determine the moles of each element or polyatomic ion in the formula:

$$C: (1.9587 \text{ g } CO_2)\left(\frac{1 \text{ mol } CO_2}{44.009 \text{ g } CO_2}\right)\left(\frac{1 \text{ mol C}}{1 \text{ mol } CO_2}\right) = 0.0445068 \text{ mole C}$$

$$H: (0.8018 \text{ g } H_2O)\left(\frac{1 \text{ mol } H_2O}{18.015 \text{ g } H_2O}\right)\left(\frac{2 \text{ mol H}}{1 \text{ mol } H_2O}\right) = 0.0890147 \text{ mole H}$$

$$S: (0.9504 \text{ g } SO_2)\left(\frac{1 \text{ mol } SO_2}{64.063 \text{ g } SO_2}\right)\left(\frac{1 \text{ mol S}}{1 \text{ mol } SO_2}\right) = 0.014835 \text{ mole S}$$

$$N: (0.2079 \text{ g } N_2)\left(\frac{1 \text{ mol } N_2}{28.028 \text{ g } N_2}\right)\left(\frac{2 \text{ mol N}}{1 \text{ mol } N_2}\right) = 0.014835 \text{ mole N}$$

We cannot determine oxygen by this procedure, because we added an unknown quantity of this element when we burned the sample in excess oxygen. The oxygen calculation will utilize the one remaining piece of information presented in the problem: the mass of the sample. The 1.7825 grams will be the sum of the masses of the elements present. We can determine the mass of four elements (C, H, S, and N) from their moles, and subtract these from the total mass of the sample; the difference will be the mass of oxygen in the original sample. The masses of carbon and hydrogen are determined as follows:

$$C: (0.0445068 \text{ mol C})\left(\frac{12.011 \text{ g C}}{1 \text{ mol C}}\right) = 0.534571 \text{ g C}$$

$$H: (0.0890147 \text{ mol H})\left(\frac{1.008 \text{ g H}}{1 \text{ mol H}}\right) = 0.0897268 \text{ g H}$$

$$S: (0.014835 \text{ mol S})\left(\frac{32.065 \text{ g S}}{1 \text{ mol S}}\right) = 0.47569 \text{ g S}$$

The mass of nitrogen could be determined in a similar manner. However, the nitrogen was originally isolated as the element not as part of a compound.

The mass of the oxygen may now be determined:

Mass of sample (C, H, N, S, O) – (mass C + mass H + mass S + mass N) = mass O
1.7825 g sample (C, H, N, S, O) – (0.534571 g C + 0.0897268 g H + 0.47569 g S + 0.2079 g N)
= 0.4746 g O

We can now convert the mass of oxygen to moles:

$$O: (0.4746 \text{ g O})\left(\frac{1 \text{ mol O}}{15.999 \text{ g O}}\right) = 0.029665 \text{ mole O}$$

Next, we must divide the moles of each element by the smallest value:

$$C: \left(\frac{0.0445068 \text{ mol C}}{0.014835 \text{ mol N}}\right) = 3.000 \text{ mol C/mol N}$$

$$H: \left(\frac{0.0890147 \text{ mol H}}{0.014835 \text{ mol N}}\right) = 6.000 \text{ mol H/mol N}$$

$$N: \left(\frac{0.014835 \text{ mol N}}{0.014835 \text{ mol N}}\right) = 1.000$$

$$S: \left(\frac{0.014835 \text{ mol S}}{0.014835 \text{ mol N}}\right) = 1.000 \text{ mol S/mol N}$$

$$O: \left(\frac{0.029665 \text{ mol O}}{0.014835 \text{ mol N}}\right) = 2.000 \text{ mol O/mol N}$$

Therefore, the empirical formula is $C_3H_6NSO_2$.

Once we have determined the empirical formula, we can use the molar mass of the compound (about 240 g/mole) to determine the molecular formula.

We need to compare the molar mass of the empirical formula to the observed molar mass of the compound. The molar mass of $C_3H_6NSO_2$ is 120 g/mol. This value is half of the molar mass (240 g/mol); therefore, the molecular formula is double the empirical formula: **$C_6H_{12}N_2S_2O_4$**.

Reality Check
The empirical formula obtained does have the simplest whole-number ratio, and the molecular formula is a simple multiple of the empirical formula.

Example Problem 3.10
In the laboratory, we may form small quantities of very reactive chlorine gas by the following reaction:

$$4 \text{ HCl(aq)} + \text{MnO}_2\text{(s)} \rightarrow \text{MnCl}_2\text{(aq)} + 2 \text{ H}_2\text{O(l)} + \text{Cl}_2\text{(g)}$$

How many grams of greenish-yellow chlorine gas will form from the reaction of a solution containing 25.000 grams of hydrochloric acid, HCl, if the black solid manganese (IV) oxide is present in excess?

Information
The balanced chemical equation, 25.000 g of HCl, and the question of how many grams of Cl_2 formed

Connections

Moles are the key. The molar mass of hydrogen and chlorine from values on the periodic table

Solution

The key to any stoichiometry problem is <u>moles</u>. This problem presents a quantity in grams and wants an answer in grams. No matter how many times grams—or most other units—appear, the key to finding a solution is <u>moles</u>. Thus, you must convert the 25.0000 grams of HCl to moles of HCl. (Note: There will be no intermediate rounding. All answers except the last answer will have extra, nonsignificant, figures. This is necessary to minimize the effects of intermediate rounding.) The required conversion factor is the molar mass of HCl (see the periodic table):

$$\text{Moles HCl} = (25.000 \text{ g HCl})\left(\frac{1 \text{ mol HCl}}{36.4606 \text{ g HCl}}\right) = 0.685671656 \text{ moles HCl}$$

The question initially gives HCl, but it requires Cl_2 in the answer, so moles of HCl must be converted to moles of Cl_2. A mole (stoichiometric) ratio (from the balanced chemical equation) is required to change from moles of HCl to moles of Cl_2:

$$\text{Moles Cl}_2 = (0.685671656 \text{ mol HCl})\left(\frac{1 \text{ mol Cl}_2}{4 \text{ mol HCl}}\right) = 0.171417914 \text{ moles Cl}_2$$

▸ To determine the correct stoichiometric ratio to use, one <u>must</u> have the balanced chemical equation.

The mole-to-mole ratio, in the second set of parentheses, comes from the balanced chemical equation. The coefficients from the balanced chemical equation yield the "1" and the "4" in the ratio. (Remember, chemists rarely write a "1" in a balanced chemical equation. You may wish to write this value into the equation as a reminder.) This mole ratio is a very important tool. Not only does it allow you to change from any substance in a balanced chemical equation to any other substance, but also it will appear in virtually every chapter in this textbook.

The final step in this problem is to change moles of chlorine gas to grams of chlorine. This conversion requires the molar mass of chlorine (see the periodic table).

$$\text{Grams Cl}_2 = (0.171417914 \text{ mol Cl}_2)\left(\frac{70.904 \text{ g Cl}_2}{1 \text{ mol Cl}_2}\right) = 12.15445577 \text{ grams Cl}_2$$

Rounding to the proper number of significant figures gives 12.154 grams Cl_2.

We may simplify this problem <u>significantly</u> by combining all the steps into one setup and doing only one calculation in place of three separate calculations. This not only saves time but also reduces the chance of an error in recopying numbers.

$$\text{Mass Cl}_2 = (25.000 \text{ g HCl})\left(\frac{1 \text{ mol HCl}}{36.4606 \text{ g HCl}}\right)\left(\frac{1 \text{ mol Cl}_2}{4 \text{ mol HCl}}\right)\left(\frac{70.904 \text{ g Cl}_2}{1 \text{ mol Cl}_2}\right) = \mathbf{12.154 \text{ grams Cl}_2}$$

Reality Check

The molar mass of Cl_2 is about double that of HCl, and 2/4 means that the mass should be about 1/2 the initial mass of HCl.

Follow-Up Problem 3.10a

Toxic hydrogen sulfide, H_2S, gas may form when sulfide-containing substances are treated with an acid. The following reaction produces hydrogen sulfide gas:

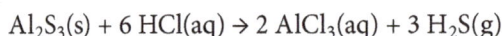

$$Al_2S_3(s) + 6 \text{ HCl(aq)} \rightarrow 2 \text{ AlCl}_3(aq) + 3 \text{ H}_2S(g)$$

How many grams of hydrogen sulfide may form if a solution containing 125.0 grams of hydrochloric acid, HCl, reacts with an excess of aluminum sulfide?

Information

The balanced chemical equation, 125.0 g of HCl, and the question of how many grams of H_2S are formed

Connections

Moles are the key. The molar mass of hydrogen, chlorine, and sulfur from values on the periodic table

Solution

Adding the known and unknown values to the balanced chemical equation may help you to visualize the problem:

$$Al_2S_3(s) + 6\ HCl(aq) \rightarrow 2\ AlCl_3(aq) + 3\ H_2S(g)$$
$$\text{125.0 g} \qquad\qquad\qquad\qquad \text{? g}$$

We will need to convert the mass of HCl to moles by using its molar mass. Use a mole ratio from the balanced chemical equation to get to moles of hydrogen sulfide. Finally, we need to use the molar mass of hydrogen sulfide to get to grams:

$$\text{Mass } H_2S = (125.0\ \text{g HCl}) \left(\frac{1\ \text{mol HCl}}{36.4606\ \text{g HCl}}\right) \left(\frac{3\ \text{mol } H_2S}{6\ \text{mol HCl}}\right) \left(\frac{34.081\ \text{g } H_2S}{1\ \text{mol } H_2S}\right) = \textbf{58.42 grams } \boldsymbol{H_2S}$$

Reality Check

The molar masses of HCl and H_2S are about the same so the mass of H_2S should be about 3/6—or 1/2 the initial mass of HCl.

Follow-Up Problem 3.10b

Colorless nitrogen oxide, NO, forms in the following reaction:

$$3\ Cu(s) + 8\ HNO_3(aq) \rightarrow 3\ Cu(NO_3)_2(aq) + 2\ NO(g) + 4\ H_2O(l)$$

How many grams of copper metal are necessary to produce 15.45 grams of nitrogen oxide in the presence of excess nitric acid?

Information

The balanced chemical equation, 15.45 g of NO, and the question of how many grams of Cu are reacted

Connections

Moles are the key. The molar mass of copper, nitrogen, and oxygen from values on the periodic table

Solution

Adding the known and unknown values to the balanced chemical equation may help you to visualize the problem:

$$3\ Cu(s) + 8\ HNO_3(aq) \rightarrow 3\ Cu(NO_3)_2(aq) + 2\ NO(g) + 4\ H_2O(l)$$
$$\text{? g} \qquad\qquad\qquad\qquad\qquad\qquad \text{15.45 g}$$

We will need to convert the mass of NO to moles by using its molar mass. Use a mole ratio from the balanced chemical equation to get to moles of copper. Finally, we need to use the molar mass of copper to get to grams:

$$\text{Mass Cu} = (15.45\ \text{g NO}) \left(\frac{1\ \text{mol NO}}{30.006\ \text{g NO}}\right) \left(\frac{3\ \text{mol Cu}}{2\ \text{mol NO}}\right) \left(\frac{63.546\ \text{g Cu}}{1\ \text{mol Cu}}\right) = \textbf{49.08 grams Cu}$$

Reality Check

The molar mass of copper is about double that of NO; therefore, the mass of copper should be about three times the mass of NO.

Example Problem 3.11

The insoluble red compound silver chromate, Ag_2CrO_4, forms when solutions of colorless silver nitrate, $AgNO_3$, and yellow sodium chromate, Na_2CrO_4, are mixed. A colorless sodium nitrate solution also forms. This reaction is

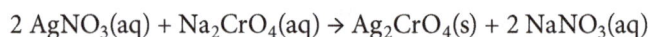

$$2\ AgNO_3(aq) + Na_2CrO_4(aq) \rightarrow Ag_2CrO_4(s) + 2\ NaNO_3(aq)$$

How many grams of silver chromate will form when a solution containing 15.00 grams of silver nitrate mixes with a solution containing 10.00 grams of sodium chromate?

Information

The balanced chemical equation, 15.00 g $AgNO_3$, 10.00 g Na_2CrO_4, and the question of how many grams of Ag_2CrO_4 will form

Connections

Moles are the key. The molar mass of silver, sodium, chromium, nitrogen, and oxygen from values on the periodic table

Solution

As with all stoichiometry problems, <u>moles</u> are the key. However, which moles are we to use? Since the amount of more than one reactant is given, this is a strong indication that the first step will be to determine the limiting reactant (reagent). In this case, this is a two-step process. It is necessary to convert each individual mass (grams) to moles, and then divide the resultant moles by the coefficient from the balanced chemical equation. The grams-to-moles conversion requires the molar mass (refer to the periodic table). (Note: There will be no intermediate rounding. All answers except the last answer will have extra, nonsignificant, figures. This minimizes the effect of intermediate rounding.)

$$\text{Moles } AgNO_3 = (15.00 \text{ g } AgNO_3)\left(\frac{1 \text{ mol } AgNO_3}{169.8731 \text{ g } AgNO_3}\right) = 0.0883012 \text{ moles } AgNO_3$$

$$\text{Moles } Na_2CrO_4 = (10.00 \text{ g } Na_2CrO_4)\left(\frac{1 \text{ mol } Na_2CrO_4}{161.9733 \text{ g } Na_2CrO_4}\right) = 0.061739 \text{ moles } Na_2CrO_4$$

Divide each of these moles of reactant by the coefficient of the compound in the balanced chemical equation:

$AgNO_3$: 0.0883012 moles $AgNO_3$ / 2 mole $AgNO_3$ = 0.0441506 *(LR)*
Na_2CrO_4: 0.061739 moles Na_2CrO_4 / 1 mole Na_2CrO_4 = 0.061737

The silver nitrate mole-to-coefficient ratio is the lower value; thus, silver nitrate is the limiting reactant. <u>All</u> subsequent calculations depend on the limiting reactant. (Note that even though there were fewer grams of sodium chromate, it was not the limiting reactant. In this case, the compound with the greater mass was limiting. Mass <u>does not</u> indicate which reactant is limiting; it only indicates the mole-to-coefficient ratio.)

To convert from the limiting reactant, $AgNO_3$, to the desired product, Ag_2CrO_4, requires the always-important mole ratio. This ratio comes from the balanced chemical equation:

$$\text{Moles } Ag_2CrO_4 = (0.0883012 \text{ mol } AgNO_3)\left(\frac{1 \text{ mol } Ag_2CrO_4}{2 \text{ mol } AgNO_3}\right) = 0.0441506 \text{ moles } Ag_2CrO_4$$

We now use the molar mass (refer to the periodic table) to convert these moles to grams:

$$\text{Grams Ag}_2\text{CrO}_4 = \left(0.0441506 \text{ mol Ag}_2\text{CrO}_4\right)\left(\frac{331.7301 \text{ g Ag}_2\text{CrO}_4}{1 \text{ mol Ag}_2\text{CrO}_4}\right) = 14.64 \text{ grams Ag}_2\text{CrO}_4$$

Combining the last two steps to simplify the calculation will help.

$$\text{Grams Ag}_2\text{CrO}_4 = \left(0.0883012 \text{ mol AgNO}_3\right)\left(\frac{1 \text{ mol Ag}_2\text{CrO}_4}{2 \text{ mol AgNO}_3}\right)\left(\frac{331.7301 \text{ g Ag}_2\text{CrO}_4}{1 \text{ mol Ag}_2\text{CrO}_4}\right)$$

$$= \textbf{14.64 grams Ag}_2\textbf{CrO}_4$$

▶ Always, when working limiting reactant problems, first determine which reactant is limiting; then work the reaction stoichiometry part of the problem.

Reality Check
There is less than 0.1 mole of $AgNO_3$, which means there will be less than $0.1 \times 330 \approx 33$ grams of Ag_2CrO_4, which must be divided in half because of the mole ratio.

Follow-Up Problem 3.11a
Acetic acid, $HC_2H_3O_2$, is the acid present in vinegar. This compound gives vinegar its characteristic odor. Bases, such as calcium hydroxide, $Ca(OH)_2$, will neutralize this acid, as shown in the reaction below:

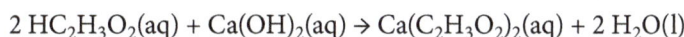

$$2 \text{ HC}_2\text{H}_3\text{O}_2(aq) + \text{Ca(OH)}_2(aq) \rightarrow \text{Ca(C}_2\text{H}_3\text{O}_2)_2(aq) + 2 \text{ H}_2\text{O}(l)$$

How many grams of water will form if a solution containing 25 grams of acetic acid reacts with a solution containing 19 grams of calcium hydroxide?

Information
The balanced chemical equation, 25 g $HC_2H_3O_2$, 19 g $Ca(OH)_2$, and the question of how many grams of H_2O will form

Connections
Moles are the key. The molar mass of calcium, carbon, hydrogen, and oxygen from values on the periodic table

Solution
Adding the known and unknown values to the balanced chemical equation may help you to visualize the problem:

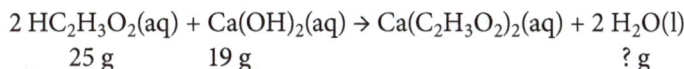

$$2 \text{ HC}_2\text{H}_3\text{O}_2(aq) + \text{Ca(OH)}_2(aq) \rightarrow \text{Ca(C}_2\text{H}_3\text{O}_2)_2(aq) + 2 \text{ H}_2\text{O}(l)$$
$$\quad 25 \text{ g} \qquad\quad 19 \text{ g} \qquad\qquad\qquad\qquad ? \text{ g}$$

The presence of more than one mass on the reactant side is a strong indicator that it will be necessary to determine which of the reactants is limiting.

We will need to convert both masses to moles by using the appropriate molar masses. Next, divide each of the moles by the appropriate coefficient from the balanced chemical equation to find the limiting reactant. Once the limiting reactant is known, finish the problem using the moles of the limiting reactant:

$$\text{Moles HC}_2\text{H}_3\text{O}_2 = \left(25 \text{ g HC}_2\text{H}_3\text{O}_2\right)\left(\frac{1 \text{ mol HC}_2\text{H}_3\text{O}_2}{60.052 \text{ g HC}_2\text{H}_3\text{O}_2}\right) = \frac{0.4163 \text{ moles HC}_2\text{H}_3\text{O}_2}{2} = 0.20815$$

$$\text{Moles Ca(OH)}_2 = \left(19 \text{ g Ca(OH)}_2\right)\left(\frac{1 \text{ mol Ca(OH)}_2}{74.092 \text{ g Ca(OH)}_2}\right) = \frac{0.2564 \text{ moles Ca(OH)}_2}{1} = 0.2564$$

The result for $HC_2H_3O_2$ is smaller than that of $Ca(OH)_2$; therefore, $HC_2H_3O_2$ is the limiting reactant. Finishing the problem with the mole of limiting reactant gives

$$\text{Mass } H_2O = (0.4163 \text{ moles } HC_2H_3O_2)\left(\frac{2 \text{ mol } H_2O}{2 \text{ mol } HC_2H_3O_2}\right)\left(\frac{18.015 \text{ g } H_2O}{1 \text{ mol } H_2O}\right) = \textbf{7.5 grams } H_2O$$

Reality Check

There is less than half a mole of $HC_2H_3O_2$; therefore, there should be less than half the molar mass of water.

Follow-Up Problem 3.11b

The rare-earth element lutetium, Lu, will precipitate (form a solid from a solution) as white lutetium hydroxide, $Lu(OH)_3$, when a solution such as lutetium nitrate is added to a solution of a base, such as lithium hydroxide. This reaction is

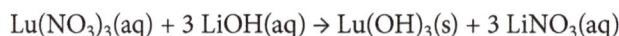

$$Lu(NO_3)_3(aq) + 3 \text{ LiOH}(aq) \rightarrow Lu(OH)_3(s) + 3 \text{ LiNO}_3(aq)$$

How many grams of lutetium hydroxide and lithium nitrate, $LiNO_3$, form when a solution containing 36.1 grams of lutetium nitrate, $Lu(NO_3)_3$, reacts with a solution containing 8.00 grams of lithium hydroxide, LiOH?

Information

The balanced chemical equation, 36.1 g $Lu(NO_3)_3$, 8.00 g LiOH, and the question of how many grams of $Lu(OH)_3$ and $LiNO_3$ will form

Connections

Moles are the key. The molar mass of lutetium, lithium, nitrogen, hydrogen, and oxygen from values on the periodic table

Solution

Adding the known and unknown values to the balanced chemical equation may help you to visualize the problem:

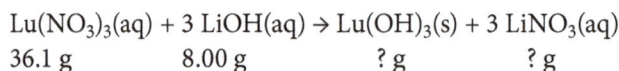

$$Lu(NO_3)_3(aq) + 3 \text{ LiOH}(aq) \rightarrow Lu(OH)_3(s) + 3 \text{ LiNO}_3(aq)$$
$$36.1 \text{ g} \qquad 8.00 \text{ g} \qquad ? \text{ g} \qquad ? \text{ g}$$

The presence of more than one mass on the reactant side is a strong indicator that it will be necessary to determine which of the reactants is limiting.

Convert both masses to moles by using the appropriate molar masses. Next, divide each of the moles by the appropriate coefficient from the balanced chemical equation to find the limiting reactant. Once the limiting reactant is known, finish the problem using the moles of the limiting reactant:

$$\text{Moles } Lu(NO_3)_3 = (36.1 \text{ g } Lu(NO_3)_3)\left(\frac{1 \text{ mol } Lu(NO_3)_3}{360.979 \text{ g } Lu(NO_3)_3}\right) = \frac{0.1000 \text{ moles } Lu(NO_3)_3}{1} = 0.1000$$

$$\text{Moles LiOH} = (8.00 \text{ g LiOH})\left(\frac{1 \text{ mol LiOH}}{23.948 \text{ g LiOH}}\right) = \frac{0.334057 \text{ moles LiOH}}{3} = 0.11135$$

The result for $Lu(NO_3)_3$ is smaller than that of $LiOH$; therefore, $Lu(NO_3)_3$ is the limiting reactant. Finishing the problem with the mole of limiting reactant gives

$$\text{Mass Lu(OH)}_3 = \left(0.1000 \text{ moles Lu(NO}_3)_3\right)\left(\frac{1 \text{ mol Lu(OH)}_3}{1 \text{ mol Lu(NO}_3)_3}\right)\left(\frac{225.988 \text{ Lu(OH)}_3}{1 \text{ mol Lu(OH)}_3}\right)$$

$$= \textbf{22.6 grams Lu(OH)}_3$$

$$\text{Mass LiNO}_3 = \left(0.1000 \text{ moles Lu(NO}_3)_3\right)\left(\frac{3 \text{ mol LiNO}_3}{1 \text{ mol Lu(NO}_3)_3}\right)\left(\frac{68.945 \text{ g LiNO}_3}{1 \text{ mol LiNO}_3}\right)$$

$$= \textbf{20.7 grams LiNO}_3$$

Reality Check

One-tenth mole of limiting reactant should give one-tenth mole of $Lu(OH)_3$ and three-tenths mole of $LiNO_3$.

Example Problem 3.12

At 1500°C, the following reaction produces elemental phosphorus:

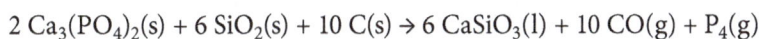

$$2 \text{ Ca}_3(\text{PO}_4)_2(s) + 6 \text{ SiO}_2(s) + 10 \text{ C}(s) \rightarrow 6 \text{ CaSiO}_3(l) + 10 \text{ CO}(g) + \text{P}_4(g)$$

The gaseous phosphorus, P_4, when cooled, becomes a waxy white solid. How many grams of phosphorus will form when 23.109 grams of calcium phosphate, $Ca_3(PO_4)_2$, 13.440 grams of silicon dioxide, SiO_2, and 4.4736 grams of carbon, C, react?

Information

The balanced chemical equation; the amounts of the starting materials—23.109 g $Ca_3(PO_4)_2$, 13.440 g SiO_2, and 4.4736 g C—and the question of how many grams of P_4 will form

Connections

Moles are the key. The atomic masses of the elements from the periodic table

Solution

As with all stoichiometry problems—<u>moles</u> are the key. However, which moles do we use? Since the amount of more than one reactant is present, this is a strong indication that we will initially need to determine the limiting reactant (reagent). In this case, this is a two-step process. First, we convert each individual mass (grams) to moles, and second, we divide the resultant moles by the coefficient from the balanced chemical equation. The grams-to-moles conversion requires the molar mass (refer to the periodic table). (Note: There will be no intermediate rounding. All answers except the last answer will have extra, nonsignificant, figures. This minimizes the effect of intermediate rounding.)

$$\text{Moles Ca}_3(\text{PO}_4)_2 = \left(23.109 \text{ g Ca}_3(\text{PO}_4)_2\right)\left(\frac{1 \text{ mol Ca}_3(\text{PO}_4)_2}{310.177 \text{ g Ca}_3(\text{PO}_4)_2}\right)$$

$$= 0.074502622 \text{ moles Ca}_3(\text{PO}_4)_2$$

$$\text{Moles SiO}_2 = \left(13.440 \text{ g SiO}_2\right)\left(\frac{1 \text{ mol SiO}_2}{60.0843 \text{ g SiO}_2}\right) = 0.22368572 \text{ moles SiO}_2$$

$$\text{Moles C} = \left(4.4736 \text{ g C}\right)\left(\frac{1 \text{ mol C}}{12.0107 \text{ g C}}\right) = 0.372467882 \text{ moles C}$$

Now divide each of these moles by the coefficient of the substance in the balanced chemical equation:

$Ca_3(PO_4)_2$:   0.074502622 moles $Ca_3(PO_4)_2$/2 moles $Ca_3(PO_4)_2$ = 0.037251

SiO_2:   0.22368572 moles SiO_2/6 moles SiO_2 = 0.037281

C: 0.372467882 moles C/10 moles C = 0.037247   (**LR**)

The carbon has the smallest mole to coefficient value, so it is limiting. (Note: If you are not careful with your significant figures, you may get the wrong limiting reactant.)

To get from the limiting reactant (**C**) to the desired product (P_4) requires the always important mole ratio. This ratio comes from the balanced chemical equation:

$$\text{Moles } P_4 = (0.372467882 \text{ mol C})\left(\frac{1 \text{ mol } P_4}{10 \text{ mol C}}\right) = 0.0372467882 \text{ mole } P_4$$

We will now use the molar mass (refer to the periodic table) to convert these moles to grams:

$$\text{Grams } P_4 = (0.0372467882 \text{ mol } P_4)\left(\frac{123.895048 \text{ g } P_4}{1 \text{ mol } P_4}\right) = 4.6189255 \text{ grams } P_4$$
$$= 4.6189 \text{ grams } P_4$$

Combining the last two steps to simplify the calculation will help:

$$\text{Grams } P_4 = (0.372467882 \text{ mol C})\left(\frac{1 \text{ mol } P_4}{10 \text{ mol C}}\right)\left(\frac{123.895048 \text{ g } P_4}{1 \text{ mol } P_4}\right) = 4.6189255 \text{ grams } P_4$$
$$= \textbf{4.6189 grams } P_4$$

Reality Check

Given the amount of limiting reactant, the mass of P_4 seems reasonable. The significant figures are correct.

Follow-Up Problem 3.12a

Potassium oxalate, $K_2C_2O_4$, reacts with deep purple potassium permanganate, $KMnO_4$, in the presence of an acid, such as sulfuric acid, H_2SO_4, according to the following equation:

$5 K_2C_2O_4(aq) + 2 KMnO_4(aq) + 8 H_2SO_4(aq) \rightarrow 10 CO_2(g) + 6 K_2SO_4(aq) + 2 MnSO_4(aq) + 8 H_2O(l)$

Suppose we added 8.311 grams of potassium oxalate, 3.150 grams of potassium permanganate, and 7.850 grams of sulfuric acid to water. According to the equation above, how many grams of potassium sulfate, K_2SO_4, form?

Information

The balanced chemical equation, the amounts of the starting materials (8.311 g $K_2C_2O_4$, 3.150 g $KMnO_4$, and 7.850 g H_2SO_4), and the question of how many grams of K_2SO_4 will form

Connections

Moles are the key. The atomic masses of the elements from the periodic table

Solution

Adding the known and unknown values to the balanced chemical equation may help you to visualize the problem.

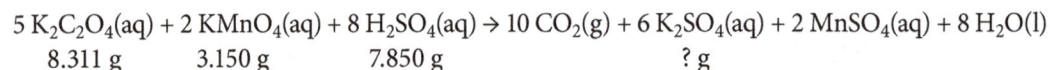

$5 K_2C_2O_4(aq) + 2 KMnO_4(aq) + 8 H_2SO_4(aq) \rightarrow 10 CO_2(g) + 6 K_2SO_4(aq) + 2 MnSO_4(aq) + 8 H_2O(l)$
　　8.311 g　　　3.150 g　　　　7.850 g　　　　　　　　　　　? g

The presence of more than one mass on the reactant side is a strong indicator that it will be necessary to determine which of the reactants is limiting.

Convert all three masses to moles by using the appropriate molar masses. Next, divide each of the moles by the appropriate coefficient from the balanced chemical equation to find the limiting reactant. Once the limiting reactant is known, finish the problem using the moles of the limiting reactant:

$$\text{Moles } K_2C_2O_4 = \left(8.311 \text{ g } K_2C_2O_4\right)\left(\frac{1 \text{ mol } K_2C_2O_4}{166.214 \text{ g } K_2C_2O_4}\right) = \frac{0.05000 \text{ moles } K_2C_2O_4}{5} = 0.01000$$

$$\text{Moles } KMnO_4 = \left(3.150 \text{ g } KMnO_4\right)\left(\frac{1 \text{ mol } KMnO_4}{158.032 \text{ g } KMnO_4}\right) = \frac{0.01993267 \text{ moles } KMnO_4}{2} = 0.009966$$

$$\text{Moles } H_2SO_4 = \left(7.850 \text{ g } H_2SO_4\right)\left(\frac{1 \text{ mol } H_2SO_4}{98.077 \text{ g } H_2SO_4}\right) = \frac{0.080039 \text{ moles } H_2SO_4}{8} = 0.01000$$

The result for $KMnO_4$ is smaller than either of the other reactants; therefore, $KMnO_4$ is the limiting reactant. Finishing the problem with the mole of limiting reactant gives

$$\text{Mass } K_2SO_4 = \left(0.01993267 \text{ moles } KMnO_4\right)\left(\frac{6 \text{ mol } K_2SO_4}{2 \text{ mol } KMnO_4}\right)\left(\frac{174.257 \text{ } K_2SO_4}{1 \text{ mol } K_2SO_4}\right)$$

$$= \textbf{10.42 grams } K_2SO_4$$

Reality Check

The answer seems reasonable given the small amount of $KMnO_4$ (< 0.02 moles), the mole ratio, and the molar mass of K_2SO_4.

Follow-Up Problem 3.12b

Using the following reaction, we may determine the quantity of iron in a sample:

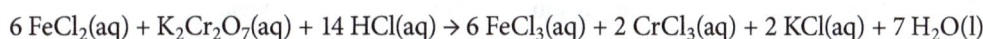

$$6 \text{ FeCl}_2(aq) + K_2Cr_2O_7(aq) + 14 \text{ HCl}(aq) \rightarrow 6 \text{ FeCl}_3(aq) + 2 \text{ CrCl}_3(aq) + 2 \text{ KCl}(aq) + 7 \text{ H}_2O(l)$$

In one experiment, these quantities are mixed: 7.605 grams of iron(II) chloride, $FeCl_2$; 2.942 grams of potassium dichromate, $K_2Cr_2O_7$; and 5.095 grams of hydrogen chloride, HCl. How many grams of chromium(III) chloride, $CrCl_3$, form?

Information

The balanced chemical equation, the amounts of the starting materials (7.605 g $FeCl_2$, 2.942 g $K_2Cr_2O_7$, and 5.095 g HCl), and the question of how many grams of $CrCl_3$ will form

Connections

Moles are the key. The atomic masses of the elements from the periodic table

Solution

Adding the known and unknown values to the balanced chemical equation may help you to visualize the problem:

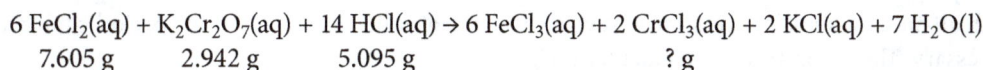

$$6 \text{ FeCl}_2(aq) + K_2Cr_2O_7(aq) + 14 \text{ HCl}(aq) \rightarrow 6 \text{ FeCl}_3(aq) + 2 \text{ CrCl}_3(aq) + 2 \text{ KCl}(aq) + 7 \text{ H}_2O(l)$$

| 7.605 g | 2.942 g | 5.095 g | | ? g | | |

The presence of more than one mass on the reactant side is a strong indicator that it will be necessary to determine which of the reactants is limiting.

Convert all three masses to moles by using the appropriate molar masses. Next, divide each of the moles by the appropriate coefficient from the balanced chemical equation to find the limiting reactant. Once the limiting reactant is known, finish the problem using the moles of the limiting reactant:

$$\text{Moles FeCl}_2 = (7.605 \text{ g FeCl}_2)\left(\frac{1 \text{ mol FeCl}_2}{126.751 \text{ g FeCl}_2}\right) = \frac{0.0599995 \text{ moles FeCl}_2}{6} = 0.0099999$$

$$\text{Moles K}_2\text{Cr}_2\text{O}_7 = (2.942 \text{ g K}_2\text{Cr}_2\text{O}_7)\left(\frac{1 \text{ mol K}_2\text{Cr}_2\text{O}_7}{294.181 \text{ g K}_2\text{Cr}_2\text{O}_7}\right) = \frac{0.010000 \text{ moles K}_2\text{Cr}_2\text{O}_7}{1}$$

$$= 0.010000$$

$$\text{Moles HCl} = (5.095 \text{ g HCl})\left(\frac{1 \text{ mol HCl}}{36.461 \text{ g HCl}}\right) = \frac{0.139738 \text{ moles HCl}}{14} = 0.0099813$$

The result for HCl is smaller than either of the other reactants; therefore, HCl is the limiting reactant. Finishing the problem with the mole of limiting reactant gives

$$\text{Mass CrCl}_3 = (0.139738 \text{ moles HCl})\left(\frac{2 \text{ mol CrCl}_3}{14 \text{ mol HCl}}\right)\left(\frac{158.352 \text{ CrCl}_3}{1 \text{ mol CrCl}_3}\right) = \textbf{3.161 grams CrCl}_3$$

Example Problem 3.13

The following reaction may be used to synthesize the useful chemical alum, $KAl(SO_4)_2 \cdot 12H_2O$:

$$2 \text{ Al(s)} + 18 \text{ H}_2\text{O(l)} + 4 \text{ K}_2\text{SO}_4\text{(aq)} \rightarrow 2 \text{ KAl(SO}_4)_2 \cdot 12\text{H}_2\text{O(s)} + 3 \text{ H}_2\text{(g)} + 6 \text{ KOH(aq)}$$

▶ The formula $KAl(SO_4)_2 \cdot 12H_2O$ indicates that there are 12 waters of hydration associated with 1 unit of $KAl(SO_4)_2$. See the Nomenclature Resource for a discussion of the rules for naming hydrates such as $KAl(SO_4)_2 \cdot 12H_2O$.

This experiment works well in the laboratory. A student weighs 3.250 grams of aluminum into a beaker and then adds an excess of the other chemicals. When finished, she isolates 48.750 grams of alum. What is the percent yield of this experiment?

Information

The balanced chemical equation, the amount of a starting material (3.250 g Al), the actual yield [48.750 g $KAl(SO_4)_2 \cdot 12H_2O$], and the question of what is the percent yield

Connections

Moles are the key. The atomic masses of the elements from the periodic table, and the definition of *percent yield*, $\left(\text{Percent yield} = \dfrac{\text{Actual yield}}{\text{Theoretical yield}} \times 100\%\right)$

Solution

We define the *percent yield* as $\dfrac{\text{Actual yield}}{\text{Theoretical yield}} \times 100\%$

The answer to this problem simply involves inserting the appropriate values into this definition. The actual yield provided in the problem is 48.750 grams of alum. Thus, the real problem here is to determine the theoretical yield.

The determination of the theoretical yield is a straight stoichiometry calculation with no surprises. As with all stoichiometry calculations, the key is moles. In this case, we must first convert the grams of aluminum (the limiting reactant) to moles; use a mole ratio from the balanced chemical equation; and, finally, convert the moles of alum to the grams of alum (theoretical yield). As with all mass-to-mole conversion, and vice versa, the atomic weights from the periodic table are necessary. The theoretical yield calculation is

$$(3.250 \text{ g Al})\left(\frac{1 \text{ mol Al}}{26.9815 \text{ g Al}}\right)\left(\frac{2 \text{ mol KAl(SO}_4)_2 \cdot 12\text{H}_2\text{O}}{2 \text{ mol Al}}\right)\left(\frac{474.384 \text{ g KAl(SO}_4)_2 \cdot 12\text{H}_2\text{O}}{1 \text{ mol KAl(SO}_4)_2 \cdot 12\text{H}_2\text{O}}\right)$$

$$= 57.1409 \text{ g KAl(SO}_4)_2 \cdot 12\text{H}_2\text{O}$$

Inserting the actual and theoretical yields into the definition of percent yield gives

$$\frac{48.750\text{g KAl}(SO_4)_2 \cdot 12H_2O}{57.1409 \text{ g KAl}(SO_4)_2 \cdot 12H_2O} \times 100\% = 85.31542 = \mathbf{85.32\%}$$

There are two additional points about these calculations. First, round only the final answer to the correct number of significant figures. Second, in this case both the actual and theoretical yields are in grams. Grams are not necessary; the actual and theoretical yields only need to be in the same units.

Reality Check

The relationship between the yields is about 50/60 = 5/6 → 83%.

Follow-Up Problem 3.13a

The isolation of gold from gold ore involves the extraction of the gold as $KAu(CN)_2$. The following simplified reaction represents how to isolate metallic gold from this compound:

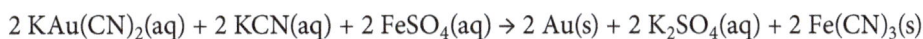

$$2 \text{ KAu}(CN)_2(aq) + 2 \text{ KCN}(aq) + 2 \text{ FeSO}_4(aq) \rightarrow 2 \text{ Au}(s) + 2 \text{ K}_2SO_4(aq) + 2 \text{ Fe}(CN)_3(s)$$

Mixing a solution of a 1.000-gram test sample of $KAu(CN)_2$ from a gold mine with an excess of potassium cyanide, KCN, and iron(II) sulfate, $FeSO_4$, produced 0.675 grams of gold. Determine the percent yield of this reaction.

Information

The balanced chemical equation, the amount of a starting material (1.000 g $KAu(CN)_2$), the actual yield (0.675 g Au), and the question of what is the percent yield

Connections

Moles are the key. The atomic masses of the elements from the periodic table; the definition of *percent yield* (Percent yield = $\dfrac{\text{Actual yield}}{\text{Theoretical yield}} \times 100\%$)

Solution

Adding the known and unknown values to the balanced chemical equation may help you to visualize the problem.

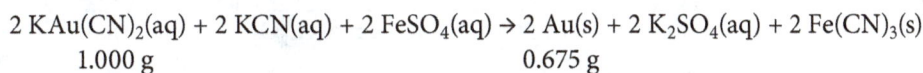

$$2 \text{ KAu}(CN)_2(aq) + 2 \text{ KCN}(aq) + 2 \text{ FeSO}_4(aq) \rightarrow 2 \text{ Au}(s) + 2 \text{ K}_2SO_4(aq) + 2 \text{ Fe}(CN)_3(s)$$

         1.000 g   0.675 g

The presence of one mass on the reactant side indicates that this is a percent yield problem. The value (0.675 g) is the actual yield.

We will need to determine the theoretical yield by converting the mass of $KAu(CN)_2$ to moles using its molar mass. Use a mole ratio from the balanced chemical equation to get to moles of Au, and finally, use the molar mass of Au to get to grams.

$$\text{Mass Au} = \left(1.000 \text{ g KAu}(CN)_2\right)\left(\frac{1 \text{ mol KAu}(CN)_2}{288.100 \text{ g KAu}(CN)_2}\right)\left(\frac{2 \text{ mol Au}}{2 \text{ mol KAu}(CN)_2}\right)\left(\frac{196.966 \text{ g Au}}{1 \text{ mol Au}}\right)$$

$$= 0.684 \text{ grams Au}$$

Inserting the actual and theoretical yields into the definition of *percent yield* gives

$$\frac{0.675 \text{ g Au}}{0.684 \text{ g Au}} \times 100\% = 98.684 = \mathbf{98.7\%}$$

Reality Check

The two yields are nearly the same; therefore, the percent yield should be near 100%.

Follow-Up Problem 3.13b

The compound aluminum chloride, $AlCl_3$, will form when aluminum oxide, Al_2O_3, reacts with hydrogen chloride gas, HCl (the other product is water). In one preparation, 25.0 grams of aluminum oxide produced 64.3 grams of aluminum chloride and excess hydrogen chloride reacted. Determine the percent yield of this reaction. (Hint: First, you will need a balanced chemical equation.)

Information

The amount of a starting material (25.0 g Al_2O_3), a hint (balance the equation), the actual yield (64.3 g $AlCl_3$), and the question of what is the percent yield

Connections

Moles are the key. The atomic masses of the elements from the periodic table; the definition of *percent yield*, (Percent yield $= \dfrac{\text{Actual yield}}{\text{Theoretical yield}} \times 100\%$)

Solution

The first step, write a balanced chemical:

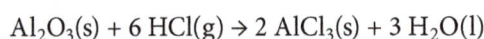

$$Al_2O_3(s) + 6\,HCl(g) \rightarrow 2\,AlCl_3(s) + 3\,H_2O(l)$$

Adding the known and unknown values to the balanced chemical equation may help you to visualize the problem:

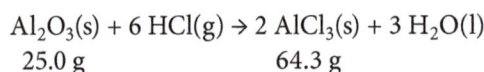

$$Al_2O_3(s) + 6\,HCl(g) \rightarrow 2\,AlCl_3(s) + 3\,H_2O(l)$$
$$25.0\text{ g}64.3\text{ g}$$

The presence of one mass on the reactant side indicates that this is a percent yield problem. The value (0.675 g) is the actual yield.

We will need to determine the theoretical yield by converting the mass of Al_2O_3 to moles using its molar mass, use a mole ratio from the balanced chemical equation to get to moles of $AlCl_3$. Finally, use the molar mass of $AlCl_3$ to get to grams:

$$\text{Mass } AlCl_3 = \left(25.0 \text{ g } Al_2O_3\right)\left(\frac{1 \text{ mol } Al_2O_3}{101.961 \text{ g } Al_2O_3}\right)\left(\frac{2 \text{ mol } AlCl_3}{1 \text{ mol } Al_2O_3}\right)\left(\frac{133.341 \text{ g } AlCl_3}{1 \text{ mol } AlCl_3}\right)$$

$$= 65.4 \text{ grams } AlCl_3$$

Inserting the actual and theoretical yields into the definition of percent yield gives

$$\frac{64.3 \text{ g } AlCl_3}{65.4 \text{ g } AlCl_3} \times 100\% = 98.318 = \textbf{98.3\%}$$

Reality Check

The two yields are nearly the same; therefore, the percent yield should be near 100%.

Example Problem 3.14

The following reaction is important to the Haber process:

$$N_2(g) + 3\,H_2(g) \rightarrow 2\,NH_3(g)$$

An industrial plant combines 3.5 metric tons of nitrogen gas and 0.68 metric ton of hydrogen gas in a Haber–Bosch reactor, and after the conditions are adjusted to optimum, 3.36 metric tons of ammonia form. What is the percent yield of ammonia? (A metric ton (t) is 1,000 kilograms.)

Information

The balanced chemical equation, the amount of the starting materials (3.5 t N_2 and 0.68 t H_2), the actual yield (3.36 t NH_3), the definition of a *metric ton*, and the question of what is the percent yield)

Connections

Moles are the key. The atomic masses of the elements from the periodic table; the definition of *percent yield*, (Percent yield $= \dfrac{\text{Actual yield}}{\text{Theoretical yield}} \times 100\%$)

Solution

Two numbers are needed to determine the percent yield: the actual yield and the theoretical yield. The actual yield is 0.85 metric tons. Thus, we need to calculate only the theoretical yield.

Since we have the quantity of more than one reactant, we need to determine the limiting reactant before calculating the theoretical yield. To calculate the limiting reactant, we convert each of the starting quantities to moles and divide by its coefficient from the balanced chemical equation.

(As always, we will carry additional digits until the very end. At the end, we will round to the proper number of significant figures.)

$$N_2: (3.5 \text{ t N}_2)\left(\frac{1{,}000 \text{ kg}}{t}\right)\left(\frac{1{,}000}{k}\right)\left(\frac{1 \text{ mol N}_2}{28.013 \text{ g N}_2}\right) = 1.2494 \times 10^5 \text{ mole N}_2$$

$$H_2: (0.68 \text{ t H}_2)\left(\frac{1{,}000 \text{ kg}}{t}\right)\left(\frac{1{,}000}{k}\right)\left(\frac{1 \text{ mol H}_2}{2.016 \text{ g H}_2}\right) = 3.37301 \times 10^5 \text{ mole H}_2$$

We must divide the moles of N_2 by 1, and the moles of H_2 by 3 (see the coefficients in the balanced chemical equation). This leaves the N_2 number unchanged, and the H_2 becomes 3.37301×10^5 mole H_2 / 3 mole H_2 = 1.12434×10^5. Thus, H_2 is the limiting reactant because it has the smaller value. Therefore, we must use the hydrogen to determine the theoretical yield.
Calculating the theoretical yield gives

$$(0.68 \text{ t H}_2)\left(\frac{1{,}000 \text{ kg}}{t}\right)\left(\frac{1{,}000}{k}\right)\left(\frac{1 \text{ mol H}_2}{2.016 \text{ g H}_2}\right)\left(\frac{2 \text{ mol NH}_3}{3 \text{ mol H}_2}\right)\left(\frac{17.031 \text{ g NH}_3}{1 \text{ mol NH}_3}\right)\left(\frac{k}{1{,}000}\right)\left(\frac{t}{1{,}000 \text{ kg}}\right)$$

$$= 3.8297 \text{ t NH}_3 \qquad \text{Unrounded (theoretical yield)}$$

Since the mass of ammonia formed was in metric tons (t), it is simplest to calculate the theoretical yield of ammonia in these units. In addition, because of the way the SI system incorporates prefixes, many of the terms are simple inverses and will cancel. Thus, the parentheses that include "1,000" all cancel, and only the remaining terms are necessary for the calculation.

Finally, plugging the actual yield and the theoretical yield into the definition of percent yield gives

$$\text{Percent yield} = \frac{\text{Actual yield}}{\text{Theoretical yield}} \times 100\%$$

$$\text{Percent yield} = \frac{3.36 \text{ t NH}_3}{3.8297 \text{ t NH}_3} \times 100\% = 87.7353 = \textbf{88.\%}$$

Reality Check

The two yields are nearly the same; therefore, the percent yield should be near 100%.

Follow-Up Problem 3.14a

The Ostwald process begins with ammonia from the Haber–Bosch process through the following reaction:

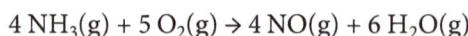

$$4 \, NH_3(g) + 5 \, O_2(g) \rightarrow 4 \, NO(g) + 6 \, H_2O(g)$$

An industrial plant combines 9.5 metric tons of ammonia gas and 19 metric tons of oxygen gas in a reactor; after the conditions are adjusted to optimum, 4.66 metric tons of nitrogen oxide form. What is the percent yield of nitrogen oxide? (A metric ton [t] is 1,000 kilograms.)

Information

The balanced chemical equation, the amount of the starting materials (9.5 t NH_3 and 19 t O_2), the actual yield (4.66 t NO), the definition of *metric ton*, and the question of what is the percent yield

Connections

Moles are the key. The atomic masses of the elements from the periodic table; the definition of *percent yield* (Percent yield = $\dfrac{\text{Actual yield}}{\text{Theoretical yield}} \times 100\%$)

Solution

Adding the known and unknown values to the balanced chemical equation may help you to visualize the problem:

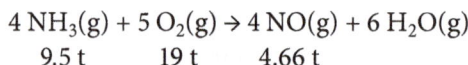

$$4 \, NH_3(g) + 5 \, O_2(g) \rightarrow 4 \, NO(g) + 6 \, H_2O(g)$$
$$ 9.5 \, t 19 \, t 4.66 \, t$$

The presence of more than one mass on the reactant side is a strong indicator that it will be necessary to determine which of the reactants is limiting.

Convert all three masses to moles by using the appropriate molar masses. Next, divide each of the moles by the appropriate coefficient from the balanced chemical equation to find the limiting reactant. Once the limiting reactant is known, find the theoretical yield using the moles of the limiting reactant:

$$\text{Moles } NH_3 = \left(9.5 \text{ t } NH_3\right)\left(\frac{1{,}000 \text{ kg}}{1 \text{ t}}\right)\left(\frac{1{,}000}{k}\right)\left(\frac{1 \text{ mol } NH_3}{17.031 \text{ g } NH_3}\right) = \frac{557806 \text{ moles } NH_3}{4} = 139452$$

$$\text{Moles } O_2 = \left(19 \text{ t } O_2\right)\left(\frac{1{,}000 \text{ kg}}{1 \text{ t}}\right)\left(\frac{1{,}000}{k}\right)\left(\frac{1 \text{ mol } O_2}{31.998 \text{ g } O_2}\right) = \frac{593787 \text{ moles } O_2}{5} = 118757$$

The result for O_2 is smaller than the other reactant; therefore, O_2 is the limiting reactant. It is now possible to determine the actual yield with the moles of limiting reactant:

$$\text{Mass NO} = \left(593787 \text{ moles } O_2\right)\left(\frac{4 \text{ mol NO}}{5 \text{ mol } O_2}\right)\left(\frac{30.006 \text{ g NO}}{1 \text{ mol NO}}\right)\left(\frac{k}{1{,}000}\right)\left(\frac{1 \text{ t}}{1{,}000 \text{ kg}}\right)$$

$$= 14.25 \text{ t NO (extra significant figures)}$$

If the last two steps in the calculation are not done, it will be necessary to convert the 4.66 t of NO in the problem to grams. Either conversion is acceptable.

Inserting the actual and theoretical yields into the definition of *percent yield* gives

$$\frac{4.66 \text{ t NO}}{14.25 \text{ t NO}} \times 100\% = 32.70 = \textbf{33\%}$$

Reality Check

The ratio of the yields is about 5/15 = 1/3 → 33%.

Follow-Up Problem 3.14b

The goal of the Ostwald process is to form nitric acid, HNO_3. This acid forms in the final step:

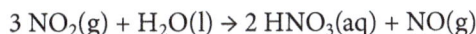

$$3\ NO_2(g) + H_2O(l) \rightarrow 2\ HNO_3(aq) + NO(g)$$

The percent yield of this reaction, in some cases, is 37.5%. Considering this percent yield, how many metric tons of nitric acid will form when 8.75 metric tons of nitrogen dioxide react with 1.00 metric ton of water? (A metric ton [t] is 1,000 kilograms.)

Information

The balanced chemical equation; the amount of the starting materials (8.75 t NO_2 and 1.00 t H_2O); the percent yield (37.5%); the question of what will be the actual yield

Connections

Moles are the key. The atomic masses of the elements from the periodic table; the definition of *percent yield*, (Percent yield = $\dfrac{\text{Actual yield}}{\text{Theoretical yield}} \times 100\%$); the definition of *metric ton* (1 metric ton = 1,000 kg)

Solution

Adding the known and unknown values to the balanced chemical equation may help you to visualize the problem:

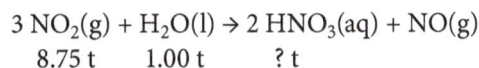

$$3\ NO_2(g) + H_2O(l) \rightarrow 2\ HNO_3(aq) + NO(g)$$
$$\quad 8.75\ t \qquad 1.00\ t \qquad\quad ?\ t$$

The presence of more than one mass on the reactant side is a strong indicator that it will be necessary to determine which of the reactants is limiting.

Convert all three masses to moles by using the appropriate molar masses. Next, divide each of the moles by the appropriate coefficient from the balanced chemical equation to find the limiting reactant. Once the limiting reactant is known, find the theoretical yield using the moles of the limiting reactant:

$$\text{Moles } NO_2 = (8.75\ t\ NO_2)\left(\frac{1{,}000\ kg}{1\ t}\right)\left(\frac{1{,}000}{k}\right)\left(\frac{1\ mol\ NO_2}{46.005\ g\ NO_2}\right) = \frac{190{,}197\ \text{moles } NO_2}{3} = 63{,}399$$

$$\text{Moles } H_2O = (1.00\ t\ H_2O)\left(\frac{1{,}000\ kg}{1\ t}\right)\left(\frac{1{,}000}{k}\right)\left(\frac{1\ mol\ H_2O}{18.015\ g\ H_2O}\right) = \frac{55{,}509\ \text{moles } H_2O}{1} = 55{,}509$$

The result for H_2O is smaller than the other reactant; therefore, H_2O is the limiting reactant. It is now possible to determine the actual yield with the moles of limiting reactant:

$$\text{Mass } HNO_3 = (55{,}509\ \text{moles } H_2O)\left(\frac{2\ mol\ HNO_3}{1\ mol\ H_2O}\right)\left(\frac{63.012\ g\ HNO_3}{1\ mol\ HNO_3}\right)\left(\frac{k}{1{,}000}\right)\left(\frac{1\ t}{1{,}000\ kg}\right)$$

$$= 6.995\ t\ HNO_3\ \text{(extra significant figures)}$$

Inserting the actual yield and percent yield into the definition of *percent yield* gives

$$\frac{?\ t\ HNO_3}{6.995\ t\ HNO_3} \times 100\% = 37.5\%$$

This rearranges to

$$\text{Actual yield} = \left(\frac{37.5\%}{100\%}\right)\left(6.995\ t\ HNO_3\right) = \mathbf{2.62\ t\ HNO_3}$$

Reality Check
The percent yield is about one-third; therefore, the amount produced should be about one-third the theoretical yield.

Example Problem 3.15
The following compounds may serve as potassium sources in fertilizer: potassium hydrogen phosphate, K_2HPO_4; potassium sulfate, K_2SO_4; potassium chloride, KCl; and potassium nitrate, KNO_3. Determine the percent K_2O from each of these substances.

Information
The formulas of the compounds (K_2HPO_4, K_2SO_4, KCl, and KNO_3); the goal of finding % K_2O for each

Connections
Moles are the key. The atomic masses of the elements from the periodic table

Solution
None of these compounds contains K_2O, so this is not a simple mass percent calculation. This calculation requires a conversion from the compound given to potassium oxide, K_2O. We will use the first compound, K_2HPO_4, to illustrate the procedure. The molar mass of K_2HPO_4, from the periodic table, is 174.174 g/mole. The normal method of determining the percent of an element in a sample would be

$$\left(\frac{2 \times 39.098\ g\ K}{174.174\ g\ K_2HPO_4}\right) \times 100\% = 44.895\%\ K$$

A modification of this procedure is necessary to find K_2O instead of K (for potassium alone). As usual, these extra steps deal with moles and a mole ratio:

$$\left(\frac{2 \times 39.098\ g\ K}{174.174\ g\ K_2HPO_4}\right)\left(\frac{1\ mol\ K}{39.098\ g\ K}\right)\left(\frac{1\ mol\ K_2O}{2\ mol\ K}\right)\left(\frac{94.195\ g\ K_2O}{1\ mol\ K_2O}\right) \times 100\% = \mathbf{54.081\%\ K_2O}$$

The other compounds give the following:

$$K_2SO_4\text{:}\left(\frac{2 \times 39.098\ g\ K}{174.258\ g\ K_2SO_4}\right)\left(\frac{1\ mol\ K}{39.098\ g\ K}\right)\left(\frac{1\ mol\ K_2O}{2\ mol\ K}\right)\left(\frac{94.195\ g\ K_2O}{1\ mol\ K_2O}\right) \times 100\% = \mathbf{54.055\%\ K_2O}$$

$$KCl\text{:}\left(\frac{39.098\ g\ K}{74.551\ g\ KCl}\right)\left(\frac{1\ mol\ K}{39.098\ g\ K}\right)\left(\frac{1\ mol\ K_2O}{2\ mol\ K}\right)\left(\frac{94.195\ g\ K_2O}{1\ mol\ K_2O}\right) \times 100\% = \mathbf{63.175\%\ K_2O}$$

$$KNO_3\text{:}\left(\frac{39.098\ g\ K}{101.102\ g\ KNO_3}\right)\left(\frac{1\ mol\ K}{39.098\ g\ K}\right)\left(\frac{1\ mol\ K_2O}{2\ mol\ K}\right)\left(\frac{94.195\ g\ K_2O}{1\ mol\ K_2O}\right) \times 100\% = \mathbf{46.584\%\ K_2O}$$

Reality Check
The values seem reasonable.

Follow-Up Problem 3.15a
The following compounds may serve as phosphorus sources in fertilizer: potassium phosphate, K_3PO_4; ammonium hydrogen phosphate, $(NH_4)_2HPO_4$; and calcium dihydrogen phosphate, $Ca(H_2PO_4)_2$. Determine the percent P_2O_5 from each of these substances.

Information

The formulas of the compounds K_3PO_4, $(NH_4)_2HPO_4$, and $Ca(H_2PO_4)_2$; the goal of finding the % P_2O_5 for each

Connections

Moles are the key. The atomic masses of the elements from the periodic table

Solution

To determine the mass percent P_2O_5, we will need to relate the given formulas to P_2O_5 and then perform a mass percent calculation:

K_3PO_4:

$$\left(\frac{30.974 \text{ g P}}{212.264 \text{ g K}_3PO_4}\right)\left(\frac{1 \text{ mol P}}{30.974 \text{ g P}}\right)\left(\frac{1 \text{ mol P}_2O_5}{2 \text{ mol P}}\right)\left(\frac{141.943 \text{ g P}_2O_5}{1 \text{ mol P}_2O_5}\right) \times 100\% = \mathbf{33.435\% \ P_2O_5}$$

$(NH_4)_2HPO_4$:

$$\left(\frac{30.974 \text{ g P}}{132.056 \text{ g } (NH_4)_2 HPO_4}\right)\left(\frac{1 \text{ mol P}}{30.974 \text{ g P}}\right)\left(\frac{1 \text{ mol P}_2O_5}{2 \text{ mol P}}\right)\left(\frac{141.943 \text{ g P}_2O_5}{1 \text{ mol P}_2O_5}\right) \times 100\% = \mathbf{53.743\% \ P_2O_5}$$

$Ca(H_2PO_4)_2$:

$$\left(\frac{2 \times 30.974 \text{ g P}}{234.050 \text{ g Ca}(H_2PO_4)_2}\right)\left(\frac{1 \text{ mol P}}{30.974 \text{ g P}}\right)\left(\frac{1 \text{ mol P}_2O_5}{2 \text{ mol P}}\right)\left(\frac{141.943 \text{ g P}_2O_5}{1 \text{ mol P}_2O_5}\right) \times 100\% = \mathbf{60.646\% \ P_2O_5}$$

Follow-Up Problem 3.15b

The following compounds may serve as nitrogen sources in fertilizer: urea, $(NH_2)_2CO$; ammonia, NH_3; ammonium nitrate, NH_4NO_3; and potassium nitrate, KNO_3. Determine the percent nitrogen in each of these substances.

Information

The formulas of the compounds $(NH_2)_2CO$, NH_3, NH_4NO_3, and KNO_3; the goal of finding the % N for each

Connections

Moles are the key. The atomic masses of the elements from the periodic table

Solution

This a mass percent problem to determine the % N.

$$(NH_2)_2CO: \left(\frac{2 \times 4.007 \text{ g N}}{60.056 \text{ g } (NH_2)_2 CO}\right) \times 100\% = \mathbf{46.646\% \ N}$$

$$NH_3: \left(\frac{14.007 \text{ g N}}{17.031 \text{ g NH}_3}\right) \times 100\% = \mathbf{82.244\% \ N}$$

$$NH_4NO_3: \left(\frac{2 \times 14.007 \text{ g N}}{80.043 \text{ g NH}_4NO_3}\right) \times 100\% = \mathbf{34.999\% \ N}$$

$$KNO_3: \left(\frac{14.007 \text{ g N}}{101.102 \text{ g KNO}_3}\right) \times 100\% = \mathbf{13.854\% \ N}$$

END-OF-CHAPTER PROBLEMS

3.1 Why is alchemy not a science in the modern sense?

Solution

Alchemy was qualitative—not quantitative like modern chemistry.

3.3 The mole is a fundamental SI unit that is the core of stoichiometry. To a chemist, what is a mole?

Solution

A mole is the SI (refer to chapter 1) unit of quantity of matter, and the definition is that a mole has the same number of particles as found in exactly 12 grams of carbon-12.

3.1 Balancing Chemical Reactions

3.4 Which fundamental law(s) require that a chemical equation be balanced?

Solution

The law of conservation of matter/mass

3.6 During a study session, one of your friends takes the following equation:

$$H_2(g) + O_2(g) \rightarrow H_2O(l)$$

Your friend balances the equation as:

$$H_2(g) + O_2(g) \rightarrow H_2O_2(l)$$

How would you explain the error your friend made?

Solution

It is not appropriate to change any of the chemical formulas in a chemical equation.

3.8 You are helping a friend understand why his grade on a recent chemistry exam was lower than he expected. One of the exam questions asked for the following equation to be balanced:

$$Fe_3O_4(s) + O_2(g) \rightarrow Fe_2O_3(s)$$

Your friend answered:

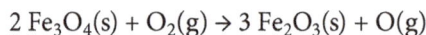

$$2\ Fe_3O_4(s) + O_2(g) \rightarrow 3\ Fe_2O_3(s) + O(g)$$

How would you explain the error to your friend?

Solution

The is no O(g) in the original equation; therefore, it cannot be in the answer.

3.10 Balance the following chemical equations by placing appropriate coefficients in the blanks:

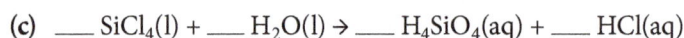

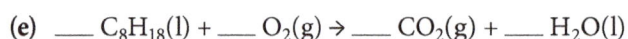

(a) ___ $Cl_2O_5(g)$ + ___ $H_2O(l)$ → ___ $HClO_3(aq)$

(b) ___ $KClO_3(s)$ → ___ $KCl(s)$ + ___ $O_2(g)$

(c) ___ $SiCl_4(l)$ + ___ $H_2O(l)$ → ___ $H_4SiO_4(aq)$ + ___ $HCl(aq)$

(d) ___ $Li_3N(s)$ + ___ $H_2SO_4(aq)$ → ___ $Li_2SO_4(aq)$ + ___ $(NH_4)_2SO_4(aq)$

(e) ___ $C_8H_{18}(l)$ + ___ $O_2(g)$ → ___ $CO_2(g)$ + ___ $H_2O(l)$

Information
The five equations to balance

Connections
The basic procedure for balancing equations (law of conservation of matter/mass)

Solution
Balance one element at a time and continue until each element has been balanced. Clear any fractions that may be present. Finally, check to make sure that each element is balanced in the final equation.

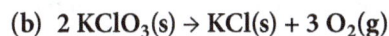

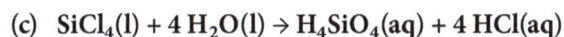

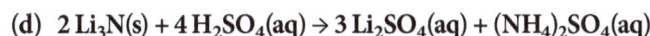

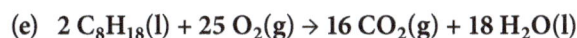

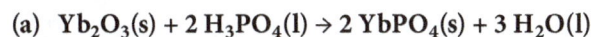

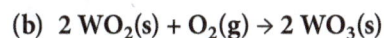

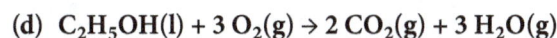

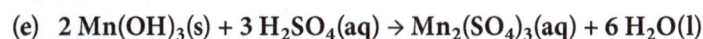

(a) $Cl_2O_5(g) + H_2O(l) \rightarrow 2\ HClO_3(aq)$

(b) $2\ KClO_3(s) \rightarrow KCl(s) + 3\ O_2(g)$

(c) $SiCl_4(l) + 4\ H_2O(l) \rightarrow H_4SiO_4(aq) + 4\ HCl(aq)$

(d) $2\ Li_3N(s) + 4\ H_2SO_4(aq) \rightarrow 3\ Li_2SO_4(aq) + (NH_4)_2SO_4(aq)$

(e) $2\ C_8H_{18}(l) + 25\ O_2(g) \rightarrow 16\ CO_2(g) + 18\ H_2O(l)$

3.12 Balance the following chemical equations by placing appropriate coefficients in the blanks:

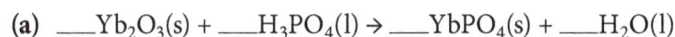

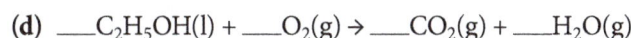

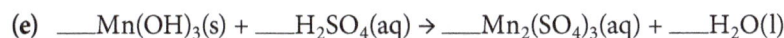

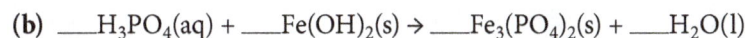

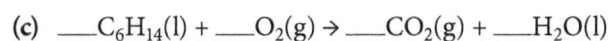

(a) ___$Yb_2O_3(s)$ + ___$H_3PO_4(l)$ → ___$YbPO_4(s)$ + ___$H_2O(l)$

(b) ___$WO_2(s)$ + ___$O_2(g)$ → ___$WO_3(s)$

(c) ___$P_4O_{10}(s)$ + ___$H_2O(l)$ → ___$H_3PO_4(aq)$

(d) ___$C_2H_5OH(l)$ + ___$O_2(g)$ → ___$CO_2(g)$ + ___$H_2O(g)$

(e) ___$Mn(OH)_3(s)$ + ___$H_2SO_4(aq)$ → ___$Mn_2(SO_4)_3(aq)$ + ___$H_2O(l)$

Information
The five equations to balance

Connections
The basic procedure for balancing equations (law of conservation of matter/mass)

Solution
Balance one element at a time and continue until each element has been balanced. Clear any fractions that may be present. Finally, check to make sure that each element is balanced in the final equation.

(a) $Yb_2O_3(s) + 2\ H_3PO_4(l) \rightarrow 2\ YbPO_4(s) + 3\ H_2O(l)$

(b) $2\ WO_2(s) + O_2(g) \rightarrow 2\ WO_3(s)$

(c) $P_4O_{10}(s) + 6\ H_2O(l) \rightarrow 4\ H_3PO_4(aq)$

(d) $C_2H_5OH(l) + 3\ O_2(g) \rightarrow 2\ CO_2(g) + 3\ H_2O(g)$

(e) $2\ Mn(OH)_3(s) + 3\ H_2SO_4(aq) \rightarrow Mn_2(SO_4)_3(aq) + 6\ H_2O(l)$

3.14 Balance the following chemical equations by placing appropriate coefficients in the blanks:

(a) ___$Al(s)$ + ___$O_2(g)$ → ___$Al_2O_3(s)$

(b) ___$H_3PO_4(aq)$ + ___$Fe(OH)_2(s)$ → ___$Fe_3(PO_4)_2(s)$ + ___$H_2O(l)$

(c) ___$C_6H_{14}(l)$ + ___$O_2(g)$ → ___$CO_2(g)$ + ___$H_2O(l)$

(d) ___$N_2O_5(s)$ + ___$H_2O(l)$ → ___$HNO_3(aq)$

(e) ___$XeF_2(s)$ + ___$H_2O(l)$ → ___$Xe(g)$ + ___$HF(g)$ + ___$O_2(g)$

Information
The five equations to balance

Connections
The basic procedure for balancing equations (law of conservation of matter/mass)

Solution
Balance one element at a time and continue until each element has been balanced. Clear any fractions that may be present. Finally, check to make sure that each element is balanced in the final equation.

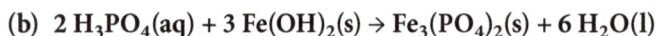

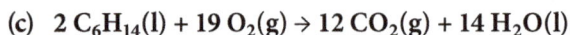

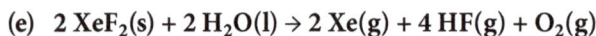

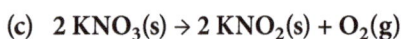

(a) $4\,Al(s) + 3\,O_2(g) → 2\,Al_2O_3(s)$

(b) $2\,H_3PO_4(aq) + 3\,Fe(OH)_2(s) → Fe_3(PO_4)_2(s) + 6\,H_2O(l)$

(c) $2\,C_6H_{14}(l) + 19\,O_2(g) → 12\,CO_2(g) + 14\,H_2O(l)$

(d) $N_2O_5(s) + H_2O(l) → 2\,HNO_3(aq)$

(e) $2\,XeF_2(s) + 2\,H_2O(l) → 2\,Xe(g) + 4\,HF(g) + O_2(g)$

3.18 Determine the formulas for all the reactants and products for the following reactions. Then write balanced chemical equations for each reaction.

(a) Carbon dioxide gas dissolves in liquid water to produce an aqueous solution of carbonic acid.

(b) Solid potassium oxide reacts with liquid water to produce an aqueous solution of potassium hydroxide.

(c) When it is heated, solid potassium nitrate decomposes to solid potassium nitrite and oxygen gas.

(d) Hydrogen sulfide gas will dissolve in an aqueous solution of lead(II) nitrate, $Pb(NO_3)_2$, to precipitate solid lead(II) sulfide, PbS, and form a dilute aqueous solution of nitric acid.

(e) Solid dichlorine heptoxide forms an aqueous perchloric acid solution when dissolved in liquid water.

Information
The five equations to balance (a, b, c, d, and e)

Connections
The basic procedure for balancing equations (law of conservation of matter/mass) and the rules for nomenclature (Nomenclature Resource)

Solution
Balance one element at a time and continue until each element has been balanced. Clear any fractions that may be present. Finally, check to make sure that each element is balanced in the final equation.

(a) $CO_2(g) + H_2O(l) → H_2CO_3(aq)$

(b) $K_2O(s) + H_2O(l) → 2\,KOH(aq)$

(c) $2\,KNO_3(s) → 2\,KNO_2(s) + O_2(g)$

(d) $H_2S(g) + Pb(NO_3)_2(aq) \rightarrow PbS(s) + 2\,HNO_3(aq)$

(e) $Cl_2O_7(s) + H_2O(l) \rightarrow 2\,HClO_4(aq)$

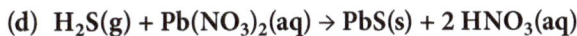

3.2 Avogadro and Moles

3.22 Define *Avogadro's number*. (Note: 6.022×10^{23} is not the definition.)

Solution

The number of particles in a mole is **Avogadro's number**.

3.24 If nitrogen molecules weigh 28 amu each, how much does a mole of nitrogen molecules weigh? Determine this without doing any calculations.

Solution

A mole would weigh 28 grams.

3.26 What information is needed to change the moles of a compound to the grams of that compound? Why is Avogadro's number not necessary?

Solution

It is only necessary to know the molar mass of the compound. It is not necessary to worry about the number of particles present.

3.28 **(a)** How many carbon-12 atoms are in each mole of carbon-12? **(b)** How many grams does each mole of carbon-12 atoms weigh? **(c)** Calculate how many grams each carbon-12 atom weighs.

Information

The three questions: number of carbon-12 atoms, mass of one mole of carbon-12, and mass of one carbon-12 atom

Connections

Avogadro's number (6.022×10^{23}/mole) and the fact that one carbon-12 atom weighs exactly 12 amu (meaning exactly 12 g/mole)

Solution

(a) There will be $\mathbf{6.022 \times 10^{23}}$ **atoms**.

(b) It is only necessary to change amu to grams: **12 g** (exactly).

(c) This is simply answer (b) divided by answer (a):

$$\frac{12\ \text{g}}{6.022 \times 10^{23}\ \text{atoms}} = 1.992693457 \times 10^{-23} = \mathbf{1.993 \times 10^{-23}}\ \textbf{g/atom}$$

Reality Check

(a) A mole of anything has Avogadro's number of that thing. **(b)** The mass of a mole of anything is numerically the same as the number of atomic mass units (amu) the object weighs. **(c)** This is just a simple ratio of the answer to (b) divided by the answer to (a).

3.30 Calculate the formula mass for each of the following: **(a)** H_2O, **(b)** Cl_2O_5, **(c)** $(NH_4)_2CrO_4$, **(d)** $Mg_3(PO_4)_2$, **(e)** $CuSO_4\cdot5H_2O$

Information

The given formulas—**(a)** H_2O, **(b)** Cl_2O_5, **(c)** $(NH_4)_2CrO_4$, **(d)** $Mg_3(PO_4)_2$, **(e)** $CuSO_4\cdot5H_2O$—and the question of what are the molar masses

Connections

The masses of the elements from the periodic table

Solution

Find the atomic mass of each element in the formula and multiply the mass by the number of atoms of that element in the formula. Finally, sum the contributions from each of the elements to give the molar mass:

(a) $(2 \times 1.008 + 1 \times 15.999)$ g/mole = **18.015 g/mole**

(b) $(2 \times 35.4537 + 5 \times 15.999)$ g/mole = **150.901 g/mole**

(c) $(2 \times 14.007 + 8 \times 1.008 + 1 \times 51.996 + 4 \times 15.999)$ g/mole = **152.070 g/mole**

(d) $(3 \times 24.305 + 2 \times 30.974 + 8 \times 15.999)$ g/mole = **262.855 g/mole**

(e) $(1 \times 63.546 + 1 \times 32.065 + 10 \times 1.008 + 9 \times 15.999)$ g/mole = **249.682 g/mole**

3.32 Morphine, $C_{17}H_{19}NO_3$, is a powerful analgesic. **(a)** What is the molar mass of morphine? **(b)** How many grams does 2.00 mole of morphine weigh? **(c)** Calculate the number of moles of morphine present in a sample weighing 0.120 grams. **(d)** How many carbon atoms are present in 5.45 µg of morphine?

Information

Four questions are given: molar mass of morphine, grams of morphine, moles of morphine, and number of carbon atoms; in addition, **(b)** 2.00 mole morphine, **(c)** 0.120 g morphine, and **(d)** 5.45 µg morphine

Connections

Moles are the key. The masses of the elements given on the periodic table; Avogadro's number $(6.022 \times 10^{23}/\text{mole})$; from chapter 1, $\mu = 10^{-6}$

Solution

(a) Find the atomic mass of each element in the formula and multiply the mass by the number of atoms of that element in the formula. Finally, sum the contributions from each of the elements to give the molar mass:

$$(17 \times 12.011 + 19 \times 1.008 + 1 \times 14.007 + 3 \times 15.999) \text{ g/mole} = \textbf{285.343 g/mole}$$

(b) Moles times molar mass gives mass (grams):

$$(2.00 \text{ mol})\left(\frac{285.343 \text{ g}}{\text{mol}}\right) = 570.686 = \textbf{571 g}$$

(c) Dividing the mass by the molar mass gives moles:

$$(0.120 \text{ g})\left(\frac{1 \text{ mol}}{285.343 \text{ g}}\right) = 0.000420547 = \textbf{4.20} \times \textbf{10}^{-4} \textbf{ mole}$$

(d) Dividing the mass by the molar mass gives moles (also, having or wanting the number of "things" implies that you will need Avogadro's number):

$$(5.45 \text{ µg})\left(\frac{10^{-6}}{\mu}\right)\left(\frac{1 \text{ mol}}{285.343 \text{ g}}\right)\left(\frac{17 \text{ mol C}}{1 \text{ mol } C_{17}H_{19}NO_3}\right)\left(\frac{6.022 \times 10^{23} \text{ atoms}}{\text{mol}}\right) = 1.95532 \times 10^{17}$$

$$= \textbf{1.96} \times \textbf{10}^{17} \textbf{ C atoms}$$

3.34 Determine the number of grams present in each of the following samples. **(a)** 0.27952 mole of calcium chloride, $CaCl_2$; **(b)** 4.37×10^{28} molecules of carbon dioxide, CO_2; **(c)** 6.95×10^{15} molecules of water; **(d)** 4.35 moles of carbon monoxide, CO; **(e)** 2.50×10^{18} atoms of xenon, Xe

Information

(a) 0.27952 mole $CaCl_2$; **(b)** 4.37×10^{28} molecules CO_2; **(c)** 6.95×10^{15} molecules H_2O; **(d)** 4.35 mole CO; **(e)** 2.50×10^{18} Xe atoms; the question of how many grams of each

Connections

Moles are the key. The masses of the elements given on the periodic table; Avogadro's number $(6.022 \times 10^{23} \text{ /mole})$

Solution

Where necessary, determine the molar mass of the substance. Find the atomic mass of each element in the formula and multiply the mass by the number of atoms of that element in the formula. Finally, sum the contributions from each of the elements to give the molar mass:

(a) Moles times molar mass gives mass (grams):

$$(0.27952 \text{ mol})\left(\frac{110.984 \text{ g}}{1 \text{ mol}}\right) = 31.02224768 = \textbf{31.022 g}$$

(b) Having or wanting the number of "things" implies that you will need Avogadro's number:

$$\left(4.37 \times 10^{27} \text{ molecules}\right)\left(\frac{1 \text{ mol}}{6.022 \times 10^{23} \text{ molecules}}\right)\left(\frac{44.009 \text{ g}}{1 \text{ mol}}\right) = 319361.2 = \textbf{3.19} \times \textbf{10}^{\textbf{5}} \textbf{ g}$$

(c) Having or wanting the number of "things" implies that you will need Avogadro's number:

$$\left(6.95 \times 10^{15} \text{ molecules}\right)\left(\frac{1 \text{ mol}}{6.022 \times 10^{23} \text{ molecules}}\right)\left(\frac{18.015 \text{ g}}{1 \text{ mol}}\right) = 2.07911 \times 10^{-7} = \textbf{2.08} \times \textbf{10}^{-\textbf{7}} \textbf{ g}$$

(d) Dividing the mass by the molar mass gives moles:

$$(4.35 \text{ mol})\left(\frac{28.010 \text{ g}}{1 \text{ mol}}\right) = 121.8435 = \textbf{122 g}$$

(e) Having or wanting the number of "things" implies that you will need Avogadro's number:

$$\left(2.50 \times 10^{18} \text{ atoms}\right)\left(\frac{1 \text{ mol}}{6.022 \times 10^{23} \text{ atoms}}\right)\left(\frac{131.293 \text{ g}}{1 \text{ mol}}\right) = 0.000545056 = \textbf{5.45} \times \textbf{10}^{-\textbf{4}} \textbf{ g}$$

3.36 Determine the number of molecules in each of the following samples: **(a)** 3.25 moles of aspirin (acetylsalicylic acid), $C_9H_8O_4$; **(b)** 0.0045 mole of table sugar (sucrose), $C_{12}H_{22}O_{11}$; **(c)** 4.55 g of water; **(d)** 2.3 ng of natural gas (methane), CH_4; **(e)** 3 kg of battery acid (sulfuric acid), H_2SO_4

Information

The questions of how many molecules are in each of the following: **(a)** 3.25 moles $C_9H_8O_4$, **(b)** 0.0045 moles $C_{12}H_{22}O_{11}$, **(c)** 4.55 g H_2O, **(d)** 2.3 ng CH_4, **(e)** 3 kg H_2SO_4

Connections

Moles are the key. The masses of the elements given on the periodic table; Avogadro's number $(6.022 \times 10^{23}/\text{mole})$; various conversions from chapter 1

Solution

Having or wanting the number of "things" implies that you will need Avogadro's number.

Where necessary, determine the molar mass of the substance. Find the atomic mass of each element in the formula and multiply the mass by the number of atoms of that element in the formula. Finally, sum the contributions from each of the elements to give the molar mass.

Where necessary, dividing the mass by the molar mass gives moles:

(a) $(3.25 \text{ mol } C_9H_8O_4)\left(\dfrac{6.022 \times 10^{23} \text{ molecules } C_9H_8O_4}{\text{mol}}\right) = 1.95715 \times 10^{24}$

$$= 1.96 \times 10^{24} \text{ molecules } C_9H_8O_4$$

(b) $(0.0045 \text{ mol } C_{12}H_{22}O_{11})\left(\dfrac{6.022 \times 10^{23} \text{ molecules } C_{12}H_{22}O_{11}}{\text{mol}}\right) = 2.7099 \times 10^{21}$

$$= 3.16 \times 10^{21} \text{ molecules } C_{12}H_{22}O_{11}$$

(c) $(4.55 \text{ g } H_2O)\left(\dfrac{\text{mol}}{18.015 \text{ g } H_2O}\right)\left(\dfrac{6.022 \times 10^{23} \text{ molecules } H_2O}{\text{mol}}\right) = 5.42305 \times 10^{22}$

$$= 2.7 \times 10^{22} \text{ molecules } H_2O$$

(d) $(2.3 \text{ ng } CH_4)\left(\dfrac{10^{-9}}{\text{n}}\right)\left(\dfrac{\text{mol}}{16.043 \text{ g } CH_4}\right)\left(\dfrac{6.022 \times 10^{23} \text{ molecules } CH_4}{\text{mol}}\right) = 8.6334 \times 10^{13}$

$$= 8.6 \times 10^{13} \text{ molecules } CH_4$$

(e) $(3 \text{ kg } H_2SO_4)\left(\dfrac{10^3}{\text{k}}\right)\left(\dfrac{\text{mol}}{98.077 \text{ g } H_2SO_4}\right)\left(\dfrac{6.022 \times 10^{23} \text{ molecules } H_2SO_4}{\text{mol}}\right) = 1.8420 \times 10^{25}$

$$= 2 \times 10^{25} \text{ molecules } H_2SO_4$$

3.40 Nickel tetracarbonyl, $Ni(CO)_4$, is used industrially in the purification of nickel. This compound is very toxic, with as little as 6.7×10^{-9} g/L in the air being dangerous. **(a)** How many moles of nickel tetracarbonyl, at 6.7×10^{-9} g/L, are present in a room 2.5 m × 3.7 m × 2.0 m? **(b)** How many molecules of nickel tetracarbonyl are in a liter?

Information

The formula, $Ni(CO)_4$, the concentration (6.7×10^{-9} g/L), and the dimensions of the room (2.5 m × 3.7 m × 2.0 m); the questions **(a)** how many moles and **(b)** how many molecules are in a liter

Connections

Moles are the key. The masses of the elements given on the periodic table; Avogadro's number (6.022×10^{23} /mole); Volume = Length × Width × Height; various conversions from chapter 1

Solution

This is a unit conversion problem.

Find the atomic mass of each element in the formula and multiply the mass by the number of atoms of that element in the formula. Finally, sum the contributions from each of the elements to give the molar mass.

Dividing the mass by the molar mass gives moles:

(a) $\left(\dfrac{6.7\times10^{-9}\text{ g Ni(CO)}_4}{L}\right)\left(\dfrac{\text{mol}}{170.733\text{ g}}\right)\left[(2.5\times3.7\times2.0)\text{m}^3\right]\left(\dfrac{d}{0.1}\right)^3\left(\dfrac{1\text{ L}}{1\text{ dm}^3}\right)=7.25987\times10^{-7}$

$= 7.3\times10^{-7}$ mole Ni(CO)$_4$

(b) $\left(\dfrac{6.7\times10^{-9}\text{ g Ni(CO)}_4}{L}\right)\left(\dfrac{\text{mol}}{170.733\text{ g}}\right)\left(\dfrac{6.022\times10^{23}\text{ molecules Ni(CO)}_4}{\text{mol}}\right)=2.363187\times10^{13}$

$= 2.4\times10^{13}$ molecules Ni(CO)$_4$/L

3.42 The mineral spinel has the formula $MgAl_2O_4$. The mineral is very hard and is occasionally used as a semiprecious gemstone. The density of spinel is 3.581 g/cm^3. Determine how many aluminum atoms are present in 7.500 cm^3 of spinel.

Information

The formula, $MgAl_2O_4$; the density (3.581 g/cm^3); the volume (7.500 cm^3); the question of how many Al atoms are present in the sample of spinel

Connections

Moles are the key. The masses of the elements given on the periodic table; Avogadro's number (6.022 × 10^{23}/mole); the definition of *density* (Density = Mass/Volume); various conversions from chapter 1

Solution

It is necessary to determine the mass of the sample from the density and the volume.

Find the atomic mass of each element in the formula and multiply the mass by the number of atoms of that element in the formula. Finally, sum the contributions from each of the elements to give the molar mass.

Dividing the mass by the molar mass gives moles:

$$\left(7.500\text{ cm}^3\right)\left(\dfrac{3.581\text{ g}}{\text{cm}^3}\right)\left(\dfrac{1\text{ mol MgAl}_2O_4}{142.2656\text{ g}}\right)\left(\dfrac{6.022\times10^{23}\text{ MgAl}_2O_4}{\text{mol}}\right)\left(\dfrac{2\text{ Al Atoms}}{1\text{ MgAl}_2O_4}\right)=2.273717\times10^{23}$$

$= 2.274\times10^{23}$ Al atoms

3.3 Percent Composition of Compounds

3.47 In addition to the chemical formula, what information is necessary to determine the percent composition of a compound?

Solution

The atomic masses of the elements present and the molar mass of the compound are needed.

3.48 For each of the following compounds, calculate the percent by mass of the indicated element: (a) carbon in octane, C_8H_{18}, a component of gasoline; (b) iodine in potassium iodide, KI, a compound used as a dietary supplement; (c) oxygen in methyl salicylate, $C_8H_8O_3$, a compound used as wintergreen flavoring; (d) sodium in sodium stearate, $NaC_{18}H_{35}O_2$, a compound in some soaps; (e) nitrogen in ammonium nitrate, NH_4NO_3, a compound used in some fertilizers

Information

The formula of the compounds **(a)** C_8H_{18}, **(b)** KI, **(c)** $C_8H_8O_3$, **(d)** $NaC_{18}H_{35}O_2$, **(e)** NH_4NO_3; the questions of what is **(a)** % C, **(b)** % I, **(c)** % O, **(d)** % Na, **(e)** % N

Connections

The masses of the elements given on the periodic table, and the definition of *percent composition*

Solution

Find the molecular mass, following the procedure introduced in section 3.2:

(a) $\dfrac{8\,\text{C atoms}\left(\dfrac{12.011\,\text{amu}}{\text{C atom}}\right)}{\dfrac{114.232\,\text{amu}}{C_8H_{18}\,\text{molecule}}} \times 100\% = 84.11653 = \mathbf{80.117\%\ C}$

(b) $\dfrac{1\,\text{I atom}\left(\dfrac{126.904\,\text{amu}}{\text{I atom}}\right)}{\dfrac{166.002\,\text{amu}}{KI}} \times 100\% = 76.44727172 = \mathbf{76.4473\%\ I}$

(c) $\dfrac{3\,\text{O atoms}\left(\dfrac{15.999\,\text{amu}}{\text{O atom}}\right)}{\dfrac{152.149\,\text{amu}}{C_8H_8O_3\,\text{molecule}}} \times 100\% = 31.54605025 = \mathbf{31.546\%\ O}$

(d) $\dfrac{1\,\text{Na atom}\left(\dfrac{22.9898\,\text{amu}}{\text{Na atom}}\right)}{\dfrac{306.4577\,\text{amu}}{NaC_{18}H_{35}O_2\,\text{molecule}}} \times 100\% = 7.50178728 = \mathbf{7.50179\%\ Na}$

(e) $\dfrac{2\,\text{N atoms}\left(\dfrac{14.007\,\text{amu}}{\text{N atom}}\right)}{\dfrac{80.043\,\text{amu}}{NH_4NO_3\,\text{molecule}}} \times 100\% = 34.998688 = \mathbf{34.999\%\ N}$

3.50 **(a)** Determine the percent by mass of each of the elements present in chlorophyll-b, $C_{55}H_{70}MgN_4O_6$. **(b)** Determine the percent by mass of each of the elements in hemoglobin, $C_{2952}H_{4664}Fe_4N_{812}O_{832}S_8$. (Yes, the numbers are correct as shown: 2,952; 4,664; 4; 812; 832; and 8.)

Information

The formulas of the compounds **(a)** $C_{55}H_{70}MgN_4O_6$ and **(b)** $C_{2952}H_{4664}Fe_4N_{812}O_{832}S_8$; the question of the mass percentages of the elements

Connections

The masses of the elements given on the periodic table, and the definition of *percent composition*

Solution

Note that using amu/molecule instead of g/mol will give identical results.

Find the molar mass, following the procedure introduced in section 3.2.

(a) Molar mass = 907.492 g/mole

$$\% \text{ C} = \frac{55\,(12.011 \text{ g/mol})}{907.462 \text{ g/mol}} \times 100\% = 72.7969876 = \mathbf{72.797\%\ C}$$

$$\% \text{ H} = \frac{70\,(1.008 \text{ g/mol})}{907.462 \text{ g/mol}} \times 100\% = 7.775532 = \mathbf{7.776\%\ H}$$

$$\% \text{ Mg} = \frac{1\,(24.305 \text{ g/mol})}{907.462 \text{ g/mol}} \times 100\% = 2.678349 = \mathbf{2.6783\%\ Mg}$$

$$\% \text{ N} = \frac{4\,(14.007 \text{ g/mol})}{907.462 \text{ g/mol}} \times 100\% = 6.174128 = \mathbf{6.1741\%\ N}$$

$$\% \text{ O} = \frac{6\,(15.999 \text{ g/mol})}{907.462 \text{ g/mol}} \times 100\% = 10.57829 = \mathbf{10.578\%\ O}$$

(b) Molar mass = 65322.536 g/mole

$$\% \text{ C} = \frac{2952\,(12.011 \text{ g/mol})}{65322.536 \text{ g/mol}} \times 100\% = 54.27908 = \mathbf{54.279\%\ C}$$

$$\% \text{ H} = \frac{4664\,(1.008 \text{ g/mol})}{65322.536 \text{ g/mol}} \times 100\% = 7.197075 = \mathbf{7.197\%\ H}$$

$$\% \text{ Fe} = \frac{4\,(55.845 \text{ g/mol})}{65322.536 \text{ g/mol}} \times 100\% = 0.341964678 = \mathbf{0.34196\%\ Fe}$$

$$\% \text{ N} = \frac{812\,(14.007 \text{ g/mol})}{65322.536 \text{ g/mol}} \times 100\% = 17.415775 = \mathbf{17.416\%\ N}$$

$$\% \text{ O} = \frac{832\,(15.999 \text{ g/mol})}{65322.536 \text{ g/mol}} \times 100\% = 20.377604 = \mathbf{20.378\%\ O}$$

$$\% \text{ S} = \frac{8\,(32.065 \text{ g/mol})}{65322.536 \text{ g/mol}} \times 100\% = 0.39269755 = \mathbf{0.39270\%\ S}$$

Reality Check

In each case, the percentages must sum to 100%.

3.53 Polymers form by joining many small molecules together to produce gigantic molecules. An example of a polymer is polypropylene, which results from joining propylene molecules, C_3H_6. A polypropylene molecule isolated at a certain factory has the formula $C_{3027}H_{6054}$. **(a)** Determine the molar mass of polypropylene. **(b)** Calculate the mass percentage of each of the elements in the polypropylene molecule. **(c)** Calculate the mass percentage of each of the elements in propylene.

Information

The formulas of two compounds (C_3H_6 and $C_{3027}H_{6054}$); the questions of **(a)** molar mass of $C_{3027}H_{6054}$, **(b)** % C and % H in $C_{3027}H_{6054}$, and **(c)** % C and % H in C_3H_6

Connections

Moles are the key. The masses of the elements given on the periodic table, and the definition of *percent composition*

Solution

Find the molar mass, following the procedure introduced in section 3.2:

(a) 3027 (12.01 g/mole C) + 6054 (1.01 g/mole H) = 42468.81 = **4.25×10^4 g/mole**

(b) $\% \, C = \dfrac{3 \left(12.01 \dfrac{g}{mol} C\right)}{3 \left(12.01 \dfrac{g}{mol} C\right) + 6 \left(1.01 \dfrac{g}{mol} H\right)} \times 100\% = 85.60228 = \mathbf{85.60\%}$

$\% \, H = \dfrac{6 \left(1.01 \dfrac{g}{mol} H\right)}{3 \left(12.01 \dfrac{g}{mol} C\right) + 6 \left(1.01 \dfrac{g}{mol} H\right)} \times 100\% = 14.397719 = \mathbf{14.40\%}$

(c) $\% \, C = \dfrac{3027 \left(12.01 \dfrac{g}{mol} C\right)}{42468.81 \ g/mol} \times 100\% = 85.60228 = \mathbf{85.60\%}$

$\% \, H = \dfrac{6054 \left(1.01 \dfrac{g}{mol} H\right)}{42468.81 \ g/mol} \times 100\% = 14.397719 = \mathbf{14.40\%}$

Reality Check

In each case, the percentages must sum to 100%.

3.55 Alstonine is a yellow solid isolated from several species of plants. A sample of alstonine weighing 1.0170 g was burned in oxygen. The reaction produced 2.6978 g of CO_2, 0.5259 g of H_2O, and 0.0818 g of N_2. The compound contained C, H, N, and O. Determine the mass percentages of each of the four elements present.

Information

The mass of alstonine (1.0170 g); the masses—2.6978 g CO_2, 0.5259 g H_2O, and 0.0818 g N_2—produced by burning in an unknown quantity of O_2; the question what are the % C, % H, % N, and % O

Connections

Moles are the key. The masses of the elements given on the periodic table

Solution

Find the molar mass, following the procedure introduced in section 3.2:

$\% \, C = \dfrac{\left(2.6978 \ g \ CO_2\right)\left(\dfrac{1 \ mol \ CO_2}{44.009 \ g \ CO_2}\right)\left(\dfrac{1 \ mol \ C}{1 \ mol \ CO_2}\right)\left(\dfrac{12.011 \ g \ C}{1 \ mol \ C}\right)}{1.0170 \ g} = 72.397982 = \mathbf{72.398\% \ C}$

$\% \, H = \dfrac{\left(0.5259 \ g \ H_2O\right)\left(\dfrac{1 \ mol \ H_2O}{18.015 \ g \ H_2O}\right)\left(\dfrac{2 \ mol \ H}{1 \ mol \ H_2O}\right)\left(\dfrac{1.008 \ g \ H}{1 \ mol \ H}\right)}{1.0170 \ g} = 5.78680 = \mathbf{5.787\% \ H}$

$$\% \, N = \frac{(0.0818 \text{ g N}_2)}{1.0170 \text{ g}} \times 100\% = 8.0432645 = \textbf{8.04\% N}$$

$$\% \, O = 100\% - (72.398 + 5.787 + 8.04)\% = 13.775 = \textbf{13.78\% O}$$

The percentages must sum to 100%.

3.4 Determination of Empirical and Molecular Formulas

3.56 Define *empirical formula* and *molecular formula*. Are there any situations where the empirical formula and the molecular formula are the same? Give an example of a compound where the empirical and molecular formulas are the same.

Solution

The **empirical formula** of a compound indicates the kind of atoms in the compound and the simplest whole-number ratio of their numbers, while the **molecular formula** indicates the kinds of atoms in the compound and the actual number of each in the smallest unit of the substance. The molecular formula may already have the simplest whole-number ratio of the numbers, which makes the empirical and molecular formulas the same. Water, H_2O, is an example of a compound for which the empirical and molecular formulas are the same.

3.58 List the types of data that you may use to determine the empirical formula of a compound.

Solution

A molecular formula, the percent composition, the masses of the elements, and the masses of compounds formed from a reaction are some of the data useful in determining the empirical formula of a compound.

Information

The given formulas—**(a)** H_2O_2, **(b)** C_6H_6, **(c)** CO_2, **(d)** P_4O_{10}, **(e)** $C_6H_{12}O_6$—and the question of finding the empirical formulas

Connections

The definition of *empirical formula*

Solution

Divide each of the molecular formulas by the largest integer that will leave integer subscripts:

(a) HO, (b) CH, (c) CO_2, (d) P_2O_5, (e) CH_2O

3.62 Three compounds—A, B, and C—were analyzed, and the following results were obtained. Convert these analyses to the empirical formulas for these three compounds. **(a)** Compound A contained 0.1248 moles of nitrogen and 0.2496 moles of hydrogen. **(b)** Compound B was found to contain 3.800 grams of iodine and 1.200 grams of oxygen. **(c)** Compound C was 39.2% phosphorus and 60.8% sulfur.

Information

Data on three compounds: **(a)** compound A contained 0.1248 moles of nitrogen and 0.2496 moles of hydrogen, **(b)** compound B contained 3.800 grams of iodine and 1.200 grams of oxygen, and **(c)** compound C contained 39.2 percent phosphorus and 60.8 percent sulfur; the question is what are the three empirical formulas

Connections

Moles are the key. For parts **(b)** and **(c)**, the atomic masses of the elements from the periodic table; dividing the mass by the molar mass gives moles

Solution

Divide by the smallest moles and find the smallest integer that will convert each to within rounding of a whole number. The whole numbers are the subscripts for the empirical formula.

It may take a little trial and error to find the lowest whole-number multiplier.

(a) 0.1248 mol N / 0.1248 = 1

0.2496 mol H / 0.1248 = 2

Empirical formula = $\mathbf{NH_2}$

(b) $(3.800 \text{ g I})\left(\dfrac{1 \text{ mol I}}{126.90 \text{ g I}}\right) = \dfrac{0.0299448 \text{ mol I}}{0.0299448} = 1.0 \times 2 = 2$

$(1.200 \text{ g O})\left(\dfrac{1 \text{ mol O}}{15.999 \text{ g O}}\right) = \dfrac{0.0750047 \text{ mol O}}{0.0299448} = 2.5 \times 2 = 5$

Empirical formula = $\mathbf{I_2O_5}$

(c) Assume 100 g, which makes the "mass" of the element numerically equal to the percent:

$(39.2 \text{ g P})\left(\dfrac{1 \text{ mol P}}{30.97 \text{ g P}}\right) = \dfrac{1.26574 \text{ mol P}}{1.26574} = 1.0 \times 2 = 2$

$(60.8 \text{ g S})\left(\dfrac{1 \text{ mol S}}{32.065 \text{ g S}}\right) = \dfrac{1.8961 \text{ mol S}}{1.26574} = 1.498 \times 2 = 3$

Empirical formula = $\mathbf{P_2S_3}$

3.64 Using the following data, determine the empirical formulas for compounds A and B:

(a) Compound A is 52.1% carbon, 13.1% hydrogen, and 34.7% oxygen.

(b) Compound B is 26.95% sulfur, 13.45% oxygen, and 59.60% chlorine.

Information

The percent composition of two compounds: compound A is 52.1% C, 13.1% H, and 34.7% O, while compound B is 26.95% S, 13.45% O, and 59.60% Cl; the question is what are the two empirical formulas.

Connections

Moles are the key. The simplest procedure is to assume 100-gram samples of each compound; in addition, data on the elements reported on the periodic table

Solution

Assume 100 grams of each compound, which means the percentages are numerically the same as the grams present.

Dividing the mass by the molar mass gives moles.

Divide by the smallest moles and find the smallest integer that will convert each to within rounding of a whole number. The whole numbers are the subscripts for the empirical formula.

(a) **Compound A** (assume 100 g)

$$(52.1 \text{ g C}) \left(\frac{1 \text{ mol C}}{12.011 \text{ g C}} \right) = \frac{4.33769 \text{ mol C}}{2.16888} = 2$$

$$(13.1 \text{ g H}) \left(\frac{1 \text{ mol H}}{1.008 \text{ g H}} \right) = \frac{12.9960 \text{ mol H}}{2.16888} = 6$$

$$(34.7 \text{ g O}) \left(\frac{1 \text{ mol O}}{15.999 \text{ g O}} \right) = \frac{2.16888 \text{ mol O}}{2.16888} = 1$$

Empirical formula = C_2H_6O

(b) **Compound B** (assume 100 g)

$$(26.95 \text{ g S}) \left(\frac{1 \text{ mol S}}{32.065 \text{ g S}} \right) = \frac{0.840480 \text{ mol S}}{0.840480} = 1$$

$$(13.45 \text{ g O}) \left(\frac{1 \text{ mol O}}{15.999 \text{ g O}} \right) = \frac{0.840678 \text{ mol O}}{0.840480} = 1$$

$$(59.60 \text{ g Cl}) \left(\frac{1 \text{ mol Cl}}{35.453 \text{ g Cl}} \right) = \frac{1.6811 \text{ mol Cl}}{0.840480} = 2$$

Empirical formula = $SOCl_2$

3.67

(a) Glucose is a sugar used by the body as the primary source of energy. This compound is blood sugar and has a molecular mass of 180.2 amu. This carbohydrate is 40.00% carbon, 6.714% hydrogen, and 53.28% oxygen. Calculate the empirical and molecular formulas for glucose.

(b) Ribose is a sugar that makes up part of the backbone of ribonucleic acid, RNA. This carbohydrate has a molecular mass of 150.1 amu. This sugar is 40.00% carbon, 6.714% hydrogen, and 53.28% oxygen. Calculate the empirical and molecular formulas for ribose.

(c) Determine the empirical formula for sucrose, cane sugar, if its molecular formula is $C_{12}H_{22}O_{11}$.

(d) The name *carbohydrate* implies the formula $C_x(H_2O)_y$. Do the empirical and molecular formulas of glucose, ribose, and sucrose have this implied formula?

Information

The molecular mass and percent composition of two compounds: (a) glucose is 180.2 amu/molecule, 40.00% C, 6.714% H, and 53.28% O; (b) ribose is 150.1 amu/molecule, 40.00% C, 6.714% H, and 53.28% O. For these two compounds, the question is what are the empirical and molecular formulas.

Part (c) gives the molecular formula of sucrose, $C_{12}H_{22}O_{11}$, and the question is what is the empirical formula.

For part (d), the question is whether the empirical and molecular formulas can be converted to the generic $C_x(H_2O)_y$ form.

Connections

Moles are the key. The simplest procedure is to assume 100-gram samples of each compound. In addition, data on the elements reported on the periodic table

Solution

Assume 100 grams of each compound, which means the percentages, are numerically the same as the grams present.

Dividing the mass by the molar mass gives moles.

Divide by the smallest moles and find the smallest integer that will convert each to within rounding of a whole number. The whole numbers are the subscripts for the empirical formula.

(a) $(40.00 \text{ g C})\left(\dfrac{1 \text{ mol C}}{12.011 \text{ g C}}\right) = \dfrac{3.33028 \text{ mol C}}{3.330208} = 1$

$(6.714 \text{ H})\left(\dfrac{1 \text{ mol H}}{1.0079 \text{ g H}}\right) = \dfrac{6.661375 \text{ mol H}}{3.330208} = 2$

$(53.28 \text{ g O})\left(\dfrac{1 \text{ mol O}}{15.999 \text{ g O}}\right) = \dfrac{3.330208 \text{ mol O}}{3.330208} = 1$

Empirical formula = CH_2O

The molecular formula must be an integer multiple of the empirical mass. The integer multiple (if not obvious) may be found by dividing the molecular formula mass by the empirical formula mass and rounding to a whole number. Multiplying the empirical formula by this whole number gives the molecular formula:

$$\text{Formula mass} \approx 1\,(12) + 2\,(1) + 1\,(16) = 30 \text{ amu}$$

The empirical formula mass is one-sixth the molecular mass given; therefore, the empirical is one-sixth the molecular formula:

$$\text{Molecular formula} = 6 \times \text{Empirical formula} = C_6H_{12}O_6$$

(b) $(40.00 \text{ g C})\left(\dfrac{1 \text{ mol C}}{12.011 \text{ g C}}\right) = \dfrac{3.33028 \text{ mol C}}{3.330208} = 1$

$(6.714 \text{ H})\left(\dfrac{1 \text{ mol H}}{1.0079 \text{ g H}}\right) = \dfrac{6.661375 \text{ mol H}}{3.330208} = 2$

$(53.28 \text{ g O})\left(\dfrac{1 \text{ mol O}}{15.999 \text{ g O}}\right) = \dfrac{3.330208 \text{ mol O}}{3.330208} = 1$

Empirical formula = CH_2O

The molecular formula must be an integer multiple of the empirical mass. The integer multiple (if not obvious) may be found by dividing the molecular formula mass by the empirical formula mass and rounding to a whole number. Multiplying the empirical formula by this whole number gives the molecular formula:

$$\text{Formula mass} \approx 1\,(12) + 2\,(1) + 1\,(16) = 30 \text{ amu}$$

The empirical formula mass is one-fifth the molecular mass given; therefore, the empirical is one-fifth the molecular formula:

$$\text{Molecular formula} = 5 \times \text{Empirical formula} = C_5H_{10}O_5$$

(c) The formula cannot be simplified, so the empirical and molecular formulas are the same:

$$C_{12}H_{22}O_{11}$$

(d) For both glucose and ribose, the empirical formula corresponds to $C_1(H_2O)_1$. (The "1" subscripts are for emphasis.)

$$\text{Glucose} = C_6(H_2O)_6$$

$$\text{Ribose} = C_5(H_2O)_5$$

$$\text{Sucrose} = C_{12}(H_2O)_{11}$$

3.69 The combustion of a 0.0168-g sample of cocaine, $C_{17}H_{21}NO_4$, in pure oxygen produced carbon dioxide, water, and nitrogen gas. How many milligrams of each of the three products formed?

Information

The mass (0.0168 g) of a sample of $C_{17}H_{21}NO_4$; the question of how many milligrams of CO_2, H_2O, and N_2 gas will form if the sample is burnt in pure oxygen

Connections

Moles are the key. Data concerning the elements present found on the periodic table

Solution

Balance the equation using the procedure discussed in section 3.1.

Find the molar mass, following the procedure introduced in section 3.2.

Dividing the mass by the molar mass gives moles.

A mole ratio is needed to convert from moles of one substance to moles of another substance.

Moles times molar mass gives mass (grams).

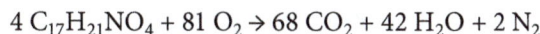

$$4\, C_{17}H_{21}NO_4 + 81\, O_2 \rightarrow 68\, CO_2 + 42\, H_2O + 2\, N_2$$

$$CO_2\ (0.0168\text{ g})\left(\frac{1\text{ mol } C_{17}H_{21}NO_4}{303.358\text{ g}}\right)\left(\frac{68\text{ mol } CO_2}{4\text{ mol } C_{17}H_{21}NO_4}\right)\left(\frac{44.009\text{ g } CO_2}{1\text{ mol } CO_2}\right) = 0.041432797 = \textbf{0.0414 g } CO_2$$

$$H_2O\ (0.0168\text{ g})\left(\frac{1\text{ mol } C_{17}H_{21}NO_4}{303.358\text{ g}}\right)\left(\frac{42\text{ mol } H_2O}{4\text{ mol } C_{17}H_{21}NO_4}\right)\left(\frac{18.015\text{ g } H_2O}{1\text{ mol } H_2O}\right) = 0.01047556 = \textbf{0.0105 g } H_2O$$

$$N_2\ (0.0168\text{ g})\left(\frac{1\text{ mol } C_{17}H_{21}NO_4}{303.358\text{ g}}\right)\left(\frac{2\text{ mol } N_2}{4\text{ mol } C_{17}H_{21}NO_4}\right)\left(\frac{28.014\text{ g } N_2}{1\text{ mol } N_2}\right) = 0.000775709 = \textbf{0.000776 g } N_2$$

3.71 To determine the formula of the compound carpiline, a 0.5572-gram sample was burned in oxygen. The reaction produced 1.5687 g of CO_2, 0.2223 g of H_2O, and 0.0384 g of N_2. The compound contained C, H, N, and O. Determine the empirical formula.

Information

The mass of a sample (0.5572 g) and the masses of the products formed from combustion of this sample—1.5687 g of CO_2, 0.2223 g of H_2O, and 0.0384 g of N_2; the fact that the compound contains only C, H, N, and O; the question is what is the empirical formula

Connections

Moles are the key. Data concerning the elements present found on the periodic table

Solution

Find the molar mass, following the procedure introduced in section 3.2.

Dividing the mass by the molar mass gives moles.

Divide by the smallest moles and find the smallest integer that will convert each to within rounding of a whole number. The whole numbers are the subscripts for the empirical formula.

A mole ratio is needed to convert from moles of one substance to moles of another substance:

$$C = \left(1.5687 \text{ g } CO_2\right)\left(\frac{1 \text{ mol } CO_2}{44.009 \text{ g } CO_2}\right)\left(\frac{1 \text{ mol } C}{1 \text{ mol } CO_2}\right) = \frac{0.03564498 \text{ mol } C}{0.002741486} = 13 \times 2 = 26$$

$$H = \left(0.2223 \text{ g } H_2O\right)\left(\frac{1 \text{ mol } H_2O}{18.015 \text{ g } H_2O}\right)\left(\frac{2 \text{ mol } H}{1 \text{ mol } H_2O}\right) = \frac{0.02466833 \text{ mol } H}{0.002741486} = 9 \times 2 = 18$$

$$N = \left(0.0384 \text{ g } N_2\right)\left(\frac{1 \text{ mol } N_2}{28.014 \text{ g } N_2}\right)\left(\frac{2 \text{ mol } N}{1 \text{ mol } N_2}\right) = \frac{0.002741486 \text{ mol } N}{0.002741486} = 1 \times 2 = 2$$

The sample was burned in an unknown quantity of oxygen; therefore, the moles of oxygen are determined by a different procedure. The mass of the sample minus the mass of each of the other elements in the compound leaves the mass of oxygen in the original compound.

$$0.5572 \text{ g} - \left[\left(0.03564498 \text{ mol } C\right)\left(\frac{12.011 \text{ g } C}{1 \text{ mol } C}\right)+\left(0.02466833 \text{ mol } H\right)\left(\frac{1.008 \text{ g } H}{1 \text{ mol } H}\right)+\left(0.0384 \text{ g } N_2\right)\right]$$

$$= 0.065802 \text{ g O}$$

Once the moles of oxygen are known, finish determining the empirical formula by dividing all the moles by the smallest number of moles:

$$O = \left(0.065802 \text{ g O}\right)\left(\frac{1 \text{ mol } O}{15.999 \text{ g } O}\right) = \frac{0.00411288 \text{ mol } O}{0.002741486} = 1.5 \times 2 = 3$$

This gives an empirical formula of $C_{26}H_{18}N_2O_3$.

3.74 Chlorophyll a is a magnesium-containing compound necessary for photosynthesis in plants. To determine the empirical formula for this compound, the magnesium was first removed, and then 0.7693 g of the remaining material was burned in oxygen. The reaction produced 2.1423 g of CO_2, 0.5740 g of H_2O, and 0.0496 g of N_2. The compound contained C, H, N, and O. Determine the empirical formula.

Information

The mass of a sample (0.7693 g); the masses of the products formed from combustion of this sample (2.1423 g of CO_2, 0.5740 g of H_2O, and 0.0496 g of N_2); the fact that the compound contains only C, H, N, and O; the question of what is the empirical formula

Connections

Moles are the key. Data concerning the elements present found on the periodic table

Solution

Find the molar mass, following the procedure introduced in section 3.2.

Dividing the mass by the molar mass gives moles.

Divide by the smallest moles and find the smallest integer that will convert each to within rounding of a whole number. The whole numbers are the subscripts for the empirical formula.

A mole ratio is needed to convert from moles of one substance to moles of another substance.

It may take a little trial and error to find the lowest whole-number multiplier.

$$C = (2.1423 \text{ g CO}_2)\left(\frac{1 \text{ mol CO}_2}{44.0095 \text{ g CO}_2}\right)\left(\frac{1 \text{ mol C}}{1 \text{ mol CO}_2}\right) = \frac{0.0486781 \text{ mol C}}{0.0035411} = 13.75 \times 20 = 275$$

$$H = (0.5740 \text{ g H}_2\text{O})\left(\frac{1 \text{ mol H}_2\text{O}}{18.015 \text{ g H}_2\text{O}}\right)\left(\frac{2 \text{ mol H}}{1 \text{ mol H}_2\text{O}}\right) = \frac{0.0764569 \text{ mol H}}{0.0035411} = 21.60 \times 20 = 432$$

$$N = (0.0496 \text{ g N}_2)\left(\frac{1 \text{ mol N}_2}{28.014 \text{ g N}_2}\right)\left(\frac{2 \text{ mol N}}{1 \text{ mol N}_2}\right) = \frac{0.0035411 \text{ mol N}}{0.0035411} = 1 \times 20 = 20$$

The sample was burned in an unknown quantity of oxygen; therefore, the moles of oxygen are determined by a different procedure. The mass of the sample minus the mass of each of the other elements in the compound leaves the mass of oxygen in the original compound.

Moles times molar mass gives mass (grams).

$$0.7693 \text{ g} - \left[(0.0486781 \text{ mol C})\left(\frac{12.011 \text{ g C}}{1 \text{ mol C}}\right) + (0.0764569 \text{ mol H})\left(\frac{1.008 \text{ g H}}{1 \text{ mol H}}\right) + (0.0496 \text{ g N}_2)\right]$$

$$= 0.0579588 \text{ g O}$$

Once the moles of oxygen are known, finish determining the empirical formula by dividing all the moles by the smallest number of moles:

$$O = (0.0579588 \text{ g O})\left(\frac{1 \text{ mol O}}{15.999 \text{ g O}}\right) = \frac{0.00362265 \text{ mol O}}{0.0035411} = 1 \times 20 = 20$$

This gives an empirical formula of $C_{275}H_{432}N_{20}O_{20}$.

3.76 Many ionic compounds exist as hydrates. The mineral mirabilite is an example of a hydrate. The general formula for mirabilite is $Na_2SO_4 \cdot xH_2O$. The value of x may be determined by calculating the difference in mass between mirabilite and sodium sulfate produced from a sample of this mineral. A 3.095-g sample of mirabilite was heated to 325°C to drive off the water. After the water was removed, the sample was cooled and weighed. The dried sample weighed 1.364 g. Determine the value of x and the complete formula for mirabilite.

Information

Mirabilite weighed 3.095 g when the sample contained H_2O, and weighed 1.364 g when water was removed; the question of what is x in the formula $Na_2SO_4 \cdot xH_2O$

Connections

Moles are the key. Data concerning the elements present found on the periodic table

Solution

Find the molar mass, following the procedure introduced in section 3.2.

$$\text{Mass of hydrate} = \text{Mass of Na}_2\text{SO}_4 + \text{Mass of H}_2\text{O}$$

$$\text{Mass of H}_2\text{O} = \text{Mass of hydrate} - \text{Mass of Na}_2\text{SO}_4 = 3.095 \text{ g} - 1.364 \text{ g} = 1.731 \text{ g H}_2\text{O}$$

Moles are needed; therefore, divide the grams of each by the molar mass.

This is like an empirical formula calculation, except the salt and water replace elements. Divide by the smallest moles and find the smallest integer that will convert each to within rounding of a whole number. The whole numbers are the subscripts for the empirical formula.

It may take a little trial and error to find the lowest whole-number multiplier.

$$\text{Na}_2\text{SO}_4\text{:} \left(1.364 \text{ g Na}_2\text{SO}_4\right)\left(\frac{1 \text{ mol Na}_2\text{SO}_4}{142.041 \text{ g Na}_2\text{SO}_4}\right) = 0.0096029 \text{ mol Na}_2\text{SO}_4$$

$$\text{H}_2\text{O:} \left(1.731 \text{ g H}_2\text{O}\right)\left(\frac{1 \text{ mol H}_2\text{O}}{18.015 \text{ g H}_2\text{O}}\right) = 0.0960866 \text{ mol H}_2\text{O}$$

To find the water to anhydrous ratio (x), divide by the moles of Na_2SO_4 (0.0096029):

Na_2SO_4: 0.0096029/0.0096029 = 1
H_2O: 0.0960866/0.0096029 = 10

Therefore, $x = 10$.

3.78 Nickel(II) sulfate is normally isolated as one of two hydrates. The general formula for the nickel(II) sulfate hydrates is $\text{NiSO}_4 \cdot x\text{H}_2\text{O}$. From the following information, determine the value of x in the formula of the two nickel(II) sulfate hydrates.

(a) A 3.781-g sample of one of the nickel(II) sulfate hydrates was heated to 150°C. At this temperature, all the water was driven off the sample, leaving anhydrous (without water) nickel(II) sulfate. The anhydrous sample weighed 2.226 g.

(b) A 4.843-g sample of one of the nickel(II) sulfate hydrates was heated to 150°C. At this temperature, all the water was driven off the sample, leaving anhydrous (without water) nickel(II) sulfate. The anhydrous sample weighed 2.669 g.

Information

Data on two compounds with the general formula $\text{NiSO}_4 \cdot x\text{H}_2\text{O}$: **(a)** sample weighed 3.781 g when containing H_2O and weighed 2.226 g when water was removed, and **(b)** sample weighed 4.843 g when containing H_2O, and weighed 2.669 g when water was removed; the question of what is x in each compound

Connections

Moles are the key. Data concerning the elements present found on the periodic table

Solution

This is like an empirical formula calculation, except the salt and water replace elements. Divide by the smallest moles and find the smallest integer that will convert each to within rounding of a whole number. The whole numbers are the subscripts for the empirical formula.

It may take a little trial and error to find the lowest whole-number multiplier.

(a) Determine the moles of $NiSO_4$ and the moles of H_2O in the sample. To get to the moles, it is necessary to begin with the grams of these two substances. The mass of $NiSO_4$ is given (2.226 g); therefore, we need to determine the grams of water:

$$\text{Mass of hydrate} = \text{Mass of } NiSO_4 + \text{Mass of } H_2O$$

$$\text{Mass of } H_2O = \text{Mass of hydrate} - \text{Mass of } NiSO_4 = 3.781 \text{ g} - 2.226 \text{ g} = 1.555 \text{ g } H_2O$$

To determine the moles, find the molar mass, following the procedure introduced in section 3.2.

Since moles are needed, divide the grams of each by the molar mass:

$$NiSO_4: \left(2.226 \text{ g } NiSO_4\right)\left(\frac{1 \text{ mol } NiSO_4}{154.994 \text{ g } NiSO_4}\right) = 0.014361846 \text{ mole } NiSO_4$$

$$H_2O: \left(1.555 \text{ g } H_2O\right)\left(\frac{1 \text{ mol } H_2O}{18.015 \text{ g } H_2O}\right) = 0.086316958 \text{ mole } H_2O$$

To find the water to anhydrous ratio (x), divide by the moles of $NiSO_4$ (0.014361846):

$NiSO_4$: 0.014361846/0.014361846 = 1
H_2O: 0.086316958/0.014361846 = 6

Therefore, $x = $ **6**.

(b) Determine the moles of $NiSO_4$ and the moles of H_2O in the sample. To get to the moles, it is necessary to begin with the grams of these two substances. The mass of $NiSO_4$ is given (2.669 g); therefore, we need to determine the grams of water:

$$\text{Mass of hydrate} = \text{Mass of } NiSO_4 + \text{Mass of } H_2O$$

$$\text{Mass of } H_2O = \text{Mass of hydrate} - \text{Mass of } NiSO_4 = 4.843 \text{ g} - 2.669 \text{ g} = 2.174 \text{ g } H_2O$$

To determine the moles, find the molar mass, following the procedure introduced in section 3.2.

Since moles are needed, divide the grams of each by the molar mass:

$$NiSO_4: \left(2.669 \text{ g } NiSO_4\right)\left(\frac{1 \text{ mol } NiSO_4}{154.994 \text{ g } NiSO_4}\right) = 0.017220021 \text{ mole } NiSO_4$$

$$H_2O: \left(2.174 \text{ g } H_2O\right)\left(\frac{1 \text{ mol } H_2O}{18.015 \text{ g } H_2O}\right) = 0.120710716 \text{ mole } H_2O$$

To find the water to anhydrous ratio (x), divide by the moles of $NiSO_4$ (0.017220021):

$NiSO_4$: 0.017220021/0.017220021 = 1
H_2O: 0.120710716/0.017220021 = 7

Therefore, $x = $ **7**.

3.5 Stoichiometric Relationships

3.79 List the six different mole ratios contained in the following equation:

$$4 \text{ Sb(s)} + 3 \text{ O}_2\text{(g)} \rightarrow 2 \text{ Sb}_2\text{O}_3\text{(s)}$$

Solution

$$\frac{4 \text{ mol Sb}}{3 \text{ mol O}_2}, \frac{4 \text{ mol Sb}}{2 \text{ mol Sb}_2\text{O}_3}, \frac{3 \text{ mol O}_2}{4 \text{ mol Sb}}, \frac{3 \text{ mol O}_2}{2 \text{ mol Sb}_2\text{O}_3}, \frac{2 \text{ mol Sb}_2\text{O}_3}{4 \text{ mol Sb}}, \frac{2 \text{ mol Sb}_2\text{O}_3}{3 \text{ mol O}_2}$$

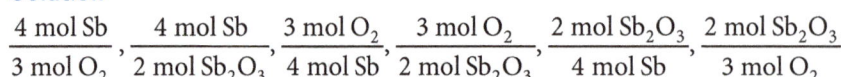

3.81 Methane, CH_4, gas burns in oxygen, O_2, gas as shown in the following equation:

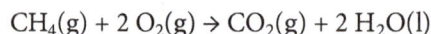

$$CH_4(g) + 2\,O_2(g) \rightarrow CO_2(g) + 2\,H_2O(l)$$

Describe this reaction on a molecular level, a molar level, and a mass level.

Solution

One molecule of CH_4 will react with two molecules of O_2 to form one molecule of CO_2 and two molecules of H_2O.

One mole of CH_4 will react with two moles of O_2 to form one mole of CO_2 and two moles of H_2O.

16.0 grams of CH_4 will react with 64.0 grams of O_2 to form 44.0 grams of CO_2 and 36.0 grams of H_2O.

3.83 Aluminum, Al, metal reacts with hydrochloric acid, HCl, to form aluminum chloride, $AlCl_3$, and hydrogen, H_2, gas. **(a)** Write a balanced chemical equation for this reaction. **(b)** Describe this reaction on a molecular level, a molar level, and a mass level.

Solution

(a) Balance the equation using the procedure discussed in section 3.1:

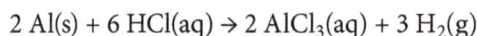

$$2\,Al(s) + 6\,HCl(aq) \rightarrow 2\,AlCl_3(aq) + 3\,H_2(g)$$

(b) Two "molecules" of Al will react with six molecules of HCl to form two "molecules" of $AlCl_3$ and three molecules of H_2.

Two moles of Al will react with six moles of HCl to form two moles of $AlCl_3$ and three moles of H_2.

On a mass level, 54 grams of Al will react with 219 grams of HCl to form 267 grams of $AlCl_3$ and 6 grams of H_2.

3.85 LP gas is liquid propane, C_3H_8. The substance vaporizes and burns as follows:

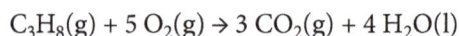

$$C_3H_8(g) + 5\,O_2(g) \rightarrow 3\,CO_2(g) + 4\,H_2O(l)$$

(a) A 2.00-mole sample of propane is burned. How many moles of oxygen are required to burn this propane? **(b)** The combustion of 10.0 g of propane requires how many grams of oxygen? **(c)** Calculate the number of grams of oxygen required to burn 15.0 cm³ of LP gas. The density of LP gas is 0.5853 g/mL. **(d)** How many grams of carbon dioxide are produced when 15.0 cm³ of LP gas combusts?

Information

The balanced chemical equations; four questions concerning this equation: **(a)** How many moles of O_2 will react with 2.00 mole C_3H_8? **(b)** How many grams of O_2 will react with 10.0 g C_3H_8? **(c)** How many grams of O_2 will react with 15.0 cm³ C_3H_8(0.5853 g/mL)? **(d)** How many grams of CO_2 will form when 15.0 cm³ C_3H_8(0.5853 g/mL)?

Connections

Moles are the key. In addition to the balanced chemical equation, information concerning the elements given on the periodic table

Solution

Find the molar mass, following the procedure introduced in section 3.2.

Where necessary, dividing the mass by the molar mass gives moles.

A mole ratio is needed to convert from moles of one substance to moles of another substance.

Moles times molar mass gives mass (grams).

(a) $\left(2.00 \text{ mol C}_3\text{H}_8\right)\left(\dfrac{5 \text{ mol O}_2}{1 \text{ mol C}_3\text{H}_8}\right) = \mathbf{10.0 \text{ mole O}_2}$

(b) Grams $O_2 = \left(10.0 \text{ g C}_3\text{H}_8\right)\left(\dfrac{1 \text{ mol C}_3\text{H}_8}{44.097 \text{ g C}_3\text{H}_8}\right)\left(\dfrac{5 \text{ mol O}_2}{1 \text{ mol C}_3\text{H}_8}\right)\left(\dfrac{31.998 \text{ g O}_2}{1 \text{ mol O}_2}\right) = 36.28138$

$$= \mathbf{36.3 \text{ g O}_2}$$

(c) Grams $O_2 = \left(15.0 \text{ cm}^3 \text{ C}_3\text{H}_8\right)\left(\dfrac{1 \text{ mL}}{1 \text{ cm}^3}\right)\left(\dfrac{0.5853 \text{ g}}{\text{mL}}\right)\left(\dfrac{1 \text{ mol C}_3\text{H}_8}{44.097 \text{ g C}_3\text{H}_8}\right)\left(\dfrac{5 \text{ mol O}_2}{1 \text{ mol C}_3\text{H}_8}\right)\left(\dfrac{31.998 \text{ g O}_2}{1 \text{ mol O}_2}\right)$

$$= 31.8532 = \mathbf{31.8 \text{ g O}_2}$$

(d) Grams $CO_2 = \left(15.0 \text{ cm}^3 \text{ C}_3\text{H}_8\right)\left(\dfrac{1 \text{ mL}}{1 \text{ cm}^3}\right)\left(\dfrac{0.5853 \text{ g}}{\text{mL}}\right)\left(\dfrac{1 \text{ mol C}_3\text{H}_8}{44.097 \text{ g C}_3\text{H}_8}\right)\left(\dfrac{3 \text{ mol CO}_2}{1 \text{ mol C}_3\text{H}_8}\right)\left(\dfrac{44.009 \text{ g CO}_2}{1 \text{ mol CO}_2}\right)$

$$= 26.2859 = \mathbf{26.3 \text{ g O}_2}$$

3.87 One form of the element phosphorus has the formula P_4. This form is prepared by heating a mixture of calcium phosphate, sand (silicon dioxide), and coke (carbon) to 1400°C–1500°C. The reaction is

$$2 \text{ Ca}_3(\text{PO}_4)_2(s) + 6 \text{ SiO}_2(s) + 10 \text{ C}(s) \rightarrow 6 \text{ CaSiO}_3(l) + 10 \text{ CO}(g) + \text{P}_4(g)$$

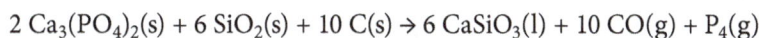

(a) Calculate the number of moles of silicon dioxide required to react with a 2.00-mole sample of calcium phosphate. (b) Calculate the number of grams of phosphorus formed from 3.50 moles of calcium phosphate. (c) Calculate the number of grams of calcium silicate that would form by the reaction of 125 g of calcium phosphate.

Information

The balanced chemical equation; three questions concerning this equation: (a) How many moles of SiO_2 are necessary to react with 2.00 moles of $Ca_3(PO_4)_2$? (b) How many grams of P_4 can form from 3.50 moles of $Ca_3(PO_4)_2$? (c) How many grams of $CaSiO_3$ would form from 125 g of $Ca_3(PO_4)_2$?

Connections

Moles are the key. In addition to the balanced chemical equation, information concerning the elements given on the periodic table

Solution

Find the molar mass, following the procedure introduced in section 3.2.

A mole ratio is needed to convert from moles of one substance to moles of another substance.

(a) $\left(2.00 \text{ mol Ca}_3(PO_4)_2\right)\left(\dfrac{6 \text{ mol SiO}_2}{2 \text{ mol Ca}_3(PO_4)_2}\right) = $ **6.00 mole SiO$_2$**

(b) $\left(3.50 \text{ mol Ca}_3(PO_4)_2\right)\left(\dfrac{1 \text{ mol P}_4}{2 \text{ mol Ca}_3(PO_4)_2}\right)\left(\dfrac{123.88 \text{ g P}_4}{1 \text{ mol P}_4}\right) = 216.79 = $ **217 g P$_4$**

(c) Dividing the mass by the molar mass gives moles.

Moles times molar mass gives mass (grams).

$\left(125 \text{ g Ca}_3(PO_4)_2\right)\left(\dfrac{1 \text{ mol Ca}_3(PO_4)_2}{310.174 \text{ g Ca}_3(PO_4)_2}\right)\left(\dfrac{6 \text{ mol CaSiO}_3}{2 \text{ mol Ca}_3(PO_4)_2}\right)\left(\dfrac{116.161 \text{ g CaSiO}_3}{1 \text{ mol CaSiO}_3}\right) = 140.43851$

$$= 1.40 \times 10^2 \text{ g CaSiO}_3$$

3.89 Rust deposits will dissolve in muriatic acid. Rust is mostly Fe_2O_3, and muriatic acid is an impure hydrochloric acid, HCl, solution. The acid will dissolve the rust to produce an aqueous solution of $FeCl_3$ and water. **(a)** What is the balanced chemical equation for this reaction? **(b)** How many grams of rust could dissolve in a sample of muriatic acid containing 4.55 g of HCl?

Information

A description of a reaction; two questions: **(a)** What is the balanced chemical equation? **(b)** How many grams of Fe_2O_3 react with 4.55 g HCl?

Connections

Moles are the key. Information concerning the elements on the periodic table

Solution

(a) Balance the equation using the procedure discussed in section 3.1.

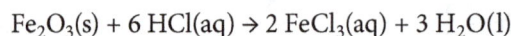

$$Fe_2O_3(s) + 6 \text{ HCl(aq)} \rightarrow 2 \text{ FeCl}_3(aq) + 3 \text{ H}_2O(l)$$

(b) Find the molar mass, following the procedure introduced in section 3.2.

Dividing the mass by the molar mass gives moles.

A mole ratio is needed to convert from moles of one substance to moles of another substance.

Moles times molar mass gives mass (grams):

$(4.55 \text{ g HCl})\left(\dfrac{1 \text{ mol HCl}}{36.461 \text{ g HCl}}\right)\left(\dfrac{1 \text{ mol Fe}_2O_3}{6 \text{ mol HCl}}\right)\left(\dfrac{159.687 \text{ g Fe}_2O_3}{1 \text{ mol Fe}_2O_3}\right) = 3.321246675 = $ **3.32 g Fe$_2$O$_3$**

3.91 Chloroform, $CHCl_3$, can be used as a sedative and as an anesthetic, but its use is not recommended because of toxicity issues. Chloroform may form during the chlorine treatment of water containing organic matter. A 1,000.0-L sample of chlorine-treated water was analyzed. Chemical treatment of the water freed the chlorine and allowed it to react with silver nitrate to form 0.0375 g of silver chloride, AgCl. How many grams of chloroform were in each liter of the treated water?

Information

Information on a 1,000.0-L water sample that produced 0.0375 g AgCl; the question of how many grams of $CHCl_3$ are in each liter of water

Connections

Moles are the key. Information concerning the elements on the periodic table

Solution

This is a unit conversion problem.

Find the molar mass, following the procedure introduced in section 3.2.

Dividing the mass by the molar mass gives moles.

A mole ratio is needed to convert from moles of one substance to moles of another substance.

Moles times molar mass gives mass (grams):

$$\frac{(0.0375 \text{ g AgCl})\left(\dfrac{1 \text{ mol AgCl}}{143.3321 \text{ g}}\right)\left(\dfrac{1 \text{ mol Cl}}{1 \text{ mol AgCl}}\right)\left(\dfrac{1 \text{ mol CHCl}_3}{3 \text{ mol Cl}}\right)\left(\dfrac{119.378 \text{ g}}{1 \text{ mol CHCl}_3}\right)}{1,000.0 \text{ L}} = 1.041096 \times 10^{-5}$$

$$= \mathbf{1.04 \times 10^{-5} \text{ g/L}}$$

3.93 A 5.782-gram sample from a fish was thought to contain mercury. Analysis of the sample produced 6.7×10^{-4} grams of mercury(II) sulfide, HgS. What was the percent mercury in the fish sample?

Information

Information on a 5.782-gram sample that produced 6.7×10^{-4} grams of HgS. The question is what is the percent of Hg in the sample.

Connections

Moles are the key. Information concerning the elements on the periodic table

Solution

This is a unit conversion problem.

Find the molar mass, following the procedure introduced in section 3.2.

Dividing the mass by the molar mass gives moles.

A mole ratio is needed to convert from moles of one substance to moles of another substance.

Moles times molar mass gives mass (grams):

$$\frac{\left[(6.7 \times 10^{-4} \text{ g HgS})\left(\dfrac{1 \text{ mol HgS}}{232.66 \text{ g HgS}}\right)\left(\dfrac{1 \text{ mol Hg}}{1 \text{ mol HgS}}\right)\left(\dfrac{200.59 \text{ g Hg}}{1 \text{ mol Hg}}\right)\right]}{5.782 \text{ g sample}} \times 100\% = 0.009990432 = \mathbf{0.010\%}$$

3.95 Highly reactive fluorine gas, F_2, will displace the less-reactive chlorine gas, Cl_2, from compounds. An example of this displacement is

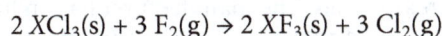

$$2 \text{ XCl}_3(s) + 3 \text{ F}_2(g) \rightarrow 2 \text{ XF}_3(s) + 3 \text{ Cl}_2(g)$$

In one experiment, 2.7825 g of XCl_3 reacted with an excess of fluorine gas to form 2.2835 g of XF_3. **(a)** Calculate the atomic weight of X. **(b)** What element is X?

Information

The balanced chemical equation; the masses of XCl_3 (2.7825 g) and XF_3 (2.2835 g); the questions of what is the atomic mass of X and what element is X

Connections

Moles are the key. Information concerning the elements on the periodic table

Solution

Find the molar mass, following the procedure introduced in section 3.2. Use X for the atomic mass of the unknown element.

A mole ratio is needed to convert from moles of one substance to moles of another substance.

(a) $(2.7825 \text{ g } XCl_3)\left(\dfrac{1 \text{ mol } XCl_3}{\left(X+(3\times 35.453)\right)\text{g } XCl_3}\right)\left(\dfrac{2 \text{ mol } XF_3}{2 \text{ mol } XCl_3}\right) = (2.2835 \text{ g } XF_3)\left(\dfrac{1 \text{ mol } XF_3}{\left(X+(3\times 18.998)\right)\text{ g } XF_3}\right)$

$$\frac{2.7825 \text{ mol } XF_3}{X+106.359} = \frac{2.2835 \text{ mol } XF_3}{X+56.994}$$

$$(2.2835)(X+106.359) = (2.7825)(X+56.994)$$

$$2.2835\,X + 242.8707765 = 2.7825\,X + 158.585805$$

$$242.8707765 - 158.585805 = (2.7825 - 2.2835)\,X$$

$$X = \frac{242.8707765 - 158.585805}{2.7825 - 2.2835} = \frac{84.2849715}{0.499}$$

$$= 168.9077585 = \textbf{169 g/mole}$$

(b) The element closest to this atomic mass is **Tm**.

3.6 The Limiting Reactant Concept

3.97 You are given the following equation:

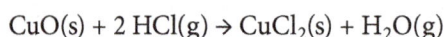

$$CuO(s) + 2\,HCl(g) \rightarrow CuCl_2(s) + H_2O(g)$$

You are then supplied with the following sets of data:

(a) 25.0 g CuO and excess HCl

(b) 25.0 g of CuO and 75.0 g of HCl

(c) 25.0 g of CuO and 39.0 g of $CuCl_2$

(d) 25.0 g of CuO, 75.0 g of HCl, and 39.0 g of $CuCl_2$

Which of these four cases will involve the limiting reactant concept?

Solution

The limiting reactant must be determined in all cases except case **(c)**, because the limiting reactant concept must be used whenever the amounts of both CuO and HCl are given.

3.99 The last step in the manufacture of tricycles requires the assembly of a frame, a front wheel, a handlebar, and two rear wheels. The manufacturer has on hand 1,725 frames, 1,700 front wheels, 1,750 handlebars, and 3,125 rear wheels. **(a)** If only the parts on hand are used, how many tricycles may be assembled? **(b)** How many frames remain? How many front wheels? How many handlebars? How many rear wheels? **(c)** In terms of concepts introduced in this chapter, which tricycle part behaves as the limiting reactant?

Information

Information of the quantities of material present: 1,725 frames, 1,700 front wheels, 1,750 handlebars, and 3,125 rear wheels; questions related to these quantities: **(a)** Using only the parts on hand, how many tricycles may be assembled? **(b)** How many frames remain? front wheels? handlebars? rear wheels? **(c)** In terms of concepts introduced in this chapter, which tricycle part behaves as the limiting reactant?

Connections

The construction of a tricycle

Solution

(a) 1,725 frames could make 1,725 tricycles; 1,700 front wheels could make 1,700 tricycles; 1,750 handlebars could make 1,750 tricycles; 3,125 rear wheels could make (3,125/2) = 1,562.5 tricycles.

The smallest number of complete tricycles is 1,562.

(b) Frames = 1,725 – 1,562 = **163**
Front wheels = 1,700 – 1,562 = **138**
Handlebars = 1,750 – 1,562 = **188**
Rear wheels = 3,125 – (2 × 1,562) = **1**

(c) The rear wheels

3.102 Chlorine dioxide, ClO_2, is used as an industrial bleach. It is prepared commercially by the following reaction:

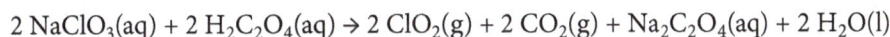

$$2\ NaClO_3(aq) + 2\ H_2C_2O_4(aq) \rightarrow 2\ ClO_2(g) + 2\ CO_2(g) + Na_2C_2O_4(aq) + 2\ H_2O(l)$$

(a) Calculate the number of grams of ClO_2 formed from 525 g of $NaClO_3$ and excess $H_2C_2O_4$. **(b)** Calculate the number of grams of $H_2C_2O_4$ needed to react completely with 525 g of $NaClO_3$. **(c)** Calculate the number of grams of ClO_2 formed when 475 g of $NaClO_3$ and 375 g of $H_2C_2O_4$ are mixed. **(d)** One of the reactants in part **(c)** was limiting, and the other was in excess. How many grams of the excess reactant remain after the reaction?

Information

The balanced chemical equation; four questions concerning the reaction: **(a)** How many grams of ClO_2 form from 525 g of $NaClO_3$? **(b)** How many grams of $H_2C_2O_4$ are necessary to react completely with 525 g of $NaClO_3$? **(c)** How many grams of ClO_2 form from the reaction of 475 g of $NaClO_3$ and 375 g of $H_2C_2O_4$? **(d)** How many grams of the excess reactant remain after the reaction?

Connections

Moles are the key. Information on the elements given on the periodic table

Solution

Find the molar mass, following the procedure introduced in section 3.2.

Dividing the mass by the molar mass gives moles.

A mole ratio is required to convert from moles of one substance to moles of another.

Moles times molar mass gives mass (grams).

(a) $(525 \text{ g NaClO}_3)\left(\dfrac{1 \text{ mol NaClO}_3}{106.440 \text{ g NaClO}_3}\right)\left(\dfrac{2 \text{ mol ClO}_2}{2 \text{ mol NaClO}_3}\right)\left(\dfrac{67.451 \text{ g ClO}_2}{1 \text{ mol ClO}_2}\right) = 332.692 = \mathbf{333 \text{ g ClO}_2}$

(b) $(525 \text{ g NaClO}_3)\left(\dfrac{1 \text{ mol NaClO}_3}{106.440 \text{ g NaClO}_3}\right)\left(\dfrac{2 \text{ mol H}_2\text{C}_2\text{O}_4}{2 \text{ mol NaClO}_3}\right)\left(\dfrac{90.034 \text{ g H}_2\text{C}_2\text{O}_4}{1 \text{ mol H}_2\text{C}_2\text{O}_4}\right) = 444.07976$

$$= \mathbf{444 \text{ g H}_2\text{C}_2\text{O}_4}$$

(c) $(475 \text{ g NaClO}_3)\left(\dfrac{1 \text{ mol NaClO}_3}{106.440 \text{ g NaClO}_3}\right) = \dfrac{4.4626 \text{ mol}}{2} = 2.23 \text{ NaClO}_3$

$(375 \text{ g H}_2\text{C}_2\text{O}_4)\left(\dfrac{1 \text{ mol H}_2\text{C}_2\text{O}_4}{90.034 \text{ g H}_2\text{C}_2\text{O}_4}\right) = \dfrac{4.16509 \text{ mol}}{2} = 2.08 \text{ H}_2\text{C}_2\text{O}_4$ Limiting reactant

$(4.16509 \text{ mol H}_2\text{C}_2\text{O}_4)\left(\dfrac{2 \text{ mol ClO}_2}{2 \text{ mol H}_2\text{C}_2\text{O}_4}\right)\left(\dfrac{67.451 \text{ g ClO}_2}{1 \text{ mol ClO}_2}\right) = 280.93970 = \mathbf{281 \text{ g ClO}_2}$

(d) $475 \text{ g NaClO}_3 - (4.16509 \text{ mol H}_2\text{C}_2\text{O}_4)\left(\dfrac{2 \text{ mol NaClO}_3}{2 \text{ mol H}_2\text{C}_2\text{O}_4}\right)\left(\dfrac{106.440 \text{ g NaClO}_3}{1 \text{ mol NaClO}_3}\right)$

$= 31.6678 = \mathbf{32 \text{ g NaClO}_3}$

3.104 Chlorine is commonly used as bleach. Sodium thiosulfate, $Na_2S_2O_3$, is used in the bleaching industry to destroy excess chlorine. Sodium thiosulfate is prepared by heating an aqueous solution of sodium sulfite, Na_2SO_3, with sulfur. The reaction is

$$Na_2SO_3(aq) + S(s) \rightarrow Na_2S_2O_3(aq)$$

Calculate the maximum number of grams of sodium thiosulfate formed when 5.25 g of sodium sulfite are reacted with 7.25 g of sulfur.

Information
The balanced chemical equation; the quantities of starting material (5.25 g Na_2SO_3, and 7.25 g S); the question of how many grams of $Na_2S_2O_3$ will form

Connections
Moles are the key. Information on the elements given on the periodic table

Solution
Find the molar mass, following the procedure introduced in section 3.2.

Dividing the mass by the molar mass gives moles.

A mole ratio is required to convert from moles of one substance to moles of another.

Moles times molar mass gives mass (grams):

$(5.25 \text{ g Na}_2\text{SO}_3)\left(\dfrac{1 \text{ mol Na}_2\text{SO}_3}{126.042 \text{ g Na}_2\text{SO}_3}\right) = \dfrac{0.041652782 \text{ mol Na}_2\text{SO}_3}{1} = 0.041652782$ LR

$$(7.25 \text{ g S})\left(\frac{1 \text{ mol S}}{32.065 \text{ g S}}\right) = \frac{0.226103228 \text{ mol S}}{1} = 0.226103228$$

$$(0.041652782 \text{ mol Na}_2\text{SO}_3)\left(\frac{1 \text{ mol Na}_2\text{S}_2\text{O}_3}{1 \text{ mol Na}_2\text{SO}_3}\right)\left(\frac{158.107 \text{ g Na}_2\text{S}_2\text{O}_3}{1 \text{ mol Na}_2\text{S}_2\text{O}_3}\right) = 6.585596 = \textbf{6.59 g Na}_2\textbf{S}_2\textbf{O}_3$$

3.106 Natural gas is primarily methane. Methane burns with the oxygen in air to produce carbon dioxide gas and water vapor. **(a)** Write a balanced chemical equation for the combustion of methane. **(b)** Calculate the maximum number of grams of water vapor that may form from the reaction of 15.2 g of methane with 15.2 g of oxygen.

Information

(a) The identities of the reactants and products in a reaction; the question of what is the balanced chemical equation; **(b)** the quantities of the reactants (15.2 g of methane and 15.2 g of oxygen), the question of how many grams of water vapor will form

Connections

Moles are the key. The rules on nomenclature covered in the Nomenclature Resource; the information on the elements given on the periodic table

Solution

(a) Balance the equation using the procedure discussed in section 3.1.

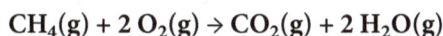

$$\textbf{CH}_4\textbf{(g)} + \textbf{2 O}_2\textbf{(g)} \rightarrow \textbf{CO}_2\textbf{(g)} + \textbf{2 H}_2\textbf{O(g)}$$

(b) Find the molar mass, following the procedure introduced in section 3.2.

Dividing the mass by the molar mass gives moles.

$$\text{Mole CH}_4 = (15.2 \text{ g CH}_4)\left(\frac{1 \text{ mol CH}_4}{16.043 \text{ g CH}_4}\right) = \left(\frac{0.94745 \text{ mol CH}_4}{1}\right) = 9.4745 \times 10^{-1}$$

$$\text{Mole O}_2 = (15.2 \text{ g O}_2)\left(\frac{1 \text{ mol O}_2}{31.998 \text{ g O}_2}\right) = \left(\frac{0.4750297 \text{ mol O}_2}{2}\right) = 2.3751 \times 10^{-1}$$

The final value for O_2 (2.3751×10^{-1}) is the smaller value; therefore, O_2 is the limiting reactant.

Finishing the problem with O_2 gives

A mole ratio is needed to convert from moles of one substance to moles of another substance.

Moles times molar mass gives mass (grams).

$$\text{Mass H}_2\text{O} = (0.4750297 \text{ mol O}_2)\left(\frac{2 \text{ mol H}_2\text{O}}{2 \text{ mol O}_2}\right)\left(\frac{18.015 \text{ g H}_2\text{O}}{1 \text{ mol H}_2\text{O}}\right) = 8.55766 = \textbf{8.56 g H}_2\textbf{O}$$

3.109 The following reaction may be used to prepare potassium iodate, KIO_3:

$$10 \text{ CrO}_3(s) + 3 \text{ I}_2(s) + 24 \text{ KCl}(s) \rightarrow 6 \text{ KIO}_3(s) + 4 \text{ K}_3\text{CrCl}_6(s) + 6 \text{ KCrO}_2(s)$$

In one experiment, the following quantities of the reactants were mixed: 0.440 g of CrO_3, 0.330 g of I_2, and 7.500 g of KCl. How many grams of KIO_3 formed?

Information

The balanced chemical equation; the quantities of starting material (0.440 g CrO_3, 0.330 g I_2, and 7.500 g KCl); the question of how many grams of KIO_3 will form

Connections

Moles are the key. Information on the elements given on the periodic table

Solution

Find the molar mass, following the procedure introduced in section 3.2.

Dividing the mass by the molar mass gives moles:

$$\text{Mole } CrO_3 = (0.440 \text{ g } CrO_3)\left(\frac{1 \text{ mol } CrO_3}{99.993 \text{ g } CrO_3}\right) = \left(\frac{0.004400308 \text{ mol } CrO_3}{10}\right) = 4.400308 \times 10^{-4}$$

$$\text{Mole } I_2 = (0.330 \text{ g } I_2)\left(\frac{1 \text{ mol } I_2}{253.808 \text{ g } I_2}\right) = \left(\frac{0.001300195 \text{ mol } I_2}{3}\right) = 4.3339847 \times 10^{-4}$$

$$\text{Mole KCl} = (7.500 \text{ g KCl})\left(\frac{1 \text{ mol KCl}}{74.551 \text{ g KCl}}\right) = \left(\frac{0.100602 \text{ mol KCl}}{24}\right) = 4.19176 \times 10^{-3}$$

The final value for I_2 (4.3339847×10^{-4}) is the smallest value; therefore, I_2 is the limiting reactant.

Finishing the problem with I_2 (limiting reactant) gives:

A mole ratio is required to convert from moles of one substance to moles of another.

Moles times molar mass gives mass (grams).

$$\text{Mass } KIO_3 = (0.001300195 \text{ mol } I_2)\left(\frac{6 \text{ mol } KIO_3}{3 \text{ mol } I_2}\right)\left(\frac{213.999 \text{ g } KIO_3}{1 \text{ mol } KIO_3}\right) = 0.55648 = \textbf{0.556 g } KIO_3$$

3.7 Percent Yield

3.112 You are given the following equation:

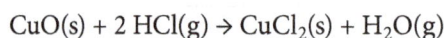

$$CuO(s) + 2 HCl(g) \rightarrow CuCl_2(s) + H_2O(g)$$

You are then supplied with the following sets of data:

(a) 25.0 g of CuO and excess HCl

(b) 25.0 g of CuO and 75.0 g of HCl

(c) 25.0 g of CuO and 39.0 g of $CuCl_2$

(d) 25.0 g of CuO, 75.0 g of HCl, and 39.0 g of $CuCl_2$

(e) 25.0 g of CuO, 75.0 g of HCl, and 4.00 g of H_2O

Which of these five cases gives you enough information to calculate the percent yield? In the cases where you can determine the percent yield, what is the actual yield in grams?

Solution

Find the molar mass, following the procedure introduced in section 3.2.

To determine the percent yield, we need to know the amount of at least one of the reactants. This situation occurs in all five cases. In addition, to determine the percent yield we need to know the amount of at least one product formed. This situation occurs in the last three cases only.

Dividing the mass by the molar mass gives moles.

A mole ratio is required to convert from moles of one substance to moles of another.

Moles times molar mass gives mass (grams).

(c) 25.0 g of CuO and 39.0 g of $CuCl_2$

$$\text{Grams } CuCl_2 = (25.0 \text{ g CuO})\left(\frac{1 \text{ mol CuO}}{79.545 \text{ g CuO}}\right)\left(\frac{1 \text{ mol } CuCl_2}{1 \text{ mol CuO}}\right)\left(\frac{134.452 \text{ g } CuCl_2}{1 \text{ mol } CuCl_2}\right)$$

$$= 42.25658 = \textbf{42.3 g } \textbf{CuCl}_2$$

(d) 25.0 g of CuO, 75.0 g of HCl, and 39.0 g of $CuCl_2$

$$\text{Mole CuO} = (25.0 \text{ g CuO})\left(\frac{1 \text{ mol CuO}}{79.545 \text{ g CuO}}\right) = \left(\frac{0.3142875 \text{ mol CuO}}{1}\right) = 0.3142875$$

$$\text{Mole HCl} = (75.0 \text{ g HCl})\left(\frac{1 \text{ mol HCl}}{36.461 \text{ g HCl}}\right) = \left(\frac{2.056992 \text{ mol HCl}}{2}\right) = 1.028496$$

The final value for CuO (0.3142875) is the smaller value; therefore, CuO is the limiting reactant.

Finishing the problem with CuO gives

$$\text{Grams } CuCl_2 = (0.3142875 \text{ mol CuO})\left(\frac{1 \text{ mol } CuCl_2}{1 \text{ mol CuO}}\right)\left(\frac{134.452 \text{ g } CuCl_2}{1 \text{ mol } CuCl_2}\right)$$

$$= 42.256584 = \textbf{42.3 g } \textbf{CuCl}_2$$

(e) 25.0 g of CuO, 75.0 g of HCl, and 4.00 g of H_2O

This involves the same limiting reactant calculation as in part (d).

$$\text{Grams } H_2O = (0.3142875 \text{ mol CuO})\left(\frac{1 \text{ mol } H_2O}{1 \text{ mol CuO}}\right)\left(\frac{18.015 \text{ g } H_2O}{1 \text{ mol } H_2O}\right)$$

$$= 5.661889 = \textbf{5.66 g } \textbf{H}_2\textbf{O}$$

3.114 Small quantities of iron(III) chloride, $FeCl_3$, may be prepared by the following reaction:

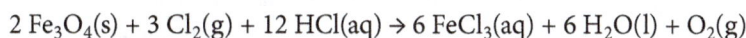

$$2 Fe_3O_4(s) + 3 Cl_2(g) + 12 HCl(aq) \rightarrow 6 FeCl_3(aq) + 6 H_2O(l) + O_2(g)$$

What is the percent yield if 16.8295 g of $FeCl_3$ are formed by reacting 15.2500 g of Fe_3O_4 with an excess of the other reactants?

Information
The balanced chemical equation; the quantities of one of the starting materials (15.2500 g of Fe_3O_4); the question of what is the percent yield if only 16.8295 g of $FeCl_3$ form

Connections
Moles are the key. Information on the elements given on the periodic table; the definition of *percent yield*, (Percent yield = $\dfrac{\text{Actual yield}}{\text{Theoretical yield}} \times 100\%$)

Solution
Find the molar mass, following the procedure introduced in section 3.2.

Dividing the mass by the molar mass gives moles.

A mole ratio is required to convert from moles of one substance to moles of another.

Moles times molar mass gives mass (grams).

$$\text{Grams FeCl}_3 = (15.2500 \text{ g Fe}_3\text{O}_4)\left(\frac{1 \text{ mol Fe}_3\text{O}_4}{231.531 \text{ g Fe}_3\text{O}_4}\right)\left(\frac{6 \text{ mol FeCl}_3}{2 \text{ mol Fe}_3\text{O}_4}\right)\left(\frac{162.204 \text{ g FeCl}_3}{1 \text{ mol FeCl}_3}\right)$$

$$= 32.05114218 = \textbf{32.0511 g FeCl}_3 \quad \text{(theoretical yield)}$$

$$\text{Percent yield} = \frac{16.8295 \text{ g FeCl}_3}{32.05114218 \text{ g FeCl}_3} \times 100\% = 52.5082695 = \textbf{52.5083\%}$$

3.116 Under certain conditions, the compound S_4N_4 may be explosive. One safe way to destroy this compound is by the following reaction:

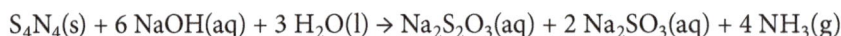

$$S_4N_4(s) + 6 \text{ NaOH}(aq) + 3 \text{ H}_2\text{O}(l) \rightarrow \text{Na}_2\text{S}_2\text{O}_3(aq) + 2 \text{ Na}_2\text{SO}_3(aq) + 4 \text{ NH}_3(g)$$

In one test reaction, 2.0000 g of S_4N_4 generated 0.5298 g of NH_3. What was the percent yield in the test reaction?

Information
The balanced chemical equation; the quantities of one of the starting materials (2.0000 g of S_4N_4); the question of what is the percent yield if only 0.5298 g of NH_3 form

Connections
Moles are the key. Information on the elements given on the periodic table; the definition of *percent yield*, (Percent yield $= \dfrac{\text{Actual yield}}{\text{Theoretical yield}} \times 100\%$)

Solution
Find the molar mass, following the procedure introduced in section 3.2.

Dividing the mass by the molar mass gives moles.

A mole ratio is required to convert from moles of one substance to moles of another.

Moles times molar mass gives mass (grams).

$$\text{Percent yield} = \frac{0.5298 \text{ g NH}_3}{(2.0000 \text{ g S}_4\text{N}_4)\left(\frac{1 \text{ mol S}_4\text{N}_4}{184.288 \text{ g S}_4\text{N}_4}\right)\left(\frac{4 \text{ mol NH}_3}{1 \text{ mol S}_4\text{N}_4}\right)\left(\frac{17.0304 \text{ g NH}_3}{1 \text{ mol NH}_3}\right)} \times 100\% = 71.662$$

$$= \textbf{71.66\%}$$

3.8 Applications
3.120 The following reaction is important to the Haber process:

$$N_2(g) + 3 \text{ H}_2(g) \rightarrow 2 \text{ NH}_3(g)$$

An industrial plant combines 13.5 metric tons of nitrogen gas and 4.0 metric tons of hydrogen gas in a Haber–Bosch reactor. After the conditions are adjusted to optimum, 7.36 metric tons of ammonia form. What is the percent yield of ammonia? (A metric ton is 1,000 kilograms.)

Information
The balanced chemical equation; the amount of starting material (13.5 metric tons N_2 and 4.0 metric tons H_2); the amount of product (7.36 metric tons NH_3); the definition of a *metric ton* (1 metric ton = 1,000 kg); the question of what is the percent yield

Connections

Moles are the key. Information on the elements given on the periodic table; the definition of *percent yield* (Percent yield = $\dfrac{\text{Actual yield}}{\text{Theoretical yield}} \times 100\%$)

Solution

Find the molar mass, following the procedure introduced in section 3.2.

Dividing the mass by the molar mass gives moles:

$$\text{Mole N}_2 = \left(13.5\ \text{t N}_2\right)\left(\frac{1,000\ \text{kg}}{1\ \text{t}}\right)\left(\frac{1\ \text{mol N}_2}{28.014\ \text{g N}_2}\right) = \left(\frac{481.9019\ \text{kmol N}_2}{1}\right) = 481.9019$$

$$\text{Mole H}_2 = \left(4.0\ \text{t H}_2\right)\left(\frac{1,000\ \text{kg}}{1\ \text{t}}\right)\left(\frac{1\ \text{mol H}_2}{2.016\ \text{g H}_2}\right) = \left(\frac{1984.12698\ \text{mol H}_2}{3}\right) = 661.37566$$

The final value for N_2 (481.9019) is the smaller value; therefore, N_2 is the limiting reactant.

Finishing the problem with N_2 gives

A mole ratio is required to convert from moles of one substance to moles of another.

Moles times molar mass gives mass (metric tons):

$$\text{Mass NH}_3 = (481.9019\ \text{kmol N}_2)\left(\frac{1\ \text{mol NH}_3}{1\ \text{mol N}_2}\right)\left(\frac{17.031\ \text{g NH}_3}{1\ \text{mol NH}_3}\right)\left(\frac{1\ \text{t}}{1,000\ \text{kg}}\right)$$

$$= 8.207271 = 8.21\ \text{t NH}_3 = \text{Theoretical yield}$$

$$\text{Percent yield} = \frac{7.36\ \text{t NH}_3}{8.207271\ \text{t NH}_3} \times 100\% = 89.6765778 = \mathbf{89.7\%}$$

3.122 The goal of the Ostwald process is to form nitric acid, HNO_3. This acid forms in the final step:

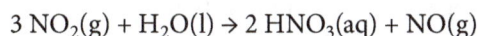

$$3\ NO_2(g) + H_2O(l) \rightarrow 2\ HNO_3(aq) + NO(g)$$

The percent yield of this reaction, in some cases, is 37.5%. Considering this percent yield, how many metric tons of nitric acid will form when 18.9 metric tons of nitrogen dioxide react with 1.75 metric tons of water? (A metric ton is 1,000 kilograms.)

Information

The balanced chemical equation; the percent yield; the amount of starting materials (18.9 metric tons NO_2 and 1.75 metric tons H_2O); the definition of a *metric ton* (1 metric ton = 1,000 kg); the question of how many metric tons of HNO_3 will form

Connections

Moles are the key. Information on the elements given on the periodic table; the definition of *percent yield*

Solution

Find the molar mass, following the procedure introduced in section 3.2.

Dividing the mass by the molar mass gives moles:

$$\text{Mole } H_2O = (1.75 \text{ t } H_2O)\left(\frac{1{,}000 \text{ kg}}{1 \text{ t}}\right)\left(\frac{1 \text{ mol } H_2O}{18.015 \text{ g } H_2O}\right) = \left(\frac{97.14147 \text{ kmol } H_2O}{1}\right) = 94.14127$$

$$\text{Mole } NO_2 = (18.9 \text{ t } NO_2)\left(\frac{1{,}000 \text{ kg}}{1 \text{ t}}\right)\left(\frac{1 \text{ mol } NO_2}{46.005 \text{ g } NO_2}\right) = \left(\frac{410.8249 \text{ kmol } NO_2}{3}\right) = 136.9416$$

The final value for H_2O (94.14127) is the smaller value; therefore, H_2O is the limiting reactant. Finishing the problem with H_2O gives

A mole ratio is required to convert from moles of one substance to moles of another.

Moles times molar mass gives mass (metric tons).

$$\text{Mass } HNO_3 = (97.14147 \text{ kmol } H_2O)\left(\frac{2 \text{ mol } HNO_3}{1 \text{ mol } H_2O}\right)\left(\frac{63.012 \text{ g } HNO_3}{1 \text{ mol } HNO_3}\right)\left(\frac{1 \text{ t}}{1{,}000 \text{ kg}}\right)\left(\frac{37.5\%}{100\%}\right)$$

$$= 4.5908 = \textbf{4.59 t } HNO_3$$

3.125 The following compounds could serve as nitrogen sources in fertilizer: calcium carbamate, $Ca(NH_2CO_2)_2$; ammonia, NH_3; calcium nitrate, $Ca(NO_3)_2$; and sodium nitrate, $NaNO_3$. Determine the percent nitrogen in each of these substances.

Information
The formulas of four compounds ($Ca(NH_2CO_2)_2$, NH_3, $Ca(NO_3)_2$ and $NaNO_3$); the question of what percent N each of the compounds represents

Connections
Information on the elements given on the periodic table; the procedure to calculate the percent composition

Solution
This is similar to determining the percent composition discussed in section 3.3.

Find the molar mass, following the procedure introduced in section 3.2:

$$\% \text{ N} = \frac{2 \text{ N atoms}\left(\dfrac{14.007 \text{ amu N}}{\text{N atom}}\right)}{160.142 \text{ amu } Ca(NH_2CO_2)_2} \times 100\% = 17.49322 = \textbf{17.493\%}$$

$$\% \text{ N} = \frac{1 \text{ N atom}\left(\dfrac{14.007 \text{ amu N}}{\text{N atom}}\right)}{17.031 \text{ amu } NH_3} \times 100\% = 82.244143 = \textbf{82.244\%}$$

$$\% \text{ N} = \frac{2 \text{ N atoms}\left(\dfrac{14.007 \text{ amu N}}{\text{N atom}}\right)}{164.086 \text{ amu } Ca(NO_3)_2} \times 100\% = 17.07275 = \textbf{17.073\%}$$

$$\% \text{ N} = \frac{1 \text{ N atom}\left(\dfrac{14.007 \text{ amu N}}{\text{N atom}}\right)}{84.794 \text{ amu } NaNO_3} \times 100\% = 16.510602 = \textbf{16.511\%}$$

Putting It All Together

3.131 One reaction that leads to the tarnishing of silverware is

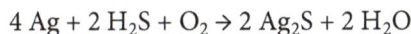

$$4\,Ag + 2\,H_2S + O_2 \rightarrow 2\,Ag_2S + 2\,H_2O$$

A chemist is investigating this reaction. She mixes the following: 1.6310 g of silver, Ag; 0.2560 g of hydrogen sulfide, H_2S; and 0.1215 g of oxygen, O_2. How many grams of silver sulfide, Ag_2S, will form?

Information

The balanced chemical equation; the masses of the three reactants (1.6310 g Ag, 0.2560 g H_2S, and 0.1215 g O_2); the question of how many grams of Ag_2S will form

Connections

Moles are the key.

Solution

Find the molar mass, following the procedure introduced in section 3.2.

Dividing the mass by the molar mass gives moles:

$$\text{Mole Ag} = (1.6310\ \text{g Au})\left(\frac{1\ \text{mol Ag}}{107.8682\ \text{g Ag}}\right) = \left(\frac{0.0151203\ \text{mol Ag}}{4}\right) = 3.780076 \times 10^{-3} = 3.7801 \times 10^{-3}$$

$$\text{Mole } H_2S = (0.2560\ \text{g } H_2S)\left(\frac{1\ \text{mol } H_2S}{34.081\ \text{g } H_2S}\right) = \left(\frac{0.0075115167\ \text{mol } H_2S}{2}\right) = 3.7557583 \times 10^{-3}$$
$$= 3.756 \times 10^{-3}$$

$$\text{Mole } O_2 = (0.1215\ \text{g } O_2)\left(\frac{1\ \text{mol } O_2}{31.9988\ \text{g } O_2}\right) = \left(\frac{0.0037970174\ \text{mol } O_2}{1}\right) = 3.797017 \times 10^{-3} = 3.797 \times 10^{-3}$$

The final value for H_2S (3.7557583×10^{-3}) is the smallest value; therefore, H_2S is the limiting reactant.

A mole ratio is required to convert from moles of one substance to moles of another.

Finishing the problem with water gives

Moles times molar mass gives mass (grams):

$$\text{Mass } Ag_2S = (0.0075115167\ \text{ml } H_2S)\left(\frac{2\ \text{mol } Ag_2S}{2\ \text{mol } H_2S}\right)\left(\frac{247.801\ \text{g } Ag_2S}{1\ \text{mol } Ag_2S}\right) = 1.86136135 = \mathbf{1.861\ g\ Ag_2S}$$

3.133 Rubies and sapphires are aluminum oxide with different colors induced by various impurities, such as chromium and manganese. The density of pure aluminum oxide is 3.96 g/cm³. How many aluminum atoms are present in a 3.50-cm³ sample of aluminum oxide?

Information

The density of Al_2O_3 (3.96 g/cm³); the volume of Al_2O_3 (3.50 cm³); the question of how many Al atoms are present

Connections

Moles are the key.

Solution

Find the molar mass, following the procedure introduced in section 3.2.

Dividing the mass by the molar mass gives moles.

A mole ratio is required to convert from moles of one substance to moles of another:

$$\text{Al atoms} = \left(3.50 \text{ cm}^3\right)\left(\frac{3.96 \text{ g Al}_2\text{O}_3}{\text{cm}^3}\right)\left(\frac{1 \text{ mol Al}_2\text{O}_3}{101.9612 \text{ g Al}_2\text{O}_3}\right)\left(\frac{2 \text{ mol Al}}{1 \text{ mol Al}_2\text{O}_3}\right)\left(\frac{6.022 \times 10^{23} \text{ Al atoms}}{1 \text{ mol Al}}\right)$$

$$= 1.6371898 \times 10^{23} = \mathbf{1.64 \times 10^{23} \text{ Al atoms}}$$

CHAPTER 4

Aqueous Solutions and Their Chemical Reactions

The successful completion of these problems requires the following nine (9) items.

1. Moles continue to be very important. (You will see that nearly every calculation in this chapter involves moles one or more times.)
2. Learn to identify the strong acids and strong bases.
3. Complete and net ionic equations contain ions; therefore, there must be charges shown.
4. Balancing ionic equations requires balancing not only the atoms, but also the charges.
5. Molarity, M, is a useful way of expressing the concentration of a solution. However, in many problems, it is better to replace M with the definition of *molarity*: $\frac{moles}{liter}$. In some cases, the inverse of the definition, $\frac{liter}{moles}$, is more useful.
6. It is normally safer to include the identity of the solute when expressing the concentration of a solution. For example, it is safer to write 2.5 M NaCl than 2.5 M.
7. Since 1 L = 1,000 mL, it is possible to use $\frac{moles}{1,000\ mL}$ in place of $\frac{moles}{liter}$ when doing calculations.
8. It is possible to express molarity as $\frac{millimoles}{milliliter}$.
9. If a calculation involves a reaction, you will probably need a mole ratio at some point.

Note: There are a larger number of problems in this chapter because, over the years, students have repeatedly asked for more practice problems.

As always, if you have trouble with a problem, try to do at least one step. For example, most calculations involve moles at some point; therefore, try to calculate moles even if you cannot do anything else. If there is a chemical equation, try to balance it, or check if the one given is balanced. Doing anything, however small, means you are making progress.

Example Problems From the Text

Example Problem 4.1

A chemist prepares a saturated sodium chloride solution, consisting of 39.12 g NaCl in 100.0 mL of solution. Calculate the molarity of NaCl in this solution.

Information

We are given 39.12 g NaCl and 100.0 mL from which to calculate the molarity of the solution.

Connections

The definition of *molarity* (mole/L) connects the given information to the desired answer, but to use it we must determine the molar mass of sodium chloride.

Solution

To determine the molarity of a solution, we need to know the moles of the solute—in this case NaCl—and the volume of the solution in liters. When, as in this case, moles are not given, we'll need to use the molar mass of the solute to determine the number of moles present. The molar mass of NaCl is 58.45 g/mole (23.00 g Na/mole + 35.45 g Cl/mole). We must also change the given milliliters to liters. It does not matter if we make the grams-to-moles conversion first or the milliliters-to-liters conversion first, since both are necessary. To save time, we can do both conversions in one calculation (setup):

$$\left(\frac{39.12 \text{ g NaCl}}{100.0 \text{ mL}}\right)\left(\frac{1 \text{ mol NaCl}}{58.45 \text{ g NaCl}}\right)\left(\frac{m}{10^{-3}}\right) = 6.6929 \quad \text{(unrounded)}$$

$$= 6.693 \, \frac{\text{mol NaCl}}{\text{L}} = \textbf{6.693 M NaCl}$$

The first set of parentheses contains the given information. The next set of parentheses contains the grams-to-mole conversion factor. The last set contains the factor for conversion to liters.

Reality Check

The units and the number of significant figures in the answer are correct. There are approximately two-thirds of a mole present ($\approx$40 g/60 g) in one-tenth of a liter of solution.

Follow-Up Problem 4.1a

Calculate the molarity of a calcium chloride, $CaCl_2$, solution containing 50.00 g of this compound in 1750.0 mL of solution.

Information

We are given 50.00 g $CaCl_2$ and 1750.0 mL from which to calculate the molarity of the solution.

Connections

The definition of *molarity* (mole/L) connects the given information to the desired answer, but to use it we must determine the molar mass of calcium chloride.

Solution

We need to use the molar mass of $CaCl_2$ to determine the moles of solute and to convert the volume to liters.

$$\left(\frac{50.00 \text{ g CaCl}_2}{1750.0 \text{ mL}}\right)\left(\frac{1 \text{ mol CaCl}_2}{110.98 \text{ g CaCl}_2}\right)\left(\frac{m}{10^{-3}}\right) = 0.257437 \quad \text{(unrounded)}$$

$$= 0.2574 \; \frac{\text{mol CaCl}_2}{\text{L}} = \textbf{0.2574 M CaCl}_2$$

Reality Check

The units and the number of significant figures in the answer are correct.

Follow-Up Problem 4.1b

A biochemist wants to prepare a potassium hydrogen phosphate, K_2HPO_4, solution. She weighs a bottle of this compound and finds its mass to be 751.32 g. After she pours some of the potassium hydrogen phosphate into a large beaker, the bottle weighs 695.32 g. She then adds some water to the beaker, dissolving the potassium hydrogen phosphate; then she continues diluting the mixture with water until the total volume of the solution is 750.0 mL. What is the molarity of the solution?

Information

The mass of a bottle containing K_2HPO_4 before (751.32 g) and after (695.32 g) the removal of some material. The volume of the solution is 750.0 mL. From this information, calculate the molarity of the solution.

Connections

The definition of *molarity* (mole/L) connects the given information to the desired answer, but to use it we must determine the molar mass of K_2HPO_4.

Solution

The mass of K_2HPO_4 used is (751.32 − 695.32) g = 56.00 grams.
We need to use the molar mass of K_2HPO_4 to determine the moles of solute and to convert the volume to liters.

$$\left(\frac{56.00 \text{ g K}_2\text{HPO}_4}{750.0 \text{ mL}}\right)\left(\frac{1 \text{ mol K}_2\text{HPO}_4}{174.174 \text{ g K}_2\text{HPO}_4}\right)\left(\frac{m}{10^{-3}}\right) = 0.428690 \quad \text{(unrounded)}$$

$$= 0.4287 \; \frac{\text{mol K}_2\text{HPO}_4}{\text{L}} = \textbf{0.4287 M K}_2\textbf{HPO}_4$$

Reality Check

The units and the number of significant figures in the answer are correct.

Example Problem 4.2

A maximum of 85.4 g of sodium sulfate, Na_2SO_4, will dissolve in enough water to give 200.0 mL of solution. In solution, this compound completely separates into individual sodium ions, Na^+, and sulfate ions, SO_4^{2-}. What is the maximum concentration (as molarity) of sodium ions in the solution?

Information

We are given the data 85.4 g Na_2SO_4 and 200.0 mL with which to find the molarity of Na^+.

Connections

The definition of *molarity* (mole/L) and the molar mass of sodium sulfate, Na_2SO_4, connect the data to the required answer.

Solution

It is necessary to determine the number of moles of sodium ions present per liter of solution. To do this, we need to change the grams of sodium sulfate to moles of sodium sulfate; then change the moles of sodium sulfate to the moles of sodium ions (since Na_2SO_4 completely separates, there are 2 Na^+ ions formed from every Na_2SO_4); and finally, convert the milliliters to liters. While it is possible to do these three calculations separately, it is faster to combine them into one step:

$$\left(\frac{85.4 \text{ g } Na_2SO_4}{200.0 \text{ mL}}\right)\left(\frac{1 \text{ mol } Na_2SO_4}{142 \text{ g } Na_2SO_4}\right)\left(\frac{2 \text{ mol } Na^+}{1 \text{ mol } Na_2SO_4}\right)\left(\frac{m}{10^{-3}}\right) = 6.01408 \frac{\text{mol } Na^+}{L} = \textbf{6.01 M } \textbf{Na}^+$$

The first term is the given information. The second term is the molar mass of sodium sulfate. The third term is a mole ratio relating the formula of the compound to one of its constituents (sodium ions). Finally, we cancel the *milli-* prefix, leaving liters in the denominator.

Reality Check

The units and the number of significant figures in the answer are correct. There is more than 1 mole of sodium ions present $[(85 \times 2)/140]$ in one-fifth of a liter of solution. This should give a concentration greater than 5 M and less than 10 M.

Follow-Up Problem 4.2a

Limewater is a saturated solution of calcium hydroxide, $Ca(OH)_2$. A chemist prepares 2.000 L of a limewater solution by dissolving 0.380 g of calcium hydroxide in enough water to yield the 2.000 L of solution. Calcium hydroxide completely separates into calcium ions and hydroxide ions in solution. Determine the molarity of hydroxide ions in this solution.

Information

We are given the data 0.380 g of calcium hydroxide and 2.000 L with which to find the molarity of OH^-.

Connections

The definition of *molarity* (mole/L) and the molar mass of $Ca(OH)_2$ connect the data to the required answer.

Solution

It is necessary to determine the moles of $Ca(OH)_2$. The moles of hydroxide come from the chemical formula.

$$\left(\frac{0.380 \text{ g } Ca(OH)_2}{2.0000 \text{ L}}\right)\left(\frac{1 \text{ mol } Ca(OH)_2}{74.092 \text{ g } Ca(OH)_2}\right)\left(\frac{2 \text{ mol } OH^-}{1 \text{ mol } Ca(OH)_2}\right) = 0.005129 \frac{\text{mol } OH^-}{L}$$

$$= \textbf{5.13} \times \textbf{10}^{-3} \textbf{ M } \textbf{OH}^-$$

Reality Check

The units and the number of significant figures in the answer are correct.

Follow-Up Problem 4.2b

When potassium arsenate, K_3AsO_4, dissolves in water, it completely separates into potassium ions and arsenate ions. What are the molarities of the potassium ions and arsenate ions in a solution made by dissolving 19.50 g of potassium arsenate in sufficient water to produce 1,625 mL of solution?

Information

We are given the data 19.50 g of potassium arsenate and 1625 mL with which to find the molarity of K^+ and AsO_4^{3-}.

Connections

The definition of *molarity* (mole/L) and the molar mass of potassium arsenate connect the data to the required answer.

Solution

We need to use the molar mass of potassium arsenate to find the moles of K_3AsO_4. We also need to convert the milliliters to liters. Finally, the chemical formula provides the appropriate mole ratios.

$$\left(\frac{19.50 \text{ g } K_3AsO_4}{1625 \text{ mL}}\right)\left(\frac{1 \text{ mol } K_3AsO_4}{256.212 \text{ g } K_3AsO_4}\right)\left(\frac{3 \text{ mol } K^+}{1 \text{ mol } K_3AsO_4}\right)\left(\frac{m}{10^{-3}}\right) = 0.1405086 \frac{\text{mol } K^+}{L}$$

$$= \textbf{0.1405 M } K^+$$

$$\left(\frac{19.50 \text{ g } K_3AsO_4}{1625 \text{ mL}}\right)\left(\frac{1 \text{ mol } K_3AsO_4}{256.212 \text{ g } K_3AsO_4}\right)\left(\frac{1 \text{ mol } AsO_4^{3-}}{1 \text{ mol } K_3AsO_4}\right)\left(\frac{m}{10^{-3}}\right) = 0.046836 \frac{\text{mol } AsO_4^{3-}}{L}$$

$$= \textbf{0.04684 M } AsO_4{}^{3-}$$

Reality Check

The units and the number of significant figures in the answer are correct.

Example Problem 4.3

How many moles of ammonium ions are in 0.100 L of a 0.20 M ammonium sulfate, $(NH_4)_2SO_4$, solution?

Information

The given information is 0.100 L of solution and 0.20 M $(NH_4)_2SO_4$, from which to determine the moles of ammonium ions.

Connections

The chemical formula and the definition of *molarity* provide the necessary relationships.

Solution

While the abbreviation for *molarity*, M, is convenient for reporting the concentration of a substance in solution, it is often much more helpful to express molarity as moles per liter (the definition of *molarity*) when solving problems. From that expression, it becomes apparent that multiplying the molarity by liters will leave an amount in moles. In this case, it will be the moles of ammonium sulfate. Then we will need to convert the moles of ammonium sulfate to the moles of ammonium ions:

$$\left(\frac{0.20 \text{ mol } (NH_4)_2SO_4}{L}\right)(0.100 \text{ L})\left(\frac{2 \text{ mol } NH_4^+}{1 \text{ mol } (NH_4)_2SO_4}\right) = \textbf{0.040 mol } NH_4{}^+$$

In this setup, the first term is the given molarity of the solution written in moles per liter. The given volume appears second, and the mole ratio appears last. These terms may be used in any order.

Reality Check

The units and the number of significant figures are correct. The value is reasonable, considering the given values ($0.2 \times 0.1 \times 2$).

Follow-Up Problem 4.3a

Calculate the number of moles of nitrate ions in 100.0 mL of a 0.1000 M solution of aluminum nitrate, $Al(NO_3)_3$.

Information

The given information is 100.0 mL of solution and 0.1000 M solution of $Al(NO_3)_3$, from which to determine the moles of nitrate ions.

Connections

The chemical formula and the definition of molarity provide the necessary relationships.

Solution

Convert M to the definition of *molarity* and enter the appropriate values to convert to the moles of nitrate ions:

$$\left(\frac{0.1000 \text{ mol } Al(NO_3)_3}{1,000 \text{ mL}}\right)(100.0 \text{ mL})\left(\frac{3 \text{ mol } NO_3^-}{1 \text{ mol } Al(NO_3)_3}\right) = \mathbf{0.03000 \text{ moles } NO_3^-}$$

Reality Check

The units and the number of significant figures are correct.

Follow-Up Problem 4.3b

Determine the number of sodium ions in 250.0 mL of a 0.0500 M sodium carbonate, Na_2CO_3, solution.

Information

The given information is 250.0 mL of solution and 0.0500 M solution of Na_2CO_3, from which to determine the moles of sodium ions.

Connections

The chemical formula and the definition of *molarity* provide the necessary relationships.

Solution

Convert M to the definition of *molarity* and enter the appropriate values to convert to the moles of nitrate ions. In addition, since we want the <u>number</u> of ions, it will be necessary to use Avogadro's <u>number</u>.

$$\left(\frac{0.0500 \text{ mol } Na_2CO_3}{1,000 \text{ mL}}\right)(250.0 \text{ mL})\left(\frac{2 \text{ mol } Na^+}{1 \text{ mol } Na_2CO_3}\right)\left(\frac{6.022 \times 10^{23} \text{ Na}^+ \text{ ions}}{1 \text{ mol } Na^+}\right)$$

$$= 1.5055 \times 10^{22} = \mathbf{1.51 \times 10^{22} \text{ sodium ions}}$$

Reality Check

The units and the number of significant figures are correct.

Example Problem 4.4

How many milliliters of a 0.20 M lithium carbonate, Li_2CO_3, solution are required to supply 1.0 mole of lithium ions?

Information

We have the solution molarity, 0.20 M, and the formula of the solute, Li_2CO_3, from which to find how many milliliters of solution contain 1.0 mole Li.

Connections

The chemical formula and the definition of *molarity* provide the necessary relationships.

Solution

This problem requires a mole ratio to relate the moles of lithium to the moles of lithium carbonate. Looking at the formula of lithium carbonate, we see that 1 mole of lithium carbonate will yield 2 mole of lithium. As in other cases, we will express the molarity as moles per liter (the definition of molarity) instead of as M. This leads to the following calculation:

$$(1.0 \text{ mol Li})\left(\frac{1 \text{ mol Li}_2\text{CO}_3}{2 \text{ mol Li}}\right)\left(\frac{L}{0.20 \text{ mol Li}_2\text{CO}_3}\right)\left(\frac{m}{10^{-3}}\right) = \mathbf{2.5 \times 10^3 \ mL}$$

The first term is the quantity of lithium given in the problem. The second term is the mole ratio. The third term is the molarity, inverted to make the units cancel as necessary. Finally, we use a conversion factor to provide the *milli-* prefix.

Reality Check

The units and the number of significant figures are correct.

Follow-Up Problem 4.4a

A saturated solution of silver chloride, AgCl, has a concentration of 1.33×10^{-5} M. What volume (in milliliters) of saturated silver chloride solution is necessary to supply 1.00 mole of silver?

Information

We have the solution molarity, 1.33×10^{-5} M, and the formula of the solute, AgCl, from which to find how many milliliters of solution contain 1.00 mole AgCl.

Connections

The chemical formula and the definition of *molarity* provide the necessary relationships.

Solution

This is a unit conversion problem beginning with moles and ending with milliliters using the definition of *molarity* to connect the two:

$$\text{Volume} = (1.00 \text{ mol AgCl})\left(\frac{1{,}000 \text{ mL}}{1.33 \times 10^{-5} \text{ mol AgCl}}\right) = 7.5188 \times 10^7 = \mathbf{7.52 \times 10^7 \ mL}$$

Reality Check

The units and the number of significant figures are correct.

Follow-Up Problem 4.4b

At one time, lithium bromide, LiBr, was a common sedative. The typical dose was about 1 g, administered orally. How many milliliters of a 0.125 M lithium bromide solution are necessary to supply 1.00 g of this compound to a patient?

Information

We have the solution molarity, 0.125 M, and the formula of the solute, LiBr, from which to find how many milliliters of solution contain 1.00 g LiBr.

Connections

The chemical formula and the definition of *molarity* provide the necessary relationships.

Solution

Change the grams to moles (using the molar mass) and then multiply by the inverse of the definition of *molarity*:

$$\text{Volume} = (1.00 \text{ g LiBr})\left(\frac{1 \text{ mol LiBr}}{86.845 \text{ g LiBr}}\right)\left(\frac{1{,}000 \text{ mL}}{0.125 \text{ mol LiBr}}\right) = 92.118 = \textbf{92.1 mL}$$

Reality Check

The units and the number of significant figures are correct.

Example Problem 4.5

How would you prepare 650.0 mL of a 0.1000 M ammonium sulfate solution?

Information

This problem gives 650.0 mL with which to make a 0.1000 M ammonium sulfate solution, and asks for directions.

Connections

The definition of *molarity* and the molar mass of ammonium sulfate provide the relationships needed to calculate the quantity of solute.

Solution

The directions should specify two numerical values: the quantity of solute (normally measured in grams) and the volume of the solution. First, we will determine the quantity of solute required:

$$\left(\frac{0.1000 \text{ mol } (NH_4)_2SO_4}{L}\right)\left(\frac{10^{-3}}{m}\right)(650.\text{mL})\left(\frac{132.14 \text{ g } (NH_4)_2SO_4}{1 \text{ mol } (NH_4)_2SO_4}\right)$$

$$= 8.5891\left(\frac{\text{moles } (NH_4)_2SO_4}{L}\right) = \textbf{8.589 g } (NH_4)_2SO_4$$

The first term in the calculation states the given molarity in moles per liter, and the second term helps cancel out the volume. The third term is the given volume of the solution. Finally, the molar mass converts moles to grams. Once we know the mass of the solute and the volume of the solution, we can write directions for the preparation of the solution. One way of stating the directions might be this: "Weigh out 8.589 g of ammonium sulfate, dissolve in a small amount of water, and dilute with more water to give a total volume of 650.0 mL."

Reality Check

The units and the number of significant figures are correct. The stated directions indicate how the solution is to be prepared.

Follow-Up Problem 4.5a

A druggist needs to prepare 250.0 mL of a 0.125 M sodium thiosulfate, $Na_2S_2O_3$, solution. What procedure should she follow?

Information

This problem gives 250.0 mL with which to make a 0.125 M sodium thiosulfate solution and asks for directions.

Connections

The definition of *molarity* and the molar mass of sodium thiosulfate provide the relationships needed to calculate the quantity of solute.

Solution

We need to first determine the moles of solute present and then convert the moles to grams using the molar mass:

$$\text{Mass} = \left(\frac{0.125 \text{ mol Na}_2\text{S}_2\text{O}_3}{1{,}000 \text{ mL}}\right)(250.0 \text{ mL})\left(\frac{158.107 \text{ g Na}_2\text{S}_2\text{O}_3}{\text{mol Na}_2\text{S}_2\text{O}_3}\right) = 4.9408$$

$$= \textbf{4.94 grams Na}_2\textbf{S}_2\textbf{O}_3$$

The druggist would need to weigh out 4.94 g of $Na_2S_2O_3$ into a container and, while stirring, add sufficient water to get a final volume of 250.0 mL of solution.

Reality Check

The units and the number of significant figures are correct. The stated directions indicate how the solution is to be prepared.

Follow-Up Problem 4.5b

What procedure will a nurse need to follow to produce 1.000 gal of 1.00% (0.0556 M) glucose, $C_6H_{12}O_6$, solution?

Information

This problem gives 1.000 gallon with which to make a 1.00 percent (0.0556 M) $C_6H_{12}O_6$ solution and asks for directions.

Connections

The definition of *molarity* and the molar mass of $C_6H_{12}O_6$ provide the relationships needed to calculate the quantity of solute. In addition, one or more volume conversions are necessary.

Solution

We need to first determine the moles of solute present and then convert the moles to grams using the molar mass:

$$(1.000 \text{ gal})\left(\frac{4 \text{ qt}}{1 \text{ gal}}\right)\left(\frac{\text{L}}{1.057 \text{ qt}}\right)\left(\frac{0.0556 \text{ mol C}_6\text{H}_{12}\text{O}_6}{\text{L}}\right)\left(\frac{180.156 \text{ g C}_6\text{H}_{12}\text{O}_6}{\text{mol C}_6\text{H}_{12}\text{O}_6}\right) = 37.9060$$

$$= \textbf{37.9 grams C}_6\textbf{H}_{12}\textbf{O}_6$$

Weigh 37.9 g of glucose into a large container, dissolve it, and dilute with sufficient water to give a final volume of 1.000 gal.

Reality Check

The units and the number of significant figures are correct. The stated directions indicate how the solution is to be prepared.

Example Problem 4.6

What volume of a 16.0 M NaOH solution is needed to prepare 1.000 L of 1.000 M NaOH?

Information

We have 16.0 M of NaOH and 1.000 L of 1.000 M NaOH, and we are asked to find the necessary volume.

Connections

$M_i V_i = M_f V_f$

Solution

We have two molarities and one volume, and we are asked to calculate another molarity:

$M = 16.0$ M NaOH $M = 1.000$ M NaOH
$V = ?$ $V = 1.000$ L

Notice that in arranging this information, we were very careful to pair each M with a V—that is, to show which volume (the 1.000-L volume or the volume that is unknown) belongs to which molarity.

The fact that we are given two concentrations of the same solute is a strong indication that the relationship $M_i V_i = M_f V_f$ might be useful for working this problem. To make sure that we insert our information into the equation properly, we need to add subscripts to identify the variables more clearly:

$M_i = 16.0$ M NaOH $M_f = 1.000$ M NaOH
$V_i = ?$ $V_f = 1.000$ L

Notice that both members of each M and V pair get the same subscript. The dilution relationship may now be rearranged to put the unknown, V_i, on one side and all the known variables on the other. After rearranging, we simply replace the known variables with their values:

▶ The use of the chemical formula—for example, "M NaOH" instead of just "M"—in calculations such as this reduces the chance of making certain common cancellation errors. For example, "M NaOH" would never cancel "M H_2SO_4."

$$V_i = \frac{M_f V_f}{M_i} = \frac{(1.000 \text{ M NaOH})(1.000 \text{ L})}{(16.0 \text{ M NaOH})} = \textbf{0.0625 L}$$

Reality Check

We were seeking a volume, and the final units are volume units, since all units except liters cancel. The number of significant figures is also correct.

Follow-Up Problem 4.6a

How many milliliters of 18.0 M sulfuric acid, H_2SO_4, are needed to prepare 4.00 L of 3.00 M sulfuric acid?

Information

We have 18.0 M H_2SO_4 (M_i) and 4.00 L of 3.00 M H_2SO_4 (V_f and M_f), and we are asked to find the volume (V_i) necessary.

Connections

$$M_i V_i = M_f V_f$$

Solution

Enter the appropriate values into the rearranged dilution equation:

$$V_i = \frac{M_f V_f}{M_i} = \frac{(3.00 \text{ M H}_2\text{SO}_4)(4.00 \text{ L})}{(18.0 \text{ M H}_2\text{SO}_4)}\left(\frac{\text{m}}{0.001}\right) = 666.67 = \textbf{667 mL}$$

Reality Check

We were seeking a volume, and the final units are volume units, since all units except milliliters cancel. The number of significant figures is also correct.

Follow-Up Problem 4.6b

The saline solution used for intravenous injection in hospitals is primarily a sodium chloride solution with a sodium chloride concentration of 0.15 M. How many milliliters of 0.750 M sodium chloride solution are needed to prepare 500.0 mL of saline solution?

Information

We have 0.750 M NaCl (M_i) and 500.0 mL of 0.150 M NaCl (V_f and M_f), and we are asked to find the volume (V_i) necessary.

Connections

$$M_i V_i = M_f V_f$$

Solution

Enter the appropriate values into the rearranged dilution equation:

$$V_i = \frac{M_f V_f}{M_i} = \frac{(0.150 \text{ M NaCl})(500.0 \text{ mL})}{(0.750 \text{ M NaCl})} = \textbf{1.0} \times \textbf{10}^2 \textbf{ mL}$$

Reality Check

We were seeking a volume, and the final units are volume units, since all units except milliliters cancel. The number of significant figures is also correct.

Example Problem 4.7

A solution is prepared by adding 450.0 mL of water to 350.0 mL of a 0.250 M sodium chloride solution. What is the final concentration of the solution?

Information

The given information is 450.0 mL H_2O added to 350.0 mL of a 0.250 M NaCl solution, from which to find the final concentration.

Connections

$$M_i V_i = M_f V_f$$

Solution

We begin by using the given information to supply the known variables in the dilution relationship and to identify the unknown variable:

M_i = 0.250 M NaCl M_f = ? M NaCl

V_i = 350.0 mL V_f = (350.0 + 450.0) mL = 800.0 mL

Notice how the final volume is derived

A common error is to fail to recognize that we are told "450.0 mL is added" to the solution, and instead to mistakenly think that the final volume is 450.0 mL. In general, the volumes in these types of problems are additive.

The presence of two concentrations for the same substance indicates that the dilution relationship is the one to use. Rearranging the dilution relationship to place the unknown on one side and the known values on the other side, and then entering the known values, gives

$$M_f = \frac{M_i V_i}{V_f} = \frac{(0.250 \text{ M NaCl})(350.0 \text{ mL})}{(800.0 \text{ mL})} = 0.109375 = \textbf{0.109 M NaCl}$$

As always, when we're using this equation, the specific volume units are unimportant as long as they agree with each other. It is not necessary to convert the volumes to liters.

Reality Check

The calculation gives us the correct final units, "M NaCl"—not just "M." The number of significant figures is also correct.

Follow-Up Problem 4.7a

Determine the final molarity of hydrochloric acid, HCl, in a solution prepared by adding 175 mL of 12.0 M hydrochloric acid to 825 mL of water.

Information

The given information is 825 mL H_2O added to 175 mL of a 12.0 M HCl (V_i and M_i) solution, from which to find the final concentration (M_f). Note that $V_f = (825 + 175) \text{ mL} = 1,000 \text{ mL}$.

Connections

$M_i V_i = M_f V_f$

Solution

Enter the appropriate values into the rearranged dilution equation:

$$M_f = \frac{M_i V_i}{V_f} = \frac{(12.0 \text{ M HCl})(175 \text{ mL})}{(1,000 \text{ mL})} = \textbf{2.10 M HCl}$$

▶ When diluting concentrated solutions of acids in the laboratory, you should *always* add the concentrated acid slowly to the water, all the while stirring—not the reverse. The dilution of acids releases a large quantity of heat and adding the acid to the water rather than vice versa minimizes the chances of splattering the hot solution.

Reality Check

We were seeking a concentration, and the final units are concentration units, since all units except molarity cancel. The number of significant figures is also correct.

Follow-Up Problem 4.7b

When magnesium nitrate, $Mg(NO_3)_2$, dissolves in water, it completely separates into magnesium ions and nitrate ions. What is the molarity of nitrate ions in a solution prepared by adding 175 mL of water to 225 mL of 2.00 M magnesium nitrate?

Information

The given information is 175 mL H_2O added to 225 mL of a 2.00 M $Mg(NO_3)_2$ solution, from which to find the final concentration. Note that $V_f = (225 + 175) \text{ mL} = 400 \text{ mL}$.

Connections

$M_i V_i = M_f V_f$

Solution

Enter the appropriate values into the rearranged dilution equation:

$$M_f = \frac{M_i V_i}{V_f} = \frac{(2.00 \text{ M Mg(NO}_3)_2)(225 \text{ mL})}{(400 \text{ mL})}\left(\frac{2 \text{ mol NO}_3^-}{1 \text{ mol Mg(NO}_3)_2}\right) = \textbf{2.25 M NO}_3^-$$

Reality Check

We were seeking a concentration, and the final units are concentration units, since all units except molarity cancel. The number of significant figures is also correct.

Example Problem 4.8

Which of the following compounds would be soluble in water? AgI, Ba(NO$_3$)$_2$, FePO$_4$, Co(OH)$_2$, SrSO$_4$

Information

The formulas of the compounds

Connections

The solubility rules

Solution

All these compounds are ionic; however, the hydroxide (Co(OH)$_2$), is not a salt but a base. Since Co(OH)$_2$ is not a strong base, it is not soluble. The remaining compounds contain the following ions: (Ag$^+$ and I$^-$), (Ba^{2+} and NO$_3^-$), (Fe^{3+} and PO$_4^{3-}$), and (Sr^{2+} and SO$_4^{2-}$). The first two compounds fall under rule 1; rule 2 covers the next compound; and rule 3 covers the last compound. Most compounds containing an IB (group 11) metal ion (e.g., Ag$^+$) are not soluble. Thus, AgI is not soluble. The presence of the nitrate ion (NO$_3^-$) indicates that Ba(NO$_3$)$_2$ is soluble. Either one of the ions in FePO$_4$ identifies the compound as insoluble. Finally, according to rule 3, SrSO$_4$ is one of the few insoluble sulfates.

Reality Check

The insolubility of weak bases provides the answer for (Co(OH)$_2$). The other compounds either follow the rules or are included in the exceptions (AgI and SrSO$_4$).

Follow-Up Problem 4.8a

Which of the following compounds would be soluble in water? Na$_3$PO$_4$, AgNO$_3$, Ca$_3$(PO$_4$)$_2$, MgO, BaCO$_3$

Information

The formulas of the compounds

Connections

The solubility rules

Solution

Na$_3$PO$_4$

> This compound contains a +1 ion (Na$^+$) and so it is soluble according to solubility rule 1.

$AgNO_3$

> This compound contains a −1 ion (NO_3^-) and so it is soluble according to solubility rule 1. Note, this is one of the few water-soluble silver compounds

$Ca_3(PO_4)_2$

> This compound contains a −3 ion (PO_4^{3-}) and so it is insoluble according to solubility rule 2.

MgO

> This compound contains a −2 ion (O^{2-}) and so it is insoluble according to solubility rule 3.

$BaCO_3$

> This compound contains a −2 ion (CO_3^{2-}) and so it is insoluble according to solubility rule 3.

Reality Check

These compounds follow the solubility rules.

Follow-Up Problem 4.8b

Which of the following compounds would be soluble in water? potassium sulfate, zinc nitrate, barium phosphate, aluminum hydroxide, magnesium acetate

Information

The names of the compounds

Connections

The solubility rules and the rules of nomenclature given in the Nomenclature Resource

Solution

Potassium sulfate, K_2SO_4

> This compound contains a +1 ion (K^+) and so it is soluble according to solubility rule 1.

Zinc nitrate, $Zn(NO_3)_2$

> This compound contains a −1 ion (NO_3^-) and so it is soluble according to solubility rule 1.

Barium phosphate, $Ba_3(PO_4)_2$

> This compound contains a −3 ion (PO_4^{3-}) and so it is insoluble according to solubility rule 2.

Aluminum hydroxide, $Al(OH)_3$

> This base is not a strong base, so it is insoluble.

Magnesium acetate, $Mg(C_2H_3O_2)_2$

> This compound contains a −1 ion ($C_2H_3O_2^-$) and so it is soluble according to solubility rule 1.

Reality Check

The insolubility of weak bases provides the answer for ($Al(OH)_3$). The other compounds follow the rules

Example Problem 4.9

Convert the following equation to net ionic form:

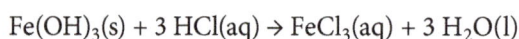

$$Fe(OH)_3(s) + 3\ HCl(aq) \rightarrow FeCl_3(aq) + 3\ H_2O(l)$$

Information
The balanced chemical equation

Connections
The solubility rules; the identities of the strong acids and bases; fundamental nomenclature rules to help with the identification of strong electrolytes

Solution
To show the participation of ions in the reaction, you need to know which substances in the balanced chemical equation are strong electrolytes:

$Fe(OH)_3$ is not a strong base, so it is not a strong electrolyte.
HCl is a strong acid, so it is a strong electrolyte.
$FeCl_3$ is a salt containing an ion with a –1 charge (Cl^-), so it is soluble (solubility rule 1) and a strong electrolyte.
H_2O is a molecular liquid and therefore a nonelectrolyte.

Next, separate all strong electrolytes into their constituent ions:

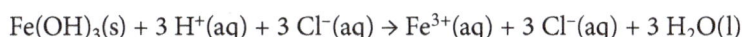

$$Fe(OH)_3(s) + 3\ H^+(aq) + 3\ Cl^-(aq) \rightarrow Fe^{3+}(aq) + 3\ Cl^-(aq) + 3\ H_2O(l)$$

There are three chloride ions on each side of the reaction arrow. Because it does not change in this reaction, the chloride ion is a spectator ion. Removing the spectator ions leaves the equation in net ionic form:

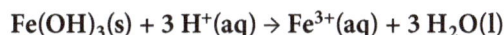

$$\mathbf{Fe(OH)_3(s) + 3\ H^+(aq) \rightarrow Fe^{3+}(aq) + 3\ H_2O(l)}$$

Reality Check
The final equation is balanced, and the only species it contains are ions and nonelectrolytes.

Follow-Up Problem 4.9a
Convert the following equation to net ionic form:

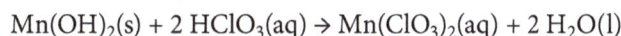

$$Mn(OH)_2(s) + 2\ HClO_3(aq) \rightarrow Mn(ClO_3)_2(aq) + 2\ H_2O(l)$$

Information
The balanced chemical equation

Connections
The solubility rules; the identities of the strong acids and bases; fundamental nomenclature rules to help with the identification of strong electrolytes

Solution
Begin by recopying the equation. Then separate the strong electrolytes, which are the strong acid ($HClO_3$) and water-soluble $Mn(ClO_3)_2$ (solubility rule 1).

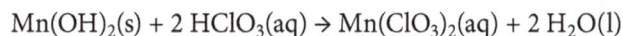

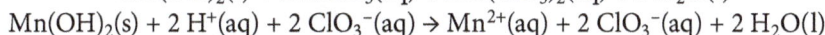

$$Mn(OH)_2(s) + 2\ HClO_3(aq) \rightarrow Mn(ClO_3)_2(aq) + 2\ H_2O(l)$$
$$Mn(OH)_2(s) + 2\ H^+(aq) + 2\ ClO_3^-(aq) \rightarrow Mn^{2+}(aq) + 2\ ClO_3^-(aq) + 2\ H_2O(l)$$

Next, cancel the spectator ion (ClO_3^-):

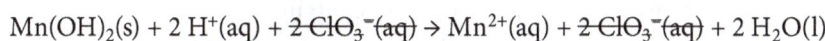

$$Mn(OH)_2(s) + 2\ H^+(aq) + \cancel{2\ ClO_3^-(aq)} \rightarrow Mn^{2+}(aq) + \cancel{2\ ClO_3^-(aq)} + 2\ H_2O(l)$$

Recopy what remains as the net ionic equation:

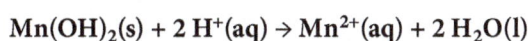

$$\mathbf{Mn(OH)_2(s) + 2\ H^+(aq) \rightarrow Mn^{2+}(aq) + 2\ H_2O(l)}$$

Check to make sure the final equation is balanced.

Reality Check
The final equation is balanced, and the only species it contains are ions and nonelectrolytes.

Follow-Up Problem 4.9b
Convert the following equation to net ionic form:

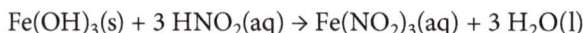

$$Fe(OH)_3(s) + 3\ HNO_2(aq) \rightarrow Fe(NO_2)_3(aq) + 3\ H_2O(l)$$

Information
The balanced chemical equation

Connections
The solubility rules; the identities of the strong acids and bases; fundamental nomenclature rules to help with the identification of strong electrolytes

Solution
Begin by recopying the equation. Then separate the strong electrolytes, which is only the water-soluble $Fe(NO_2)_3$ (solubility rule 1). The HNO_2 is a weak acid and will not separate. $Fe(OH)_3$ is not a strong base, so it is not soluble (not an electrolyte). Water is not an electrolyte.

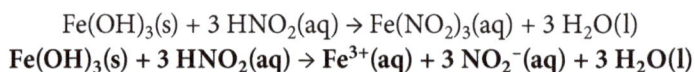

$$Fe(OH)_3(s) + 3\ HNO_2(aq) \rightarrow Fe(NO_2)_3(aq) + 3\ H_2O(l)$$
$$\mathbf{Fe(OH)_3(s) + 3\ HNO_2(aq) \rightarrow Fe^{3+}(aq) + 3\ NO_2{}^-(aq) + 3\ H_2O(l)}$$

There are no spectator ions; therefore, this is the net ionic equation.

Check to make sure the final equation is balanced.

Reality Check
The final equation is balanced, and the only species it contains are ions and nonelectrolytes.

Example Problem 4.10
Convert the following equation to net ionic form:

$$Na_2CO_3(aq) + 2\ HNO_3(aq) \rightarrow 2\ NaNO_3(aq) + CO_2(g) + H_2O(l)$$

Information
The balanced chemical equation

Connections
The solubility rules; the identities of the strong acids and bases; rules of nomenclature, to help with the identification of strong electrolytes

Solution
We need to identify which substances in the balanced chemical equation are strong electrolytes:

- Na_2CO_3 contains an ion with a +1 charge (Na^+), so according to solubility rule 1, it is soluble (a strong electrolyte).
- HNO_3 is a strong acid, so it is a strong electrolyte.
- $NaNO_3$ contains an ion with a +1 charge (Na^+), so according to solubility rule 1, it is soluble (a strong electrolyte). [This compound also contains an ion with a –1 charge ($NO_3{}^-$), which also means, according to solubility rule 1, that it is soluble.]
- CO_2 and H_2O are molecular compounds, and therefore nonelectrolytes.

Next, separate all strong electrolytes into their constituent ions:

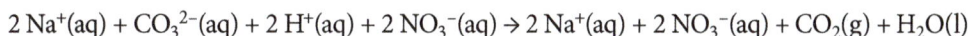

$$2\,Na^+(aq) + CO_3^{2-}(aq) + 2\,H^+(aq) + 2\,NO_3^-(aq) \rightarrow 2\,Na^+(aq) + 2\,NO_3^-(aq) + CO_2(g) + H_2O(l)$$

There are two sodium ions (Na^+) on each side of the reaction arrow, so the sodium ions are spectator ions. There are two nitrate ions (NO_3^-) on each side of the reaction arrow, so the nitrate ions are spectator ions.

Removing the spectator ions leaves this net ionic equation:

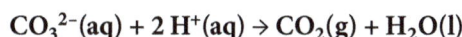

$$CO_3^{2-}(aq) + 2\,H^+(aq) \rightarrow CO_2(g) + H_2O(l)$$

Reality Check

The final equation remains balanced after the spectator ions are removed, and the only species left are ions and nonelectrolytes.

Follow-Up Problem 4.10a

Convert the following equation to net ionic form:

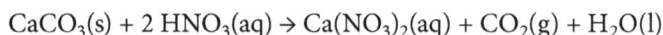

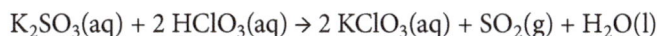

$$CaCO_3(s) + 2\,HNO_3(aq) \rightarrow Ca(NO_3)_2(aq) + CO_2(g) + H_2O(l)$$

Information

The balanced chemical equation

Connections

The solubility rules, the identities of the strong acids and bases, and rules of nomenclature, to help with the identification of strong electrolytes.

Solution

Begin by recopying the equation and then separate the strong electrolytes, which are the strong acid (HNO_3) and, according to solubility rule 1, the water-soluble ($Ca(NO_3)_2$).

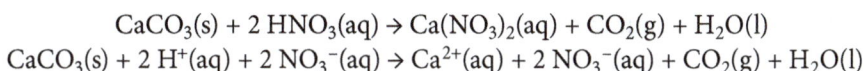

$$CaCO_3(s) + 2\,HNO_3(aq) \rightarrow Ca(NO_3)_2(aq) + CO_2(g) + H_2O(l)$$
$$CaCO_3(s) + 2\,H^+(aq) + 2\,NO_3^-(aq) \rightarrow Ca^{2+}(aq) + 2\,NO_3^-(aq) + CO_2(g) + H_2O(l)$$

Next, cancel the spectator ion (NO_3^-)

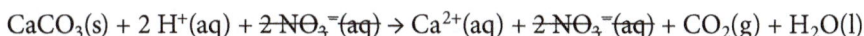

$$CaCO_3(s) + 2\,H^+(aq) + \cancel{2\,NO_3^-(aq)} \rightarrow Ca^{2+}(aq) + \cancel{2\,NO_3^-(aq)} + CO_2(g) + H_2O(l)$$

Recopy what remains as the net ionic equation:

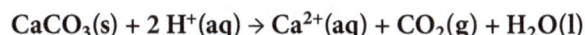

$$CaCO_3(s) + 2\,H^+(aq) \rightarrow Ca^{2+}(aq) + CO_2(g) + H_2O(l)$$

Check to make sure the final equation is balanced.

Reality Check

The final equation is balanced, and the only species it contains are ions and nonelectrolytes.

Follow-Up Problem 4.10b

Convert the following equation to net ionic form:

$$K_2SO_3(aq) + 2\,HClO_3(aq) \rightarrow 2\,KClO_3(aq) + SO_2(g) + H_2O(l)$$

Information

The balanced chemical equation

Connections

The solubility rules; the identities of the strong acids and bases; rules of nomenclature, to help with the identification of strong electrolytes

Solution

Begin by recopying the equation. Then separate the strong electrolytes, which are the strong acid ($HClO_3$) and, according to solubility rule 1, the water-soluble (K_2SO_3 and $KClO_3$).

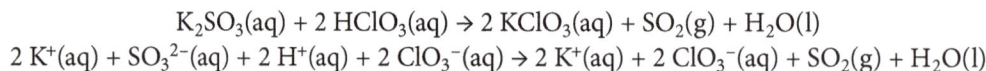

$$K_2SO_3(aq) + 2\ HClO_3(aq) \rightarrow 2\ KClO_3(aq) + SO_2(g) + H_2O(l)$$
$$2\ K^+(aq) + SO_3{}^{2-}(aq) + 2\ H^+(aq) + 2\ ClO_3{}^-(aq) \rightarrow 2\ K^+(aq) + 2\ ClO_3{}^-(aq) + SO_2(g) + H_2O(l)$$

Next, cancel the spectator ions (K^+ and $ClO_3{}^-$):

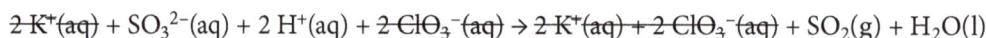

$$\cancel{2\ K^+(aq)} + SO_3{}^{2-}(aq) + 2\ H^+(aq) + \cancel{2\ ClO_3{}^-(aq)} \rightarrow \cancel{2\ K^+(aq)} + \cancel{2\ ClO_3{}^-(aq)} + SO_2(g) + H_2O(l)$$

Recopy what remains as the net ionic equation:

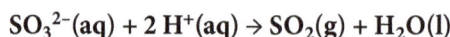

$$SO_3{}^{2-}(aq) + 2\ H^+(aq) \rightarrow SO_2(g) + H_2O(l)$$

Check to make sure the final equation is balanced.

Reality Check

The final equation is balanced, and the only species it contains are ions and nonelectrolytes.

Example Problem 4.11

Convert the following equation to net ionic form:

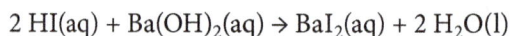

$$2\ HI(aq) + Ba(OH)_2(aq) \rightarrow BaI_2(aq) + 2\ H_2O(l)$$

Information

The balanced chemical equation

Connections

The solubility rules; the identities of the strong acids and bases; rules of nomenclature to help with the identification of strong electrolytes

Solution

We need to identify which substances in the balanced chemical equation are strong electrolytes.

HI is a strong acid, so it is a strong electrolyte.
$Ba(OH)_2$ is a strong base, so it is a strong electrolyte.
BaI_2 contains an ion with a –1 charge (I^-), so according to solubility rule 1, it is soluble and therefore a strong electrolyte.
H_2O is a molecular liquid and therefore a nonelectrolyte.

Next, separate all strong electrolytes into their constituent ions:

$$2\ H^+(aq) + 2\ I^-(aq) + Ba^{2+}(aq) + 2\ OH^-(aq) \rightarrow Ba^{2+}(aq) + 2\ I^-(aq) + 2\ H_2O(l)$$

We have one barium ion (Ba^{2+}) and two iodide ions (I^-) on each side of the reaction arrow. Thus, these ions (Ba^{2+} and I^-) are spectator ions.

▶ Do not forget to simplify the equation if the coefficients are larger than necessary.

Removing the spectator ions leaves

$$2\ H^+(aq) + 2\ OH^-(aq) \rightarrow 2\ H_2O(l)$$

It is possible to divide the coefficients in this equation by the same whole number. To obtain the final (correct) net ionic equation, you must divide the equation by 2:

$$H^+(aq) + OH^-(aq) \rightarrow H_2O(l)$$

Reality Check
The final equation is balanced, and the only species it contains are ions and nonelectrolytes.

Follow-Up Problem 4.11a
Convert the following equation to net ionic form:

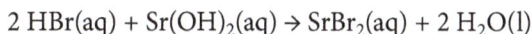

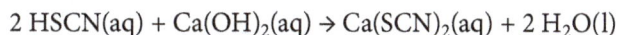

$$2\ HBr(aq) + Sr(OH)_2(aq) \rightarrow SrBr_2(aq) + 2\ H_2O(l)$$

Information
The balanced chemical equation

Connections
The solubility rules; the identities of the strong acids and bases; rules of nomenclature to help with the identification of strong electrolytes

Solution
Begin by recopying the equation. Then separate the strong electrolytes, which are the strong acid (HBr), the strong base ($Sr(OH)_2$), and according to solubility rule 1, the water-soluble ($SrBr_2$).

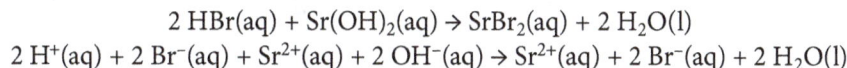

$$2\ HBr(aq) + Sr(OH)_2(aq) \rightarrow SrBr_2(aq) + 2\ H_2O(l)$$
$$2\ H^+(aq) + 2\ Br^-(aq) + Sr^{2+}(aq) + 2\ OH^-(aq) \rightarrow Sr^{2+}(aq) + 2\ Br^-(aq) + 2\ H_2O(l)$$

Next, cancel the spectator ions (Sr^{2+} and Br^-):

$$2\ H^+(aq) + \cancel{2\ Br^-(aq)} + \cancel{Sr^{2+}(aq)} + 2\ OH^-(aq) \rightarrow \cancel{Sr^{2+}(aq)} + \cancel{2\ Br^-(aq)} + 2\ H_2O(l)$$

Recopy what remains as the net ionic equation:

$$2\ H^+(aq) + 2\ OH^-(aq) \rightarrow 2\ H_2O(l)$$

Since all the coefficients are the same (2), it is possible to simplify the equation:

$$H^+(aq) + OH^-(aq) \rightarrow H_2O(l)$$

Check to make sure the final equation is balanced.

Reality Check
The final equation is balanced, and the only species it contains are ions and nonelectrolytes.

Follow-Up Problem 4.11b
Convert the following equation to net ionic form:

$$2\ HSCN(aq) + Ca(OH)_2(aq) \rightarrow Ca(SCN)_2(aq) + 2\ H_2O(l)$$

Information
The balanced chemical equation

Connections

The solubility rules; the identities of the strong acids and bases; rules of nomenclature to help with the identification of strong electrolytes

Solution

Begin by recopying the equation. Then separate the strong electrolytes, which are the strong base $(Ca(OH)_2)$ and, according to solubility rule 1, the water-soluble $(Ca(SCN)_2)$.

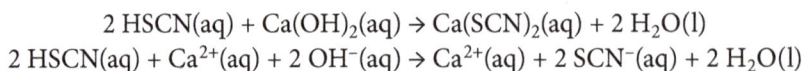

$$2\ HSCN(aq) + Ca(OH)_2(aq) \rightarrow Ca(SCN)_2(aq) + 2\ H_2O(l)$$
$$2\ HSCN(aq) + Ca^{2+}(aq) + 2\ OH^-(aq) \rightarrow Ca^{2+}(aq) + 2\ SCN^-(aq) + 2\ H_2O(l)$$

Next, cancel the spectator ion (Ca^{2+}):

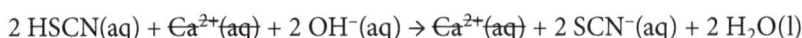

$$2\ HSCN(aq) + \cancel{Ca^{2+}(aq)} + 2\ OH^-(aq) \rightarrow \cancel{Ca^{2+}(aq)} + 2\ SCN^-(aq) + 2\ H_2O(l)$$

Recopy what remains as the net ionic equation:

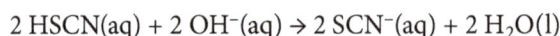

$$2\ HSCN(aq) + 2\ OH^-(aq) \rightarrow 2\ SCN^-(aq) + 2\ H_2O(l)$$

Since all the coefficients are the same (2), it is possible to simplify the equation:

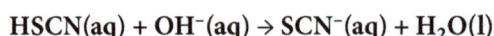

$$\mathbf{HSCN(aq) + OH^-(aq) \rightarrow SCN^-(aq) + H_2O(l)}$$

Check to make sure the final equation is balanced.

Reality Check

The final equation is balanced, and the only species it contains are ions and nonelectrolytes.

Example Problem 4.12

Predict the products and write a net ionic equation for the reaction

$$K_3PO_4(aq) + HI(aq) \rightarrow$$

Information

The formulas of the reactants

Connections

The solubility rules; the identities of the strong acids and bases; basic nomenclature rules to help identify the reacting ions and predict their behavior

Solution

In order to identify the charges on the ions, we need to predict the formulas of the products. The compounds contain the potassium ion (K^+), the phosphate ion (PO_4^{3-}), the hydrogen ion (H^+), and the iodide ion (I^-). The formulas of the products come from switching the ion pairs so that K^+ leaves PO_4^{3-} and pairs with I^-, while H^+ leaves I^- and pairs with PO_4^{3-}. This gives the products KI and H_3PO_4 (we derive their formulas from the requirement that the products must be neutral compounds). Inserting the products into the original equation gives

$$K_3PO_4(aq) + HI(aq) \rightarrow KI + H_3PO_4$$

Assigning states of matter and balancing gives

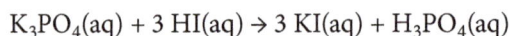

$$K_3PO_4(aq) + 3\ HI(aq) \rightarrow 3\ KI(aq) + H_3PO_4(aq)$$

To create the total ionic equation, we need to know which substances in the balanced chemical equation are strong electrolytes. Both potassium compounds are soluble (strong electrolytes), because they contain an ion with a +1 charge. HI is a strong acid (strong electrolyte). H_3PO_4 is a weak acid (weak electrolyte).

Creating the total ionic equation gives

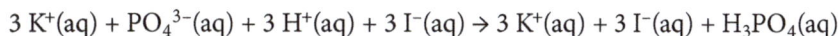

$$3\ K^+(aq) + PO_4{}^{3-}(aq) + 3\ H^+(aq) + 3\ I^-(aq) \rightarrow 3\ K^+(aq) + 3\ I^-(aq) + H_3PO_4(aq)$$

Removing the spectator ions leaves

$$\mathbf{PO_4{}^{3-}(aq) + 3\ H^+(aq) \rightarrow H_3PO_4(aq)} \qquad \text{(net ionic equation)}$$

Reality Check

The final equation is balanced, and the only species remaining in it are ions and weak electrolytes (the weak acid).

Follow-Up Problem 4.12a

Predict the products and write a net ionic equation for the reaction

$$K_2C_2O_4(aq) + HNO_3(aq) \rightarrow$$

Information

The formulas of the reactants

Connections

The solubility rules; the identities of the strong acids and bases; basic nomenclature rules to help us identify the reacting ions and predict their behavior

Solution

The ions involved are K^+, $C_2O_4{}^{2-}$, H^+, and $NO_3{}^-$. Each of these will "switch" partners to produce $H_2C_2O_4$ and KNO_3. No other combinations will work, since each compound must contain oppositely charged ions. Adding these potential products to the given equation gives

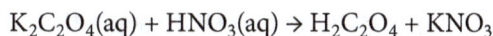

$$K_2C_2O_4(aq) + HNO_3(aq) \rightarrow H_2C_2O_4 + KNO_3$$

The next step is to balance the equation as done previously:

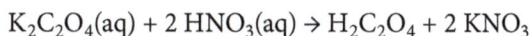

$$K_2C_2O_4(aq) + 2\ HNO_3(aq) \rightarrow H_2C_2O_4 + 2\ KNO_3$$

Now separate the strong electrolytes, which are the strong acid (HNO_3) and, according to solubility rule 1, the water-soluble ($K_2C_2O_4$ and KNO_3):

$$2\ K^+(aq) + C_2O_4{}^{2-}(aq) + 2\ H^+(aq) + 2\ NO_3{}^-(aq) \rightarrow H_2C_2O_4 + 2\ K^+(aq) + 2\ NO_3{}^-(aq)$$

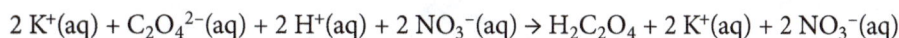

Next, cancel the spectator ions (K^+ and $NO_3{}^-$):

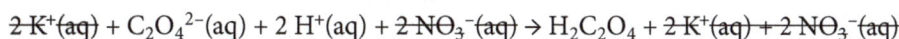

$$\cancel{2\ K^+(aq)} + C_2O_4{}^{2-}(aq) + 2\ H^+(aq) + \cancel{2\ NO_3{}^-(aq)} \rightarrow H_2C_2O_4 + \cancel{2\ K^+(aq)} + \cancel{2\ NO_3{}^-(aq)}$$

Recopy what remains as the net ionic equation:

$$\mathbf{C_2O_4{}^{2-}(aq) + 2\ H^+(aq) \rightarrow H_2C_2O_4}$$

Check to make sure the final equation is balanced.

Reality Check

The final equation is balanced, and the only species it contains are ions and nonelectrolytes.

Follow-Up Problem 4.12b

Predict the products and write a net ionic equation for the reaction

$$NaOH(aq) + HOCN(aq) \rightarrow$$

Information

The formulas of the reactants

Connections

The solubility rules; the identities of the strong acids and bases; basic nomenclature rules to help us identify the reacting ions and predict their behavior

Solution

The ions involved are Na^+, OH^-, H^+, and OCN^-. Note that in this step it does not matter that HOCN is a weak acid. Each of these will "switch" partners to produce NaOCN and H_2O. No other combinations will work, since each compound must contain oppositely charged ions. Adding these potential products to the given equation gives

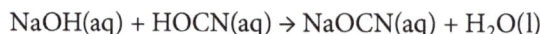

$$NaOH(aq) + HOCN(aq) \rightarrow NaOCN(aq) + H_2O(l)$$

The next step is normally to balance the equation as done previously; however, the equation is already balanced.

Now separate the strong electrolytes, which are the strong base (NaOH) and, according to solubility rule 1, the water-soluble (NaOCN):

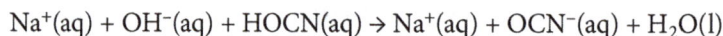

$$Na^+(aq) + OH^-(aq) + HOCN(aq) \rightarrow Na^+(aq) + OCN^-(aq) + H_2O(l)$$

Next, cancel the spectator ion (Na^+):

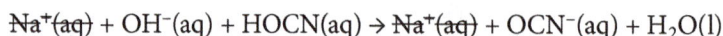

$$\cancel{Na^+(aq)} + OH^-(aq) + HOCN(aq) \rightarrow \cancel{Na^+(aq)} + OCN^-(aq) + H_2O(l)$$

Recopy what remains as the net ionic equation:

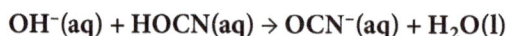

$$\mathbf{OH^-(aq) + HOCN(aq) \rightarrow OCN^-(aq) + H_2O(l)}$$

Check to make sure the final equation is balanced.

Reality Check

The final equation is balanced, and the only species it contains are ions and nonelectrolytes.

Example Problem 4.13

Predict the products and write a net ionic equation for the reaction

$$NaBr(aq) + (NH_4)_3PO_4(aq) \rightarrow$$

Information

The formulas of the reactants

Connections

The solubility rules; the identities of the strong acids and bases; basic nomenclature rules

Solution

We need to identify the charges on the ions in order to predict the formulas of the products. The compounds contain sodium ions (Na^+), bromide ions (Br^-), ammonium ions (NH_4^+), and phosphate ions (PO_4^{3-}). The product formulas result from exchanging the ions' partners and balancing the charges to give Na_3PO_4 and NH_4Br. Inserting the products into the original equation gives

$$NaBr(aq) + (NH_4)_3PO_4(aq) \rightarrow NH_4Br + Na_3PO_4$$

Assigning states of matter and balancing gives

$$3\ NaBr(aq) + (NH_4)_3PO_4(aq) \rightarrow 3\ NH_4Br(aq) + Na_3PO_4(aq)$$

Writing the total ionic equation gives

$$3\ Na^+(aq) + 3\ Br^-(aq) + 3\ NH_4^+(aq) + PO_4^{3-}(aq) \rightarrow 3\ NH_4^+(aq) + 3\ Br^-(aq) + 3\ Na^+(aq) + PO_4^{3-}(aq)$$

Removing the spectator ions leaves

$$\text{No Reaction (NR)}$$

Reality Check

All ions were spectator ions, so no reaction occurs.

Follow-Up Problem 4.13a

Predict the products and write a net ionic equation for the reaction

$$CaBr_2(aq) + NH_4NO_3(aq) \rightarrow$$

Information

The formulas of the reactants

Connections

The solubility rules; the identities of the strong acids and bases; basic nomenclature rules

Solution

The ions involved are Ca^{2+}, Br^-, NH_4^+, and NO_3^-. Each of these will "switch" partners to produce $Ca(NO_3)_2$ and NH_4Br. No other combinations will work, since each compound must contain oppositely charged ions. Adding these potential products to the given equation gives

$$CaBr_2(aq) + NH_4NO_3(aq) \rightarrow Ca(NO_3)_2(aq) + NH_4Br(aq)$$

The next step is normally to balance the equation as done previously:

$$CaBr_2(aq) + 2\ NH_4NO_3(aq) \rightarrow Ca(NO_3)_2(aq) + 2\ NH_4Br(aq)$$

Now separate the strong electrolytes, which are, according to solubility rule 1, the water-soluble ($CaBr_2$, NH_4NO_3, $Ca(NO_3)_2$, and NH_4Br):

$$Ca^{2+}(aq) + 2\ Br^-(aq) + 2\ NH_4^+(aq) + 2\ NO_3^-(aq) \rightarrow Ca^{2+}(aq) + 2\ NO_3^-(aq) + 2\ NH_4^+(aq) + 2\ Br^-(aq)$$

Next, cancel the spectator ions (Ca^{2+}, Br^-, NH_4^+, and NO_3^-):

$$Ca^{2+}(aq) + 2\ Br^-(aq) + 2\ NH_4^+(aq) + 2\ NO_3^-(aq) \rightarrow Ca^{2+}(aq) + 2\ NO_3^-(aq) + 2\ NH_4^+(aq) + 2\ Br^-(aq)$$

Since all ions cancel, there is no net ionic equation and this combination should be considered no reaction (NR).

Reality Check

There is nothing remaining to check.

Follow-Up Problem 4.13b

Predict the products and write a net ionic equation for the reaction

$$KBr(aq) + HNO_3(aq) \rightarrow$$

Information

The formulas of the reactants

Connections

The solubility rules; the identities of the strong acids and bases; basic nomenclature rules

Solution

The ions involved are K^+, Br^-, H^+, and NO_3^-. Each of these will "switch" partners to produce KNO_3 and HBr. No other combinations will work, since each compound must contain oppositely charged ions. Adding these potential products to the given equation gives

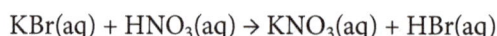

$$KBr(aq) + HNO_3(aq) \rightarrow KNO_3(aq) + HBr(aq)$$

The next step is normally to balance the equation; however, this equation is already balanced. Now separate the strong electrolytes, which are the two strong acids (HNO_3 and HBr) and, according to solubility rule 1, the water-soluble (KBr and KNO_3):

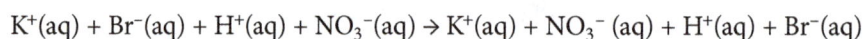

$$K^+(aq) + Br^-(aq) + H^+(aq) + NO_3^-(aq) \rightarrow K^+(aq) + NO_3^-(aq) + H^+(aq) + Br^-(aq)$$

Next, cancel the spectator ions ($K^+ + Br^- + H^+$, and NO_3^-):

$$\cancel{K^+(aq)} + \cancel{Br^-(aq)} + \cancel{H^+(aq)} + \cancel{NO_3^-(aq)} \rightarrow \cancel{K^+(aq)} + \cancel{NO_3^-(aq)} + \cancel{H^+(aq)} + \cancel{Br^-(aq)}$$

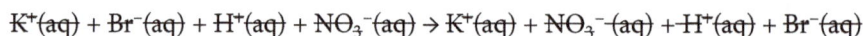

Since all ions cancel, there is no net ionic equation and this combination should be considered no reaction (NR).

Reality Check

There is nothing remaining to check.

Example Problem 4.14

Predict the products and write a net ionic equation for the reaction

$$Ca(C_2H_3O_2)_2(aq) + FeSO_4(aq) \rightarrow$$

Information

The formulas of the reactants

Connections

The solubility rules; the identities of the strong acids and bases; basic nomenclature rules

Solution

We need to identify the charges on the ions in order to predict the formulas of the products. The compounds contain the calcium ion (Ca^{2+}), acetate ion ($C_2H_3O_2^-$), iron(II) ion (Fe^{2+}), and sulfate ion (SO_4^{2-}). The product formulas result from changing partners and balancing charges to give $CaSO_4$ and $Fe(C_2H_3O_2)_2$. Inserting the product formulas into the original reaction gives

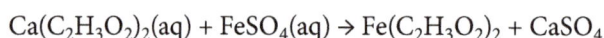

$$Ca(C_2H_3O_2)_2(aq) + FeSO_4(aq) \rightarrow Fe(C_2H_3O_2)_2 + CaSO_4$$

Assigning states of matter and balancing the reaction gives

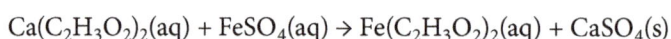

$$Ca(C_2H_3O_2)_2(aq) + FeSO_4(aq) \rightarrow Fe(C_2H_3O_2)_2(aq) + CaSO_4(s)$$

Calcium sulfate ($CaSO_4$) is one of the few sulfates that is insoluble. All the other species are soluble (strong electrolytes).

Generating the total ionic equation gives

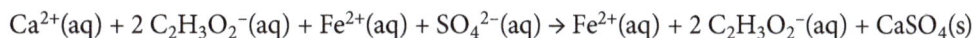

$$Ca^{2+}(aq) + 2\ C_2H_3O_2^-(aq) + Fe^{2+}(aq) + SO_4^{2-}(aq) \rightarrow Fe^{2+}(aq) + 2\ C_2H_3O_2^-(aq) + CaSO_4(s)$$

Removing the spectator ions leaves

$$\mathbf{Ca^{2+}(aq) + SO_4^{2-}(aq) \rightarrow CaSO_4(s)} \quad \text{(net ionic equation)}$$

Reality Check

The final equation is balanced, and the only species remaining in it are ions and nonelectrolytes (an insoluble salt).

Follow-Up Problem 4.14a

Predict the products and write a net ionic equation for the reaction

$$AgNO_3(aq) + FeCl_2(aq) \rightarrow$$

Information

The formulas of the reactants

Connections

The solubility rules; the identities of the strong acids and bases; basic nomenclature rules

Solution

The ions involved are Ag^+, NO_3^-, Fe^{2+}, and Cl^-. Each of these will "switch" partners to produce AgCl and $Fe(NO_3)_2$. No other combinations will work, since each compound must contain oppositely charged ions. Adding these potential products to the given equation gives

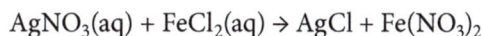

$$AgNO_3(aq) + FeCl_2(aq) \rightarrow AgCl + Fe(NO_3)_2$$

The next step is to balance the equation as done previously:

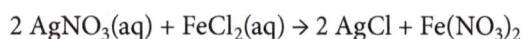

$$2\ AgNO_3(aq) + FeCl_2(aq) \rightarrow 2\ AgCl + Fe(NO_3)_2$$

Now separate the strong electrolytes, which are, according to solubility rule 1, the water-soluble ($AgNO_3$, $FeCl_2$, and $Fe(NO_3)_2$). The insoluble AgCl should be labeled as a solid, and the soluble $Fe(NO_3)_2$ should be labeled as aqueous.

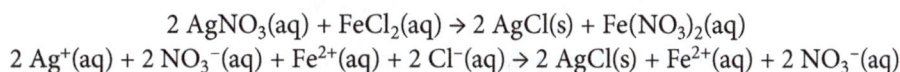

$$2\ AgNO_3(aq) + FeCl_2(aq) \rightarrow 2\ AgCl(s) + Fe(NO_3)_2(aq)$$
$$2\ Ag^+(aq) + 2\ NO_3^-(aq) + Fe^{2+}(aq) + 2\ Cl^-(aq) \rightarrow 2\ AgCl(s) + Fe^{2+}(aq) + 2\ NO_3^-(aq)$$

Next, cancel the spectator ions (Fe^{2+} and $2\ NO_3^-$):

$$2\ Ag^+(aq) + \cancel{2\ NO_3^-(aq)} + \cancel{Fe^{2+}(aq)} + 2\ Cl^-(aq) \rightarrow 2\ AgCl(s) + \cancel{Fe^{2+}(aq)} + \cancel{2\ NO_3^-(aq)}$$

Recopy what remains as the net ionic equation:

$$2\ Ag^+(aq) + 2\ Cl^-(aq) \rightarrow 2\ AgCl(s)$$

Since all the coefficients are the same (they are both 2), it is possible to simplify the equation to

$$\mathbf{Ag^+(aq) + Cl^-(aq) \rightarrow AgCl(s)}$$

Check to make sure the final equation is balanced.

Reality Check

The final equation is balanced, and the only species it contains are ions and nonelectrolytes.

Follow-Up Problem 4.14b

Predict the products and write a net ionic equation for the reaction

$$BaCl_2(aq) + H_3PO_4(aq) \rightarrow$$

Information

The formulas of the reactants

Connections

The solubility rules; the identities of the strong acids and bases; basic nomenclature rules

Solution

The ions involved are H^+, PO_4^{3-}, Ba^{2+}, and Cl^-. Each of these will "switch" partners to produce $Ba_3(PO_4)_2$ and HCl. No other combinations will work, since each compound must contain oppositely charged ions. Adding these potential products to the given equation gives

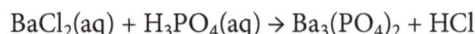

$$BaCl_2(aq) + H_3PO_4(aq) \rightarrow Ba_3(PO_4)_2 + HCl$$

The next step is to balance the equation as done previously:

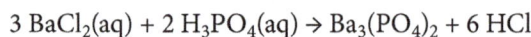

$$3\ BaCl_2(aq) + 2\ H_3PO_4(aq) \rightarrow Ba_3(PO_4)_2 + 6\ HCl$$

Now separate the strong electrolytes, which are, according to solubility rule 1, the water-soluble ($BaCl_2$) and the strong acid (HCl). The insoluble $Ba_3(PO_4)_2$ should be labeled as a solid, and the soluble HCl should be labeled as aqueous.

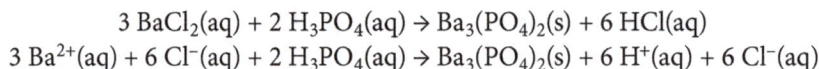

$$3\ BaCl_2(aq) + 2\ H_3PO_4(aq) \rightarrow Ba_3(PO_4)_2(s) + 6\ HCl(aq)$$
$$3\ Ba^{2+}(aq) + 6\ Cl^-(aq) + 2\ H_3PO_4(aq) \rightarrow Ba_3(PO_4)_2(s) + 6\ H^+(aq) + 6\ Cl^-(aq)$$

Next, cancel the spectator ion (Cl^-):

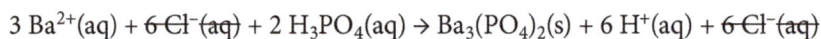

$$3\ Ba^{2+}(aq) + \cancel{6\ Cl^-(aq)} + 2\ H_3PO_4(aq) \rightarrow Ba_3(PO_4)_2(s) + 6\ H^+(aq) + \cancel{6\ Cl^-(aq)}$$

Recopy what remains as the net ionic equation:

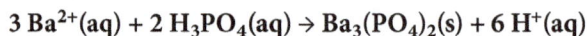

$$\mathbf{3\ Ba^{2+}(aq) + 2\ H_3PO_4(aq) \rightarrow Ba_3(PO_4)_2(s) + 6\ H^+(aq)}$$

Check to make sure the final equation is balanced.

Reality Check

The final equation is balanced, and the only species it contains are ions and nonelectrolytes.

Example Problem 4.15

Predict the products of and write a molecular equation for the reaction

$$Fe(aq) + H_2SO_4(aq) \rightarrow$$

Information

The formulas of the potential reactants

Connections

The activity series (**table 4.3**)

Solution

Locating iron, Fe, and hydrogen ions, H^+, on the activity series shows that H^+ is lower (less active) than iron. Therefore, a reaction will occur.

From the activity series, we can extract the following equations. It is necessary to reverse the hydrogen equation:

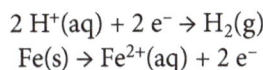

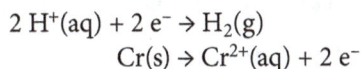

$$2 \, H^+(aq) + 2 \, e^- \rightarrow H_2(g)$$
$$Fe(s) \rightarrow Fe^{2+}(aq) + 2 \, e^-$$

Adding the two equations and canceling the electrons produces the net ionic equation for the reaction:

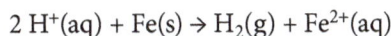

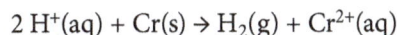

$$2 \, H^+(aq) + Fe(s) \rightarrow H_2(g) + Fe^{2+}(aq)$$

Adding the spectator ions (sulfate in this case) and writing the species in molecular form yields the molecular equation:

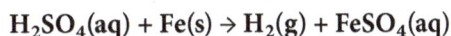

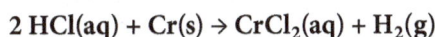

$$\mathbf{H_2SO_4(aq) + Fe(s) \rightarrow H_2(g) + FeSO_4(aq)}$$

Reality Check

The equation is balanced, and there are no charges left over.

Follow-Up Problem 4.15a

Predict the products and write a molecular equation for the reaction

$$HCl(aq) + Cr(s) \rightarrow$$

Information

The formulas of the potential reactants

Connections

The activity series (**table 4.3**)

Solution

Locating chromium, Cr, and hydrogen ions, H^+, on the activity series shows that H^+ is lower (less active) than chromium. Therefore, a reaction will occur. From the activity series, we can extract the following equations. It is necessary to reverse the hydrogen equation.

$$2 \, H^+(aq) + 2 \, e^- \rightarrow H_2(g)$$
$$Cr(s) \rightarrow Cr^{2+}(aq) + 2 \, e^-$$

Adding the two equations and canceling the electrons produces the net ionic equation for the reaction:

$$2 \, H^+(aq) + Cr(s) \rightarrow H_2(g) + Cr^{2+}(aq)$$

Adding the spectator ions (sulfate in this case) and writing the species in molecular form yields the molecular equation:

$$\mathbf{2 \, HCl(aq) + Cr(s) \rightarrow CrCl_2(aq) + H_2(g)}$$

Reality Check

The equation is balanced, and there are no charges left over.

Follow-Up Problem 4.15b

Predict the products and write a molecular equation for the reaction

$$HCl(aq) + Au(s) \rightarrow$$

Information

The formulas of the potential reactants

Connections

The activity series (**table 4.3**)

Solution

Locating gold, Au, and hydrogen ions, H^+, on the activity series shows that Au is lower (less active) than H^+. Therefore, no reaction will occur.

Example Problem 4.16

Predict the products and write a molecular equation for the reaction

$$AgNO_3(aq) + Zn(s) \rightarrow$$

Information

The formulas of the potential reactants

Connections

The activity series (**table 4.3**)

Solution

Locating zinc, Zn, and silver ions, Ag^+, on the activity series, we see that Ag^+ is lower (less active) than zinc. This tells us that a reaction will occur.

From the activity series, we get the following equations. We reverse the silver equation, to provide the reduction half reaction; then we multiply it by 2 to produce equal numbers of electrons on each side of the reaction arrows:

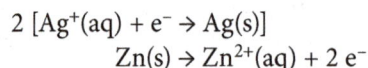

$$2\ [Ag^+(aq) + e^- \rightarrow Ag(s)]$$
$$Zn(s) \rightarrow Zn^{2+}(aq) + 2\ e^-$$

Adding the two equations and canceling the electrons produces the net ionic equation:

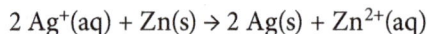

$$2\ Ag^+(aq) + Zn(s) \rightarrow 2\ Ag(s) + Zn^{2+}(aq)$$

Adding the spectator ions (nitrate in this case) and writing the species in molecular form yield the molecular equation:

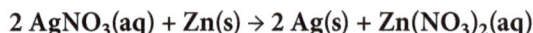

$$\mathbf{2\ AgNO_3(aq) + Zn(s) \rightarrow 2\ Ag(s) + Zn(NO_3)_2(aq)}$$

Reality Check

The equation is balanced, and all chemical species are in the molecular or elemental form.

Follow-Up Problem 4.16a

Predict the products and write a molecular equation for the reaction

$$HNO_3(aq) + V(s) \rightarrow$$

Information

The formulas of the potential reactants

Connections

The activity series (**table 4.3**)

Solution

Locating vanadium, V, and hydrogen ions, H^+, on the activity series shows H^+ to be lower (less active) than vanadium and tells us that a reaction will occur. From the activity series, we get the following equations. We reverse the vanadium equation, to provide the reduction half reaction; and we multiply it by 2 and multiple the hydrogen half-reaction by 3, to produce equal numbers of electrons on each side of the reaction arrows:

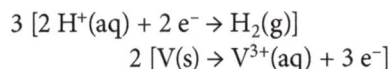

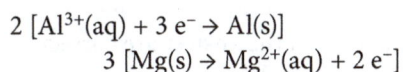

$$3 \, [2 \, H^+(aq) + 2 \, e^- \rightarrow H_2(g)]$$
$$2 \, [V(s) \rightarrow V^{3+}(aq) + 3 \, e^-]$$

Adding the two equations and canceling the electrons produces the net ionic equation:

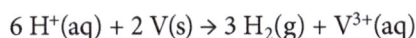

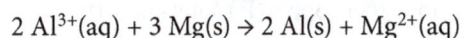

$$6 \, H^+(aq) + 2 \, V(s) \rightarrow 3 \, H_2(g) + V^{3+}(aq)$$

Adding the spectator ions (nitrate in this case) and writing the species in molecular form yields the molecular equation:

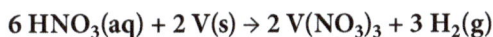

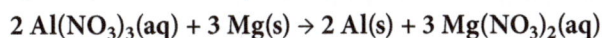

$$\textbf{6 HNO}_3\textbf{(aq) + 2 V(s)} \rightarrow \textbf{2 V(NO}_3\textbf{)}_3 + \textbf{3 H}_2\textbf{(g)}$$

Reality Check

The equation is balanced, and all chemical species are in the molecular or elemental form.

Follow-Up Problem 4.16b

Predict the products and write a molecular equation for the reaction

$$Al(NO_3)_3(aq) + Mg(s) \rightarrow$$

Information

The formulas of the potential reactants

Connections

The activity series (**table 4.3**)

Solution

Locating magnesium, Mg, and aluminum ions, Al^{3+}, on the activity series shows Al^{3+} to be lower (less active) than magnesium and tells us that a reaction will occur. From the activity series, we get the following equations. We reverse the magnesium equation, to provide the reduction half reaction; and we multiply it by 3 and the aluminum half-reaction by 2 to produce equal numbers of electrons on each side of the reaction arrows:

$$2 \, [Al^{3+}(aq) + 3 \, e^- \rightarrow Al(s)]$$
$$3 \, [Mg(s) \rightarrow Mg^{2+}(aq) + 2 \, e^-]$$

Adding the two equations and canceling the electrons produces the net ionic equation:

$$2 \, Al^{3+}(aq) + 3 \, Mg(s) \rightarrow 2 \, Al(s) + Mg^{2+}(aq)$$

Adding the spectator ions (nitrate in this case) and writing the species in molecular form yields the molecular equation:

$$\textbf{2 Al(NO}_3\textbf{)}_3\textbf{(aq) + 3 Mg(s)} \rightarrow \textbf{2 Al(s) + 3 Mg(NO}_3\textbf{)}_2\textbf{(aq)}$$

Reality Check

The equation is balanced and all chemical species are in the molecular or elemental form.

Example Problem 4.17

The result of adding chloride ions to solutions containing lead(II) ions is the precipitation of lead(II) chloride, $PbCl_2$. How many grams of sodium chloride are needed to precipitate all the lead ions from 0.750 L of a 0.150 M solution of lead(II) nitrate? The reaction is

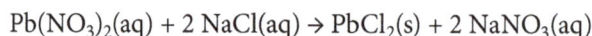

$$Pb(NO_3)_2(aq) + 2\ NaCl(aq) \rightarrow PbCl_2(s) + 2\ NaNO_3(aq)$$

Information

The balanced chemical equation; the data 0.750 L of 0.150 M $Pb(NO_3)_2$ with which to find the grams of sodium chloride

Connections

Moles are the key to solving stoichiometry problems.

Solution

One useful method for organizing the information given and required in a stoichiometry problem is to place the known and needed values beneath the corresponding substances in the balanced chemical equation:

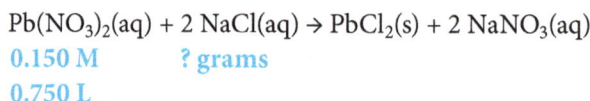

$$Pb(NO_3)_2(aq) + 2\ NaCl(aq) \rightarrow PbCl_2(s) + 2\ NaNO_3(aq)$$

$\qquad$ 0.150 M $\qquad\qquad$? grams

$\qquad$ 0.750 L

Most of the known information is associated with the lead(II) nitrate, which indicates that we would be wise to begin our calculations with that compound. Since this is a stoichiometry problem, the key to solving it will be to convert the given data into moles. To clarify how to find the moles of a substance, it helps to use the definition of *molarity* in place of the abbreviation M.

$$\left(\frac{0.150\ mol\ Pb(NO_3)_2}{L}\right)(0.750\ L)\left(\frac{2\ mol\ NaCl}{1\ mol\ Pb(NO_3)_2}\right)\left(\frac{58.45\ g\ NaCl}{1\ mol\ NaCl}\right) = 13.151 = \mathbf{13.2\ g\ NaCl}$$

$\qquad\qquad$ **1** $\qquad\qquad\qquad$ **2** $\qquad\qquad$ **3** $\qquad\qquad$ **4**

The first and second terms are the molarity and the volume, respectively, which multiply to give the moles of lead(II) nitrate. The third term is the mole ratio from the balanced chemical equation, used to convert from moles of lead(II) nitrate to moles of sodium chloride. At the fourth term, the molar mass of the sodium chloride converts the moles of sodium chloride to the mass of sodium chloride.

Reality Check

The units and significant figures in the answer are correct.

Follow-Up Problem 4.17a

The result of adding arsenate ions to a copper(II) solution is the precipitation of copper(II) arsenate. How many grams of sodium arsenate are needed to precipitate all the copper(II) ions in 1.00 L of a 0.100 M copper(II) sulfate solution? The reaction is

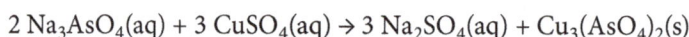

$$2\ Na_3AsO_4(aq) + 3\ CuSO_4(aq) \rightarrow 3\ Na_2SO_4(aq) + Cu_3(AsO_4)_2(s)$$

Information

We are given the balanced chemical equation and the data 1.00 L of 0.100 M $CuSO_4$, with which to find the grams of Na_3AsO_4.

Connections

Moles are the key to solving stoichiometry problems.

Solution

Begin by recopying the chemical equation. Then enter the given information beneath the appropriate substance in the chemical equation.

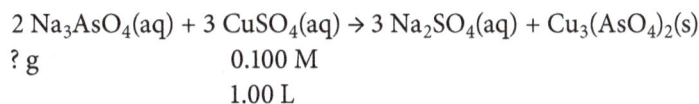

$$2\ Na_3AsO_4(aq) + 3\ CuSO_4(aq) \rightarrow 3\ Na_2SO_4(aq) + Cu_3(AsO_4)_2(s)$$

? g	0.100 M
	1.00 L

Most of the known information is associated with the copper(II) sulfate, an indication that we would be wise to begin our calculations with that compound. Since this is a stoichiometry problem, the key to solving it will be to convert the given data into moles. To clarify how to find the moles of a substance, it helps to use the definition of *molarity* in place of the abbreviation M.

$$\left(\frac{0.100\ \text{mol } CuSO_4}{L}\right)(1.00\ L)\left(\frac{2\ \text{mol } Na_3AsO_4}{3\ \text{mol } CuSO_4}\right)\left(\frac{207.888\ \text{g } Na_3AsO_4}{1\ \text{mol } Na_3AsO_4}\right) = 13.8592 = \mathbf{13.9\ g\ Na_3AsO_4}$$

The first two terms are the molarity and the volume, which multiply to give the moles of copper(II) sulfate. The third term is the mole ratio from the balanced chemical equation, used to convert from moles of copper(II) sulfate to moles of sodium arsenate. Finally, the molar mass of the sodium arsenate converts the moles to the mass of sodium arsenate.

Reality Check

The units and significant figures in the answer are correct.

Follow-Up Problem 4.17b

The result of adding hydrogen sulfide gas to a bismuth(III) nitrate solution is the precipitation of bismuth(III) sulfide. How many grams of hydrogen sulfide are needed to precipitate all the bismuth(III) ions in 1.50 L of a 0.125 M bismuth(III) nitrate solution?

Information

Information to write a balanced chemical equation; data 1.50 L of 0.125 M bismuth(III) nitrate with which to find the grams of hydrogen sulfide

Connections

Moles are the key to solving stoichiometry problems.

Solution

We need to derive a balanced chemical equation for the reaction. To do this, begin by writing down the formulas of the reactants and products (this may require reference to the Nomenclature Resource). This gives

$$Bi(NO_3)_3(aq) + H_2S(g) \rightarrow Bi_2S_3(s)$$

The hydrogen and nitrate ions must combine to make nitric acid the other product, which gives

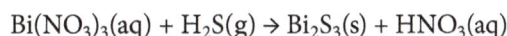

$$Bi(NO_3)_3(aq) + H_2S(g) \rightarrow Bi_2S_3(s) + HNO_3(aq)$$

It is necessary to balance this equation by the procedure introduced previously:

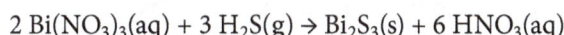

$$2\ Bi(NO_3)_3(aq) + 3\ H_2S(g) \rightarrow Bi_2S_3(s) + 6\ HNO_3(aq)$$

Begin by recopying the balanced chemical equation. Then enter the given information beneath the appropriate substance in the chemical equation:

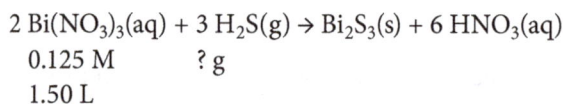

$$2\ Bi(NO_3)_3(aq) + 3\ H_2S(g) \rightarrow Bi_2S_3(s) + 6\ HNO_3(aq)$$

0.125 M	? g
1.50 L	

Most of the known information is associated with the bismuth(III) nitrate, an indication that we would be wise to begin our calculations with that compound. Since this is a stoichiometry problem, the key to solving it will be to convert the given data into moles. To clarify how to find the moles of a substance, it helps to use the definition of *molarity* in place of the abbreviation M:

$$\left(\frac{0.125\ mol\ Bi(NO_3)_3}{L}\right)(1.50\ L)\left(\frac{3\ mol\ H_2S}{2\ mol\ Bi(NO_3)_3}\right)\left(\frac{34.081\ g\ H_2S}{1\ mol\ H_2S}\right) = 9.585281 = \mathbf{9.58\ g\ H_2S}$$

The first two terms are the molarity and the volume, which multiply to give the moles of bismuth(III) nitrate. The third term is the mole ratio from the balanced chemical equation, used to convert from moles of bismuth(III) nitrate to moles of hydrogen sulfide. Finally, the molar mass of the hydrogen sulfide converts the moles to the mass of hydrogen sulfide.

Reality Check
The units and significant figures in the answer are correct.

Example Problem 4.18
You are asked to analyze a solution that may contain one or more of the following ions: Al^{3+}, Ca^{2+}, Co^{2+}, Cu^{2+}, Fe^{3+}, Mg^{2+}, Mn^{2+}, and Sr^{2+}. (Refer to the flowchart in **figure 4.6** to help keep track of your progress through the separations.) A precipitate will form when you add a small amount of ammonia to the sample, but no precipitate forms when you add some ammonium carbonate. The addition of ammonia and sodium hydrogen phosphate does not result in the formation of a precipitate. The addition of sodium hydroxide solution to the ammonia precipitate does result in a solution; no new precipitate forms when acetic acid is added. The addition of nitric acid to the ammonia precipitate gives a solution, which you divide into two portions. You add ammonium thiocyanate to one portion and cerium(IV) ammonium nitrate to the other portion. The ammonium thiocyanate solution turns red, and the cerium(IV) solution turns purple. You take the solution remaining from the ammonia and sodium hydrogen phosphate test and split it into two portions; you add ammonium thiocyanate to one and potassium iodide to the other. The thiocyanate portion turns blue-green, and the iodide portion forms a tan precipitate. What ions are present in the solution?

Information
Presence of one or more of the following ions—Al^{3+}, Ca^{2+}, Co^{2+}, Cu^{2+}, Fe^{3+}, Mg^{2+}, Mn^{2+}, Sr^{2+}; the question of which ions are present

Connections
The flowchart in **figure 4.6**, based on the solubility rules

Solution
The initial precipitation means that one or more of the following ions are present: Al^{3+}, Fe^{3+}, and Mn^{2+}. The lack of a precipitate when ammonium carbonate is added eliminates Ca^{2+} and Sr^{2+}. Since the addition of ammonia and sodium hydrogen phosphate does not give a precipitate, Mg^{2+} is absent. Since the addition of acetic acid to the sodium hydroxide solution gave no new precipitate, the sample must not contain any aluminum. The red color from the addition of thiocyanate

confirms the presence of iron, and the purple solution from the addition of cerium(IV) confirms the presence of manganese. The blue-green thiocyanate solution means that cobalt is present, while the tan precipitate from the addition of potassium iodide confirms the presence of copper. The ions present are therefore Co^{2+}, Cu^{2+}, Fe^{3+}, and Mn^{2+}.

Reality Check

The observations are consistent with the presence of these ions.

Follow-Up Problem 4.18a

You have a solution that may contain one or more of the following ions: Al^{3+}, Ca^{2+}, Co^{2+}, Cu^{2+}, Fe^{3+}, Mg^{2+}, Mn^{2+}, and Sr^{2+}. A precipitate will form when you add a small amount of ammonia to the sample, and a white precipitate will form when you add some ammonium carbonate. The addition of ammonia and sodium hydrogen phosphate also gives a white precipitate. The addition of sodium hydroxide solution to the ammonia precipitate gives a solution that forms a new precipitate when acetic acid is added. The result of adding nitric acid to the ammonia precipitate is a solution that you divide into two portions. To one portion you add ammonium thiocyanate, and to the other portion you add cerium(IV) ammonium nitrate. The ammonium thiocyanate solution does not change color, but the cerium(IV) solution turns purple. You dissolve the white precipitate from the carbonate precipitation in hydrochloric acid. The addition of ammonium sulfate to the hydrochloric acid solution does not give a precipitate, but the addition of ammonia and ammonium oxalate gives a white precipitate. You take the solution remaining from the ammonia and sodium hydrogen phosphate test and split it into two portions. You add ammonium thiocyanate to one portion and potassium iodide to the other portion. The thiocyanate portion turns blue-green, and the iodide portion does not form a precipitate. What ions are present in the solution?

Information

The possible presence of one or more of the following ions: Al^{3+}, Ca^{2+}, Co^{2+}, Cu^{2+}, Fe^{3+}, Mg^{2+}, Mn^{2+}, and Sr^{2+}; the question of which ions are present

Connections

The flowchart in **figure 4.6**, which is based on the solubility rules

Solution

Examining each of the tests in each step leads to the following conclusions. In addition, following through the flow chart with each step will help you keep track of what you are trying to find. The first precipitate is one or more of the following: $Al(OH)_3$, $Fe(OH)_3$, and $Mn(OH)_2$. The second precipitate is one or both of the following: $CaCO_3$ and $SrCO_3$. The precipitate with ammonia and sodium hydrogen phosphate proves magnesium is present. The addition of acetic acid to give a precipitate from the sodium hydroxide solution proves that aluminum is present. The purple color generated by cerium(IV) ammonium nitrate proves that manganese is present. The precipitate formed by the addition of ammonium oxalate proves the presence of calcium. The blue-green color generated by ammonium thiocyanate proves that cobalt is present. The ions present are Al^{3+}, Ca^{2+}, Co^{2+}, Mg^{2+}, and Mn^{2+}.

Reality Check

The observations are consistent with the presence of these ions.

Follow-Up Problem 4.18b

You have a solution that may contain one or more of the following ions: Cu^{2+}, Fe^{3+}, and Sr^{2+}. Devise a shortened qualitative analysis scheme that will allow you to determine which of these ions is present.

Information

The possible presence of one or more of the following ions: Cu^{2+}, Fe^{3+}, and Sr^{2+}; the question of how to determine which ions are present

Connections

The flowchart in **figure 4.6**, which is based on the solubility rules

Solution

Iron is the only one of the three that will precipitate with the addition of ammonia; therefore, if a precipitate forms when ammonia is added, iron must be present. After the addition of ammonia, the addition of ammonium carbonate will only precipitate strontium, so the formation of a precipitate indicates this ion. The only ion that might remain is copper, which will give a precipitate and a brown solution upon the addition of potassium iodide.

The shorted qualitative analysis scheme is as follows: (1) Add ammonia and look for a precipitate (iron). (2) Add ammonium carbonate to the solution that remains after you add the ammonia; then look for a precipitate (strontium). (3) After completing the first two steps, add potassium iodide and look for a precipitate and color change of the solution (copper).

Reality Check

The tests are consistent with the flowchart in **figure 4.6**.

Example Problem 4.19

Chemists often find the quantity of sulfur in a sample by converting the sulfur to sulfate and then precipitating the sulfate as barium sulfate. The mineral molybdenite, MoS_2, is a common ore of molybdenum. A 0.6524-g sample of molybdenite ore produced 0.3352 g of barium sulfate, $BaSO_4$. What was the percentage of MoS_2 in the sample?

Information

The mass of the sample (0.6524 g) and the mass of $BaSO_4$ precipitate (0.3352 g) from which to calculate the percentage of MoS_2

Connections

The chemical formulas and the molar masses from the periodic table, which provide the factors for conversion between mole and mass

Solution

To get the answer requires two steps: (1) determine the mass of MoS_2 in the sample, and (2) determine the percentage.

We begin by converting the mass of barium sulfate to moles of barium sulfate. Be careful not to try converting the mass of the entire sample (0.6524 g) to moles. In fact, it is not possible to convert this value directly to moles, since the composition of the sample is not fully known.

$$(0.3352 \text{ g } BaSO_4)\left(\frac{1 \text{ mol } BaSO_4}{233.40 \text{ g } BaSO_4}\right)\left(\frac{1 \text{ mol S}}{1 \text{ mol } BaSO_4}\right)\left(\frac{1 \text{ mol } MoS_2}{2 \text{ mol S}}\right)\left(\frac{160.07 \text{ g } MoS_2}{1 \text{ mol } MoS_2}\right)$$

$$= 0.114943 \text{ g } MoS_2 \quad \text{(unrounded)}$$

Once we know the mass of the substance of interest, we can determine the percent of the substance in the sample. To determine the percentage of one substance in another, we need to divide the mass of molybdenite by the mass of the ore:

$$\left(\frac{0.114943 \text{ g}}{0.6524 \text{ g}}\right) \times 100\% = 17.6185 = \textbf{17.62\%}$$

To minimize the effect of intermediate rounding, we round only the last answer to the proper number of significant figures.

Reality Check
The units and the number of significant figures in the answer are correct. The value should be about $(1/7) \times 100$ (the approximate values in the final equation).

Follow-Up Problem 4.19a
The mineral chromite, $FeCr_2O_4$, is a common ore of chromium. Chemists can determine the quantity of chromium in chromite samples by converting the chromium to chromate and then precipitating the chromate as barium chromate, $BaCrO_4$. A 0.8236-g sample of chromite ore produced 1.5929 g of barium chromate. What was the percentage of $FeCr_2O_4$ in the sample?

Information
The mass of the sample (0.8236 g) and the mass of $BaCrO_4$ precipitate (1.5929 g), from which to calculate the percentage of $FeCr_2O_4$

Connections
The chemical formulas and the molar masses from the periodic table provide the factors for conversion between mole and mass.

Solution
To get the answer requires two steps: (1) determine the mass of $FeCr_2O_4$ in the sample, and (2) determine the percentage.

We begin by converting the mass of barium chromate to moles of barium chromate. It is not possible to convert this value directly to moles since the composition of the sample is not fully known.

$$(1.5929 \text{ g BaCrO}_4)\left(\frac{1 \text{ mol BaCrO}_4}{253.319 \text{ g BaCrO}_4}\right)\left(\frac{1 \text{ mol Cr}}{1 \text{ mol BaCrO}_4}\right)\left(\frac{1 \text{ mol FeCr}_2\text{O}_4}{2 \text{ mol Cr}}\right)\left(\frac{223.833 \text{ g FeCr}_2\text{O}_4}{1 \text{ mol FeCr}_2\text{O}_4}\right)$$

$$= 0.703744 \text{ g FeCr}_2\text{O}_4 \quad \text{(unrounded)}$$

Once we know the mass of the substance of interest, we can determine the percent of the substance in the sample. To determine the percentage of one substance in another, we need to divide the mass of $FeCr_2O_4$ by the mass of the ore:

$$\left(\frac{0.703744 \text{ g}}{0.8236 \text{ g}}\right) \times 100\% = 85.4473 = \textbf{85.45\%}$$

To minimize the effect of intermediate rounding, we round only the last answer to the proper number of significant figures.

Reality Check
The units and the number of significant figures in the answer are correct.

Follow-Up Problem 4.19b
One of the common lead ores is the mineral cerussite, $PbCO_3$. This mineral dissolves in nitric acid to produce a solution of lead(II) nitrate, carbon dioxide gas, and liquid water. The addition of sodium chloride to the solution precipitates lead(II) chloride. Determine the percent $PbCO_3$ in a 0.5529-g sample of lead ore if 0.1094 g of sodium chloride were needed to precipitate the lead.

Information

The mass of the sample (0.5529 g) and the mass of NaCl added (0.1094 g), from which to calculate the percentage of $PbCO_3$

Connections

The chemical formulas and the molar masses from the periodic table provide the factors for conversion between mole and mass.

Solution

To get the answer requires two steps: (1) determine the mass of $PbCO_3$ in the sample, and (2) determine the percentage.

We begin by converting the mass of lead(II) chloride to moles of lead(II) chloride. It is not possible to convert this value directly to moles, since the composition of the sample is not fully known.

$$(0.1094 \text{ g NaCl})\left(\frac{1 \text{ mol NaCl}}{58.443 \text{ g NaCl}}\right)\left(\frac{1 \text{ mol Pb}}{2 \text{ mol NaCl}}\right)\left(\frac{1 \text{ mol } PbCO_3}{1 \text{ mol Pb}}\right)\left(\frac{267.2 \text{ g } PbCO_3}{1 \text{ mol } PbCO_3}\right)$$

$$= 0.250087 \text{ g } PbCO_3 \text{ (unrounded)}$$

Once we know the mass of the substance of interest, we can determine the percent of the substance in the sample. To determine the percentage of one substance in another, we need to divide the mass of $PbCO_3$ by the mass of the ore:

$$\left(\frac{0.250087 \text{ g}}{0.5529 \text{ g}}\right) \times 100\% = 45.231885 = \textbf{45.23\%}$$

To minimize the effect of intermediate rounding, we round only the last answer to the proper number of significant figures.

Reality Check

The units and the number of significant figures in the answer are correct.

Example Problem 4.20

We commonly use sodium carbonate, Na_2CO_3, to determine the concentration of strong acids such as nitric acid, HNO_3. A sodium carbonate solution containing 0.3025 g of Na_2CO_3 in 75.00 mL of water required 45.32 mL of a nitric acid solution to reach the equivalence point in a titration. What was the concentration of the acid? The reaction was

$$Na_2CO_3(aq) + 2 \text{ } HNO_3(aq) \rightarrow 2 \text{ } NaNO_3(aq) + H_2O(l) + CO_2(g)$$

Information

The balanced equation and measures of 0.3025 g Na_2CO_3, 75.00 mL H_2O, and 45.32 mL HNO_3 from which to find the concentration of the acid

Connections

Molar masses provide the necessary conversion factors.

Solution

We begin by organizing the known measurements under the balanced chemical equation:

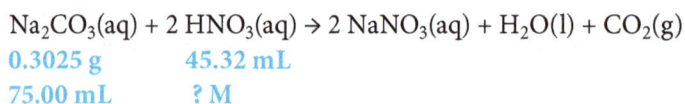

$$Na_2CO_3(aq) + 2 \text{ } HNO_3(aq) \rightarrow 2 \text{ } NaNO_3(aq) + H_2O(l) + CO_2(g)$$

0.3025 g   45.32 mL

75.00 mL   ? M

We proceed by treating this problem as a normal stoichiometry problem; that is, we convert the mass of sodium carbonate to moles and then take the mole ratio relating the sodium carbonate to the nitric acid from the balanced chemical equation. To find the concentration of the acid, we need the moles of acid and the liters of solution, so we'll need to change the milliliters of acid to liters:

$$(0.3025 \text{ g Na}_2\text{CO}_3)\left(\frac{1 \text{ mol Na}_2\text{CO}_3}{105.99 \text{ g Na}_2\text{CO}_3}\right)\left(\frac{2 \text{ mol HNO}_3}{1 \text{ mol Na}_2\text{CO}_3}\right)\left(\frac{1}{48.47 \text{ mL}}\right)\left(\frac{\text{m}}{10^{-3}}\right) = 0.1177653$$

$$= \textbf{0.1178 M HNO}_3$$

In this problem, it is not necessary to use the 75.00-mL measurement; only the volume of the acid is important for determining the concentration of the acid.

Reality Check
The units and the number of significant figures in the answer are correct.

Follow-Up Problem 4.20a
Vinegar is a dilute solution of acetic acid, $HC_2H_3O_2$. Typically, the concentration of acetic acid is near 1 M. A 15.00-mL sample thought to be vinegar was titrated with 1.150 M sodium hydroxide, NaOH. The titration required 42.50 mL of sodium hydroxide. What was the actual concentration of acetic acid in the vinegar? Was the sample typical vinegar?

Information
The information to write a balanced equation; 42.50 mL of 1.150 M NaOH and 15.00 mL of vinegar, from which to find the concentration of the acid and determine if the solution was typical vinegar (1 M)

Connections
Molar masses provide the necessary conversion factors.

Solution
Write the chemical equation and balance it:

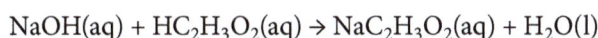

$$\text{NaOH(aq)} + \text{HC}_2\text{H}_3\text{O}_2\text{(aq)} \rightarrow \text{NaC}_2\text{H}_3\text{O}_2\text{(aq)} + \text{H}_2\text{O(l)}$$

The equation is already balanced, so transfer the information from the problem to the balanced chemical equation:

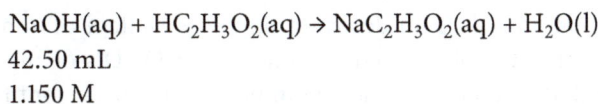

$$\text{NaOH(aq)} + \text{HC}_2\text{H}_3\text{O}_2\text{(aq)} \rightarrow \text{NaC}_2\text{H}_3\text{O}_2\text{(aq)} + \text{H}_2\text{O(l)}$$
42.50 mL
1.150 M

As usual, moles are the key. Note that the two *mL* cancel; therefore, no volume conversions are necessary. Use the molarity and volume to determine the moles of NaOH; then use a mole ratio to determine the moles of acid; finally, divide by the volume of the solution:

$$\text{M HC}_2\text{H}_3\text{O}_2 = \left(\frac{1.150 \text{ mol NaOH}}{\text{L}}\right)(42.50 \text{ mL})\left(\frac{1 \text{ mol HC}_2\text{H}_3\text{O}_2}{1 \text{ mol NaOH}}\right)\left(\frac{1}{15.00 \text{ mL}}\right) = 3.25833$$

$$= \textbf{3.258 M HC}_2\textbf{H}_3\textbf{O}_2$$

The actual molarity (3.258 M) is significantly greater than the typical value (1 M).

Reality Check
The units and the number of significant figures in the answer are correct.

Follow-Up Problem 4.20b

Barium sulfate is used in medical imaging because of its relative opacity to X-rays. One method of preparing this compound is to dissolve the barium mineral witherite (barium carbonate) in hydrochloric acid and then to precipitate the barium as barium sulfate using sodium sulfate. It is important to know the concentration of the hydrochloric acid to calculate the amount of acid necessary to dissolve the mineral. In an experiment similar to a titration, 45.33 mL of hydrochloric acid was used to dissolve 53.25 g of solid barium carbonate. What was the concentration of the acid?

Information

The information to write a balanced equation; 45.33 mL of HCl and 53.25 g of barium carbonate, from which to find the concentration of the acid

Connections

Molar masses provide the necessary conversion factors.

Solution

Write the chemical equation and balance it:

$$BaCO_3(s) + 2\ HCl(aq) \rightarrow BaCl_2(aq) + H_2O(l) + CO_2(g)$$

Transfer the information from the problem to the balanced chemical equation:

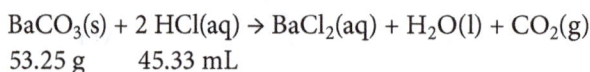

$$BaCO_3(s) + 2\ HCl(aq) \rightarrow BaCl_2(aq) + H_2O(l) + CO_2(g)$$
$$\text{53.25 g} \qquad \text{45.33 mL}$$

As usual, moles are the key. Convert the mass of $BaCO_3$ to moles using the molar mass; then use a mole ratio to convert to moles of HCl; finally, divide by the volume (converted to liters):

$$\text{M HCl} = (53.25\ \text{g BaCO}_3)\left(\frac{1\ \text{mol BaCO}_3}{197.335\ \text{g BaCO}_3}\right)\left(\frac{2\ \text{mol HCl}}{1\ \text{mol BaCO}_3}\right)\left(\frac{1}{45.33\ \text{mL}}\right)\left(\frac{\text{m}}{0.001}\right) = 11.90583$$

$$= \mathbf{11.91\ M\ HCl}$$

Reality Check

The units and the number of significant figures in the answer are correct.

Example Problem 4.21

In the past, the common procedure for determining the percentage of iron in a sample of iron ore was to titrate the iron with potassium dichromate, $K_2Cr_2O_7$. Dissolving the iron ore in acid, followed by reducing all the iron to Fe^{2+}, gave a sample that was ready for titration. The titration used the following reaction:

$$14\ HCl(aq) + 6\ FeCl_2(aq) + K_2Cr_2O_7(aq) \rightarrow 6\ FeCl_3(aq) + 2\ CrCl_3(aq) + 2\ KCl(aq) + 7\ H_2O(l)$$

In one analysis, 0.5072 g of iron ore required 44.25 mL of 0.01726 M potassium dichromate for the titration. What was the percentage of iron in the sample?

Information

The balanced chemical equation; the measurements 0.5072 g of iron ore and 44.25 mL of 0.01726 M $K_2Cr_2O_7$, from which to find the percentage of iron

Connections

The molar masses provide the necessary conversion factors.

Solution

Take the balanced chemical equation and add the information from the problem:

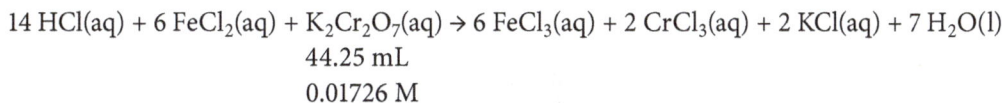

$$14 \, HCl(aq) + 6 \, FeCl_2(aq) + K_2Cr_2O_7(aq) \rightarrow 6 \, FeCl_3(aq) + 2 \, CrCl_3(aq) + 2 \, KCl(aq) + 7 \, H_2O(l)$$
$$44.25 \text{ mL}$$
$$0.01726 \text{ M}$$

The following equation leads to the percentage of iron in the sample:

$$\left(\frac{\text{Grams of iron}}{\text{Grams of sample}} \right) \times 100\%$$

The grams of sample are given (0.5072 g). Therefore, only the grams of iron are needed to complete the expression. Determining the amount of iron is a straightforward stoichiometry calculation using the balanced chemical equation and the molarity and volume of the potassium dichromate solution:

$$\left(\frac{0.01726 \text{ mol } K_2Cr_2O_7}{L} \right)\left(\frac{10^{-3}}{m} \right)(44.25 \text{ mL})\left(\frac{6 \text{ mol } FeCl_2}{1 \text{ mol } K_2Cr_2O_7} \right)\left(\frac{1 \text{ mol } Fe}{1 \text{ mol } FeCl_2} \right)\left(\frac{55.845 \text{ g } Fe}{1 \text{ mol } Fe} \right)$$

$$= 0.255911 \text{ g Fe} \quad \text{(unrounded)}$$

In this calculation, the first term is the molarity of the potassium dichromate solution, expressed as the definition of *molarity* (mol/L). The second term converts the liters to milliliters, so the volume of the solution (44.25 mL) will cancel those units. The third term is the given volume, followed by the moles of potassium dichromate. The 6-to-1 mole ratio comes from the balanced equation and gives the moles of iron(II) chloride. The last mole ratio converts the chemical formula of iron(II) chloride to give the moles of iron. The last term in the calculation is the molar mass of iron, from the periodic table.

Now that we have the grams of iron, we can insert them and the mass of the sample into the percentage equation to obtain the percent of iron in the sample:

$$\left(\frac{0.255911 \text{ g Fe}}{0.5072 \text{ g sample}} \right) \times 100\% = 50.4556 = \mathbf{50.46\% \ Fe}$$

Reality Check

The units and the number of significant figures are correct. The value determined by the last calculation [(26/51) × 100 > 50] is reasonable.

Follow-Up Problem 4.21a

Another method for determining the percentage of iron in a sample of iron ore is to do a redox titration of the iron with potassium permanganate, $KMnO_4$. A 0.5381-g sample of iron ore from the previous problem (Example problem 4.21) dissolves in excess sulfuric acid. Reduction of the iron in the solution with tin(II) sulfate leaves all the iron as Fe^{2+}. Titration of the resultant acid solution required 42.55 mL of 0.02285 M potassium permanganate. The reaction is

$$10 \, FeSO_4(aq) + 2 \, KMnO_4(aq) + 8 \, H_2SO_4(aq) \rightarrow 5 \, Fe_2(SO_4)_3(aq) + 2 \, MnSO_4(aq) + K_2SO_4(aq) + 8 \, H_2O(l)$$

What is the percent iron in the ore?

Information

The balanced chemical equation; the measurements 0.5381 g iron ore and 44.25 mL of 0.02285 M $KMnO_4$ from which to find the percentage of iron

Connections

The molar masses provide the necessary conversion factors.

Solution

Take the balanced chemical equation and add the measurement information from the problem:

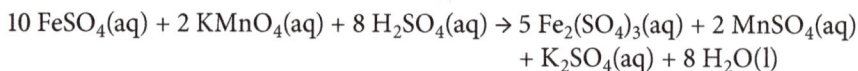

$$10 \ FeSO_4(aq) + 2 \ KMnO_4(aq) + 8 \ H_2SO_4(aq) \rightarrow 5 \ Fe_2(SO_4)_3(aq) + 2 \ MnSO_4(aq)$$
$$+ \ K_2SO_4(aq) + 8 \ H_2O(l)$$

44.55 mL
0.02285 M

The following equation leads to the percentage of iron in the sample:

$$\left(\frac{\text{Grams of iron}}{\text{Grams of sample}} \right) \times 100\%$$

The grams of sample are given (0.5381 g). Therefore, only the grams of iron are still needed to complete the expression. The determination of the amount of iron is a straightforward stoichiometry calculation using the balanced chemical equation and the molarity and volume of the potassium dichromate solution:

$$\left(\frac{0.02285 \ \text{mol KMnO}_4}{1,000 \ \text{mL}} \right)(42.55 \ \text{mL})\left(\frac{10 \ \text{mol FeSO}_4}{2 \ \text{mol KMnO}_4} \right)\left(\frac{1 \ \text{mol Fe}}{1 \ \text{mol FeSO}_4} \right)\left(\frac{55.845 \ \text{g Fe}}{1 \ \text{mol Fe}} \right)$$

= 0.271481 g Fe   (unrounded)

In this calculation, the first term is the molarity of the potassium permanganate solution, expressed as the definition of *molarity* (mole/L) with L replaced by 1,000 mL. The second term is the given volume, followed by the moles of potassium permanganate. The 10-to-5 mole ratio comes from the balanced equation and gives the moles of iron(II) sulfate. The last mole ratio converts the chemical formula of iron(II) sulfate to give the moles of iron. The last term in the calculation is the molar mass of iron, from the periodic table.

Now that we have the grams of iron, we can insert them and the mass of the sample into the percentage equation to obtain the percent of iron in the sample:

$$\left(\frac{0.271481 \ \text{g Fe}}{0.5381 \ \text{g sample}} \right) \times 100\% = 50.4518 = \textbf{50.45\% Fe}$$

Reality Check

The units and the number of significant figures are correct.

Follow-Up Problem 4.21b

The element europium, Eu, is important in color television technology. It occurs, in combination with several other elements, in ores such as the mineral gadolinite. To measure the amount of europium in an ore, it is necessary to dissolve a sample and convert the europium to the divalent (+2) state, to prevent the other elements present from interfering with the titration. Analysis of a 26.023-g sample of gadolinite required 47.85 mL of 0.005245 M potassium bromate, $KBrO_3$, solution for the titration. The titration reaction was

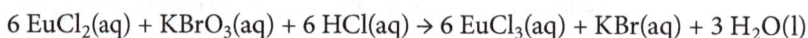

$$6 \ EuCl_2(aq) + KBrO_3(aq) + 6 \ HCl(aq) \rightarrow 6 \ EuCl_3(aq) + KBr(aq) + 3 \ H_2O(l)$$

Determine the percentage of europium in the sample.

Information

The balanced chemical equation; the measurements 26.023 g gadolinite and 47.85 mL of 0.005245 M $KBrO_3$ from which to find the percentage of europium

Connections

The molar masses provide the necessary conversion factors.

Solution

Take the balanced chemical equation and add the information from the problem:

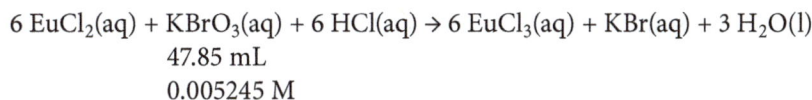

$$6\ EuCl_2(aq) + KBrO_3(aq) + 6\ HCl(aq) \rightarrow 6\ EuCl_3(aq) + KBr(aq) + 3\ H_2O(l)$$
$$47.85\ mL$$
$$0.005245\ M$$

The following equation leads to the percentage of europium in the sample:

$$\left(\frac{\text{Grams of europium}}{\text{Grams of sample}}\right) \times 100\%$$

The grams of sample are given (26.023 g). Therefore, only the grams of europium are still needed to complete the expression. The determination of the amount of europium is a straightforward stoichiometry calculation using the balanced chemical equation and the molarity and volume of the potassium bromate solution:

$$\left(\frac{0.005245\ mol\ KBrO_3}{1{,}000\ mL}\right)(47.85\ mL)\left(\frac{6\ mol\ EuCl_2}{1\ mol\ KBrO_3}\right)\left(\frac{1\ mol\ Eu}{1\ mol\ EuCl_2}\right)\left(\frac{151.964\ g\ Eu}{1\ mol\ Eu}\right)$$
$$= 0.228833\ g\ Eu \quad \text{(unrounded)}$$

In this calculation, the first term is the molarity of the potassium bromate solution, expressed as the definition of *molarity* (mole/L) with L replaced by 1,000 mL. The second term is the given volume, followed by the moles of potassium bromate. The 6-to-1 mole ratio comes from the balanced equation and gives the moles of europium(II) chloride. The last mole ratio converts the chemical formula of europium(II) chloride to give the moles of europium. The last term in the calculation is the molar mass of europium, from the periodic table.

Now that we have the grams of europium, we can insert them and the mass of the sample into the percentage equation to obtain the percent of europium in the sample:

$$\left(\frac{0.228833\ g\ Eu}{26.023\ g\ sample}\right) \times 100\% = 0.87935055 = \mathbf{0.8794\%\ Eu}$$

Reality Check

The units and the number of significant figures are correct.

END-OF-CHAPTER PROBLEMS

4.1 Solution Fundamentals

4.1 A solution forms when sugar dissolves in water. What is the solute and what is the solvent? Is this an aqueous solution?

Solution

The sugar is the solute, and the water is the solvent. This is an aqueous solution because water is the solvent.

4.3 Define the terms (a) *unsaturated solution*, (b) *saturated solution*, and (c) *supersaturated solution*.

Solution

(a) An **unsaturated solution** has less solute present than will normally dissolve.
(b) A **saturated solution** contains the maximum amount of solute that will normally dissolve.
(c) A **supersaturated solution** contains more solute than will normally dissolve.

4.2 Molarity

4.6 Define *molarity*.

Solution

Molarity is the moles of solute divided by the liters (or cubic decimeters) of solution.

4.8 When you are performing a dilution, which of the following increases? moles of solute, volume of solution, concentration of solute

Solution

Only the volume of the solution increases. The moles of solute remain constant, and the concentration of the solute decreases.

4.10 (a) What is the molarity of a solution containing 0.0335 mol of potassium dichromate, $K_2Cr_2O_7$, in 450.0 mL of solution? (b) Determine the number of milliliters of a 1.05 M calcium bromide, $CaBr_2$, solution required to supply 0.500 mol of solute. (c) Calculate the number of moles of sodium chloride, NaCl, in 125 mL of a 2.75 M solution of sodium chloride. (d) How many milliliters of a 0.100 M iron(III) chloride, $FeCl_3$, solution are required to supply 0.575 mol of chloride ion, Cl^-?

Information

(a) The moles (0.0335 mol) and volume (450.0 mL) of a $K_2Cr_2O_7$ solution, and the question is to find the molarity. (b) A concentration (1.05 M), and the question is what volume (mL) will contain 0.500 mol $CaBr_2$. (c) A concentration (2.75 M), a volume (125 mL), and the question is to determine the number on moles of NaCl. (d) A concentration (0.100 M $FeCl_3$), and the question of what volume (mL) contains 0.575 mol Cl^-.

Connections

The definition of *molarity* is the key.

Solution

In each case, the solution involves the definition of *molarity* ($M = \frac{moles}{liter}$ or $\frac{moles}{1,000 \text{ mL}}$). This series of calculations are the basic molarity problems that will appear in this chapter. Obviously, many problems will have additional parts.

(a) In this case, it is necessary to convert the milliliters to liters.

$$M = \left(\frac{0.0335 \text{ mol } K_2Cr_2O_7}{450.0 \text{ mL}} \right) \left(\frac{m}{0.001} \right) = 0.74444 = \mathbf{0.744 \ M}$$

(b) It is necessary to invert the definition of *molarity* so that moles will cancel

$$V = (0.500 \text{ mol CaBr}_2)\left(\frac{1,000 \text{ mL}}{1.05 \text{ mol CaBr}_2}\right) = 476.19 = \textbf{476 mL}$$

(c) This is a straight application of the definition of *molarity*.

$$\text{Moles} = \left(\frac{2.75 \text{ mole NaCl}}{1,000 \text{ mL}}\right)(125 \text{ mL}) = 0.34375 = \textbf{0.344 mole NaCl}$$

(d) This part involves a mole ratio in addition to the definition of *density*.

$$V = (0.575 \text{ mol Cl}^-)\left(\frac{1 \text{ mol FeCl}_3}{3 \text{ mol Cl}^-}\right)\left(\frac{1,000 \text{ mL}}{0.100 \text{ mol FeCl}_3}\right) = 1916.67 = \textbf{1.92} \times \textbf{10}^3 \text{ \textbf{mL}}$$

4.12 How many grams of solute are required to make each of the following solutions? **(a)** 0.250 L of 0.250 M nitric acid, HNO_3; **(b)** 175 mL of 0.500 M sulfuric acid, H_2SO_4; **(c)** 100.0 mL of 1.25 M phosphoric acid, H_3PO_4; **(d)** 250.0 mL of 1.55×10^{-6} M hydrofluoric acid, HF; **(e)** 1250 mL of 10.0 M perchloric acid, $HClO_4$

Information
(a) A volume (0.250 L) and a concentration (0.250 M HNO_3). **(b)** A volume (175 mL) and a concentration (0.500 M H_2SO_4). **(c)** A volume (100.0 mL) and a concentration (1.25 M H_3PO_4). **(d)** A volume (250.0 mL) and a concentration (1.55×10^{-6} M HF). **(e)** A volume (1250 mL) and a concentration (10.0 M $HClO_4$). In all cases, the question is how many grams.

Connections
The definition of *molarity* and the molar masses

Solution
Moles are the key. Once moles are found (from the molarity and volume), we only need to multiply by the molar mass to determine the grams present.

(a) $\text{Mass} = \left(\frac{0.250 \text{ mol HNO}_3}{\text{L}}\right)(0.250 \text{ L})\left(\frac{63.08 \text{ g HNO}_3}{1 \text{ mol HNO}_3}\right) = 3.9425 = \textbf{3.94 g HNO}_3$

(b) $\text{Mass} = \left(\frac{0.500 \text{ mol H}_2\text{SO}_4}{1,000 \text{ mL}}\right)(175 \text{ mL})\left(\frac{98.08 \text{ g H}_2\text{SO}_4}{1 \text{ mol H}_2\text{SO}_4}\right) = 8.582 = \textbf{8.58 g H}_2\textbf{SO}_4$

(c) $\text{Mass} = \left(\frac{1.25 \text{ mol H}_3\text{PO}_4}{1,000 \text{ mL}}\right)(100.0 \text{ mL})\left(\frac{97.45 \text{ g H}_3\text{PO}_4}{1 \text{ mol H}_3\text{PO}_4}\right) = 12.182 = \textbf{12.2 g H}_3\textbf{PO}_4$

(d) $\text{Mass} = \left(\frac{1.55 \times 10^{-6} \text{ mol HF}}{1,000 \text{ mL}}\right)(250.0 \text{ mL})\left(\frac{20.0063 \text{ g HF}}{1 \text{ mol HF}}\right) = 7.7524 \times 10^{-6} = \textbf{7.75} \times \textbf{10}^{-6} \text{ \textbf{g HF}}$

(e) $\text{Mass} = \left(\frac{10.0 \text{ mol HClO}_4}{1,000 \text{ mL}}\right)(1,250 \text{ mL})\left(\frac{100.457 \text{ g HClO}_4}{1 \text{ mol HClO}_4}\right) = 1,255.71 = \textbf{1.26} \times \textbf{10}^3 \text{ \textbf{g HClO}}_4$

4.14 You have a bottle of pure magnesium chloride, $MgCl_2$, and you need to prepare 250.0 mL of a 0.100 M solution of magnesium chloride. Calculate how much solute you would need and tell how you would make the solution.

Information

A volume (250.0 mL), a concentration (0.100 M $MgCl_2$); two questions: how much solute is needed, and what is the procedure for making the solution

Connections

The definition of *molarity* and the molar mass

Solution

Moles are the key. Once moles are found (from the molarity and volume), we only need to multiply by the molar mass to determine the grams that are needed to prepare the solution.

$$\text{Mass} = \left(\frac{0.100 \text{ mol MgCl}_2}{1,000 \text{ mL}}\right)(250.0 \text{ mL})\left(\frac{95.211 \text{ g MgCl}_2}{1 \text{ mol MgCl}_2}\right) = 2.285064 = 2.28 \text{ g MgCl}_2$$

To finish the problem, we furnish the directions:

Directions: Dissolve 2.28 g of $MgCl_2$ in a little water and add water to get a final volume of 250.0 mL.

4.16 Concentrated sulfuric acid is supplied in 4-L bottles of 18.0 M H_2SO_4. Outline the steps you would take and show the calculations necessary for preparing 500.0 mL of 3.0 M sulfuric acid.

Information

The available amount of H_2SO_4 solution (4 L of 18.0 M); the desired amount of H_2SO_4l solution (500.0 mL of 3.0 M); two questions: what amount is needed, and what is the procedure for making the solution

Connections

$M_iV_i = M_fV_f$

Solution

Some of the concentrated sulfuric acid is necessary to prepare the diluted solution. We must determine the amount (V_i) of concentrated acid (M_i = 18.0 M) that will be needed to dilute to 500.0 mL (V_f) of 3.0 M (M_f).

$$V_i = \frac{M_fV_f}{M_i} = \frac{(3.0 \text{ M})(500.0 \text{ mL})}{18.0 \text{ M}} = 83.3333 = \textbf{83 mL}$$

4.18 Calculate the final molarity of acid in each of the following solutions: **(a)** 0.125 L of 1.50 M acetic acid, $HC_2H_3O_2$, mixed with sufficient water to prepare 1.00 L of solution; **(b)** 475 mL of 5.00 M nitric acid, HNO_3, added to 725 mL of water (assume the volumes are additive); **(c)** 5.33 g of dinitrogen pentoxide added to sufficient water to prepare 750.0 mL of solution (be careful, the acid is HNO_3)

Information

(a) The original volume and concentration (0.125 L of 1.50 M $HC_2H_3O_2$) and the final volume (1.00 L). **(b)** The original volume and concentration (475 mL of 5.00 M HNO_3) and the amount of water added (725 mL). **(c)** The mass of solute (5.33 g N_2O_5) and the volume of solution (750.0 mL). In all cases, the question is what is the final molarity.

Connections

$M_i V_i = M_f V_f$

The definition of *molarity*; for part (c), a balanced chemical equation and a molar mass

Solution

For parts **(a)** and **(b)**, we need to rearrange the dilution equation to find the missing quantity (M_f):

(a) $M_f = \dfrac{(0.125 \text{ L})(1.50 \text{ M HC}_2\text{H}_3\text{O}_2)}{(1.00 \text{ L})} = 0.1875 = \textbf{0.188 M HC}_2\textbf{H}_3\textbf{O}_2$

(b) $M_f = \dfrac{(475 \text{ mL})(5.00 \text{ M HNO}_3)}{(475 + 725)\text{mL}} = 1.9791667 = \textbf{1.98 M HNO}_3$

(c) This part if different from the other two parts in that the starting material is not an acid. So, we need to convert the N_2O_5 to an acid (HNO_3), beginning with a balanced chemical equation. Using the mass of the N_2O_5 and the balanced chemical equation, it is possible to determine the moles of acid using a chapter 3 stoichiometry calculation (numerator in first fraction in the calculation).

$$N_2O_5(s) + H_2O(l) \rightarrow 2\ HNO_3(aq)$$

$$M = \dfrac{(5.33 \text{ g N}_2\text{O}_5)\left(\dfrac{1 \text{ mol N}_2\text{O}_5}{108.009 \text{ g N}_2\text{O}_5}\right)\left(\dfrac{2 \text{ mol HNO}_3}{1 \text{ mol N}_2\text{O}_5}\right)}{750.0 \text{ mL}}\left(\dfrac{m}{0.001}\right) = 0.13159397 = \textbf{0.132 M HNO}_3$$

4.3 Electrolytes and Nonelectrolytes

4.20 **(a)** What is a cation? **(b)** What is an anion?

Solution

(a) A cation is an atom or a group of atoms that has a positive charge due to a loss of electrons.
(b) An anion is an atom or a group of atoms that has a negative charge due to a gain of electrons.

4.22 What is the difference between a strong electrolyte and a weak electrolyte? Give an example of each.

Solution

A strong electrolyte is 100% dissociated in solution, and a weak electrolyte is less than 100% dissociated in a solution. Strong acids, such as HCl, are strong electrolytes; weak acids, such as $HC_2H_3O_2$, are weak electrolytes.

4.24 Which of the following is an example of a strong base solution: 10.0 M NH_3 or 0.001 M NaOH? Why?

Solution

Even though it is less concentrated, the NaOH solution is an example of a strong base solution. Whether a solution is strong or weak depends in the identity of the base, not on its concentration.

4.26 Each of the following substances will dissolve, to a greater or lesser extent, in water. Predict which are nonelectrolytes and which are electrolytes. Then predict which of the electrolytes are strong and which are weak. **(a)** potassium chloride (KCl, a salt substitute); **(b)** sucrose ($C_{12}H_{22}O_{11}$, table sugar); **(c)** acetic acid ($HC_2H_3O_2$, in vinegar); **(d)** hydrochloric acid (HCl, stomach acid); **(e)** sodium bicarbonate ($NaHCO_3$, baking soda); **(f)** ethylene glycol ($C_2H_4(OH)_2$, in antifreeze); **(g)** ammonia (NH_3, in some household cleaners); **(h)** isopropyl alcohol ($CH_3CHOHCH_3$, rubbing alcohol); **(i)** copper(II) sulfate ($CuSO_4$, used as an algaecide); **(j)** oxalic acid ($H_2C_2O_4$, in some rust removers)

Information
The names and formulas of several compounds

Connections
Strong electrolytes are strong acids and bases and soluble salts. Weak electrolytes are weak acids and bases.

Solution
(a) KCl   **Strong electrolyte** because it is a soluble salt.

(b) $C_{12}H_{22}O_{11}$ **Nonelectrolyte** this is a molecular compound that is not an acid.

(c) $HC_2H_3O_2$ **Weak electrolyte** this is an acid, but not a strong acid.

(d) HCl   **Strong electrolyte** this is one of the few strong acids.

(e) $NaHCO_3$ **Strong electrolyte** because it is a soluble salt.

(f) $C_2H_4(OH)_2$ **Nonelectrolyte** this is a molecular compound that is not an acid.

(g) NH_3 **Weak electrolyte** this is one of the few weak bases.

(h) $CH_3CHOHCH_3$ **Nonelectrolyte** this is a molecular compound that is not an acid.

(i) $CuSO_4$ **Strong electrolyte** because it is a soluble salt.

(j) $H_2C_2O_4$ **Weak electrolyte** this is an acid, but not a strong acid.

4.4 Precipitation Reactions
4.32 (a) To which ions does the first solubility rule apply? **(b)** To which ions does the second solubility rule apply? **(c)** To which ions does the third solubility rule apply?

Solution
(a) The first rule applies to ions with a +1 or a –1 charge.

(b) The second rule applies to ions with a ±3 or greater charge.

(c) The third rule applies to ions with a –2 charge.

4.33 (a) List the exceptions to the first solubility rule. **(b)** List the exceptions to the second solubility rule. **(c)** List the exceptions to the third solubility rule.

Solution
(a) Compounds containing ions with a +1 charge involving metals in group 11 (1B) on the periodic table and the halides combined with lead(II). **(b)** Compounds containing ions with a +3 or greater charge combined with sulfate ion or dichromate ions. **(c)** Compounds containing the sulfate ion or dichromate ion other than the sulfates of calcium, strontium, barium, lead or mercury.

4.35 Which of the following are soluble in water? **(a)** potassium nitrate, KNO_3; **(b)** silver bromide, AgBr; **(c)** iron(III) phosphate, $FePO_4$; **(d)** barium hydroxide, $Ba(OH)_2$; **(e)** zinc hydroxide, $Zn(OH)_2$;

(**f**) aluminum sulfate, $Al_2(SO_4)_3$; (**g**) lead(II) iodide, PbI_2; (**h**) ammonium oxalate, $(NH_4)_2C_2O_4$; (**i**) sodium permanganate, $NaMnO_4$; (**j**) mercury(I) chloride, Hg_2Cl_2

Information
The names and formulas of several compounds.

Connections
The solubility rules

Solution

Substance	Solubility	Applicable Rule
(**a**) KNO_3	Soluble	Rule 1 (+1 and –1)
(**b**) $AgBr$	Not soluble	This is an exception to Rule 1
(**c**) $FePO_4$	Not soluble	Rule 2 (+3 and –3).
(**d**) $Ba(OH)_2$	Soluble	Because this is a strong base
(**e**) $Zn(OH)_2$	Not soluble	Because this is not a strong base
(**f**) $Al_2(SO_4)_3$	Soluble	Because sulfates are exceptions to Rule 2
(**g**) PbI_2	Not soluble	An exception to Rule 1
(**h**) $(NH_4)_2C_2O_4$	Soluble	Because of Rule 1 (+1)
(**i**) $NaMnO_4$	Soluble	Rule 1 (+1 and –1)
(**j**) Hg_2Cl_2	Not soluble	An exception to Rule 1

4.5 Acid–Base Reactions

4.38 Which, if any, of the following would not be a neutralization reaction? (**a**) a strong acid with a strong base; (**b**) a strong acid with a weak base; (**c**) a weak acid with a strong base; (**d**) a weak acid with a weak base

Solution
These are all neutralization reactions. Each involves an acid reacting with a base. Strong or weak makes no difference.

4.40 Label each of the following as an acid or a base; then label them as weak or strong: (**a**) HCl (**b**) $HClO_2$; (**c**) $Ba(OH)_2$; (**d**) $HC_2H_3O_2$ (**e**) NH_3

Solution
Check **table 4.1** to find the strong acids or bases; assume all other acids or bases are weak.

(**a**) HCl, strong acid; (**b**) $HClO_2$, weak acid; (**c**) $Ba(OH)_2$, strong base; (**d**) $HC_2H_3O_2$, weak acid; (**e**) NH_3, weak base

4.43 Write balanced chemical equations showing how each of the following acidic oxides forms a strong acid when added to water: (**a**) SO_3; (**b**) Cl_2O_5; (**c**) dinitrogen pentoxide; (**d**) dichlorine heptoxide

Information
The names or formulas of several compounds; the directions to add each to water and show how they produce an acid

Connections

All the nonmetal oxides will produce an acid; the Nomenclature Resource

Solution

The problem says that each of these compounds plus water will give an acid. So, write down the formula for each compound, and add water to the oxide (as directed). On the product side of the reaction will be the acid containing the nonmetal in the same oxidation state. Finally, balance the equation. Note: The nonmetal will normally not change its oxidation state.

(a) $SO_3(s) + H_2O(l) \rightarrow H_2SO_4(aq)$

(b) $Cl_2O_5(s) + H_2O(l) \rightarrow 2\,HClO_3(aq)$

(c) $N_2O_5(s) + H_2O(l) \rightarrow 2\,HNO_3(aq)$

(d) $Cl_2O_7(s) + H_2O(l) \rightarrow 2\,HClO_4(aq)$

▶ **Note:** It may be useful for you to either book-mark **table 4.3** or make a copy for reference while working the problems in this section.

4.6 Redox Reactions

4.47 If copper undergoes oxidation in a reaction, is copper the oxidizing agent or the reducing agent?

Solution

The substance that undergoes oxidation is the reducing agent.

4.49 What is the relationship between the electrons lost and the electrons gained in a redox reaction?

Solution

The total number of electrons lost must be equal to the total number of electrons gained.

4.51 Based on their positions on the periodic table, list the maximum and minimum oxidation numbers expected for each of the following elements: **(a)** As, **(b)** S, **(c)** Cr, **(d)** Ba, **(e)** Cu

Information

The symbols of several elements; the instruction to determine the maximum and minimum oxidation number for each

Connections

The rules in the Nomenclature Resource for assigning oxidation numbers

Solution

(a) As　+5 to –3

(b) S　　+6 to –2

(c) Cr　+6 to 0

(d) Ba　+2 to 0

(e) Cu　+2 to 0

4.53 Give the name or the formula, as appropriate, for each of the following: **(a)** $Cu(NO_3)_2$; **(b)** $TiCl_3$; **(c)** $NiCO_3$; **(d)** Ag_2O_3; **(e)** $Fe_3(AsO_4)_2$; **(f)** tin(II) fluoride; **(g)** molybdenum(IV) oxide; **(h)** chromium(III) hydroxide; **(i)** manganese(II) sulfate; **(j)** cobalt(II) phosphate

Information

The names or formula of several compounds and the directions to give the name or formula of each.

Connections

The rules in the Nomenclature Resource for assigning names or formulas

Solution

(a) Copper(II) nitrate; (b) Titanium((III) chloride; (c) Nickel(II) carbonate; (d) Silver(III) oxide; (e) Iron(II) arsenate; (f) SnF_2; (g) MoO_2; (h) $Cr(OH)_3$; (i) $MnSO_4$; (j) $Co_3(PO_4)_2$

4.7 Complete and Net Ionic Equations

4.55 Define *molecular equation*, *total ionic equation*, and *net ionic equation*, and give an example of each.

Solution

A **molecular equation** is a chemical equation where species are treated as molecules.

A *total* **ionic equation** is a chemical equation where all strong electrolytes are dissociated into the appropriate ions.

A **net ionic equation** is a total ionic equation with the spectator ions removed.

4.57 List the types of substances that dissociate in a total ionic equation. Give one example of each type.

Solution

Strong electrolytes dissociate in a total ionic equation. Strong electrolytes include strong acids, such as HCl; strong bases, such as NaOH; and soluble salts, such as NaCl.

4.59 Convert the following balanced chemical reactions to net ionic equations and list the spectator ions, if any.

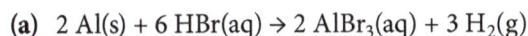

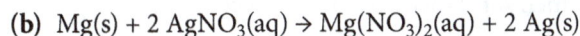

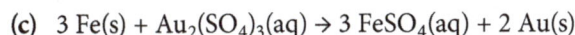

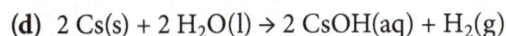

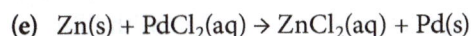

(a) $2\,Al(s) + 6\,HBr(aq) \rightarrow 2\,AlBr_3(aq) + 3\,H_2(g)$

(b) $Mg(s) + 2\,AgNO_3(aq) \rightarrow Mg(NO_3)_2(aq) + 2\,Ag(s)$

(c) $3\,Fe(s) + Au_2(SO_4)_3(aq) \rightarrow 3\,FeSO_4(aq) + 2\,Au(s)$

(d) $2\,Cs(s) + 2\,H_2O(l) \rightarrow 2\,CsOH(aq) + H_2(g)$

(e) $Zn(s) + PdCl_2(aq) \rightarrow ZnCl_2(aq) + Pd(s)$

Information

Several balanced equations; the instructions to convert each to net ionic form and identify the spectator ions

Connections

Need to determine which substances are strong electrolytes

Solution

Convert each molecular equation to a complete ionic equation before converting the equation to net ionic form. You may need the Nomenclature Resource to help with this.

(a) $2 Al(s) + 6 HBr(aq) \rightarrow 2 AlBr_3(aq) + 3 H_2(g)$

$2 Al(s) + 6 H^+(aq) + 6 Br^-(aq) \rightarrow 2 Al^{3+}(aq) + 6 Br^-(aq) + 3 H_2(g)$

$2 Al(s) + 6 H^+(aq) \rightarrow 2 Al^{3+}(aq) + 3 H_2(g)$ Spectator: Br^-

(b) $Mg(s) + 2 AgNO_3(aq) \rightarrow Mg(NO_3)_2(aq) + 2 Ag(s)$

$Mg(s) + 2 Ag^+(aq) + 2 NO_3^-(aq) \rightarrow Mg^{2+}(aq) + 2 NO_3^-(aq) + 2 Ag(s)$

$Mg(s) + 2 Ag^+(aq) \rightarrow Mg^{2+}(aq) + 2 Ag(s)$ Spectator: NO_3^-

(c) $3 Fe(s) + Au_2(SO_4)_3(aq) \rightarrow 3 FeSO_4(aq) + 2 Au(s)$

$3 Fe(s) + 2 Au^{3+}(aq) + 3 SO_4^{2-}(aq) \rightarrow 3 Fe^{2+}(aq) + 3 SO_4^{2-}(aq) + 2 Au(s)$

$3 Fe(s) + 2 Au^{3+}(aq) \rightarrow 3 Fe^{2+}(aq) + 2 Au(s)$ Spectator: SO_4^{2-}

(d) $2 Cs(s) + 2 H_2O(l) \rightarrow 2 CsOH(aq) + H_2(g)$

$Cs(s) + 2 H_2O(l) \rightarrow 2 Cs^+(aq) + OH^-(aq) + H_2(g)$ Spectator: None

(e) $Zn(s) + PdCl_2(aq) \rightarrow ZnCl_2(aq) + Pd(s)$

$Zn(s) + Pd^{2+}(aq) + 2 Cl^-(aq) \rightarrow Zn^{2+}(aq) + 2 Cl^-(aq) + Pd(s)$

$Zn(s) + Pd^{2+}(aq) \rightarrow Zn^{2+}(aq) + Pd(s)$ Spectator: Cl^-

4.62 Complete and balance the following equations using the activity series (**table 4.3**). Write molecular and net ionic equations for each. (**a**) Copper metal is added to an aqueous silver nitrate solution. (**b**) Zinc metal is added to an aqueous sulfuric acid solution. (**c**) Iron metal is added to an aqueous aluminum nitrate solution. (**d**) Tin metal is added to an aqueous copper(II) sulfate solution. (**e**) Potassium metal is added to water.

Information
The reactants for several chemical equations; the directions to complete and balance the chemical equation and then convert the equation to net ionic form

Connections
The activity series (**table 4.3**); recognizing which substances are strong electrolytes

Solution
Unlike in the preceding examples, in this problem we need to predict the products using the activity series. Convert each molecular equation to a complete ionic equation before converting the equation to net ionic form. You may need the Nomenclature Resource to help with this.

(a) $Cu(s) + 2 AgNO_3(aq) \rightarrow Cu(NO_3)_2(aq) + 2 Ag(s)$

$Cu(s) + 2 Ag^+(aq) + 2 NO_3^-(aq) \rightarrow Cu^{2+}(aq) + 2 NO_3^-(aq) + 2 Ag(s)$

$Cu(s) + 2 Ag^+(aq) \rightarrow Cu^{2+}(aq) + 2 Ag(s)$

(b) $Zn(s) + H_2SO_4(aq) \rightarrow ZnSO_4(aq) + H_2(g)$

$Zn(s) + 2 H^+(aq) + SO_4^{2-}(aq) \rightarrow Zn^{2+}(aq) + SO_4^{2-}(aq) + H_2(g)$

$Zn(s) + 2 H^+(aq) \rightarrow Zn^{2+}(aq) + H_2(g)$

(c) $Fe(s) + Al(NO_3)_3(aq) \rightarrow$ No Reaction because $Fe(s)$ is below $Al^{3+}(aq)$ on the activity series

$Fe(s) + Al^{3+}(aq) \rightarrow$ No Reaction

(d) $Sn(s) + CuSO_4(aq) \rightarrow SnSO_4(aq) + Cu(s)$

$Sn(s) + Cu^{2+}(aq) + SO_4^{2-}(aq) \rightarrow Sn^{2+}(aq) + SO_4^{2-}(aq) + Cu(s)$

$Sn(s) + Cu^{2+}(aq) \rightarrow Sn^{2+}(aq) + Cu(s)$

(e) $2\ K(s) + 2\ H_2O(l) \rightarrow 2\ KOH(aq) + H_2(g)$

$2\ K(s) + 2\ H_2O(l) \rightarrow 2\ K^+(aq) + 2\ OH^-(aq) + H_2(g)$

4.65 Complete and balance the following equations using the activity series (**table 4.3**). Write both molecular and net ionic equations.

(a) $Zn(s) + CuSO_4(aq) \rightarrow$

(b) $Mg(s) + ZnSO_4(aq) \rightarrow$

(c) $H_2(g) + AuCl_3(aq) \rightarrow$

(d) $Fe(s) + HCl(aq) \rightarrow$

(e) $Cu(s) + AgNO_3(aq) \rightarrow$

(f) $Au(s) + Al_2(SO_4)_3(aq) \rightarrow$

(g) $Ba(s) + H_2O(l) \rightarrow$

(h) $Sn(s) + Pb(C_2H_3O_2)_2(aq) \rightarrow$

(i) $Hg(l) + AgClO_3(aq) \rightarrow$

(j) $Cr(s) + NiI_2(aq) \rightarrow$

Information
The reactants for several chemical equations; the directions to complete and balance the chemical equation and then convert the equation to net ionic form

Connections
The activity series (**table 4.3**); recognizing which substances are strong electrolytes

Solution
Unlike in the preceding examples, in this problem we need to predict the products using the activity series. Convert each molecular equation to a complete ionic equation before converting the equation to net ionic form. You may need the Nomenclature Resource to help with this.

(a) $Zn(s) + CuSO_4(aq) \rightarrow Cu(s) + ZnSO_4(aq)$

$Zn(s) + Cu^{2+}(aq) + SO_4^{2-}(aq) \rightarrow Cu(s) + Zn^{2+}(aq) + SO_4^{2-}(aq)$

$Zn(s) + Cu^{2+}(aq) \rightarrow Cu(s) + Zn^{2+}(aq)$

(b) $Mg(s) + ZnSO_4(aq) \rightarrow Zn(s) + MgSO_4(aq)$

$Mg(s) + Zn^{2+}(aq) + SO_4^{2-}(aq) \rightarrow Zn(s) + Mg^{2+}(aq) + SO_4^{2-}(aq)$

$Mg(s) + Zn^{2+}(aq) \rightarrow Zn(s) + Mg^{2+}(aq)$

(c) $3\ H_2(g) + 2\ AuCl_3(aq) \rightarrow 2\ Au(s) + 6\ HCl(aq)$

$3\ H_2(g) + 2\ Au^{3+}(aq) + 6\ Cl^-(aq) \rightarrow 2\ Au(s) + 6\ H^+(aq) + 6\ Cl^-(aq)$

$3\ H_2(g) + 2\ Au^{3+}(aq) \rightarrow 2\ Au(s) + 6\ H^+(aq)$

(d) $Fe(s) + 2\ HCl(aq) \rightarrow FeCl_2(aq) + H_2(g)$

$Fe(s) + 2\ H^+(aq) + 2\ Cl^-(aq) \rightarrow Fe^{2+}(aq) + 2\ Cl^-(aq) + H_2(g)$

$Fe(s) + 2\ H^+(aq) \rightarrow Fe^{2+}(aq) + H_2(g)$

(e) $Cu(s) + 2\ AgNO_3(aq) \rightarrow Cu(NO_3)_2(aq) + 2\ Ag(s)$

$Cu(s) + 2\ Ag^+(aq) + 2\ NO_3^-(aq) \rightarrow Cu^{2+}(aq) + 2\ NO_3^-(aq) + 2\ Ag(s)$

$Cu(s) + 2\ Ag^+(aq) \rightarrow Cu^{2+}(aq) + 2\ Ag(s)$

(f) $Au(s) + Al_2(SO_4)_3(aq) \rightarrow$ No Reaction because Au is below $Al^{3+}(aq)$ on the activity series.

$Au(s) + 2\ Al^{3+}(aq) + 3\ SO_4^{2-}(aq) \rightarrow$ No Reaction

(g) $Ba(s) + 2\ H_2O(l) \rightarrow Ba(OH)_2(aq) + H_2(g)$

$Ba(s) + 2\ H_2O(l) \rightarrow Ba^{2+}(aq) + 2\ OH^-(aq) + H_2(g)$

(There are no spectator ions, so the complete and net ionic equations are the same.)

(h) $Sn(s) + Pb(C_2H_3O_2)_2(aq) \rightarrow Pb(s) + Sn(C_2H_3O_2)_2(aq)$

$Sn(s) + Pb^{2+}(aq) + 2\ C_2H_3O_2^-(aq) \rightarrow Pb(s) + Sn^{2+}(aq) + 2\ C_2H_3O_2^-(aq)$

$Sn(s) + Pb^{2+}(aq) \rightarrow Pb(s) + Sn^{2+}(aq)$

(i) $Hg(l) + 2\ AgClO_3(aq) \rightarrow Hg(ClO_3)_2(aq) + 2\ Ag(s)$

$Hg(l) + 2\ Ag^+(aq) + 2\ ClO_3^-(aq) \rightarrow Hg^{2+}(aq) + 2\ ClO_3^-(aq) + 2\ Ag(s)$

$Hg(l) + 2\ Ag^+(aq) \rightarrow Hg^{2+}(aq) + 2\ Ag(s)$

(j) $Cr(s) + NiI_2(aq) \rightarrow CrI_2(aq) + Ni(s)$

$Cr(s) + Ni^{2+}(aq) + 2\ I^-(aq) \rightarrow Cr^{2+}(aq) + 2\ I^-(aq) + Ni(s)$

$Cr(s) + Ni^{2+}(aq) \rightarrow Cr^{2+}(aq) + Ni(s)$

4.8 Metathesis and Gas Formation Reactions

4.69 What is a *metathesis reaction*?

Solution

A **metathesis reaction** is a double replacement reaction.

4.71 Balance the following reactions; convert them to net ionic equations; and list the spectator ions, if any.

(a) $KOH(aq) + (NH_4)_2SO_4(aq) \rightarrow K_2SO_4(aq) + H_2O(l) + NH_3(g)$

(b) $H_3PO_4(aq) + CaSO_3(s) \rightarrow Ca_3(PO_4)_2(s) + H_2O(l) + SO_2(g)$

(c) $FeS(s) + HCl(aq) \rightarrow FeCl_2(aq) + H_2S(g)$

(d) $HCl(aq) + CaCO_3(s) \rightarrow CaCl_2(aq) + H_2O(l) + CO_2(g)$

(e) $NH_4NO_3(aq) + K_2CO_3(aq) \rightarrow KNO_3(aq) + H_2O(l) + NH_3(g) + CO_2(g)$

Information

Several chemical reactions to balance and then to convert to net ionic form; the instruction to identify the spectator ions

Connections

The rules for balancing chemical equations; recognizing which substances are strong electrolytes

Solution

Convert each molecular equation to a complete ionic equation before converting the equation to net ionic form. You may need the Nomenclature Resource to help with this.

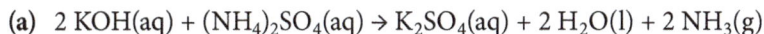

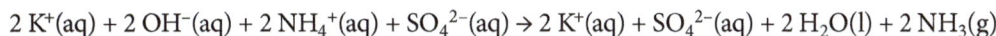

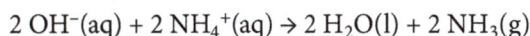

(a) $2 KOH(aq) + (NH_4)_2SO_4(aq) \rightarrow K_2SO_4(aq) + 2 H_2O(l) + 2 NH_3(g)$

$2 K^+(aq) + 2 OH^-(aq) + 2 NH_4^+(aq) + SO_4^{2-}(aq) \rightarrow 2 K^+(aq) + SO_4^{2-}(aq) + 2 H_2O(l) + 2 NH_3(g)$

$2 OH^-(aq) + 2 NH_4^+(aq) \rightarrow 2 H_2O(l) + 2 NH_3(g)$

This should be simplified because all the coefficients are the same (2).

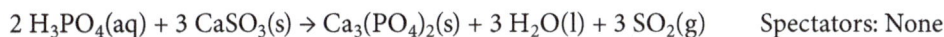

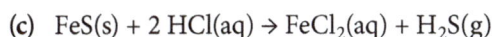

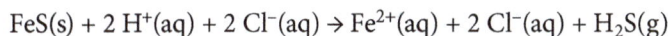

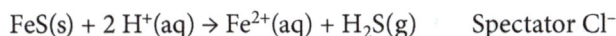

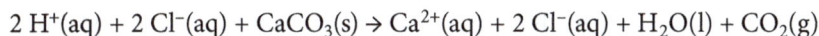

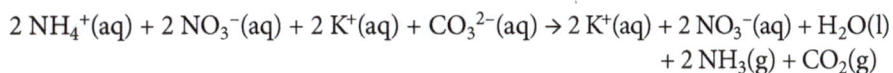

$OH^-(aq) + NH_4^+(aq) \rightarrow H_2O(l) + NH_3(g)$ Spectators: K^+ and SO_4^{2-}

(b) $2 H_3PO_4(aq) + 3 CaSO_3(s) \rightarrow Ca_3(PO_4)_2(s) + 3 H_2O(l) + 3 SO_2(g)$

$2 H_3PO_4(aq) + 3 CaSO_3(s) \rightarrow Ca_3(PO_4)_2(s) + 3 H_2O(l) + 3 SO_2(g)$ Spectators: None

(c) $FeS(s) + 2 HCl(aq) \rightarrow FeCl_2(aq) + H_2S(g)$

$FeS(s) + 2 H^+(aq) + 2 Cl^-(aq) \rightarrow Fe^{2+}(aq) + 2 Cl^-(aq) + H_2S(g)$

$FeS(s) + 2 H^+(aq) \rightarrow Fe^{2+}(aq) + H_2S(g)$ Spectator Cl^-

(d) $2 HCl(aq) + CaCO_3(s) \rightarrow CaCl_2(aq) + H_2O(l) + CO_2(g)$

$2 H^+(aq) + 2 Cl^-(aq) + CaCO_3(s) \rightarrow Ca^{2+}(aq) + 2 Cl^-(aq) + H_2O(l) + CO_2(g)$

$2 H^+(aq) + CaCO_3(s) \rightarrow Ca^{2+}(aq) + H_2O(l) + CO_2(g)$ Spectator: Cl^-

(e) $2 NH_4NO_3(aq) + K_2CO_3(aq) \rightarrow 2 KNO_3(aq) + H_2O(l) + 2 NH_3(g) + CO_2(g)$

$2 NH_4^+(aq) + 2 NO_3^-(aq) + 2 K^+(aq) + CO_3^{2-}(aq) \rightarrow 2 K^+(aq) + 2 NO_3^-(aq) + H_2O(l)$
$+ 2 NH_3(g) + CO_2(g)$

$2 NH_4^+(aq) + CO_3^{2-}(aq) \rightarrow H_2O(l) + 2 NH_3(g) + CO_2(g)$ Spectators: NO_3^- and K^+

4.73 Complete the molecular equations for any reactions resulting when the following substances are mixed, then write the net ionic equations for each. If there is no reaction, label the answer as NR.

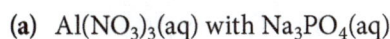

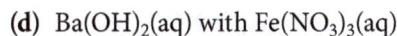

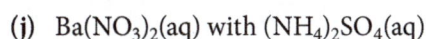

(a) $Al(NO_3)_3(aq)$ with $Na_3PO_4(aq)$

(b) $KOH(aq)$ with $H_2CO_3(aq)$

(c) $Pb(NO_3)_2(aq)$ with $HBr(aq)$

(d) $Ba(OH)_2(aq)$ with $Fe(NO_3)_3(aq)$

(e) $AgClO_4(aq)$ with $SrBr_2(aq)$

(f) $NH_4NO_3(aq)$ with $KOH(aq)$

(g) $NaNO_3(aq)$ with $CaCl_2(aq)$

(h) $NiBr_2(aq)$ with $H_2S(aq)$

(i) $HNO_2(aq)$ with $Mn(OH)_2(s)$

(j) $Ba(NO_3)_2(aq)$ with $(NH_4)_2SO_4(aq)$

Information

The reactants for several chemical equations; the directions to complete and balance the chemical equation and then convert the equation to net ionic form. The choice of No Reaction, NR, is possible.

Connections

After predicting the products and balancing, we need to recognize the strong electrolytes (strong acids, strong bases, soluble ionic compounds).

Solution

We need to predict the products using the solubility rules or identifying the strong/weak acids/bases. Convert each molecular equation to a complete ionic equation before converting the equation to net ionic form. You may need the Nomenclature Resource to help with this.

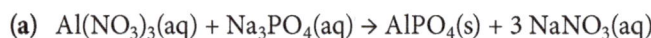

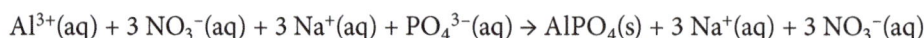

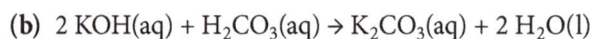

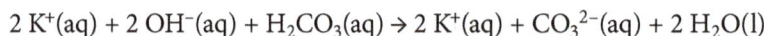

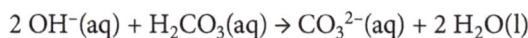

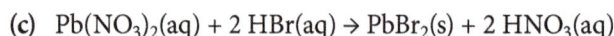

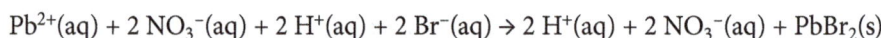

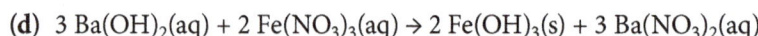

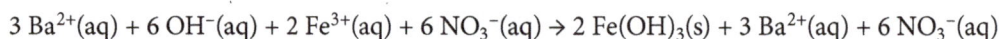

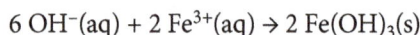

(a) $Al(NO_3)_3(aq) + Na_3PO_4(aq) \rightarrow AlPO_4(s) + 3\ NaNO_3(aq)$

$Al^{3+}(aq) + 3\ NO_3^-(aq) + 3\ Na^+(aq) + PO_4^{3-}(aq) \rightarrow AlPO_4(s) + 3\ Na^+(aq) + 3\ NO_3^-(aq)$

$Al^{3+}(aq) + PO_4^{3-}(aq) \rightarrow AlPO_4(s)$

(b) $2\ KOH(aq) + H_2CO_3(aq) \rightarrow K_2CO_3(aq) + 2\ H_2O(l)$

$2\ K^+(aq) + 2\ OH^-(aq) + H_2CO_3(aq) \rightarrow 2\ K^+(aq) + CO_3^{2-}(aq) + 2\ H_2O(l)$

$2\ OH^-(aq) + H_2CO_3(aq) \rightarrow CO_3^{2-}(aq) + 2\ H_2O(l)$

(c) $Pb(NO_3)_2(aq) + 2\ HBr(aq) \rightarrow PbBr_2(s) + 2\ HNO_3(aq)$

$Pb^{2+}(aq) + 2\ NO_3^-(aq) + 2\ H^+(aq) + 2\ Br^-(aq) \rightarrow 2\ H^+(aq) + 2\ NO_3^-(aq) + PbBr_2(s)$

$Pb^{2+}(aq) + 2\ Br^-(aq) \rightarrow PbBr_2(s)$

(d) $3\ Ba(OH)_2(aq) + 2\ Fe(NO_3)_3(aq) \rightarrow 2\ Fe(OH)_3(s) + 3\ Ba(NO_3)_2(aq)$

$3\ Ba^{2+}(aq) + 6\ OH^-(aq) + 2\ Fe^{3+}(aq) + 6\ NO_3^-(aq) \rightarrow 2\ Fe(OH)_3(s) + 3\ Ba^{2+}(aq) + 6\ NO_3^-(aq)$

$6\ OH^-(aq) + 2\ Fe^{3+}(aq) \rightarrow 2\ Fe(OH)_3(s)$

This should be simplified by dividing by 2.

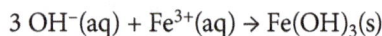

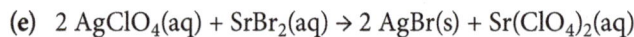

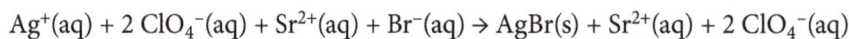

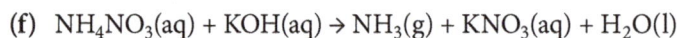

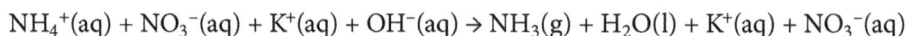

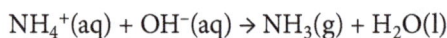

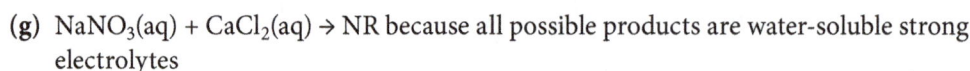

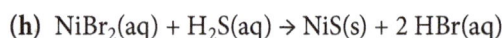

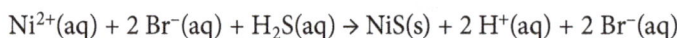

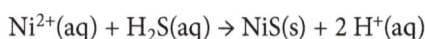

$3\ OH^-(aq) + Fe^{3+}(aq) \rightarrow Fe(OH)_3(s)$

(e) $2\ AgClO_4(aq) + SrBr_2(aq) \rightarrow 2\ AgBr(s) + Sr(ClO_4)_2(aq)$

$Ag^+(aq) + 2\ ClO_4^-(aq) + Sr^{2+}(aq) + Br^-(aq) \rightarrow AgBr(s) + Sr^{2+}(aq) + 2\ ClO_4^-(aq)$

$Ag^+(aq) + Br^-(aq) \rightarrow AgBr(s)$

(f) $NH_4NO_3(aq) + KOH(aq) \rightarrow NH_3(g) + KNO_3(aq) + H_2O(l)$

$NH_4^+(aq) + NO_3^-(aq) + K^+(aq) + OH^-(aq) \rightarrow NH_3(g) + H_2O(l) + K^+(aq) + NO_3^-(aq)$

$NH_4^+(aq) + OH^-(aq) \rightarrow NH_3(g) + H_2O(l)$

(g) $NaNO_3(aq) + CaCl_2(aq) \rightarrow$ NR because all possible products are water-soluble strong electrolytes

(h) $NiBr_2(aq) + H_2S(aq) \rightarrow NiS(s) + 2\ HBr(aq)$

$Ni^{2+}(aq) + 2\ Br^-(aq) + H_2S(aq) \rightarrow NiS(s) + 2\ H^+(aq) + 2\ Br^-(aq)$

$Ni^{2+}(aq) + H_2S(aq) \rightarrow NiS(s) + 2\ H^+(aq)$

(i) $2\ HNO_2(aq) + Mn(OH)_2(s) \rightarrow Mn(NO_2)_2(aq) + 2\ H_2O(l)$

$2\ HNO_2(aq) + Mn(OH)_2(s) \rightarrow Mn^{2+}(aq) + 2\ NO_2^-(aq) + 2\ H_2O(l)$

(j) $Ba(NO_3)_2(aq) + (NH_4)_2SO_4(aq) \rightarrow BaSO_4(s) + 2\ NH_4NO_3(aq)$

$Ba^{2+}(aq) + 2\ NO_3^-(aq) + 2\ NH_4^+(aq) + SO_4^{2-}(aq) \rightarrow BaSO_4(s) + 2\ NH_4^+(aq) + 2\ NO_3^-(aq)$

$Ba^{2+}(aq) + SO_4^{2-}(aq) \rightarrow BaSO_4(s)$

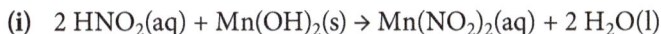

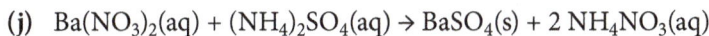

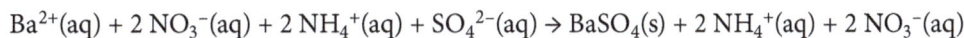

4.75 Balance the following chemical equations by placing appropriate coefficients in the blanks. Then classify the type of reaction for each as decomposition, combination, combustion, or "other."

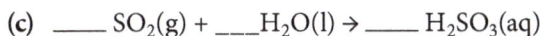

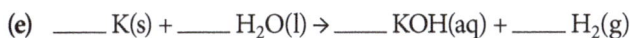

(a) ＿＿ $Mg(s) +$ ＿＿ $O_2(g) \rightarrow$ ＿＿ $MgO(s)$

(b) ＿＿ $Mg(s) +$ ＿＿ $N_2(g) \rightarrow$ ＿＿ $Mg_3N_2(s)$

(c) ＿＿ $SO_2(g) +$ ＿＿$H_2O(l) \rightarrow$ ＿＿ $H_2SO_3(aq)$

(d) ＿＿ $HgO(s) \rightarrow$ ＿＿ $Hg(l) +$ ＿＿ $O_2(g)$

(e) ＿＿ $K(s) +$ ＿＿ $H_2O(l) \rightarrow$ ＿＿ $KOH(aq) +$ ＿＿$H_2(g)$

Information
Several chemical equations to balance and classify

Connections
The procedure for balancing chemical equations; the definitions of the different types of reactions

Solution

(a) $2\ Mg(s) + O_2(g) \rightarrow 2\ MgO(s)$ Combination and Combustion

(b) $3\ Mg(s) + N_2(g) \rightarrow Mg_3N_2(s)$ Combination

(c) $SO_2(g) + H_2O(l) \rightarrow H_2SO_3(aq)$ Combination

(d) $2\ HgO(s) \rightarrow 2\ Hg(l) + O_2(g)$ Decomposition

(e) $2\ K(s) + 2\ H_2O(l) \rightarrow 2\ KOH(aq) + H_2(g)$ "Other"

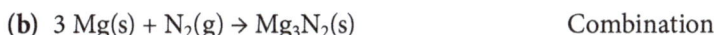

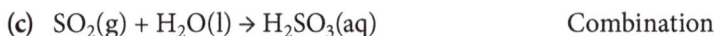

4.77 Write balanced molecular and net ionic equations for the reaction of aqueous phosphoric acid, H_3PO_4, with each of the following: **(a)** a potassium hydroxide, KOH, solution; **(b)** solid aluminum hydroxide, $Al(OH)_3$; **(c)** a calcium chloride, $CaCl_2$, solution; **(d)** a sodium carbonate, Na_2CO_3, solution; **(e)** a cesium fluoride, CsF, solution

Information
Phosphoric acid and five compounds that might react with this acid; directions to complete and balance the chemical equations and then convert to net ionic form

Connections
Predict the products and balance the equation, then look for any strong electrolytes

Solution
We need to predict the products using the solubility rules or identifying the strong/weak acids/bases. Convert each molecular equation to a complete ionic equation before converting the equation to net ionic form. You may need the Nomenclature Resource to help with this.

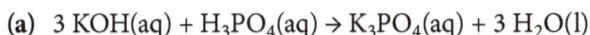

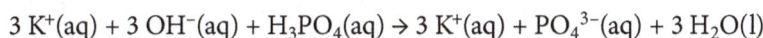

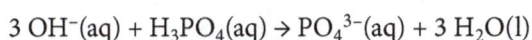

(a) $3\ KOH(aq) + H_3PO_4(aq) \rightarrow K_3PO_4(aq) + 3\ H_2O(l)$

$3\ K^+(aq) + 3\ OH^-(aq) + H_3PO_4(aq) \rightarrow 3\ K^+(aq) + PO_4^{3-}(aq) + 3\ H_2O(l)$

$3\ OH^-(aq) + H_3PO_4(aq) \rightarrow PO_4^{3-}(aq) + 3\ H_2O(l)$

(b) $Al(OH)_3(s) + H_3PO_4(aq) \rightarrow AlPO_4(s) + 3\ H_2O(l)$

$Al(OH)_3(s) + H_3PO_4(aq) \rightarrow AlPO_4(s) + 3\ H_2O(l)$

(c) $3\ CaCl_2(aq) + 2\ H_3PO_4(aq) \rightarrow Ca_3(PO_4)_2(s) + 6\ HCl(aq)$

$3\ Ca^{2+}(aq) + 6\ Cl^-(aq) + 2\ H_3PO_4(aq) \rightarrow Ca_3(PO_4)_2(s) + 6\ H^+(aq) + 6\ Cl^-(aq)$

(d) $3\ Na_2CO_3(aq) + 2\ H_3PO_4(aq) \rightarrow 2\ Na_3PO_4(aq) + 3\ H_2CO_3(aq)$

$6\ Na^+(aq) + 3\ CO_3^{2-}(aq) + 2\ H_3PO_4(aq) \rightarrow 6\ Na^+(aq) + 2\ PO_4^{3-}(aq) + 3\ H_2CO_3(aq)$

$3\ CO_3^{2-}(aq) + 2\ H_3PO_4(aq) \rightarrow 2\ PO_4^{3-}(aq) + 3\ H_2CO_3(aq)$

As an alternative, it is possible to use $H_2CO_3(aq) \rightarrow H_2O(l) + CO_2(g)$

(e) $3\ CsF(aq) + H_3PO_4(aq) \rightarrow Cs_3PO_4(aq) + 3\ HF(aq)$

$3\ Cs^+(aq) + 3\ F^-(aq) + H_3PO_4(aq) \rightarrow 3\ Cs^+(aq) + PO_4^{3-}(aq) + 3\ HF(aq)$

$3\ F^-(aq) + H_3PO_4(aq) \rightarrow PO_4^{3-}(aq) + 3\ HF(aq)$

4.9 Solution Stoichiometry

4.79 How many milliliters of 0.2300 M $Na_2C_2O_4$ solution are required to react as follows with 17.00 g of $ThCl_4$?

$$ThCl_4(aq) + 2\ Na_2C_2O_4(aq) \rightarrow Th(C_2O_4)_2(s) + 4\ NaCl(aq)$$

Information

The balanced chemical equation; the question of how many milliliters of 0.2300 M Na_2CO_3 will react with 17.00 g $ThCl_4$

Connections

Moles are the key, in addition to the definition of *molarity*

Solution

It will help to recopy the balanced chemical equation and place the given information directly below the appropriate substance in the equation.

$$ThCl_4(aq) + 2\ Na_2C_2O_4(aq) \rightarrow Th(C_2O_4)_2(s) + 4\ NaCl(aq)$$
$$\text{17.00 g} \qquad \text{0.2300 M}$$
$$\underline{\qquad ?\quad} \text{mL}$$

Convert the mass of $ThCl_4$ to moles (using the molar mass); use a moles ratio to get to moles of $Na_2C_2O_4$; finally, use the inverted definition of *molarity* to determine the volume:

$$\text{Volume} = (17.00\,\text{g}\,ThCl_4)\left(\frac{1\,\text{mol}\,ThCl_4}{373.850\,\text{g}\,ThCl_4}\right)\left(\frac{2\,\text{mol}\,Na_2C_2O_4}{1\,\text{mol}\,ThCl_4}\right)\left(\frac{1{,}000\,\text{mL}}{0.2300\,\text{mol}\,Na_2C_2O_4}\right)$$

$$= 395.4155 = \textbf{395.4 mL}$$

4.82 How many milliliters of a 1.125 M $K_2C_2O_4$ solution are required to produce 5.000 g of $U(C_2O_4)_2$ in the following reaction?

$$UCl_4(aq) + 2\ K_2C_2O_4(aq) \rightarrow U(C_2O_4)_2(s) + 4\ KCl(aq)$$

Information

The balanced chemical equation; the question of how many milliliters of 1.125 M $K_2C_2O_4$ are necessary to form 5.000 g $U(C_2O_4)_2$

Connections

Moles are the key, in addition to the definition of *molarity*

Solution

It will help to recopy the balanced chemical equation and place the given information directly below the appropriate substance in the equation:

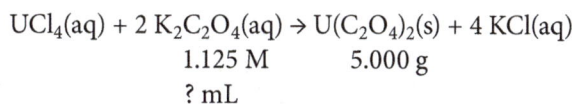

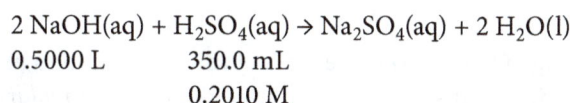

$$UCl_4(aq) + 2\ K_2C_2O_4(aq) \rightarrow U(C_2O_4)_2(s) + 4\ KCl(aq)$$

	1.125 M	5.000 g
	? mL	

Using its molar mass, convert the mass of $U(C_2O_4)_2$ to moles and use a mole ratio to get to moles of $K_2C_2O_4$; finish with the inverted definition of *molarity*:

$$\text{Volume} = \left(5.000\ \text{g U}(C_2O_4)_2\right)\left(\frac{1\ \text{mol U}(C_2O_4)_2}{414.065\ \text{g U}(C_2O_4)_2}\right)\left(\frac{2\ \text{mol K}_2C_2O_4}{1\ \text{mol U}(C_2O_4)_2}\right)\left(\frac{1{,}000\ \text{mL}}{1.125\ \text{mol K}_2C_2O_4}\right)$$

$$= 21.467 = \mathbf{21.47\ mL}$$

4.84 What is the concentration of base when 350.0 mL of 0.2010 M sulfuric acid reacts with 0.5000 L of sodium hydroxide?

Information

The question of what is the concentration of the base if 350.0 mL of 0.2010 M sulfuric acid reacts with 0.5000 L of sodium hydroxide

Connections

Moles are the key, in addition to the definition of *molarity*

Solution

It will help to recopy the balanced chemical equation and place the given information directly below the appropriate substance in the equation:

$$2\ NaOH(aq) + H_2SO_4(aq) \rightarrow Na_2SO_4(aq) + 2\ H_2O(l)$$

0.5000 L	350.0 mL
	0.2010 M

Determine the moles of H_2SO_4 from the volume and molarity of the acid; use a mole ratio to determine the moles of NaOH; and finish by dividing the mole by the volume (in liters):

$$\text{M NaOH} = (350.0\ \text{mL})\left(\frac{0.2010\ \text{mol H}_2SO_4}{1{,}000\ \text{mL}}\right)\left(\frac{2\ \text{mol NaOH}}{1\ \text{mol H}_2SO_4}\right)\left(\frac{1}{0.5000\ \text{L}}\right) = \mathbf{0.2814\ M\ NaOH}$$

4.87 What is the concentration of base when 350.0 mL of 0.2010 M sulfuric acid react with 0.1500 L of lithium hydroxide?

Information

The question of what is the concentration of the base if 350.0 mL of 0.2010 M sulfuric acid react with 0.1500 L of lithium hydroxide

Connections

Moles are the key, in addition to the definition of *molarity*

Solution

It will help to recopy the balanced chemical equation and place the given information directly below the appropriate substance in the equation:

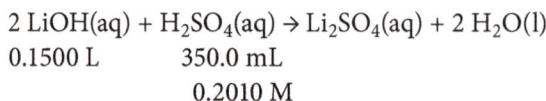

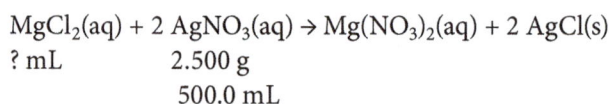

$$2 \text{ LiOH(aq)} + \text{H}_2\text{SO}_4\text{(aq)} \rightarrow \text{Li}_2\text{SO}_4\text{(aq)} + 2 \text{ H}_2\text{O(l)}$$

0.1500 L   350.0 mL

0.2010 M

More is known about the H_2SO_4, so begin with this compound. Determine the moles of H_2SO_4 from the volume and the concentration of the H_2SO_4 solution; use a mole ratio to determine the moles of LiOH; finally, divide by the volume of the LiOH solution (in liters):

$$\text{M LiOH} = (350.0 \text{ mL})\left(\frac{0.2010 \text{ mol H}_2\text{SO}_4}{1{,}000 \text{ mL}}\right)\left(\frac{2 \text{ mol LiOH}}{1 \text{ mol H}_2\text{SO}_4}\right)\left(\frac{1}{0.1500 \text{ L}}\right) = \textbf{0.9380 M LiOH}$$

4.90 How many milliliters of 0.1550 M magnesium chloride are needed to precipitate the silver ion completely from a solution made by dissolving 2.500 g of silver nitrate in 500.0 mL of water?

Information

The question of how many milliliters of 0.1550 M magnesium chloride will precipitate the silver ion from a solution of 2.500 g of silver nitrate in 500.0 mL of water

Connections

Moles are the key, in addition to the definition of *molarity*

Solution

It will help to recopy the balanced chemical equation and place the given information directly below the appropriate substance in the equation:

$$\text{MgCl}_2\text{(aq)} + 2 \text{ AgNO}_3\text{(aq)} \rightarrow \text{Mg(NO}_3)_2\text{(aq)} + 2 \text{ AgCl(s)}$$

? mL   2.500 g

500.0 mL

Use the molar mass of AgNO_3 to convert the mass of this compound to moles; then use a mole ratio to get to moles of MgCl_2; finally, use the inverted definition of *molarity* to determine the volume of the solution:

$$\text{Volume} = (2.500 \text{ g AgNO}_3)\left(\frac{1 \text{ mole AgNO}_3}{169.8731 \text{ g AgNO}_3}\right)\left(\frac{1 \text{ mole MgCl}_2}{2 \text{ mole AgNO}_3}\right)\left(\frac{1{,}000 \text{ mL}}{0.1550 \text{ mole MgCl}_2}\right)$$

$$= 47.4738 = \textbf{47.47 mL}$$

4.93 The following reaction produced 2.875 g of KNO_3. Assume the HNO_3 is in excess. **(a)** How many milliliters of a 0.1400 M K_2CO_3 solution were required to do this? **(b)** How many grams of $\text{CO}_2\text{(g)}$ will escape?

$$\text{K}_2\text{CO}_3\text{(aq)} + 2 \text{ HNO}_3\text{(aq)} \rightarrow 2 \text{ KNO}_3\text{(aq)} + \text{CO}_2\text{(g)} + \text{H}_2\text{O(l)}$$

Information

A balanced chemical equation; these two questions: **(a)** How many milliliters of 0.1400 M K_2CO_3 will produce 2.875 g KNO_3? and **(b)** How many grams of CO_2 escape?

Connections

Moles are the key, in addition to the *definition* of molarity

Solution

It will help to recopy the balanced chemical equation and place the given information directly below the appropriate substance in the equation:

(a) $K_2CO_3(aq) + 2\ HNO_3(aq) \rightarrow 2\ KNO_3(aq) + CO_2(g) + H_2O(l)$
 0.1400 M   2.875 g
 ? mL

Convert the mass of KNO_3 formed to moles by using the molar mass; then use a mole ratio to get to moles of K_2CO_3; finally, use the inverted definition of *molarity* to determine the volume:

$$\text{Volume} = (2.875\ \text{g KNO}_3)\left(\frac{1\ \text{mol KNO}_3}{101.102\ \text{g KNO}_3}\right)\left(\frac{1\ \text{mol K}_2\text{CO}_3}{2\ \text{mol KNO}_3}\right)\left(\frac{1{,}000\ \text{mL}}{0.1400\ \text{mol K}_2\text{CO}_3}\right)$$

$$= 101.5593 = \textbf{101.6 mL}$$

(b) Recopy the chemical equation, and put the given information (including the question) below the appropriate substance:

$$K_2CO_3(aq) + 2\ HNO_3(aq) \rightarrow 2\ KNO_3(aq) + CO_2(g) + H_2O(l)$$
$$\qquad\qquad\qquad\qquad\qquad\qquad 2.875\ \text{g} \qquad\quad ?\ \text{g}$$

Convert the mass of KNO_3 formed to moles by using the molar mass; then use a mole ratio to get to moles of CO_2; finally, use the molar mass of CO_2 to determine the mass:

$$\text{Mass} = (2.875\ \text{g KNO}_3)\left(\frac{1\ \text{mol KNO}_3}{101.102\ \text{g KNO}_3}\right)\left(\frac{1\ \text{mol CO}_2}{2\ \text{mol KNO}_3}\right)\left(\frac{44.009\ \text{g}}{1\ \text{mol CO}_2}\right) = 0.62573$$

$$= \textbf{0.6257 g CO}_2$$

4.10 Applications and Extensions

4.94 Someone gives you two unlabeled beakers. You know that one beaker contains a barium nitrate solution and one beaker contains a magnesium nitrate solution. Since solutions containing barium ions are toxic, it is important to know which of the beakers contains barium ions. Which of the following substances could be used to distinguish between barium ions and magnesium ions: $NaNO_3$, $CaCl_2$, $(NH_4)_2SO_4$, KBr, or HBr? Write a balanced chemical equation for any reactions that occur.

Information

Two solutions (barium nitrate and magnesium nitrate) and five test reagents ($NaNO_3$, $CaCl_2$, $(NH_4)_2SO_4$, KBr, or HBr) to choose from; the question of which of the test reagents will react with one or the other of the test solutions; also, what is the balanced chemical equation for any reactions

Connections

The solubility rules

Solution

$(NH_4)_2SO_4$ will cause barium, but not magnesium, ions to precipitate from solution.

No other substance will give a noticeable reaction.

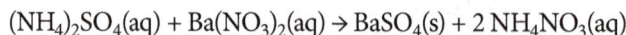

$$(NH_4)_2SO_4(aq) + Ba(NO_3)_2(aq) \rightarrow BaSO_4(s) + 2\,NH_4NO_3(aq)$$

4.96 Toxic mercury ions may be removed from a solution by precipitating mercury(II) sulfide, HgS. A solution of sodium sulfide, Na_2S, is made by dissolving 50.00 g in sufficient water to prepare 0.7500 L of solution. How many milliliters of the sodium sulfide solution are needed to precipitate the mercury ions from 10.00 L of a solution that is 1.58×10^{-3} M Hg^{2+}?

Information

The fact that HgS will precipitate from solution; a Na_2S solution (50.00 g in 0.7500 L of solution); the question of how many milliliters of the solution are needed to precipitate the mercury in a solution (10.00 L of 1.58×10^{-3} M Hg^{2+})

Connections

Moles are the key, in addition to the definition of *molarity*

Solution

It will help to recopy the balanced chemical equation and place the given information directly below the appropriate substance in the equation:

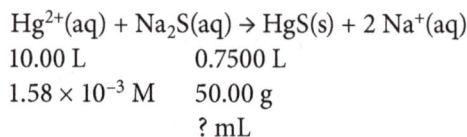

$$Hg^{2+}(aq) + Na_2S(aq) \rightarrow HgS(s) + 2\,Na^+(aq)$$

10.00 L   0.7500 L

1.58×10^{-3} M   50.00 g

           ? mL

Determine the moles of Hg^{2+} from the volume and concentration of the solution; use a mole ratio to determine the moles of Na_2S; convert moles to grams using the molar mass; then use the number of grams of Na_2S present in 0.7500 L; finally, convert to milliliters:

$$Volume = (10.00\ L)\left(\frac{1.58 \times 10^{-3}\ mol\ Hg^{2+}}{L}\right)\left(\frac{1\ mol\ Na_2S}{1\ mol\ Hg^{2+}}\right)\left(\frac{78.045\ g\ Na_2S}{1\ mol\ Na_2S}\right)\left(\frac{0.7500\ L}{50.00\ g\ Na_2S}\right)\left(\frac{m}{0.001}\right)$$

$$= 18.496665 = \textbf{18.5 mL}$$

4.98 Vinegar is normally 5%–6% acetic acid. A 5.00-g sample of vinegar is titrated with 0.2243 M sodium hydroxide, NaOH, solution. If the titration requires 44.32 mL of base to neutralize the vinegar, what is the percentage of acetic acid in the vinegar in the following reaction?

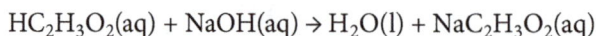

$$HC_2H_3O_2(aq) + NaOH(aq) \rightarrow H_2O(l) + NaC_2H_3O_2(aq)$$

Information

The statement that vinegar is normally 5%–6% $HC_2H_3O_2$; a 5.00 g vinegar sample that is titrated with (0.2243 M NaOH and 44.32 mL); the question of what is the percent $HC_2H_3O_2$ in the sample

Connections

Moles are the key, in addition to the definition of *molarity*

Solution

It will help to recopy the balanced chemical equation and place the given information directly below the appropriate substance in the equation:

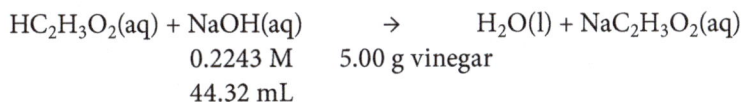

$$HC_2H_3O_2(aq) + NaOH(aq) \rightarrow H_2O(l) + NaC_2H_3O_2(aq)$$

0.2243 M   5.00 g vinegar
44.32 mL

The percent in the mass of acetic acid (to be calculated) divided by the mass of the sample (given), all times 100%. Determine the mass of acetic acid present (numerator in the following calculation). The mass comes from the volume and concentration of the base (NaOH) solution, times a mole ratio times the molar mass of the acid.

$$Percent = \frac{(44.32 \text{ mL})\left(\frac{0.2243 \text{ mol NaOH}}{1{,}000 \text{ mL}}\right)\left(\frac{1 \text{ mol HC}_2\text{H}_3\text{O}_2}{1 \text{ mol NaOH}}\right)\left(\frac{60.052 \text{ g HC}_2\text{H}_3\text{O}_2}{1 \text{ mol HC}_2\text{H}_3\text{O}_2}\right)}{5.00 \text{ g}} \times 100\%$$

$$= 11.9395098 = \mathbf{11.9\%}$$

Putting It All Together

4.101 **(a)** Calculate the molarity of nitrate ion, NO_3^-, in a solution made by mixing 500.0 mL of 0.2500 M sodium nitrate, $NaNO_3$, with 750.0 mL of 0.1250 M potassium nitrate, KNO_3. **(b)** Calculate the molarity of nitrate ion in a solution made by mixing 75.0 mL of 0.2500 M sodium nitrate with 75.0 mL of 0.3750 M calcium nitrate, $Ca(NO_3)_2$. In both cases, assume that the volumes are additive.

Information

The question is to calculate the molarity of NO_3^- in two solutions made by mixing **(a)** 500.0 mL of 0.2500 M $NaNO_3$ with 750.0 mL of 0.1250 M KNO_3, and **(b)** 75.0 mL of 0.2500 M $NaNO_3$ with 75.0 mL of 0.3750 M $Ca(NO_3)_2$.

Connections

Moles are the key, in addition to the definition of *molarity*

Solution

(a) There are two sources of nitrate ion, so it is necessary to determine the moles of NO_3^- from each source and sum the two. This is done in the numerator of the following calculation. For each source ($NaNO_3$ and KNO_3) use its volume time concentration to get the moles. Then use a moles ratio to get the moles of nitrate ion. Next, add the two moles together. Finally, divide the total moles by the total volume (converted to liters):

$$\frac{\left[(500.0 \text{ mL})\left(\frac{0.2500 \text{ mol NaNO}_3}{1{,}000 \text{ mL}}\right)\left(\frac{1 \text{ mol NO}_3^-}{1 \text{ mol NaNO}_3}\right)\right] + \left[(750.0 \text{ mL})\left(\frac{0.1250 \text{ mol KNO}_3}{1{,}000 \text{ mL}}\right)\left(\frac{1 \text{ mol NO}_3^-}{1 \text{ mol KNO}_3}\right)\right]}{(500.0 + 750.0) \text{ mL}}$$

$$\times \left(\frac{m}{0.001}\right) = \mathbf{0.1750 \text{ M}}$$

(b) This is like (a) except that the KNO_3 is replaced by $Ca(NO_3)_2$, which changes one of the mole ratios:

$$\left[\frac{\left[(75.0\text{ mL})\left(\dfrac{0.2500\text{ mol NaNO}_3}{1{,}000\text{ mL}}\right)\left(\dfrac{1\text{ mol NO}_3^-}{1\text{ mol NaNO}_3}\right)\right]+\left[(75.0\text{ mL})\left(\dfrac{0.3750\text{ mol Ca(NO}_3)_2}{1{,}000\text{ mL}}\right)\left(\dfrac{2\text{ mol NO}_3^-}{1\text{ mol Ca(NO}_3)_2}\right)\right]}{(75.0+75.0)\text{ mL}}\right]$$

$$\times\left(\frac{m}{0.001}\right) = \textbf{0.5000 M}$$

4.103 Give the formula and the name of the salt produced in each of the following neutralization reactions: **(a)** aqueous potassium hydroxide reacts with aqueous nitric acid; **(b)** solid magnesium hydroxide dissolves in aqueous hydrochloric acid; **(c)** aqueous acetic acid reacts with aqueous barium hydroxide; **(d)** aqueous arsenic acid, H_3AsO_4, reacts with solid zinc hydroxide; **(e)** gaseous ammonia dissolves in aqueous phosphoric acid

Information

The questions are to give the formula and name of the salt produced by each of the five reactions: **(a)** aqueous potassium hydroxide with aqueous nitric acid; **(b)** solid magnesium hydroxide in aqueous hydrochloric acid; **(c)** aqueous acetic acid with aqueous barium hydroxide; **(d)** H_3AsO_4, with solid zinc hydroxide; **(e)** gaseous ammonia in aqueous phosphoric acid.

Connections

Acids react with bases to produce salts.

Solution

For some people, it may be easier to write a balanced chemical equation for this problem.

(a) Aqueous potassium hydroxide reacts with aqueous nitric acid to form **potassium nitrate, KNO_3.**

(b) Solid magnesium hydroxide dissolves in aqueous hydrochloric acid to form **magnesium chloride, $MgCl_2$.**

(c) Aqueous acetic acid reacts with aqueous barium hydroxide to form **barium acetate, $Ba(C_2H_3O_2)_2$.**

(d) Aqueous arsenic acid, H_3AsO_4, reacts with solid zinc hydroxide to form **zinc arsenate, $Zn_3(AsO_4)_2$.**

(e) Gaseous ammonia dissolves in aqueous phosphoric acid to form **ammonium phosphate, $(NH_4)_3PO_4$.**

4.106 Determine the molarity of each solute particle in the following solutions: **(a)** 0.250 M hydrochloric acid, HCl; **(b)** 0.500 M sodium fluoride, NaF; **(c)** 0.125 M strontium bromide, $SrBr_2$; **(d)** 5.00 M ethyl alcohol, C_2H_5OH; **(e)** a solution prepared by mixing 125 mL of 0.100 M potassium chloride, KCl, solution with 275 mL of a 0.0500 M calcium chloride, $CaCl_2$, solution

Information

The question is to determine the molarity of each solute particle in five solutions: **(a)** 0.250 M HCl; **(b)** 0.500 M NaF; **(c)** 0.125 M $SrBr_2$; **(d)** 5.00 M C_2H_5OH; **(e)** a solution prepared by mixing 125 mL of 0.100 M KCl solution and 275 mL of a 0.0500 M $CaCl_2$

Connections

Moles are the key, in addition to the definition of *molarity*

Solution

(a) According to **table 4.1**, HCl is a strong acid (strong electrolyte); therefore, HCl completely dissociates to $H^+(aq)$ and $Cl^-(aq)$. The mole ratio accounts for the dissociation:

$$M\ H^+ = \left(\frac{0.250\ mol\ HCl}{L}\right)\left(\frac{1\ mol\ H^+}{1\ mol\ HCl}\right) = \textbf{0.250 M } \textbf{H}^+$$

$$M\ Cl^- = \left(\frac{0.250\ mol\ HCl}{L}\right)\left(\frac{1\ mol\ Cl^-}{1\ mol\ HCl}\right) = \textbf{0.250 M } \textbf{Cl}^-$$

(b) According to the solubility rules, NaF should be soluble (strong electrolyte); therefore, NaF completely dissociates to $Na^+(aq)$ and $F^-(aq)$. The mole ratio accounts for the dissociation:

$$M\ Na^+ = \left(\frac{0.500\ mol\ NaF}{L}\right)\left(\frac{1\ mol\ Na^+}{1\ mol\ NaF}\right) = \textbf{0.500 M } \textbf{Na}^+$$

$$M\ F^- = \left(\frac{0.500\ mol\ NaF}{L}\right)\left(\frac{1\ mol\ F^-}{1\ mol\ NaF}\right) = \textbf{0.500 M } \textbf{F}^-$$

(c) According to the solubility rules, $SrBr_2$ should be soluble (strong electrolyte); therefore, $SrBr_2$ completely dissociates to $Sr^{2+}(aq)$ and $Br^-(aq)$. The mole ratio accounts for the dissociation:

$$M\ Sr^{2+} = \left(\frac{0.125\ mol\ SrBr_2}{L}\right)\left(\frac{1\ mol\ Sr^{2+}}{1\ mol\ SrBr_2}\right) = \textbf{0.125 M } \textbf{Sr}^{2+}$$

$$M\ Br^- = \left(\frac{0.125\ mol\ SrBr_2}{L}\right)\left(\frac{2\ mol\ Br^-}{1\ mol\ SrBr_2}\right) = \textbf{0.250 M } \textbf{Br}^-$$

(d) This compound is a nonelectrolyte, so C_2H_5OH remains unchanged:

$$M\ C_2H_5OH = \textbf{5.00 M } \textbf{C}_2\textbf{H}_5\textbf{OH}$$

(e) According to the solubility rules, $CaCl_2$ should be soluble (strong electrolyte); therefore, $CaCl_2$ completely dissociates to $Ca^{2+}(aq)$ and $Cl^-(aq)$. The mole ratio accounts for the dissociation. The concentration of Ca^{2+} is

$$M\ Ca^{2+} = \left(\frac{\left(\frac{0.0500\ mol\ CaCl_2}{1,000\ mL}\right)(275\ mL)\left(\frac{1\ mol\ Ca^{2+}}{1\ mol\ CaCl_2}\right)}{(125+275)\ mL}\right)\left(\frac{m}{0.001}\right) = 0.034375 = \textbf{0.0344 M } \textbf{Ca}^{2+}$$

According to the solubility rules, KCl should be soluble (strong electrolyte); therefore, KCl completely dissociates to $K^+(aq)$ and $Cl^-(aq)$. The mole ratio accounts for the dissociation:

$$M\ K^+ = \left(\frac{\left(\frac{0.100\ mol\ KCl}{1,000\ mL}\right)(125\ mL)\left(\frac{1\ mol\ K^+}{1\ mol\ KCl}\right)}{(125+275)\ mL}\right)\left(\frac{m}{0.001}\right) = 0.03125 = \textbf{0.0312 M } \textbf{K}^+$$

The chloride ion comes from two sources. The concentration of Cl^- may be calculated like the concentrations of K^+ and Ca^{2+}, with the final answers summed (which is perfectly correct if you did it this way) or it may be determined as shown in the following: In the numerator, determine the moles of Cl^- from each of the electrolytes and sum the two values. Next, divide by the total volume of solution (convert to liters):

$$M\ Cl^- = \left(\frac{\left(\frac{0.100\ mol\ KCl}{1,000\ mL}\right)(125\ mL)\left(\frac{1\ mol\ Cl^-}{1\ mol\ KCl}\right) + \left(\frac{0.0500\ mol\ CaCl_2}{1,000\ mL}\right)(275\ mL)\left(\frac{2\ mol\ Cl^-}{1\ mol\ CaCl_2}\right)}{(125+275)\ mL}\right)$$

$$\times \left(\frac{m}{0.001}\right) = \textbf{0.100 M Cl}^-$$

4.109

(a) How many grams of solid could you produce by the following reaction if 100.00 mL of a 0.2000 M $CoCl_2$ solution was reacted with an excess of a 0.5000 M K_3AsO_4 solution?

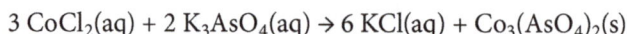

$$3\ CoCl_2(aq) + 2\ K_3AsO_4(aq) \rightarrow 6\ KCl(aq) + Co_3(AsO_4)_2(s)$$

(b) How many grams of solid could you produce by the above reaction if 100.00 mL of a 0.2000 M $CoCl_2$ solution was reacted with 25.00 mL of a 0.5000 M K_3AsO_4 solution?

Information

A balanced chemical equation; the questions of (a) how many grams of solid form if 100.00 mL of 0.2000 M $CoCl_2$ reacts with excess 0.5000 M K_3AsO_4, and (b) how many grams of solid form if 100.00 mL of 0.2000 M $CoCl_2$ reacts with 25.00 mL of 0.5000 M K_3AsO_4

Connections

Moles are the key, in addition to the definition of *molarity*

Solution

It will help to recopy the balanced chemical equation and place the given information directly below the appropriate substance in the equation:

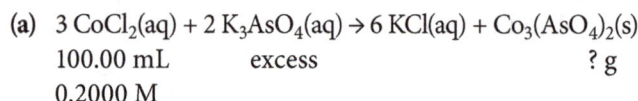

(a) $3\ CoCl_2(aq) + 2\ K_3AsO_4(aq) \rightarrow 6\ KCl(aq) + Co_3(AsO_4)_2(s)$
   100.00 mL   excess   ? g
   0.2000 M

The mass of precipitate comes from the molarity of the $CoCl_2$ solution times its volume, times a mole ratio, times the molar mass:

$$Mass\ Co_3(AsO_4)_2 = \left(\frac{0.2000\ mol\ CoCl_2}{1,000\ mL}\right)(100.00\ mL)\left(\frac{1\ mol\ Co_3(AsO_4)_2}{3\ mol\ CoCl_2}\right)\left(\frac{454.635\ g\ Co_3(AsO_4)_2}{1\ mol\ Co_3(AsO_4)_2}\right)$$

$$= 3.0309 = \textbf{3.031 g Co}_3\textbf{(AsO}_4\textbf{)}_2$$

(b) Recopy the chemical equation, and put the given information (including the question) below the appropriate substance:

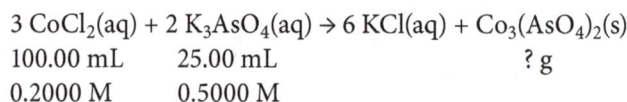

$$3\ CoCl_2(aq) + 2\ K_3AsO_4(aq) \rightarrow 6\ KCl(aq) + Co_3(AsO_4)_2(s)$$
   100.00 mL   25.00 mL   ? g
   0.2000 M   0.5000 M

The quantity of more than one reactant is given; therefore, we need to determine the limiting reactant before moving on. As seen in chapter 3, to determine the limiting reactant, the first step is to find the moles of each and then to divide the moles by the coefficient from the balanced chemical equation. The moles of each reactant are found from the molarity and the volume of the solution:

$$\text{Moles CoCl}_2 = \left(\frac{0.2000 \text{ mol CoCl}_2}{1,000 \text{ mL}}\right)(100.00 \text{ mL}) = \frac{0.02000 \text{ mol CoCl}_2}{3} = 0.0066667$$

$$\text{Moles K}_3\text{AsO}_4 = \left(\frac{0.5000 \text{ mol K}_3\text{AsO}_4}{1,000 \text{ mL}}\right)(25.00 \text{ mL}) = \frac{0.01250 \text{ mol K}_3\text{AsO}_4}{2} = 0.006250 \text{ LR}$$

We can now complete the problem, beginning with the moles of the limiting reactant. Take the moles of the LR times a mole ratio (from the balanced chemical equation), times the molar mass of the precipitate:

$$\text{Mass Co}_3(\text{AsO}_4)_2 = (0.01250 \text{ mol K}_3\text{AsO}_4)\left(\frac{1 \text{ mol Co}_3(\text{AsO}_4)_2}{2 \text{ mol K}_3\text{AsO}_4}\right)\left(\frac{454.635 \text{ g Co}_3(\text{AsO}_4)_2}{1 \text{ mol Co}_3(\text{AsO}_4)_2}\right)$$

$$= 2.84146875 = \textbf{2.841 g Co}_3(\textbf{AsO}_4)_2$$

4.112 How many milliliters of 0.1300 M $Na_2C_2O_4$ solution are required to react with 17.00 g of $FeCl_3$? The reaction is

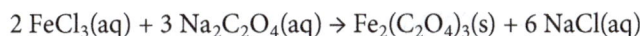

$$2 \text{ FeCl}_3(aq) + 3 \text{ Na}_2\text{C}_2\text{O}_4(aq) \rightarrow \text{Fe}_2(\text{C}_2\text{O}_4)_3(s) + 6 \text{ NaCl}(aq)$$

Information
A balanced chemical equation; the question of any how milliliters of 0.1300 M $Na_2C_2O_4$ will react with 17.00 g $FeCl_3$

Connections
Moles are the key, in addition to the definition of *molarity*

Solution
It will help to recopy the balanced chemical equation and place the given information directly below the appropriate substance in the equation:

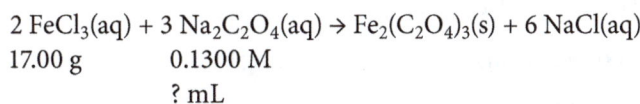

$$2 \text{ FeCl}_3(aq) + 3 \text{ Na}_2\text{C}_2\text{O}_4(aq) \rightarrow \text{Fe}_2(\text{C}_2\text{O}_4)_3(s) + 6 \text{ NaCl}(aq)$$
$$\phantom{2 \text{ FeCl}}17.00 \text{ g} \qquad\quad 0.1300 \text{ M}$$
$$\phantom{2 \text{ FeCl}_3(aq) + 3 \text{ Na}}\text{? mL}$$

Determine the moles of $FeCl_3$ from the mass (17.00 g $FeCl_3$) and its molar mass; then use a mole ratio; finish by multiplying by the inverse of the definition of *molarity*:

$$\text{Volume Na}_2\text{C}_2\text{O}_4 = (17.00 \text{ g FeCl}_3)\left(\frac{1 \text{ mol FeCl}_3}{162.204 \text{ g FeCl}_3}\right)\left(\frac{3 \text{ mol Na}_2\text{C}_2\text{O}_4}{2 \text{ mol FeCl}_3}\right)\left(\frac{1,000 \text{ mL}}{0.1300 \text{ mol Na}_2\text{C}_2\text{O}_4}\right)$$

$$= 1209.303 = \textbf{1209 mL Na}_2\textbf{C}_2\textbf{O}_4$$

4.115 Write balanced molecular and net ionic equations for each of the following combinations. (Assume that all reactions take place in aqueous solution.) **(a)** hydrochloric acid plus calcium acetate; **(b)** sulfuric acid plus ammonium thiocyanate; **(c)** sodium oxalate plus barium hydroxide; **(d)** barium hydroxide plus perchloric acid; **(e)** potassium phosphate plus strontium bromide

Information

The names of five pairs of aqueous reactants: **(a)** hydrochloric acid plus calcium acetate, **(b)** sulfuric acid plus ammonium thiocyanate, **(c)** sodium oxalate plus barium hydroxide, **(d)** barium hydroxide plus perchloric acid, **(e)** potassium phosphate plus strontium bromide; in each case, the instruction to write to write a molecular equation and to write a net ionic equation

Connections

How to predict the products and how to recognize strong electrolytes

Solution

Convert each molecular equation to a complete ionic equation before converting the equation to net ionic form. You may need the Nomenclature Resource to help with this.

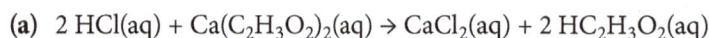

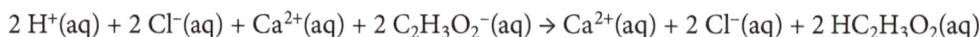

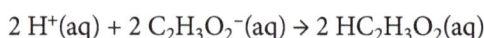

(a) $2\ HCl(aq) + Ca(C_2H_3O_2)_2(aq) \rightarrow CaCl_2(aq) + 2\ HC_2H_3O_2(aq)$

$2\ H^+(aq) + 2\ Cl^-(aq) + Ca^{2+}(aq) + 2\ C_2H_3O_2^-(aq) \rightarrow Ca^{2+}(aq) + 2\ Cl^-(aq) + 2\ HC_2H_3O_2(aq)$

$2\ H^+(aq) + 2\ C_2H_3O_2^-(aq) \rightarrow 2\ HC_2H_3O_2(aq)$

It is necessary to simplify this equation by dividing by 2.

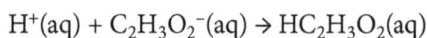

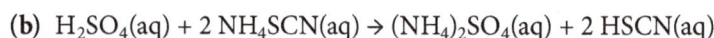

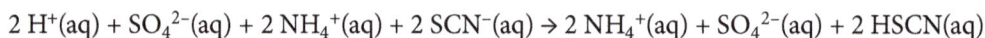

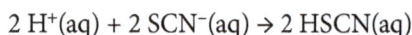

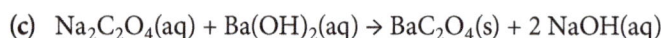

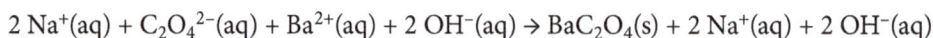

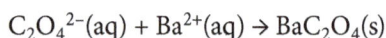

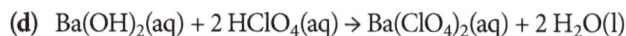

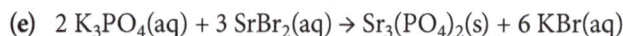

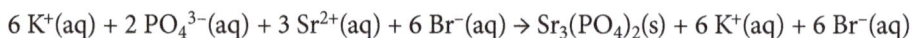

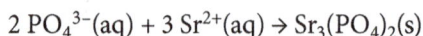

$H^+(aq) + C_2H_3O_2^-(aq) \rightarrow HC_2H_3O_2(aq)$

(b) $H_2SO_4(aq) + 2\ NH_4SCN(aq) \rightarrow (NH_4)_2SO_4(aq) + 2\ HSCN(aq)$

$2\ H^+(aq) + SO_4^{2-}(aq) + 2\ NH_4^+(aq) + 2\ SCN^-(aq) \rightarrow 2\ NH_4^+(aq) + SO_4^{2-}(aq) + 2\ HSCN(aq)$

$2\ H^+(aq) + 2\ SCN^-(aq) \rightarrow 2\ HSCN(aq)$

It is necessary to simplify this equation by dividing by 2.

$H^+(aq) + SCN^-(aq) \rightarrow HSCN(aq)$

(c) $Na_2C_2O_4(aq) + Ba(OH)_2(aq) \rightarrow BaC_2O_4(s) + 2\ NaOH(aq)$

$2\ Na^+(aq) + C_2O_4^{2-}(aq) + Ba^{2+}(aq) + 2\ OH^-(aq) \rightarrow BaC_2O_4(s) + 2\ Na^+(aq) + 2\ OH^-(aq)$

$C_2O_4^{2-}(aq) + Ba^{2+}(aq) \rightarrow BaC_2O_4(s)$

(d) $Ba(OH)_2(aq) + 2\ HClO_4(aq) \rightarrow Ba(ClO_4)_2(aq) + 2\ H_2O(l)$

$Ba^{2+}(aq) + 2\ OH^-(aq) + 2\ H^+(aq) + 2\ ClO_4^-(aq) \rightarrow Ba^{2+}(aq) + 2\ ClO_4^-(aq) + 2\ H_2O(l)$

$2\ OH^-(aq) + 2\ H^+(aq) \rightarrow 2\ H_2O(l)$

It is necessary to simplify this equation by dividing by 2.

$OH^-(aq) + H^+(aq) \rightarrow H_2O(l)$

(e) $2\ K_3PO_4(aq) + 3\ SrBr_2(aq) \rightarrow Sr_3(PO_4)_2(s) + 6\ KBr(aq)$

$6\ K^+(aq) + 2\ PO_4^{3-}(aq) + 3\ Sr^{2+}(aq) + 6\ Br^-(aq) \rightarrow Sr_3(PO_4)_2(s) + 6\ K^+(aq) + 6\ Br^-(aq)$

$2\ PO_4^{3-}(aq) + 3\ Sr^{2+}(aq) \rightarrow Sr_3(PO_4)_2(s)$

4.117 Seawater contains an average of 65 mg Br^- per kilogram of seawater. If the density of seawater is 1.025 g/mL, what is the molarity of bromide ion?

Information
Seawater contains 65 mg Br⁻ per kilogram and has a density of 1.025 g/mL; the question of what is the molarity of Br⁻

Connections
Moles are the key, in addition to the definition of *molarity*

Solution
Begin with the given concentration $\left(\frac{65 \text{ mg Br}^-}{\text{kg}}\right)$ (do not worry about converting the mg at this point); convert to moles of Br⁻ using the molar mass; use the kilo equality $\left(\frac{k}{1,000}\right)$ to convert kg to g; finally, use the density of the solution. After cancelling, the result is moles per liter, which is equal to molarity. (Note: The m from mg is cancelled by the m from mL.)

$$\left(\frac{65 \text{ mg Br}^-}{\text{kg}}\right)\left(\frac{1 \text{ mol Br}^-}{79.904 \text{ g Br}^-}\right)\left(\frac{k}{1,000}\right)\left(\frac{1.025 \text{ g}}{\text{mL}}\right) = 8.33813 \times 10^{-4} = \mathbf{8.3 \times 10^{-4} \text{ M}}$$

4.120 The following reaction generates HCl. **(a)** How many grams of HCl could we produce by reacting 50.00 mL of a 0.2000 M $ZnCl_2$ solution with an excess of a 0.3000 M H_2CrO_4 solution? **(b)** Titration of the generated HCl with 1.000 M NaOH required 13.70 mL of base. What was the percent yield of HCl?

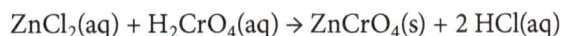

$$ZnCl_2(aq) + H_2CrO_4(aq) \rightarrow ZnCrO_4(s) + 2 \text{ HCl}(aq)$$

Information
The balanced chemical equation; the questions of **(a)** how many grams of HCl could form from 50.00 mL of 0.2000 M $ZnCl_2$ and excess 0.3000 M H_2CrO_4 and **(b)** what was the percent yield if the HCl reacted with 13.70 mL of 1.000 M NaOH

Connections
Moles are the key, in addition to the definition of *molarity*

Solution
It will help to recopy the balanced chemical equation and place the given information directly below the appropriate substance in the equation:

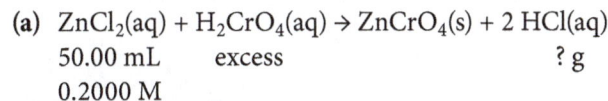

(a) $ZnCl_2(aq) + H_2CrO_4(aq) \rightarrow ZnCrO_4(s) + 2 \text{ HCl}(aq)$
    50.00 mL   excess   ? g
    0.2000 M

We can determine the moles of $ZnCl_2$ from the molarity and volume of the solution, then use a mole ratio (from the balanced chemical equation) and complete the calculation with the molar mass of HCl (this is the theoretical (calculated) yield):

$$\text{Mass HCl} = \left(\frac{0.2000 \text{ mol ZnCl}_2}{1,000 \text{ mL}}\right)(50.00 \text{ mL})\left(\frac{2 \text{ mol HCl}}{1 \text{ mol ZnCl}_2}\right)\left(\frac{36.461 \text{ g HCl}}{1 \text{ mol HCl}}\right) = 0.72922$$

$$= \mathbf{0.7292 \text{ g HCl}}$$

(b) $NaOH(aq) + HCl(aq) \rightarrow NaCl(aq) + H_2O(l)$
13.70 mL
1.000 M

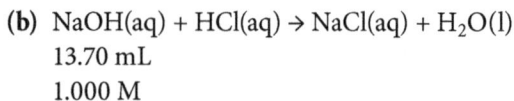

The moles of the base, NaOH, comes from the molarity times the volume of the NaOH solution. Multiplying this by the mole ratio gives the moles of acid, HCl. Multiplying the moles of acid by its molar mass gives the mass of HCl (this is the actual yield):

$$\text{Mass HCl} = \left(\frac{1.000 \text{ mol NaOH}}{1,000 \text{ mL}}\right)(13.70 \text{ mL})\left(\frac{1 \text{ mol HCl}}{1 \text{ mol NaOH}}\right)\left(\frac{36.461 \text{ g HCl}}{1 \text{ mol HCl}}\right) = 0.4995157$$

$$= 0.4995 \text{ g HCl}$$

We need to enter the appropriate values into the definition of *percent yield*. The theoretical yield is from part **(a)**, and the actual yield is from part (b):

$$\text{Percent yield} = \frac{\text{Actual yield}}{\text{Theoretical yield}} \times 100\% = \frac{0.4995157 \text{ g HCl}}{0.72922 \text{ g HCl}} \times 100\% = \textbf{68.50\%}$$

CHAPTER 5

Gases

The successful completion of these problems requires the following ten (10) items.

1. **All temperatures used in any calculation in this chapter <u>must</u> be in Kelvin units.** There are no exceptions. If a Celsius temperature is present, convert it to K as soon as reasonably possible (K = °C + 273.15). It may be necessary to reverse this conversion later in the problem.

2. The basic information, including the definitions and discussions in chapter 5, is necessary.

3. Four core equations are needed to solve the problems in this chapter:

   $$PV = nRT$$

   $$\frac{P_1 V_1}{n_1 T_1} = \frac{P_2 V_2}{n_2 T_2}$$

   $$\frac{Rate_A}{Rate_B} = \sqrt{\frac{MM_B}{MM_A}}$$

   $$P_{total} = P_a + P_b + P_c + \ldots$$

4. Another useful equation is the van der Waals equation:

   $$\left(P + \frac{an^2}{V^2} \right)(V - nb) = nRT$$

5. The following definitions are also useful (treat them as definitions and not as equations):

   $$P = \frac{F}{A} \qquad X_A = \frac{n_A}{n_{Total}} \qquad X_A = \frac{P_A}{P_{Total}} \qquad \text{(for gases only)}$$

6. The following constant is necessary in many cases (it will save you time if you learn it and not have to look it up every time you need it):

$$R = \frac{0.08206 \text{ L} \cdot \text{atm}}{\text{mol} \cdot \text{K}}$$

7. Some pressure conversions—such as 1 atm = 760 torr and mmHg = torr—are used very often.

8. The information in the tables for the vapor pressure of water and the van der Waals constants are necessary in some problems.

9. The information contained in the periodic table and in all previous chapters of this textbook are important references. This includes such information as how to relate mass and molar mass to moles, and conversions such as 1 in = 2.54 cm.

10. Moles continue to be extremely important. In this chapter, moles are usually indicated by the variable n.

Example Problems From the Text

Example Problem 5.1

During the early 1900s, Alfred Stock determined that magnesium boride, Mg_3B_2, would react with phosphoric acid, H_3PO_4, to give a variety of gaseous boron hydrides. In one experiment, 0.500 moles of B_2H_6, 0.221 moles of B_5H_9, and 0.158 moles of B_6H_{10} formed. If the total pressure of these three gases was 775 torr, what was the partial pressure of each of the three gases expressed in torr?

Information

Collect and label the information from the problem:

B_2H_6 = 0.500 mole	P = ?
B_5H_9 = 0.221 mole	P = ?
B_6H_{10} = 0.158 mole	P = ?
	P_{total} = 775 torr

Connections

$$P_A = X_A P_{total}; \quad X_A = \frac{n_A}{n_{total}}$$

Solution

To find the partial pressure of each of the gases, we need to find the mole fraction of each gas. The *mole fraction* is, by definition, the moles of a component divided by the total moles present. The total moles are

$$n_{total} = (0.500 + 0.221 + 0.158) \text{ moles} = 0.879 \text{ moles}$$

The mole fraction for each component is

$$X_{B_2H_6} = \frac{n_{B_2H_6}}{n_{total}} = \frac{0.100969 \text{ mol}}{0.879 \text{ mol}} = 0.5688328 \quad \text{(unrounded)}$$

$$X_{B_5H_9} = \frac{n_{B_5H_9}}{n_{total}} = \frac{0.100969 \text{ mol}}{0.879 \text{ mol}} = 0.251422 \quad \text{(unrounded)}$$

$$X_{B_6H_{10}} = \frac{n_{B_6H_{10}}}{n_{total}} = \frac{0.100969 \text{ mol}}{0.879 \text{ mol}} = 0.179750 \quad \text{(unrounded)}$$

(A temporary check to see if these calculations are reasonable is to sum the values for the mole fractions. The total of all the fractions should be 1.)

To determine the partial pressure of each of the gases, multiply the mole fraction of the gas by the total pressure:

$$P_{B_2H_6} = (0.568828)\,(775\text{ torr}) = 440.8417 = \textbf{441 torr}$$
$$P_{B_5H_9} = (0.251422)\,(775\text{ torr}) = 194.85205 = \textbf{195 torr}$$
$$P_{B_6H_{10}} = (0.179750)\,(775\text{ torr}) = 139.30625 = \textbf{139 torr}$$

Reality Check

The units and the number of significant figures are correct. The final check is that the total of the three partial pressures equals the total pressure of 775 torr.

Follow-Up Problem 5.1a

A gas mixture contains 0.175 moles of nitrogen, 0.455 moles of hydrogen, and 0.110 moles of ammonia. The total pressure of the mixture is 0.785 atm. Determine the partial pressure of each gas expressed in atmospheres.

Information

The moles of each gas (0.175 moles of nitrogen, 0.455 moles of hydrogen, and 0.110 moles of ammonia); the total pressure (0.785 atm); the questions of the pressure of N_2, pressure of hydrogen, and pressure of ammonia

Connections

$$X_A = \frac{n_A}{n_{Total}}; X_A = \frac{P_A}{P_{total}}$$

Solution

The total moles (n_{Total}) are (0.175 + 0.455 + 0.110) moles = 0.740 moles
Substituting into the definition gives the following mole fractions:

$$X_{N_2} = \frac{n_{N_2}}{n_{total}} = \frac{0.175\text{ mol}}{0.740\text{ mol}} = 0.236486 \qquad \text{(unrounded)}$$

$$X_{H_2} = \frac{n_{H_2}}{n_{total}} = \frac{0.455\text{ mol}}{0.740\text{ mol}} = 0.61486 \qquad \text{(unrounded)}$$

$$X_{NH_3} = \frac{n_{NH_3}}{n_{total}} = \frac{0.110\text{ mol}}{0.740\text{ mol}} = 0.1486486 \qquad \text{(unrounded)}$$

(An optional check for consistency is to add the mole fractions (the total must be 1), 0.236486 + 0.61486 + 0.1486486 = 0.999995.)

Rearranging the alternate mole fraction definition gives $P_A = X_A P_{total}$
Using the total pressures and the pressure definition of mole fraction gives

$$P_{N_2} = (0.23686)\,(0.785\text{ atm}) = 0.185935 \qquad = \textbf{0.186 atm } N_2$$
$$P_{H_2} = (0.61486)\,(0.785\text{ atm}) = 0.482665 \qquad = \textbf{0.483 atm } H_2$$
$$P_{NH_3} = (0.1486486)\,(0.785\text{ atm}) = 0.116689 \qquad = \textbf{0.117 atm } NH_3$$

Reality Check

As a check, the total pressure should be the sum of the partial pressures: (0.186 + 0.483 + 0.117) atm = 0.786 atm (0.785 atm if using the unrounded values). The units and the number of significant figures are correct.

Follow-Up Problem 5.1b

A gas mixture contains 45.2 g of hydrogen chloride, 75.3 g of hydrogen bromide, and 116 g of hydrogen iodide. The total pressure of the mixture is 555 mmHg. Determine the partial pressure of each of the gases in millimeters of mercury.

Information

The mass of each gas (45.2 grams of hydrogen chloride, 75.3 grams of hydrogen bromide, and 116 grams of hydrogen iodide), the total pressure (555 mmHg); the questions of the pressure hydrogen chloride, pressure of hydrogen bromide, and pressure of hydrogen iodide

Connections

$$X_A = \frac{n_A}{n_{total}}; X_A = \frac{P_A}{P_{total}}$$

Solution

To determine the partial pressure of each component, we need to know the mole fraction of each. To determine the mole fraction, we must start by determining the moles of each compound, using the grams given and the molar mass of each substance:

$$\text{Moles HCl} = (45.2 \text{ g HCl})\left(\frac{1 \text{ mol HCl}}{36.461 \text{ g HCl}}\right) = 1.23968 \text{ mol HCl} \qquad \text{(unrounded)}$$

$$\text{Moles HBr} = (75.3 \text{ g HBr})\left(\frac{1 \text{ mol HBr}}{80.912 \text{ g HBr}}\right) = 0.93064 \text{ mol HBr} \qquad \text{(unrounded)}$$

$$\text{Moles HI} = (116 \text{ g HI})\left(\frac{1 \text{ mol HI}}{127.912 \text{ g HI}}\right) = 0.90687 \text{ mol HI} \qquad \text{(unrounded)}$$

The next step is to determine the total moles (n_{total}) by adding the individual moles:

$$\text{Total moles} = n_{total} = (1.23968 + 0.93064 + 0.90687) \text{ mol} = 3.07719 \text{ mol} \qquad \text{(unrounded)}$$

It is now possible to combine the individual moles and the total moles with the definition of *mole fraction* $(X_A = \frac{n_A}{n_{total}})$ to determine the mole fractions of each compound:

$$X_{HCl} = \frac{n_A}{n_{total}} = \frac{1.23968 \text{ mol}}{3.07719 \text{ mol}} = 0.40286 \qquad \text{(unrounded)}$$

$$X_{HBr} = \frac{n_A}{n_{total}} = \frac{0.93064 \text{ mol}}{3.07719 \text{ mol}} = 0.30243 \qquad \text{(unrounded)}$$

$$X_{HI} = \frac{n_A}{n_{total}} = \frac{0.90687 \text{ mol}}{3.07719 \text{ mol}} = 0.29471 \qquad \text{(unrounded)}$$

From the alternate definition of *mole fraction*, $(X_A = \frac{P_A}{P_{total}})$, the mole fractions, and the total pressure, it is possible to determine the separate partial pressures. To begin, we need to rewrite the alternate definition of *mole fraction* as

$$P_A = X_A P_{total}$$

Using the total pressure and the individual mole fractions gives

$$P_{HCl} = X_{HCl}\, P_{total} = (0.40286)\,(555\text{ mmHg}) = 223.587 = \textbf{224 mmHg HCl}$$

$$P_{HBr} = X_{HBr}\, P_{total} = (0.30243)\,(555\text{ mmHg}) = 167.849 = \textbf{168 mmHg HBr}$$

$$P_{HI} = X_{HI}\, P_{total} = (0.29471)\,(555\text{ mmHg}) = 163.564 = \textbf{164 mmHg HI}$$

Reality Check

The total of the mole fractions is 1, and the total of the partial pressures is the total pressure (555 mmHg, using the unrounded values). The units and the number of significant figures are correct.

Example Problem 5.2

Determine the pressure in atmospheres of a sample of gas containing 2.50 moles of gas at 27°C in a 10.0 L container.

Information

The most important first step in a gas law problem is to extract all the numbers, including their units, and the actual question (Be very careful to label everything correctly.):

$P = ?$ atm
$V = 10.0$ L
$n = 2.50$ moles
$T = 27°C = 300.$ K   (Recall from chapter 1 that the decimal points means there are three significant figures present.)

The pressure, P, is what we are seeking—therefore, the "?" The temperature is in degrees Celsius, which is not acceptable in any gas law calculation: thus, it immediately becomes a kelvin unit (°C + 273).

Connections

Since there is only one value for each of the variable types, it seems logical that the ideal gas equation is necessary to solve this problem. Rearranging $PV = nRT$ gives $P = \dfrac{nRT}{V}$.

Solution

Inserting the given values into the ideal gas equation gives

$$P = \frac{(2.50\ \cancel{mol})\left(\dfrac{0.08206\ \cancel{L}\bullet atm}{\cancel{mol}\bullet\cancel{K}}\right)(300.\ \cancel{K})}{(10.0\ \cancel{L})} = 6.1545 = \textbf{6.15 atm}$$

Reality Check

The units (pressure) and the number of significant figures are correct. We can round the values in the equation and determine an approximate answer:

$$P = \frac{(2.50)(0.1)(300.)}{(10.0)} = (0.250 \times 30) = 7.5$$

(This, as expected, is high, because 0.08206 was rounded up.) Ideally, you should round until you can approximate the answer in your head.

Follow-Up Problem 5.2a

Determine the pressure in atmospheres of a sample of gas containing 5.50 moles of helium gas at 37°C in a 15.0-L container.

Information

The number of moles (5.50 moles); the temperature (37°C); the volume (15.0 L); the question of how many atmospheres of pressure

Connections

$PV = nRT$

Solution

Collect and label the information from the problem:

$P = ?$ atm
$V = 15.0$ L
$n = 5.50$ mol
$T = 37°C = 310.$ K
$R = \dfrac{0.08206 \text{ L} \bullet \text{atm}}{\text{mol} \bullet \text{K}}$

Rearrange the ideal gas equation to $P = \dfrac{nRT}{V}$

Enter the appropriate values into the equation and cancel:

$$P = \frac{(5.50 \text{ mol})\left(\dfrac{0.08206 \text{ L} \bullet \text{atm}}{\text{mol} \bullet \text{K}}\right)(310.\text{ K})}{(15.0 \text{ L})} = 9.327487 = \mathbf{9.33 \text{ atm}}$$

Reality Check

The units and the number of significant figures are correct. It is possible to approximate this answer by rounding the values as $P = \dfrac{(5.50)(0.1)(300)}{(15.0)} = (0.550 \times 20)$. Ideally, you should round until you can approximate the answer in your head.

Follow-Up Problem 5.2b

Determine the pressure in atmospheres of a sample of gas containing 2.75 moles of gas at 17°C in a 1.50×10^3 mL container.

Information

The number of moles (2.75 moles); the temperature (17°C); the volume (1.50×10^3 mL); the question of how many atmospheres of pressure

Connections

$PV = nRT$

Solution

Collect and label the information from the problem:

$P = ?$ atm

$V = 1.50 \times 10^3$ mL

$n = 2.75$ mol

$T = 17°C = 290.$ K

$R = \dfrac{0.08206 \text{ L} \bullet \text{atm}}{\text{mol} \bullet \text{K}}$

Rearrange the ideal gas equation to $P = \dfrac{nRT}{V}$

Enter the appropriate values into the equation and cancel:

$$P = \frac{(2.75 \text{ mol})\left(\dfrac{0.08206 \text{ L} \bullet \text{atm}}{\text{mol} \bullet \text{K}}\right)(290. \text{ K})}{(1.50 \times 10^3 \text{ mL})}$$

The need for an additional conversion is now apparent. The *milli-* conversion ($m = 0.001 = 10^{-3}$) is appropriate:

$$P = \frac{(2.75 \text{ mol})\left(\dfrac{0.08206 \text{ L} \bullet \text{atm}}{\text{mol} \bullet \text{K}}\right)(290. \text{ K})}{(1.50 \times 10^3 \text{ mL})}\left(\frac{m}{0.001}\right) = 43.62857 = \textbf{43.6 atm}$$

Reality Check

The units and the number of significant figures are correct. It is possible to approximate this answer by rounding the values as $P = \dfrac{(2.75)(0.10)(300)}{(1.50)} = \dfrac{(0.275)(300)}{(1.50)}$.

Example Problem 5.3

Determine the volume in liters of a sample of gas containing 2.50 moles of gas at 27°C at 745 torr.

Information

The most important first step in a gas law problem is to extract all the numbers, including their units, and the actual question (Be very careful to label everything correctly.):

$P = 745$ torr
$V = ?$ L
$n = 2.50$ moles
$T = 27°C = 300.$ K

The volume, V, is what we are seeking—therefore, the "?" The temperature was in degrees Celsius, which is not acceptable in any gas law calculation; therefore, it immediately becomes a kelvin unit (°C + 273).

Connections

Since there is only one value for each of the variables, it seems reasonable that the ideal gas equation is necessary to solve this problem. Rearranging $PV = nRT$ gives $V = \dfrac{nRT}{P}$.

Solution

Enter the appropriate values into the equation and cancel:

$$V = \frac{(2.50 \text{ mol})\left(\dfrac{0.08206 \text{ L} \bullet \text{atm}}{\text{mol} \bullet \text{K}}\right)(300. \text{ K})}{745 \text{ torr}}$$

The need for an additional conversion is now apparent. Adding the appropriate pressure conversion (1 atm = 760 torr) gives this:

$$V = \frac{(2.50 \text{ mol})\left(\dfrac{0.08206 \text{ L} \cdot \text{atm}}{\text{mol} \cdot \text{K}}\right)(300. \text{K})}{745 \text{ torr}}\left(\frac{760 \text{ torr}}{1 \text{ atm}}\right) = 62.784 = \mathbf{62.8 \ L}$$

Reality Check

The units (volume) and the number of significant figures are correct. The value may be estimated by rounding the values. In this case, the pressure conversion (760/745) ≈ 1. Ideally, you should round until you can approximate the answer in your head.

Follow-Up Problem 5.3a

Determine the volume in liters of a sample of gas containing 7.50 moles of gas at 127°C at 74.5 torr.

Information

The number of moles (7.50 moles); the temperature (127°C); the pressure (74.5 torr); the question of how many liters volume

Connections

$PV = nRT$

Solution

Collect and label the information from the problem:

$P = 74.5$ torr
$V = ?$ L
$n = 7.50$ mol
$T = 127°C = 400. \text{K}$
$R = \dfrac{0.08206 \text{ L} \cdot \text{atm}}{\text{mol} \cdot \text{K}}$

Rearrange the ideal gas equation to $V = \dfrac{nRT}{P}$

Enter the appropriate values into the equation and cancel:

$$V = \frac{(7.50 \text{ mol})\left(\dfrac{0.08206 \text{ L} \cdot \text{atm}}{\text{mol} \cdot \text{K}}\right)(400. \text{K})}{74.5 \text{ torr}}$$

The necessity of an additional conversion is now apparent. Adding the appropriate pressure conversion (1 atm = 760 torr) gives

$$V = \frac{(7.50 \text{ mol})\left(\dfrac{0.08206 \text{ L} \cdot \text{atm}}{\text{mol} \cdot \text{K}}\right)(400. \text{K})}{74.5 \text{ torr}}\left(\frac{760 \text{ torr}}{1 \text{ atm}}\right) = 2511.366 = \mathbf{2.51 \times 10^3 \ L}$$

Reality Check

The units and the number of significant figures are correct. The value may be estimated by rounding the values. In this case, the pressure conversion is (760/74.5) ≈ 10.

Follow-Up Problem 5.3b

Determine the volume, in milliliters, of a sample of gas containing 6.50 moles of gas at 17°C at 645 torr.

Information

The number of moles (6.50 moles); the temperature (17°C); the pressure (645 torr); the question (how many milliliters volume)

Connections

$PV = nRT$

Solution

Collect and label the information from the problem:

$P = 645$ torr
$V = ?$ mL
$n = 6.50$ mol
$T = 17°C = 290.$ K
$R = \dfrac{0.08206 \text{ L} \cdot \text{atm}}{\text{mol} \cdot \text{K}}$

Rearrange the ideal gas equation to $V = \dfrac{nRT}{P}$

Enter the appropriate values into the equation and cancel:

$$V = \frac{(6.50 \text{ mol})\left(\dfrac{0.08206 \text{ L} \cdot \text{atm}}{\text{mol} \cdot \text{K}}\right)(290. \text{ K})}{645 \text{ torr}}$$

The necessity of an additional conversion is now apparent. The *milli-* conversion ($m = 0.001 = 10^{-3}$) is appropriate:

$$V = \frac{(6.50 \text{ mol})\left(\dfrac{0.08206 \text{ L} \cdot \text{atm}}{\text{mol} \cdot \text{K}}\right)(290. \text{ K})}{645 \text{ torr}}\left(\frac{m}{0.001}\right)$$

Adding the appropriate pressure conversion (1 atm = 760 torr) gives

$$V = \frac{(6.50 \text{ mol})\left(\dfrac{0.08206 \text{ L} \cdot \text{atm}}{\text{mol} \cdot \text{K}}\right)(290. \text{ K})}{645 \text{ torr}}\left(\frac{m}{0.001}\right)\left(\frac{760 \text{ torr}}{1 \text{ atm}}\right) = 182262.257 = \mathbf{1.82 \times 10^5 \text{ mL}}$$

Reality Check

The units and the number of significant figures are correct. The value may be estimated by rounding the values. In this case, it is possible to assume $(6.50/645) \approx 0.01$.

Example Problem 5.4

Determine the moles of gas present in a sample of gas at 27°C and a pressure of 655 mmHg in a container with a volume of 755 mL.

Information

The most important first step in a gas law problem is to extract all the numbers, including their units, and the actual question (Be very careful to label everything correctly.):

$P = 655$ mmHg
$V = 755$ mL
$n = ?$ moles
$T = 27°C = 300.$ K

The moles, n, is what we are seeking—therefore, the "?" The temperature is in degrees Celsius, which is not acceptable in any gas law calculation; therefore, it immediately needs to become a kelvin unit (°C + 273).

Connections

Having only one value for each of the variable types is again a strong indication that the ideal gas equation is needed in order to solve this problem. Rearranging $PV = nRT$ gives $n = \dfrac{PV}{RT}$.

Solution

Enter the appropriate values into the equation and cancel:

$$n = \frac{(655 \text{ mmHg})(755 \text{ m\cancel{L}})}{\left(\dfrac{0.08206 \text{ \cancel{L}} \cdot \text{atm}}{\text{mol} \cdot \text{\cancel{K}}}\right)(300.\text{ \cancel{K}})}$$

The need for additional conversions is now apparent. The *milli-* conversion ($m = 0.001 = 10^{-3}$) is appropriate:

$$n = \frac{(655 \text{ mmHg})(755 \text{ \cancel{mL}})}{\left(\dfrac{0.08206 \text{ \cancel{L}} \cdot \text{atm}}{\text{mol} \cdot \text{\cancel{K}}}\right)(300.\text{ \cancel{K}})}\left(\frac{0.001}{\text{\cancel{m}}}\right)$$

Adding the appropriate pressure conversion (1 atm = 760 mmHg) gives us this:

$$n = \frac{(655 \text{ \cancel{mmHg}})(755 \text{ \cancel{mL}})}{\left(\dfrac{0.08206 \text{ \cancel{L}} \cdot \text{\cancel{atm}}}{\text{mol} \cdot \text{\cancel{K}}}\right)(300.\text{ \cancel{K}})}\left(\frac{0.001}{\text{\cancel{m}}}\right)\left(\frac{1 \text{ \cancel{atm}}}{760 \text{ \cancel{mmHg}}}\right) = 0.0264315 = \textbf{0.0264 mol}$$

Reality Check

The units (moles) and the number of significant figures are correct. As always, it is possible to simplify the final calculation and estimate the answer:

$$n = \frac{(655)(755)}{(0.10)(300)}\left(\frac{0.001}{1}\right)\left(\frac{1}{760}\right) = \frac{(655)}{(300)}\left(\frac{0.01}{1}\right) = \frac{(600)}{(300)}\left(\frac{0.01}{1}\right) = 0.02$$

Ideally, you should round until you can approximate the answer in your head.

Follow-Up Problem 5.4a

Determine the moles of gas present in a sample of gas at 37.0°C and a pressure of 635 mmHg in a container with a volume of 1,755 mL.

Information

The temperature (37.0°C); the pressure (635 mmHg); the volume (1755 mL); the question of how many moles

Connections

$PV = nRT$

Solution

Collect and label the information from the problem:

$P = 635 \text{ mmHg}$

$V = 1755 \text{ mL}$

$n = \text{? mol}$

$T = 37.0°C = 310.2$ K

$$R = \frac{0.08206 \text{ L} \cdot \text{atm}}{\text{mol} \cdot \text{K}}$$

Rearrange the ideal gas equation to $n = \dfrac{PV}{RT}$

Enter the appropriate values into the equation and cancel:

$$n = \frac{(635 \text{ mmHg})(1755 \text{ mL})}{\left(\dfrac{0.08206 \text{ L} \cdot \text{atm}}{\text{mol} \cdot \text{K}}\right)(310.2 \text{ K})}$$

The necessity of additional conversions is now apparent. The *milli-* conversion ($m = 0.001 = 10^{-3}$) is appropriate:

$$n = \frac{(635 \text{ mmHg})(1755 \text{ mL})}{\left(\dfrac{0.08206 \text{ L} \cdot \text{atm}}{\text{mol} \cdot \text{K}}\right)(310.2 \text{ K})}\left(\frac{0.001}{m}\right)$$

Adding the appropriate pressure conversion (1 atm = 760 mmHg) gives

$$n = \frac{(635 \text{ mmHg})(1755 \text{ mL})}{\left(\dfrac{0.08206 \text{ L} \cdot \text{atm}}{\text{mol} \cdot \text{K}}\right)(310.2 \text{ K})}\left(\frac{0.001}{m}\right)\left(\frac{1 \text{ atm}}{760 \text{ mmHg}}\right) = 0.057605 = \textbf{0.0576 mol}$$

Reality Check

The units and the number of significant figures are correct. As always, it is possible to simplify the final calculation and estimate the answer.

Follow-Up Problem 5.4b

Determine the moles of gas present in a sample of gas at 47.0°C and a pressure of 825 mmHg in a container with a volume of 1.75 L.

Information

The temperature (47.0°C); the pressure (855 mmHg); the volume (1.75 L); the question of how many moles

Connections

$PV = nRT$

Solution

Collect and label the information from the problem:

$P = 855$ mmHg
$V = 1.75$ L
$n = ?$ mol
$T = 47°C = 320.2$ K
$$R = \frac{0.08206 \text{ L} \cdot \text{atm}}{\text{mol} \cdot \text{K}}$$

Rearrange the ideal gas equation to $n = \dfrac{PV}{RT}$

Enter the appropriate values into the equation and cancel:

$$n = \frac{(855 \text{ mmHg})(1.75 \cancel{L})}{\left(\dfrac{0.08206\ \cancel{L} \cdot \text{atm}}{\text{mol} \cdot \cancel{K}}\right)(320.2\ \cancel{K})}$$

The necessity of an additional conversion is now apparent. Adding the appropriate pressure conversion (1 atm = 760 mmHg) gives

$$n = \frac{(855\ \cancel{\text{mmHg}})(1.75\ \cancel{L})}{\left(\dfrac{0.08206\ \cancel{L} \cdot \cancel{\text{atm}}}{\text{mol} \cdot \cancel{K}}\right)(320.2\ \cancel{K})}\left(\frac{1\ \cancel{\text{atm}}}{760\ \cancel{\text{mmHg}}}\right) = 0.07492689 = \mathbf{0.0749\ mol}$$

Reality Check

The units and the number of significant figures are correct. As always, it is possible to simplify the final calculation and estimate the answer.

Example Problem 5.5

Determine the temperature, in °C, of the gas present in 2.525 grams of oxygen gas, O_2, at a pressure of 1,075 mmHg in a container with a volume of 755.5 mL.

Information

The most important first step in a gas law problem is to extract all the numbers, including their units, along with the actual question (Be very careful to label everything correctly.):

$P = 1075$ mmHg
$V = 755.5$ mL
Mass $= 2.525$ g O_2
$T = ?°C$

The temperature, T, is what we are seeking—therefore, the "?"

Connections

Since there is only one value for each of the variable types, the ideal gas equation is needed to solve this problem. Rearranging $PV = nRT$ gives $T = \dfrac{PV}{nR}$.

Solution

It is necessary to begin by determining the moles of oxygen gas. This requires the mass given and the molar mass of oxygen (32.00 g/mol):

$$\text{Moles } O_2 = 2.525\ \cancel{\text{g } O_2}\left(\frac{1 \text{ mol } O_2}{32.00\ \cancel{\text{g } O_2}}\right)$$

Enter the appropriate values into the equation and cancel:

$$T = \frac{(1075 \text{ mmHg})(755.5\ \cancel{\text{mL}})}{\left(2.525\ \cancel{\text{g } O_2}\left(\dfrac{1\ \cancel{\text{mol } O_2}}{32.00\ \cancel{\text{g } O_2}}\right)\right)\left(\dfrac{0.08206\ \cancel{L} \cdot \text{atm}}{\cancel{\text{mol}} \cdot \text{K}}\right)}$$

The need for an additional conversion is now apparent. The *milli-* conversion ($m = 0.001 = 10^{-3}$) is appropriate:

$$T = \frac{(1075 \text{ mmHg})(755.5\ \cancel{\text{mL}})}{\left(2.525\ \cancel{\text{g } O_2}\left(\dfrac{1\ \cancel{\text{mol } O_2}}{32.00\ \cancel{\text{g } O_2}}\right)\right)\left(\dfrac{0.08206\ \cancel{L} \cdot \text{atm}}{\cancel{\text{mol}} \cdot \text{K}}\right)}\left(\frac{0.001}{\cancel{m}}\right)$$

Adding the appropriate pressure conversion (1 atm = 760 mmHg) gives this:

$$T = \frac{(1075 \ \cancel{mmHg})(755.5 \ \cancel{mL})}{\left(2.525 \ \cancel{g \, O_2} \left[\dfrac{1 \ \cancel{mol \, O_2}}{32.00 \ \cancel{g \, O_2}}\right]\right)\left(\dfrac{0.08206 \ \cancel{L} \bullet \cancel{atm}}{\cancel{mol} \bullet K}\right)} \left(\frac{0.001}{\cancel{m}}\right)\left|\frac{1 \ \cancel{atm}}{760 \ \cancel{mmHg}}\right)$$

= 165.0389 K   (unrounded)

Finally, we need to convert K to °C:

$$T = (165.0389 - 273.15)°C = -108.1111 = \textbf{-108.1°C}$$

Reality Check

The units (°C) and the number of significant figures are correct. As always, it is possible to simplify the final calculation and estimate the answer. Ideally, you should round until you can approximate the answer in your head.

Follow-Up Problem 5.5a

Determine the temperature, in °C, of the gas present in 2.375 grams of chlorine gas, Cl_2, at a pressure of 975.7 mmHg in a container with a volume of 855.5 mL.

Information

The mass of chlorine (2.375 g); the pressure (975.7 mmHg); the volume (855.5 mL); the question of what is the temperature in °C

Connections

$PV = nRT$

Solution

Collect and label the information from the problem:

Mass = 2.375 g Cl_2
P = 975.7 mmHg
V = 855.5 mL
T = ? °C
$R = \dfrac{0.08206 \ L \bullet atm}{mol \bullet K}$

Rearrange the ideal gas equation to $T = \dfrac{PV}{nR}$

To use this equation, it is necessary to determine the moles of chlorine. To determine this value, we need the mass of chlorine (2.375 g) and the molar mass of chlorine (70.906 g/mol):

$$\text{Moles chlorine} = 2.375 \ \cancel{g \, Cl_2}\left(\frac{1 \ mol \ Cl_2}{70.906 \ \cancel{g \, Cl_2}}\right)$$

Enter the appropriate values into the equation and cancel:

$$T = \frac{(975.7 \ mmHg)(855.5 \ \cancel{mL})}{\left(2.375 \ \cancel{g \, Cl_2}\left[\dfrac{1 \ \cancel{mol \, Cl_2}}{70.906 \ \cancel{g \, Cl_2}}\right]\right)\left(\dfrac{0.08206 \ \cancel{L} \bullet atm}{\cancel{mol} \bullet K}\right)}$$

The need for an additional conversion is now apparent. The *milli-* conversion ($m = 0.001 = 10^{-3}$) is appropriate:

$$T = \frac{(975.7 \text{ mmHg})(855.5 \text{ mL})}{\left(2.375 \text{ g Cl}_2 \left(\dfrac{1 \text{ mol Cl}_2}{70.906 \text{ g Cl}_2}\right)\right)\left(\dfrac{0.08206 \text{ L} \cdot \text{atm}}{\text{mol} \cdot \text{K}}\right)}\left(\dfrac{0.001}{m}\right)$$

Adding the appropriate pressure conversion (1 atm = 760 mmHg) gives

$$T = \frac{(975.7 \text{ mmHg})(855.5 \text{ mL})}{\left(2.375 \text{ g Cl}_2 \left(\dfrac{1 \text{ mol Cl}_2}{70.906 \text{ g Cl}_2}\right)\right)\left(\dfrac{0.08206 \text{ L} \cdot \text{atm}}{\text{mol} \cdot \text{K}}\right)}\left(\dfrac{0.001}{m}\right)\left(\dfrac{1 \text{ atm}}{760 \text{ mmHg}}\right)$$

$$= 399.5868 \text{ K} \quad \text{(unrounded)}$$

It is necessary to convert K to °C:

$$T = (399.586 - 273.15)°C = 126.436 = \mathbf{126.4°C}$$

Reality Check

The units and the number of significant figures are correct. As always, it is possible to simplify the final calculation and estimate the answer.

Follow-Up Problem 5.5b

Determine the temperature in kelvins of the gas present in 4.375 grams of iodine vapor at a pressure of 175.7 mmHg in a container with a volume of 8555 mL.

Information

The mass of iodine (4.375 g); the pressure (175.7 mmHg); the volume (8555 mL); the question of what is the temperature in K

Connections

$PV = nRT$

Solution

Collect and label the information from the problem:

Mass = 4.375 g I_2
P = 175.7 mmHg
V = 8555 mL
T = ? K
$R = \dfrac{0.08206 \text{ L} \cdot \text{atm}}{\text{mol} \cdot \text{K}}$

Rearrange the ideal gas equation to $T = \dfrac{PV}{nR}$

It is necessary to determine the moles of iodine. To determine this value, we need the mass of iodine (4.375 g) and the molar mass of iodine (253.808 g/mol):

$$\text{Moles chlorine} = 4.375 \text{ g I}_2\left(\frac{1 \text{ mol I}_2}{253.808 \text{ g I}_2}\right)$$

Enter the appropriate values into the equation and cancel:

$$T = \frac{(175.7 \text{ mmHg})(8555 \text{ mL})}{\left(4.375 \text{ gI}_2 \left(\dfrac{1 \text{ mol I}_2}{253.808 \text{ gI}_2}\right)\right)\left(\dfrac{0.08206 \text{ L} \cdot \text{atm}}{\text{mol} \cdot \text{K}}\right)}$$

The necessity of an additional conversion is now apparent. The *milli-* conversion $(m = 0.001 = 10^{-3})$ is appropriate:

$$T = \frac{(175.7 \text{ mmHg})(8555 \text{ mL})}{\left(4.375 \text{ gI}_2 \left(\dfrac{1 \text{ mol I}_2}{253.808 \text{ gI}_2}\right)\right)\left(\dfrac{0.08206 \text{ L} \cdot \text{atm}}{\text{mol} \cdot \text{K}}\right)}\left(\dfrac{0.001}{m}\right)$$

Adding the appropriate pressure conversion (1 atm = 760 mmHg) gives

$$T = \frac{(175.7 \text{ mmHg})(8555 \text{ mL})}{\left(4.375 \text{ gI}_2 \left(\dfrac{1 \text{ mol I}_2}{253.808 \text{ gI}_2}\right)\right)\left(\dfrac{0.08206 \text{ L} \cdot \text{atm}}{\text{mol} \cdot \text{K}}\right)}\left(\dfrac{0.001}{m}\right)\left(\dfrac{1 \text{ atm}}{760 \text{ mmHg}}\right)$$

$$= 1398.21 = \textbf{1,398 K}$$

Reality Check

The units and the number of significant figures are correct. As always, it is possible to simplify the final calculation and estimate the answer.

Example Problem 5.6

A sample of a gas has a volume of 675 mL at a pressure of 555 torr. What is the volume of the gas sample in milliliters if the pressure increases to 755 torr?

Information

The most important first step in a gas law problem is to extract all the numbers, including their units, and the actual question. (Be very careful to label everything correctly.):

$P_1 = 555$ torr $P_2 = 755$ torr
$V_1 = 675$ mL $V_2 = ?$ mL
$n_1 = -$ $n_2 = -$
$T_1 = -$ $T_2 = -$

Connections

The presence of two volumes, or two of any variable, is a strong indication that this problem is most effectively solved using the combined gas law, $\dfrac{P_1 V_1}{n_1 T_1} = \dfrac{P_2 V_2}{n_2 T_2}$.

Solution

Neither the moles nor the temperatures were present in the question; therefore, there are no values given. When there are no values, assume that the values are constant. Group each pressure with the appropriate volume. Deleting the unnecessary values, and labeling of the remaining variables as initial and final, gives this:

$V_1 = 675$ mL $V_2 = ?$ mL
$P_1 = 555$ torr $P_2 = 755$ torr

Using the simplified table allows us to simplify the combined gas law to

$$P_1V_1 = P_2V_2$$

The simplified combined gas law rearranges to

$$V_2 = \frac{(P_1)(V_1)}{(P_2)}$$

The solution begins with the substitution of the appropriate values into the labeled positions in the rearranged gas law equation:

$$V_2 = \frac{(555 \ \cancel{torr})(675 \ mL)}{(755 \ \cancel{torr})} = 496.19 = \textbf{496 mL}$$

Reality Check
The units of the answer are the volume units that we were seeking. In addition, the increase in pressure leads to a decrease in volume, which is in accordance with Boyle's law.

Follow-Up Problem 5.6a
A sample of a gas has a volume of 1,675 mL at a pressure of 825.5 torr. What is the volume of the gas sample in mL if the pressure decreases to 755.2 torr?

Information
The volume (1,675 mL); the pressures [825.5 torr (initial) and 755.2 torr (final)]; the question of what is the volume in milliliters

Connections
$$\frac{P_1V_1}{n_1T_1} = \frac{P_2V_2}{n_2T_2}$$

Solution
Collect and label the information from the problem:

$P_1 = 825.5$ torr $P_2 = 755.2$ torr
$V_1 = 1675$ mL $V_2 = ?$ mL
$n_1 = -$ $n_2 = -$
$T_1 = -$ $T_2 = -$

Based on the available information, the combined gas law simplifies to $P_1V_1 = P_2V_2$.

The simplified combined gas law rearranges to $V_2 = \dfrac{P_1V_1}{P_2}$.

Enter the appropriate values into the equation and cancel:

$$V_2 = \frac{(825.5 \ \cancel{torr})(1675 \ mL)}{(755.2 \ \cancel{torr})} = 1830.922 = \textbf{1,831 mL}$$

Reality Check
The units and the number of significant figures are correct. In addition, the decrease in pressure leads to an increase in volume, which is in accordance with Boyle's law.

Follow-Up Problem 5.6b
A sample of a gas has a volume of 125 mL at a pressure of 815 torr. What is the volume of the gas sample in liters if the pressure decreases to 0.985 atm?

Information

The volume (125 mL); the pressures 815 torr (initial) and 0.985 atm (final); the question of what is the volume in liters

Connections

$$\frac{P_1 V_1}{n_1 T_1} = \frac{P_2 V_2}{n_2 T_2}$$

Solution

Collect and label the information from the problem:

$P_1 = 815$ torr	$P_2 = 0.985$ atm
$V_1 = 125$ mL	$V_2 = ?$ L
$n_1 = -$	$n_2 = -$
$T_1 = -$	$T_2 = -$

Based on the available information, the combined gas law simplifies to $P_1 V_1 = P_2 V_2$.

The simplified combined gas law rearranges to $V_2 = \dfrac{P_1 V_1}{P_2}$.

Enter the appropriate values into the equation:

$$V_2 = \frac{(815 \text{ torr})(125 \text{ mL})}{(0.985 \text{ atm})}$$

The necessity of additional conversions is now apparent. The *milli-* conversion ($m = 0.001 = 10^{-3}$) is appropriate, because liters, not milliliters, are necessary in the answer:

$$V_2 = \frac{(815 \text{ torr})(125 \text{ \cancel{mL}})}{(0.985 \text{ atm})}\left(\frac{0.001}{\cancel{m}}\right)$$

Adding the appropriate pressure conversion (1 atm = 760 torr) gives

$$V_2 = \frac{(815 \text{ \cancel{torr}})(125 \text{ \cancel{mL}})}{(0.985 \text{ \cancel{atm}})}\left(\frac{0.001}{\cancel{m}}\right)\left(\frac{1 \text{ \cancel{atm}}}{760 \text{ \cancel{torr}}}\right) = 0.136087 = \mathbf{0.0136 \text{ L}}$$

Reality Check

The magnitude of the answer is reasonable, and the increase in volume with increasing pressure is in accordance with Boyle's Law. The units and the number of significant figures are correct.

Example Problem 5.7

Determine the final temperature, in °C, of a sample of gas that initially had a volume of 125 mL at 25°C, and a final volume of 175 mL.

Information

The most important first step in a gas law problem is to extract all the numbers, including their units, and the actual question (Be very careful to label everything correctly.):

$P_1 = -$	$P_2 = -$
$V_1 = 125$ mL	$V_2 = 175$ mL
$n_1 = -$	$n_2 = -$
$T_1 = 25°C = 298$ K	$T_2 = ?°C$

Connections

$$\frac{P_1 V_1}{n_1 T_1} = \frac{P_2 V_2}{n_2 T_2}$$

Solution

Neither the moles nor the pressures were present in the question, thus, there are no values. When there are no values, assume the values are constant. It is usually best, as shown in this case, to change immediately any temperature to kelvin units. This is the only required conversion in all gas law calculations. Group each temperature with the appropriate volume. Deleting the unnecessary values, and labeling the remaining variables as initial and final, gives

$V_1 = 125$ mL $\qquad\qquad\qquad V_2 = 175$ mL
$T_1 = 25°C = 298$ K $\qquad\qquad T_2 = ?°C$

The presence of two volumes, or two of any of the variables, again is a strong indication that this problem requires the combined gas law, $\dfrac{P_1 V_1}{n_1 T_1} = \dfrac{P_2 V_2}{n_2 T_2}$. Simplify the combined gas law by eliminating any variable not in the table. This gives $\dfrac{V_1}{T_1} = \dfrac{V_2}{T_2}$. Rearranging the simplified equation gives

$T_2 = \dfrac{V_2\, T_1}{V_1}$

Enter the appropriate values into the equation, and cancel:

$$T_2 = \frac{(175 \;\cancel{mL})(298 \text{ K})}{(125 \;\cancel{mL})} = 417.2 \text{ K} \qquad \text{(unrounded)}$$

$T_2 = (417.2 - 273.2)°C = 144.0 = \mathbf{0.0136\ L}$

Reality Check

The units and the number of significant figures are correct. The calculated increase in temperature as predicted from Charles's law when there is an increase in volume.

Follow-Up Problem 5.7a

Determine the final temperature, in °C, of a sample of gas that initially had a volume of 225 mL at 27°C and a final volume of 175 mL.

Information

The initial volume (225 mL); the initial temperature (27°C); the final volume (175 mL); the question of what is the final temperature in °C

Connections

$\dfrac{P_1 V_1}{n_1 T_1} = \dfrac{P_2 V_2}{n_2 T_2}$

Solution

Collect and label the information from the problem:

$P_1 = -$ $\qquad\qquad\qquad\qquad P_2 = -$
$V_1 = 225$ mL $\qquad\qquad\qquad V_2 = 175$ mL
$n_1 = -$ $\qquad\qquad\qquad\qquad n_2 = -$
$T_1 = 27°C = 300.\ \text{K}$ $\qquad\qquad T_2 = ?\ °C$

Based on the available information, the combined gas law simplifies to $\dfrac{V_1}{T_1} = \dfrac{V_2}{T_2}$.

The simplified combined gas law rearranges to $T_2 = \dfrac{V_2\, T_1}{V_1}$

Enter the appropriate values into the equation and cancel:

$$T_2 = \frac{(175 \;\cancel{mL})(300.\ \text{K})}{(225 \;\cancel{mL})} = 233.3333 \text{ K} \qquad \text{(unrounded)}$$

The problem requests a temperature in °C, so one more conversion is necessary:

$$T_2 = (233.3333 - 273.15)°C = -39.8167 = \mathbf{-40.°C}$$

Reality Check

The units and the number of significant figures are correct. The volume decreases; therefore, according to Charles's law the temperature should decrease.

Follow-Up Problem 5.7b

Determine the final volume, in liters, of a sample of gas that initially had a volume of 325 mL at 27°C, and a final temperature of 127°C.

Information

The initial volume (325 mL); the initial temperature (27°C); the final temperature (127°C); and the question of what is the final volume in liters

Connections

$$\frac{P_1 V_1}{n_1 T_1} = \frac{P_2 V_2}{n_2 T_2}$$

Solution

Collect and label the information from the problem:

$P_1 = —$ $P_2 = —$
$V_1 = 325$ mL $V_2 = ?$ L
$n_1 = —$ $n_2 = —$
$T_1 = 27°C = 300.$ K $T_2 = 127°C = 400.$ K

Based on the available information, the combined gas law simplifies to $\dfrac{V_1}{T_1} = \dfrac{V_2}{T_2}$

The simplified combined gas law rearranges to $V_2 = \dfrac{T_2 V_1}{T_1}$

Enter the appropriate values into the equation and cancel:

$$V_2 = \frac{(400.\,\cancel{K})(325 \text{ mL})}{(300.\,\cancel{K})}$$

The necessity of an additional conversion is now apparent. The *milli-* conversion ($m = 0.001 = 10^{-3}$) is appropriate, because the question asks for liters not milliliters:

$$V_2 = \frac{(400.\,\cancel{K})(325 \,\cancel{\text{mL}})}{(300.\,\cancel{K})}\left(\frac{0.001}{\cancel{m}}\right) = 0.433333 = \mathbf{0.433 \text{ L}}$$

Reality Check

The units and the number of significant figures are correct. The increase in volume is in accordance to Charles's law, which states that there is a direct relationship between volume and temperature.

Example Problem 5.8

A sample of gas with a volume of 475 mL at a temperature of 45°C and a pressure of 745 mmHg is cooled to 25°C while the pressure is changed to 0.775 atm. What is the new volume in milliliters of the sample of gas?

Information

The most important first step in a gas law problem is to extract all the numbers, including their units, and the actual question (Be very careful to label everything correctly.):

$P_1 = 745$ mmHg $\qquad\qquad$ $P_2 = 0.775$ atm

$V_1 = 475$ mL $\qquad\qquad$ $V_2 = ?$ mL

$n_1 = —$ $\qquad\qquad$ $n_2 = —$

$T_1 = 45°C = 318$ K $\qquad\qquad$ $T_2 = 25°C = 298$ K

Connections

The presence of two volumes, or two of any variable, is a strong indication that this problem requires the use of the combined gas law, $\dfrac{P_1 V_1}{n_1 T_1} = \dfrac{P_2 V_2}{n_2 T_2}$. Simplify the combined gas law by eliminating any variable that is not in the table. This gives $\dfrac{P_1 V_1}{T_1} = \dfrac{P_2 V_2}{T_2}$. Rearranging the simplified equation gives $V_2 = \dfrac{T_2 P_1 V_1}{T_1 P_2}$.

Solution

Enter the appropriate values into the equation and cancel:

$$V_2 = \frac{(298 \ \cancel{K})(745 \text{ mmHg})(475 \text{ mL})}{(318 \ \cancel{K})(0.775 \text{ atm})}$$

The necessity of an additional conversion is now apparent. Adding the appropriate pressure conversion (1 atm = 760 mmHg) gives

$$V_2 = \frac{(298 \ \cancel{K})(745 \ \cancel{\text{mmHg}})(475 \text{ mL})}{(318 \ \cancel{K})(0.775 \ \cancel{\text{atm}})}\left(\frac{1 \ \cancel{\text{atm}}}{760 \ \cancel{\text{mmHg}}}\right) = 563.0199 = \mathbf{563 \text{ mL}}$$

Reality Check

The units and the number of significant figures are correct. As always, it is possible to round the values and estimate an answer. Ideally, you should round until you can approximate the answer in your head.

Follow-Up Problem 5.8a

A sample of gas with a volume of 4.75 L at a temperature of 25°C and a pressure of 785 mmHg is warmed to 55°C while the pressure is changed to 1.08 atm. What is the new volume in liters of the sample of gas?

Information

The initial volume temperature and pressure (4.75 L, 25°C, and 785 mmHg); the final temperature and pressure (55°C and 1.08 atm); the question of what is the final volume in liters

Connections

$$\frac{P_1 V_1}{n_1 T_1} = \frac{P_2 V_2}{n_2 T_2}$$

Solution

Collect and label the information from the problem:

$P_1 = 785$ mmHg $\qquad\qquad$ $P_2 = 1.08$ atm

$V_1 = 4.75$ L $\qquad\qquad$ $V_2 = ?$ L

$n_1 = —$ $\qquad\qquad$ $n_2 = —$

$T_1 = 25°C = 298$ K $\qquad\qquad$ $T_2 = 55°C = 328$ K

Based on the available information, the combined gas law simplifies to $\dfrac{P_1V_1}{T_1} = \dfrac{P_2V_2}{T_2}$

The simplified combined gas law rearranges to $V_2 = \dfrac{T_2P_1V_1}{T_1P_2}$

Enter the appropriate values into the equation and cancel:

$$V_2 = \frac{(328\ \cancel{K})(785\ \text{mmHg})(4.75\ \text{L})}{(298\ \cancel{K})(1.08\ \text{atm})}$$

The necessity of an additional conversion is now apparent. Adding the appropriate pressure conversion (1 atm = 760 mmHg) gives

$$V_2 = \frac{(328\ \cancel{K})(785\ \cancel{\text{mmHg}})(4.75\ \text{L})}{(298\ \cancel{K})(1.08\ \cancel{\text{atm}})}\left(\frac{1\ \cancel{\text{atm}}}{760\ \cancel{\text{mmHg}}}\right) = 5.000155 = \mathbf{5.00\ L}$$

Reality Check

The units and the number of significant figures are correct. As always, it is possible to round the values and estimate an answer.

Follow-Up Problem 5.8b

A sample of gas with a volume of 4.75 L at a temperature of 27°C and a pressure of 745 torr is cooled to –33°C while the volume is changed to 1,080 mL. What is the new pressure, in atmospheres, of the sample of gas?

Information

The initial volume temperature and pressure (4.75 L, 27°C, and 745 torr); the final temperature and volume (–33°C and 1080 mL); the question of what is the final pressure in atmospheres

Connections

$$\frac{P_1V_1}{n_1T_1} = \frac{P_2V_2}{n_2T_2}$$

Solution

Collect and label the information from the problem:

$P_1 = 745$ torr	$P_2 = ?$ atm
$V_1 = 4.75$ L	$V_2 = 1080$ mL
$n_1 = -$	$n_2 = -$
$T_1 = 27°C = 300.\ K$	$T_2 = -33°C = 240.\ K$

Based on the available information, the combined gas law simplifies to $\dfrac{P_1V_1}{T_1} = \dfrac{P_2V_2}{T_2}$

The simplified combined gas law rearranges to $P_2 = \dfrac{P_1\ V_1\ T_2}{T_1\ V_2}$

Enter the appropriate values into the equation and cancel:

$$P_2 = \frac{(745\ \text{torr})(4.75\ \cancel{\text{L}})(240.\cancel{K})}{(300.\cancel{K})(1080\ \text{mL})}$$

The necessity of additional conversions is now apparent. The *milli-* conversion ($m = 0.001 = 10^{-3}$) is appropriate:

$$P_2 = \frac{(745\ \text{torr})(4.75\ \cancel{\text{L}})(240.\cancel{K})}{(300.\cancel{K})(1080\ \cancel{\text{mL}})}\left(\frac{\cancel{m}}{0.001}\right)$$

Finally, add the appropriate pressure conversion (1 atm = 760 torr), because the question requests an answer in atmospheres instead of torr:

$$P_2 = \frac{(745 \text{ torr})(4.75 \text{ L})(240. \text{K})}{(300. \text{ K})(1080 \text{ mL})} \left(\frac{\text{m}}{0.001}\right)\left(\frac{1 \text{ atm}}{760 \text{ torr}}\right) = 3.44907 = \textbf{3.45 atm}$$

Reality Check

The units and the number of significant figures are correct. As always, it is possible to round the values and estimate an answer.

Example Problem 5.9

Determine the volume of oxygen gas, in L, at 27°C and 775 torr that is released from the decomposition of 10.45 g of potassium nitrate. The reaction is

$$2 \text{ KNO}_3(s) \rightarrow 2 \text{ KNO}_2(s) + \text{O}_2(g)$$

Information

The balanced chemical equation; the temperature (27°C); the pressure (775 torr); the mass of potassium nitrate (10.45 g); the question of what is the volume of oxygen

Connections

There is only one value for each variable, thus, the ideal gas equation, $PV = nRT$, is probably the equation most appropriate for this problem. This equation needs to be rearranged to $V = nRT/P$.

Solution

Recopy the balanced chemical equation, and include the information about each substance below its formula:

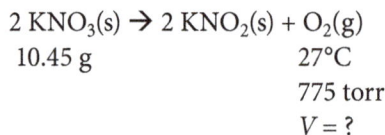

$$2 \text{ KNO}_3(s) \rightarrow 2 \text{ KNO}_2(s) + \text{O}_2(g)$$

10.45 g		27°C
		775 torr
		$V = ?$

Extract the variables and the question and label everything:

$V = ? \text{ L}$
$T = 27°C = 300. \text{ K}$
$P = 775 \text{ torr}$
$\text{Mass} = 10.45 \text{ g KNO}_3$

To use a gas law equation, we need to know the moles of gas. Potassium nitrate is not a gas, so a conversion is necessary to get to moles of gas (O_2). (Be careful not to skip this step. The gas law equations are for gases, not for solids such as potassium nitrate, so there must be a conversion to give the moles of gas.):

$$\text{Moles O}_2 = (10.45 \text{ gKNO}_3)\left(\frac{1 \text{ mol KNO}_3}{101.102 \text{ gKNO}_3}\right)\left(\frac{1 \text{ mol O}_2}{2 \text{ mol KNO}_3}\right) = n$$

Substituting the appropriate values into the equation gives

$$V = \frac{\left[(10.45 \text{ gKNO}_3)\left(\dfrac{1 \text{ mol KNO}_3}{101.102 \text{ gKNO}_3}\right)\left(\dfrac{1 \text{ mol O}_2}{2 \text{ mol KNO}_3}\right)\right]\left(\dfrac{0.08206 \text{ L} \cdot \text{atm}}{\text{mol} \cdot \text{K}}\right)(300. \text{ K})}{775 \text{ torr}}$$

The need for additional conversions is now apparent. Adding the appropriate pressure conversion (1 atm = 760 torr) gives

$$V = \frac{\left(10.45 \ \cancel{g\ KNO_3}\right)\left(\dfrac{1 \ \cancel{mol\ KNO_3}}{101.102 \ \cancel{g\ KNO_3}}\right)\left(\dfrac{1 \ \cancel{mol\ O_2}}{2 \ \cancel{mol\ KNO_3}}\right)\left(\dfrac{0.08206 \ L \bullet \cancel{atm}}{\cancel{mol} \bullet \cancel{K}}\right)(300. \ \cancel{K})}{775 \ \cancel{torr}\left(\dfrac{760 \ \cancel{torr}}{1 \ \cancel{atm}}\right)}$$

$$= 1.24764 = \textbf{1.25 L}$$

Reality Check

The units and the number of significant figures are correct. As always, it is possible to round the values and estimate an answer. Ideally, you should round until you can approximate the answer in your head.

Follow-Up Problem 5.9a

The compound xenon trioxide (XeO_3) is very unstable. This compound decomposes to the elements with explosive violence. The reaction is

$$2 \ XeO_3(s) \rightarrow 2 \ Xe(g) + 3 \ O_2(g)$$

What volume of oxygen gas in milliliters will form when 1.50 grams of xenon trioxide decompose? The final oxygen partial pressure is 555 mmHg, and the final temperature is 47°C.

Information

The balanced chemical equation; the mass of xenon trioxide (1.50 g); the oxygen pressure (555 mmHg), the temperature (47°C); the question of how many milliliters of oxygen form

Connections

$PV = nRT$

Solution

Recopy the balanced chemical equation, and include the information about each substance below its formula:

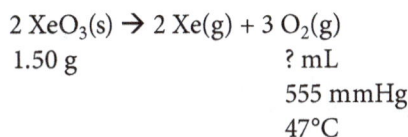

$$2 \ XeO_3(s) \rightarrow 2 \ Xe(g) + 3 \ O_2(g)$$

1.50 g		? mL
		555 mmHg
		47°C

Collect and label the information from the problem:

Mass = 1.50 g XeO_3
P = 555 mmHg
V = ? mL
T = 47°C = 320. K
$R = \dfrac{0.08206 \ L \bullet atm}{mol \bullet K}$

Rearrange the ideal gas equation to $V = \dfrac{nRT}{P}$

To use a gas law equation, the moles of gas are necessary. Xenon trioxide is not a gas, so a conversion is necessary to get to moles of gas (O_2):

$$\text{Moles } O_2 = (1.50 \ \cancel{g\ XeO_3})\left(\frac{1 \ \cancel{mol\ XeO_3}}{179.3 \ \cancel{g\ XeO_3}}\right)\left(\frac{3 \ mol \ O_2}{2 \ \cancel{mol\ XeO_3}}\right) = n$$

Enter the appropriate values into the ideal gas equation and cancel:

$$V = \frac{\left(1.50\ \text{g XeO}_3\right)\left(\dfrac{1\ \text{mol XeO}_3}{179.3\ \text{g XeO}_3}\right)\left(\dfrac{3\ \text{mol O}_2}{2\ \text{mol XeO}_3}\right)\left(\dfrac{0.08206\ \text{L} \cdot \text{atm}}{\text{mol} \cdot \text{K}}\right)(320.\ \text{K})}{555\ \text{mmHg}}$$

The necessity of additional conversions is now apparent. The *milli-* conversion ($m = 0.001 = 10^{-3}$) is appropriate because the problem asks for milliliters:

$$V = \frac{\left(1.50\ \text{g XeO}_3\right)\left(\dfrac{1\ \text{mol XeO}_3}{179.3\ \text{g XeO}_3}\right)\left(\dfrac{3\ \text{mol O}_2}{2\ \text{mol XeO}_3}\right)\left(\dfrac{0.08206\ \text{L} \cdot \text{atm}}{\text{mol} \cdot \text{K}}\right)(320.\ \text{K})}{555\ \text{mmHg}}\left(\dfrac{m}{0.001}\right)$$

Adding the appropriate pressure conversion (1 atm = 760 mmHg) gives

$$V = \frac{\left(1.50\ \text{g XeO}_3\right)\left(\dfrac{1\ \text{mol XeO}_3}{179.3\ \text{g XeO}_3}\right)\left(\dfrac{3\ \text{mol O}_2}{2\ \text{mol XeO}_3}\right)\left(\dfrac{0.08206\ \text{L} \cdot \text{atm}}{\text{mol} \cdot \text{K}}\right)(320.\ \text{K})}{555\ \text{mmHg}}\left(\dfrac{m}{0.001}\right)\left(\dfrac{760\ \text{mmHg}}{1\ \text{atm}}\right)$$

$$= 451.2366 = \textbf{451 mL}$$

Reality Check

The units and the number of significant figures are correct. As always, it is possible to round the values and estimate an answer.

Follow-Up Problem 5.9b

Thermal decomposition of nickel tetracarbonyl ($Ni(CO)_4$) is the last step in the purification of nickel by the Mond process. The reaction is

$$Ni(CO)_4(g) \rightarrow Ni(s) + 4\ CO(g)$$

Determine the volume of CO gas in liters that forms at 375°C and 0.750 atm from the decomposition of a sample of nickel tetracarbonyl originally in a 10.0-L container at 125°C and 855 torr.

Information

The balanced chemical equation; the volume, temperature, and pressure of nickel tetracarbonyl (10.0 liter, 125°C, and 855 torr); the carbon monoxide pressure and temperature (0.750 atm and 375°C); the question of how many liters of carbon monoxide form

Connections

$PV = nRT$

Solution

Recopy the balanced chemical equation, and include the information about each substance below its formula:

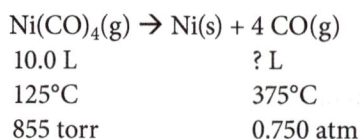

$$Ni(CO)_4(g) \rightarrow Ni(s) + 4\ CO(g)$$

10.0 L		? L
125°C		375°C
855 torr		0.750 atm

Collect and label the information from the problem:

For Ni(CO)$_4$

$P = 855$ torr

$V = 10.0$ L

$n = ?$ mol

$T = 125°C = 398$ K

$R = \dfrac{0.08206 \text{ L} \cdot \text{atm}}{\text{mol} \cdot \text{K}}$

Rearrange the ideal gas equation to $n = \dfrac{PV}{RT}$

Enter the appropriate values into the ideal gas equation and cancel:

$$n = \frac{(855 \text{ torr})(10.0 \text{ L})}{\left(\dfrac{0.08206 \text{ L} \cdot \text{atm}}{\text{mol} \cdot \text{K}}\right)(398 \text{ K})}$$

The necessity of an additional conversion is now apparent. Adding the appropriate pressure conversion (1 atm = 760 torr) gives

$$n = \frac{(855 \text{ torr})(10.0 \text{ L})}{\left(\dfrac{0.08206 \text{ L} \cdot \text{atm}}{\text{mol} \cdot \text{K}}\right)(398 \text{ K})}\left(\frac{1 \text{ atm}}{760 \text{ torr}}\right) = 0.344459 \text{ mol Ni(CO)}_4 \qquad \text{(unrounded)}$$

To convert from moles of Ni(CO)$_4$ to moles of CO, we need to use the mole ratio from the balanced chemical equation:

$$\text{Moles CO} = (0.344459 \text{ mol Ni(CO)}_4)\left(\frac{4 \text{ mol CO}}{1 \text{ mol Ni(CO)}_4}\right) = 1.377836 \text{ mol CO} \quad \text{(unrounded)}$$

For CO

$P = 0.750$ atm

$V = ?$ L

$T = 375°C = 648$ K

$n = 1.377836$ mol CO

Rearrange the ideal gas equation to $V = \dfrac{nRT}{P}$

Enter the appropriate values into the equation and cancel:

$$V = \frac{(1.377836 \text{ mol})\left(\dfrac{0.08206 \text{ L} \cdot \text{atm}}{\text{mol} \cdot \text{K}}\right)(648 \text{ K})}{0.750 \text{ atm}} = 97.68835 = \mathbf{97.7 \text{ L}}$$

Reality Check
The units and the number of significant figures are correct. As always, it is possible to round the values and estimate an answer.

Example Problem 5.10
The reaction of aluminum metal with hydrochloric acid produces aluminum chloride and hydrogen gas. The reaction is

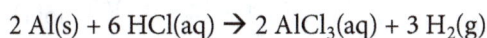

$$2 \text{ Al(s)} + 6 \text{ HCl(aq)} \rightarrow 2 \text{ AlCl}_3\text{(aq)} + 3 \text{ H}_2\text{(g)}$$

A 2.550-gram sample of aluminum metal reacts with excess hydrochloric acid. The generated hydrogen is collected over water and has a total pressure of 745.5 torr at a temperature of 25.00°C. Determine the volume in liters of dry hydrogen collected.

Information

The balanced chemical equation; the mass of aluminum (2.550 g); the total pressure (745.5 torr); the temperature (25.00°C); the presence of water; the question of how many liters of dry hydrogen will be collected

Connections

The collection of the sample over water means we need one more piece of information: the vapor pressure of water at 25°C. The vapor pressure of water at this temperature is 23.756 torr (from the vapor pressure table, **table 5.2**). We will also need to use the ideal gas equation and Dalton's law.

Solution

Recopy the balanced chemical equation, and include the information about each substance below its formula:

$$2\ Al(s) + 6\ HCl(aq) \rightarrow 2\ AlCl_3(aq) + 3\ H_2(g)$$
$$2.550\ g \qquad\qquad\qquad\qquad\qquad 25.00°C$$
$$P_{total} = 745.5\ torr$$

Collecting and labeling the variables from the problem gives

Mass Al = 2.550 grams Al
P_{total} = 745.5 torr
T = 25.00°C = 298.15 K
V = ? L

It is necessary to subtract the partial pressure of the water vapor from the total pressure to get the partial pressure of the dry gas. This is an application of Dalton's law:

$$P_{total} = P_{dry} + P_{H_2O}$$

Rearranging this equation gives

$$P_{dry} = P_{total} - P_{H_2O}$$

Using the values from the problem and the vapor pressure table (**table 5.2**) gives

P_{dry} = 745.5 torr – 23.756 torr = 721.744 torr   (unrounded)

We can now substitute the partial pressure of dry hydrogen into the variable table from earlier:

Mass Al = 2.550 grams Al
P_{H_2} = 721.744 torr   (unrounded)
T = 25.00°C = 298.15 K
V = ? L

The presence of only one pressure, temperature, and volume value is strongly indicative that you should use the ideal gas equation, $PV = nRT$. Rearranging the ideal gas equation to find the volume gives $V = nRT/P$.

To use a gas law equation, we need to determine the moles of gas. Aluminum is not a gas, so a conversion is necessary to get to moles of gas (H_2):

$$\text{Moles } H_2 = (2.550\ \cancel{g\ Al})\left(\frac{1\ \cancel{mol\ Al}}{26.9815\ \cancel{g\ Al}}\right)\left(\frac{3\ mol\ H_2}{2\ \cancel{mol\ Al}}\right) = n$$

Enter the appropriate values into the equation and cancel:

$$V = \frac{\left(2.550\ \cancel{g\ Al}\right)\left(\dfrac{1\ \cancel{mol\ Al}}{26.9815\ \cancel{g\ Al}}\right)\left(\dfrac{3\ \cancel{mol\ H_2}}{2\ \cancel{mol\ Al}}\right)\left(\dfrac{0.08206\ L \cdot atm}{\cancel{mol} \cdot \cancel{K}}\right)(298.15\ \cancel{K})}{721.444\ torr}$$

The necessity of an additional conversion is now apparent. Adding the appropriate pressure conversion (1 atm = 760 torr) gives

$$V = \frac{\left(2.550\ \cancel{g\ Al}\right)\left(\dfrac{1\ \cancel{mol\ Al}}{26.9815\ \cancel{g\ Al}}\right)\left(\dfrac{3\ \cancel{mol\ H_2}}{2\ \cancel{mol\ Al}}\right)\left(\dfrac{0.08206\ L \cdot \cancel{atm}}{\cancel{mol} \cdot \cancel{K}}\right)(298.15\ \cancel{K})}{721.444\ \cancel{torr}}\left(\dfrac{760\ \cancel{torr}}{1\ \cancel{atm}}\right)$$

$$= 3.65378 = \mathbf{3.654\ L}$$

Since all the original data contained four significant figures, all values in the calculation have at least four significant figures. This is why 0.08206 is the R-value, and why the kelvin conversion used 273.15 instead of the usual 273.

Reality Check

The units and the number of significant figures are correct. As always, it is possible to round the values and estimate an answer. Ideally, you should round until you can approximate the answer in your head.

Follow-Up Problem 5.10a

Acetylene gas, C_2H_2, forms when calcium carbide, CaC_2, reacts with water. The reaction is

$$CaC_2(s) + 2\ H_2O(l) \rightarrow Ca(OH)_2(aq) + C_2H_2(g)$$

A 4.858-gram sample of calcium carbide reacts with excess water. The acetylene that was generated was collected over water. The total pressure of the collected gas was 655.5 mmHg at 30.00°C. Determine the volume in liters of dry acetylene formed.

Information

The balanced chemical equation; the mass of calcium carbide (4.858 g); the total pressure (655.5 mmHg); the temperature (30.00°C); the question of what is the volume of acetylene in liters

Connections

$PV = nRT$; $P_{total} = P_a + P_b + P_c + ...$; the vapor pressure of water from **table 5.2** in the textbook (31.824 torr)

Solution

Recopy the balanced chemical equation, and include the information about each substance below its formula:

$$CaC_2(s) + 2\ H_2O(l) \rightarrow Ca(OH)_2(aq) + C_2H_2(g)$$

4.858 g   ? L
                                                       30.00°C

$$P_{total} = 655.5\ mmHg\ (= 655.5\ torr)$$

It is necessary to subtract the partial pressure of the water vapor from the total pressure to get the partial pressure of the dry gas. This is an application of Dalton's law.

$$P_{total} = P_{dry} + P_{H_2O}$$

Rearranging this equation gives

$$P_{dry} = P_{total} - P_{H_2O}$$

Using the values from the problem and the vapor pressure table (**table 5.2**) gives

$$P_{dry} = 655.5 \text{ torr} - 31.824 \text{ torr} = 623.676 \text{ torr} \qquad \text{(unrounded)}$$

We can now substitute the partial pressure of dry hydrogen into the variable table from earlier:

Collect and label the information from the problem:

Mass = 4.858 g CaC_2
P = 623.67 torr (1 extra significant figure)
V = ? L
T = 30.00°C = 303.15 K
$R = \dfrac{0.08206 \text{ L} \cdot \text{atm}}{\text{mol} \cdot \text{K}}$

Rearrange the ideal gas equation to $V = \dfrac{nRT}{P}$

To use a gas law equation, we need to know the moles of gas. Calcium carbide is not a gas, so a conversion is needed to get to moles of gas (C_2H_2):

$$\text{Moles } C_2H_2 = (4.858 \text{ g } CaC_2)\left(\frac{1 \text{ mol } CaC_2}{64.100 \text{ g } CaC_2}\right)\left(\frac{1 \text{ mol } C_2H_2}{1 \text{ mol } CaC_2}\right) = n$$

Enter the appropriate values into the equation and cancel:

$$V = \frac{\left[(4.858 \text{ g } CaC_2)\left(\frac{1 \text{ mol } CaC_2}{64.100 \text{ g } CaC_2}\right)\left(\frac{1 \text{ mol } C_2H_2}{1 \text{ mol } CaC_2}\right)\right]\left(\frac{0.08206 \text{ L} \cdot \text{atm}}{\text{mol} \cdot \text{K}}\right)(303.15 \text{ K})}{623.67 \text{ torr}}$$

The necessity of an additional conversion is now apparent. Adding the appropriate pressure conversion (1 atm = 760 torr) gives

$$V = \frac{\left[(4.858 \text{ g } CaC_2)\left(\frac{1 \text{ mol } CaC_2}{64.100 \text{ g } CaC_2}\right)\left(\frac{1 \text{ mol } C_2H_2}{1 \text{ mol } CaC_2}\right)\right]\left(\frac{0.08206 \text{ L} \cdot \text{atm}}{\text{mol} \cdot \text{K}}\right)(303.15 \text{ K})}{623.67 \text{ torr}}\left(\frac{760 \text{ torr}}{1 \text{ atm}}\right)$$

$$= 2.2974565 = \mathbf{2.297 \text{ L}}$$

Reality Check
The units and the number of significant figures are correct. As always, it is possible to round the values and estimate an answer.

Follow-Up Problem 5.10b
The thermal decomposition of ammonium nitrate generates dinitrogen oxide and water vapor. The decomposition of a 10.175-gram sample of ammonium nitrate produced dinitrogen oxide, which was collected over water at 20.00°C. The total pressure of the sample was 8.515×10^4 Pa. What is the volume in liters of dry dinitrogen oxide in the sample?

Information
Information on the reaction (ammonium nitrate generates dinitrogen oxide and water vapor), the mass of ammonium nitrate (10.175 g), the temperature (20.00°C), the total pressure (8.515×10^4 Pa), and the question (what is the volume of dinitrogen oxide in liters)

Connections

$PV = nRT$; $P_{total} = P_a + P_b + P_c + \ldots$; the vapor pressure of water from **table 5.2** in the textbook (17.535 torr)

Solution

Write the skeleton equation:

$$\underline{\qquad} NH_4NO_3(s) \rightarrow \underline{\qquad} N_2O(g) + \underline{\qquad} H_2O(g)$$

Balance the equation:

$$NH_4NO_3(s) \rightarrow N_2O(g) + 2\,H_2O(g)$$

Recopy the balanced chemical equation, and include the information about each substance below its formula:

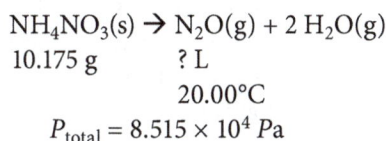

$$NH_4NO_3(s) \rightarrow N_2O(g) + 2\,H_2O(g)$$
$$\text{10.175 g} \qquad \text{? L}$$
$$\text{20.00°C}$$
$$P_{total} = 8.515 \times 10^4\ Pa$$

We need to subtract the partial pressure of the water vapor from the total pressure to get the partial pressure of the dry gas. This is an application of Dalton's law.

$$P_{total} = P_{dry} + P_{H_2O}$$

Rearranging this equation gives

$$P_{dry} = P_{total} - P_{H_2O}$$

We need to convert the pressure from pascals to torr (or vice versa). Then, using the values from the problem and the vapor pressure table (**table 5.2**) gives

$$P_{dry} = 8.515 \times 10^4\ \cancel{Pa} \left(\frac{760\ \text{torr}}{1.01325 \times 10^5\ \cancel{Pa}}\right) - 17.535\ \text{torr} = 621.142\ \text{torr} \qquad \text{(unrounded)}$$

We can now substitute the partial pressure of dry hydrogen into the variable table from earlier: Collect and label the information from the problem:

Mass = 10.175 g NH_4NO_3
P = 621.142 torr (2 extra significant figure)
V = ? L
T = 20.00°C = 293.15 K
$R = \dfrac{0.08206\ \text{L} \cdot \text{atm}}{\text{mol} \cdot \text{K}}$

Rearrange the ideal gas equation to $V = \dfrac{nRT}{P}$

To use a gas law equation, we need the moles of gas. Ammonium nitrate is not a gas, so a conversion is needed to get to moles of gas (N_2O):

$$\text{Moles } N_2O = (10.175\ \text{g } NH_4NO_3)\left(\frac{1\ \text{mol } NH_4NO_3}{80.043\ \text{g } NH_4NO_3}\right)\left(\frac{1\ \text{mol } N_2O}{1\ \text{mol } NH_4NO_3}\right) = n$$

Enter the appropriate values into the equation and cancel:

$$V = \frac{\left(10.175\ \cancel{\text{g } NH_4NO_3}\right)\left(\dfrac{1\ \cancel{\text{mol } NH_4NO_3}}{80.043\ \cancel{\text{g } NH_4NO_3}}\right)\left(\dfrac{1\ \cancel{\text{mol } N_2O}}{1\ \cancel{\text{mol } NH_4NO_3}}\right)\left(\dfrac{0.08206\ \text{L} \cdot \cancel{\text{atm}}}{\cancel{\text{mol}} \cdot \cancel{K}}\right)(293.15\ \cancel{K})}{621.142\ \cancel{\text{torr}}}$$

The need for an additional conversion is now apparent. Adding the appropriate pressure conversion (1 atm = 760 torr) gives

$$V = \frac{\left(10.175 \text{ g } NH_4NO_3\right)\left(\dfrac{1 \text{ mol } NH_4NO_3}{80.043 \text{ g } NH_4NO_3}\right)\left(\dfrac{1 \text{ mol } N_2O}{1 \text{ mol } NH_4NO_3}\right)\left(\dfrac{0.08206 \text{ L} \cdot \text{atm}}{\text{mol} \cdot \text{K}}\right)(293.15 \text{ K})}{621.142 \text{ torr}} \left(\dfrac{760 \text{ torr}}{1 \text{ atm}}\right)$$

$$= 3.741581 = \textbf{3.742 L}$$

Reality Check

The units and the number of significant figures are correct. As always, it is possible to round the values and estimate an answer.

Example Problem 5.11

The rate of effusion of a sample of oxygen gas was measured along with the initial pressure and temperature of the sample. The oxygen diffused at a rate of 155.5 mL in 101.5 seconds. A sample of an unknown gas, at the same initial pressure and temperature, effused in the same apparatus at a rate of 225.3 mL in 172.5 seconds. What is the molar mass of the unknown gas?

Information

Collecting and labeling the variables gives the following (Be careful to keep the oxygen values separate from the unknown gas values.):

Oxygen
V = 155.5 mL
t = 101.5 s
Molar mass = 31.998 g/mole

Unknown
V = 225.3 mL
t = 172.5 s
Molar mass = ? g/mole

Connections

Graham's law gives the relationship between the rates of effusion and the molar masses:

$$\frac{Rate_A}{Rate_B} = \sqrt{\frac{MM_B}{MM_A}}$$

Solution

We can find the rates, R_A and R_B, by dividing the volume by the time for each sample. We will assume that gas A is the oxygen and gas B is the unknown. Entering this information into Graham's law gives

$$\frac{R_A}{R_B} = \frac{\dfrac{155.5 \text{ mL}}{101.5 \text{ s}}}{\dfrac{225.3 \text{ mL}}{172.5 \text{ s}}} = \sqrt{\frac{MM_B}{MM_A}} = \sqrt{\frac{MM_B}{31.998 \text{ g/mol}}}$$

$$= \frac{1.5320197}{1.3060870} = 1.172984 = \sqrt{\frac{MM_B}{31.998 \text{ g/mol}}}$$

$$1.375891 = \frac{MM_B}{31.998 \text{ g/mol}}$$

$$MM_B = (1.375891)(31.998 \text{ g/mol}) = 44.02576 = \textbf{44.03 g/mol}$$

This relationship is valid only if the initial pressures and temperatures are the same.

Reality Check

The units and the number of significant figures are correct. It is helpful to remember that the lightest molecule (H_2) has a molar mass of 2 g/mol, and any value less than this is clearly in error. Very large molar masses (greater than 500 g/mol) are unlikely for gases.

Follow-Up Problem 5.11a

The rate of effusion of a sample of argon gas was measured. The argon diffused at a rate of 135.2 mL in 103.5 seconds. A sample of an unknown gas effused in the same apparatus at a rate of 101.3 mL in 230.2 seconds. Determine the molar mass of the unknown gas. The initial temperatures and pressures of the two samples were the same.

Information

The diffusion rate of argon (135.2 milliliters in 103.5 seconds); the diffusion rate of an unknown gas (101.3 milliliters in 230.2 seconds); the question of what is the molar mass of the unknown gas

Connections

$$\frac{Rate_A}{Rate_B} = \sqrt{\frac{MM_B}{MM_A}}$$

Solution

The rates will be in terms of milliliters per second. In this solution, we will assume gas A = argon (MM_A = 39.948 g/mol) and gas B is the unknown. Entering the appropriate values into Graham's Law gives

$$\frac{Rate_A}{Rate_B} = \frac{\dfrac{135.2 \text{ mL}}{103.5 \text{ s}}}{\dfrac{101.3 \text{ mL}}{230.2 \text{ s}}} = \sqrt{\frac{MM_B}{MM_A}} = \sqrt{\frac{MM_B}{39.948 \text{ g/mol}}}$$

$$= \frac{1.306280}{0.4400521} = 2.968466688 = \sqrt{\frac{MM_B}{39.948 \text{ g/mol}}}$$

$$8.811794 = \frac{MM_B}{39.948 \text{ g/mol}}$$

$$MM_B = (8.811794)(39.948 \text{ g/mol}) = 352.0135 = \textbf{352.0 g/mol}$$

Reality Check

The magnitude of the answer is reasonable. All values <u>must</u> be greater than 2 g/mol and are usually less than 500 g/mole. The units and the number of significant figures are correct.

Follow-Up Problem 5.11b

The effusion of a chlorine gas sample, at a certain temperature and pressure, was determined to be 110.2 mL in 10.52 minutes. This rate was compared to that of an unknown silicon hydride. The silicon hydride might be SiH_4, Si_2H_6, Si_3H_8, Si_4H_{10}, Si_5H_{12}, or Si_6H_{14}. The silicon hydride, at the same temperature and pressure as the chlorine, effused at a rate of 99.98 mL in 752.5 seconds. Which silicon hydride was present in the unknown sample?

Information

The diffusion rate of chlorine (110.2 mL in 10.52 minutes); the diffusion rate of an unknown gas (99.98 mL in 752.5 seconds); the formulas for several possible products (SiH_4, Si_2H_6, Si_3H_8, Si_4H_{10}, Si_5H_{12}, or Si_6H_{14}); the question of what is the identity of the unknown gas

Connections

$$\frac{Rate_A}{Rate_B} = \sqrt{\frac{MM_B}{MM_A}}$$

Solution

To determine which of the six choices has a molecular weight nearest the value determined from Graham's law, a minute/second conversion is necessary.

The rates will be in terms of milliliters per second (or milliliters per minute). In this solution, we will assume gas A = chlorine (MM_A = 70.906 g/mol) and gas B is the unknown. Entering the appropriate values into Graham's Law gives

$$\frac{Rate_A}{Rate_B} = \frac{\dfrac{110.2 \text{ mL}}{10.52 \text{ min}}}{\dfrac{99.98 \text{ mL}}{752.5 \text{ s}}} \left(\frac{1 \text{ min}}{60 \text{ s}}\right) = \sqrt{\frac{MM_B}{MM_A}} = \sqrt{\frac{MM_B}{70.906 \text{ g/mol}}}$$

$$= \frac{10.475285}{0.1328638}\left(\frac{1}{60}\right) = 1.314038 = \sqrt{\frac{MM_B}{70.906 \text{ g/mol}}}$$

$$1.72669589 = \frac{MM_B}{70.906 \text{ g/mol}}$$

$$MM_B = (1.72669589)\,(70.906 \text{ g/mol}) = 122.433 = 122.4 \text{ g/mol}$$

The approximate molar masses of the silicon hydrides are

SiH_4 (32 g/mol)	Si_2H_6 (62 g/mol)	Si_3H_8 (92 g/mol)
Si_4H_{10} (122 g/mol)	Si_5H_{12} (152 g/mol)	Si_6H_{14} (182 g/mol)

The best match in molar masses is **Si_4H_{10}**.

Reality Check

The magnitude of the answer is reasonable. All values must be greater than 2 g/mol and are usually less than 500 g/mole. The units and the number of significant figures are correct.

Example Problem 5.12

A 2.50-mole sample of ammonia gas was contained in a 1.10-liter container at 27°C. Determine the pressure in atmospheres of the ammonia using (a) the ideal gas equation and (b) the van der Waals equation.

Information

(a) Collect and label the data from the problem:

$n = 2.50$ mol
$V = 1.10$ L
$T = 27°C = 300.$ K
$P = ?$ atm

(b) To use the van der Waals equation, add the van der Waals constants (**table 5.3**) to the above table of variables:

$a = 4.17 \ L^2atm/mol^2$
$b = 0.138 \ L/mol$
$n = 2.50 \ mol$
$V = 1.10 \ L$
$T = 27°C = 300. \ K$
$P = ? \ atm$

Connections

(a) Rearranging the ideal gas equation to find pressure gives $P = nRT/V$.

(b) The van der Waals equation $\left(P + \dfrac{an^2}{V^2}\right)(V - nb) = nRT$, which rearranges to find pressure

$$P = \left(\frac{nRT}{(V - nb)}\right) - \left(\frac{an^2}{V^2}\right)$$

Solution

(a) Substituting the values from the table into this equation gives this (Enter the appropriate values into the equation and cancel.):

$$P = \frac{(2.50 \ \cancel{mol})\left(\dfrac{0.08206 \ \cancel{L} \bullet atm}{\cancel{mol} \bullet \cancel{K}}\right)(300. \ \cancel{K})}{(1.10 \ \cancel{L})} = 55.9772 = \mathbf{56.0 \ atm}$$

(b) Substituting the values from the table into the rearranged van der Waals equation gives

$$P = \left(\frac{(2.50 \ \cancel{mol})\left(\dfrac{0.08206 \ L \bullet atm}{\cancel{mol} \bullet \cancel{K}}\right)(300. \cancel{K})}{\left[1.10 \ L - (2.50 \ \cancel{mol})\left(\dfrac{0.138 \ L}{\cancel{mol}}\right)\right]}\right) - \left(\frac{\left(\dfrac{4.17 \ \cancel{L}^2 \ atm}{\cancel{mol}^2}\right)(2.50 \ \cancel{mol})^2}{(1.10 \ \cancel{L})^2}\right)$$

To make the equation simpler, we will remove the cancelled units from the above equation:

$$P = \left(\frac{(2.50)\left(\dfrac{0.08206 \ L \bullet atm}{1}\right)(300.)}{\left[1.10 \ L - (2.50)\left(\dfrac{0.138 \ L}{1}\right)\right]}\right) - \left(\frac{\left(\dfrac{4.17 \ atm}{1}\right)(2.50)^2}{(1.10)^2}\right)$$

Now we will do some preliminary calculations and the final unit cancellation:

$$P = \left(\frac{\left(\dfrac{61.545 \ \cancel{L} \bullet atm}{1}\right)}{(1.10 - (0.345))\cancel{L}}\right) - \left(\frac{\left(\dfrac{4.17 \ atm}{1}\right)6.25}{1.21}\right)$$

Both terms on the right have the same units (atm), which indicates that the cancellation was correct. The units for the two terms _must_ be identical if we are to subtract one from the other. Finishing the calculation gives

$$P = 60.017 = \mathbf{60.0 \ atm}$$

Reality Check

The units and the number of significant figures are correct. As always, it is possible to round the values and estimate an answer. Ideally, you should round until you can approximate the answer in your head.

Follow-Up Problem 5.12a

A 2.00-liter steel cylinder contains 1.85 moles of sulfur dioxide (SO_2) at 21°C. Determine the pressure in atmospheres of this sample using **(a)** the ideal gas equation and **(b)** the van der Waals equation.

Information

The volume (2.00 L); moles (1.85 mol); the temperature (21°C); the questions of what is the pressure in atmospheres using **(a)** the ideal gas equation and **(b)** the van der Waals equation

Connections

(a) $PV = nRT$; **(b)** $\left(P + \dfrac{an^2}{V^2}\right)(V - nb) = nRT$

Solution

(a) Collect and label the information from the problem:

$P = ?$ atm
$V = 2.00$ L
$n = 1.85$ mol
$T = 21°C = 294$ K
$R = \dfrac{0.08206 \text{ L} \cdot \text{atm}}{\text{mol} \cdot \text{K}}$

Rearrange the ideal gas equation to $P = \dfrac{nRT}{V}$

Enter the appropriate values into the equation and cancel:

$$P = \frac{(1.85 \text{ \sout{mol}})\left(\dfrac{0.08206 \text{ \sout{L}} \cdot \text{atm}}{\text{\sout{mol}} \cdot \text{\sout{K}}}\right)(294 \text{ \sout{K}})}{(2.00 \text{ \sout{L}})} = 22.3162 = \textbf{22.3 atm}$$

(b) To use the van der Waals equation, we must add the van der Waals constants (**table 5.3**) to the above table of variables. The new table is this:

$a = 6.865$ L^{2}atm/mol^2
$b = 0.05679$ L/mol
$n = 1.85$ mol
$V = 2.00$ L
$T = 21°C = 294$ K
$P = ?$ atm

Substituting the values from the table into the rearranged van der Waals' equation gives

$$P = \left[\frac{(1.85 \text{ \sout{mol}})\left(\dfrac{0.08206 \text{ L} \cdot \text{atm}}{\text{\sout{mol}} \cdot \text{\sout{K}}}\right)(294\text{\sout{K}})}{\left(2.00 \text{ L} - (1.85 \text{ \sout{mol}})\left(\dfrac{0.05679 \text{ L}}{\text{\sout{mol}}}\right)\right)}\right] - \left[\frac{\left(\dfrac{6.865 \text{ \sout{L}}^2\text{atm}}{\text{\sout{mol}}^2}\right)(1.85 \text{ \sout{mol}})^2}{(2.00 \text{ \sout{L}})^2}\right]$$

To make the equation simpler, we will remove the cancelled units from the above equation:

$$P = \frac{\left((1.85)\left(\dfrac{0.08206 \text{ L} \bullet \text{atm}}{1}\right)(294)\right)}{\left(2.00 \text{ L} - (1.85)\left(\dfrac{0.05679 \text{ L}}{1}\right)\right)} - \left(\frac{\left(\dfrac{6.865 \text{ atm}}{1}\right)(1.85)^2}{(2.00)^2}\right)$$

Now we will do some preliminary calculations and the final unit cancellation:

$$P = \frac{\left(\dfrac{44.632 \text{ L} \bullet \text{atm}}{1}\right)}{(2.00 - (0.10506))\text{ L}} - \left(\frac{\left(\dfrac{6.865 \text{ atm}}{1}\right)3.4225}{4.00}\right)$$

Both terms on the right have the same units (atm), which indicates that the cancellation was correct. The units for the two terms <u>must</u> be identical if we are to subtract one from the other. Finishing the calculation gives

$$P = 17.679 = \mathbf{17.7 \text{ atm}}$$

Reality Check

The units and the number of significant figures are correct. As always, it is possible to round the values and estimate an answer

Follow-Up Problem 5.12b

The gas in an automobile airbag is nitrogen. This nitrogen forms when sodium azide, NaN_3, undergoes thermal decomposition. The products are sodium metal and nitrogen gas. The sodium metal reacts with other components in the airbag to form nonvolatile sodium compounds. Use the van der Waals equation to determine the pressure in atmospheres of nitrogen gas produced by 75.0 grams of sodium azide in a 1.100-liter container at 45°C.

Information

Information on the reaction (sodium azide undergoes thermal decomposition to form sodium metal and nitrogen gas); the mass of sodium azide (75.0 g); the volume (1.100 L); the temperature (45°C); the van der Waals equation; the question of what is the pressure of nitrogen in atmospheres

Connections

The van der Waals equation $\left(P + \dfrac{an^2}{V^2}\right)(V - nb) = nRT$; the van der Waals constants for nitrogen

(a) $= 1.39 \text{ L}^2\text{atm/mol}^2$ and **(b)** $= 0.0391 \text{ L/mol}$

Solution

Collecting the information gives

$a = 1.39 \text{ L}^2\text{atm/mol}^2$
$b = 0.0391 \text{ L/mol}$
Mass $= 75.0 \text{ g NaN}_3$
$V = 1.100 \text{ L}$
$T = 45°C = 318 \text{ K}$
$P = ? \text{ atm}$

Before we can use the van der Waals equation, we need the moles of gas (N_2). To determine this value, we need to use the balanced chemical equation for the reaction. The skeleton equation is

$$NaN_3(s) \rightarrow Na(s) + N_2(g)$$

Balancing this equation gives

$$2\,NaN_3(s) \rightarrow 2\,Na(s) + 3\,N_2(g)$$

Adding the stoichiometric information to this equation gives

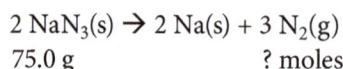

$$2\,NaN_3(s) \rightarrow 2\,Na(s) + 3\,N_2(g)$$
$$75.0\ g \qquad\qquad\qquad ?\ moles$$

To determine the moles of nitrogen, we combine the molar mass of sodium azide (65.011 g/mol) with the information from the balanced chemical equation:

$$\text{Moles } N_2 = (75.0\ g\ NaN_3)\left(\frac{1\ mol\ NaN_3}{65.011\ g\ NaN_3}\right)\left(\frac{3\ mol\ N_2}{2\ mol\ NaN_3}\right) = 1.730476\ mol\ N_2 \quad \text{(unrounded)}$$

To find the pressure, we need to rearrange the van der Waals equation:

$$P = \left(\frac{nRT}{(V-nb)}\right) - \left(\frac{an^2}{V^2}\right)$$

Substituting the values from the table into the rearranged van der Waals equation gives

$$P = \left| \frac{(1.730476\ \cancel{mol})\left(\dfrac{0.08206\ L \cdot atm}{\cancel{mol} \cdot \cancel{K}}\right)(318\,\cancel{K})}{\left(1.100\ L - (1.730476\ \cancel{mol})\left(\dfrac{0.0391\ L}{\cancel{mol}}\right)\right)} \right| - \left| \frac{\left(\dfrac{1.39\ \cancel{L}^2\ atm}{\cancel{mol}^2}\right)(1.730476\ \cancel{mol})^2}{(1.100\ \cancel{L})^2} \right|$$

To make the equation simpler, we remove the cancelled units from the above equation:

$$P = \left| \frac{(1.730476)\left(\dfrac{0.08206\ L \cdot atm}{1}\right)(318)}{\left(1.100\ L - (1.730476)\left(\dfrac{0.0391\ L}{1}\right)\right)} \right| - \left| \frac{\left(\dfrac{1.39\ atm}{1}\right)(1.730476)^2}{(1.100)^2} \right|$$

Now we do some preliminary calculations and the final unit cancellation:

$$P = \left| \frac{\left(\dfrac{45.1569\ \cancel{L} \cdot atm}{1}\right)}{(1.100 - (0.06766))\cancel{L}} \right| - \left| \frac{\left(\dfrac{1.39\ atm}{1}\right)2.9945}{1.210} \right|$$

Both terms on the right have the same units (atm), which indicates that the cancellation was correct. The terms <u>must</u> be identical if we are to subtract one from the other. Finishing the calculation gives

$$P = 40.3023 = \textbf{40.3 atm}$$

Reality Check

The units and the number of significant figures are correct. As always, it is possible to round the values and estimate an answer

Example Problem 5.13

A diver is planning a dive to a depth of 100 feet. What is the minimum pressure, in psi, required in her diving tank?

Information

Collect the information from the problem: Depth = 100 feet and P = ? psi

Connections

14.7 psi/atm

Solution

This leads to the following series of conversions:
To use the conversion 2.54 cm = 1 in, we need to start with

$$(100 \text{ ft})\left(\frac{12 \text{ in}}{1 \text{ ft}}\right)\left(\frac{2.54 \text{ cm}}{1 \text{ in}}\right)$$

Changing to meters (to take advantage of the 1 atm = 10 m conversion) gives

$$(100 \text{ ft})\left(\frac{12 \text{ in}}{1 \text{ ft}}\right)\left(\frac{2.54 \text{ cm}}{1 \text{ in}}\right)\left(\frac{0.01}{\text{c}}\right)$$

Introducing pressure gives

$$(100 \text{ ft})\left(\frac{12 \text{ in}}{1 \text{ ft}}\right)\left(\frac{2.54 \text{ cm}}{1 \text{ in}}\right)\left(\frac{0.01}{\text{c}}\right)\left(\frac{1 \text{ atm}}{10 \text{ m}}\right)$$

Converting from atmospheres to pounds per square inch (psi) gives

$$(100 \text{ ft})\left(\frac{12 \text{ in}}{1 \text{ ft}}\right)\left(\frac{2.54 \text{ cm}}{1 \text{ in}}\right)\left(\frac{0.01}{\text{c}}\right)\left(\frac{1 \text{ atm}}{10 \text{ m}}\right)\left(\frac{14.7 \text{ psi}}{1 \text{ atm}}\right) = 44.8056 = \textbf{40 psi}$$

At a depth of 100 ft, only a pressure greater than 40 psi is available to the diver.

Reality Check

The units and the number of significant figures are correct. From the reading, we know that 10 meters in depth is roughly equivalent to 1 atm. As always, it is possible to round the values and estimate an answer. Ideally, you should round until you can approximate the answer in your head. The values in the problem and in the reading justify reporting the answer to only one significant figure.

Follow-Up Problem 5.13a

A diver is planning on making a deep dive. He is planning to dive to 300 feet. What is the minimum pressure, in torr, required in the air tank?

Information

The depth (300 ft); the question of what is minimum pressure in torr

Connections

The external pressure increases by 1 atmosphere for each 10 meters of descent and 760 torr/atm

Solution

This leads to the following series of conversions:

To use the conversion 2.54 cm = 1 in, we need to start with

$$(300 \text{ ft})\left(\frac{12 \text{ in}}{1 \text{ ft}}\right)\left(\frac{2.54 \text{ cm}}{1 \text{ in}}\right)$$

Changing to meters (to take advantage of the 1 atm = 10 m conversion):

$$(300 \text{ ft})\left(\frac{12 \text{ in}}{1 \text{ ft}}\right)\left(\frac{2.54 \text{ cm}}{1 \text{ in}}\right)\left(\frac{0.01}{\text{c}}\right)$$

Introducing pressure:

$$(300 \text{ ft})\left(\frac{12 \text{ in}}{1 \text{ ft}}\right)\left(\frac{2.54 \text{ cm}}{1 \text{ in}}\right)\left(\frac{0.01}{\text{c}}\right)\left(\frac{1 \text{ atm}}{10 \text{ m}}\right)$$

Converting from atmospheres to pounds per square inch (psi):

$$(300 \text{ ft})\left(\frac{12 \text{ in}}{1 \text{ ft}}\right)\left(\frac{2.54 \text{ cm}}{1 \text{ in}}\right)\left(\frac{0.01}{\text{c}}\right)\left(\frac{1 \text{ atm}}{10 \text{ m}}\right)\left(\frac{760 \text{ torr}}{1 \text{ atm}}\right) = 6949.44 = 7 \times 10^3 \text{ torr}$$

Reality Check

The units and the number of significant figures are correct. From the reading, we know that 10 meters in depth is roughly equivalent to 1 atm. As always, it is possible to round the values and estimate an answer. The values in the problem and in the reading only justify reporting the answer to one significant figure.

Follow-Up Problem 5.13b

The deepest point in the ocean is about 36,000 feet. Determine the pressure, in atmospheres, at this depth.

Information

The depth (36,000 ft); the question of what is the pressure in atmospheres

Connections

The external pressure increases by 1 atm for each 10 meters of descent

Solution

This leads to the following series of conversions:
To use the conversion 2.54 cm = 1 in, we need to start with

$$(36{,}000 \text{ ft})\left(\frac{12 \text{ in}}{1 \text{ ft}}\right)\left(\frac{2.54 \text{ cm}}{1 \text{ in}}\right)$$

Changing to meters (to take advantage of the 1 atm = 10 m conversion):

$$(36{,}000 \text{ ft})\left(\frac{12 \text{ in}}{1 \text{ ft}}\right)\left(\frac{2.54 \text{ cm}}{1 \text{ in}}\right)\left(\frac{0.01}{\text{c}}\right)$$

Introducing pressure:

$$(36{,}000 \text{ ft})\left(\frac{12 \text{ in}}{1 \text{ ft}}\right)\left(\frac{2.54 \text{ cm}}{1 \text{ in}}\right)\left(\frac{0.01}{\text{c}}\right)\left(\frac{1 \text{ atm}}{10 \text{ m}}\right)$$

$$= 1097.28 = 1.1 \times 10^3 \text{ atm}$$

Reality Check

The units and the number of significant figures are correct. From the reading, we know that 10 meters in depth is roughly equivalent to 1 atm. As always, it is possible to round the values and estimate an answer. The values in the problem and in the reading only justify reporting the answer to one significant figure.

END-OF-CHAPTER PROBLEMS

5.1 Characteristics of Gases

5.2 List the two types of condensed phases.

Solution

The two types of condensed phases (the constituent particles are in contact) are **solids** and **liquids.**

5.2 Pressure and Dalton's Law

5.4 A 125-lb woman places her entire weight on one heel. If she is wearing high heels with an area of 0.75 in^2 at the heel's end, what is the pressure under her heel in pascals?

Information

The weight (125 lb); the area (0.75 in^2); the question of what is the pressure in pascals

Connections

$P = F/A$; the definition of *pascal* in terms of base units (Kg/m•s^2); 9.8 m/s^2 (gravity)

Solution

Using the definition of *pressure*, the force (= weight), and area gives

$$P = \left(\frac{125 \text{ lbs}}{0.75 \text{ in}^2} \right)$$

From the definition of *pascal*, we can see that it will be necessary to convert the pounds to kilograms. There are several ways to make this conversion; the following is only one:

$$P = \left(\frac{125 \text{ lbs}}{0.75 \text{ in}^2} \right)\left(\frac{1 \text{ kg}}{2.205 \text{ lbs}} \right)$$

The definition of *pascal* includes meters instead of inches (at this time, do not be concerned that the meters are not squared), so it is necessary to convert inches squared to meters squared. Again, there are multiple ways to make the conversion.

$$P = \left(\frac{125 \text{ lbs}}{0.75 \text{ in}^{\,2}} \right)\left(\frac{1 \text{ kg}}{2.205 \text{ lbs}} \right)\left(\frac{1 \text{ in}}{2.54 \text{ cm}} \right)^2\left(\frac{c}{0.01} \right)^2$$

This leaves kg/m^2. Adding the acceleration due to gravity (9.8 m/s^2) gives

$$P = \left(\frac{125 \text{ lbs}}{0.75 \text{ in}^{\,2}} \right)\left(\frac{1 \text{ kg}}{2.205 \text{ lbs}} \right)\left(\frac{1 \text{ in}}{2.54 \text{ cm}} \right)^2\left(\frac{c}{0.01} \right)^2\left(\frac{9.8 \text{ m}}{s^2} \right)$$

The meters from m/s^2 cancel one of the meters from kg/m^2 to leave kg/ms^2. We can finish the problem by adding the definition of *pascal*:

$$P = \left(\frac{125 \text{ lbs}}{0.75 \text{ in}^{\,2}} \right)\left(\frac{1 \text{ kg}}{2.205 \text{ lbs}} \right)\left(\frac{1 \text{ in}}{2.54 \text{ cm}} \right)^2\left(\frac{c}{0.01} \right)^2\left(\frac{9.8 \text{ m}}{s^2} \right)\left(\frac{1 \text{ Pa}}{\frac{1 \text{ kg}}{\text{m} \cdot s^2}} \right) = 1148150.4 = \mathbf{1.1 \times 10^6} \text{ Pa}$$

Reality Check

The magnitude of the answer is reasonable (check by estimating the final answer). The units and the number of significant figures are correct.

5.6 Make the following conversions: **(a)** 1.5×10^5 Pa to atmospheres; **(b)** 852 torr to atmospheres; **(c)** 1.95 kPa to atmospheres; **(d)** 127 mmHg to torr; **(e)** 827 torr to pascals

Information
The initial and final units for **(a)** 1.5×10^5 Pa to atmospheres; **(b)** 852 torr to atmospheres; **(c)** 1.95 kPa to atmospheres; **(d)** 127 mmHg to torr; **(e)** 827 torr to pascals)

Connections
Various pressure conversions (see **table 5.1**).

Solution
Write the given unit, followed by the appropriate conversion(s):

(a) $1.5 \text{ a } 10^5 \text{ Pa} \left(\dfrac{1 \text{ atm}}{1.01325 \times 10^5 \text{ Pa}} \right) = 1.4803849 = \textbf{1.5 atm}$

(b) $852 \text{ torr} \left(\dfrac{1 \text{ atm}}{760 \text{ torr}} \right) = 1.1210526 = \textbf{1.12 atm}$

(c) $1.95 \text{ kPa} \left(\dfrac{1 \text{ atm}}{1.01325 \times 10^5 \text{ Pa}} \right) \left(\dfrac{1,000}{k} \right) = 0.0192450 = \textbf{0.0192 atm}$

(d) $127 \text{ mmHg} \left(\dfrac{1 \text{ torr}}{1 \text{ mmHg}} \right) = \textbf{127 torr}$

(e) $827 \text{ torr} \left(\dfrac{1.01325 \times 10^5 \text{ Pa}}{760 \text{ torr}} \right) = 1.102575987 \times 10^5 = \textbf{1.10} \times \textbf{10}^\textbf{5} \text{ \textbf{pascals}}$

Reality Check
The magnitudes of the answers seem reasonable. The units and the number of significant figures are correct.

5.8 Determine the total pressure, in atmospheres, in a balloon that contains 0.950 atm of nitrogen gas, 181 torr of oxygen gas, and 9 mmHg of argon.

Information
The individual pressures 0.950 atm nitrogen gas, 181 torr of oxygen gas, and 9 mmHg of argon; the question of what is the total pressure in atmospheres

Connections
$P_{total} = P_a + P_b + P_c + \ldots$ and the appropriate unit conversions

Solution
The equivalency of mmHg and torr means that 9 mmHg = 9 torr:

$P_a = 0.950 \text{ atm } N_2$
$P_b = 181 \text{ torr } O_2$
$P_c = 9 \text{ torr } Ar$

Entering the values into Dalton's law gives

$$P_{total} = 0.985 \text{ atm} + 181 \text{ torr} + 9 \text{ torr}$$

The units must agree before addition; therefore, the following conversion factor is necessary:

$$\left(\frac{1 \text{ atm}}{760 \text{ torr}} \right)$$

Including the conversion gives

$$P_{total} = 0.985 \text{ atm} + 181 \text{ torr} \left(\frac{1 \text{ atm}}{760 \text{ torr}} \right) + 9 \text{ torr} \left(\frac{1 \text{ atm}}{760 \text{ torr}} \right) = 1.235 = \textbf{1.24 atm}$$

Reality Check

The magnitude of the answer seems reasonable. The units and the number of significant figures are correct. The two torr conversions could be combined as $(181 + 9) \text{ torr} \left(\dfrac{1 \text{ atm}}{760 \text{ torr}} \right)$.

5.10 Determine the mole fraction of each component in a gas mixture with a nitrogen partial pressure of 0.855 atm, an oxygen partial pressure of 0.220 atm, and a carbon dioxide partial pressure of 0.100 atm.

Information

The partial pressures of nitrogen = 0.855 atm, oxygen = 0.220 atm, and carbon dioxide = 0.100 atm; the questions of what are the mole fractions of each gas

Connections

$$X_A = \frac{P_A}{P_{total}}; P_{total} = P_a + P_b + P_c + \ldots$$

Solution

Using Dalton's law, we can determine the total pressure:

$$P_{total} = P_a + P_b + P_c + \ldots = 0.855 \text{ atm} + 0.220 \text{ atm} + 0.100 \text{ atm} = 1.175 \text{ atm}$$

Entering the values into the pressure definition of *mole fraction* $\left(X_A = \dfrac{P_A}{P_{total}} \right)$ gives

$$X_{N_2} = \frac{0.855 \text{ atm}}{1.175 \text{ atm}} = 0.7276596 = \textbf{0.728}$$

$$X_{O_2} = \frac{0.220 \text{ atm}}{1.175 \text{ atm}} = 0.1872340 = \textbf{0.187}$$

$$X_{CO_2} = \frac{0.100 \text{ atm}}{1.175 \text{ atm}} = 0.085106 = \textbf{0.0851}$$

Reality Check

The magnitudes of the answers seem reasonable. The sum of the mole fractions is correct (1.000). The units (none) and the number of significant figures are correct.

5.3 The Development of Gas Law Relationships

5.14 You place a small piece of dry ice (solid carbon dioxide) into a balloon and then seal the balloon. The balloon slowly expands, even though neither the temperature nor the pressure changes. Why does the volume of the balloon increase?

Solution

Avogadro's gas law explains the observation. As the dry ice sublimes, the moles of gas will increase. The increase in moles results in an increase in volume.

5.4 The Ideal Gas Equation

5.19 The ideal gas constant has a value of 0.08206 L•atm/mol•K. What is the value of the ideal gas constant in ft^3•psi/mol•K?

Information

The value of the gas constant (0.08206 L•atm/mol•K); the question of what is the value of the gas constant in ft^3•psi/mol•K

Connections

The conversion factors to relate L to ft^3 and atm to psi

Solution

This is a conversion problem. We can begin with any conversion, so we will start with a pressure conversion (1 atm = 14.7 psi):

$$R = \left(\frac{0.08206 \; L \bullet \text{atm}}{\text{mol} \bullet K}\right)\left(\frac{14.7 \; \text{psi}}{1 \; \text{atm}}\right)$$

We will do the volume conversion (L → ft^3) in steps. We begin by converting the liters to milliliters followed by the equivalence of a mL to a cm^3:

$$R = \left(\frac{0.08206 \; \text{L} \bullet \text{atm}}{\text{mol} \bullet K}\right)\left(\frac{14.7 \; \text{psi}}{1 \; \text{atm}}\right)\left(\frac{\text{m}}{0.001}\right)\left(\frac{\text{cm}^3}{\text{mL}}\right)$$

Next, we will use the relationship that 2.54 cm = 1 in:

$$R = \left(\frac{0.08206 \; \text{L} \bullet \text{atm}}{\text{mol} \bullet K}\right)\left(\frac{14.7 \; \text{psi}}{1 \; \text{atm}}\right)\left(\frac{\text{m}}{0.001}\right)\left(\frac{\text{cm}^3}{\text{mL}}\right)\left(\frac{1 \; \text{in}}{2.54 \; \text{cm}}\right)^3$$

Finally, after using 12 in = 1 ft, we are ready to determine the value:

$$R = \left(\frac{0.08206 \; \text{L} \bullet \text{atm}}{\text{mol} \bullet K}\right)\left(\frac{14.7 \; \text{psi}}{1 \; \text{atm}}\right)\left(\frac{\text{m}}{0.001}\right)\left(\frac{\text{cm}^3}{\text{mL}}\right)\left(\frac{1 \; \text{in}}{2.54 \; \text{cm}}\right)^3\left(\frac{1 \; \text{ft}}{12 \; \text{in}}\right)^3$$

$$= 0.042599447 = \textbf{0.0426 ft}^3\textbf{•psi/mol•K}$$

Reality Check

The units and the number of significant figures are correct. Based upon an estimation, the answer seems reasonable.

5.21 Your body heats the air in your lungs to body temperature (37°C). If you exhaled 1075 mL of air at a pressure at 755 mmHg, how many molecules of air did you exhale?

Information

The temperature (37°C); the volume (1075 mL); the pressure (755 mmHg); the question of how many molecules of air you would exhale

Connections

$PV = nRT$; Avogadro's number

Solution

Collect and label the information from the problem:

$P = 755$ mmHg

$V = 1075$ mL

Number of molecules = ? molecules

$T = 37°C = 310.$ K

$R = \dfrac{0.08206 \text{ L} \cdot \text{atm}}{\text{mol} \cdot \text{K}}$

Rearrange the ideal gas equation to $n = \dfrac{PV}{RT}$

Enter the appropriate values into the equation and cancel:

$$n = \frac{(755 \text{ mmHg})(1075 \text{ m\cancel{L}})}{\left(\dfrac{0.08206 \text{ \cancel{L}} \cdot \text{atm}}{\text{mol} \cdot \text{\cancel{K}}}\right)(310. \text{ \cancel{K}})}$$

The necessity of an additional conversion is now apparent. The *milli-* conversion ($m = 0.001 = 10^{-3}$) is appropriate:

$$n = \frac{(755 \text{ mmHg})(1075 \text{ \cancel{mL}})}{\left(\dfrac{0.08206 \text{ \cancel{L}} \cdot \text{atm}}{\text{mol} \cdot \text{\cancel{K}}}\right)(310. \text{ \cancel{K}})}\left(\frac{0.001}{\cancel{m}}\right)$$

Adding the appropriate pressure conversion (1 atm = 760 mmHg) gives

$$n = \frac{(755 \text{ \cancel{mmHg}})(1075 \text{ \cancel{mL}})}{\left(\dfrac{0.08206 \text{ \cancel{L}} \cdot \text{\cancel{atm}}}{\text{mol} \cdot \text{\cancel{K}}}\right)(310. \text{ \cancel{K}})}\left(\frac{0.001}{\cancel{m}}\right)\left(\frac{1 \text{ \cancel{atm}}}{760 \text{ \cancel{mmHg}}}\right)$$

This gives the moles; however, the problem wants molecules. To get from moles to molecules, we need to use Avogadro's number (6.022×10^{23} molecules/mol):

$$\text{Molecules} = \frac{(755 \text{ \cancel{mmHg}})(1075 \text{ \cancel{mL}})}{\left(\dfrac{0.08206 \text{ \cancel{L}} \cdot \text{\cancel{atm}}}{\cancel{\text{mol}} \cdot \text{\cancel{K}}}\right)(310. \text{\cancel{K}})}\left(\frac{0.001}{\cancel{m}}\right)\left(\frac{1 \text{ \cancel{atm}}}{760 \text{ \cancel{mmHg}}}\right)\left(\frac{6.022 \times 10^{23} \text{ molecules}}{1 \text{ \cancel{mol}}}\right)$$

$$= 2.52807 \times 10^{22} = \mathbf{2.53 \times 10^{22} \text{ molecules}}$$

Reality Check

The units and the number of significant figures are correct. The answer is close to the estimated answer.

5.23 **(a)** What is the density (in grams per liter) of gaseous carbon dioxide (CO_2) at 0.893 atm and 47°C? **(b)** A sample of an unknown gas weighing 0.144 g has a volume of 275 mL at 755 mmHg and 97°C. What is the molar mass of the gas?

Information

(a) The identity of the gas (CO_2); the pressure (0.893 atm); the temperature (47°C); the question of what is the density in g/L

(b) The mass (0.144 g); the volume (275 mL); the pressure (755 mmHg); the temperature (97°C); the question of what is the molar mass

Connections

$PV = nRT$

Solution

(a) Collect and label the information from the problem:

$P = 0.893$ atm
$V =$ assume 1.000 L (It is possible to assume any volume.)
$n = ?$ mol
$T = 47°C = 320.$ K
$R = \dfrac{0.08206 \text{ L} \cdot \text{atm}}{\text{mol} \cdot \text{K}}$

Rearrange the ideal gas equation to $n = \dfrac{PV}{RT}$

Enter the appropriate values into the equation and cancel:

$$n = \frac{(0.893 \text{ \sout{atm}})(1.000 \text{ \sout{L}})}{\left(\dfrac{0.08206 \text{ \sout{L}} \cdot \text{\sout{atm}}}{\text{mol} \cdot \text{\sout{K}}}\right)(320.\text{\sout{K}})}$$

This gives the moles; however, we need the mass. Adding the molar mass of CO_2 (44.0 g/mol) to the calculation gives the grams:

$$n = \frac{(0.893 \text{ \sout{atm}})(1.000 \text{ \sout{L}})}{\left(\dfrac{0.08206 \text{ \sout{L}} \cdot \text{\sout{atm}}}{\text{\sout{mol}} \cdot \text{\sout{K}}}\right)(320.\text{\sout{K}})}\left(\frac{44.0 \text{ g}}{\text{\sout{mol}}}\right) = 1.49631 \text{ g} \qquad \text{(unrounded)}$$

Using the definition of *density* from chapter 1 (Density = Mass/Volume), we can combine the calculated mass with the assumed volume:

$$\text{Density} = \frac{1.49631 \text{ g}}{1.000 \text{ L}} = 1.49631 = \mathbf{1.50 \text{ g/L}}$$

(b) Collect and label the information from the problem:

Mass = 0.144 g
$P = 755$ mmHg
$V = 275$ mL
$T = 97°C = 370.$ K
Molar mass = ? g/mol
$R = \dfrac{0.08206 \text{ L} \cdot \text{atm}}{\text{mol} \cdot \text{K}}$
Molar mass = ? g/mol

Rearrange the ideal gas equation to $n = \dfrac{PV}{RT}$

Enter the appropriate values into the equation and cancel:

$$n = \frac{(755 \text{ mmHg})(275 \text{ m\sout{L}})}{\left(\dfrac{0.08206 \text{ \sout{L}} \cdot \text{atm}}{\text{mol} \cdot \text{\sout{K}}}\right)(370. \text{ \sout{K}})}$$

The necessity of additional conversions is now apparent. The *milli-* conversion ($m = 0.001 = 10^{-3}$) is appropriate:

$$n = \frac{(755 \text{ mmHg})(275 \text{ \sout{mL}})}{\left(\dfrac{0.08206 \text{ \sout{L}} \cdot \text{atm}}{\text{mol} \cdot \text{\sout{K}}}\right)(370. \text{ \sout{K}})}\left(\frac{0.001}{\text{\sout{m}}}\right)$$

Adding the appropriate pressure conversion (1 atm = 760 mmHg) gives

$$n = \frac{(755 \; \cancel{mmHg})(275 \; \cancel{mL})}{\left(\dfrac{0.08206 \; \cancel{L} \bullet atm}{mol \bullet \cancel{K}}\right)(370. \; \cancel{K})}\left(\dfrac{0.001}{\cancel{m}}\right)\left(\dfrac{1 \; \cancel{atm}}{760 \; \cancel{mmHg}}\right) = 0.0089977 \; mol \qquad \text{(unrounded)}$$

To determine the molar mass, we need to use the definition of *molar mass* (g/mol):

$$\text{Molar mass} = \left(\frac{0.144 \; g}{0.0089977 \; mol}\right) = 16.0041 = \mathbf{16.0 \; g/mol}$$

Reality Check

The magnitude of the answer seems reasonable. The molar mass must be greater than or equal to the lightest molecule (H_2 = 2 g/mole), and most gases are less than 500 g/mole. The units and the number of significant figures are correct.

5.25 A student used the Dumas method (see Problem 5.24) to determine the molecular weight of an unknown liquid he was assigned to identify. At a temperature of 98°C and a pressure of 743 torr, 1.220 g of the liquid's vapor occupied 375 mL. Determine the molecular weight of the unknown.

Information

The mass (1.220 g); the volume (375 mL); the pressure (743 torr); the temperature (98°C); the question of what is the molecular weight

Connections

$PV = nRT$

Solution

Collect and label the information from the problem:

Mass = 1.220 g
P = 743 torr
V = 375 mL
T = 98°C = 371 K
$R = \dfrac{0.08206 \; L \bullet atm}{mol \bullet K}$
Molecular weight = ? g/mol

Rearrange the ideal gas equation to $n = \dfrac{PV}{RT}$

Enter the appropriate values into the equation and cancel:

$$n = \frac{(743 \; torr)(375 \; \cancel{mL})}{\left(\dfrac{0.08206 \; \cancel{L} \bullet atm}{mol \bullet \cancel{K}}\right)(371 \cancel{K})}$$

The necessity of additional conversions is now apparent. The *milli-* conversion ($m = 0.001 = 10^{-3}$) is appropriate:

$$n = \frac{(743 \; torr)(375 \; \cancel{mL})}{\left(\dfrac{0.08206 \; \cancel{L} \bullet atm}{mol \bullet \cancel{K}}\right)(371 \; \cancel{K})}\left(\dfrac{0.001}{\cancel{m}}\right)$$

Adding the appropriate pressure conversion (1 atm = 760 torr) gives

$$n = \frac{(743 \ \cancel{torr})(375 \ \cancel{mL})}{\left(\dfrac{0.08206 \ \cancel{L} \bullet \cancel{atm}}{mol \bullet \cancel{K}}\right)(371 \ \cancel{K})}\left(\frac{0.001}{\cancel{m}}\right)\left(\frac{1 \ atm}{760 \ \cancel{torr}}\right) = 1.2042 \times 10^{-2} \ mol \qquad \text{(unrounded)}$$

To determine the molar mass, we need to use the definition of *molar mass* (g/mol):

$$\text{Molar mass} = \left(\frac{1.220 \ g}{1.2042 \times 10^{-2} \ mol}\right) = 101.31 = \textbf{101 g/mol}$$

Reality Check

The magnitude of the answer seems reasonable. The molar mass must greater than or equal to the lightest molecule (H_2 = 2 g/mole), and most gases are less than 500 g/mole. The units and the number of significant figures are correct.

5.27 A sample of neon gas, Ne, was placed in a 1250.0-mL container at a temperature of 17.00°C and a pressure of 795.0 mmHg. How many grams of neon were in the sample?

Information

The identity of the gas (Ne); the volume (1250.0 mL); the temperature (17.00°C); the pressure (795.0 mmHg); the question of how many grams

Connections

$PV = nRT$

Solution

Collect and label the information from the problem:

$P = 795.0 \ mmHg$
$V = 1250.0 \ mL$
$T = 17.00°C = 290.15 \ K$
$R = \dfrac{0.08206 \ L \bullet atm}{mol \bullet K}$
$\text{Mass} = ? \ g \ Ne$

Rearrange the ideal gas equation to $n = \dfrac{PV}{RT}$

Enter the appropriate values into the equation and cancel:

$$n = \frac{(795.0 \ mmHg)(1250.0 \ m\cancel{L})}{\left(\dfrac{0.08206 \ \cancel{L} \bullet atm}{mol \bullet \cancel{K}}\right)(290.15 \ \cancel{K})}$$

The necessity of additional conversions is now apparent. The *milli-* conversion ($m = 0.001 = 10^{-3}$) is appropriate:

$$n = \frac{(795.0 \ mmHg)(1250.0 \ \cancel{mL})}{\left(\dfrac{0.08206 \ \cancel{L} \bullet atm}{mol \bullet \cancel{K}}\right)(290.15 \ \cancel{K})}\left(\frac{0.001}{\cancel{m}}\right)$$

Adding the appropriate pressure conversion (1 atm = 760 mmHg) gives

$$n = \frac{(795.0 \ \cancel{mmHg})(1250.0 \ \cancel{mL})}{\left(\dfrac{0.08206 \ \cancel{L} \bullet \cancel{atm}}{mol \bullet \cancel{K}}\right)(290.15 \ \cancel{K})}\left(\frac{0.001}{\cancel{m}}\right)\left(\frac{1 \ \cancel{atm}}{760 \ \cancel{mmHg}}\right)$$

This gives the number of moles present. We need to use the molar mass (20.18 g/mol) to convert from moles to grams:

$$\text{Mass Ne} = \frac{(795.0 \; \cancel{\text{mmHg}})(1250.0 \; \cancel{\text{mL}})}{\left(\dfrac{0.08206 \; \cancel{\text{L}} \bullet \cancel{\text{atm}}}{\cancel{\text{mol}} \bullet \cancel{\text{K}}}\right)(290.15 \; \cancel{\text{K}})} \left(\frac{0.001}{\cancel{\text{m}}}\right) \left(\frac{1 \; \cancel{\text{atm}}}{760 \; \cancel{\text{mmHg}}}\right) \left(\frac{20.18 \; \text{g}}{\cancel{\text{mol}}}\right) = 1.10823$$

$$= \textbf{1.108 g Ne}$$

Reality Check

The magnitude of the answer seems reasonable based upon an estimate. The units and the number of significant figures are correct.

5.29 The first binary compound of krypton to be prepared was KrF_2. A sample of this compound was prepared having a volume of 500.0 mL at a pressure of 795.0 mmHg and a temperature of 17.00°C. How many grams of KrF_2 were in the sample?

Information

The identity of the gas (KrF_2); the volume (500.0 mL); the temperature (17.00°C); the pressure (795.0 torr); the question of how many grams

Connections

$PV = nRT$

Solution

Collect and label the information from the problem:

$P = 795.0$ torr
$V = 500.0$ mL
$T = 17.00°C = 290.15$ K
$R = \dfrac{0.08206 \; \text{L} \bullet \text{atm}}{\text{mol} \bullet \text{K}}$
Mass = ? g KrF_2

Rearrange the ideal gas equation to $n = \dfrac{PV}{RT}$

Enter the appropriate values into the equation and cancel:

$$n = \frac{(795.0 \; \text{torr})(500.0 \; \cancel{\text{mL}})}{\left(\dfrac{0.08206 \; \cancel{\text{L}} \bullet \text{atm}}{\text{mol} \bullet \cancel{\text{K}}}\right)(290.15 \; \cancel{\text{K}})}$$

The necessity of additional conversions is now apparent. The *milli-* conversion ($m = 0.001 = 10^{-3}$) is appropriate:

$$n = \frac{(795.0 \; \text{torr})(500.0 \; \cancel{\text{mL}})}{\left(\dfrac{0.08206 \; \cancel{\text{L}} \bullet \text{atm}}{\text{mol} \bullet \cancel{\text{K}}}\right)(290.15 \; \cancel{\text{K}})} \left(\frac{0.001}{\cancel{\text{m}}}\right)$$

Adding the appropriate pressure conversion (1 atm = 760 torr) gives

$$n = \frac{(795.0 \; \cancel{\text{torr}})(500.0 \; \cancel{\text{mL}})}{\left(\dfrac{0.08206 \; \cancel{\text{L}} \bullet \cancel{\text{atm}}}{\text{mol} \bullet \cancel{\text{K}}}\right)(290.15 \; \cancel{\text{K}})} \left(\frac{0.001}{\cancel{\text{m}}}\right)\left(\frac{1 \; \cancel{\text{atm}}}{760 \; \cancel{\text{torr}}}\right)$$

This gives the number of moles present. We need to use the molar mass (121.794 g/mol) to convert from moles to grams:

$$\text{Mass KrF}_2 = \frac{(795.0 \text{ torr})(500.0 \text{ mL})}{\left(\dfrac{0.08206 \text{ L} \cdot \text{atm}}{\text{mol} \cdot \text{K}}\right)(290.15 \text{ K})}\left(\frac{0.001}{\text{m}}\right)\left(\frac{1 \text{ atm}}{760 \text{ torr}}\right)\left(\frac{121.794 \text{ g KrF}_2}{1 \text{ mol}}\right) = 2.67544$$

$$= \textbf{2.675 g KrF}_2$$

Reality Check
The magnitude of the answer seems reasonable. The units and the number of significant figures are correct.

5.5 The Combined Gas Equation
5.31 A sample of a gas occupying a volume of 5.72 L exerts a pressure of 725 mmHg. **(a)** What would be the volume in milliliters of the sample if you increased the pressure to 1.25 atm? **(b)** What would be the pressure in torr exerted by the gas if you decreased the volume to 3.76 L?

Information
(a) The initial volume and pressure (5.72 L and 725 mmHg); the final pressure (1.25 atm); the question of what is the final volume in liters

(b) The initial volume and pressure (5.72 L and 725 mmHg); the final volume (3.76 L); the question of what is the pressure in torr

Connections
$$\frac{P_1 V_1}{n_1 T_1} = \frac{P_2 V_2}{n_2 T_2}$$

Solution
(a) $\dfrac{P_1 V_1}{n_1 T_1} = \dfrac{P_2 V_2}{n_2 T_2} \rightarrow V_2 = \dfrac{P_1 V_1}{P_2} = \left(\dfrac{(725 \text{ mmHg})(5.72 \text{ L})}{1.25 \text{ atm}}\right)\left(\dfrac{1 \text{ atm}}{760 \text{ mmHg}}\right)\left(\dfrac{\text{m}}{0.001}\right)$

$$= 4365 = \textbf{4360 mL}$$

(b) Collect and label the information from the problem:

$P_1 = 725 \text{ mmHg}$ $P_2 = ? \text{ torr}$
$V_1 = 5.72 \text{ L}$ $V_2 = 3.76 \text{ L}$
$n_1 = -$ $n_2 = -$
$T_1 = -$ $T_2 = -$

Based on the available information, the combined gas law simplifies to $P_1 V_1 = P_2 V_2$.
The simplified combined gas law rearranges to $P_2 = \dfrac{P_1 V_1}{V_2}$
Enter the appropriate values into the equation and cancel:

$$P_2 = \frac{(725 \text{ mmHg})(5.72 \text{ L})}{(3.76 \text{ L})} = 1102.9255 = 1.10 \times 10^3 \text{ mmHg} = \textbf{1.10} \times \textbf{10}^3 \textbf{ torr}$$

Reality Check
The magnitudes of the answers seem reasonable. The units and the number of significant figures are correct.

5.33 A sample of a gas at a temperature of 15.5°C and a pressure of 0.895 atm occupies 14.3 L. (a) Determine the volume in milliliters of the gas at STP. (b) Determine the volume in liters of the gas at a pressure of 0.752 atm and a temperature of 31.0°C.

Information

(a) The initial temperature, pressure, and volume (15.5°C, 0.895 atm, and 14.3 L); the final temperature and pressure (STP); the question of what is the final volume in milliliters

(b) The initial temperature, pressure, and volume (15.5°C, 0.895 atm, and 14.3 L); the final pressure and temperature (0.752 atm and 31.0°C); the question of what is the final volume in liters

Connections

$$\frac{P_1 V_1}{n_1 T_1} = \frac{P_2 V_2}{n_2 T_2}$$

Solution

(a) Collect and label the information from the problem:

$P_1 = 0.895$ atm $\qquad$ $P_2 = 1.00$ atm

$V_1 = 14.3$ L $\qquad$ $V_2 = ?$ mL

$n_1 = -$ $\qquad$ $n_2 = -$

$T_1 = 15.5°C = 288.7$ K $\qquad$ $T_2 = 0.00°C = 273.15$ K

Based on the available information, the combined gas law simplifies to $\dfrac{P_1 V_1}{T_1} = \dfrac{P_2 V_2}{T_2}$

The simplified combined gas law rearranges to $V_2 = \dfrac{T_2 P_1 V_1}{T_1 P_2}$

Enter the appropriate values into the equation and cancel:

$$V_2 = \frac{(273.15\ \cancel{K})(0.895\ \cancel{atm})(14.3\ \text{L})}{(288.7\ \cancel{K})(1.00\ \cancel{atm})}$$

The necessity of an additional conversion is now apparent. The *milli-* conversion ($m = 0.001 = 10^{-3}$) is appropriate because the problem requests milliliters.

$$V_2 = \frac{(273.15\ \cancel{K})(0.895\ \cancel{atm})(14.3\ \text{L})}{(288.7\ \cancel{K})(1.00\ \cancel{atm})}\left(\frac{m}{0.001}\right) = 12109.1 = \mathbf{1.21 \times 10^4\ mL}$$

(b) Collect and label the information from the problem:

$P_1 = 0.895$ atm $\qquad$ $P_2 = 0.752$ atm

$V_1 = 14.3$ L $\qquad$ $V_2 = ?$ L

$n_1 = -$ $\qquad$ $n_2 = -$

$T_1 = 15.5°C = 288.7$ K $\qquad$ $T_2 = 31.0°C = 304.2$ K

Based on the available information, the combined gas law simplifies to $\dfrac{P_1 V_1}{T_1} = \dfrac{P_2 V_2}{T_2}$

The simplified combined gas law rearranges to $V_2 = \dfrac{T_2 P_1 V_1}{T_1 P_2}$

Enter the appropriate values into the equation and cancel:

$$V_2 = \frac{(304.2\ \cancel{K})(0.895\ \cancel{atm})(14.3\ \text{L})}{(288.7\ \cancel{K})(0.752\ \cancel{atm})} = 17.9330 = \mathbf{17.9\ L}$$

Reality Check

The magnitudes of the answers seem reasonable. The units and the number of significant figures are correct.

5.35 An engineer collected a sample of nitrogen gas in a 7.50 L container at a pressure of 575 torr and a temperature of 37°C. Later she found that the pressure had changed to 0.6000 atm, and the volume had changed to 7750.0 mL. What was the new Celsius temperature of the gas?

Information

The initial volume, pressure, and temperature (7.50 L, 575 mmHg, 37°C); the final pressure and volume (0.6000 atm 7500.0 mL); the question of what is the final temperature in °C

Connections

$$\frac{P_1 V_1}{n_1 T_1} = \frac{P_2 V_2}{n_2 T_2}$$

Solution

Collect and label the information from the problem:

$P_1 = 575$ mmHg $\qquad P_2 = 0.6000$ atm
$V_1 = 7.50$ L $\qquad V_2 = 7500.0$ mL
$n_1 = -$ $\qquad n_2 = -$
$T_1 = 37°C = 310.$ K $\qquad T_2 = ?$

Based on the available information, the combined gas law simplifies to $\frac{P_1 V_1}{T_1} = \frac{P_2 V_2}{T_2}$

The simplified combined gas law rearranges to $T_2 = \frac{P_2 V_2 T_1}{P_1 V_1}$

Enter the appropriate values into the equation and cancel:

$$T_2 = \frac{(0.6000 \text{ atm})(7500.0 \text{ mL})(310. \text{ K})}{(575 \text{ mmHg})(7.50 \text{ L})}$$

The necessity of additional conversions is now apparent. The *milli-* conversion ($m = 0.001 = 10^{-3}$) is appropriate:

$$T_2 = \frac{(0.6000 \text{ atm})(7500.0 \text{ mL})(310. \text{ K})}{(575 \text{ mmHg})(7.50 \text{ L})}\left(\frac{m}{0.001}\right)$$

Adding the appropriate pressure conversion (1 atm = 760 mmHg) gives

$$T_2 = \frac{(0.6000 \text{ atm})(7500.0 \text{ mL})(310. \text{ K})}{(575 \text{ mmHg})(7.50 \text{ L})}\left(\frac{0.001}{m}\right)\left(\frac{760 \text{ mmHg}}{1 \text{ atm}}\right) = 245.84 - 273.15$$

$$= -27.31 = \mathbf{-27°C}$$

5.37 A sample of air had all the oxygen removed to leave nearly pure nitrogen gas. Initially, the nitrogen gas had a volume of 15.00 L at 0.952 atm and 25°C. Later, the volume was 17.25 L and the pressure was 785 mmHg. What was the later temperature in degrees Celsius?

Information

The initial volume, pressure, and temperature (15.00 L, 0.952 atm, 25°C), the final pressure and volume (785 mmHg, 17.25 L); the question of what is the final temperature in °C

Connections

$$\frac{P_1 V_1}{n_1 T_1} = \frac{P_2 V_2}{n_2 T_2}$$

Solution

Collect and label the information from the problem:

$P_1 = 0.952$ atm $\qquad$ $P_2 = 785$ mmHg
$V_1 = 15.00$ L $\qquad$ $V_2 = 17.25$ L
$n_1 = -$ $\qquad\qquad$ $n_2 = -$
$T_1 = 25°C = 298$ K $\qquad$ $T_2 = ?\ °C$

Based on the available information, the combined gas law simplifies to $\dfrac{P_1 V_1}{T_1} = \dfrac{P_2 V_2}{T_2}$

The simplified combined gas law rearranges to $T_2 = \dfrac{P_2\ V_2\ T_1}{P_1\ V_1}$

Enter the appropriate values into the equation and cancel:

$$T_2 = \frac{(785\ \text{mmHg})(17.25\ \cancel{\text{L}})(298\ \text{K})}{(0.952\ \text{atm})(15.00\ \cancel{\text{L}})}$$

The necessity of an additional conversion is now apparent. Adding the appropriate pressure conversion (1 atm = 760 mmHg) gives

$$T_2 = \frac{(785\ \cancel{\text{mmHg}})(17.25\ \cancel{\text{L}})(298\ \text{K})}{(0.952\ \cancel{\text{atm}})(15.00\ \cancel{\text{L}})}\left(\frac{1\ \cancel{\text{atm}}}{760\ \cancel{\text{mmHg}}}\right) = 371.82\ \text{K} \qquad \text{(unrounded)}$$

In addition to the above, a temperature conversion is necessary:

$$T_2 = (371.82 - 273.15)°C = 98.67 = \textbf{99°C}$$

Reality Check

The magnitude of the answer seems reasonable. The units and the number of significant figures are correct.

5.39 A 250.00-mL sample of helium gas was collected at a temperature of 25°C and a pressure of 1.15 atm. At what Celsius temperature will the sample of gas have a volume of 225.0 mL and a pressure of 725 torr?

Information

The initial volume, temperature, and pressure (250.00 mL, 25°C, 1.15 atm); the final volume and pressure (225.0 mL, 725 torr); the question of what is the final temperature in °C

Connections

$$\frac{P_1 V_1}{n_1 T_1} = \frac{P_2 V_2}{n_2 T_2}$$

Solution

Collect and label the information from the problem:

$P_1 = 1.15$ atm $\qquad$ $P_2 = 725$ torr
$V_1 = 250.00$ mL $\qquad$ $V_2 = 225.0$ mL
$n_1 = -$ $\qquad\qquad$ $n_2 = -$
$T_1 = 25°C = 298$ K $\qquad$ $T_2 = ?\ °C$

Based on the available information, the combined gas law simplifies to $\dfrac{P_1 V_1}{T_1} = \dfrac{P_2 V_2}{T_2}$

The simplified combined gas law rearranges to $T_2 = \dfrac{P_2\ V_2\ T_1}{P_1\ V_1}$

Enter the appropriate values into the equation and cancel:

$$T_2 = \frac{(725 \text{ torr})(225.0 \text{ mL})(298 \text{ K})}{(1.15 \text{ atm})(250.00 \text{ mL})}$$

The necessity of an additional conversion is now apparent. Adding the appropriate pressure conversion (1 atm = 760 torr) gives

$$T_2 = \frac{(725 \text{ torr})(225.0 \text{ mL})(298 \text{ K})}{(1.15 \text{ atm})(250.00 \text{ mL})} \left(\frac{1 \text{ atm}}{760 \text{ torr}} \right) = 222.477 \text{ K} \qquad \text{(unrounded)}$$

In addition to the above, a temperature conversion is necessary:

$$T_2 = (222.477 - 273.15)°\text{C} = -50.673 = \mathbf{-51°C}$$

Reality Check

The magnitude of the answer seems reasonable. The units and the number of significant figures are correct.

5.40 A sample of a gas occupies 15.55 L at a temperature of 27.85°C. At what temperature, in degrees Celsius, would the volume of the gas be 10.00 L?

Information

The initial volume and temperature (15.55 L, 27.85°C); the final volume (10.00 L); the question of what is the final temperature in °C

Connections

$$\frac{P_1 V_1}{n_1 T_1} = \frac{P_2 V_2}{n_2 T_2}$$

Solution

Collect and label the information from the problem:

$P_1 = \text{—}$ $\qquad\qquad\qquad$ $P_2 = \text{—}$
$V_1 = 15.55 \text{ L}$ $\qquad\qquad$ $V_2 = 10.00 \text{ L}$
$n_1 = \text{—}$ $\qquad\qquad\qquad$ $n_2 = \text{—}$
$T_1 = 27.85°\text{C} = 301.00 \text{ K}$ $\qquad$ $T_2 = ? \text{ °C}$

Based on the available information, the combined gas law simplifies to $\dfrac{V_1}{T_1} = \dfrac{V_2}{T_2}$
The simplified combined gas law rearranges to $T_2 = \dfrac{V_2 T_1}{V_1}$

Enter the appropriate values into the equation and cancel; then convert to °C:

$$T_2 = \frac{(10.00 \text{ L})(301.00 \text{ K})}{(15.55 \text{ L})} = 193.5691 \text{ K} \quad \text{(unrounded)}$$

$$T_2 = (193.5691 - 273.15)°\text{C} = -79.580868 = \mathbf{-79.6°C}$$

Reality Check

The magnitude of the answer seems reasonable. The units and the number of significant figures are correct.

5.42 A mixture of gases made of 3.525 g C_5H_{12}, 2.528 g C_3H_8, and 3.056 g C_4H_{10} was contained in a flask. The total pressure of the gases was 1.385 atm. Determine the partial pressure of each gas, in atmospheres.

Information

The masses of the compounds (3.525 g C_5H_{12}, 2.528 g C_3H_8, and 3.056 g C_4H_{10}); the total pressure (1.385 atm); the question of what are the partial pressures of the gases

Connections

The definition *of mole fraction* in two forms: $X_A = \dfrac{P_A}{P_{total}}$ and $X_A = \dfrac{n_A}{n_{total}}$

Solution

Before we attempt to find the partial pressures (using $X_A = \dfrac{P_A}{P_{total}}$), we need to determine the

mole fraction of the individual gases. To determine the mole fraction of each component, we must determine the moles of each. To determine the moles, we need the mass of each component and the molar mass:

$$\text{Moles } C_5H_{12} = (3.525 \text{ g } C_5H_{12})\left(\frac{1 \text{ mol } C_5H_{12}}{72.151 \text{ g } C_5H_{12}}\right) = 0.04885587 \text{ mol } C_5H_{12} \quad \text{(unrounded)}$$

$$\text{Moles } C_3H_8 = (2.528 \text{ g } C_3H_8)\left(\frac{1 \text{ mol } C_3H_8}{44.097 \text{ g } C_3H_8}\right) = 0.05732816 \text{ mol } C_3H_8 \quad \text{(unrounded)}$$

$$\text{Moles } C_4H_{10} = (3.056 \text{ g } C_4H_{10})\left(\frac{1 \text{ mol } C_4H_{10}}{58.124 \text{ g } C_4H_{10}}\right) = 0.05257715 \text{ mol } C_4H_{10} \quad \text{(unrounded)}$$

We need to know the total moles (n_{total}) present:

$$\text{Total moles} = n_{total} = (0.04885587 + 0.05732816 + 0.05257715) \text{ mol}$$
$$= 0.15876118 \text{ mol (unrounded)}$$

Using the definition of *mole fraction* ($X_A = \dfrac{n_A}{n_{total}}$), the individual moles, and the total moles it is

possible to determine the mole fraction of each gas:

$$X_{C_5H_{12}} = \frac{n_{C_5H_{12}}}{n_{total}} = \frac{0.04885587 \text{ mol}}{0.15876118 \text{ mol}} = 0.30773184 \quad \text{(unrounded)}$$

$$X_{C_3H_8} = \frac{n_{C_3H_8}}{n_{total}} = \frac{0.05732816 \text{ mol}}{0.15876118 \text{ mol}} = 0.361096837 \quad \text{(unrounded)}$$

$$X_{C_4H_{10}} = \frac{n_{C_4H_{10}}}{n_{total}} = \frac{0.05257715 \text{ mol}}{0.15876118 \text{ mol}} = 0.331171323 \quad \text{(unrounded)}$$

We can rearrange the other definition of *mole fraction* ($X_A = \dfrac{P_A}{P_{total}}$) to give $P_A = X_A P_{total}$ and use the individual mole fractions and the total pressure to find the partial pressures.

$$P_{C_5H_{12}} = X_{C_5H_{12}} P_{total} = (0.30773184)(1.385 \text{ atm}) = 0.4262086 = \textbf{0.4262 atm } C_5H_{12}$$

$$P_{C_3H_8} = X_{C_3H_8} P_{total} = (0.361096837)(1.385 \text{ atm}) = 0.5001191 = \textbf{0.5001 atm } C_3H_8$$

$$P_{C_4H_{10}} = X_{C_4H_{10}} P_{total} = (0.331171323)(1.385 \text{ atm}) = 0.458672 = \textbf{0.4587 atm } C_4H_{10}$$

Reality Check

The sum of the mole fraction equals 1, and the sum of the partial pressures equals the total pressure.

5.6 Gas Stoichiometry

5.44 The catalytic decomposition of hydrogen peroxide generates small quantities of oxygen gas by the reaction

$$2 H_2O_2(aq) \rightarrow 2 H_2O(l) + O_2(g)$$

The generated oxygen acts as a disinfectant; this is why we use hydrogen peroxide to cleanse minor injuries. Calculate the number of grams of hydrogen peroxide necessary to generate 15.25 L of oxygen gas at 24.35°C, if the partial pressure of the oxygen is 745.0 torr.

Information

The balanced chemical equation; the volume, temperature, and pressure of the oxygen (15.25 L, 24.35°C, 745.0 torr); the question of how many grams of hydrogen peroxide

Connections

$PV = nRT$

Solution

Recopy the balanced chemical equation, and include the information about each substance below its formula:

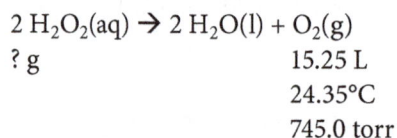

$$2 H_2O_2(aq) \rightarrow 2 H_2O(l) + O_2(g)$$
? g   15.25 L
                         24.35°C
                         745.0 torr

Collect and label the information from the problem:

$P = 745.0$ torr
$V = 15.25$ L
Mass = ? g H_2O_2
$T = 24.35°C = 297.50$ K
$R = \dfrac{0.08206 \text{ L} \cdot \text{atm}}{\text{mol} \cdot \text{K}}$

Rearrange the ideal gas equation to $n = \dfrac{PV}{RT}$

Enter the appropriate values into the equation and cancel:

$$n = \frac{(745.0 \text{ torr})(15.25\,\cancel{L})}{\left(\dfrac{0.08206\,\cancel{L} \cdot \text{atm}}{\text{mol} \cdot \cancel{K}}\right)(297.50\,\cancel{K})}$$

The necessity of an additional conversion is now apparent. Adding the appropriate pressure conversion (1 atm = 760 torr) gives

$$n = \frac{(745.0\,\cancel{\text{torr}})(15.25\,\cancel{L})}{\left(\dfrac{0.08206\,\cancel{L} \cdot \cancel{\text{atm}}}{\text{mol} \cdot \cancel{K}}\right)(297.50\,\cancel{K})}\left(\frac{1\,\cancel{\text{atm}}}{760\,\cancel{\text{torr}}}\right)$$

Since this is a gas law equation, this gives the number of moles of gas (O_2). We need to convert from moles of O_2 to moles of H_2O_2 using the mole ratio from the balanced chemical equation:

$$n = \frac{(745.0 \text{ torr})(15.25 \text{ L})}{\left(\frac{0.08206 \text{ L} \cdot \text{atm}}{\text{mol} \cdot \text{K}}\right)(297.50 \text{ K})}\left(\frac{1 \text{ atm}}{760 \text{ torr}}\right)\left(\frac{2 \text{ mol } H_2O_2}{1 \text{ mol } O_2}\right)$$

We can convert the moles of H_2O_2 to grams by using the molar mass (34.014 g/mol):

$$n = \frac{(745.0 \text{ torr})(15.25 \text{ L})}{\left(\frac{0.08206 \text{ L} \cdot \text{atm}}{\text{mol} \cdot \text{K}}\right)(297.50 \text{ K})}\left(\frac{1 \text{ atm}}{760 \text{ torr}}\right)\left(\frac{2 \text{ mol } H_2O_2}{1 \text{ mol } O_2}\right)\left(\frac{34.014 \text{ g } H_2O_2}{1 \text{ mol } H_2O_2}\right)$$

$$= 41.65640 = \textbf{41.66 g } \mathbf{H_2O_2}$$

Reality Check

The magnitude of the answer seems reasonable. The units and the number of significant figures are correct.

5.47 In the following reaction, how many grams of $Mg(NH_2)_2$ are required to generate 5.00 L of NH_3 gas at 27°C and 675 torr?

$$3 \text{ Mg(NH}_2)_2(s) \rightarrow Mg_3N_2(s) + 4 \text{ NH}_3(g)$$

Information

The balanced chemical equation; the volume, temperature, and pressure of ammonia (5.00 L, 27°C, 675 torr); the question of how many grams of $Mg(NH_2)_2$

Connections

$PV = nRT$

Solution

Recopy the balanced chemical equation, and include the information about each substance below its formula:

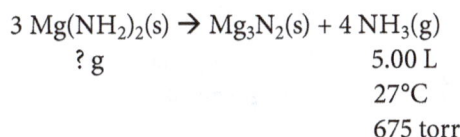

$$3 \text{ Mg(NH}_2)_2(s) \rightarrow Mg_3N_2(s) + 4 \text{ NH}_3(g)$$
$$? \text{ g} \qquad\qquad\qquad 5.00 \text{ L}$$
$$27°C$$
$$675 \text{ torr}$$

Collect and label the information from the problem:

$P = 675$ torr
$V = 5.00$ L
Mass = ? g $Mg(NH_2)$
$T = 27°C = 300.$ K
$R = \dfrac{0.08206 \text{ L} \cdot \text{atm}}{\text{mol} \cdot \text{K}}$

This is a stoichiometry problem, which means that moles are the key. Therefore, the first step is to determine moles. Based upon the given information, we need to rearrange the ideal gas equation to $n = \dfrac{PV}{RT}$

Enter the appropriate values into the equation and cancel:

$$n = \frac{(675 \text{ torr})(5.00 \cancel{\text{L}})}{\left(\dfrac{0.08206 \cancel{\text{L}} \cdot \text{atm}}{\text{mol} \cdot \cancel{\text{K}}}\right)(300. \cancel{\text{K}})}$$

The need for an additional conversion is now apparent. Adding the appropriate pressure conversion (1 atm = 760 torr) gives

$$n = \frac{(675 \cancel{\text{torr}})(5.00 \cancel{\text{L}})}{\left(\dfrac{0.08206 \cancel{\text{L}} \cdot \cancel{\text{atm}}}{\text{mol} \cdot \cancel{\text{K}}}\right)(300. \cancel{\text{K}})}\left(\frac{1 \cancel{\text{atm}}}{760 \cancel{\text{torr}}}\right)$$

This gives us moles. We used a gas law; therefore, this is the moles of gas (NH_3). To get to the compound of interest ($Mg(NH_2)_2$), we need a mole ratio:

$$n = \frac{(675 \cancel{\text{torr}})(5.00 \cancel{\text{L}})}{\left(\dfrac{0.08206 \cancel{\text{L}} \cdot \cancel{\text{atm}}}{\cancel{\text{mol}} \cdot \cancel{\text{K}}}\right)(300. \cancel{\text{K}})}\left(\frac{1 \cancel{\text{atm}}}{760 \cancel{\text{torr}}}\right)\left(\frac{3 \text{ mol } Mg(NH_2)_2}{4 \cancel{\text{mol }NH_3}}\right)$$

We now need the molar mass of $Mg(NH_2)_2$ to reach the desired units (grams):

$$\text{Mass} = \frac{(675 \cancel{\text{torr}})(5.00 \cancel{\text{L}})}{\left(\dfrac{0.08206 \cancel{\text{L}} \cdot \cancel{\text{atm}}}{\cancel{\text{mol}} \cdot \cancel{\text{K}}}\right)(300. \cancel{\text{K}})}\left(\frac{1 \cancel{\text{atm}}}{760 \cancel{\text{torr}}}\right)\left(\frac{3 \cancel{\text{mol }Mg(NH_2)_2}}{4 \cancel{\text{mol }NH_3}}\right)\left(\frac{56.351 \text{ g } Mg(NH_2)_2}{1 \cancel{\text{mol }Mg(NH_2)_2}}\right)$$

$$= 7.623779 = \textbf{7.62 g } \textbf{Mg(NH}_2\textbf{)}_2$$

Reality Check

The magnitude of the answer seems reasonable. The units and the number of significant figures are correct.

5.49 According to the reaction below, how many grams of NH_2Cl would we use if we collected 12.3 L of N_2 over water at 30.0°C and a total pressure of 795 mmHg?

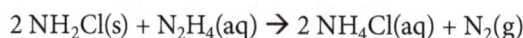

$$2 \text{ NH}_2\text{Cl(s)} + \text{N}_2\text{H}_4\text{(aq)} \rightarrow 2 \text{ NH}_4\text{Cl(aq)} + \text{N}_2\text{(g)}$$

Information

The balanced chemical equation; the volume, temperature, and pressure of nitrogen (12.3 L, 30.0°C, 795 torr); the question of how many grams of NH_2Cl

Connections

$PV = nRT$, $P_{total} = P_a + P_b + P_c + \ldots$; the vapor pressure of water from **table 5.2** in the textbook (31.824 torr)

Solution

Recopy the balanced chemical equation, and include the information about each substance below its formula:

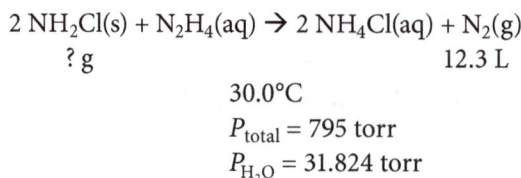

$$2 \text{ NH}_2\text{Cl(s)} + \text{N}_2\text{H}_4\text{(aq)} \rightarrow 2 \text{ NH}_4\text{Cl(aq)} + \text{N}_2\text{(g)}$$

$$\begin{array}{ccc} ? \text{ g} & & 12.3 \text{ L} \\ & 30.0°\text{C} & \\ & P_{total} = 795 \text{ torr} & \\ & P_{H_2O} = 31.824 \text{ torr} & \end{array}$$

We need to subtract the partial pressure of the water vapor from the total pressure to get the partial pressure of the dry gas. This is an application of Dalton's law.

$$P_{total} = P_{dry} + P_{H_2O}$$

Rearranging this equation gives

$$P_{dry} = P_{total} - P_{H_2O}$$

Using the values from the problem and the vapor pressure table (**table 5.2**) gives

$$P_{dry} = 795 \text{ torr} - 31.824 \text{ torr} = 763.176 \text{ torr} \qquad \text{(unrounded)}$$

We can now substitute the partial pressure of dry nitrogen into the variable table from earlier: Collect and label the information from the problem:

$P = 763.2$ torr (1 extra significant figure)
$V = 12.3$ L
Mass = ? g NH_2Cl
$T = 30.0°C = 303.2$ K
$R = \dfrac{0.08206 \text{ L} \cdot \text{atm}}{\text{mol} \cdot \text{K}}$

This is a stoichiometry problem, which means that moles are the key. Therefore, the first step is to determine moles. Based upon the given information, we will need to rearrange the ideal gas equation to $n = \dfrac{PV}{RT}$

Enter the appropriate values into the equation and cancel:

$$n = \frac{(763.2 \text{ torr})(12.3\text{ L})}{\left(\dfrac{0.08206 \text{ L} \cdot \text{atm}}{\text{mol} \cdot \text{K}}\right)(303.2\text{ K})}$$

The need for an additional conversion is now apparent. Adding the appropriate pressure conversion (1 atm = 760 torr) gives

$$n = \frac{(763.2 \text{ torr})(12.3 \text{ L})}{\left(\dfrac{0.08206 \text{ L} \cdot \text{atm}}{\text{mol} \cdot \text{K}}\right)(303.2\text{ K})}\left(\frac{1 \text{ atm}}{760 \text{ torr}}\right)$$

This gives us moles. We used a gas law; therefore, this is the moles of gas (N_2). To get to the substance of interest (NH_2Cl), we need a mole ratio:

$$n = \frac{(763.2 \text{ torr})(12.3 \text{ L})}{\left(\dfrac{0.08206 \text{ L} \cdot \text{atm}}{\text{mol} \cdot \text{K}}\right)(303.2\text{ K})}\left(\frac{1 \text{ atm}}{760 \text{ torr}}\right)\left(\frac{2 \text{ mol } NH_2Cl}{1 \text{ mol } N_2}\right)$$

We now need the molar mass of NH_2Cl to reach the desired units (grams):

$$\text{Mass} = \frac{(763.2 \text{ torr})(12.3 \text{ L})}{\left(\dfrac{0.08206 \text{ L} \cdot \text{atm}}{\text{mol} \cdot \text{K}}\right)(303.2\text{ K})}\left(\frac{1 \text{ atm}}{760 \text{ torr}}\right)\left(\frac{2 \text{ mol } NH_2Cl}{1 \text{ mol } N_2}\right)\left(\frac{51.476 \text{ g } NH_2Cl}{1 \text{ mol } NH_2Cl}\right)$$

$$= 51.10977 = \textbf{51.1 g } NH_2Cl$$

Reality Check

The magnitude of the answer seems reasonable. The units and the number of significant figures are correct.

5.51 Chemists can use the reaction below to generate PH_3 gas. In one experiment, a chemist collected 2.75 L of PH_3 gas over water at 20.0°C with a total pressure of 785 torr. How many grams of KH_2PO_2 did the chemist produce at the same time?

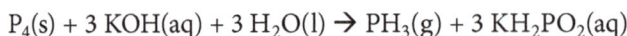

$$P_4(s) + 3\ KOH(aq) + 3\ H_2O(l) \rightarrow PH_3(g) + 3\ KH_2PO_2(aq)$$

Information

The balanced chemical equation; the volume and temperature of PH_3 (2.75 L and 20.0°C); the total pressure (785 torr); and the question of how many grams of KH_2PO_2

Connections

$PV = nRT$; $P_{total} = P_a + P_b + P_c + \ldots$; the vapor pressure of water from **table 5.2** in the textbook (17.535 torr)

Solution

Recopy the balanced chemical equation, and include the information about each substance below its formula:

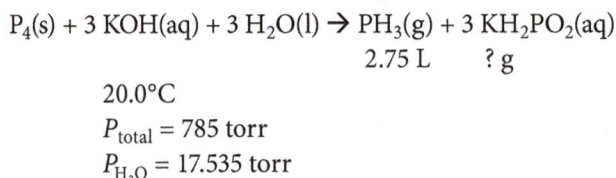

$$P_4(s) + 3\ KOH(aq) + 3\ H_2O(l) \rightarrow PH_3(g) + 3\ KH_2PO_2(aq)$$

$$2.75\ L \qquad ?\ g$$

$$20.0°C$$
$$P_{total} = 785\ torr$$
$$P_{H_2O} = 17.535\ torr$$

We need to subtract the partial pressure of the water vapor from the total pressure to get the partial pressure of the dry gas. This is an application of Dalton's law.

$$P_{total} = P_{dry} + P_{H_2O}$$

Rearranging this equation gives

$$P_{dry} = P_{total} - P_{H_2O}$$

Using the values from the problem and the vapor pressure table (**table 5.2**) gives

$$P_{dry} = 785\ torr - 17.535\ torr = 767.465\ torr\ (unrounded)$$

We can now substitute the partial pressure of dry hydrogen into the variable table from earlier: Collect and label the information from the problem:

$P = 767.5$ torr (1 extra significant figure)
$V = 2.75$ L
Mass = ? g KH_2PO_2
$T = 20.0°C = 293.2$ K
$R = \dfrac{0.08206\ L \cdot atm}{mol \cdot K}$

This is a stoichiometry problem, which means that moles are the key. Therefore, the first step is to determine moles. Based upon the given information, we need to rearrange the ideal gas equation to $n = \dfrac{PV}{RT}$

Enter the appropriate values into the equation and cancel:

$$n = \frac{(767.5\ torr)(2.75\ \cancel{L})}{\left(\dfrac{0.08206\ \cancel{L} \cdot atm}{mol \cdot \cancel{K}}\right)(293.2\ \cancel{K})}$$

The need for an additional conversion is now apparent. Adding the appropriate pressure conversion (1 atm = 760 torr) gives

$$n = \frac{(767.5 \ \text{torr})(2.75 \ \text{L})}{\left(\dfrac{0.08206 \ \text{L} \bullet \text{atm}}{\text{mol} \bullet \text{K}}\right)(293.2 \ \text{K})}\left(\frac{1 \ \text{atm}}{760 \ \text{torr}}\right)$$

This gives us moles. We used a gas law; therefore, this is the moles of gas (PH_3). To get to the substance of interest (KH_2PO_2), we need a mole ratio:

$$n = \frac{(767.5 \ \text{torr})(2.75 \ \text{L})}{\left(\dfrac{0.08206 \ \text{L} \bullet \text{atm}}{\text{mol} \bullet \text{K}}\right)(293.2 \ \text{K})}\left(\frac{1 \ \text{atm}}{760 \ \text{torr}}\right)\left(\frac{3 \ \text{mol} \ KH_2PO_2}{1 \ \text{mol} \ PH_3}\right)$$

We now need the molar mass of KH_2PO_2 to reach the desired units (grams):

$$\text{Mass} = \frac{(767.5 \ \text{torr})(2.75 \ \text{L})}{\left(\dfrac{0.08206 \ \text{L} \bullet \text{atm}}{\text{mol} \bullet \text{K}}\right)(293.2 \ \text{K})}\left(\frac{1 \ \text{atm}}{760 \ \text{torr}}\right)\left(\frac{3 \ \text{mol} \ KH_2PO_2}{1 \ \text{mol} \ PH_3}\right)\left(\frac{104.086 \ \text{g} \ KH_2PO_2}{1 \ \text{mol} \ KH_2PO_2}\right)$$

$$= 36.042556 = \textbf{36.0 g} \ \mathbf{KH_2PO_2}$$

Reality Check

The magnitude of the answer seems reasonable. The units and the number of significant figures are correct.

5.53 A student used the reaction below to generate H_2 gas. After some Si_2H_6 was reacted with an excess of H_2O, she collected a total of 7.75 L of H_2 over water at 30.0°C. The total pressure of the gas sample was 685 torr. How many grams of Si_2H_6 did she use in this reaction?

$$Si_2H_6(aq) + 4 \ H_2O(l) \rightarrow 2 \ SiO_2(s) + 7 \ H_2(g)$$

Information

The balanced chemical equation; the volume and temperature of H_2 (7.75 L, 30.0°C); the total pressure (685 mmHg); the question of how many grams of Si_2H_6

Connections

$PV = nRT$; $P_{total} = P_a + P_b + P_c + \ldots$; the vapor pressure of water from **table 5.2** in the textbook (31.824 torr)

Solution

Recopy the balanced chemical equation, and include the information about each substance below its formula:

$$Si_2H_6(aq) + 4 \ H_2O(l) \rightarrow 2 \ SiO_2(s) + 7 \ H_2(g)$$

$$? \ g \qquad\qquad\qquad\qquad\qquad\qquad 7.75 \ L$$

$$30.0°C$$

$$P_{total} = 685 \ \text{mmHg} = 685 \ \text{torr}$$

$$P_{H_2O} = 31.824 \ \text{torr}$$

We need to subtract the partial pressure of the water vapor from the total pressure to get the partial pressure of the dry gas. This is an application of Dalton's law.

$$P_{total} = P_{dry} + P_{H_2O}$$

Rearranging this equation gives

$$P_{dry} = P_{total} - P_{H_2O}$$

Using the values from the problem and the vapor pressure table (**table 5.2**) gives

$$P_{dry} = 685 \text{ torr} - 31.824 \text{ torr} = 653.176 \text{ torr} \qquad \text{(unrounded)}$$

We can now substitute the partial pressure of dry hydrogen into the variable table from earlier:
Collect and label the information from the problem:

$P = 653.2$ torr (1 extra significant figure)
$V = 7.75$ L
Mass = ? g Si_2H_6
$T = 30.0°C = 303.2$ K
$R = \dfrac{0.08206 \text{ L} \cdot \text{atm}}{\text{mol} \cdot \text{K}}$

This is a stoichiometry problem, which means that moles are the key. Therefore, the first step is to determine moles. Based upon the given information, we will need to rearrange the ideal gas equation to: $n = \dfrac{PV}{RT}$

Enter the appropriate values into the equation and cancel:

$$n = \frac{(653.2 \text{ torr})(7.75 \text{ L})}{\left(\dfrac{0.08206 \text{ L} \cdot \text{atm}}{\text{mol} \cdot \text{K}}\right)(303.2 \text{ K})}$$

The need for an additional conversion is now apparent. Adding the appropriate pressure conversion (1 atm = 760 torr) gives

$$n = \frac{(653.2 \text{ torr})(7.75 \text{ L})}{\left(\dfrac{0.08206 \text{ L} \cdot \text{atm}}{\text{mol} \cdot \text{K}}\right)(303.2 \text{ K})}\left(\frac{1 \text{ atm}}{760 \text{ torr}}\right)$$

This gives us moles. We used a gas law; therefore, this is the moles of gas (H_2). To get to the substance of interest (Si_2H_6), we need a mole ratio:

$$n = \frac{(653.2 \text{ torr})(7.75 \text{ L})}{\left(\dfrac{0.08206 \text{ L} \cdot \text{atm}}{\text{mol} \cdot \text{K}}\right)(303.2 \text{ K})}\left(\frac{1 \text{ atm}}{760 \text{ torr}}\right)\left(\frac{1 \text{ mol } Si_2H_6}{7 \text{ mol } H_2}\right)$$

We now need the molar mass of Si_2H_6 to reach the desired units (grams):

$$\text{Mass} = \frac{(653.2 \text{ torr})(7.75 \text{ L})}{\left(\dfrac{0.08206 \text{ L} \cdot \text{atm}}{\text{mol} \cdot \text{K}}\right)(303.2 \text{ K})}\left(\frac{1 \text{ atm}}{760 \text{ torr}}\right)\left(\frac{1 \text{ mol } Si_2H_6}{7 \text{ mol } H_2}\right)\left(\frac{62.220 \text{ g } Si_2H_6}{1 \text{ mol } Si_2H_6}\right)$$

$$= 2.3796 = \textbf{2.38 g } Si_2H_6$$

Reality Check

The magnitude of the answer seems reasonable. The units and the number of significant figures are correct.

5.55 The **reaction below** may be used to generate $(CN)_2$ gas. The two products of the reaction are much more stable than the highly unstable $Cu(CN)_2$. If 2.85 L of $(CN)_2$ produced by this reaction was collected over water at 40.0°C with a total pressure of 475 torr, how many grams of $Cu(CN)_2$ were decomposed?

$$2\ Cu(CN)_2(s) \rightarrow 2\ CuCN(s) + (CN)_2(g)$$

Information

The balanced chemical equation; the volume and temperature of $(CN)_2$ (2.85 L, 40.0°C); the total pressure (475 mmHg); the question of how many grams of $Cu(CN)_2$

Connections

$PV = nRT$; $P_{total} = P_a + P_b + P_c + \ldots$; the vapor pressure of water from **table 5.2** in the textbook (55.324 torr)

Solution

Recopy the balanced chemical equation, and include the information about each substance below its formula:

$$2\ Cu(CN)_2(s) \rightarrow 2\ CuCN(s) + (CN)_2(g)$$

$$? g \qquad\qquad\qquad\qquad\qquad 2.85\ L$$
$$40.0°C$$

$$P_{total} = 475\ mmHg = 475\ torr$$

$$P_{H_2O} = 55.324\ torr$$

We need to subtract the partial pressure of the water vapor from the total pressure to get the partial pressure of the dry gas. This is an application of Dalton's law.

$$P_{total} = P_{dry} + P_{H_2O}$$

Rearranging this equation gives

$$P_{dry} = P_{total} - P_{H_2O}$$

Using the values from the problem and the vapor pressure table (**table 5.2**) gives

$$P_{dry} = 475\ torr - 55.324\ torr = 419.676\ torr \qquad (unrounded)$$

We can now substitute the partial pressure of dry hydrogen into the variable table from earlier: Collect and label the information from the problem:

$P = 419.7$ torr (1 extra significant figure)
$V = 2.85$ L
Mass = ? g $Cu(CN)_2$
$T = 40.0°C = 313.2$ K

$$R = \frac{0.08206\ L \cdot atm}{mol \cdot K}$$

This is a stoichiometry problem, which means that moles are the key. Therefore, the first step is to determine moles. Based upon the given information, we need to rearrange the ideal gas equation to $n = \dfrac{PV}{RT}$

Enter the appropriate values into the equation and cancel:

$$n = \frac{(419.7\ torr)(2.85\ \cancel{L})}{\left(\dfrac{0.08206\ \cancel{L} \cdot atm}{mol \cdot \cancel{K}}\right)(313.2\ \cancel{K})}$$

The need for an additional conversion is now apparent. Adding the appropriate pressure conversion (1 atm = 760 torr) gives

$$n = \frac{(419.7 \ \cancel{torr})(2.85 \ \cancel{L})}{\left(\dfrac{0.08206 \ \cancel{L} \bullet \cancel{atm}}{mol \bullet \cancel{K}}\right)(313.2 \ \cancel{K})}\left(\frac{1 \ atm}{760 \ \cancel{torr}}\right)$$

This gives us moles. We used a gas law; therefore, this is the moles of gas: $(CN)_2$. To get to the substance of interest—$Cu(CN)_2$—we need a mole ratio:

$$n = \frac{(419.7 \ \cancel{torr})(2.85 \ \cancel{L})}{\left(\dfrac{0.08206 \ \cancel{L} \bullet \cancel{atm}}{\cancel{mol} \bullet \cancel{K}}\right)(313.2 \ \cancel{K})}\left(\frac{1 \ \cancel{atm}}{760 \ \cancel{torr}}\right)\left(\frac{2 \ mol \ Cu(CN)_2}{1 \ \cancel{mol \ (CN)_2}}\right)$$

We now need the molar mass of $Cu(CN)_2$ to reach the desired units (grams):

$$Mass = \frac{(419.7 \ \cancel{torr})(2.85 \ \cancel{L})}{\left(\dfrac{0.08206 \ \cancel{L} \bullet \cancel{atm}}{\cancel{mol} \bullet \cancel{K}}\right)(313.2 \ \cancel{K})}\left(\frac{1 \ \cancel{atm}}{760 \ \cancel{torr}}\right)\left(\frac{2 \ \cancel{mol \ Cu(CN)_2}}{1 \ \cancel{mol \ (CN)_2}}\right)\left(\frac{115.582 \ g \ Cu(CN)_2}{1 \ \cancel{mol \ Cu(CN)_2}}\right)$$

$$= 14.1559 = \textbf{14.2 g } Cu(CN)_2$$

Reality Check

The magnitude of the answer seems reasonable. The units and the number of significant figures are correct.

5.57 A student in a general chemistry class used the reaction below to generate $KClO_3$. How many grams of $KClO_3$ could be prepared from 8.75 L of Cl_2 gas, if the gas was originally at a pressure of 1,275 mmHg and a temperature of 57°C?

$$3 \ Cl_2(g) + 6 \ KOH(aq) \rightarrow KClO_3(aq) + 5 \ KCl(aq) + 3 \ H_2O(l)$$

Information

The balanced chemical equation; the volume, pressure, and temperature of Cl_2 (8.75 L, 1,275 mmHg, 57°C); the question of how many grams of $KClO_3$

Connections

$PV = nRT$

Solution

Recopy the balanced chemical equation, and include the information about each substance below its formula:

$$3 \ Cl_2(g) + 6 \ KOH(aq) \rightarrow KClO_3(aq) + 5 \ KCl(aq) + 3 \ H_2O(l)$$

8.75 L   ? g

1,275 mmHg

57°C

Collect and label the information from the problem:

$P = 1,275 \ mmHg$

$V = 8.75 \ L$

$Mass = ? \ g \ KClO_3$

$T = 57°C = 330. \ K$

$R = \dfrac{0.08206 \ L \bullet atm}{mol \bullet K}$

This is a stoichiometry problem, which means that moles are the key. Therefore, the first step is to determine moles. Based upon the given information, we need to rearrange the ideal gas equation to $n = \dfrac{PV}{RT}$

Enter the appropriate values into the equation and cancel:

$$n = \frac{(1275 \text{ mmHg})(8.75 \cancel{\text{ L}})}{\left(\dfrac{0.08206 \cancel{\text{ L}} \cdot \text{atm}}{\text{mol} \cdot \cancel{\text{K}}}\right)(330. \cancel{\text{ K}})}$$

The need for an additional conversion is now apparent. Adding the appropriate pressure conversion (1 atm = 760 mmHg) gives

$$n = \frac{(1275 \cancel{\text{ mmHg}})(8.75 \cancel{\text{ L}})}{\left(\dfrac{0.08206 \cancel{\text{ L}} \cdot \cancel{\text{atm}}}{\text{mol} \cdot \cancel{\text{K}}}\right)(330. \cancel{\text{ K}})}\left(\frac{1 \cancel{\text{ atm}}}{760 \cancel{\text{ mmHg}}}\right)$$

This gives us moles. We used a gas law; therefore, this is the moles of gas (Cl_2). To get to the substance of interest ($KClO_3$), we need a mole ratio:

$$n = \frac{(1275 \cancel{\text{ mmHg}})(8.75 \cancel{\text{ L}})}{\left(\dfrac{0.08206 \cancel{\text{ L}} \cdot \cancel{\text{atm}}}{\cancel{\text{mol}} \cdot \cancel{\text{K}}}\right)(330. \cancel{\text{ K}})}\left(\frac{1 \cancel{\text{ atm}}}{760 \cancel{\text{ mmHg}}}\right)\left(\frac{1 \text{mol } KClO_3}{3 \cancel{\text{ mol } Cl_2}}\right)$$

We now need the molar mass of $KClO_3$ to reach the desired units (grams):

$$\text{Mass} = \frac{(1275 \cancel{\text{ mmHg}})(8.75 \cancel{\text{ L}})}{\left(\dfrac{0.08206 \cancel{\text{ L}} \cdot \cancel{\text{atm}}}{\cancel{\text{mol}} \cdot \cancel{\text{K}}}\right)(330. \cancel{\text{ K}})}\left(\frac{1 \cancel{\text{ atm}}}{760 \cancel{\text{ mmHg}}}\right)\left(\frac{1 \cancel{\text{ mol } KClO_3}}{3 \cancel{\text{ mol } Cl_2}}\right)\left(\frac{122.548 \text{ g } KClO_3}{1 \cancel{\text{ mol } KClO_3}}\right)$$

$$= 22.14339 = \textbf{22.1 g } KClO_3$$

Reality Check

The magnitude of the answer seems reasonable. The units and the number of significant figures are correct.

5.59 Students use the reaction below to generate O_2 gas. In one experiment, 8.25 L of gas was collected over water at 35°C and a total pressure of 895 mmHg. How many grams of $Ba(IO_3)_2$ were used in this experiment?

$$5 \, Ba(IO_3)_2(s) \rightarrow Ba_5(IO_6)_2(s) + 4 \, I_2(s) + 9 \, O_2(g)$$

Information

The balanced chemical equation; the volume and temperature of oxygen (8.25 L, 35°C); the total pressure (895 mmHg); the question of how many grams of $Ba(IO_3)_2$

Connections

$PV = nRT$, $P_{\text{total}} = P_a + P_b + P_c + \ldots$; the vapor pressure of water from **table 5.2** in the textbook (41.175 torr)

Solution

Recopy the balanced chemical equation, and include the information about each substance below its formula:

$$5\ Ba(IO_3)_2(s) \rightarrow Ba_5(IO_6)_2(s) + 4\ I_2(s) + 9\ O_2(g)$$

$$? g \qquad\qquad\qquad\qquad\qquad\qquad 8.25\ L$$

$$35°C$$

$$P_{total} = 895\ mmHg = 895\ torr$$

$$P_{H_2O} = 41.175\ torr$$

We need to subtract the partial pressure of the water vapor from the total pressure to get the partial pressure of the dry gas. This is an application of Dalton's law.

$$P_{total} = P_{dry} + P_{H_2O}$$

Rearranging this equation gives

$$P_{dry} = P_{total} - P_{H_2O}$$

Using the values from the problem and the vapor pressure table (**table 5.2**) gives

$$P_{dry} = 895\ torr - 41.175\ torr = 853.825\ torr \qquad (unrounded)$$

We can now substitute the partial pressure of dry hydrogen into the variable table from earlier: Collect and label the information from the problem:

$P = 853.8$ torr (1 extra significant figure)
$V = 8.25$ L
Mass $= ?$ g $Ba(IO_3)_2$
$T = 35°C = 308$ K
$R = \dfrac{0.08206\ L \cdot atm}{mol \cdot K}$

This is a stoichiometry problem, which means that moles are the key. Therefore, the first step is to determine moles. Based upon the given information, we will need to rearrange the ideal gas equation to $n = \dfrac{PV}{RT}$

Enter the appropriate values into the equation and cancel:

$$n = \frac{(853.8\ torr)(8.25\ \cancel{L})}{\left(\dfrac{0.08206\ \cancel{L} \cdot atm}{mol \cdot \cancel{K}}\right)(308\ \cancel{K})}$$

The need for an additional conversion is now apparent. Adding the appropriate pressure conversion (1 atm = 760 torr) gives

$$n = \frac{(853.8\ \cancel{torr})(8.25\ \cancel{L})}{\left(\dfrac{0.08206\ \cancel{L} \cdot \cancel{atm}}{mol \cdot \cancel{K}}\right)(308\ \cancel{K})}\left(\frac{1\ \cancel{atm}}{760\ \cancel{torr}}\right)$$

This gives us moles. We used a gas law; therefore, this is the moles of gas (O_2). To get to the substance of interest ($Ba(IO_3)_2$), we need a mole ratio:

$$n = \frac{(853.8\ \cancel{torr})(8.25\ \cancel{L})}{\left(\dfrac{0.08206\ \cancel{L} \cdot \cancel{atm}}{\cancel{mol} \cdot \cancel{K}}\right)(308\ \cancel{K})}\left(\frac{1\ \cancel{atm}}{760\ \cancel{torr}}\right)\left(\frac{5\ mol\ Ba(IO_3)_2}{9\ \cancel{mol\ O_2}}\right)$$

We now need the molar mass of $Ba(IO_3)_2$ to reach the desired units (grams):

$$Mass = \frac{(853.8 \text{ torr})(8.25 \text{ L})}{\left(\dfrac{0.08206 \text{ L} \cdot \text{atm}}{\text{mol} \cdot \text{K}}\right)(308 \text{ K})}\left(\frac{1 \text{ atm}}{760 \text{ torr}}\right)\left(\frac{5 \text{ mol Ba(IO}_3)_2}{9 \text{ mol O}_2}\right)\left(\frac{487.129 \text{ g Ba(IO}_3)_2}{1 \text{ mol Ba(IO}_3)_2}\right)$$

$$= 99.23977 = \textbf{99.2 g Ba(IO}_3)_2$$

Reality Check

The magnitude of the answer seems reasonable. The units and the number of significant figures are correct.

5.61 An engineer used the reaction below to generate SiF_4 gas. How many liters of SiF_4 gas could she generate by reacting 75.00 g of HF with an excess of SiO_2 if the pressure of the SiF_4 is 745 torr at a temperature of 27°C?

$$SiO_2(s) + 4 HF(aq) \rightarrow 2 H_2O(l) + SiF_4(g)$$

Information

The balanced chemical equation; the mass of HF (75.00 g); the pressure and temperature of SiF_4 (745 torr, 27°C); the question of how many liters of SiF_4

Connections

$PV = nRT$

Solution

Recopy the balanced chemical equation, and include the information about each substance below its formula:

$$SiO_2(s) + 4 HF(aq) \rightarrow 2 H_2O(l) + SiF_4(g)$$

$$\qquad\qquad\quad 75.00 \text{ g} \qquad\qquad\qquad\qquad\quad ? \text{ L}$$

$$\qquad\qquad\qquad\qquad\qquad\qquad\qquad\qquad 745 \text{ torr}$$

$$\qquad\qquad\qquad\qquad\qquad\qquad\qquad\qquad 27°C$$

Collect and label the information from the problem:

$P = 745$ torr SiF_4

$V = ?$ L SiF_4

Mass = 75.00 g HF

$T = 27°C = 300.$ K

$R = \dfrac{0.08206 \text{ L} \cdot \text{atm}}{\text{mol} \cdot \text{K}}$

Rearrange the ideal gas equation to $V = \dfrac{nRT}{P}$

To use a gas law equation, the moles of gas are necessary. Hydrogen fluoride is not the substance of interest, so a conversion is necessary to get to moles of gas (SiF_4).

$$\text{Moles SiF}_4 = (75.00 \text{ g HF})\left(\frac{1 \text{ mol HF}}{20.006 \text{ g HF}}\right)\left(\frac{1 \text{ mol SiF}_4}{4 \text{ mol HF}}\right) = n$$

Enter the appropriate values into the equation and cancel:

$$V = \frac{\left(75.00 \text{ g HF}\right)\left(\dfrac{1 \text{ mol HF}}{20.006 \text{ g HF}}\right)\left(\dfrac{1 \text{ mol SiF}_4}{4 \text{ mol HF}}\right)\left(\dfrac{0.08206 \text{ L} \cdot \text{atm}}{\text{mol} \cdot \text{K}}\right)\left(300. \text{ K}\right)}{745 \text{ torr}}$$

The need for an additional conversion is now apparent. Adding the appropriate pressure conversion (1 atm = 760 torr) gives

$$V = \frac{\left(75.00 \text{ g HF}\right)\left(\dfrac{1 \text{ mol HF}}{20.006 \text{ g HF}}\right)\left(\dfrac{1 \text{ mol SiF}_4}{4 \text{ mol HF}}\right)\left(\dfrac{0.08206 \text{ L} \cdot \text{atm}}{\text{mol} \cdot \text{K}}\right)\left(300. \text{ K}\right)}{745 \text{ torr}}\left(\dfrac{760 \text{ torr}}{1 \text{ atm}}\right)$$

$$= 23.536999 = \textbf{23.5 L}$$

Reality Check

The magnitude of the answer seems reasonable. The units and the number of significant figures are correct.

5.63 Chemists produce chlorine gas, Cl_2, by the electrolysis of a saltwater solution. A 0.7500-L sample of chlorine was prepared in this manner; it had a pressure of 0.9500 atm and a temperature of 37.0°C. Later the volume had changed to 500.0 mL and the pressure had changed to 695.0 mmHg. What was the temperature at the new volume and pressure?

Information

The initial volume, pressure, and temperature (0.7500 L, 0.9500 atm, 37.0°C); the final volume and pressure (500.0 mL and 695.0 mmHg); the question of what is the final temperature

Connections

$$\frac{P_1 V_1}{n_1 T_1} = \frac{P_2 V_2}{n_2 T_2}$$

Solution

Collect and label the information from the problem:

$P_1 = 0.9500$ atm $P_2 = 695.0$ mmHg
$V_1 = 0.7500$ L $V_2 = 500.0$ mL
$n_1 = -$ $n_2 = -$
$T_1 = 37.0°C = 310.2$ K $T_2 = ?$

Based on the available information, the combined gas law simplifies to $\dfrac{P_1 V_1}{T_1} = \dfrac{P_2 V_2}{T_2}$

The simplified combined gas law rearranges to $T_2 = \dfrac{P_2 \, V_2 \, T_1}{P_1 \, V_1}$

Enter the appropriate values into the equation and cancel:

$$T_2 = \frac{(695.0 \text{ mmHg})(500.0 \text{ mL})(310.2 \text{ K})}{(0.9500 \text{ atm})(0.7500 \text{ L})}$$

The need for additional conversions is now apparent. The *milli-* conversion ($m = 0.001 = 10^{-3}$) is appropriate:

$$T_2 = \frac{(695.0 \text{ mmHg})(500.0 \text{ mL})(310.2 \text{ K})}{(0.9500 \text{ atm})(0.7500 \text{ L})}\left(\frac{0.001}{m}\right)$$

Adding the appropriate pressure conversion (1 atm = 760 mmHg) gives

$$T_2 = \frac{P_2 V_2 T_1}{P_1 V_1} = \left[\frac{(695.0 \text{ mmHg})(500.0 \text{ mL})(310.2 \text{ K})}{(0.7500 \text{ L})(0.9500 \text{ atm})}\right]\left(\frac{0.001}{\text{m}}\right)\left(\frac{1 \text{ atm}}{760 \text{ mmHg}}\right) = 199.066 = \mathbf{199.1 \text{ K}}$$

Reality Check

The magnitude of the answer seems reasonable. The units and the number of significant figures are correct.

5.7 Kinetic Molecular Theory and Graham's Law

5.65 In an effusion experiment that was set up to determine the molecular weight of an unknown gas, 39.71 mL of the gas effused through a porous barrier in 262.0 s. When the experiment was repeated using oxygen gas, 47.92 mL of oxygen effused through the same barrier in 148.0 s. What was the molecular weight of the unknown gas?

Information

The rate of effusion of the unknown gas (39.71 mL in 262.0 s); the rate of effusion of the oxygen (47.92 mL in 148.0 s); the question of what is the molecular weight of the unknown gas

Connections

$$\frac{Rate_A}{Rate_B} = \sqrt{\frac{MM_B}{MM_A}}$$

Solution

The rates will be in terms of milliliters per second. In this solution, we will assume gas A = oxygen (MM_A = 31.9988 g/mol) and gas B is the unknown. Entering the appropriate values into Graham's law gives

$$\frac{Rate_A}{Rate_B} = \frac{\dfrac{47.92 \text{ mL}}{148.0 \text{ s}}}{\dfrac{39.71 \text{ mL}}{262.0 \text{ s}}} = \sqrt{\frac{MM_B}{MM_A}} = \sqrt{\frac{MM_B}{31.9988 \text{ g/mol}}}$$

$$= \frac{0.323783784}{0.151564885} = 2.136271755 = \sqrt{\frac{MM_B}{31.9988 \text{ g/mol}}}$$

$$4.563657 = \frac{MM_B}{31.9988 \text{ g/mol}}$$

$$MM_B = (4.563657)(31.9988 \text{ g/mol}) = 146.0315 = \mathbf{146.0 \text{ g/mol}}$$

Reality Check

The magnitude of the answer seems reasonable; molar masses of gases must be at least 2 g/mol and may be up to 500 g/mol. The units and the number of significant figures are correct.

5.8 The van der Waals Equation

5.70 You place a sample of 2.50 mol of chlorine gas, Cl_2, in a 1.00-L steel container at 25°C. **(a)** Calculate the pressure exerted by the gas if it behaved ideally. **(b)** Calculate the pressure exerted by the gas if it did not behave ideally. The van der Waals constants for chlorine gas are

$a = 6.49 \text{ L}^2 \text{ atm/mol}^2$
$b = 0.0562 \text{ L/mol}$

Information

(a) The moles (2.50 mol); the volume (1.00 L); the temperature (25°C); the question of what is the pressure if the gas is ideal

(b) The moles (2.50 mol); the volume (1.00 L); the temperature (25°C); the van der Waals constants for chlorine (a = 6.49 L^2 atm/mol^2 and b = 0.0562 L/mol); the question of what is the pressure if the gas is not ideal

Connections

$$PV = nRT; \quad \left(P + \frac{an^2}{V^2}\right)(V - nb) = nRT$$

Solution

(a) Collect and label the information from the problem:

$P = ?$
$V = 1.00 \text{ L}$
$n = 2.50 \text{ mol}$
$T = 25°C = 298 \text{ K}$
$R = \dfrac{0.08206 \text{ L} \cdot \text{atm}}{\text{mol} \cdot \text{K}}$

Rearrange the ideal gas equation to $P = \dfrac{nRT}{V}$

Enter the appropriate values into the equation and cancel:

$$P = \frac{(2.50 \ \cancel{\text{mol}})\left(\dfrac{0.08206 \ \cancel{\text{L}} \cdot \text{atm}}{\cancel{\text{mol}} \cdot \cancel{\text{K}}}\right)(298 \ \cancel{\text{K}})}{(1.00 \ \cancel{\text{L}})} = 61.1347 = \mathbf{61.1 \text{ atm}}$$

(b) Substituting the values from the table into the rearranged van der Waals equation gives

$$P = \left|\frac{(2.50 \ \cancel{\text{mol}})\left(\dfrac{0.08206 \text{ L} \cdot \text{atm}}{\cancel{\text{mol}} \cdot \cancel{\text{K}}}\right)(298 \ \cancel{\text{K}})}{\left(1.00 \text{ L} - (2.50 \ \cancel{\text{mol}})\left(\dfrac{0.0562 \text{ L}}{\cancel{\text{mol}}}\right)\right)}\right| - \left|\frac{\left(\dfrac{6.49 \ \cancel{\text{L}}^2 \text{atm}}{\cancel{\text{mol}}^2}\right)(2.50 \ \cancel{\text{mol}})^2}{(1.00 \ \cancel{\text{L}})^2}\right|$$

To make the equation simpler, we remove the cancelled units from the above equation:

$$P = \left|\frac{(2.50)\left(\dfrac{0.08206 \text{ L} \cdot \text{atm}}{1}\right)(298.)}{\left(1.00 \text{ L} - (2.50)\left(\dfrac{0.0.562 \text{ L}}{1}\right)\right)}\right| - \left|\frac{\left(\dfrac{6.49 \text{ atm}}{1}\right)(2.50)^2}{(1.00)^2}\right|$$

Now we do some preliminary calculations and the final unit cancellation:

$$P = \left|\frac{\left(\dfrac{61.1247 \ \cancel{\text{L}} \cdot \text{atm}}{1}\right)}{(1.00 - (0.1405))\cancel{\text{L}}}\right| - \left|\frac{\left(\dfrac{6.49 \text{ atm}}{1}\right)6.25}{1.00}\right|$$

Both terms on the right have the same units (atm), which indicates that the cancellation was correct. The terms <u>must</u> be identical if we are to subtract one from the other. Finishing the calculation gives

$$P = 30.55408 = \mathbf{30.6 \text{ atm}}$$

Reality Check

The magnitudes of the answers seem reasonable. The units and the number of significant figures are correct.

5.9 Air Pollution

5.72 List the five major types of air pollutants.

Solution

The major types of air pollutants are carbon monoxide, oxides of nitrogen, sulfur dioxide, hydrocarbons, and particulates.

5.74 Define *greenhouse effect*. List three gases that contribute to the greenhouse effect.

Solution

Various gases in the atmosphere—such as carbon dioxide, water vapor, and methane—absorb the heat reflected into the atmosphere by the Earth. This process warms the atmosphere and helps to moderate temperature fluctuations of the atmosphere and the Earth.

5.76 If the air in an urban area contains 175 µg of suspended particulates per cubic meter, how many particles do people inhale in one breath? Assume the particles are spherical with a radius of 0.50 mm and a density of 1.05 g/cm³. The average human breath is 0.50 L.

Information

The concentration (175 µg per cubic meter); radius (0.50 µm); density (1.05 g/cm³); volume (0.50 L); and the question of how many particles

Connections

$V = \dfrac{4}{3}\pi r^3$ (volume of a sphere)

Solution

Collect and label the information from the problem:

Concentration = 175 mg per cubic meter
V = 0.50 L
Density = 1.05 g/cm³
Radius = 0.50 µm
Number of particles = ?

This problem requires several conversions. It is acceptable to do these conversions in any order, and in some cases, alternate conversions are acceptable.

We will begin by using the volume equation to determine the volume of a particle:

$$V = \frac{4}{3}\pi r^3 = \frac{4}{3}(3.14159)\,(0.50\ \mu m)^3 = 0.523598\ \mu m^3 \text{ (unrounded)}$$

Next, we convert the micrograms per cubic meter to grams per cubic meter:

$$\left(\frac{175\ \cancel{\mu g}}{m^3}\right)\left(\frac{10^{-6}}{\cancel{\mu}}\right)$$

We can now convert the volume. To do this, we may use any of the following relationships: 1 mL = 1 cm³, 1 L = 1 dm³, or 1,000 L = 1 m³. If you use either of the first two conversions, additional steps will be necessary to convert m³ to either cm³ or dm³. Using the third conversion gives

$$\left(\frac{175\ \cancel{\mu g}}{\cancel{m^3}}\right)\left(\frac{10^{-6}}{\cancel{\mu}}\right)\left(\frac{1\ \cancel{m^3}}{1{,}000\ L}\right)$$

Using the volume of one breath (0.50 L) gives the mass of particles in one breath:

$$\left(\frac{175 \ \mu g}{m^3}\right)\left(\frac{10^{-6}}{\mu}\right)\left(\frac{1 \ m^3}{1,000 \ L}\right)\left(\frac{0.50 \ L}{1 \ \text{breath}}\right)$$

From the density, it is possible to find the volume of the particles in one breath:

$$\left(\frac{175 \ \mu g}{m^3}\right)\left(\frac{10^{-6}}{\mu}\right)\left(\frac{1 \ m^3}{1,000 \ L}\right)\left(\frac{0.50 \ L}{1 \ \text{breath}}\right)\left(\frac{cm^3}{1.05 \ g}\right)$$

In this case, the volume units are in centimeters (actually cm^3), while the size of the particles is in micrometers (μm). We need to resolve this difference in units. There are several ways to do this; here, however, we will do so by changing centimeters to micrometers:

$$\left(\frac{175 \ \mu g}{m^3}\right)\left(\frac{10^{-6}}{\mu}\right)\left(\frac{1 \ m^3}{1,000 \ L}\right)\left(\frac{0.50 \ L}{1 \ \text{breath}}\right)\left(\frac{cm^3}{1.05 \ g}\right)\left(\frac{0.01}{c}\right)^3\left(\frac{\mu}{10^{-6}}\right)^3$$

Finally, we need to use the volume of each particle (0.523598 μm^3) to get the number of particles:

$$\left(\frac{175 \ \mu g}{m^3}\right)\left(\frac{10^{-6}}{\mu}\right)\left(\frac{1 \ m^3}{1,000 \ L}\right)\left(\frac{0.50 \ L}{1 \ \text{breath}}\right)\left(\frac{cm^3}{1.05 \ g}\right)\left(\frac{0.01}{c}\right)^3\left(\frac{\mu}{10^{-6}}\right)^3\left(\frac{1 \ \text{particle}}{0.523598 \ \mu m^3}\right)$$

$$= 159155.2 = \mathbf{1.6 \times 10^5 \ particles/breath}$$

An alternative cancelling is

$$\left(\frac{175 \ \mu g}{m^3}\right)\left(\frac{10^{-6}}{\mu}\right)\left(\frac{1 \ m^3}{1,000 \ L}\right)\left(\frac{0.50 \ L}{1 \ \text{breath}}\right)\left(\frac{cm^3}{1.05 \ g}\right)\left(\frac{0.01}{c}\right)^3\left(\frac{\mu}{10^{-6}}\right)^3\left(\frac{1 \ \text{particle}}{0.523598 \ \mu m^3}\right)$$

$$= 159155.2 = \mathbf{1.6 \times 10^5 \ particles/breath}$$

Reality Check

The magnitude of the answer seems reasonable. The units and the number of significant figures are correct.

5.10 Applications and Extensions

5.78 The solubility of which gas contributes to the bends?

Solution

Nitrogen is the cause of the bends.

5.80 What are the two main purposes of a catalytic converter?

Solution

The catalytic converter has two main purposes: (1) oxidation of carbon monoxide and unburned hydrocarbons to carbon dioxide and water and (2) the reduction of the oxides of nitrogen (primarily NO and NO_2) to nitrogen gas and oxygen gas.

Putting It All Together

5.83 In the following reaction, how many grams of $NaBH_4$ are required to produce 4.85 L of B_2H_6 at a pressure of 685 torr and a temperature of 37°C?

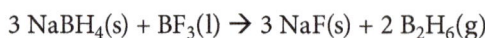

$$3 \ NaBH_4(s) + BF_3(l) \rightarrow 3 \ NaF(s) + 2 \ B_2H_6(g)$$

Information

The balanced chemical equation; the volume, pressure, and temperature of B_2H_6 (4.85 L, 685 torr, 37°C); the question of how many grams of $NaBH_4$

Connections

$PV = nRT$

Solution

Recopy the balanced chemical equation, and include the information about each substance below its formula:

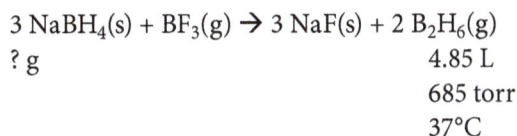

$$3\ NaBH_4(s) + BF_3(g) \rightarrow 3\ NaF(s) + 2\ B_2H_6(g)$$

? g		4.85 L
		685 torr
		37°C

Collect and label the information from the problem:

$P = 685$ torr
$V = 4.85$ L
Mass = ? g $NaBH_4$
$T = 37°C = 310.\ K$
$R = \dfrac{0.08206\ L \bullet atm}{mol \bullet K}$

This is a stoichiometry problem, which means that moles are the key. Therefore, the first step is to determine moles. Based upon the given information, we will need to rearrange the ideal gas equation to $n = \dfrac{PV}{RT}$

Enter the appropriate values into the equation and cancel:

$$n = \frac{(685\ torr)(4.85\ \cancel{L})}{\left(\dfrac{0.08206\ \cancel{L} \bullet atm}{mol \bullet \cancel{K}}\right)(310.\ \cancel{K})}$$

The need for an additional conversion is now apparent. Adding the appropriate pressure conversion (1 atm = 760 torr) gives

$$n = \frac{(685\ \cancel{torr})(4.85\ \cancel{L})}{\left(\dfrac{0.08206\ \cancel{L} \bullet \cancel{atm}}{mol \bullet \cancel{K}}\right)(310.\ \cancel{K})}\left(\frac{1\ \cancel{atm}}{760\ \cancel{torr}}\right)$$

This gives us moles. We used a gas law; therefore, this is the moles of gas (B_2H_6). To get to the substance of interest ($NaBH_4$), we need a mole ratio:

$$n = \frac{(685\ \cancel{torr})(4.85\ \cancel{L})}{\left(\dfrac{0.08206\ \cancel{L} \bullet \cancel{atm}}{\cancel{mol} \bullet \cancel{K}}\right)(310.\ \cancel{K})}\left(\frac{1\ \cancel{atm}}{760\ \cancel{torr}}\right)\left(\frac{3\ mol\ NaBH_4}{2\ \cancel{mol\ B_2H_6}}\right)$$

We now need the molar mass of $NaBH_4$ to reach the desired units (grams):

$$Mass = \frac{(685\ \cancel{torr})(4.85\ \cancel{L})}{\left(\dfrac{0.08206\ \cancel{L} \bullet \cancel{atm}}{\cancel{mol} \bullet \cancel{K}}\right)(310.\ \cancel{K})}\left(\frac{1\ \cancel{atm}}{760\ \cancel{torr}}\right)\left(\frac{3\ \cancel{mol\ NaBH_4}}{2\ \cancel{mol\ B_2H_6}}\right)\left(\frac{37.833\ g\ NaBH_4}{1\ \cancel{mol\ NaBH_4}}\right)$$

$$= 9.75186 = \textbf{9.75 g NaBH}_4$$

Reality Check

The magnitude of the answer seems reasonable. The units and the number of significant figures are correct.

5.85 A student produced hydrogen gas from the reaction of hydrochloric acid, HCl, with zinc metal, Zn, collecting the gas by the displacement of water from an inverted 500.0-mL flask. The temperature of the flask was 35.0°C. The total pressure in the flask was 0.885 atm. Determine the partial pressure of hydrogen in the flask.

Information

The chemical reaction (hydrogen gas may be prepared from HCl and Zn); the volume and temperature of the hydrogen (500.0 mL, 35.0°C); the total pressure (0.885 atm); the question of what is the partial pressure of hydrogen

Connections

$P_{total} = P_a + P_b + P_c + ...$; the vapor pressure of water from **table 5.2** in the textbook (41.175 torr), and 1 atm = 760 torr

Solution

Collect and label the information from the problem:

$$P_{total} = 0.855 \text{ atm}$$
$$P = ?$$
$$V = 500.0 \text{ mL}$$
$$T = 35.0°C = 308.2 \text{ K}$$
$$R = \frac{0.08206 \text{ L} \bullet \text{atm}}{\text{mol} \bullet \text{K}}$$

Setting a = H_2 and b = H_2O and using Dalton's law gives

$$P_{total} = P_a + P_b = 0.855 \text{ atm} = P_a + 41.175 \text{ torr}$$

The presence of mixed units will require a conversion (1 atm = 760 torr). Rearranging Dalton's law and incorporating this conversion gives

$$P_a = P_{total} - P_b = 0.855 \text{ atm} - (41.175 \text{ torr})\left(\frac{1 \text{ atm}}{760 \text{ torr}}\right) = 0.800822 = \textbf{0.801 atm}$$

Reality Check

The magnitude of the answer seems reasonable. The units and the number of significant figures are correct.

5.88 The final step in the Ostwald process for the industrial synthesis of nitric acid is

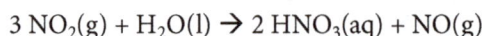

$$3 \text{ NO}_2(g) + \text{H}_2O(l) \rightarrow 2 \text{ HNO}_3(aq) + \text{NO}(g)$$

How many liters of nitrogen dioxide (NO_2) at 75.35°C and 2.750 atm are required to produce 225.0 kg of nitric acid?

Information

The balanced chemical equation; the temperature and pressure (75.35°C, 2.750 atm); the mass of nitric acid (225.0 kg); the question of how many liters of NO_2

Connections

$PV = nRT$

Solution

Recopy the balanced chemical equation, and include the information about each substance below its formula:

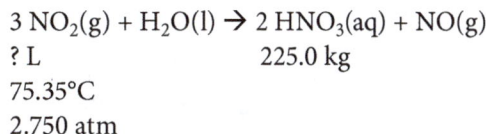

$$3\ NO_2(g) + H_2O(l) \rightarrow 2\ HNO_3(aq) + NO(g)$$

? L	225.0 kg
75.35°C	
2.750 atm	

Collect and label the information from the problem:

$P = 2.750$ atm

$V = ?$ L NO_2

Mass $= 225.0$ kg HNO_3

$T = 75.35°C = 348.50$ K

$$R = \frac{0.08206\ L \cdot atm}{mol \cdot K}$$

Rearrange the ideal gas equation to $V = \dfrac{nRT}{P}$

To use a gas law equation, we need to know the moles of gas. Nitric acid is not a gas, so a conversion is needed to get to moles of gas (NO_2).

$$\text{Moles } NO_2 = (225.0\ \text{kg HNO}_3)\left(\frac{1\ \text{mol HNO}_3}{63.012\ \text{g HNO}_3}\right)\left(\frac{3\ \text{mol } NO_2}{2\ \text{mol HNO}_3}\right)\left(\frac{1{,}000}{k}\right) = n$$

Enter the appropriate values into the equation and cancel:

$$V = \frac{\left(225.0\ \text{kg HNO}_3\right)\left(\dfrac{1\ \text{mol HNO}_3}{63.012\ \text{g HNO}_3}\right)\left(\dfrac{3\ \text{mol } NO_2}{2\ \text{mol HNO}_3}\right)\left(\dfrac{1{,}000}{k}\right)\left(\dfrac{0.08206\ L \cdot atm}{mol \cdot K}\right)(348.50\ K)}{2.750\ \text{atm}}$$

$$= 55{,}699.60 = \mathbf{5.570 \times 10^4\ L}$$

Reality Check

The magnitude of the answer seems reasonable. The units and the number of significant figures are correct.

5.90 **(a)** Determine the mass in kilograms of ammonia gas in a 1.00×10^3-liter tank at 35°C and a pressure of 925 mmHg. **(b)** What would be the volume of this gas, in liters, at 27°C and 1.00 atm?

Information

The volume, temperature, and pressure of ammonia (1.00×10^3 L, 35°C, 925 mmHg); the question of how many kilograms of ammonia

Connections

$PV = nRT$

Solution

(a) Collect and label the information from the problem:

$P = 925$ mmHg

$V = 1.00 \times 10^3$ L

Mass = ? kg NH_3

$T = 35°C = 308$ K

$$R = \frac{0.08206 \text{ L} \cdot \text{atm}}{\text{mol} \cdot \text{K}}$$

This is a stoichiometry problem, which means that moles are the key. Therefore, the first step is to determine moles. Based upon the given information, we will need to rearrange the ideal gas equation to $n = \dfrac{PV}{RT}$

Enter the appropriate values into the equation and cancel:

$$n = \frac{(925 \text{ mmHg})(1.00 \times 10^3 \text{ L})}{\left(\dfrac{0.08206 \text{ L} \cdot \text{atm}}{\text{mol} \cdot \text{K}}\right)(308 \text{ K})}$$

The need for an additional conversion is now apparent. Adding the appropriate pressure conversion (1 atm = 760 mmHg) gives

$$n = \frac{(925 \text{ mmHg})(1.00 \times 10^3 \text{ L})}{\left(\dfrac{0.08206 \text{ L} \cdot \text{atm}}{\text{mol} \cdot \text{K}}\right)(308 \text{ K})}\left(\frac{1 \text{ atm}}{760 \text{ mmHg}}\right)$$

This gives the moles of gas (NH_3). To transform moles to mass, we need the molar mass of NH_3:

$$\text{Mass} = \frac{(925 \text{ mmHg})(1.00 \times 10^3 \text{ L})}{\left(\dfrac{0.08206 \text{ L} \cdot \text{atm}}{\text{mol} \cdot \text{K}}\right)(308 \text{ K})}\left(\frac{1 \text{ atm}}{760 \text{ mmHg}}\right)\left(\frac{17.031 \text{ g } NH_3}{1 \text{ mol } NH_3}\right)$$

Finally, we need to add a *kilo-* conversion ($k = 1,000 = 10^3$)

$$\text{Mass} = \frac{(925 \text{ mmHg})(1.00 \times 10^3 \text{ L})}{\left(\dfrac{0.08206 \text{ L} \cdot \text{atm}}{\text{mol} \cdot \text{K}}\right)(308 \text{ K})}\left(\frac{1 \text{ atm}}{760 \text{ mmHg}}\right)\left(\frac{17.031 \text{ g } NH_3}{1 \text{ mol } NH_3}\right)\left(\frac{k}{1,000}\right)$$

$$= 0.820136 = \textbf{0.820 kg } NH_3$$

(b) $V_2 = \dfrac{(925 \text{ mmHg})(1.00 \times 10^3 \text{ L})(300. \text{ K})}{(1.00 \text{ atm})(308 \text{ K})}\left(\dfrac{1 \text{ atm}}{760 \text{ mmHg}}\right) = 1185.492 = \textbf{1.19} \times \textbf{10}^\textbf{3} \textbf{ L}$

Reality Check

The magnitude of the answer seems reasonable. The units and the number of significant figures are correct.

5.93 A student collected a sample of xenon gas in a 5.000-L container at a pressure of 225.0 mmHg and a temperature of 27.0°C. Later, she found that the pressure had changed to 1.000 atm, and the temperature had changed to 295 K. What was the new volume of the gas in milliliters?

Information

The initial volume, pressure, and temperature (5.000 L, 225.0 mmHg, 27.0°C); the final pressure and temperature (1.000 atm, 295 K); the question of how many milliliters of gas

Connections

$$\frac{P_1 V_1}{n_1 T_1} = \frac{P_2 V_2}{n_2 T_2}$$

Solution

Collect and label the information from the problem:

$P_1 = 225.0 \text{ mmHg}$ $P_2 = 1.000 \text{ atm}$

$V_1 = 5.000 \text{ L}$ $V_2 = ? \text{ L}$

$n_1 = \text{---}$ $n_2 = \text{---}$

$T_1 = 27.0°\text{C} = 300.2 \text{ K}$ $T_2 = 295 \text{ K}$

Based on the available information, the combined gas law simplifies to $\frac{P_1 V_1}{T_1} = \frac{P_2 V_2}{T_2}$

The simplified combined gas law rearranges to $V_2 = \frac{T_2 P_1 V_1}{T_1 P_2}$

Enter the appropriate values into the equation and cancel:

$$V_2 = \frac{(295 \text{ K})(225.0 \text{ mmHg})(5.000 \text{ L})}{(300.2 \text{ K})(1.000 \text{ atm})}$$

The need for additional conversions is now apparent. Adding the appropriate pressure conversion (1 atm = 760 mmHg) gives

$$V_2 = \frac{(295 \text{ K})(225.0 \text{ mmHg})(5.000 \text{ L})}{(300.2 \text{ K})(1.000 \text{ atm})}\left(\frac{1 \text{ atm}}{760 \text{ mmHg}}\right)\left(\frac{m}{0.001}\right) = 1454.622 = \mathbf{1.45 \times 10^3 \text{ mL}}$$

Reality Check

The magnitude of the answer seems reasonable. The units and the number of significant figures are correct.

5.95 You prepared a sample of carbon dioxide by burning pure carbon in oxygen gas. After the reaction, you found that 1.25 L of gas had been collected at a pressure of 1.000 atm, and that the burning had heated the sample to 127°C. Later, you found the volume to be 125 mL and the temperature to be 175°C. What was the pressure in millimeters of mercury at the new volume and temperature?

Information

The initial pressure, volume, and temperature of the gas (1.000 atm, 1.25 L at 127°C); the final volume and temperature (125 mL, 175°C); the question of what is the final pressure in mmHg

Connections

$$\frac{P_1 V_1}{n_1 T_1} = \frac{P_2 V_2}{n_2 T_2}$$

Solution

Collect and label the information from the problem:

$P_1 = 1.000 \text{ atm}$ $P_2 = ? \text{ mmHg}$

$V_1 = 1.25 \text{ L}$ $V_2 = 125 \text{ mL}$

$n_1 = \text{---}$ $n_2 = \text{---}$

$T_1 = 127°\text{C} = 400. \text{ K}$ $T_2 = 448 \text{ K}$

Based on the available information, the combined gas law simplifies to $\frac{P_1 V_1}{T_1} = \frac{P_2 V_2}{T_2}$

The simplified combined gas law rearranges to $P_2 = \dfrac{P_1 \, V_1 \, T_2}{T_1 \, V_2}$

Enter the appropriate values into the equation and cancel:

$$P_2 = \frac{(1.000 \text{ atm})(1.25 \text{ } \cancel{L})(448 \text{ } \cancel{K})}{(400.\cancel{K})(125 \text{ m}\cancel{L})}$$

The need for additional conversions is now apparent. We will begin with a *milli-* conversion ($m = 0.001 = 10^{-3}$):

$$P_2 = \frac{(1.000 \text{ atm})(1.25 \text{ } \cancel{L})(448 \text{ } \cancel{K})}{(400.\cancel{K})(125 \text{ } \cancel{mL})}\left(\frac{m}{0.001}\right)$$

Finally, we need to convert atmospheres to mmHg, using 1 atm = 760 mmHg:

$$P_2 = \frac{(1.000 \text{ } \cancel{atm})(1.25 \text{ } \cancel{L})(448 \text{ } \cancel{K})}{(400.\cancel{K})(125 \text{ } \cancel{mL})}\left(\frac{m}{0.001}\right)\left(\frac{760 \text{ mmHg}}{1 \text{ } \cancel{atm}}\right) = 8512 = \textbf{8.51} \times \textbf{10}^3 \textbf{ mmHg}$$

Reality Check

The magnitude of the answer seems reasonable. The units and the number of significant figures are correct.

5.98 Students use the reaction below to generate O_2 gas. The O_2 was collected over water at a temperature of 30.0°C. The total pressure was 875 mmHg. If the students found that 1.75 L of O_2 gas was generated, how many grams of $KMnO_4$ were used?

$$2 \text{ KMnO}_4(s) \rightarrow \text{K}_2\text{MnO}_4(s) + \text{MnO}_2(s) + \text{O}_2(g)$$

Information

The balanced chemical equation; the temperature (30.0°C); the total pressure (875 mmHg); the volume of oxygen (1.75 L); the question of how many grams of $KMnO_4$

Connections

$PV = nRT$; $P_{total} = P_a + P_b + P_c + \dots$; the vapor pressure of water from **table 5.2** in the textbook (31.824 torr)

Solution

Recopy the balanced chemical equation, and include the information about each substance below its formula:

$$2 \text{ KMnO}_4(s) \rightarrow \text{K}_2\text{MnO}_4(s) + \text{MnO}_2(s) + \text{O}_2(g)$$

$$\text{? g} \qquad\qquad\qquad\qquad\qquad\qquad 1.75 \text{ L}$$
$$30.0°C$$

$$P_{total} = 875 \text{ mmHg} = 875 \text{ torr}$$
$$P_{H_2O} = 31.824 \text{ torr}$$

We need to subtract the partial pressure of the water vapor from the total pressure to get the partial pressure of the dry gas. This is an application of Dalton's law.

$$P_{total} = P_{dry} + P_{H_2O}$$

Rearranging this equation gives

$$P_{dry} = P_{total} - P_{H_2O}$$

Using the values from the problem and the vapor pressure table (**table 5.2**) gives

$$P_{dry} = 875 \text{ torr} - 31.824 \text{ torr} = 843.176 \text{ torr} \qquad \text{(unrounded)}$$

We can now substitute the partial pressure of dry oxygen into the variable table from earlier:

Collect and label the information from the problem:

$P = 843.2$ torr (1 extra significant figure)
$V = 1.75$ L
Mass = ? g $KMnO_4$
$T = 30.0°C = 303.2$ K
$$R = \frac{0.08206 \text{ L} \cdot \text{atm}}{\text{mol} \cdot \text{K}}$$

This is a stoichiometry problem, which means that moles are the key. Therefore, the first step is to determine moles. Based upon the given information, we will need to rearrange the ideal gas equation to $n = \dfrac{PV}{RT}$

Enter the appropriate values into the equation and cancel:

$$n = \frac{(843.2 \text{ torr})(1.75 \text{ L})}{\left(\dfrac{0.08206 \text{ L} \cdot \text{atm}}{\text{mol} \cdot \text{K}}\right)(303.2 \text{ K})}$$

The need for an additional conversion is now apparent. Adding the appropriate pressure conversion (1 atm = 760 torr) gives

$$n = \frac{(843.2 \text{ torr})(1.75 \text{ L})}{\left(\dfrac{0.08206 \text{ L} \cdot \text{atm}}{\text{mol} \cdot \text{K}}\right)(303.2 \text{ K})}\left(\frac{1 \text{ atm}}{760 \text{ torr}}\right)$$

This gives us moles. We used a gas law; therefore, this is the moles of gas (O_2). To get to the substance of interest ($KMnO_4$), we need a mole ratio:

$$n = \frac{(843.2 \text{ torr})(1.75 \text{ L})}{\left(\dfrac{0.08206 \text{ L} \cdot \text{atm}}{\text{mol} \cdot \text{K}}\right)(303.2 \text{ K})}\left(\frac{1 \text{ atm}}{760 \text{ torr}}\right)\left(\frac{2 \text{ mol } KMnO_4}{1 \text{ mol } O_2}\right)$$

We now need the molar mass of $KMnO_4$ to reach the desired units (grams):

$$\text{Mass} = \frac{(843.2 \text{ torr})(1.75 \text{ L})}{\left(\dfrac{0.08206 \text{ L} \cdot \text{atm}}{\text{mol} \cdot \text{K}}\right)(303.2 \text{ K})}\left(\frac{1 \text{ atm}}{760 \text{ torr}}\right)\left(\frac{2 \text{ mol } KMnO_4}{1 \text{ mol } O_2}\right)\left(\frac{158.032 \text{ g } KMnO_4}{1 \text{ mol } KMnO_4}\right)$$

$$= 24.66433 = \textbf{24.7 g } KMnO_4$$

Reality Check

The magnitude of the answer seems reasonable. The units and the number of significant figures are correct.

5.100 When it comes in contact with air, sodium hydroxide, NaOH, slowly loses its purity by reacting with carbon dioxide, CO_2, to produce sodium carbonate, Na_2CO_3:

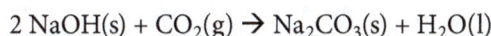

$$2 \text{ NaOH(s)} + CO_2(g) \rightarrow Na_2CO_3(s) + H_2O(l)$$

How many milliliters of carbon dioxide at 725 torr and 25.0°C will react with 2.50 g of sodium hydroxide?

Information

The balanced chemical equation; the pressure and temperature of the CO_2 (725 torr, 25.0°C); the mass of NaOH (2.50 g); the question of how many milliliters of CO_2

Connections

$PV = nRT$

Solution

Recopy the balanced chemical equation, and include the information about each substance below its formula:

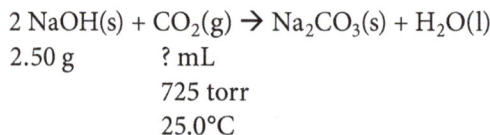

$$2\ NaOH(s) + CO_2(g) \rightarrow Na_2CO_3(s) + H_2O(l)$$

2.50 g   ? mL
725 torr
25.0°C

Collect and label the information from the problem:

$P = 725$ torr
$V = ?$ mL CO_2
Mass $= 2.50$ g NaOH
$T = 25.0°C = 298.2$ K
$R = \dfrac{0.08206\ L \cdot atm}{mol \cdot K}$

Rearrange the ideal gas equation to $V = \dfrac{nRT}{P}$

To use a gas law equation, we need to know the moles of gas. Sodium hydroxide is not the substance of interest, so a conversion is necessary to get to moles of gas (CO_2).

$$\text{Moles H}_2 = (2.50\ \cancel{\text{g NaOH}})\left(\frac{1\ \cancel{\text{mol NaOH}}}{39.9971\ \cancel{\text{g NaOH}}}\right)\left(\frac{1\ \text{mol CO}_2}{2\ \cancel{\text{mol NaOH}}}\right) = n$$

Enter the appropriate values into the equation and cancel:

$$V = \frac{\left(2.50\ \cancel{\text{g NaOH}}\right)\left(\dfrac{1\ \cancel{\text{mol NaOH}}}{39.9971\ \cancel{\text{g NaOH}}}\right)\left(\dfrac{1\ \cancel{\text{mol CO}_2}}{2\ \cancel{\text{mol NaOH}}}\right)\left(\dfrac{0.08206\ L \cdot atm}{\cancel{mol} \cdot \cancel{K}}\right)(298.2\ \cancel{K})}{725\ \text{torr}}$$

The need for an additional conversion is now apparent. The *milli-* conversion ($m = 0.001 = 10^{-3}$) is appropriate because the problem requests milliliters.

$$V = \frac{\left(2.50\ \cancel{\text{g NaOH}}\right)\left(\dfrac{1\ \cancel{\text{mol NaOH}}}{39.9971\ \cancel{\text{g NaOH}}}\right)\left(\dfrac{1\ \cancel{\text{mol CO}_2}}{2\ \cancel{\text{mol NaOH}}}\right)\left(\dfrac{0.08206\ L \cdot atm}{\cancel{mol} \cdot \cancel{K}}\right)(298.2\ \cancel{K})}{725\ \text{torr}} \left(\dfrac{m}{0.001}\right)$$

Adding the appropriate pressure conversion (1 atm = 760 torr) gives

$$V = \frac{\left(2.50\ \cancel{\text{g NaOH}}\right)\left(\dfrac{1\ \cancel{\text{mol NaOH}}}{39.9971\ \cancel{\text{g NaOH}}}\right)\left(\dfrac{1\ \cancel{\text{mol CO}_2}}{2\ \cancel{\text{mol NaOH}}}\right)\left(\dfrac{0.08206\ L \cdot \cancel{atm}}{\cancel{mol} \cdot \cancel{K}}\right)(298.2\ \cancel{K})}{725\ \cancel{\text{torr}}}$$

$$\times \left(\frac{m}{0.001}\right)\left(\frac{760\ \cancel{\text{torr}}}{1\ \cancel{\text{atm}}}\right)$$

$$= 801.6711 = \textbf{802 mL}$$

Reality Check

The magnitude of the answer seems reasonable. The units and the number of significant figures are correct.

5.103 A chemist performed an analysis on a gas sample with a density of 1.80 g/L at 25°C and 0.955 atm and found it to be 52.2% carbon, 13.0% hydrogen, and 34.8% oxygen. Assuming there was only one compound in the gas sample, what is its molecular formula?

Information

The density (1.80 g/L); the temperature (25°C); the pressure (0.955 atm); the composition (52.2 % C, 13.0 % H, and 34.8 % O); the question of what is the molecular formula

Connections

$PV = nRT$

Solution

Collect and label the information from the problem:

Density = 1.80 g/L
$P = 0.955$ atm
$V = ?$ (Assume = 1.000 L)
$n = ?$
$T = 25°C = 298$ K
$R = \dfrac{0.08206 \text{ L} \cdot \text{atm}}{\text{mol} \cdot \text{K}}$
52.2% C
13.0% H
34.8% O

To get the molecular formula, we must first determine the empirical formula.

To determine the empirical formula, we need to determine the moles of each element present in the compound. We need the mass of each element and its molar mass to determine the moles. Since the problem gives percentages, we will need to convert the values to mass. Percentage is an intensive quantity; therefore, we can choose any sample mass. The simplest sample mass is 100 g (exactly). With this mass, the numerical values of the percentages (52.2, 13.0, and 34.8) are the same as the numerical values of the masses (52.2, 13.0, and 34.8). Converting the masses to moles gives

$$\text{Mol C} = (52.2 \text{ g C})\left(\frac{1 \text{ mol C}}{12.011 \text{ g C}}\right) = 4.346016 \text{ mol C} \quad \text{(unrounded)}$$

$$\text{Mol H} = (13.0 \text{ g H})\left(\frac{1 \text{ mol H}}{1.0079 \text{ g H}}\right) = 12.89810 \text{ mol H} \quad \text{(unrounded)}$$

$$\text{Mol O} = (34.8 \text{ g O})\left(\frac{1 \text{ mol O}}{15.999 \text{ g O}}\right) = 2.1751359 \text{ mol O} \quad \text{(unrounded)}$$

The next step is to divide each mole value by the lowest value (2.1751359):

$$C = \left(\frac{4.346016 \text{ mol C}}{2.1751359} \right) = 2.00 \text{ C}$$

$$H = \left(\frac{12.89810 \text{ mol H}}{2.1751359} \right) = 5.93 \text{ H}$$

$$O = \left(\frac{2.1751359 \text{ mol H}}{2.1751359} \right) = 1.00 \text{ O}$$

The values must be whole numbers (or close to whole numbers). The value for hydrogen is close to a whole number; therefore, rounding to 6 is acceptable. This gives C = 2, H = 6, and O = 1, which makes the empirical formula C_2H_6O.

To find the molecular formula, the second thing we need is the molecular weight. This calculation begins with the rearrangement of the ideal gas equation to $n = \dfrac{PV}{RT}$

Enter the appropriate values into the equation and cancel:

$$n = \frac{(0.955 \text{ atm})(1.000 \text{ L})}{\left(\dfrac{0.08206 \text{ L} \cdot \text{atm}}{\text{mol} \cdot \text{K}} \right)(298 \text{ K})} = 0.0390531 \text{mol} \qquad \text{(unrounded)}$$

The volume (1.000 L) and the density (1.80 g/L) combine to give the mass of the sample:

$$\text{Mass} = \left(\frac{1.80 \text{ g}}{\text{L}} \right)(1.000 \text{ L}) = 1.80 \text{ g}$$

The units of molecular weight are amu/molecule or g/mole. Using the mass given (1.80 g) and the moles calculated (0.0390531 mol), we can determine the molecular weight:

$$\text{Molecular weight} = \left(\frac{1.80 \text{ g}}{0.0390531 \text{ mol}} \right) = 46.09109 \text{ g/mol} \quad \text{(unrounded)}$$

The empirical formula (C_2H_6O) weight is about 46 g/mol. Since the two masses are the same, the empirical formula is the same as the molecular formula, so the molecular formula is C_2H_6O.

Reality Check
The magnitude of the molecular weight seems reasonable: Molecular weights cannot be less than hydrogen (2 g/mol), and for volatile materials the values are usually below 500 g/mol. The units and the number of significant figures are correct.

5.105 An engineer submitted a sample of an unknown gas for analysis. The first step toward determining the molecular weight of the unknown gas was to allow the gas to effuse through a porous barrier. The technicians found that 30.90 mL of the gas effused in 408.0 s. A sample of nitrogen gas was then tested under the same pressure and at the same temperature, as a standard of comparison, and 45.84 mL of it effused in 152.0s. What was the molecular weight of the unknown gas?

Information
The rate of effusion of the unknown gas (30.90 mL in 408.0 s); the rate of effusion of the nitrogen (45.84 mL in 152.0 s); the question of what is the molecular weight of the unknown gas

Connections

$$\frac{Rate_A}{Rate_B} = \sqrt{\frac{MW_B}{MW_A}}$$

Solution

The rates will be in terms of milliliters per second. In this solution, we will assume gas A = nitrogen (MM_A = 28.0134 g/mol) and gas B is the unknown. Entering the appropriate values into Graham's law gives

$$\frac{Rate_A}{Rate_B} = \frac{\dfrac{45.84 \; \cancel{mL}}{152.0 \; \cancel{s}}}{\dfrac{30.90 \; \cancel{mL}}{408.0 \; \cancel{s}}} = \sqrt{\frac{MW_B}{MW_A}} = \sqrt{\frac{MW_B}{28.0134 \; g/mol}}$$

$$= \frac{0.3015789}{0.075735} = 3.98201 = \sqrt{\frac{MW_B}{28.0134 \; g/mol}}$$

$$15.85642 = \frac{MW_B}{28.0134 \; g/mol}$$

$$MM_B = (15.85642)(28.0134 \; g/mol) = 444.19237 = \textbf{444.2 g/mol}$$

Reality Check

The magnitude of the answer seems reasonable. The units and the number of significant figures are correct.

5.107 Most aerosol cans contain a gas or gases under pressure. If you heat the can sufficiently, it will explode. If the pressure in such a can is 1.9 atm at 25°C, how high will the temperature need to be to cause the can to explode, assuming it will explode when the internal pressure reaches 3.1 atm?

Information

The initial pressure and temperature (1.9 atm, 25°C); the final pressure (3.1 atm), the question of what is the final temperature

Connections

$$\frac{P_1 V_1}{n_1 T_1} = \frac{P_2 V_2}{n_2 T_2}$$

Solution

Collect and label the information from the problem:

P_1 = 1.9 atm	P_2 = 3.1 atm
V_1 = —	V_2 = —
n_1 = —	n_2 = —
T_1 = 25°C = 298 K	T_2 = ?

Based on the available information, the combined gas law simplifies to $\dfrac{P_1}{T_1} = \dfrac{P_2}{T_2}$

The simplified combined gas law rearranges to $T_2 = \dfrac{P_2 \, T_1}{P_1}$

Enter the appropriate values into the equation and cancel:

$$T_2 = \frac{(3.1 \ \cancel{atm})(298 \ K)}{(1.9 \ \cancel{atm})} = 486.2105 = \textbf{486 K (or 213°C)}$$

Reality Check

The magnitude of the answer seems reasonable. The units and the number of significant figures are correct.

5.111 A chemist wishes to identify an unknown liquid and must therefore determine its molecular weight. She chose the Dumas method (see Problem 5.24) and found that at a temperature of 98°C and a pressure of 715 torr, 1.668 g of vapor occupied 415 mL. Determine the molecular weight of the unknown.

Information

The temperature (98°C); the pressure (715 torr); the mass (1.668 g); the volume (415 mL); the question of what is the molecular weight

Connections

$PV = nRT$

Solution

Collect and label the information from the problem:

$P = 715$ torr
$V = 415$ mL
Mass $= 1.668$ g
$T = 98°C = 371$ K
$R = \dfrac{0.08206 \ L \bullet atm}{mol \bullet K}$
Molecular weight $=$? g/mol

Rearrange the ideal gas equation to $n = \dfrac{PV}{RT}$

Enter the appropriate values into the equation and cancel:

$$n = \frac{(715 \ torr)(415 \ \cancel{mL})}{\left(\dfrac{0.08206 \ \cancel{L} \bullet atm}{mol \bullet \cancel{K}}\right)(371 \ \cancel{K})}$$

The need for an additional conversion is now apparent. The *milli-* conversion ($m = 0.001 = 10^{-3}$) is appropriate:

$$n = \frac{(715 \ torr)(415 \ \cancel{mL})}{\left(\dfrac{0.08206 \ \cancel{L} \bullet atm}{mol \bullet \cancel{K}}\right)(371 \ \cancel{K})}\left(\frac{0.001}{\cancel{m}}\right)$$

Adding the appropriate pressure conversion (1 atm = 760 torr) gives

$$n = \frac{(715 \ \cancel{torr})(415 \ \cancel{mL})}{\left(\dfrac{0.08206 \ \cancel{L} \bullet atm}{mol \bullet \cancel{K}}\right)(371 \ \cancel{K})}\left(\frac{0.001}{\cancel{m}}\right)\left(\frac{1 \ \cancel{atm}}{760 \ \cancel{torr}}\right) = 0.012824343 \ mol \qquad \text{(unrounded)}$$

The units of molecular weight are amu/molecule or g/mole. Using the mass given (1.668 g) and the moles calculated (0.012824343 mol), we can determine the molecular weight:

$$\text{Molecular weight} = \left(\frac{1.668 \text{ g}}{0.012824343 \text{ mol}}\right) = 130.065 = \mathbf{1.30 \times 10^2 \text{ g/mol}}$$

Reality Check

The magnitude of the molecular weight seems reasonable. Molecular weights cannot be less than hydrogen (2 g/mol), and for volatile materials the values are usually below 500 g/mol. The units and the number of significant figures are correct.

5.112 Name each of the following compounds: **(a)** Na_2SO_4, **(b)** KNO_3, **(c)** $CaCO_3$, **(d)** $Mg_3(PO_4)_2$, **(e)** Al_2O_3, **(f)** Li_2SO_3, **(g)** NH_4Br, **(h)** $BaCl_2$, **(i)** $Sr(OH)_2$, **(j)** CsI

Solution

As shown in the Nomenclature Resource,

(a) Na_2SO_4 = **sodium sulfate**

(b) KNO_3 = **potassium nitrate**

(c) $CaCO_3$ = **calcium carbonate**

(d) $Mg_3(PO_4)_2$ = **magnesium phosphate**

(e) Al_2O_3 = **aluminum oxide**

(f) Li_2SO_3 = **lithium sulfite**

(g) NH_4Br = **ammonium bromide**

(h) $BaCl_2$ = **barium chloride**

(i) $Sr(OH)_2$ = **strontium hydroxide**

(j) CsI = **cesium iodide**

5.114 What is the name or the formula of each of the following compounds: **(a)** nitric acid, **(b)** HNO_2, **(c)** H_2SO_4, **(d)** carbonic acid, **(e)** $HC_2H_3O_2$, **(f)** phosphoric acid, **(g)** chromic acid, **(h)** sulfurous acid, **(i)** H_3AsO_4, **(j)** $H_2C_2O_4$

Solution

As shown in the Nomenclature Resource,

(a) nitric acid = $\mathbf{HNO_3}$

(b) HNO_2 = **nitrous acid**

(c) H_2SO_4 = **sulfuric acid**

(d) carbonic acid = $\mathbf{H_2CO_3}$

(e) $HC_2H_3O_2$ = **acetic acid**

(f) phosphoric acid = $\mathbf{H_3PO_4}$

(g) chromic acid = $\mathbf{H_2CrO_4}$

(h) sulfurous acid = $\mathbf{H_2SO_3}$

(i) H_3AsO_4 = **arsenic acid**

(j) $H_2C_2O_4$ = **oxalic acid**

5.116 Many chemicals are known by their common names. Give the chemical names for each of the following substances. **(a)** lime (CaO); **(b)** blue vitriol ($CuSO_4·5H_2O$); **(c)** saltpeter (KNO_3); **(d)** baking soda ($NaHCO_3$); **(e)** muriatic acid (HCl); **(f)** milk of magnesia ($Mg(OH)_2$); **(g)** battery acid (H_2SO_4); **(h)** Epsom salts ($MgSO_4·7H_2O$); **(i)** smelling salts (($NH_4)_2CO_3$); **(j)** table salt (NaCl)

Solution

As shown in the Nomenclature Resource,

(a) lime, CaO = **calcium oxide**

(b) blue vitriol, $CuSO_4·5H_2O$ = **copper(II) sulfate pentahydrate**

(c) saltpeter, KNO_3 = **potassium nitrate**

(d) baking soda, $NaHCO_3$ = **sodium hydrogen carbonate or sodium bicarbonate**

(e) muriatic acid, HCl = **hydrochloric acid**

(f) milk of magnesia, $Mg(OH)_2$ = **magnesium hydroxide**

(g) battery acid, H_2SO_4 = **sulfuric acid**

(h) Epsom salts, $MgSO_4·7H_2O$ = **magnesium sulfate heptahydrate**

(i) smelling salts, $(NH_4)_2CO_3$ = **ammonium carbonate**

(j) table salt, $NaCl$ = **sodium chloride**

5.118 Write balanced chemical equations for each of the following reactions: **(a)** Sulfur, in coal, burns to produce sulfur dioxide gas. **(b)** Sulfur dioxide gas, from burning coal, reacts with atmospheric oxygen gas to form gaseous sulfur trioxide. **(c)** Gaseous sulfur trioxide, from the air oxidation of sulfur dioxide, dissolves in raindrops to form an aqueous solution of sulfuric acid. **(d)** Acid rain, containing an aqueous solution of sulfuric acid, falls on a marble (calcium carbonate) statue and forms solid calcium sulfate, gaseous carbon dioxide, and liquid water.

Solution

As shown in the Nomenclature Resource,

(a) Sulfur, in coal, burns to produce sulfur dioxide gas:

$$S(s) + O_2(g) \rightarrow SO_2(g)$$

(b) Sulfur dioxide gas, from burning coal, reacts with atmospheric oxygen gas to form gaseous sulfur trioxide:

$$2\,SO_2(g) + O_2(g) \rightarrow 2\,SO_3(g)$$

(c) Gaseous sulfur trioxide, from the air oxidation of sulfur dioxide, dissolves in raindrops to form an aqueous solution of sulfuric acid:

$$SO_3(g) + H_2O(l) \rightarrow H_2SO_4(aq)$$

(d) Acid rain, containing an aqueous solution of sulfuric acid, falls on a marble (calcium carbonate) statue and forms solid calcium sulfate, gaseous carbon dioxide, and liquid water:

$$H_2SO_4(aq) + CaCO_3(s) \rightarrow CaSO_4(s) + CO_2(g) + H_2O(l)$$

CHAPTER 6

Thermochemistry—The Study of Energy Changes

The successful completion of these problems requires the following eleven (11) items.

1. Be <u>extra careful</u> with the units in this chapter. This is a conversion intensive chapter.
2. Watch the phases of the substances involved in any chemical reactions.
3. In Hess's law problems, remember that $H_2O(g)$ is not the same as $H_2O(l)$, and neither of these is the same as $H_2O(s)$.
4. When working Hess's law problems, you can avoid many errors by rewriting the equations as you modify them.
5. Unlike "normal" chemical equations, thermochemical equations deal only with moles.
6. According to the law of conservation of energy (the first law of thermodynamics), heat (energy) lost must equal heat gained.
7. Moles are still the key to many problems.
8. Energy is normally expressed as joules (or kilojoules); however, calories or Calories may appear in some cases (rarely in combination with other energy units).
9. Exothermic processes are always negative (–), and endothermic processes are always positive (+). The correct sign may not be obvious from the calculation.
10. See appendix C for Standard Heats of Formation.
11. Temperature changes are numerically the same in both °C and K. For example, $T_f - T_i$ for a change from 25°C to 0°C is 25°C or 25 K (from 298 K – 273 K).

Example Problems From the Text

Example Problem 6.1

We learned in chapter 5 that the average velocity of a hydrogen gas molecule at room temperature is about 1,500 m/s. What is the kinetic energy, in joules, of a molecule of hydrogen gas travelling this average speed at room temperature?

Information

The only given value is the molecule's average velocity: 1,500 m/s.

Connections

The equation for kinetic energy ($KE = \dfrac{1}{2}\, mv^2$) requires both velocity (which we are given) and mass. We can use the periodic table on the inside front cover of this textbook to find the mass of a hydrogen molecule. Remember that the answer must be in joules, the SI unit for kinetic energy.

Solution

An individual hydrogen molecule, H_2, has a mass of 2×1.008 amu $= 2.016$ amu. We begin our calculation by inserting the appropriate values into the kinetic energy equation:

$$KE = \frac{1}{2}(2.016 \text{ amu})\left(\frac{1,500 \text{ m}}{\text{s}}\right)^2$$

The next step is to apply the appropriate unit conversions that lead to joules:

$$KE = \frac{1}{2}(2.016 \text{ amu})\left(\frac{1,500 \text{ m}}{\text{s}}\right)^2\left(\frac{1 \text{ g}}{6.02 \times 10^{23} \text{ amu}}\right)\left(\frac{\text{k}}{10^3}\right)\left(\frac{\text{J}}{\text{kg m}^2 / \text{s}^2}\right)$$

$$= 3.76619 \times 10^{-21} = \mathbf{3.8 \times 10^{-21} \text{ J}}$$

Reality Check

The units and significant figures are correct. The extremely small size of a hydrogen molecule explains the very small quantity of kinetic energy it possesses.

Follow-Up Problem 6.1a

Determine the kinetic energy, in joules, of a 5.0-ounce baseball traveling at 95 miles per hour.

Information

The mass (5.0 oz); the speed (95 mph); the question of what is the kinetic energy (? J)

Connections

The equation for kinetic energy ($KE = \dfrac{1}{2}\, mv^2$) requires both velocity (which we are given) and mass. We need to use the appropriate conversions. Remember that the answer must be in joules, the SI unit for kinetic energy.

Solution

We begin our calculation by inserting the appropriate values into the kinetic energy equation:

$$KE = \frac{1}{2}(5.0 \text{ oz})\left(\frac{95 \text{ mi}}{\text{h}}\right)^2$$

The next step is to apply the appropriate unit conversions that lead to joules:

$$KE = \frac{1}{2}(5.0 \text{ oz})\left(\frac{28.35 \text{ g}}{1 \text{ oz}}\right)\left(\frac{k}{10^3}\right)\left(\frac{95 \text{ mi}}{h}\right)^2\left[\left(\frac{1609 \text{ m}}{1 \text{ mi}}\right)\left(\frac{1 \text{ h}}{3600 \text{ s}}\right)\right]^2\left(\frac{J}{kg \text{ m}^2 \big/ s^2}\right)$$

$$= 127.775 = \mathbf{1.3 \times 10^2 \text{ J}}$$

Reality Check

The units and the significant figures are correct.

Follow-Up Problem 6.1b

One of the basic postulates of kinetic molecular theory is that molecules of different gases have the same average kinetic energy at the same temperature. Using the kinetic energy of hydrogen found in Example Problem 6.1, determine the velocity, in meters per second, of an oxygen molecule at the same temperature.

Information

The kinetic energy for a hydrogen molecule (3.8×10^{-21} J); the question of what is the velocity (? m/s) of an oxygen molecule with the same kinetic energy

Connections

The equation for kinetic energy ($KE = \frac{1}{2} mv^2$); the masses of a hydrogen and oxygen molecule using information from the periodic table and the relationship between grams (kilograms) and atomic mass units (1 g = 6.02×10^{23} amu) (Do not forget that oxygen normally exists as diatomic molecules.)

Solution

We need to rearrange the kinetic energy equation to find the velocity:

$$\text{Velocity} = v = \sqrt{\frac{KE}{\frac{1}{2} m}}$$

Now enter the appropriate values into the "new" equation:

$$\text{Velocity} = \sqrt{\frac{3.8 \times 10^{-21} \text{ J}}{\frac{1}{2}(2 \times 16.0 \text{ amu})}}$$

The next step is to apply the appropriate unit conversions that lead to velocity (m/s):

$$\text{Velocity} = \sqrt{\frac{3.8 \times 10^{-21} \text{ J} \left(\frac{kg \text{ m}^2 \big/ s^2}{J}\right)}{\frac{1}{2}(2 \times 16.0 \text{ amu})\left(\frac{1 \text{ g}}{6.02 \times 10^{23} \text{ amu}}\right)\left(\frac{k}{10^3}\right)}} = 378.120 = \mathbf{3.8 \times 10^2 \text{ m/s}}$$

Reality Check

The units and the significant figures are correct.

Example Problem 6.2

How many joules of heat does it take to warm 25 g of iron from 273 K to 298 K?

Information

Given the mass of iron (25 g) and its change in temperature (273 K to 298 K), we are asked to provide the needed amount of heat in joules.

Connections

The heat capacity of iron, from table 6.2 (0.44 J/g °C), connects the number of joules to the change in temperature.

Solution

We know to use the specific heat capacity to answer this question, because the given data include joules, grams, and temperatures, which is the same combination of units and properties used to describe the specific heat capacity. We will begin constructing our solution by stating the specific heat capacity of iron:

$$\text{Joules} = \left(\frac{0.44 \text{ J}}{\text{g} \,^\circ\text{C}}\right) \quad \text{(incomplete solution)}$$

To arrive at an answer in joules, we must eliminate the grams and the degrees Celsius. We will start this process by inserting the amount of substance in grams (which will cause the "g" unit to cancel):

$$\text{Joules} = \left(\frac{0.44 \text{ J}}{\text{g} \,^\circ\text{C}}\right)(25 \text{ g}) \quad \text{(incomplete solution)}$$

The remaining units are joules and degrees Celsius, and we wish to cancel out the degrees Celsius. The temperature change is in kelvins, but degrees Celsius have the same magnitude as kelvins. Therefore, the numerical value of a temperature change is the same whether reported in kelvins or in degrees Celsius. In this case, the temperature change is 298 K − 273 K = 25 K = 25°C. Incorporating the Celsius temperature change into the calculation gives

$$\text{Joules} = \left(\frac{0.44 \text{ J}}{\text{g} \,^\circ\text{C}}\right)(25 \text{ g})(25^\circ\text{C}) = 275 = \mathbf{2.8 \times 10^2 \text{ J}}$$

Reality Check

The final answer has the correct units and seems reasonable in magnitude. The value should be less than half of 625 (= 25^2) × (less than 0.5). This is an endothermic process, so the answer should be positive.

Follow-Up Problem 6.2a

Determine the number of joules necessary to warm 175 g of copper metal from 25°C to 75°C.

Information

The mass of copper (175 g) and its change in temperature (25°C to 75°C); the question of the needed amount of heat in joules

Connections

The heat capacity of iron, from table 6.2 (0.39 J/g °C), connects the number of joules to the change in temperature

Solution

We will begin with the specific heat capacity of iron and use the other information in the problem to achieve the desired conversions:

$$\text{Joules} = \left(\frac{0.39 \text{ J}}{\text{g} \,°\text{C}}\right)(175 \text{ g})(75-25)°\text{C} = 3412.5 = \mathbf{3.4 \times 10^3 \text{ J}}$$

Reality Check

The final answer has the correct units and seems reasonable in magnitude. This is an endothermic process, so the answer should be positive.

Follow-Up Problem 6.2b

Calculate the energy change, in joules, when 75 g of aluminum metal cools from 45°C to 15°C.

Information

The mass of aluminum (75 g) and its change in temperature (45°C to 15°C); the question of the amount of heat lost in joules

Connections

The heat capacity of aluminum, from table 6.2 (0.90 J/g °C), connects the number of joules to the change in temperature

Solution

We will begin with the specific heat capacity of aluminum and use the other information in the problem to achieve the desired conversions"

$$\text{Joules} = \left(\frac{0.90 \text{ J}}{\text{g} \,°\text{C}}\right)(75 \text{ g})(15-45)°\text{C} = -2025 = \mathbf{-2.0 \times 10^3 \text{ J}}$$

Reality Check

The final answer has the correct units and seems reasonable in magnitude. The loss of heat is exothermic; therefore, the final answer must be negative.

Example Problem 6.3

A 1.5886-g sample of glucose, $C_6H_{12}O_6$, was combusted in a bomb calorimeter. The temperature increased from 20.000°C to 23.682°C. The heat capacity of the calorimeter was 3.562 kJ/°C, and the calorimeter contained 1.000 kg of water. Find the molar heat of reaction for the reaction

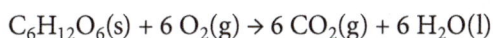

$$C_6H_{12}O_6(s) + 6\,O_2(g) \rightarrow 6\,CO_2(g) + 6\,H_2O(l)$$

Information

Along with a reaction equation, we have a mass of 1.5886 g $C_6H_{12}O_6$; a temperature change from 20.000°C to 23.682°C; and a calorimeter with a heat capacity of 3.562 kJ/°C, containing 1.000 kg H_2O. We want to calculate the molar heat of reaction.

Connections

The molar mass of glucose (180.16 g/mol) is the needed conversion factor, because molar heats of reaction are in units of joules per mole (or kilojoules per mole). The specific heat of water (4.18 J/g °C).

Solution

The reaction released heat, causing the increase in temperature; therefore, the process was exothermic. The generated heat went to two destinations: some of it to the calorimeter, and the remainder of it to the water in the calorimeter. To determine the amount of heat energy that went to the calorimeter, we need the temperature change and the heat capacity of the calorimeter. The calculation of the calorimeter portion of the heat energy is

$$q_{calorimeter} = \left(\frac{3.562 \text{ kJ}}{°C} \right)(23.682 - 20.000)°C = 13.115284 \text{ kJ} \qquad \text{(unrounded)}$$

To determine the heat energy that went to the water, we need the temperature change, the mass of the water, and the specific heat of water.
The calculation of the energy portion of the heat energy is

$$q_{water} = \left(\frac{4.18 \text{ J}}{g°C} \right)(1.000 \text{ kg})(23.682 - 20.000)°C = 15.39076 \text{ kJ} \qquad \text{(unrounded)}$$

Note that the gram unit ("g") from the specific heat cancels only the gram part of the unit from the mass of water, leaving the "kilo" to combine with the joules (J) to give the desired unit: kilojoules.

The total amount of energy released is the sum of the energy that went to the calorimeter and the energy that went to the water. This value is

$$q_{total} = (13.115284 + 15.39076) \text{ kJ} = 28.506044 \text{ kJ} \qquad \text{(unrounded)}$$

Since the process was exothermic, the sign must be negative, giving –28.506044 kJ. The sign change is necessitated by the definition of *exothermic* and does not come directly from the calculations. The final step is to divide the energy by the moles of glucose:

$$\frac{-28.506044 \text{ kJ}}{(1.5886 \text{ g } C_6H_{12}O_6)\left(\dfrac{1 \text{ mol } C_6H_{12}O_6}{180.16 \text{ g } C_6H_{12}O_6} \right)} = -3{,}232.814357 = \mathbf{-3.23 \times 10^3 \text{ kJ/mol}}$$

The specific heat of water limits the significant figures in the answer.

Reality Check

The units and the significant figures are correct. The amount of reactant was less than 0.01 mole (~2/200), so it makes sense that the final answer is more than 100 times the amount of energy released (100 × 28.5). This (burning) is an exothermic process; therefore, the final answer is negative.

Follow-Up Problem 6.3a

A sample of $C_2H_5OH(l)$ weighing 1.42 g was burned with excess $O_2(g)$ in a bomb calorimeter. After completion of the reaction, the temperature of the calorimeter had increased from 24.00°C to 28.36°C. The calorimeter contained 0.500 kg of water. The heat capacity of the calorimeter was 7.54 kJ/°C. Calculate the heat of reaction in kilojoules per mole of C_2H_5OH. The reaction was

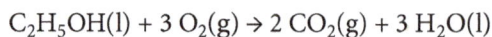

$$C_2H_5OH(l) + 3 O_2(g) \rightarrow 2 CO_2(g) + 3 H_2O(l)$$

Information

A reaction equation; a mass of 1.42 g C_2H_5OH; a temperature change from 24.00°C to 28.36°C; a calorimeter with a heat capacity of 7.54 kJ/°C, containing 0.500 kg H_2O; the question of the molar heat of reaction.

Connections

The molar mass of glucose (46.069 g/mol) is the needed conversion factor, because molar heats of reaction are in units of joules per mole (or kilojoules per mole). The specific heat of H_2O is 4.184 J/g °C.

Solution

Unlike in Example Problem 6.3, here many of the calculations are combined.

The calculation involves finding the energy and finding the moles. In the following calculation, the numerator is the energy and the denominator is the moles. The energy is divided into two portions: the heat going to the calorimeter (first in the numerator) plus the heat going to the water (second in the numerator). To find the moles (denominator), multiply the mass by the inverse of the molar mass. Convert the final answer to negative:

$$\frac{\left(\dfrac{7.54 \text{ kJ}}{°C}\right)(28.36 - 24.00)°C + \left(\dfrac{4.184 \text{ J}}{\text{g} °C}\right)(0.500 \text{ kg})(28.36 - 24.00)°C}{(1.42 \text{ g } C_2H_5OH)\left(\dfrac{1 \text{ mol } C_2H_5OH}{46.069 \text{ g } C_2H_5OH}\right)}$$

$$= -1362.46 = \mathbf{-1.36 \times 10^3 \text{ kJ/mol}}$$

Reality Check

The units and the significant figures are correct. This (burning) is an exothermic process; therefore, the final answer is negative.

Follow-Up Problem 6.3b

When a 24.8-g sample of sodium nitrate, $NaNO_3$, dissolves in 250.0 g of water in a coffee-cup calorimeter, the temperature changes from 28.37°C to 22.79°C. Determine the enthalpy change, in kilojoules per mole of $NaNO_3$, for sodium nitrate dissolving in water. Assume that the specific heat of the solution is the same as that of pure water, and that the heat capacity of the calorimeter is negligible.

Information

The mass of the solute (24.8 g $NaNO_3$); the mass of the solvent (250.0 g H_2O); the temperature change (28.37°C to 22.79°C); the specific heat of the solution equals the specific heat of H_2O (4.184 J/g °C) and the heat capacity of the calorimeter is zero; the question of what is the enthalpy change in kJ/mol $NaNO_3$

Connections

The molar mass of $NaNO_3$ (84.998 g/mol) is the needed conversion factor, because molar heats of reaction are in units of joules per mole (or kilojoules per mole); the mass of the solution will equal the mass of the solvent plus the mass of the solute (274.8 g).

Solution

Unlike in Example Problem 6.3, here many of the calculations are combined.

The calculation involves finding the energy and finding the moles. In the following calculation, the numerator is the energy and the denominator is the moles. The energy is the specific heat of the solution times the mass of the solution (solute plus solvent, or 24.8 g + 250.0 g) times the temperature change and a unit conversion. To find the moles (denominator), multiply the mass by the inverse of the molar mass. Convert the final answer to negative:

$$\frac{\left(\dfrac{4.184\ J}{g\ °C}\right)(274.8\ g)\left(\dfrac{k}{10^3}\right)(22.79 - 28.37)°C}{\left(24.8\ g\ NaNO_3\right)\left(\dfrac{1\ mol\ NaNO_3}{84.998\ g\ NaNO_3}\right)} = +21.9887 = \textbf{+22.0 kJ/mol}$$

Reality Check

The units and the significant figures are correct. The temperature decrease indicates that this is an endothermic process; therefore, the enthalpy change must be positive.

Example Problem 6.4

Calculate the heat of reaction for

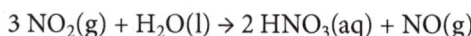

$$3\ NO_2(g) + H_2O(l) \rightarrow 2\ HNO_3(aq) + NO(g)$$

using the following thermochemical equations:

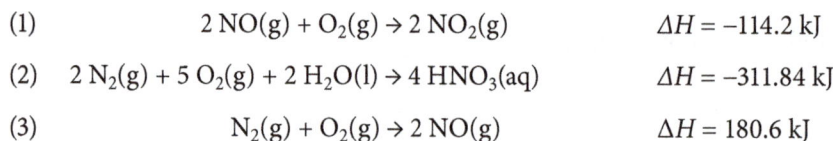

(1) $\qquad\qquad 2\ NO(g) + O_2(g) \rightarrow 2\ NO_2(g)$ $\qquad\qquad \Delta H = -114.2\ kJ$

(2) $\quad 2\ N_2(g) + 5\ O_2(g) + 2\ H_2O(l) \rightarrow 4\ HNO_3(aq)$ $\qquad \Delta H = -311.84\ kJ$

(3) $\qquad\qquad N_2(g) + O_2(g) \rightarrow 2\ NO(g)$ $\qquad\qquad \Delta H = 180.6\ kJ$

Information

We have three thermochemical equations with their associated enthalpy values to use in determining the enthalpy value of a fourth chemical equation.

Connections

Hess's law provides the connection between the given data and desired heat of reaction.

Solution

A Hess's law problem of this type becomes an exercise in mixing and matching: The goal is to combine the given alternative reaction equations in such a way that their sum will match the target reaction. It is possible to examine the alternative equations in any order for ways of matching the individual reactants and products to those in the target equation. In this example, we will begin by matching the components of the target equation from left to right.

The first compound we will try to match is nitrogen dioxide. This substance appears in equation 1. Two changes must take place for the nitrogen dioxide in equation 1 to exactly match the nitrogen dioxide in the target equation. The coefficient must change from 2 to 3, and the nitrogen dioxide must change from a product to a reactant. We can achieve these changes by reversing reaction 1 and multiplying it by 3/2:

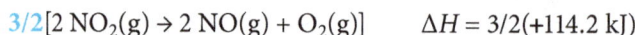

$$3/2[2\ NO_2(g) \rightarrow 2\ NO(g) + O_2(g)] \qquad \Delta H = 3/2(+114.2\ kJ)$$

The reversal of the reaction reverses the sign on the enthalpy change. Then multiplication gives

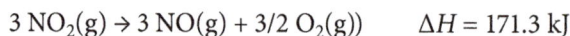

$$3\ NO_2(g) \rightarrow 3\ NO(g) + 3/2\ O_2(g)) \qquad \Delta H = 171.3\ kJ$$

The next substance in the target equation is water. Water appears in equation 2. We'll need to multiply equation 2 by 1/2 to get the desired coefficient of 1:

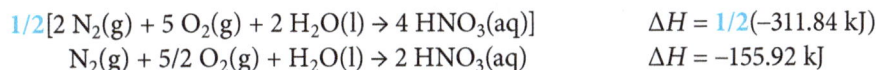

$$1/2[2\,N_2(g) + 5\,O_2(g) + 2\,H_2O(l) \rightarrow 4\,HNO_3(aq)] \qquad \Delta H = 1/2(-311.84\text{ kJ})$$
$$N_2(g) + 5/2\,O_2(g) + H_2O(l) \rightarrow 2\,HNO_3(aq) \qquad \Delta H = -155.92\text{ kJ}$$

By coincidence, the change in equation 2 not only makes the water match but also makes the nitric acid match. Thus, only NO(g) needs matching to the target equation. The reversal of equation 1 gave us two NO on the right, and we must reduce them to one. The reversal of equation 3 will put two NOs on the left to cancel two of the three on the right:

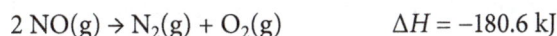

$$2\,NO(g) \rightarrow N_2(g) + O_2(g) \qquad \Delta H = -180.6\text{ kJ}$$

We now collect the three modified equations into a list. It is not necessary to determine the "new" enthalpy values now.

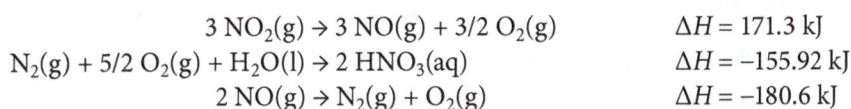

$$3\,NO_2(g) \rightarrow 3\,NO(g) + 3/2\,O_2(g) \qquad \Delta H = 171.3\text{ kJ}$$
$$N_2(g) + 5/2\,O_2(g) + H_2O(l) \rightarrow 2\,HNO_3(aq) \qquad \Delta H = -155.92\text{ kJ}$$
$$2\,NO(g) \rightarrow N_2(g) + O_2(g) \qquad \Delta H = -180.6\text{ kJ}$$

> ► We have found that when students do not recopy all the "new" equations, numerous errors commonly result. A few seconds spent in recopying can save a lot of grief.

The next step is to cancel equal amounts of any substance appearing on both sides of the reaction arrows:

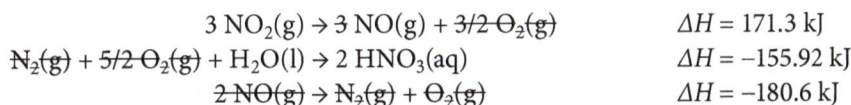

$$3\,NO_2(g) \rightarrow 3\,NO(g) + \cancel{3/2\,O_2(g)} \qquad \Delta H = 171.3\text{ kJ}$$
$$\cancel{N_2(g)} + \cancel{5/2\,O_2(g)} + H_2O(l) \rightarrow 2\,HNO_3(aq) \qquad \Delta H = -155.92\text{ kJ}$$
$$\cancel{2\,NO(g) \rightarrow N_2(g) + O_2(g)} \qquad \Delta H = -180.6\text{ kJ}$$

Notice that the amounts of oxygen are 5/2 on the reactant side and 3/2 + 1 = 5/2 on the product side, cancelling out oxygen entirely. The two NO(g) on the reactant side cancel two of the NOs on the product side, leaving one.

Combining the remaining components of the three equations gives

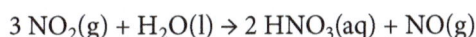

$$3\,NO_2(g) + H_2O(l) \rightarrow 2\,HNO_3(aq) + NO(g)$$

This is our target equation. Thus, we seem to have found a path to the desired enthalpy state. Now we must sum the three energies to produce the thermochemical equation, containing the enthalpy value we were seeking:

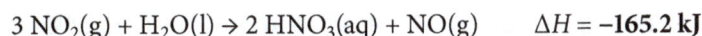

$$3\,NO_2(g) + H_2O(l) \rightarrow 2\,HNO_3(aq) + NO(g) \qquad \Delta H = \textbf{-165.2 kJ}$$

Reality Check

The units and the significant figures are correct. The equation we have produced is an exact match to the target equation. The values for the first equation and the last equation are nearly equal in magnitude; therefore, they will cancel, leaving the second equation. Consequently, the final answer should be near the value for the second equation. The most common error is to cancel species that appear on the same side instead of on opposite sides.

Follow-Up Problem 6.4a

Using

$$NH_3(g) + HCl(g) \rightarrow NH_4Cl(s) \qquad \Delta H = -176.0\text{ kJ}$$
$$N_2(g) + 3\,H_2(g) \rightarrow 2\,NH_3(g) \qquad \Delta H = -92.22\text{ kJ}$$
$$N_2(g) + 4\,H_2(g) + Cl_2(g) \rightarrow 2\,NH_4Cl(s) \qquad \Delta H = -628.86\text{ kJ}$$

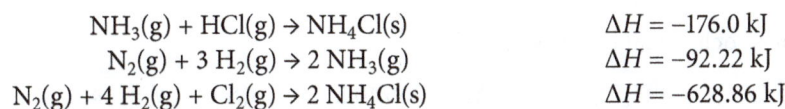

determine the heat of reaction for

$$H_2(g) + Cl_2(g) \rightarrow 2\,HCl(g)$$

Information

Three thermochemical equations with their associated enthalpy values; the question of determining the enthalpy value of a fourth chemical equation

Connections

Hess's law provides the connection between the given data and desired heat of reaction.

Solution

As with other Hess's law problems, this is a matching problem. The last equation has the correct amount of $Cl_2(g)$ on the reactant side; therefore, it is a good place to start.

$$N_2(g) + 4\,H_2(g) + Cl_2(g) \rightarrow 2\,NH_4Cl(s) \qquad \Delta H = -628.86 \text{ kJ}$$

Reversing the first equation and multiplying by 2 matches the 2 HCl(g) on the product side. Do not forget that reversing the equation requires a sign change of the enthalpy change:

$$2\,NH_4Cl(s) \rightarrow 2\,NH_3(g) + 2\,HCl(g) \qquad \Delta H = -2(-176.0 \text{ kJ})$$

While it may not be obvious, the final step is to reverse the second equation:

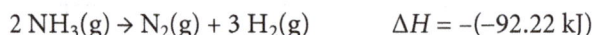

$$2\,NH_3(g) \rightarrow N_2(g) + 3\,H_2(g) \qquad \Delta H = -(-92.22 \text{ kJ})$$

The equations are now

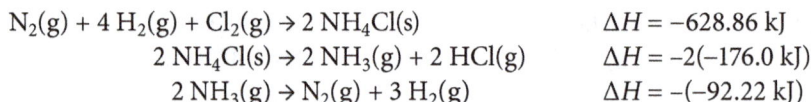

$$
\begin{aligned}
N_2(g) + 4\,H_2(g) + Cl_2(g) &\rightarrow 2\,NH_4Cl(s) & \Delta H &= -628.86 \text{ kJ} \\
2\,NH_4Cl(s) &\rightarrow 2\,NH_3(g) + 2\,HCl(g) & \Delta H &= -2(-176.0 \text{ kJ}) \\
2\,NH_3(g) &\rightarrow N_2(g) + 3\,H_2(g) & \Delta H &= -(-92.22 \text{ kJ})
\end{aligned}
$$

It is now possible to cancel (note that the 3 $H_2(g)$ in the third equation cancel only 3 of the 4 $H_2(g)$ in the first equation):

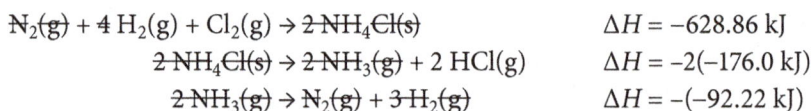

$$
\begin{aligned}
\cancel{N_2(g)} + 4\,H_2(g) + Cl_2(g) &\rightarrow \cancel{2\,NH_4Cl(s)} & \Delta H &= -628.86 \text{ kJ} \\
\cancel{2\,NH_4Cl(s)} &\rightarrow \cancel{2\,NH_3(g)} + 2\,HCl(g) & \Delta H &= -2(-176.0 \text{ kJ}) \\
\cancel{2\,NH_3(g)} &\rightarrow \cancel{N_2(g)} + \cancel{3\,H_2(g)} & \Delta H &= -(-92.22 \text{ kJ})
\end{aligned}
$$

After cancelling, what remains is the desired equation, which means that we need to add only the enthalpy changes to get the final answer:

$$H_2(g) + Cl_2(g) \rightarrow 2\,HCl(g) \qquad \Delta H = -628.86 \text{ kJ} -2(-176.0 \text{ kJ}) - (-92.22 \text{ kJ}) = -184.64$$

$$= \mathbf{-184.6 \text{ kJ}}$$

Reality Check

The units and the significant figures are correct. The equation we have produced is an exact match to the target equation.

Follow-Up Problem 6.4b

Calculate ΔH for the reaction

$$O_2(g) + 2\,CH_4(g) \rightarrow 2\,CH_3OH(l)$$

using the following thermochemical equations:

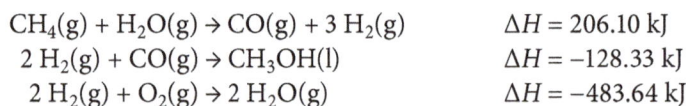

$$
\begin{aligned}
CH_4(g) + H_2O(g) &\rightarrow CO(g) + 3\,H_2(g) & \Delta H &= 206.10 \text{ kJ} \\
2\,H_2(g) + CO(g) &\rightarrow CH_3OH(l) & \Delta H &= -128.33 \text{ kJ} \\
2\,H_2(g) + O_2(g) &\rightarrow 2\,H_2O(g) & \Delta H &= -483.64 \text{ kJ}
\end{aligned}
$$

Information

Three thermochemical equations with their associated enthalpy values; the question of determining the enthalpy value of a fourth chemical equation

Connections

Hess's law provides the connection between the given data and desired heat of reaction.

Solution

As with other Hess's law problems, this is a matching problem. The last equation has the correct amount of $O_2(g)$ on the reactant side; therefore, it is a good place to start:

$$2\ H_2(g) + O_2(g) \rightarrow 2\ H_2O(g) \qquad\qquad \Delta H = -483.64\ kJ$$

Multiplying the first equation by 2 will match the $CH_4(g)$:

$$2\ CH_4(g) + 2\ H_2O(g) \rightarrow 2\ CO(g) + 6\ H_2(g) \qquad\qquad \Delta H = 2(206.10\ kJ)$$

Multiplying the second equation by 2 will match the $CH_3OH(l)$:

$$4\ H_2(g) + 2\ CO(g) \rightarrow 2\ CH_3OH(l) \qquad\qquad \Delta H = 2(-128.33\ kJ)$$

The equations are now

$$2\ H_2(g) + O_2(g) \rightarrow 2\ H_2O(g) \qquad\qquad \Delta H = -483.64\ kJ$$
$$2\ CH_4(g) + 2\ H_2O(g) \rightarrow 2\ CO(g) + 6\ H_2(g) \qquad\qquad \Delta H = 2(206.10\ kJ)$$
$$4\ H_2(g) + 2\ CO(g) \rightarrow 2\ CH_3OH(l) \qquad\qquad \Delta H = 2(-128.33\ kJ)$$

It is now possible to cancel. Note that the 6 $H_2(g)$ in the second equation requires the $H_2(g)$ from both the first and third equations.

$$\cancel{2\ H_2(g)} + O_2(g) \rightarrow \cancel{2\ H_2O(g)} \qquad\qquad \Delta H = -483.64\ kJ$$
$$2\ CH_4(g) + \cancel{2\ H_2O(g)} \rightarrow \cancel{2\ CO(g)} + \cancel{6\ H_2(g)} \qquad\qquad \Delta H = 2(206.10\ kJ)$$
$$\cancel{4\ H_2(g)} + \cancel{2\ CO(g)} \rightarrow 2\ CH_3OH(l) \qquad\qquad \Delta H = 2(-128.33\ kJ)$$

Combing the un-cancelled substances gives

$$O_2(g) + 2\ CH_4(g) \rightarrow 2\ CH_3OH(l)$$

This is the desired equation; therefore, we only need to combine the enthalpy changes to finish the problem:

$$O_2(g) + 2\ CH_4(g) \rightarrow 2\ CH_3OH(l) \qquad \Delta H = -483.64\ kJ + 2(206.10\ kJ) + 2(-128.33\ kJ)$$
$$= \mathbf{-328.10\ kJ}$$

Reality Check

The units and the significant figures are correct. The equation we have produced is an exact match to the target equation.

Example Problem 6.5

Determine the standard enthalpy change for the following reaction:

$$8\ CO(g) + 10\ H_2O(l) \rightarrow 2\ C_4H_{10}(g) + 9\ O_2(g)$$

Information

We have a chemical equation and want to calculate the enthalpy change ($\Delta H_{rxn}°$).

Connections

The table in appendix C and the relationship $\Delta H_{rxn}° = \sum \Delta H_f°(products) - \sum \Delta H_f°(reactants)$ provide the needed connections.

Solution

The initial step in solving a problem such as this is to locate the standard heats of formation for each reactant and product. It will not be necessary to look for the value of oxygen gas, since the standard heat of formation for an element in its standard state is, by definition, exactly 0. We find the remaining values in tables such as the one in appendix C, being careful to consider the physical state:

$$\Delta H_f°$$

$C_4H_{10}(g)$	−125.0 kJ/mol
$CO(g)$	−110.5 kJ/mol
$H_2O(l)$	−285.840 kJ/mol
$O_2(g)$	0.0 kJ/mol

Take care that you do not use the value for $H_2O(g) = -241.826$ kJ/mol and, in addition, that you do refer to the appropriate column of appendix C. (We will need the information in the other columns for the discussion in chapter 20.) Insert the heat-of-formation values into the following relationship:

$$\Delta H_{rxn}° = \sum \Delta H_f°(products) - \sum \Delta H_f°(reactants)$$

$$\Delta H_{rxn}° = [2 \text{ mole } C_4H_{10} (-125.0 \text{ kJ/mol}) + 9 \text{ mole } O_2 (0.000 \text{ kJ/mol})]$$
$$- [8 \text{ mole CO} (-110.5 \text{ kJ/mol}) + 10 \text{ mole } H_2O (-285.840 \text{ kJ/mol})]$$

$$\Delta H_{rxn}° = [-250.0 + 0.000] \text{ kJ} - [-884.0 + (-2858.40)] \text{ kJ} = \textbf{3,492.4 kJ}$$

> ▸ We have found that including the value for oxygen, even if it is 0, helps prevent errors in this type of problem. This is especially true on exams.

> ▸ The most common error committed in this type of problem is to forget that the minus sign before the second set of brackets applies to everything within the brackets.

Reality Check

The units and the significant figures are correct. The magnitude of the answer is comparable to the other numbers in the calculation.

Follow-Up Problem 6.5a

Determine the standard enthalpy change for the reaction

$$CaCO_3(s) \rightarrow CaO(s) + CO_2(g)$$

Information

A chemical equation; the question of determining the enthalpy change $\left(\Delta H_{rxn}°\right)$

Connections

The table in appendix C and the relationship $\Delta H_{rxn}° = \sum \Delta H_f°(products) - \sum \Delta H_f°(reactants)$ provide the needed connections.

Solution

To begin, we need to locate the heats of formation for the substances involved in the reaction:

$$\Delta H_f°$$

$CaCO_3(s)$	−1,206.9 kJ/mol
$CaO(s)$	−635.1 kJ/mol
$CO_2(g)$	−393.5 kJ/mol

Next, begin with the heat of reaction relationship and insert the appropriate information:

$$\Delta H_{rxn}° = \sum \Delta H_f°(products) - \sum \Delta H_f°(reactants)$$

$$\Delta H_{rxn}° = [1 \text{ mole CaO } (-635.1 \text{ kJ/mol}) + 1 \text{ mole CO}_2 (-393.5 \text{ kJ/mol})]$$
$$- [1 \text{ mole CaCO}_3 (-1.206.9 \text{ kJ/mol})]$$
$$\Delta H_{rxn}° = [-635.1 + -393.5] \text{ kJ} - [-1206.9] \text{ kJ} = \textbf{178.3 kJ}$$

Reality Check
The units and the significant figures are correct. The magnitude of the answer is comparable to the other numbers in the calculation.

Follow-Up Problem 6.5b
Determine the enthalpy change for the reaction

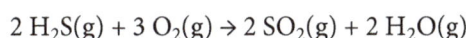

$$2 \text{ H}_2\text{S(g)} + 3 \text{ O}_2\text{(g)} \rightarrow 2 \text{ SO}_2\text{(g)} + 2 \text{ H}_2\text{O(g)}$$

Information
A chemical equation; the question of determining the enthalpy change $\Delta H_{rxn}°$)

Connections
The table in appendix C and the relationship $\Delta H_{rxn}° = \sum \Delta H_f°(products) - \sum \Delta H_f°(reactants)$ provide the needed connections.

Solution
To begin, we need to locate the heats of formation for the substances involved in the reaction:

	$\Delta H_f°$
H$_2$S(g)	–20.2 kJ/mol
O$_2$(g)	0.0 kJ/mol
SO$_2$(g)	–296.9 kJ/mol
H$_2$O(g)	–241.826 kJ/mol [Be careful not to use the value for H$_2$O(l).]

Next, begin with the heat of reaction relationship and insert the appropriate information:

$$\Delta H_{rxn}° = \sum \Delta H_f°(products) - \sum \Delta H_f°(reactants)$$

$$\Delta H_{rxn}° = [2 \text{ mole SO}_2 (-296.9 \text{ kJ/mol}) + 2 \text{ mole H}_2\text{O} (-241.826 \text{ kJ/mol})]$$
$$- [2 \text{ mole H}_2\text{S} (-20.2 \text{ kJ/mol}) + 3 \text{ mole O}_2 (0.0 \text{ kJ/mol})]$$
$$\Delta H_{rxn}° = [-593.8 + -483.652] \text{ kJ} - [-40.4 + 0.0] \text{ kJ} = -1,037.052 = \textbf{-1,037.1 kJ}$$

Reality Check
The units and the significant figures are correct. The magnitude of the answer is comparable to the other numbers in the calculation.

Example Problem 6.6
The nutrition label on a brand of sardines lists 12 g of fat, 2 g of carbohydrate, and 17 g of protein. How many nutritional calories does this represent?

Information
We need to convert the given data—12 g fat, 2 g carbohydrates, and 17 g proteins—into nutritional calories.

Connections
The fuel values of different food categories are given in table 6.5.

Solution
The Calorie values from table 6.5 are carbohydrate = 4 Cal/g, fat = 9 Cal/g, and protein = 4 Cal/g.

Calories from carbohydrate = (2 g carb) (4 Cal/g carb)	=	8 Cal
Calories from fat = (12 g fat) (9 Cal/g fat)	=	108 Cal
Calories from protein = (17 g prot) (4 Cal/g prot)	=	68 Cal
	Total	**184 Cal**

The total rounds to 200 Cal according to the addition–subtraction rule for significant figures. (The 108 Cal has only 1 significant figure, so the addition is really 8 + 100 + 70.) The value reported on the nutrition label should be 200 Calories.

Reality Check
The units and the significant figures are correct. The magnitude of the answer is reasonable.

Follow-Up Problem 6.6a
The nutrition label on a brand of cream-style corn lists 1 g of fat, 22 g of carbohydrate, and 2 g of protein. How many nutritional calories does this represent?

Information
The given data 1 g fat, 22 g carbohydrates, and 2 g proteins; the question of converting these into nutritional calories

Connections
The fuel values of different food categories in table 6.5

Solution
The Calorie values from table 6.5 are carbohydrate = 4 Cal/g, fat = 9 Cal/g, and protein = 4 Cal/g:

Calories from carbohydrate = (22 g carb) (4 Cal/g carb)	= 88 Cal
Calories from fat = (1 g fat) (9 Cal/g fat)	= 9 Cal
Calories from protein = (2 g prot) (4 Cal/g prot)	= 8 Cal
Total	105 Cal = **110 Cal**

According to the addition–subtraction rule for significant figures, the total rounds to 110 Cal. As the 88 Cal should have only one significant figure, the value reported on the nutrition label should be 110 Calories.

Reality Check
The units and the significant figures are correct. The magnitude of the answer is reasonable.

Follow-Up Problem 6.6b
The nutrition label on a brand of rice reports 1 g of fat, 46 g of carbohydrate, and 5 g of protein in every serving. How many kilojoules does this represent?

Information
The given data 1 g fat, 46 g carbohydrates, and 5 g proteins; the question of converting these into kilojoules.

Connections

The fuel values of different food categories in table 6.5; the equality 4.184 kJ = 1 Cal

Solution

The Calorie values from table 6.5 are carbohydrate = 4 Cal/g, fat = 9 Cal/g, and protein = 4 Cal/g:

Calories from carbohydrate = (46 g carb) (4 Cal/g carb)   = 184 Cal
Calories from fat = (1 g fat) (9 Cal/g fat)   = 9 Cal
Calories from protein = (5 g prot) (4 Cal/g prot)   = 20 Cal
Total   213 Cal

According to the addition–subtraction rule for significant figures, the total rounds to 200 Cal. To finish the problem, we need to convert the Calories to kilojoules. It is preferable to use the unrounded value (213 Cal) to minimize potential rounding errors:

$$(213 \text{ Cal})\left(\frac{4.184 \text{ kJ}}{1 \text{ Cal}}\right) = 891.192 = \mathbf{9 \times 10^2 \text{ kJ}}$$

Reality Check

The units and the significant figures are correct. The magnitude of the answer is reasonable.

Example Problem 6.7

The combustion of methane ideally produces carbon dioxide and water vapor. However, the combustion of methane in an oxygen-deficient environment may yield the following alternate reaction:

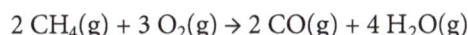

$$2 \text{ CH}_4(g) + 3 \text{ O}_2(g) \rightarrow 2 \text{ CO}(g) + 4 \text{ H}_2\text{O}(g)$$

Calculate the enthalpy change for this reaction per mole of methane.

Information

We have a chemical equation, and we want to predict the associated enthalpy change ($\Delta H_{rxn}°$).

Connections

Appendix C provides the heats of formation that, when inserted into the relationship

$\Delta H_{rxn}° = \sum \Delta H_f°(products) - \sum \Delta H_f°(reactants)$, will yield the desired answer.

Solution

As explained in section 6.6, it is not necessary to look for the heat of formation of oxygen gas. The values for the other reactants and products come from appendix C:

$$\mathbf{\Delta H_f°}$$

$CH_4(g)$	–74.87 kJ/mol
$CO(g)$	–110.5 kJ/mol
$H_2O(g)$	–241.826 kJ/mol
$O_2(g)$	0.0 kJ/mol

Inserting the values into the heat-of-formation relationship gives

$$\Delta H_{rxn}° = \sum \Delta H_f°(products) - \sum \Delta H_f°(reactants)$$

$$\Delta H_{rxn}° = [2 \text{ mole CO } (-110.5 \text{ kJ/mol}) + 4 \text{ mole H}_2\text{O } (-241.826 \text{ kJ/mol})]$$
$$- [2 \text{ mole CH}_4 (-74.87 \text{ kJ/mol}) + 3 \text{ mole O}_2 (0.000 \text{ kJ/mol})]$$
$$\Delta H_{rxn}° = [-221.0 + (-967.304)] \text{ kJ} - [-149.74 + 0.000] \text{ kJ} = -1,038.564 \text{ kJ} \quad \textbf{(unrounded)}$$

This value is for 2 moles of methane; thus, division by 2 is necessary to give the final answer:

$$-1038.564 \text{ kJ} \div 2 = -519.3 \text{ kJ}$$

When methane combustion produces carbon monoxide instead of carbon dioxide, less energy is released. To ensure maximum energy output as well as to avoid producing toxic carbon monoxide, we must always be careful to burn methane in the presence of adequate oxygen.

Reality Check
The units and the significant figures are correct. The value is negative, as expected for a combustion reaction. The magnitude is in keeping with the other values in the calculation.

Follow-Up Problem 6.7a
When sufficient oxygen is present, the combustion of methane produces carbon dioxide and water vapor; in an oxygen-restricted environment, the products are carbon monoxide and water vapor. However, methane combustion in a *severely* oxygen-deficient environment may yield elemental carbon and water vapor by the reaction

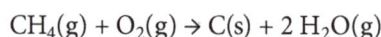

$$CH_4(g) + O_2(g) \rightarrow C(s) + 2\ H_2O(g)$$

Calculate the enthalpy change for this reaction per mole of methane.

Information
A chemical equation; the question of the associated enthalpy change ($\Delta H_{rxn}°$)

Connections
Appendix C provides the heats of formation that, when inserted into the relationship $\Delta H_{rxn}° = \sum \Delta H_f°(\text{products}) - \sum \Delta H_f°(\text{reactants})$, will yield the desired answer.

Solution
As explained in section 6.6, it is not necessary to look for the heat of formation of oxygen gas or solid carbon. The values for the reactants and products come from appendix C:

	$\Delta H_f°$
$CH_4(g)$	–74.87 kJ/mol
$C(s)$	0.0 kJ/mol
$H_2O(g)$	–241.826 kJ/mol
$O_2(g)$	0.0 kJ/mol

Inserting the values into the heat-of-formation relationship gives

$$\Delta H_{rxn}° = \sum \Delta H_f°(products) - \sum \Delta H_f°(reactants)$$

$$\Delta H_{rxn}° = [1 \text{ mole C } (0.0 \text{ kJ/mol}) + 2 \text{ mole } H_2O\ (-241.826 \text{ kJ/mol})]$$
$$- [1 \text{ mole } CH_4\ (-74.87 \text{ kJ/mol}) + 1 \text{ mole } O_2\ (0.000 \text{ kJ/mol})]$$

$$\Delta H_{rxn}° = [0.0 -483.652] \text{ kJ} - [-74.87 + 0.000] \text{ kJ} = -408.782 = \textbf{-408.78 kJ}$$

This value is for 1 mole of methane; therefore, this is the final answer.

When methane combustion produces carbon instead of carbon dioxide, less energy is released. To ensure maximum energy output, one must always be careful to burn methane in the presence of adequate oxygen.

Reality Check

The units and the significant figures are correct. The value is negative, as expected for a combustion reaction. The magnitude is in keeping with the other values in the calculation.

Follow-Up Problem 6.7b

Acetylene, C_2H_2, is a frequent fuel choice when high temperatures are desired. Determine the enthalpy change per mole of acetylene gas when it is combusted to produce carbon dioxide gas and water vapor.

Information

Information about the chemical reaction; ; the question of the associated enthalpy change (ΔH_{rxn}°)

Connections

Appendix C provides the heats of formation that, when inserted into the relationship

$$\Delta H_{rxn}^{\circ} = \sum \Delta H_f^{\circ}(products) - \sum \Delta H_f^{\circ}(reactants) \text{ will yield the desired answer.}$$

Solution

We need to write a balanced chemical equation:

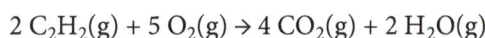

$$2\ C_2H_2(g) + 5\ O_2(g) \rightarrow 4\ CO_2(g) + 2\ H_2O(g)$$

As explained in section 6.6, it is not necessary to look for the heat of formation of oxygen gas or solid carbon. The values for the reactants and products come from appendix C:

	ΔH_f°
$C_2H_2(g)$	227 kJ/mol
$CO_2(g)$	–393.5 kJ/mol
$H_2O(g)$	–241.826 kJ/mol
$O_2(g)$	0.0 kJ/mol

Inserting the values into the heat-of-formation relationship gives

$$\Delta H_{rxn}^{\circ} = \sum \Delta H_f^{\circ}(products) - \sum \Delta H_f^{\circ}(reactants)$$

$$\Delta H_{rxn}^{\circ} = [4 \text{ moles } CO_2\ (-393.5 \text{ kJ/mol}) + 2 \text{ moles } H_2O\ (-241.826 \text{ kJ/mol})]$$
$$- [2 \text{ moles } C_2H_2\ (227 \text{ kJ/mol}) + 5 \text{ mole } O_2\ (0.0 \text{ kJ/mol})]$$

$$\Delta H_{rxn}^{\circ} = [-1,574 - 483.652] \text{ kJ} - [454 + 0.000] \text{ kJ} = -2,511.652 = -2,512 \text{ kJ}$$

This value is for 2 moles of acetylene, thus division by 2 is necessary to give the final answer:

$$-2,511.652 \text{ kJ} \div 2 = -1,255.826 = \textbf{–1,256 kJ}$$

When methane combustion produces carbon instead of carbon dioxide, less energy is released. To ensure maximum energy output, one must always be careful to burn methane in the presence of adequate oxygen.

Reality Check

The units and the significant figures are correct. The value is negative, as expected for a combustion reaction. The magnitude is in keeping with the other values in the calculation.

END-OF-CHAPTER PROBLEMS

6.1 System and Surroundings

6.2 List three common energy units.

Solution

There are many choices, some of which are Joule, calorie, Calorie, and BTU (British thermal unit). (Note that a calorie and a Calorie are different units, with 1 Calorie = 1,000 calories.)

6.2 Energy

6.5 **(a)** A baseball is heavier than a tennis ball. If both balls are traveling with the same velocity, which ball has the greater kinetic energy? **(b)** How fast must a 0.0750-kg ball travel to have the same kinetic energy as a 0.175-kg ball traveling at 45.0 m/s?

Information

(a) The relative masses of two balls. The question is which ball has the greater kinetic energy.
(b) The mass of one ball (0.0750 kg) and the mass and velocity of another ball (0.175 kg and 45.0 m/s.) The question is what is the velocity of the first ball.

Connections

$$KE = \frac{1}{2}mv^2$$

Solution

(a) If the velocities are the same, then the more massive ball has more kinetic energy.

(b) The two balls have the same kinetic energy. If they are labelled ball 1 and ball 2, this means

$$KE_1 = KE_2 \quad \text{The subscripts refer to the different balls.}$$

Substituting into the KE equation,

$$\frac{1}{2}m_1v_1^2 = \frac{1}{2}m_2v_2^2$$

Multiplying through by 2,

$$m_1v_1^2 = m_2v_2^2$$

Substituting the given values,

$$(0.0750 \text{ kg})v_1^2 = (0.175 \text{ kg})\left(\frac{45.0 \text{ m}}{\text{s}}\right)^2$$

Rearranging and solving gives

$$v_1 = \sqrt{\frac{(0.175 \text{ kg})\left(\frac{45.0 \text{ m}}{\text{s}}\right)^2}{0.0750 \text{ kg}}} = 68.7386 = \textbf{68.7 m/s}$$

Reality Check

The answer is reasonable since the lighter ball must be travelling faster to have the same kinetic energy.

6.7 A 200.0-grain bullet may leave the barrel of a .44 Magnum pistol with a velocity as high as 1,475 ft/s (7,000 grains are exactly equal to 1 pound). **(a)** Calculate the maximum velocity in meters per second. **(b)** Calculate the kinetic energy of the bullet in joules.

Information

The mass (200.0 grains) and velocity (1475 ft/s) of a .44 Magnum bullet; a conversion of 7,000 grains = 1 pound; the questions **(a)** What is the velocity in m/s? and **(b)** What is the kinetic energy in joules?

Connections

$KE = \frac{1}{2}mv^2$; J = kg m/s^2

Solution

(a) This is a unit conversion problem, using relationships from chapter 1:

$$\left[\left(\frac{1,475 \text{ ft}}{s}\right)\left(\frac{12 \text{ in}}{1 \text{ ft}}\right)\left(\frac{2.54 \text{ cm}}{1 \text{ in}}\right)\left(\frac{0.01}{c}\right)\right] = 449.58 = \textbf{449.6 m/s}$$

(b) This part is a matter of substituting values into the kinetic energy equation:

$$KE = \frac{1}{2}mv^2 = \frac{1}{2}\left[(200.0 \text{ gr})\left(\frac{1 \text{ lb}}{7,000 \text{ gr}}\right)\left(\frac{1 \text{ kg}}{2.205 \text{ lb}}\right)\right]\left[\left(\frac{1475 \text{ ft}}{s}\right)\left(\frac{12 \text{ in}}{1 \text{ ft}}\right)\left(\frac{2.54 \text{ cm}}{1 \text{ in}}\right)\left(\frac{0.01}{c}\right)\right]^2\left(\frac{J}{\text{kg m}^2/\text{s}^2}\right)$$

$$= 1,309.5055 = \textbf{1,309 J}$$

The answer to part (a) can be used in place of the values in the second set of brackets. The last term is the SI definition of *joule*.

Reality Check

The final answer has the correct units and seems reasonable in magnitude.

6.9 What is the sign of the indicated variable in each of the following situations? **(a)** The internal energy increases. **(b)** The system loses heat. **(c)** The system does work on the surroundings.

Solution

Everything done is relative to the system.

(a) An increase in the internal energy is positive (+).

(b) A loss of heat is negative (–).

(c) Doing work on the surroundings is negative (–).

6.11 Determine how much the internal energy changes in each of the following cases: **(a)** A balloon bursts, and the released air expands without any significant heat exchange and does 125 J of work on the surroundings. **(b)** A pan of water on a stove absorbs 1,250 J of heat. **(c)** A sample of a gas is compressed; during compression, the sample has 375 J of work done on it, and 125 J of heat energy are removed from the sample.

Information

(a) $q = 0$ and $w = 125$ J (on surroundings); **(b)** $q = 1,250$ J and $w = 0$ (assumed); **(c)** $q = 125$ J (lost) and $w = 375$ J (on system). In each case, the question is what is the change in internal energy (ΔE).

Connections

$\Delta E = q + w$

Solution

The solutions involve entering values into the equation with, where necessary, sign changes:

(a) $q = 0$ and $w = -125$ J (change sign because it acts on the surroundings):

$$\Delta E = q + w = 0 + (-125 \text{ J}) = \textbf{-125 J}$$

(b) $q = 1{,}250$ J (positive because heat was added to the system) and $w = 0$ (assumed):

$$\Delta E = q + w = 1{,}250 \text{ J} + 0 = \textbf{1,250 J}$$

(c) $q = -125$ J (negative because heat was removed) and $w = 375$ J (positive because work was done on the system):

$$\Delta E = q + w = -125 \text{ J} + 375 \text{ J} = \textbf{250 J}$$

6.3 Energy Conservation and the First Law

6.13 State the first law of thermodynamics.

Solution

The total energy is constant; that is, or energy can neither be created nor destroyed.

6.15 If the pressure is in pascals and the volume is in liters, what conversions are necessary to determine pressure–volume work in joules?

Solution

Pressure volume work is $w = -P\,\Delta V$. The units are pascals (N m^{-2} = kg m^{-1} s^{-2}) and liters.

It is possible to convert a liter to m^3 using the conversion 1 L = 0.001 m^3.

Substituting the base units in the work equation gives

$$w = -P\,\Delta V = (\text{kg m}^{-1}\text{ s}^{-2})\,(\text{m}^3) = (\text{kg m}^2\text{ s}^{-2}), \text{ which is equal to a joule.}$$

6.17 Decide whether each of the following processes is exothermic or endothermic: **(a)** Water in a water heater becomes warmer. **(b)** Water in a freezer turns into ice. **(c)** Water in a glass on a table evaporates. **(d)** A sample of charcoal burns. **(e)** When ice is removed from the freezer, the ice melts.

Solution

(a) **Endothermic**, because heat is gained by the water

(b) **Exothermic**, because heat must be removed for the water to freeze

(c) **Endothermic**, because the water molecules must gain energy to escape

(d) **Exothermic**, because burning gives off heat

(e) **Endothermic**, because the ice must absorb energy to melt

6.4 Calorimetry

6.19 List the common units for each of the following properties: **(a)** heat capacity, **(b)** specific heat capacity, **(c)** molar heat capacity

Solution

(a) Heat capacity has units of J/°C or J/K.

(b) Specific heat capacity has units of J/g °C or J/g K.

(c) Molar heat capacity has units of J/mol °C or J/mol K.

6.22 Which type of calorimeter directly yields the enthalpy change?

Solution

A constant-pressure calorimeter directly yields the enthalpy change. An example of this type of calorimeter is the "coffee-cup" calorimeter discussed in the book.

6.24 Determine the specific heat of an unknown metal from the following data: A 39.2-g sample (at 61.67°C) was dropped into 53.4 g of water (at 20.00°C). The final temperature was 30.00°C.

Information

The unknown metal's mass of 39.2 grams and initial temperature of 61.67°C; the water's mass of 53.4 grams and initial temperature of 20.00°C; the metal and water both have a final temperature of 30.00°C; the question of what is the specific heat of the metal

Connections

The definition of specific heat: J/g °C or J/g K; the specific heat of water (4.184 J/g °C); the law of conservation of energy (the first law of thermodynamics); $\Delta T = T_{final} - T_{initial}$

Solution

The water is cooler; therefore, it will gain heat while the metal loses heat. Applying the law of conservation of energy leads to the heat lost (by the metal) must be the same as the heat gained (by the water): that is,

$$\text{Heat gained (water)} = -\text{ Heat lost (metal)}$$

Beginning with the specific heat of water, we can determine the heat (joules) gained by the water with two conversion steps. A similar set of steps will give the heat lost by the metal:

$$\left(\frac{4.184 \text{ J}}{\text{g} \,^\circ\text{C}}\right)(53.4 \text{ g})(30.00 - 20.00)^\circ\text{C} = -\left(\frac{? \text{ J}}{\text{g} \,^\circ\text{C}}\right)(39.2 \text{ g})(30.00 - 61.67)^\circ\text{C}$$

Rearranging the above gives

$$\frac{\left(\frac{4.184 \text{ J}}{\text{g} \,^\circ\text{C}}\right)(53.4 \text{ g})(30.00 - 20.00)^\circ\text{C}}{-(39.2 \text{ g})(30.00 - 61.67)^\circ\text{C}} = \frac{? \text{ J}}{\text{g} \,^\circ\text{C}}$$

$$\frac{(2{,}231.256 \text{ J})}{(1{,}241.464 \text{ g} \,^\circ\text{C})} = \frac{1.79969\text{J}}{\text{g} \,^\circ\text{C}} = \frac{\textbf{1.80 J}}{\textbf{g} \,^\circ\textbf{C}} \text{ or } \frac{\textbf{1.80 J}}{\textbf{g K}}$$

Reality Check

The Celsius and kelvin answers are the same because the temperature changes are numerically the same. For water, the change is 10.00°C or 10.00 K; for the metal, the change is –31.67°C or –31.67 K.

6.26 Gold has a specific heat of 0.129 J/g · °C. **(a)** What is the specific heat of gold in J/g · K? **(b)** Calculate the change in enthalpy when 0.3251 troy ounces of gold cools from 37.0°C to 25.0°C. (1 troy ounce = 31.103 g)

Information

The specific heat of gold (0.129 J/g · °C); **(a)** the question of what is the specific heat of gold in J/g · K; **(b)** the question of the change in enthalpy when a 0.3251 troy ounce sample of gold cools from 37.0°C to 25.0°C

Connections

1 troy ounce = 31.103 g; $\Delta T = T_{final} - T_{initial}$

Solution

(a) Numerically, the specific heat is the same when °C or kelvins are used. Therefore, the answer is **0.129 J/g K**.

(b) We only need to begin with the specific heat and carry out three unit conversions:

$$\left(\frac{0.129\ J}{g°C}\right)(0.3251\ \text{tr.oz})\left(\frac{31.103\ g}{1\ \text{tr. oz}}\right)(25.0 - 37.0)°C = 15.6527 = \textbf{-15.6 J}$$

Reality Check

The final answer has the correct units and seems reasonable in magnitude. Part (b) is an exothermic process, so the answer should be negative.

6.28 When a 12.4-g sample of sodium nitrate dissolves in 250.0 g of water in a coffee-cup calorimeter, the temperature changes from 25.30°C to 22.51°C. Determine the enthalpy change in kJ/mol of sodium nitrate for the dissolution of sodium nitrate in water. Assume that the specific heat of the solution is the same as that of pure water.

Information

The masses of $NaNO_3$ (12.4 g) and water (250.0 g); the temperature change (25.30°C to 22.51°C); the question of what is the enthalpy change in kJ/mole $NaNO_3$

Connections

The specific heat of water is 4.184 J/g · °C, or 4.184 J/g · K (which is the same as that of the solution); $\Delta T = T_{final} - T_{initial}$

Solution

The solution is the mass of solvent (H_2O) plus the mass of solute ($NaNO_3$), or (12.4 + 250.0) grams.

The calculation has two parts. We need to determine the kilojoules of heat and (2) determine the moles of $NaNO_3$. In the numerator below is the first calculation, which begins with the specific heat of the solution followed by three unit conversions. The denominator contains the second calculation, which begins with the mass of $NaNO_3$ and uses the molar mass of $NaNO_3$ to convert to moles $NaNO_3$:

$$\frac{\left(\dfrac{4.184\ J}{g\ °C}\right)(12.4 + 250.0)g(22.51 - 25.30)°C\left(\dfrac{k}{1,000}\right)}{(12.4\ g\ NaNO_3)\left(\dfrac{1\ mol\ NaNO_3}{84.9947\ g\ NaNO_3}\right)} = 20.99568 = \textbf{21.0 kJ/mol}$$

Reality Check

The final answer has the correct units and seems reasonable in magnitude. This is an endothermic process, so the answer should be positive.

6.31 Naphthalene is used in mothballs. To measure naphthalene's heat of combustion, a 2.870-g sample was combined with an excess of O_2 and burned in a bomb calorimeter. After the reaction, the temperature of the calorimeter had increased from 23.00°C to 34.34°C. The calorimeter contained 2.000 kg of water. The heat capacity of the empty calorimeter was 1.80 kJ/°C. Determine the heat of reaction in kJ/mol of naphthalene for the reaction

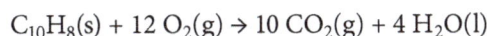

$$C_{10}H_8(s) + 12 \, O_2(g) \rightarrow 10 \, CO_2(g) + 4 \, H_2O(l)$$

Information

A 2.870-gram sample of $C_{10}H_8$ burned in a bomb calorimeter with a heat capacity of 1.80 kJ/°C and containing 2.000 kg H_2O; the temperature change from 23.00°C to 34.34°C; the question of what is the heat of reaction in kJ/mol $C_{10}H_8$

Connections

The specific heat of water is 4.184 J/g · °C, or 4.184 J/g · K; $\Delta T = T_{final} - T_{initial}$

Solution

The calculation has two parts: We need to (1) determine the kilojoules of heat and (2) determine the moles of $C_{10}H_8$. In the numerator below is the first calculation, which begins with the heat capacity of the calorimeter followed by a unit conversion plus a calculation using the specific heat of water and two unit conversions. The denominator contains the second calculation, which begins with the mass of $C_{10}H_8$ and uses the molar mass of $C_{10}H_8$ to convert to moles $C_{10}H_8$. Remember, this is an exothermic process, so the final answer must be negative (this comes from the definition, not the calculation):

$$\frac{\left(\dfrac{1.80 \text{ kJ}}{°C}\right)(34.34 - 23.00)°C + \left(\dfrac{4.184 \text{ J}}{g°C}\right)(2.000 \text{ kg})(34.34 - 23.00)°C}{\left(2.870 \text{ g } C_{10}H_8\right)\left(\dfrac{1 \text{ mol } C_{10}H_8}{128.174 \text{ g } C_{10}H_8}\right)} = 5{,}149.5186$$

$$= \mathbf{-5.150 \times 10^3 \text{ kJ/mol } C_{10}H_8}$$

This calculation is a simplified form of the following example:

$$\left(\frac{4.184 \text{ J}}{g \, °C}\right)(2.000 \text{ kg})(34.34 - 23.00)°C$$

$$\left(\frac{4.184 \text{ J}}{g \, °C}\right)\left(\frac{1 \text{ kJ}}{1{,}000 \text{ J}}\right)\left(\frac{1{,}000 \text{ g}}{1 \text{ kg}}\right)(2.000 \text{ kg})(34.34 - 23.00)°C$$

The second approach is the first calculation times $\left(\dfrac{1{,}000}{1{,}000}\right)$.

Reality Check

The final answer has the correct units and seems reasonable in magnitude. This (burning) is an exothermic process, so the answer should be negative.

6.33 The reaction of 3.986 g of Fe_2O_3 with an excess of Al was carried out in a bomb calorimeter. The heat capacity of the empty calorimeter was 1.96 kJ/°C, and the calorimeter contained 1.97 kg of water. After the reaction, it was determined that the temperature had increased from 25.00 to 27.58°C. Determine the heat of reaction per mole of Al for the following reaction:

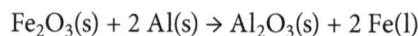

$$Fe_2O_3(s) + 2\ Al(s) \rightarrow Al_2O_3(s) + 2\ Fe(l)$$

Information

A 3.986-gram sample of Fe_2O_3 reacted in a bomb calorimeter with a heat capacity of 1.96 kJ/°C and containing 1.97 kg H_2O; a temperature change from 25.00°C to 27.58°C; the question of what is the heat of reaction in kJ/mol Al

Connections

The specific heat of water is 4.184 J/g · °C, or 4.184 J/g · K; $\Delta T = T_{final} - T_{initial}$

Solution

The calculation has two parts. We need to determine the kilojoules of heat and (2) determine the moles of Al. In the numerator below is the first calculation, which begins with the specific heat capacity of the calorimeter followed by a unit conversion plus a calculation using the specific heat of water and two unit conversions. The denominator contains the second calculation, which begins with the mass of Fe_2O_3 and uses the molar mass of Fe_2O_3; next, a mole ratio from the balanced chemical equation gives the moles Al. Remember, this is an exothermic process, so the final answer must be negative (this comes from the definition, not the calculation):

$$\frac{\left(\dfrac{1.96\ kJ}{°C}\right)(27.58-25.00)°C + \left(\dfrac{4.184\ J}{g\ °C}\right)(1.97\ kg)(27.58-25.00)°C}{(3.986\ g\ Fe_2O_3)\left(\dfrac{1\ mol\ Fe_2O_3}{159.687\ g\ Fe_2O_3}\right)\left(\dfrac{2\ mol\ Al}{1\ mol\ Fe_2O_3}\right)} = -527.2635 = \mathbf{-527\ kJ/mol\ Al}$$

Reality Check

The final answer has the correct units and seems reasonable in magnitude. This is an exothermic process, so the answer should be negative.

6.35 Lactic acid, $C_3H_6O_3$, generated in the body by the partial oxidation of glucose, can be further oxidized in the body to produce energy. Combustion of a 5.24-g sample with an excess of O_2 in a bomb calorimeter raised the temperature of the calorimeter from 22.000°C to 25.600°C. The calorimeter contained 2.000 kg of water. The heat capacity of the empty calorimeter was 13.33 kJ/°C. Determine the heat of reaction in kJ/mole lactic acid for the following reaction:

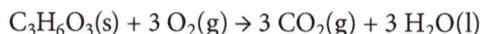

$$C_3H_6O_3(s) + 3\ O_2(g) \rightarrow 3\ CO_2(g) + 3\ H_2O(l)$$

Information

A 5.24-gram sample of $C_3H_6O_3$ burned in a bomb calorimeter with a heat capacity of 13.33 kJ/°C and containing 2.000 kg H_2O; a temperature change from 22.000°C to 25.600°C; the question of what is the heat of reaction in kJ/mol $C_3H_6O_3$

Connections

The specific heat of water is 4.184 J/g · °C, or 4.184 J/g · K; $\Delta T = T_{final} - T_{initial}$

Solution

The calculation has two parts. We need to (1) determine the kilojoules of heat and (2) determine the moles of $C_3H_6O_3$. In the numerator below is the first calculation, which begins with the heat capacity of the calorimeter followed by a unit conversion plus a calculation using the specific heat of water and two unit conversions. The denominator contains the second calculation, which begins with the mass of $C_3H_6O_3$ and uses the molar mass of $C_3H_6O_3$ to convert to moles $C_3H_6O_3$. Remember, this is an exothermic process, so the final answer must be negative (this comes from the definition, not the calculation):

$$\frac{\left(\dfrac{13.33\ kJ}{°C}\right)(25.600 - 22.000)°C + \left(\dfrac{4.184\ J}{g°C}\right)(2.000\ kg)(25.600 - 22.000)°C}{(5.24\ g\ C_3H_6O_3)\left(\dfrac{1\ mol\ C_3H_6O_3}{90.078\ g\ C_3H_6O_3}\right)} = 1{,}342.7948$$

$$= -1.34 \times 10^3\ kJ/mol\ C_3H_6O_3$$

Reality Check

The final answer has the correct units and seems reasonable in magnitude. This (burning) is an exothermic process, so the answer should be negative.

6.37 Butane, C_4H_{10}, is used as a fuel. Combustion of a 2.000-g sample with an excess of O_2 increased the temperature of a bomb calorimeter from 23.00°C to 34.34°C. The calorimeter contained 1.000 kg of water. The heat capacity of the empty calorimeter was 3.88 kJ/°C. Determine the heat of reaction in kJ/mol C_4H_{10} for the following reaction:

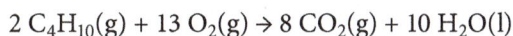

$$2\ C_4H_{10}(g) + 13\ O_2(g) \rightarrow 8\ CO_2(g) + 10\ H_2O(l)$$

Information

A 2.000-gram sample of C_4H_{10} burned in a bomb calorimeter with a heat capacity of 3.88 kJ/°C and containing 1.000 kg H_2O; a temperature change from 23.00°C to 34.34°C; the question of what is the heat of reaction in kJ/mol C_4H_{10}

Connections

The specific heat of water is 4.184 J/g · °C, or 4.184 J/g · K; $\Delta T = T_{final} - T_{initial}$

Solution

The calculation has two parts. We need to (1) determine the kilojoules of heat and (2) determine the moles of C_4H_{10}. In the numerator below is the first calculation, which begins with the heat capacity of the calorimeter followed by a unit conversion plus a calculation using the specific heat of water and two unit conversions. The denominator contains the second calculation, which begins with the mass of C_4H_{10} and uses the molar mass of C_4H_{10} to convert to moles C_4H_{10}. Remember, this is an exothermic process, so the final answer must be negative (this comes from the definition, not the calculation).

$$\frac{\left(\dfrac{3.88\ kJ}{°C}\right)(34.34 - 23.00)°C + \left(\dfrac{4.184\ J}{g\ °C}\right)(1.000\ kg)(34.34 - 23.00)°C}{(2.000\ g\ C_4H_{10})\left(\dfrac{1\ mol\ C_4H_{10}}{58.124\ g\ C_4H_{10}}\right)} = 2{,}657.5967$$

$$= -2.66 \times 10^3\ kJ/mol\ C_4H_{10}$$

Reality Check

The final answer has the correct units and seems reasonable in magnitude. This (burning) is an exothermic process, so the answer should be negative.

6.5 Heats of Reaction

6.42 What is the expected sign for ΔH in each of the following cases?

(a) $H_2O(l) \rightarrow H_2O(g)$

(b) $CH_4(g) + 2\,O_2(g) \rightarrow CO_2(g) + 2\,H_2O(l)$ Methane (CH_4) is natural gas.

(c) $CO_2(g) + 2\,H_2O(l) \rightarrow CH_4(g) + 2\,O_2(g)$

(d) $NH_4NO_3(s) \rightarrow NH_4NO_3(aq)$ The temperature of the solution is lowered.

(e) $CO_2(g) \rightarrow CO_2(s)$

Solution

(a) **Positive**, as it is necessary to add heat to boil water

(b) **Negative**, as burning releases heat

(c) **Positive**, as this is the reverse of the reaction in part (b), and reversing a reaction reverses the sign

(d) **Positive** heat energy went from the water to dissolve the solid.

(e) **Negative**, as it is necessary to remove heat energy from a gas to convert it to a solid

6.45 The combustion of octane in gasoline proceeds by the following reaction:

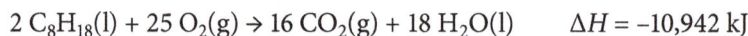

$$2\,C_8H_{18}(l) + 25\,O_2(g) \rightarrow 16\,CO_2(g) + 18\,H_2O(l) \qquad \Delta H = -10{,}942 \text{ kJ}$$

How much energy is released when 175 g of $CO_2(g)$ are formed by this reaction?

Information

The balanced thermochemical chemical equation; the enthalpy change of the reaction (-10942 kJ); the question of what is the enthalpy change from 175 g of CO_2

Solution

The amount of heat released was for 16 moles of CO_2 (or 2 moles of C_8H_{18} or 25 moles of O_2 or 18 moles of H_2O).

$$\text{Energy} = \left(175 \text{ g } CO_2\right)\left(\frac{1 \text{ mol } CO_2}{44.009 \text{ g } CO_2}\right)\left(\frac{-10942 \text{ kJ}}{16 \text{ mol } CO_2}\right) = -2719.40 = \mathbf{-2.72 \times 10^3 \text{ kJ}}$$

Reality Check

The final answer has the correct units and seems reasonable in magnitude. This (burning) is an exothermic process, so the answer should be negative.

6.47 Carbon monoxide reacts with nitrogen oxide as follows:

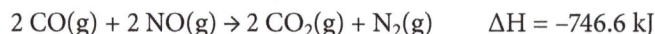

$$2\,CO(g) + 2\,NO(g) \rightarrow 2\,CO_2(g) + N_2(g) \qquad \Delta H = -746.6 \text{ kJ}$$

(a) Calculate the enthalpy change when 0.250 mole of carbon dioxide forms. **(b)** Calculate the enthalpy change when 50.0 g of $NO(g)$ are consumed. **(c)** What would be the enthalpy change if 0.3750 mole of $CO(g)$ is produced by the reverse of the above reaction?

Information

There is a balanced thermochemical equation that applies to all parts. **(a)** 0.250 moles CO_2 forms **(b)** 50.0 g NO forms **(c)** 0.3750 moles CO forms. What is the energy (enthalpy) change in each part?

Solution

(a) This is a unit conversion.

$$(0.250 \text{ mol CO}_2)\left(\frac{-746.6 \text{ kJ}}{2 \text{ mol CO}_2}\right) = -93.325 = \textbf{-93.3 kJ}$$

(b) This is a unit conversion, which includes a gram to mole conversion.

$$(50.0 \text{ g NO})\left(\frac{1 \text{ mol NO}}{30.006 \text{ g NO}}\right)\left(\frac{-746.6 \text{ kJ}}{2 \text{ mol NO}}\right) = -622.04 = \textbf{-622 kJ}$$

(c) This is a unit conversion. Do not forget to reverse the sign on the enthalpy change because the reaction is reversed.

$$(0.3750 \text{ mol CO})\left(\frac{+746.6 \text{ kJ}}{2 \text{ mol CO}}\right) = +139.9875 = \textbf{+140.0 kJ}$$

6.49 The following thermochemical equation is exothermic by 1037 kJ:

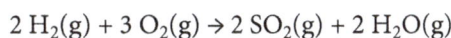

$$2 \text{ H}_2(g) + 3 \text{ O}_2(g) \rightarrow 2 \text{ SO}_2(g) + 2 \text{ H}_2\text{O}(g)$$

Calculate the enthalpy change when 125.0 g of $SO_2(g)$ gas react as follows:

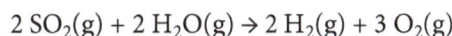

$$2 \text{ SO}_2(g) + 2 \text{ H}_2\text{O}(g) \rightarrow 2 \text{ H}_2(g) + 3 \text{ O}_2(g)$$

Information

A balanced chemical equation; the enthalpy change of the reaction (–1037 kJ); the question of what is the enthalpy change from 125.0 g of SO_2 according to a different equation

Connections

The two given equations

Solution

This is a unit conversion calculation, which includes a gram to mole conversion. Do not forget to reverse the sign on the enthalpy change because the reaction is reversed.

$$(125.0 \text{ g SO}_2)\left(\frac{1 \text{ mol SO}_2}{64.063 \text{ g SO}_2}\right)\left(\frac{1037 \text{ kJ}}{2 \text{ mol SO}_2}\right) = 1011.699 = \textbf{1012 kJ}$$

Reality Check

The final answer has the correct units and seems reasonable in magnitude. This is an endothermic process, so the answer should be positive.

6.51 The following exothermic reaction is used in the altitude-control engines of the space shuttle:

$$4 \text{ CH}_3\text{N}_2(l) + 5 \text{ N}_2\text{O}_4(l) \rightarrow 4 \text{ CO}_2(g) + 3 \text{ H}_2\text{O}(l) + 5 \text{ N}_2(g)$$

The molar heat of reaction is 1,384 kJ. What is the energy change when 25 g of $N_2O_4(l)$ reacts?

Information

A balanced chemical equation and the molar heat of reaction (–1384 kJ). The question is, what is the enthalpy change when 25 grams of N_2O_4 react.

Solution

This is a unit conversion, which includes a gram to mole conversion.

$$\left(25 \text{ g N}_2\text{O}_4\right)\left(\frac{1 \text{ mol N}_2\text{O}_4}{92.011 \text{ g N}_2\text{O}_4}\right)\left(\frac{-1384 \text{ kJ}}{5 \text{ mol N}_2\text{O}_4}\right) = -75.208 = \mathbf{-75 \text{ kJ}}$$

Reality Check

The final answer has the correct units and seems reasonable in magnitude. This is an exothermic process, so the answer should be negative.

6.53 How many grams of $C_2H_4(g)$ must be burned to produce 3,250.0 kJ of heat? The heat of combustion of $C_2H_4(g)$ is –1,410.0 kJ/mol C_2H_4.

Information

The heat of combustion (–1410.0 kJ/mol C_2H_4) and the question is, how many grams of C_2H_4 will produce 3250.0 kJ.

Solution

This is a unit conversion, which includes a gram to mole conversion. The way the problem is stated, a balanced equation is unnecessary.

$$\left(-3250.0 \text{ kJ}\right)\left(\frac{1 \text{ mol C}_2\text{H}_4}{-1410.0 \text{ kJ}}\right)\left(\frac{28.054 \text{ g C}_2\text{H}_4}{1 \text{ mol C}_2\text{H}_4}\right) = 64.663475 = \mathbf{64.663 \text{ g}}$$

6.55 Using the thermochemical equations

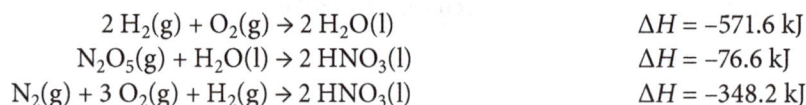

$2 \text{ H}_2(g) + \text{O}_2(g) \rightarrow 2 \text{ H}_2\text{O}(l)$	$\Delta H = -571.6 \text{ kJ}$
$\text{N}_2\text{O}_5(g) + \text{H}_2\text{O}(l) \rightarrow 2 \text{ HNO}_3(l)$	$\Delta H = -76.6 \text{ kJ}$
$\text{N}_2(g) + 3 \text{ O}_2(g) + \text{H}_2(g) \rightarrow 2 \text{ HNO}_3(l)$	$\Delta H = -348.2 \text{ kJ}$

determine ΔH for the following reaction:

$$2 \text{ N}_2(g) + 5 \text{ O}_2(g) \rightarrow 2 \text{ N}_2\text{O}_5(g)$$

Information

Three balanced thermochemical equations and another equation with no enthalpy change. The question is, what is the enthalpy change for the first equation.

Connections

Hess's law

Solution

It is necessary to reverse the first equation (including the sign ΔH). Next both reverse and double the second equation. Then double the third equation. Now make the indicated cancellations. These steps may be done in any order.

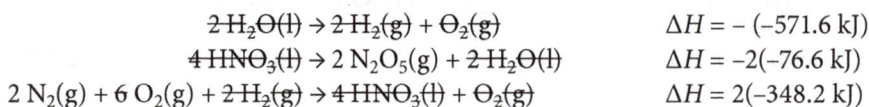

$2 \text{ H}_2\text{O}(l) \rightarrow 2 \text{ H}_2(g) + \text{O}_2(g)$	$\Delta H = - (-571.6 \text{ kJ})$
$4 \text{ HNO}_3(l) \rightarrow 2 \text{ N}_2\text{O}_5(g) + 2 \text{ H}_2\text{O}(l)$	$\Delta H = -2(-76.6 \text{ kJ})$
$2 \text{ N}_2(g) + 6 \text{ O}_2(g) + 2 \text{ H}_2(g) \rightarrow 4 \text{ HNO}_3(l) + \text{O}_2(g)$	$\Delta H = 2(-348.2 \text{ kJ})$

Add the remaining material from the equations. This matches the original equation; therefore, to finish the problem, add the three enthalpy changes.

$$2 \text{ N}_2(g) + 5 \text{ O}_2(g) \rightarrow 2 \text{ N}_2\text{O}_5(g) \qquad \mathbf{\Delta H = 28.4 \text{ kJ}}$$

Reality Check

A common error is to correctly double the third equation and then both reverse the first equation and then multiple by five to balance the O_2; however, the reversed first equation will not cancel the O_2 from the third equation correctly.

6.57 Using the thermochemical equations

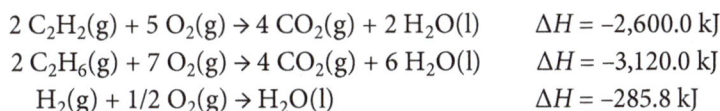

$$2\,C_2H_2(g) + 5\,O_2(g) \rightarrow 4\,CO_2(g) + 2\,H_2O(l) \qquad \Delta H = -2{,}600.0\ kJ$$
$$2\,C_2H_6(g) + 7\,O_2(g) \rightarrow 4\,CO_2(g) + 6\,H_2O(l) \qquad \Delta H = -3{,}120.0\ kJ$$
$$H_2(g) + 1/2\,O_2(g) \rightarrow H_2O(l) \qquad \Delta H = -285.8\ kJ$$

calculate the heat of reaction for

$$C_2H_2(g) + 2\,H_2(g) \rightarrow C_2H_6(g)$$

Information

Three balanced thermochemical equations and another equation with no enthalpy change. The question is, what is the enthalpy change for the final equation.

Connections

Hess's law

Solution

Multiply the first equation by one-half. Both reverse and divide the second equation by one-half. Then double the third equation. Now make the indicated cancellations. [Notice that the $O_2(g)$ appears twice on the reactant side and once on the product side; these three cancel because $5/2 + 1 = 7/2$.] These steps may be done in any order.

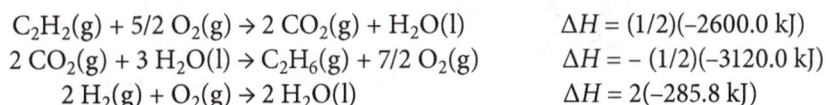

$$C_2H_2(g) + 5/2\,O_2(g) \rightarrow 2\,CO_2(g) + H_2O(l) \qquad \Delta H = (1/2)(-2600.0\ kJ)$$
$$2\,CO_2(g) + 3\,H_2O(l) \rightarrow C_2H_6(g) + 7/2\,O_2(g) \qquad \Delta H = -(1/2)(-3120.0\ kJ)$$
$$2\,H_2(g) + O_2(g) \rightarrow 2\,H_2O(l) \qquad \Delta H = 2(-285.8\ kJ)$$

Add the remaining material from the equations. This matches the original equation; therefore, to finish the problem, add the three enthalpy changes.

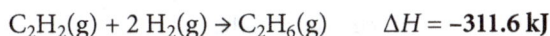

$$C_2H_2(g) + 2\,H_2(g) \rightarrow C_2H_6(g) \qquad \Delta H = -311.6\ kJ$$

Reality Check

The final answer has the correct units and seems reasonable in magnitude. The final equation matches the one being sought exactly.

6.59 Calculate the heat of reaction for

$$2\,N_2(g) + 5\,O_2(g) \rightarrow 2\,N_2O_5(g)$$

using the following thermochemical equations:

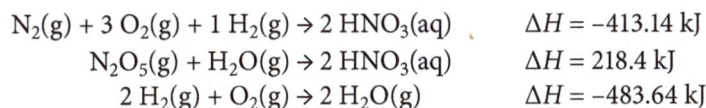

$$N_2(g) + 3\,O_2(g) + 1\,H_2(g) \rightarrow 2\,HNO_3(aq) \qquad \Delta H = -413.14\ kJ$$
$$N_2O_5(g) + H_2O(g) \rightarrow 2\,HNO_3(aq) \qquad \Delta H = 218.4\ kJ$$
$$2\,H_2(g) + O_2(g) \rightarrow 2\,H_2O(g) \qquad \Delta H = -483.64\ kJ$$

Information

Three balanced thermochemical equations and another equation with no enthalpy change. The question is, what is the enthalpy change for the final equation.

Connections

Hess's law

Solution

Make the indicated changes.

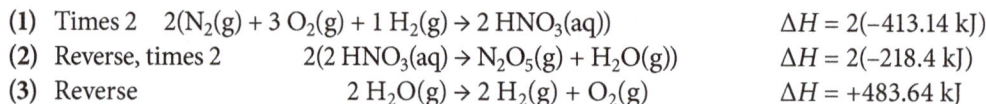

(1)	Times 2	$2(N_2(g) + 3 O_2(g) + 1 H_2(g) \rightarrow 2 HNO_3(aq))$	$\Delta H = 2(-413.14 \text{ kJ})$
(2)	Reverse, times 2	$2(2 HNO_3(aq) \rightarrow N_2O_5(g) + H_2O(g))$	$\Delta H = 2(-218.4 \text{ kJ})$
(3)	Reverse	$2 H_2O(g) \rightarrow 2 H_2(g) + O_2(g)$	$\Delta H = +483.64 \text{ kJ}$

Now make the indicated cancellations.

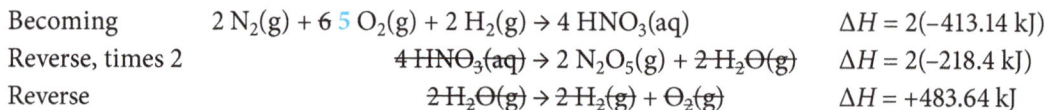

Becoming	$2 N_2(g) + 6\ 5\ O_2(g) + 2 H_2(g) \rightarrow 4 HNO_3(aq)$	$\Delta H = 2(-413.14 \text{ kJ})$
Reverse, times 2	$4\,HNO_3(aq) \rightarrow 2 N_2O_5(g) + 2\,H_2O(g)$	$\Delta H = 2(-218.4 \text{ kJ})$
Reverse	$2\,H_2O(g) \rightarrow 2\,H_2(g) + O_2(g)$	$\Delta H = +483.64 \text{ kJ}$

Add the remaining material from the equations. This matches the original equation; therefore, to finish the problem, add the three enthalpy changes.

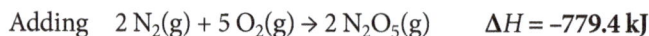

$$\text{Adding} \quad 2 N_2(g) + 5 O_2(g) \rightarrow 2 N_2O_5(g) \qquad \Delta H = -779.4 \text{ kJ}$$

Reality Check

The final answer has the correct units and seems reasonable in magnitude. The final equation matches the one being sought exactly.

6.6 Enthalpies of Formation

6.62 For each of the following substances, derive a balanced thermochemical equation for the standard heat of formation of one mole of the substance from its constituent elements. Assume all materials are in their standard states. Use appendix C to determine the enthalpy change for each reaction. **(a)** solid calcium iodide, $CaI_2(s)$; **(b)** gaseous sulfur trioxide, $SO_3(g)$; **(c)** solid sodium carbonate, $Na_2CO_3(s)$; **(d)** liquid ethanol, $C_2H_5OH(l)$; **(e)** solid sodium bicarbonate, $NaHCO_3(s)$

Information

The formulas for several compounds: **(a)** $CaI_2(s)$, **(b)** $SO_3(g)$, **(c)** $Na_2CO_3(s)$, **(d)** $C_2H_5OH(l)$, **(e)** $NaHCO_3(s)$; the question of a balanced thermochemical equation for each compound

Connections

The definition of *standard heat of formation*; appendix C

Solution

Only elements (in their standard states) can appear on the reactant site. <u>Only one</u> mole of product can appear on the product side. Balance the equation with new coefficients on the reactant side only (the product side must remain unchanged and equal to 1). Since these are thermochemical equations, fractional coefficients are allowed. The ΔH_f° come from appendix C.

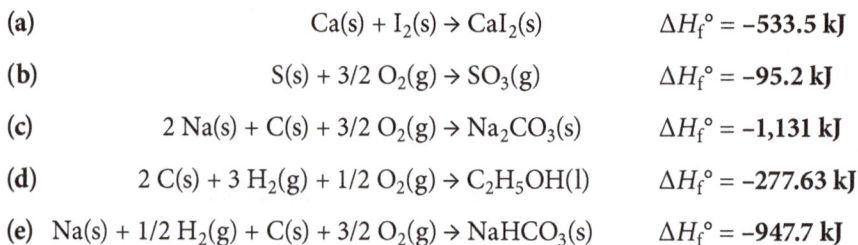

(a)	$Ca(s) + I_2(s) \rightarrow CaI_2(s)$	$\Delta H_f^\circ = \textbf{-533.5 kJ}$
(b)	$S(s) + 3/2\ O_2(g) \rightarrow SO_3(g)$	$\Delta H_f^\circ = \textbf{-95.2 kJ}$
(c)	$2 Na(s) + C(s) + 3/2\ O_2(g) \rightarrow Na_2CO_3(s)$	$\Delta H_f^\circ = \textbf{-1,131 kJ}$
(d)	$2 C(s) + 3 H_2(g) + 1/2\ O_2(g) \rightarrow C_2H_5OH(l)$	$\Delta H_f^\circ = \textbf{-277.63 kJ}$
(e)	$Na(s) + 1/2\ H_2(g) + C(s) + 3/2\ O_2(g) \rightarrow NaHCO_3(s)$	$\Delta H_f^\circ = \textbf{-947.7 kJ}$

6.64 Calculate the standard heat of formation for $HC_2H_3O_2(l)$ using the following thermochemical equations:

$$C(s) + O_2(g) \rightarrow CO_2(g) \qquad\qquad \Delta H° = -393.5 \text{ kJ}$$
$$H_2(g) + 1/2\ O_2(g) \rightarrow H_2O(l) \qquad\qquad \Delta H° = -285.8 \text{ kJ}$$
$$HC_2H_3O_2(l) + 2\ O_2(g) \rightarrow 2\ CO_2(g) + 2\ H_2O(l) \qquad\qquad \Delta H° = -871 \text{ kJ}$$

Information

Three balanced thermochemical equations; the question of what is the enthalpy change for the standard heat of formation for $HC_2H_3O_2(l)$

Connections

Hess's law; the definition of *standard heat of formation*

Solution

The standard heat of formation for $HC_2H_3O_2(l)$ (from the definition) is

$$2\ C(s) + 2\ H_2(g) + O_2(g) \rightarrow HC_2H_3O_2(l)$$

This now becomes a Hess's law problem. Reverse the third equation, double both remaining equations, then make the indicated cancellations:

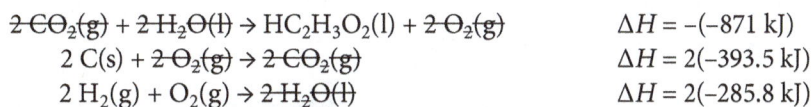

$$\cancel{2\ CO_2(g)} + \cancel{2\ H_2O(l)} \rightarrow HC_2H_3O_2(l) + \cancel{2\ O_2(g)} \qquad \Delta H = -(-871 \text{ kJ})$$
$$2\ C(s) + \cancel{2\ O_2(g)} \rightarrow \cancel{2\ CO_2(g)} \qquad \Delta H = 2(-393.5 \text{ kJ})$$
$$2\ H_2(g) + O_2(g) \rightarrow \cancel{2\ H_2O(l)} \qquad \Delta H = 2(-285.8 \text{ kJ})$$

Add the remaining material from the equations. This matches the standard heat of formation equation for $HC_2H_3O_2(l)$; therefore, to finish the problem, add the three enthalpy changes:

$$2\ C(s) + 2\ H_2(g) + O_2(g) \rightarrow HC_2H_3O_2(l) \qquad \Delta H = -487.6 = \mathbf{-488\ kJ}$$

Reality Check

The final answer has the correct units and seems reasonable in magnitude. The final equation matches the one being sought (based upon the definition of *standard heat of formation*) exactly.

6.66 Calculate the heat of formation for $ZnO(s)$, using the following thermochemical equations:

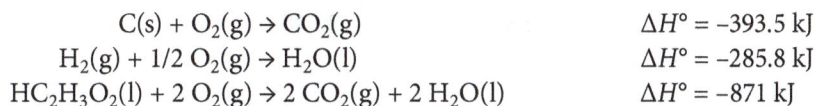

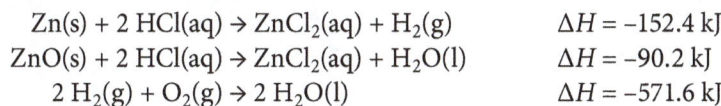

$$Zn(s) + 2\ HCl(aq) \rightarrow ZnCl_2(aq) + H_2(g) \qquad \Delta H = -152.4 \text{ kJ}$$
$$ZnO(s) + 2\ HCl(aq) \rightarrow ZnCl_2(aq) + H_2O(l) \qquad \Delta H = -90.2 \text{ kJ}$$
$$2\ H_2(g) + O_2(g) \rightarrow 2\ H_2O(l) \qquad \Delta H = -571.6 \text{ kJ}$$

Information

Three balanced thermochemical equations; the question of what is the enthalpy change for the standard heat of formation for $ZnO(s)$

Connections

Hess's law; the definition of *standard heat of formation*

Solution

The standard heat of formation for $ZnO(s)$ (from the definition) is

$$Zn(s) + 1/2\ O_2(g) \rightarrow ZnO(s)$$

This now becomes a Hess's law problem. Reverse the second equation. Use the first equation unchanged. Divide the third equation by 2. Then make the indicated cancellations.

$$ZnCl_2(aq) + H_2O(l) \rightarrow ZnO(s) + 2\,HCl(aq) \qquad \Delta H = 90.2 \text{ kJ}$$
$$Zn(s) + 2\,HCl(aq) \rightarrow ZnCl_2(aq) + H_2(g) \qquad \Delta H = -152.4 \text{ kJ}$$
$$H_2(g) + 1/2\,O_2(g) \rightarrow H_2O(l) \qquad \Delta H = 1/2(-571.6 \text{ kJ})$$

Add the remaining material from the equations. This matches the standard heat of formation equation for ZnO(s); therefore, to finish the problem, add the three enthalpy changes.

$$Zn(s) + 1/2\,O_2(g) \rightarrow ZnO(s) \qquad \Delta H = \textbf{--348.0 kJ}$$

Reality Check

The final answer has the correct units and seems reasonable in magnitude. The final equation matches the one being sought (based upon the definition of standard heat of formation) exactly.

6.68 Determine the enthalpy change for each of the following:

(a) $Ca(OH)_2(s) \rightarrow CaO(s) + H_2O(g)$

(b) $2\,Cu(s) + O_2(g) \rightarrow 2\,CuO(s)$

(c) $C_6H_{12}(l) + 6\,O_2(g) \rightarrow 6\,CO(g) + 6\,H_2O(l)$

Information

The balanced chemical equations; in all cases, the question of what is the enthalpy change

Connections

The thermodynamic values in appendix C; ΔH = Products – Reactants

Solution

(a) $Ca(OH)_2(s) \rightarrow CaO(s) + H_2O(g)$

    –986.09   –635.1   –241.826   kJ/mole

    $[-635.1 \text{ kJ} - 241.826 \text{ kJ}] - [(-986.09 \text{ kJ})] = 109.164 = \textbf{+109.7 kJ}$

(b) $2\,Cu(s) + O_2(g) \rightarrow 2\,CuO(s)$

    0   0   –157.1   kJ/mole

    $[2(-157.1 \text{ kJ})] - [2\,(0.000) + (0.000 \text{ kJ})] = -314.2 = \textbf{--314.2 kJ}$

(c) $C_6H_{12}(l) + 6\,O_2(g) \rightarrow 6\,CO(g) + 6\,H_2O(l)$

    –123.1   0   –110.5   –285.840 kJ/mole

    $[6\,(-110.5 \text{ kJ}) + 6\,(-285.840 \text{ kJ})] - [(-123.1 \text{ kJ}) + 6\,(0.000 \text{ kJ})] = -2254.94 = \textbf{--2,254.9 kJ}$

Reality Check

The final answer has the correct units and seems reasonable in magnitude. Recall that the standard heat for elements (in their states) is exactly 0.

6.71 Ethyl alcohol—$C_2H_5OH(l)$—undergoes the following combustion reaction:

$$C_2H_5OH(l) + 3\,O_2(g) \rightarrow 2\,CO_2(g) + 3\,H_2O(l) \qquad \Delta H = -1,366.8 \text{ kJ}$$

Determine the enthalpy change when 5.00 g of ethyl alcohol burn according to this reaction.

Information
The heat of combustion (–1,366.8 kJ/mol C_2H_5OH); the question of how much energy 5.00 g of C_2H_5OH will produce

Solution
This is a unit conversion, which includes a gram to mole conversion. The way the problem is stated, a balanced equation is unnecessary:

$$\text{Enthalpy change} = (5.00 \text{ g } C_2H_5OH)\left(\frac{1 \text{ mol } C_2H_5OH}{46.069 \text{ g } C_2H_5OH}\right)\left(\frac{-1{,}366.8 \text{ kJ}}{1 \text{ mol } C_2H_5OH}\right) = -148.3427 = \mathbf{-148 \text{ kJ}}$$

Reality Check
The final answer has the correct units and seems reasonable in magnitude. This is an exothermic process, so the final answer must be negative.

6.73 At one time, manganese metal was produced by the reaction

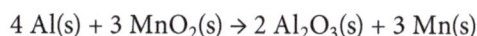

$$4 \text{ Al(s)} + 3 \text{ MnO}_2\text{(s)} \rightarrow 2 \text{ Al}_2O_3\text{(s)} + 3 \text{ Mn(s)}$$

Determine $\Delta H°$ for this reaction using data from appendix C.

Information
The balanced chemical equation; the question of what is the enthalpy change

Connections
The thermodynamic values in appendix C; ΔH = Products – Reactants

Solution
$$4 \text{ Al(s)} + 3 \text{ MnO}_2\text{(s)} \rightarrow 2 \text{ Al}_2O_3\text{(s)} + 3 \text{ Mn(s)}$$
$$0 \qquad -520.9 \qquad -1{,}676 \qquad 0 \qquad \text{kJ/mole}$$
$$[2(-1{,}676 \text{ kJ}) + 3(0.000 \text{ kJ})] - [3(-520.9 \text{ kJ}) + 4(0.000 \text{ kJ})] = -1{,}789.3 = \mathbf{-1{,}789 \text{ kJ}}$$

Reality Check
The final answer has the correct units and seems reasonable in magnitude. Recall that the standard heat for elements (in their states) is exactly 0.

6.75 Diborane (B_2H_6) reacts with oxygen as follows:

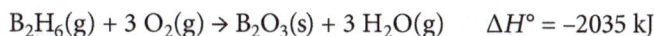

$$B_2H_6\text{(g)} + 3 \text{ O}_2\text{(g)} \rightarrow B_2O_3\text{(s)} + 3 \text{ H}_2O\text{(g)} \qquad \Delta H° = -2035 \text{ kJ}$$

Using the above reaction and appendix C, determine $\Delta H_f°$ for diborane.

Information
The balanced thermochemical equation; the heat of reaction; the question of what is the standard enthalpy of formation for B_2H_6

Connections
The thermodynamic values in appendix C; ΔH = Products – Reactants

Solution

This is like the other problems dealing with the calculation of the heat of reaction. However, in this case, the heat of reaction is known and the value for one of the substances is missing.

$$\Delta H°(\text{rxn}) = [\Delta H_f°(B_2O_3(s)) + 3\,\Delta H_f°(H_2O(g))] - [\Delta H_f°(B_2H_6(g)) + 3\,\Delta H_f°(O_2(g))]$$

$$\Delta H_f°(B_2H_6(g)) = [\Delta H_f°(B_2O_3(s)) + 3\,\Delta H_f°(H_2O(g))] - [3\,\Delta H_f°(O_2(g))] - \Delta H°(\text{rxn})$$

$$\Delta H_f°(B_2H_6(g)) = [(-1272) + 3\,(-241.826\text{ kJ})] - [3\,(0.0)] - (-2{,}035\text{ kJ})$$

$$\Delta H_f°(B_2H_6(g)) = 37.522 = \textbf{38 kJ/mol}$$

6.7 Phase Transitions

6.76 Identify the type of phase transition occurring in each of the following changes: **(a)** dew forms on grass; **(b)** ice cubes in a freezer slowly disappear; **(c)** when warmed in a pan on a stove, butter changes to a liquid; **(d)** water in a glass slowly disappears; **(e)** gaseous carbon dioxide forms dry ice (solid carbon dioxide)

Solution

(a) This is a change from a gas to a liquid; therefore, it is **Condensation**.

(b) This is a change from a solid to a gas; therefore, it is **Sublimation**.

(c) This is a change from a solid to a liquid; therefore, it is **Melting (Fusion)**.

(d) This is a change from a liquid to a gas; therefore, it is **Evaporation (Vaporization)**.

(e) This is a change from a gas to a solid; therefore, it is **Deposition**.

6.78 In the desert, water may be cooled by evaporation. The evaporation of water from the surface of a water bag cools the liquid in the bag. Calculate the number of milliliters of water that may be cooled from 40.0°C to 25°C by the evaporation of 15 g of water. The density of water is 1.0 g/cm3, the specific heat of water is 4.18 J/g · °C, and the heat of vaporization of water is 41 kJ/mol.

Information

A temperature change (40.0°C to 25°C); mass (15 g H_2O); some properties of H_2O (density = 1.0 g/cm³, specific heat = 4.18J/g · °C, and $\Delta H_{\text{vaporization}}$ = 41 kJ/mol); the question of how many milliliters of water must evaporate

Connections

The law of conservation of energy (first law of thermodynamics); $\Delta T = T_{\text{final}} - T_{\text{initial}}$

Solution

According to the law of conservation of energy, the energy gained by the evaporating water (positive) must be the same as the energy lost by the cooling water (negative). The energy may be in either joules or kilojoules. In the following calculation, the unit conversions on the left is the energy (kJ) absorbed by the evaporating water, and the unit conversions on the right is the energy (kJ) lost by the cooling water:

$$(15\text{ g }H_2O)\left(\frac{1\text{ mol }H_2O}{18.015\text{ g }H_2O}\right)\left(\frac{41\text{ kJ}}{\text{mol }H_2O}\right) = -\left(\frac{4.18\text{ J}}{\text{g}\,°C}\right)\left(\frac{k}{1{,}000}\right)\left(\frac{1.0\text{ g}}{cm^3}\right)\left(\frac{cm^3}{mL}\right)(25.0-40.0)°C(?\text{ mL})$$

Removing the cancelled units to make the calculation simpler:

$$(15)\left(\frac{41 \text{ kJ}}{18.015}\right) = -\left(\frac{4.18 \text{ kJ}}{1,000 \text{ mL}}\right)(-15.0)(?\text{mL})$$

Rearrange to find ? mL:

$$?\text{ mL} = \frac{(15)\left(\dfrac{41 \text{ kJ}}{18.015}\right)}{-\left(\dfrac{4.18 \text{ kJ}}{1,000 \text{ mL}}\right)(-15.0)} = 544.469 = \textbf{540 mL}$$

6.80 Gallium, Ga, melts at 29°C and boils at 2,403°C. The enthalpy of fusion of gallium is 5.590 kJ/mol, and its enthalpy of vaporization is 295.8 kJ/mol. The specific heats of solid, liquid, and gaseous gallium are 0.381 J/g · °C, 0.409 J/g · °C, and 0.364 J/g · °C, respectively. How much heat is required to convert 135.0 g of gallium solid at 0.00°C to the vapor phase at 2,600.0°C?

Information

There are many properties plus other necessary material. It will help to tabulate the data or to sketch a heating curve. In this case, we will construct a table. The question is, how much heat (energy) is required. (It may help to refer to the **figure accompanying Problem 6.79**.)

	Heat of fusion (vaporization)	Transition T	Specific heat
Solid	5.590 kJ/mol	29°C	0.381 J/g °C
Liquid	295.8 kJ/mol	2,403°C	0.409 J/g °C
Gas			0.364 J/g °C

Start: 0.00°C   End: 2,600.0°C

Mass: 135.0 g

Connections

$\Delta T = T_{\text{final}} - T_{\text{initial}}$

Solution

To get from the "start" to the "end," we need to do five sets of unit conversions. The calculations below are for kilojoules; however, any energy unit will work. Significant figures in the preliminary answers are underlined.

Warming the solid: $\left(\dfrac{0.381 \text{ J}}{\text{g} \,^\circ\text{C}}\right)\left(\dfrac{\text{k}}{1,000}\right)(135.0 \text{ g})(29 - 0.00)^\circ\text{C} = \underline{1.49}16 \text{ kJ}$

Melting the solid: $\left(\dfrac{5.590 \text{ kJ}}{\text{mol}}\right)(135.0 \text{ g})\left(\dfrac{1 \text{ mol}}{69.723 \text{ g}}\right) = 10.\underline{82}354 \text{ kJ}$

Warming the liquid: $\left(\dfrac{0.409 \text{ J}}{\text{g} \,^\circ\text{C}}\right)\left(\dfrac{\text{k}}{1,000}\right)(135.0 \text{ g})(2403 - 29)^\circ\text{C} = \underline{131.0}80 \text{ kJ}$

Boiling the liquid: $\left(\dfrac{295.8 \text{ kJ}}{\text{mol}}\right)(135.0 \text{ g})\left(\dfrac{1 \text{ mol}}{69.723 \text{ g}}\right) = \underline{572.7}378 \text{ kJ}$

Warming the vapor: $\left(\dfrac{0.364 \text{ J}}{\text{g} \,^\circ\text{C}}\right)\left(\dfrac{\text{k}}{1,000}\right)(135.0 \text{ g})(2600.0 - 2403)^\circ\text{C} = \underline{9.68}058 \text{ kJ}$

The energy required is the sum of the five steps:

Total = (1.4916 + 10.82354 + 131.080 + 572.7378 + 9.68058) kJ = 725.81352 = **726 kJ**

Reality Check

The final answer has the correct units and seems reasonable in magnitude. This is an endothermic process, so the answer must be positive.

6.82 Sulfur dioxide melts at –73°C and boils at –10.0°C. The enthalpy of fusion of sulfur dioxide is 8.619 kJ/mol, and its enthalpy of vaporization is 25.73 kJ/mol. The specific heats of liquid and gaseous sulfur dioxide are 0.995 J/g · °C and 0.622 J/g · °C, respectively. How much heat is required to convert 2.50 kg of solid sulfur dioxide at the melting point to the vapor phase at 60.0°C?

Information

There are many properties plus other necessary material. It will help to tabulate the data or to sketch a heating curve. In this case, we will construct a heating curve. The question is, how much heat (energy) is required.

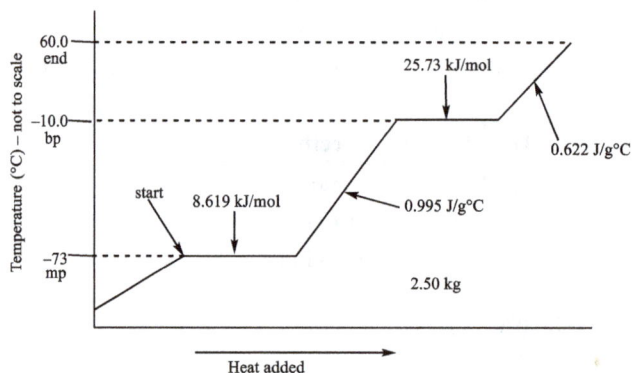

Connections

$\Delta T = T_{final} - T_{initial}$

Solution

To get from the "start" to the "end," we need to do four sets of unit conversions. The calculations below are for kilojoules; however, any energy unit will work. Significant figures in the preliminary answers are underlined.

Melting the solid: $\left(\dfrac{8.619 \text{ kJ}}{\text{mol}}\right)(2.50 \text{ kg})\left(\dfrac{1,000}{\text{k}}\right)\left(\dfrac{1 \text{ mol}}{64.063 \text{ g}}\right) = 336.34859 \text{ kJ}$

Heating the liquid: $\left(\dfrac{0.995 \text{ J}}{\text{g °C}}\right)(2.50 \text{ kg})(-10. - (-73))°C = 156.7125 \text{ kJ}$

Boiling the liquid: $\left(\dfrac{25.73 \text{ kJ}}{\text{mol}}\right)(2.50 \text{ kg})\left(\dfrac{1,000}{\text{k}}\right)\left(\dfrac{1 \text{ mol}}{64.063 \text{ g}}\right) = 1,004.0897 \text{ kJ}$

Heating the vapor: $\left(\dfrac{0.622 \text{ J}}{\text{g °C}}\right)(2.50 \text{ kg})(60.0 - (-10.0))°C = 108.85 \text{ kJ}$

The energy required is the sum of the four steps:

Total = (336.34859 + 156.7125 + 1,004.0897 + 108.85) kJ = 1,606.00079 = **1.61 × 10³ kJ**

Reality Check
The final answer has the correct units and seems reasonable in magnitude. This is an endothermic process, so the answer must be positive.

6.84 Benzene (C_6H_6) melts at –6°C and boils at 80.0°C. The enthalpy of fusion of benzene is 9.937 kJ/mol, and its enthalpy of vaporization is 42.90 kJ/mol. The specific heats of liquid and gaseous benzene are 1.74 J/g · °C and 1.05 J/g · °C, respectively. How much heat is required to convert 150.0 g of solid benzene at the melting point to the vapor phase at 125°C?

Information
There are many properties plus other necessary material. It will help to tabulate the data or to sketch a heating curve. In this case, we will construct a table. The question is, how much heat (energy) is required. (It may help to refer to the figure accompanying Problem 6.79.)

	Heat of fusion (vaporization)	Transition T	Specific heat
Solid	9.937 kJ/mol	–6°C	
Liquid	42.90 kJ/mol	80.0°C	1.74 J/g °C
Gas			1.05 J/g °C

Start: –6°C   End: 125°C

Mass: 150.0 g

Connections
$\Delta T = T_{final} - T_{initial}$

Solution
To get from the "start" to the "end," we need to do four sets of unit conversions. The calculations below are for kilojoules; however, any energy unit will work. Significant figures in the preliminary answers are underlined.

Melting the solid: $\left(\frac{9.937\ kJ}{mol}\right)(150.0\ g)\left(\frac{1\ mol}{78.114\ g}\right) = \underline{19.08}1727\ kJ$

Heating the liquid: $\left(\frac{1.74\ J}{g°C}\right)\left(\frac{k}{1,000}\right)(150.0\ g)(80.0 - (-6))°C = \underline{19.3}14\ kJ$

Boiling the vapor: $\left(\frac{42.90\ kJ}{mol}\right)(150.0\ g)\left(\frac{1\ mol}{78.114\ g}\right) = \underline{82.37}9599\ kJ$

Heating the vapor: $\left(\frac{1.05\ J}{g°C}\right)\left(\frac{k}{1,000}\right)(150.0\ g)(125 - (80.0))°C = \underline{7.0}875\ kJ$

The energy required is the sum of the four steps:

Total = (19.081727+ 19.314 + 82.379599 + 7.0875) kJ = 127.862826 = **128 kJ**

Reality Check

The final answer has the correct units and seems reasonable in magnitude. This is an endothermic process, so the answer must be positive.

6.86 Dimethyl sulfide—$(CH_3)_2S$—melts at –98°C and boils at 37°C. The enthalpy of fusion of dimethyl sulfide is 7.97 kJ/mol, and its enthalpy of vaporization is 28.21 kJ/mol. The specific heats of liquid and gaseous dimethyl sulfide are 1.91 J/g· °C and 1.16 J/g· °C, respectively. How much heat is required to convert 375.0 g of solid dimethyl sulfide at the melting point to the vapor phase at 77°C?

Information

There are many properties plus other necessary material. It will help to tabulate the data or to sketch a heating curve. In this case, we will construct a table. The question is, how much heat (energy) is required. (It may help to refer to the figure accompanying Problem 6.79.)

	Heat of fusion (vaporization)	Transition T	Specific heat
Solid	7.97 kJ/mol	–98°C	
Liquid	28.21 kJ/mol	37°C	1.91 J/g °C
Gas			1.16 J/g °C

Start: –98°C   End: 77°C

Mass: 375.0 g

Connections

$\Delta T = T_{final} - T_{initial}$

Solution

To get from the "start" to the "end," we need to do four sets of unit conversions. The calculations below are for kilojoules; however, any energy unit will work. Significant figures in the preliminary answers are underlined.

Melting the solid: $\left(\dfrac{7.97\ kJ}{mol}\right)(375.0\ g)\left(\dfrac{1\ mol}{62.135\ g}\right) = 48.100909\ kJ$

Heating the liquid: $\left(\dfrac{1.91\ J}{g°C}\right)\left(\dfrac{k}{1,000}\right)(375.0\ g)(37-(-98))°C = 96.69375\ kJ$

Boiling the liquid: $\left(\dfrac{28.21\ kJ}{mol}\right)(375.0\ g)\left(\dfrac{1\ mol}{62.135\ g}\right) = 170.25428\ kJ$

Heating the vapor: $\left(\dfrac{1.16\ J}{g°C}\right)\left(\dfrac{k}{1,000}\right)(375.0\ g)(77-(37))°C = 17.4\ kJ$

The energy required is the sum of the four steps:

Total = (48.100909+ 96.69375 + 170.25428 + 17.4) kJ = 332.448939 = **332 kJ**

Reality Check

The final answer has the correct units and seems reasonable in magnitude. This is an endothermic process, so the answer must be positive.

6.8 Thermal Pollution and Henry's Law

6.89 How does the solubility of a gas vary with temperature?

Solution

The solubility of a gas decreases with increasing temperature.

6.92 If the air pressure is 1.00 atm and the mole fraction of oxygen in the atmosphere is 0.209, calculate the molar solubility of oxygen in the water in a lake at 20°C. At this temperature, the Henry's law constant for oxygen is 1.38×10^{-3} M/atm.

Information

The 20°C Henry's law constant for O_2 (1.38×10^{-3} M/atm); the total pressure (1.00 atm); the mole fraction of O_2 (0.209); the question of what is the solubility of O_2

Connections

The partial pressure of a gas of a gas is the mole fraction of the gas times the total pressure. Henry's law states that the solubility of a gas is proportional to its partial pressure.

Solution

A unit-conversion calculation is necessary:

$$\text{Solubility } O_2 = (0.209)(1.00 \text{ atm})\left(\frac{1.38 \times 10^{-3} \text{ M}}{\text{atm}}\right) = 2.8842 \times 10^{-4} = \mathbf{2.88 \times 10^{-4} \text{ M } O_2}$$

6.9 Applications and Extensions

6.94 A package of a brand of instant oatmeal contains 2 g of fat, 34 g of carbohydrate, and 5 g of protein. Fats typically produce 38 kJ/g, and both proteins and carbohydrates typically produce 17 kJ/g. How many nutritional calories (Calories) are present in the package of instant oatmeal?

Information

The mass and energy content of fat (2 g and 38 kJ/g), of carbohydrate (34 g and 17 kJ/g), and of protein (5 g and 17 kg/g); the question of how many Calories are present in the food

Connections

1 Calorie = 1,000 calories = 4.184 kJ

Solution

The sum of three unit conversions times the Calorie unit conversion gives the answer:

[(2 g fat) (38 kJ/g) + (34 g carbohydrate) (17 kJ/g) + (5 g protein) (17 kJ/g)] (1 Calorie/4.184 kJ)

$= 176.6252 = \mathbf{1.8 \times 10^2 \text{ Calories}}$

6.96 Nitrogen may be oxidized in automobile engines by the following reaction:

$$N_2(g) + O_2(g) \rightarrow 2 \text{ NO}(g) \qquad \Delta H = 180.6 \text{ kJ}$$

How many grams of nitrogen are required to absorb 125 kJ?

Information

A balanced thermochemical equation; the question of how many grams of N_2 are necessary to absorb 125 kJ

Solution

Two unit conversions are necessary—one from the thermochemical equation and one involving the molar mass:

$$\text{Mass } N_2 = (125 \text{ kJ})\left(\frac{1 \text{ mol } N_2}{180.6 \text{ kJ}}\right)\left(\frac{28.014 \text{ g } N_2}{1 \text{ mol } N_2}\right) = 19.3895 = \textbf{19.4 g } N_2$$

6.99 Propane gas, C_3H_8, is sometimes used as a fuel. To measure its energy output as a fuel, a 1.860-g sample was combined with an excess of O_2 and ignited in a bomb calorimeter, causing the temperature of the calorimeter to increase from 25.000°C to 26.061°C. The calorimeter contained 1.000 kg of water. The heat capacity of the empty calorimeter was 4.643 kJ/°C. Determine the heat of reaction in kJ/mol propane. The reaction was

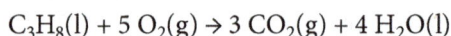

$$C_3H_8(l) + 5\ O_2(g) \rightarrow 3\ CO_2(g) + 4\ H_2O(l)$$

Information

A 1.860-gram sample of C_3H_8 burned in a bomb calorimeter with a heat capacity of 4.643 kJ/°C and containing 1.000 kg H_2O; a temperature change from 25.000°C to 26.061°C; the question of what is the heat of reaction in kJ/mol C_3H_8

Connections

The specific heat of water is 4.184 J/g · °C, or 4.184 J/g · K; $\Delta T = T_{final} - T_{initial}$

Solution

The calculation has two parts. We need to (1) determine the kilojoules of heat and (2) determine the moles of C_3H_8. In the numerator below is the first calculation, which begins with the heat capacity of the calorimeter followed by two unit conversions plus a calculation using the specific heat of water and two unit conversions. The denominator contains the second calculation, which begins with the mass of C_3H_8 and uses the molar mass of C_3H_8 to convert to moles C_3H_8. Remember, this is an exothermic process, so the final answer must be negative (this comes from the definition, not the calculation).

$$\frac{\left(\frac{4.643 \text{ kJ}}{°C}\right)(26.061 - 25.000)°C + \left(\frac{4.184 \text{ J}}{g\,°C}\right)(1.000 \text{ kg})(26.061 - 25.000)°C}{(1.860 \text{ g } C_3H_8)\left(\frac{1 \text{ mol } C_3H_8}{44.097 \text{ g } C_3H_8}\right)} = -222.0366$$

$$= \textbf{-2.220} \times \textbf{10}^2 \textbf{ kJ/mol}$$

Putting It All Together

6.103 Write a thermochemical equation for the standard heat of formation of solid sodium carbonate, Na_2CO_3.

Information

The formula for a compound: $Na_2CO_3(s)$; the question of a balanced thermochemical equation for Na_2CO_3

Connections

The definition of *standard heat of formation*; appendix C

Solution

Only elements (in their standard states) can appear on the reactant site. <u>Only one</u> mole of product can appear on the product side. Balance the equation with new coefficients on the reactant side only (the product side must remain unchanged). Since these are thermochemical equations, fractional coefficients are allowed. The $\Delta H_f°$ comes from appendix C.

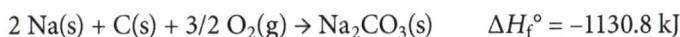

$$2 \text{ Na(s)} + \text{C(s)} + 3/2 \text{ O}_2\text{(g)} \rightarrow \text{Na}_2\text{CO}_3\text{(s)} \qquad \Delta H_f° = -1130.8 \text{ kJ}$$

6.105 A 100.0-g sample of water is heated to boiling, 100.00°C, and removed from the heat source. A 45.0-g sample of manganese, at 25.00°C, was immediately dropped into the hot water. The final temperature of the water plus manganese was 98.49°C. Assuming no heat was lost, what is the specific heat of manganese?

Information

Information on water (100.0 g, 100.00°C) and manganese (45.0 g, 25.00°C); the final temperature (98.49°C) of the sample; the question of what is the specific heat of manganese

Connections

The definition of *specific heat* (J/g °C or J/g K); the specific heat of water (4.184 J/g °C); the law of conservation of energy (the first law of thermodynamics); $\Delta T = T_{final} - T_{initial}$

Solution

The metal is cooler; therefore, it will gain heat while the water loses heat. Applying the law of conservation of energy means that the heat lost (by the water) must be the same as the heat gained (by the metal). That is,

$$\text{Heat gained (metal)} = - \text{ Heat lost (water)}$$

Beginning with the specific heat of water, we can determine the heat (joules) gained by the water with two conversion steps. A similar set of steps will give the heat lost by the metal:

$$\left(\frac{? \text{ J}}{\text{g}°\text{C}}\right)(45.0 \text{ g})(98.49 - 25.00)°\text{C} = -\left(\frac{4.184 \text{ J}}{\text{g}°\text{C}}\right)(100.0 \text{ g})(98.49 - 100.00)°\text{C}$$

Rearranging gives

$$\left(\frac{? \text{ J}}{\text{g}°\text{C}}\right) = \frac{-\left(\dfrac{4.184 \text{ J}}{\text{g}°\text{C}}\right)(100.0 \text{ g})(98.49 - 100.00)°\text{C}}{(45.0 \text{ g})(98.49 - 25.00)°\text{C}} = 0.19104156 = \textbf{0.191 J/g °C}$$

Reality Check

The final units are correct for a specific heat.

6.107 A 15.00-g sample of lead metal was heated to 65.00°C. This sample was clamped in contact with a 27.00 g sample of magnesium metal at 25.00°C. The specific heat of lead metal is 0.127 J/g °C, and the specific heat of magnesium metal is 1.024 J/g °C. Assuming no heat is lost to the surroundings, what was the final temperature of the two metals?

Information

Information on lead (15.00 g, 65.00°C, 0.127 J/g · °C) and magnesium (27.00 g, 25.00°C, 1.024 J/g· °C); the question of what is the final temperature

Connections

The definition of *specific heat* (J/g °C or J/g K); the specific heat of water (4.184 J/g °C); the law of conservation of energy (the first law of thermodynamics); $\Delta T = T_{final} - T_{initial}$

Solution

The magnesium is cooler; therefore, it will gain heat while the lead loses heat. Applying the law of conservation of energy means that the heat lost (by the lead) must be the same as the heat gained (by the magnesium). That is,

$$\text{Heat gained (magnesium)} = -\text{Heat lost (lead)}$$

Beginning with the specific heat of lead, we can determine the heat (joules) lost by the lead with two conversion steps. A similar set of steps will give the heat gained by the beryllium.

$$-\left[\left(\frac{0.127 \text{ J}}{\text{g}°\text{C}}\right)(15.00 \text{ g})(T_f - 65.00)°\text{C}\right] = +\left[\left(\frac{1.024 \text{ J}}{\text{g}°\text{C}}\right)(27.00 \text{ g})(T_f - 25.00)°\text{C}\right]$$

Significant figures are underlined:

$$-[(\underline{1.90}5 \text{ J}) (T_f - \underline{65.00})] = + [(\underline{27.64}8 \text{ J}) (T_f - \underline{25.00})]$$

Distributing gives

$$-[\underline{1.90}5 \, T_f - \underline{123.8}25] = + [\underline{27.64}8 \, T_f - \underline{691.2}]$$

Collecting terms gives

$$\underline{691.2} + \underline{123.8}25 = (\underline{27.64}8 + 1.905) \, T_f$$

$$\underline{815.0}25 = (\underline{29.55}3) \, T_f$$

Rearranging gives

$$T_f = \underline{815.0}25 \, / \, \underline{29.55}3 = \underline{27.57}84 = \textbf{27.6°C}$$

6.109 A house may be kept warm by solar heating. Normally, water, with its high specific heat capacity, is used to store the heat. For example, a volume of 1,500 gallons of water will store enough heat to keep a house warm overnight. Wood, on the other hand, is not as efficient for heat storage. A typical piece of wood has a density of 0.865 g/cm^3 and a specific heat of 1.76 J/g °C. Wood is measured in board feet. A *board foot* is the volume of a piece of wood measuring exactly 12 in × 12 in × 1 in. How many board feet of wood would be required to replace the 1,500 gallons of water for heat storage? Hint: The heat capacity of the wood will equal the heat capacity of the water.

Information

The information 1,500 gallons of water; some properties of wood (density = 0.865 g/cm^3, specific heat of wood = 1.76 J/g °C); the definition of *board foot* (12 in × 12 in × 1 in); the question of how many board feet of wood are equivalent to 1,500 gallons of water

Connections

A variation of the law of conservation of energy (first law of thermodynamics); the density of water (1.00 $g/cm^{3)}$; the specific heat of water (4.184 J/g °C); the need for several unit conversions

Solution

The series of conversions in the square brackets is a determination of the heat capacity of the water (same as the heat capacity of the wood, which allows us to switch over to wood using the specific heat of the wood):

$$\left[(1{,}500 \text{ gal})\left(\frac{4 \text{ qt}}{1 \text{ gal}}\right)\left(\frac{1 \text{ L}}{1.057 \text{ qt}}\right)\left(\frac{m}{0.001}\right)\left(\frac{1.00 \text{ g}}{mL}\right)\left(\frac{4.184 \text{ J}}{g\,°C}\right)\right]\left(\frac{g\,°C}{1.76 \text{ J}}\right)\left(\frac{cm^3}{0.865 \text{ g}}\right)\left(\frac{1 \text{ in}}{2.54 \text{ cm}}\right)^3\left(\frac{1 \text{ bf}}{(12 \times 12 \times 1) \text{ in}^3}\right)$$

$$= 6{,}611.127 = \mathbf{6.6 \times 10^3 \text{ board feet}}$$

6.112 A sample of benzoic acid, $HC_7H_5O_2$, weighing 0.286 g is burned in a bomb calorimeter (that is, at constant volume), raising the calorimeter temperature from 21.487°C to 23.485°C. A sample of caffeine, $C_8H_{10}N_4O_2$, weighing 0.323 g was burned in the same calorimeter, and the temperature increased from 22.352°C to 24.208°C. The heat of combustion for benzoic acid is reported to be 3,221.6 kJ/mol. Determine the heat of combustion, in kJ/mol, for caffeine.

Information

Two sets of data: (1) 0.286 g $HC_7H_5O_2$ caused the temperature to change from 21.487°C to 23.485°C; the heat of combustion of $HC_7H_5O_2$ (3221.6 kJ/mol); (2) 0.323 g $C_8H_{10}N_4O_2$ caused the temperature to change from 22.352°C to 24.208°C; the question of what is the heat of combustion, in kJ/mol, for caffeine

Connections

$\Delta T = T_{final} - T_{initial}$

Solution

From the first set of data, we can determine the heat capacity of the calorimeter:

$$C_{calorimeter} = \frac{(0.286 \text{ g } HC_7H_5O_2)\left(\dfrac{1 \text{ mol } HC_7H_5O_2}{122.123 \text{ g } HC_7H_5O_2}\right)\left(\dfrac{3{,}221.6 \text{ kJ}}{1 \text{ mol } HC_7H_5O_2}\right)}{(23.485 - 21.487)°C} = 3.77611 = 3.78 \text{ kJ/}°C$$

From the heat capacity of the calorimeter and the second set of data, we can determine the heat of the combustion of caffeine:

$$\frac{\left(\dfrac{3.77611 \text{ kJ}}{°C}\right)(24.208 - 22.352)°C}{(0.323 \text{ g } C_8H_{10}N_4O_2)\left(\dfrac{1 \text{ mol } C_8H_{10}N_4O_2}{194.194 \text{ g } C_8H_{10}N_4O_2}\right)} = -4{,}213.625 = \mathbf{-4.21 \times 10^3 \text{ kJ/mol}}$$

6.114 Chloroform, $CHCl_3$, melts at –64°C and boils at 62°C. The enthalpy of fusion of chloroform is 8.798 kJ/mol, and its enthalpy of vaporization is 31.38 kJ/mol. The specific heats of liquid and gaseous chloroform are 0.967 J/g · K and 0.550 J/g · K, respectively. How much heat is required to convert 175.0 g of solid chloroform at the melting point to the vapor phase at 82°C?

Information

There are many properties plus other necessary material. It will help to tabulate the data or to sketch a heating curve. In this case, we will construct a table. The question is, how much heat (energy) is required.

	Heat of fusion (vaporization)	Transition T	Specific heat
Solid	8.798 kJ/mol	−64°C	
Liquid	31.38 kJ/mol	62°C	0.967 J/g °C
Gas			0.550 J/g °C

Start: −64°C   End: 82°C

Mass: 175.0 g

Connections

$\Delta T = T_{final} - T_{initial}$

Solution

To get from the "start" to the "end," we need to do four sets of unit conversions. The calculations below are for kilojoules; however, any energy unit will work. Substitute °C for K. Significant figures in the preliminary answers are underlined.

Melting the solid $\left(\dfrac{8.798 \text{ kJ}}{\text{mol}}\right)(175.0 \text{ g})\left(\dfrac{1 \text{ mol}}{119.378 \text{ g}}\right) = \underline{12.89}727 \text{ kJ}$

Heating the liquid $\left(\dfrac{0.967 \text{ J}}{\text{g}°\text{C}}\right)\left(\dfrac{k}{1{,}000}\right)(175.0 \text{ g})(62 - (-64))°\text{C} = \underline{21.3}22 \text{ kJ}$

Boiling the liquid $\left(\dfrac{31.38 \text{ kJ}}{\text{mol}}\right)(175.0 \text{ g})\left(\dfrac{1 \text{ mol}}{119.378 \text{ g}}\right) = \underline{46.00}09 \text{ kJ}$

Heating the vapor $\left(\dfrac{0.550 \text{ J}}{\text{g}°\text{C}}\right)\left(\dfrac{k}{1{,}000}\right)(175.0 \text{ g})(82 - (62))°\text{C} = \underline{1.9}25 \text{ kJ}$

The energy required is the sum of the four steps:

Total = ($\underline{12.89}727 + \underline{21.3}22 + \underline{46.00}09 + \underline{1.9}25$) kJ = 82.14517 = **82.1 kJ**

6.116 Isopropyl alcohol, C_3H_7OH, melts at −90.0°C and boils at 82°C. The enthalpy of fusion of isopropyl alcohol is 5.36 kJ/mol, and its enthalpy of vaporization is 42.11 kJ/mol. The specific heats of liquid and gaseous isopropyl alcohol are 2.68 J/g · K and 1.54 J/g · K, respectively. How much heat is required to convert 150.0 g of solid isopropyl alcohol at the melting point to the vapor phase at 122°C?

Information

There are many properties plus other necessary material. It will help to tabulate the data or to sketch a heating curve. In this case, we will construct a table. The question is, how much heat (energy) is required.

	Heat of fusion (vaporization)	Transition T	Specific heat
Solid	5.36 kJ/mol	−90°C	
Liquid	42.11 kJ/mol	82°C	2.68 J/g °C
Gas			1.54 J/g °C

Start: −90°C   End: 122°C

Mass: 150.0 g

Connections

$\Delta T = T_{final} - T_{initial}$

Solution

To get from the "start" to the "end," we need to do four sets of unit conversions. The calculations below are for kilojoules; however, any energy unit will work. Substitute °C for K. Significant figures in the preliminary answers are underlined.

Melting the solid
$$\left(\frac{5.36 \text{ kJ}}{\text{mol}}\right)(150.0 \text{ g})\left(\frac{1 \text{ mol}}{60.096 \text{ g}}\right) = \underline{13.37859} \text{ kJ}$$

Heating the liquid
$$\left(\frac{2.68 \text{ J}}{\text{g}°\text{C}}\right)\left(\frac{k}{1,000}\right)(150.0 \text{ g})(82-(-90.0))°\text{C} = \underline{69.144} \text{ kJ}$$

Boiling the liquid
$$\left(\frac{42.11 \text{ kJ}}{\text{mol}}\right)(150.0 \text{ g})\left(\frac{1 \text{ mol}}{60.096 \text{ g}}\right) = \underline{105.106829} \text{ kJ}$$

Heating the vapor
$$\left(\frac{1.54 \text{ J}}{\text{g}°\text{C}}\right)\left(\frac{k}{1,000}\right)(150.0 \text{ g})(122-(82))°\text{C} = \underline{9.24} \text{ kJ}$$

The energy required is the sum of the four steps:

$$\text{Total} = (\underline{13.37859} + \underline{69.144} + \underline{105.106829} + \underline{9.24}) \text{ kJ} = 196.869482 = \mathbf{196.9 \text{ kJ}}$$

6.120 Natural gas is primarily methane (CH_4). Methane burns with the oxygen in air to produce carbon dioxide gas and water vapor. The reaction is

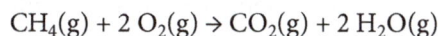

$$CH_4(g) + 2 \, O_2(g) \rightarrow CO_2(g) + 2 \, H_2O(g)$$

(a) Calculate the maximum number of grams of carbon dioxide that may form from the reaction of 15.2 g of methane with 15.2 g of oxygen. **(b)** What is the percent yield if the mixture in part (a) produces only 9.75 g of carbon dioxide?

Solution

(a) This is a limiting reagent problem, which begins with a determination of the limiting reactant (LR):

$$\text{Mole } CH_4 = \left(15.2 \text{ g } CH_4\right)\left(\frac{1 \text{ mol } CH_4}{16.043 \text{ g } CH_4}\right) = \left(\frac{0.94745 \text{ mol } CH_4}{1}\right) = 9.4745 \times 10^{-1}$$

$$\text{Mole } O_2 = \left(15.2 \text{ g } O_2\right)\left(\frac{1 \text{ mol } O_2}{31.998 \text{ g } O_2}\right) = \left(\frac{0.4750297 \text{ mol } O_2}{2}\right) = 2.3751 \times 10^{-1}$$

The final value for O_2 (2.3751×10^{-1}) is the smaller value; therefore, O_2 is the limiting reagent. Finishing the problem with O_2 (LR) gives

$$\text{Mass } H_2O = \left(0.4750297 \text{ mol } O_2\right)\left(\frac{1 \text{ mol } CO_2}{2 \text{ mol } O_2}\right)\left(\frac{44.009 \text{ g } CO_2}{1 \text{ mol } CO_2}\right) = 10.45279 = \mathbf{10.4 \text{ g } CO_2}$$

(b) Entering the values into the definition of *percent yield* gives the percent yield:

$$\frac{Actual \; yield}{Theoretical \; yield} \times 100\% = \frac{9.75 \text{ g } CO_2}{10.4 \text{ g } CO_2} \times 100\% = 93.75 = \mathbf{93.8\%}$$

CHAPTER 7

Electrons in Atoms

The successful completion of these problems requires the following six (6) items.

1. Wavelength may be in any length unit (meters, centimeters, or miles—or any other length unit, such as Å). A common mistake is to use measures other than units of length.
2. Do not confuse frequency, v, and velocity, v.
3. The de Broglie relationship is the only equation in this chapter that uses velocity, v.
4. The definition of *joule* ($J = kg\ m^2/s^2$) is a useful unit conversion for this chapter.
5. Carefully labeling the variables (E, m, λ, v, and v) can help you organize your thoughts. For example, if a problem contains any combination (known or unknown) of m, λ, and v, you will probably need to use the de Broglie relation ($\lambda = \dfrac{h}{mv}$).
6. Frequency, v, is measured in $1/s = s^{-1}$. Velocity, v, is measured in units of length/time, such as m/s, mph, or km per h).

Note: It will help you to work through the unit conversions in the following solutions to make sure you understand how they work in these problems.

Example Problems From the Text

Example Problem 7.1
What is the wavelength, in meters, of light with a frequency of 900.0 kHz?

Information

We have the frequency (900.0 kHz) of a certain kind of light, and we want to find the wavelength.

Connections

Using the equation $\lambda v = c$ and the speed of light (2.9979×10^8 m/s), we can convert the frequency to the wavelength.

Solution

Begin by listing and labeling the information in the problem. We need to find the wavelength (λ) given the frequency (v):

$$v = 900.0 \text{ kHz} = (900.0 \text{ ks}^{-1}) \qquad \lambda = ?$$

The equation $\lambda v = c$ relates these two variables to the speed of light ($c = 2.9979 \times 10^8$ m/s). Rearranging this equation to isolate the unknown gives

$$\lambda = c / v$$

Inserting the values for the speed of light and the frequency gives

$$\lambda = \left(\frac{2.9979 \times 10^8 \text{ m}/_{\text{s}}}{900.0 \text{ ks}^{-1}} \right)$$

Next, add a conversion factor to cancel the prefix *kilo-*. Now we can cancel all units except the desired unit of meters:

$$\lambda = \left(\frac{2.9979 \times 10^8 \text{ m}/_{\text{s}}}{900.0 \text{ ks}^{-1}} \right) \left(\frac{\text{k}}{10^3} \right) = \textbf{333.1 m}$$

Reality Check

The magnitude of the answer seems reasonable. The units and significant figures are correct.

Follow-Up Problem 7.1a

FM radio frequencies are measured in megahertz (MHz). Determine the wavelength in microns (μm) of a 98.2-MHz radio signal.

Information

The frequency of an FM radio wave (98.2 MHz = 98.2 Ms^{-1}); the question of what is the wavelength in microns (μm)

Connections

Using the equation $\lambda v = c$ and the speed of light (2.9979×10^8 m/s), we can convert the frequency to the wavelength.

Solution

Rearrange the equation $\lambda v = c$ and enter the appropriate values, including the appropriate conversions:

$$\lambda = \left(\frac{2.9979 \times 10^8 \text{ m}/_{\text{s}}}{98.2 \text{ Ms}^{-1}} \right) \left(\frac{\text{M}}{10^6} \right) \left(\frac{\propto}{10^{-6}} \right) = 3052851.3 = \textbf{3.05} \times \textbf{10}^6 \text{ } \boldsymbol{\mu}\textbf{m}$$

Reality Check

The magnitude of the answer seems reasonable. The units and significant figures are correct.

Follow-Up Problem 7.1b

Determine the frequency, in s^{-1}, of a radio wave with a wavelength of 0.250 miles.

Information

The wavelength of a radio wave—0.250 miles; the question of what is the frequency (s^{-1})

Connections

Using the equation $\lambda v = c$ and the speed of light (2.9979×10^8 m/s) to convert the wavelength to the frequency

Solution

Rearrange the equation $\lambda v = c$ and enter the appropriate values, including the appropriate conversion:

$$v = \left(\frac{2.9979 \times 10^8 \ ^m/_s}{0.250 \ \text{mi}} \right) \left(\frac{\text{mi}}{1609 \ \text{m}} \right) = 745282.78 = \mathbf{7.45 \times 10^5 \ s^{-1}}$$

Reality Check

The magnitude of the answer seems reasonable. The units and significant figures are correct.

Example Problem 7.2

Calculate the energy, in joules, of a photon having a frequency of $3.12 \times 10^{12} \ s^{-1}$.

Information

The frequency of the photon; the question of the photon's energy in joules

Connections

The equation $E = hv$ relates the energy of light to its frequency. (The value of Planck's constant, h, is 6.626×10^{-34} J $\cdot$ s.)

Solution

You are to find the photon's energy (E) given the frequency (v). The relationship $E = hv$ relates these two variables to Planck's constant. Inserting the given values into the equation gives

$$E = hv = (6.626 \times 10^{-34} \ \text{J} \cdot \text{s}) \ (3.12 \times 10^{12} \ s^{-1}) = 2.067312 \times 10^{-21}$$
$$= \mathbf{2.07 \times 10^{-21} \ J}$$

Reality Check

The magnitude of the answer seems reasonable. The units and significant figures are correct.

Follow-Up Problem 7.2a

What is the frequency, in s^{-1}, of a photon with an energy of 1.75×10^{-19} J?

Information

A photon that has an energy of 1.75×10^{-19} J; the question of what is the frequency (s^{-1}) of this photon

Connections

The equation $E = h\nu$ relates the energy of light to its frequency. (The value of Planck's constant, h, is 6.626×10^{-34} J · s.)

Solution

Rearrange the equation $E = h\nu$ and enter the appropriate values:

$$\text{Frequency} = \nu = \frac{E}{h} = \frac{1.75 \times 10^{-19}\ \text{J}}{6.626 \times 10^{-34}\ \text{J} \cdot \text{s}} = 2.64111 \times 10^{14} = \mathbf{2.64 \times 10^{14}\ s^{-1}}$$

Reality Check

The magnitude of the answer seems reasonable. The units and significant figures are correct.

Follow-Up Problem 7.2b

Calculate the energy, in joules, of a photon of light having a wavelength of 475 nm.

Information

A photon that has a wavelength of 475 nm; the question of what is the energy (J) of this photon

Connections

The equations $E = h\nu$ and $\lambda\nu = c$ and the speed of light $(2.9979 \times 10^8$ m/s) relate the energy of light to its frequency. (The value of Planck's constant, h, is 6.626×10^{-34} J · s.) It is possible to combine these two equations to $E = hc/\lambda$.

Solution

Using the combined equation, $E = hc/\lambda$, rearrange and enter the appropriate values, including a conversion.

$$E = \frac{hc}{\lambda} = \frac{\left(6.626 \times 10^{-34}\ \text{J} \cdot \text{s}\right)\left(2.9979 \times 10^8\ \text{m}/_{\text{s}}\right)}{475\ \text{nm}}\left(\frac{\text{n}}{10^{-9}}\right) = 4.18191 \times 10^{-19} = \mathbf{4.18 \times 10^{-19}\ J}$$

Reality Check

The magnitude of the answer seems reasonable. The units and significant figures are correct.

Example Problem 7.3

Calculate the wavelength, in meters, of a 125-pound sprinter running at 15.0 miles per hour.

Information

We have the sprinter's weight (125 pounds) and velocity (15.0 miles per hour) from which to discover the wavelength in meters.

Connections

The de Broglie relationship $(\lambda = \dfrac{h}{m\nu})$ relates the given data to wavelength. (The value of Planck's constant is 6.626×10^{-34} J · s.)

Solution

Assigning values to the terms in the de Broglie relationship gives

$$\lambda = ? \qquad h = 6.626 \times 10^{-34} \text{ J} \cdot \text{s} \qquad m = 125 \text{ lb} \qquad v = 15.0 \text{ mi/h}$$

Inserting these values into the equation yields

$$\lambda = \frac{6.626 \times 10^{-34} \text{ J} \cdot \text{s}}{(125 \text{ lb})\left(15.0 \text{ mi/h}\right)}$$

At this point, none of the units will cancel, so we need to insert conversion factors until only the meters remain. It is possible to add the conversion factors in any order. We will begin with the definition of *joule* ($J = kg \cdot m^2/s^2$):

$$\lambda = \frac{6.626 \times 10^{-34} \text{ J} \cdot \text{s}}{(125 \text{ lb})\left(15.0 \text{ mi/h}\right)} \left(\frac{kg\,m^2/s^2}{J}\right)$$

This eliminates joules (J) from the equation. The seconds in Planck's constant and one of the seconds in the *joule* definition cancel. We will now use 1 h = 3,600 seconds to construct another conversion factor:

$$\lambda = \frac{6.626 \times 10^{-34} \text{ J} \cdot \text{s}}{(125 \text{ lb})\left(15.0 \text{ mi/h}\right)} \left(\frac{kg\,m^2/s^2}{J}\right)\left(\frac{3,600 \text{ s}}{1 \text{ h}}\right)$$

This removes the remaining second from the *joule* definition and the hour from the velocity. The remaining units are $kg \cdot m^2 / lb \cdot mi$. Using 1 mile = 1.6093 km, we get

$$\lambda = \frac{6.626 \times 10^{-34} \text{ J} \cdot \text{s}}{(125 \text{ lb})\left(15.0 \text{ mi/h}\right)} \left(\frac{kg\,m^2/s^2}{J}\right)\left(\frac{3,600 \text{ s}}{1 \text{ h}}\right)\left(\frac{1 \text{ mi}}{1.6093 \text{ km}}\right)$$

This conversion cancels the miles unit, one of the meter units in the *joule* definition, and the kilo in the *joule* definition. We now have $g \cdot m/lb$ as our units. Our next conversion factor makes use of 1 lb = 453.59 g:

$$\lambda = \frac{6.626 \times 10^{-34} \text{ J} \cdot \text{s}}{(125 \text{ lb})\left(15.0 \text{ mi/h}\right)} \left(\frac{kg\,m^2/s^2}{J}\right)\left(\frac{3,600 \text{ s}}{1 \text{ h}}\right)\left(\frac{1 \text{ mi}}{1.6093 \text{ km}}\right)\left(\frac{1 \text{ lb}}{453.59 \text{ g}}\right)$$

This final conversion factor cancels all units except length (meters). (The k from kg cancels the k from km; otherwise, you need to multiply your result by 1,000 to change kilograms to grams and divide the result by 1,000 to change kilometers to meters—the same as multiplying by 1,000/1,000). Now we have achieved the desired unit, a good indication that the setup is correct. Multiplying and dividing the numerical values with a calculator gives

$$\lambda = 1.742818565 \times 10^{-36} = \mathbf{1.74 \times 10^{-36} \text{ m}}$$

Reality Check

The magnitude of the answer is reasonable. The units are as requested, and the significant figures are correct. (See chapter 1 "The Tools of Chemistry" for a review of the kilogram/kilometer cancellation.)

Follow-Up Problem 7.3a

Determine the wavelength, in meters, of a sodium atom traveling at 1.75×10^3 m/s.

Information

A sodium atom moving at 1.75×10^3 m/s; the question of what is the wavelength (m) of this sodium atom

Connections

The de Broglie relationship ($\lambda = \dfrac{h}{mv}$) relates the given data to wavelength. (The value of Planck's constant is 6.626×10^{-34} J · s.)

Solution

Using $\lambda = \dfrac{h}{mv}$, rearrange and enter the appropriate values, including conversions:

$$\lambda = \frac{6.626 \times 10^{-34} \text{ J} \cdot \text{s}}{(22.99 \text{ amu})\left(1.75 \times 10^3 \text{ }{}^{m}\!/\!{}_{s}\right)} \left| \frac{{}^{kg\,m^2}\!/\!{}_{s^2}}{J} \right| \left(\frac{6.022 \times 10^{23} \text{ amu}}{1 \text{ g}} \right) \left(\frac{1{,}000}{k} \right) = 9.9177958 \times 10^{-12}$$

$$= 9.92 \times 10^{-12} \text{ m}$$

Reality Check

The magnitude of the answer is reasonable. The units are as requested, and the significant figures are correct.

Follow-Up Problem 7.3b

What is the velocity, in meters per second, of an electron with a wavelength of 0.500 Å? The mass of an electron is 5.486×10^{-4} amu.

Information

An electron with a wavelength of 0.500 Å and a mass of 5.486×10^{-4} amu; the question of what is the velocity (m/s) of this electron

Connections

The de Broglie relationship ($\lambda = \dfrac{h}{mv}$) relates the given data to velocity. (The value of Planck's constant is 6.626×10^{-34} J · s.)

Solution

Using $\lambda = \dfrac{h}{m\lambda}$, rearrange and enter the appropriate values, including conversions:

$$\text{Velocity} = v = \frac{h}{m\lambda}$$

$$= \frac{6.626 \times 10^{-34} \text{ J} \cdot \text{s}}{\left(5.486 \times 10^{-4} \text{ amu}\right)\left(0.500 \text{ Å}\right)} \left| \frac{{}^{kg\,m^2}\!/\!{}_{s^2}}{J} \right| \left(\frac{6.022 \times 10^{23} \text{ amu}}{1 \text{ g}} \right) \left(\frac{1000}{k} \right) \left(\frac{1 \text{ Å}}{10^{-10} \text{ m}} \right)$$

$$= 14546763 = 1.45 \times 10^7 \text{ m/s}$$

Reality Check

The magnitude of the answer is reasonable. The units are as requested, and the significant figures are correct.

Example Problem 7.4

What are the possible values of m_l if $n = 5$ and $l = 3$?

Information

We have the values of n (5) and l (3) from which we need to find the values of m_l.

Connections

The rules for assigning quantum numbers will lead us to the answer.

Solution

The values of m_l depend directly upon l, so the value of n is unimportant in this case. Since $l = 3$ and $m_l = -l$ to 0 to $+l$, $m_l = $ **−3, −2, −1, 0, +1, +2, and +3**.

Reality Check

The results are consistent with the rules for assigning quantum numbers.

Follow-Up Problem 7.4a

Predict the possible values of l when $n = 4$.

Information

The value of n, which is 4; the question of what are the possible values of l

Connections

The rules for assigning quantum numbers

Solution

The rule for the l quantum number is $l = 0, 1, 2, \ldots (n - 1)$; therefore, if $n = 4$, then $(n - 1) = 3$. This leads to $l = $ **0, 1, 2, 3 (= n −1)**.

Reality Check

The results are consistent with the rules for assigning quantum numbers.

Follow-Up Problem 7.4b

Determine the possible values of m_s when $n = 5$, $l = 2$, and $m_l = 0$.

Information

The given quantum numbers $n = 5$, $l = 2$, and $m_l = 0$; the question of what are the possible values of m_s

Connections

The rules for assigning quantum numbers

Solution

The values for m_s can be only **+1/2 or −1/2**.

Reality Check

The results are consistent with the rules for assigning quantum numbers.

Example Problem 7.5

The emission spectrum of cesium, Cs, has a blue line located at 455.5 nm. Determine the frequency of this light in s^{-1}.

Information

We have the wavelength (455.5 nm) and want to determine the frequency in s^{-1}.

Connections

The equation $\lambda v = c$ connects wavelength to frequency (given the speed of light, 2.9979×10^8 m/s).

Solution

Summarizing the information from the problem gives

$$\lambda = 455.5 \text{ nm} \qquad v = ? \qquad c = 2.9979 \times 10^8 \text{ m/s}$$

We need to rearrange the equation to isolate the frequency (v):

$$v = c / \lambda$$

Then we enter the values:

$$v = \left(\frac{2.9979 \times 10^8 \, ^m\!/_s}{455.5 \text{ nm}} \right)$$

To get the correct final units, we need to eliminate the *nano-*, creating a conversion factor from $n = 10^{-9}$:

$$v = \left(\frac{2.9979 \times 10^8 \, ^m\!/_s}{455.5 \text{ nm}} \right)\left(\frac{n}{10^{-9}} \right) = 6.581558727 \times 10^{14} = \mathbf{6.582 \times 10^{14} \text{ s}^{-1}}$$

Reality Check

The answer has a reasonable magnitude. The units are as requested, and the significant figures are correct.

Follow-Up Problem 7.5a

The emission spectrum of thallium, Tl, has a green line at 535.0 nm. Calculate the frequency of this light in 1/s.

Information

In the emission spectrum, a green line appears at 535.0 nm; the question of what is the frequency (1/s) of the light

Connections

The equation $\lambda v = c$ connects wavelength to frequency (given the speed of light, 2.9979×10^8 m/s).

Solution

Rearrange $\lambda v = c$ and enter the appropriate values, including a conversion:

$$v = \left(\frac{2.9979 \times 10^8 \, ^m\!/_s}{535.0 \text{ nm}} \right)\left(\frac{n}{10^{-9}} \right) = 5.60355 \times 10^{14} = \mathbf{5.604 \times 10^{14} \text{ s}^{-1}}$$

Reality Check

The answer has a reasonable magnitude. The units are as requested, and the significant figures are correct.

Follow-Up Problem 7.5b

The absorption spectrum of indium, In, has an indigo line at 410.2 nm. What is the energy of a photon of this light in joules?

Information

In the emission spectrum, an indigo line appears at 410.2 nm; the question of what is the energy (J) of the photon

Connections

The equation $E = hc/\lambda$ connects energy to wavelength (given the speed of light, 2.9979×10^8 m/s, and Planck's constant, 6.626×10^{-34} J · s)

Solution

Use $E = hc/\lambda$ and enter the appropriate values, including a conversion:

$$E = \frac{hc}{\lambda} = \frac{\left(6.626 \times 10^{-34} \text{ J} \cdot \text{s}\right)\left(2.9979 \times 10^8 \text{ m}/\text{s}\right)}{410.2 \text{ nm}}\left(\frac{\text{n}}{10^{-9}}\right) = 4.8425 \times 10^{-19} = \mathbf{4.843 \times 10^{-19} \text{ J}}$$

Reality Check

The answer has a reasonable magnitude. The units are as requested, and the significant figures are correct.

Example Problem 7.6

Determine the percent by mass of oxygen in potassium chlorate.

Information

We have the name of the compound (potassium chlorate) from which to calculate the percent by mass of oxygen.

Connections

Useful connections are the definition (equation) for *mass percent* from chapter 3, nomenclature rules from which to discover the chemical formula, and the periodic table from which to obtain atomic weights.

Solution

To determine the percent by mass of an element, you need to know how much of that element is present in a mole of the compound (section 3.4). The relationship is

$$\text{Mass \% of element} = \frac{(Moles\ element)(Molar\ mass\ element)}{(Molar\ mass\ compound)} \times 100\%$$

For oxygen in potassium chlorate, this relationship becomes

$$\text{Mass \% of element} = \left(\frac{(3 \text{ mol oxygen})\left(\dfrac{16.00 \text{ g oxygen}}{\text{mol oxygen}}\right)}{122.55 \text{ g KClO}_3}\right)(100\%)$$

$$= 39.16768666 = \textbf{39.17\% oxygen}$$

Reality Check
The magnitude of the calculated value is reasonable, and the units and significant figures are correct.

Follow-Up Problem 7.6a
Calculate the percent by mass of oxygen in potassium perchlorate.

Information
The question of what is the mass percent of oxygen in potassium perchlorate

Connections
Moles are the key.

Solution
To determine the percent by mass of an element, you need to know how much of that element is present in a mole of the compound (section 3.4). The relationship is

$$\text{Mass \% of element} = \frac{(\textit{Moles element})(\textit{Molar mass element})}{(\textit{Molar mass compound})} \times 100\%$$

For oxygen in potassium chlorate, this relationship becomes

$$\text{Mass \% of element} = \left(\frac{(4 \text{ mol oxygen})\left(\dfrac{16.00 \text{ g oxygen}}{\text{mol oxygen}}\right)}{138.55 \text{ g KClO}_4}\right)(100\%) = 46.1927 = \textbf{46.19\% oxygen}$$

Reality Check
The magnitude of the calculated value is reasonable, and the units and significant figures are correct.

Follow-Up Problem 7.6b
How many grams of oxygen gas will 1.00 g of potassium chlorate produce, and how many grams of oxygen gas will 1.00 g of potassium perchlorate produce? Assume all the oxygen in the solid becomes oxygen gas.

Information
Two samples: 1.00 g of potassium chlorate and 1.00 g of potassium perchlorate; the questions of how many grams of oxygen each sample can produce

Connections
Moles are the key.

Solution

$KClO_3$:

$$\text{Mass O} = \left(1.00 \text{ g } KClO_3\right)\left(\frac{1 \text{ mol } KClO_3}{122.55 \text{ g } KClO_3}\right)\left(\frac{3 \text{ mol O}}{1 \text{ mol } KClO_3}\right)\left(\frac{16.00 \text{ g O}}{1 \text{ mol O}}\right) = 0.391677 = \mathbf{0.392 \text{ g}}$$

$KClO_4$:

$$\text{Mass O} = \left(1.00 \text{ g } KClO_4\right)\left(\frac{1 \text{ mol } KClO_4}{138.55 \text{ g } KClO_4}\right)\left(\frac{4 \text{ mol O}}{1 \text{ mol } KClO_4}\right)\left(\frac{16.00 \text{ g O}}{1 \text{ mol O}}\right) = 0.461927 = \mathbf{0.462 \text{ g}}$$

Reality Check

The magnitude of the calculated value is reasonable, and the units and significant figures are correct. Note: We can determine the answers using the answers to Example Problem 7.6 and Follow-Up Problem 7.6a.

END-OF-CHAPTER PROBLEMS

7.1 Properties of Light

7.1 Explain why electrons are the key to understanding the behavior of atoms.

Solution

The interactions of the outer electrons on an atom are the basis of all chemical reactions.

7.2 Spectroscopy

7.3 Name three examples of radiant energy.

Solution

Three examples would be light from a light bulb, heat from a heater, and gamma rays from a radioactive substance. (Obviously, there are many other examples.)

7.6 What is an angstrom?

Solution

An angstrom is a unit of length: $1 \text{ Å} = 10^{-10} \text{ m}$.

7.8 Give the relationship between wavelength and frequency for light.

Solution

The product of wavelength and frequency is the speed of light, or $c = \lambda v$.

7.9 If the wavelength doubles, by what factor does the frequency change?

Solution

If the wavelength doubles, the frequency must be halved for the relationship $c = \lambda v$ to hold, as there is an inverse relationship between the wavelength and the frequency.

7.11 FM radio transmissions range from 87.5 to 108.0 MHz. Calculate the range of wavelengths that this represents in centimeters.

Information
Two frequencies (87.5 MHz and 108.0 MHz); the question of what wavelengths these frequencies represent

Connections
$c = \lambda v$

Solution
Rearrange $c = \lambda v$ and enter the appropriate values and conversions:

$$\lambda = \frac{c}{v} = \left(\frac{2.9979 \times 10^8 \text{ ms}^{-1}}{87.5 \text{ MHz}}\right)\left(\frac{M}{10^6}\right)\left(\frac{Hz}{s^{-1}}\right)\left(\frac{c}{0.01}\right) = 3.42617 \times 10^2 = \mathbf{3.43 \times 10^2 \text{ cm}}$$

$$\lambda = \frac{c}{v} = \left(\frac{2.9979 \times 10^8 \text{ ms}^{-1}}{108.0 \text{ MHz}}\right)\left(\frac{M}{10^6}\right)\left(\frac{Hz}{s^{-1}}\right)\left(\frac{c}{0.01}\right) = 2.775833 \times 10^2 = \mathbf{2.776 \times 10^2 \text{ cm}}$$

7.13 (a) A beam of light has a frequency of 3.55×10^{13}/s. What is the wavelength of this light in nanometers? **(b)** Calculate the frequency of a light wave with a wavelength of 0.500 pm.

Information
(a) The frequency of 3.55×10^{13}/s; the question of what is the wavelength (nm). **(b)** The wavelength of 0.500 pm; the question of what is the frequency

Connections
$c = \lambda v$

Solution
Rearrange $c = \lambda v$ and enter the appropriate values and conversions:

(a) $\lambda = \dfrac{c}{v} = \left(\dfrac{2.9979 \times 10^8 \text{ ms}^{-1}}{3.55 \times 10^{13} \text{ s}^{-1}}\right)\left(\dfrac{n}{10^{-9}}\right) = 8.4447887 \times 10^3 = \mathbf{8.44 \times 10^3 \text{ nm}}$

(b) $v = \dfrac{c}{\lambda} = \left(\dfrac{2.9979 \times 10^8 \text{ ms}^{-1}}{0.500 \text{ pm}}\right)\left(\dfrac{p}{10^{-12}}\right) = 5.9958 \times 10^{20} = \mathbf{6.00 \times 10^{20} \text{ s}^{-1}}$

7.16 (a) How long does it take a radio wave to travel 3,000 miles across the United States? **(b)** How does the time it takes a radio wave to travel this distance compare to the time it takes a microwave to cross the United States?

Solution
(a) This is a unit conversion calculation using the speed of light:

$$\text{Time} = (3{,}000 \text{ mi})\left(\frac{1{,}609 \text{ m}}{1 \text{ mi}}\right)\left(\frac{s}{3.00 \times 10^8 \text{ m}}\right) = 1.609 \times 10^{-2} = \mathbf{1.6 \times 10^{-2} \text{ s}}$$

(b) Both radio waves and microwaves take the same amount of time since they are traveling at the same speed.

7.3 Emission and Absorption Spectra

7.18 **(a)** Give the relationship between frequency and energy. **(b)** Give the relationship between energy and wavelength.

Solution

The two equations are

(a) $E = h\nu$ and **(b)** $E = \dfrac{hc}{\lambda}$

7.21 What does *quantized* mean?

Solution

Quantized means that only certain values are allowed.

7.23 You get an answer of 5.0×10^{19} J for a single photon of light. Explain why this is an unreasonable value.

Solution

Photons normally have very small amounts of energy; 5.0×10^{19} J is a very large amount of energy, which makes the value incompatible with normal photon energies.

7.25 The emission spectrum of sodium has a line with a wavelength of 589.0 nm. **(a)** What color is this light? **(b)** How does this wavelength compare to the wavelength of the corresponding transition in the absorption spectrum?

Solution

(a) Yellow (see **figure 7.2a**); **(b)** It is the same as the other wavelength, as the transition involves the same two energy states.

7.27 In addition to the wavelength, what information is needed to calculate the energy of a photon of light?

Solution

The values of Planck's constant and the speed of light are needed, because the equation is $E = \dfrac{hc}{\lambda}$.

7.30 Waves used for AM radio transmissions are between 530 kHz and 1,710 kHz. Determine the energy of each of these limiting values in joules.

Information

The two frequencies 530 kHz and 1710 kHz; the questions of what are the energies (J)

Connections

$E = h\nu$

Solution

Enter the appropriate values and conversions into $E = h\nu$:

$$E = h\nu = \left(6.626 \times 10^{-34}\ \text{Js}\right)\left(530\ \text{kHz}\right)\left(\frac{10^3}{k}\right)\left(\frac{s^{-1}}{Hz}\right) = 3.51178 \times 10^{-28} = \mathbf{3.5 \times 10^{-28}\ J}$$

$$E = h\nu = \left(6.626 \times 10^{-34}\ \text{Js}\right)\left(1{,}710\ \text{kHz}\right)\left(\frac{10^3}{k}\right)\left(\frac{s^{-1}}{Hz}\right) = 1.133046 \times 10^{-27} = \mathbf{1.13 \times 10^{-27}\ J}$$

7.33 Many organic compounds have a hydrogen atom attached to an oxygen atom. This arrangement absorbs infrared radiation with a wavelength near 3.0 µm. How many joules does a photon of 3.0 µm radiation supply?

Information

A wavelength of 3.0 µm; the question of how much energy (J) this is

Connections

$$E = \frac{hc}{\lambda}$$

Solution

Enter the appropriate values and conversion into $E = \frac{hc}{\lambda}$:

$$E = \frac{hc}{\lambda} = \left[\frac{\left(6.63 \times 10^{-34} \text{ Js}\right)\left(3.00 \times 10^8 \text{ ms}^{-1}\right)}{3.0 \text{ µm}} \right]\left(\frac{\mu}{10^{-6}} \right) = 6.63 \times 10^{-20} = \mathbf{6.6 \times 10^{-20} \text{ J}}$$

7.36 Electromagnetic radiation may be used to break the bonds between atoms. This process is known as photodissociation. To photodissociate carbon monoxide (CO) requires 1,072 kJ/mol. Determine the wavelength of a photon of radiation with sufficient energy to break up a single carbon monoxide molecule.

Information

Energy of 1,072 kJ/mol; the question of what is the necessary wavelength

Connections

$$E = \frac{hc}{\lambda}$$

Solution

Rearrange the equation $E = hc/\lambda$, and enter the appropriate values (Avogadro's number is necessary to convert from a mole to a single photon):

$$\lambda = \frac{hc}{E} = \frac{\left(6.626 \times 10^{-34} \text{ Js}\right)\left(2.9979 \times 10^8 \text{ m/s}\right)}{1,072 \text{ kJ/mol}}\left(\frac{k}{10^3} \right)\left(\frac{6.022 \times 10^{23}}{\text{mol}} \right) = 1.11587 \times 10^{-7}$$

$$= \mathbf{1.116 \times 10^{-7} \text{ m}}$$

7.38 High-powered lasers emit exceedingly intense beams of high-energy light for very short periods. A high-powered laser emits a 75-ps pulse (75 picoseconds), which has a total energy of 25 joules. The wavelength emitted by the laser has a wavelength of 7500 Å. How many photons are in the pulse?

Information

Information about a laser: 75-ps pulse, 25 J, and 7500 Å; the question of how many photons are present

Connections

$$E = \frac{hc}{\lambda}$$

Solution

The energy per photon comes from the equation $E = \dfrac{hc}{\lambda}$. Enter the appropriate values and the conversion:

$$E = \frac{hc}{\lambda} = \left| \frac{\left(6.626 \times 10^{-34} \text{ Js}\right)\left(2.9979 \times 10^{8} \text{ ms}^{-1}\right)}{7{,}500 \text{ Å photons}} \right| \left(\frac{1 \text{ Å}}{10^{-10} \text{ m}} \right) = 2.64854 \times 10^{-19}$$

$$= 2.6 \times 10^{-19} \text{ J/photon}$$

The total energy (25 J) divided by the energy per photon gives the number of photons:

$$\text{Photons} = \frac{25 \text{ J}}{2.64854 \times 10^{-19} \text{ J/photon}} = 9.4391 \times 10^{19} = \mathbf{9.4 \times 10^{19} \text{ photons}}$$

7.4 Bohr's Atomic Model

7.41 **(a)** What type of spectrum results when an electron moves from the ground state to an excited state? **(b)** What type of spectrum results when an electron moves from an excited state to the ground state?

Solution

(a) The movement from the ground state (lowest) to an excited state (higher) gives an absorption spectrum. **(b)** The movement from an excited state (higher) to the ground state (lowest) gives an emission spectrum.

7.43 Each of the following processes is accompanied by the gain or loss of energy. Decide if energy is gained or lost in each case. **(a)** An electron in the $n = 3$ shell of iron is completely removed from the atom. **(b)** An electron moves from the $n = 2$ shell to the $n = 1$ shell in a copper atom. **(c)** An electron moves from an orbital with a radius of 0.537 nm to one with a radius of 0.062 nm.

Solution

(a) There is a <u>gain</u> in energy because the electron is moving away from the nucleus. **(b)** Energy is <u>lost</u> because the electron is moving closer to the nucleus. **(c)** Energy is <u>lost</u> because the electron is moving closer to the nucleus.

7.5 The de Broglie Relationship

7.46 **(a)** What is the difference between v and ν? **(b)** What are typical units for v and ν?

Solution

(a) The symbol v represents the velocity, while the symbol ν represents the frequency.

(b) Velocity typically has units of m/s, while frequency usually has the unit 1/s.

7.48 **(a)** If two objects with different masses are moving at the same velocity, which one will have the shorter wavelength? **(b)** If two objects with different velocities have the same mass, which one will have the shorter wavelength?

Solution

The relationship is $\lambda = \dfrac{h}{mv}$, so both mass and velocity are inversely related to the wavelength.
(a) The heavier object will have the shorter wavelength. **(b)** The object with the greater velocity will have the shorter wavelength.

7.50 State the uncertainty principle.

Solution

The **uncertainty principle** states that it is impossible to accurately determine both the position and the momentum of an electron simultaneously.

7.53 The de Broglie relationship may be used to determine the wavelength of any object. Determine the de Broglie wavelength of each of the following: **(a)** a 68-kg person sprinting at 10.0 km per hour; **(b)** a 5.25-ounce baseball traveling at 95 mph; **(c)** a helium atom traveling at 2,500 mph

Information

The data **(a)** $m = 68$ kg and $v = 10.0$ km/h, **(b)** $m = 5.25$ oz and $v = 95$ mi/h, and **(c)** a He atom with $v = 2,500$ mi/h; the questions of what is the de Broglie wavelength in each case

Connections

$$\lambda = \frac{h}{mv}$$

Solution

In all three parts, enter the appropriate values into $\lambda = \dfrac{h}{mv}$ and add the appropriate conversions:

(a) $\lambda = \dfrac{h}{mv} = \left[\dfrac{6.626 \times 10^{-34} \text{ Js}}{(68 \text{ kg})\left(\dfrac{10.0 \text{ km}}{h}\right)}\right]\left[\dfrac{\left(\dfrac{\text{kg m}^2}{\text{s}^2}\right)}{J}\right]\left(\dfrac{3,600 \text{ s}}{h}\right)\left(\dfrac{k}{1,000}\right) = 3.507882 \times 10^{-36} = \mathbf{3.5 \times 10^{-36} \text{ m}}$

(b) $\lambda = \dfrac{h}{mv} = \left[\dfrac{6.626 \times 10^{-34} \text{ Js}}{(5.25 \text{ oz})\left(\dfrac{95 \text{ mi}}{h}\right)}\right]\left[\dfrac{\left(\dfrac{\text{kg m}^2}{\text{s}^2}\right)}{J}\right]\left(\dfrac{3,600 \text{ s}}{h}\right)\left(\dfrac{1 \text{ mi}}{1,609 \text{ m}}\right)\left(\dfrac{16 \text{ oz}}{1 \text{ lb}}\right)\left(\dfrac{2.205 \text{ lb}}{1 \text{ kg}}\right)$

$= 1.048681 \times 10^{-34} = \mathbf{1.0 \times 10^{-34} \text{ m}}$

(c) $\lambda = \dfrac{h}{mv} = \left[\dfrac{6.626 \times 10^{-34} \text{ Js}}{(4.0026 \text{ amu})\left(\dfrac{2,500 \text{ mi}}{h}\right)}\right]\left[\dfrac{\left(\dfrac{\text{kg m}^2}{\text{s}^2}\right)}{J}\right]\left(\dfrac{3,600 \text{ s}}{h}\right)\left(\dfrac{6.022 \times 10^{23} \text{ amu}}{1 \text{ g}}\right)\left(\dfrac{1,000}{k}\right)\left(\dfrac{1 \text{ mi}}{1,609 \text{ m}}\right)$

$= 8.92188 \times 10^{-11} = \mathbf{8.9 \times 10^{-11} \text{ m}}$

Only part (c) is long enough to be measured directly.

7.55 A transmission electron microscope may accelerate electrons to speeds nearly that of light. In one experiment, the electrons were found to have a de Broglie wavelength of 0.037 Å. How fast were these electrons moving (in m/s)? The mass of an electron is 9.109×10^{-28} g.

Information

An electron's wavelength (0.037 Å) and mass (9.109×10^{-28} g); the question of what is the velocity (m/s)

Connections

$$\lambda = \frac{h}{mv}$$

Solution

Rearrange $\lambda = \dfrac{h}{mv}$ and enter the appropriate values plus the appropriate conversions:

$$v = \frac{h}{m\lambda} = \left[\frac{6.626 \times 10^{-34} \text{ Js}}{(9.109 \times 10^{-28} \text{ g})(0.037 \text{ Å})}\right]\left[\frac{\left(\frac{\text{kg m}^2}{\text{s}^2}\right)}{\text{J}}\right]\left(\frac{1{,}000}{\text{k}}\right)\left(\frac{1 \text{ Å}}{10^{-10} \text{ m}}\right) = 1.96598 \times 10^8$$

$$= 2.0 \times 10^8 \text{ m/s}$$

7.6 Schrödinger's Wave Equation

7.58 What is an electron cloud?

Solution

Scientists commonly calculate probability densities at the 90% probability level, meaning that the size of the orbital is such that the electron is likely to be found within that volume of space 90% of the time (or some other convenient percentage). We sometimes call these electron density plots **electron clouds,** and we quite commonly use them in representing the probabilities of finding various electrons within an atom.

7.7 Quantum Numbers

7.59 List the names and symbols for the four quantum numbers.

Solution

1. The **principal quantum number, n**
2. The **angular momentum quantum number, l**
3. The **magnetic quantum number, m_l**
4. The **electron spin quantum number, m_s**

7.61 Each of the quantum numbers gives information on the features of an orbital or an electron. **(a)** What feature of an orbital does the principal quantum number, n, describe? **(b)** What feature of an orbital does the angular momentum quantum number, l, describe? **(c)** What feature of an orbital does the magnetic quantum number, m_l, describe? **(d)** What feature of an electron does the electron spin quantum number, m_s, describe?

Solution

(a) The principle quantum number gives the energy of the electron (energy level).

(b) The angular momentum quantum number gives the shape of the orbital occupied by the electron.

(c) The magnetic quantum number gives the orientation of the orbital occupied by the electron.

(d) The electron-spin quantum number gives the "direction" the electron is spinning.

7.65 Give the letter designation for each of the following values of l: 0, 1, 2, and 3.

Solution
The designations are $l = 0$ is s, $l = 1$ is p, $l = 2$ is d, and $l = 3$ is f.

7.67 **(a)** List the allowed values for n, l, and m_l for each electron in a 5d subshell. **(b)** List the allowed values for n, l, and m_l for each electron in the third shell.

Information
For **(a)**, a 5d subshell; for **(b)**, the third shell; for each, the question of what are the allowed values for n, l, and m_l for each electron

Connections
The rules for quantum numbers

Solution
(a) The value of n is 5 for all electrons. The values of l are 0, 1, 2, 3, and 4.

If $l = 0$, then $m_l = 0$.
If $l = 1$, then $m_l = -1$, 0, or +1.
If $l = 2$, then $m_l = -2, -1, 0, +1$, or +2.
If $l = 3$, then $m_l = -3, -2, -1, 0, +1, +2$, or +3.
If $l = 4$, then $m_l = -4, -3, -2, -1, 0, +1, +2, +3$, or +4.

The value of m_s may be +1/2 or $-1/2$.

(b) The value of n is 3 for all electrons, which allows the values of l to be 0, 1, and 2.

If $l = 0$, then $m_l = 0$.
If $l = 1$, then $m_l = -1$, 0, or +1.
If $l = 2$, then $m_l = -2, -1, 0, +1$, or +2.

The value of m_s may be +1/2 or $-1/2$.

7.8 Applications and Extensions
7.73 How does the calcium spectrum of a sample of calcium chloride compare to the calcium spectrum of a sample of calcium nitrate?

Solution
The calcium spectrum will always be the same, regardless of the source of the calcium.

7.75 In addition to a line at 455.5 nm, the spectrum of cesium, Cs, has a line at 459.3 nm. **(a)** Determine the frequency in 1/s for the 459.3-nm line. **(b)** Determine the energy, in joules, for a photon of the 459.3-nm emission line.

Information
The two wavelengths 455.5 nm and 459.3 nm; the questions of what is the frequency (1/s) of the 455.5-nm line and what is the energy (J) of the 459.3-nm line

Connections
$c = \lambda v$; $E = hv$

Solution

(a) Rearrange $c = \lambda v$ and enter the appropriate values and a conversion:

$$v = \frac{c}{\lambda} = \left(\frac{2.9979 \times 10^8 \text{ ms}^{-1}}{459.3 \text{ nm}}\right)\left(\frac{n}{10^{-9}}\right) = 6.527106 \times 10^{14} = \mathbf{6.527 \times 10^{14} \text{ s}^{-1}}$$

(b) Enter the appropriate values, including the answer to part (a), into $E = hv$ (or use $E = hc/\lambda$):

$$E = hv = \left(6.626 \times 10^{-34} \text{ Js}\right)\left(6.527106 \times 10^{14} \text{ s}^{-1}\right) = 4.32486 \times 10^{-19} = \mathbf{4.325 \times 10^{-19} \text{ J}}$$

7.77 Scientists use atomic absorption spectroscopy to analyze various materials. The sample is vaporized by various means, and the amounts of light of specific wavelengths absorbed by the vapor indicate what elements are present in what amounts. The wavelengths that indicate the presence of the alkali and alkaline earth metals are

Li	670.8 nm	Be	234.9 nm
Na	589.0 nm	Mg	285.2 nm
K	766.5 nm	Ca	422.7 nm
Rb	780.0 nm	Sr	460.7 nm
Cs	852.1 nm	Ba	553.6 nm

(a) For the elements absorbing light in the visible portion of the spectrum, determine the color of the radiation absorbed. **(b)** Rank these elements in order of increasing energy of the absorbed radiation.

Solution

(a) Wavelengths in the infrared or ultraviolet portions of the spectrum do not have color.

Li	red	Be	ultraviolet
Na	yellow	Mg	ultraviolet
K	infrared	Ca	indigo
Rb	infrared	Sr	blue
Cs	infrared	Ba	green

(b) Increasing energy means decreasing wavelength. Therefore, **Cs < Rb < K < Li < Na < Ba <Sr < Ca < Mg < Be.**

7.80 Potassium chlorate, $KClO_3$, may substitute for the potassium nitrate in gunpowder (see Problem 7.79). Unlike potassium nitrate, which releases only some of its oxygen to produce potassium nitrite, potassium chlorate decomposes to release all its oxygen. How many grams of potassium chlorate are needed to supply the same quantity of oxygen as 15.0 g of potassium nitrate?

Information

15.0 grams of KNO_3; the question of how many grams of $KClO_3$ are needed

Connections

Moles are the key.

Solution

We need to determine the balanced chemical equations. Use the Nomenclature Resource and follow the normal rules for balancing chemical equations:

$$2 \, KNO_3(s) \rightarrow 2 \, KNO_2(s) + O_2(g)$$

$$2 \, KClO_3(s) \rightarrow 2 \, KCl(s) + 3 \, O_2(g)$$

The stoichiometry requires a gram to mole conversion (using the molar mass), several mole-to-mole conversions, and finally a mole to gram conversion (using the molar mass):

$$\text{Mass } KClO_3 = \left(15.0 \, g \, KNO_3\right)\left(\frac{1 \, mol \, KNO_3}{101.102 \, g \, KNO_3}\right)\left(\frac{1 \, mol \, O_2}{2 \, mol \, KNO_3}\right)\left(\frac{2 \, mol \, KClO_3}{3 \, mol \, O_2}\right)\left(\frac{122.548 \, g \, KClO_3}{1 \, mol \, KClO_3}\right)$$

$$= 6.060612 = \textbf{6.06 g } \textbf{KClO}_3$$

Putting It All Together

7.82 How many joules are there in a mole of photons with a frequency of $1.01 \times 10^{16} \, s^{-1}$?

Information

A mole of photons with a frequency of $1.01 \times 10^{16} \, s^{-1}$; the question of how much energy (J) is present

Connections

$E = h\nu$

Solution

Simply enter the given values into $E = h\nu$:

$$E = h\nu = (6.63 \times 10^{-34} \, Js) \, (1.01 \times 10^{16} \, s^{-1})\left(\frac{6.022 \times 10^{23}}{1 \, mol}\right) = 4.03251 \times 10^6 = \textbf{4.03} \times \textbf{10}^6 \textbf{ J/mol}$$

7.84 The element cesium, Cs, was discovered before scientists knew about electrons, protons, or neutrons in atoms. We now know that natural cesium consists entirely of cesium-132. How many protons, electrons, and neutrons are present in a cesium-132 atom?

Solution

Cesium has **55 protons** (as do all Cs atoms, because 55 is the atomic number of Cs), **55 electrons** (if #p ≠ #e, this would be an ion and not an atom), and **77 neutrons** (#p + #n = 132).

7.86 Name or give the formula for each of the following compounds: **(a)** $XeF_2(s)$; **(b)** $BrCl(g)$; **(c)** $S_2Cl_2(s)$; **(d)** $PBr_3(l)$; **(e)** $CI_4(s)$; **(f)** disilicon hexachloride; **(g)** nitrogen trifluoride; **(h)** oxygen difluoride; **(i)** iodine pentafluoride; **(j)** diboron tetrachloride

Solution

See the Nomenclature Resource.

(a) $XeF_2(s)$ xenon difluoride

(b) $BrCl(g)$ bromine chloride

(c) $S_2Cl_2(s)$ disulfur dichloride

(d) $PBr_3(l)$ phosphorus tribromide

(e) $CI_4(s)$ carbon tetraiodide

(f) disilicon hexachloride Si_2Cl_6

(g) nitrogen trifluoride NF_3

(h) oxygen difluoride OF_2

(i) iodine pentafluoride IF_5

(j) diboron tetrachloride B_2Cl_4

7.88 Name or give the formula for each of the following compounds: **(a)** lithium nitrate; **(b)** magnesium phosphate; **(c)** aluminum sulfate; **(d)** barium fluoride; **(e)** zinc acetate; **(f)** SrH_2; **(g)** AlP; **(h)** CdS; **(i)** $(NH_4)HSO_4$; **(j)** $NaHCO_3$

Solution
See the Nomenclature Resource.

(a) lithium nitrate $LiNO_3$

(b) magnesium phosphate $Mg_3(PO_4)_2$

(c) aluminum sulfate $Al_2(SO_4)_3$

(d) barium fluoride BaF_2

(e) zinc acetate $Zn(C_2H_3O_2)_2$

(f) SrH_2 strontium hydride

(g) AlP aluminum phosphide

(h) CdS cadmium sulfide

(i) $(NH_4)HSO_4$ ammonium hydrogen sulfate or ammonium bisulfate

(j) $NaHCO_3$ sodium hydrogen carbonate or sodium bicarbonate

7.92 Provide the name or formula for each of the following compounds: **(a)** iron(III) oxide; **(b)** $SnCl_4$; **(c)** CuCN; **(d)** tin(II) nitrate; **(e)** PbI_2; **(f)** nickel(II) sulfate; **(g)** MnO_2; **(h)** iron(II) carbonate; **(i)** vanadium(V) oxide; **(j)** Co_2O_3

Solution
See the Nomenclature Resource.

(a) iron(III) oxide Fe_2O_3

(b) $SnCl_4$ tin(IV) chloride

(c) CuCN copper(I) cyanide

(d) tin(II) nitrate $Sn(NO_3)_2$

(e) PbI_2 lead(II) iodide

(f) nickel(II) sulfate $NiSO_4$

(g) MnO_2 manganese(IV) oxide

(h) iron(II) carbonate $FeCO_3$

(i) vanadium(V) oxide V_2O_5

(j) Co_2O_3 cobalt(III) oxide

7.94 The highest-energy gamma-ray photon emitted by americium-240 has an energy of 0.98764 MeV (see **Problem 7.93** for the definition of this unit). Determine the wavelength of the photon in meters.

Information

Americium-240 emits photons with $E = 0.98764$ MeV; the question of what is the wavelength (m)

Connections

$$E = \frac{hc}{\lambda}$$

Solution

Rearrange $E = \dfrac{hc}{\lambda}$ and enter the appropriate values:

$$\lambda = \frac{hc}{E} = \left[\frac{\left(6.62607 \times 10^{-34}\ \text{Js}\right)\left(2.99792 \times 10^{8}\ \text{ms}^{-1}\right)}{0.98764\ \text{MeV}} \right]\left(\frac{\text{M}}{10^{6}}\right)\left(\frac{1\ \text{eV}}{1.602176\ \times\ 10^{-19}\ \text{J}}\right)$$

$$= 1.25535676 \times 10^{-12} = \mathbf{1.2554 \times 10^{-12}\ m}$$

7.96 A mixture of charcoal, sulfur, and potassium chlorate, all of which are solids, is used as a gunpowder substitute. This mixture will react to form gaseous carbon dioxide and sulfur dioxide along with solid potassium chloride. The following balanced chemical equation illustrates one of the possible reaction mixtures. Determine the standard heat of reaction per mole of potassium chlorate.

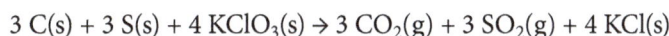

$$3\ C(s) + 3\ S(s) + 4\ KClO_3(s) \rightarrow 3\ CO_2(g) + 3\ SO_2(g) + 4\ KCl(s)$$

Information

A balanced chemical equation; the question of what is the standard heat of reaction (kJ/mol $KClO_3$)

Connections

ΔH_{rxn} = Products – Reactants; the values from appendix C

Solution

The heat of reaction depends upon the standard heats of formation for the substances involved (elements in their standard states are exactly 0):

ΔH_{rxn} = Products – Reactants

$$= [3(\Delta H_f^\circ\ CO_2(g)) + 3(\Delta H_f^\circ\ SO_2(g)) + 4(\Delta H_f^\circ\ KCl(s))]$$
$$- [3(\Delta H_f^\circ\ C(s)) + 3(\Delta H_f^\circ\ S(s)) + 4(\Delta H_f^\circ\ KClO_3(s))]$$

$$= [3(-393.5) + 3(-296.9) + 4(-436)]\ kJ - [3(0.000) + 3(0.000) + 4(-391)]\ kJ$$
$$- 2251.2 = -2251\ kJ/4\ \text{mol}\ KClO_3 \qquad \text{or} \qquad \mathbf{-562.8\ kJ/mol\ KClO_3}$$

7.99 Ozone, O_3, helps to protect the Earth's surface from high-energy photons of ultraviolet light. The energy from a photon of light can cause the following photodissociation process:

$$O_3(g) \rightarrow O_2(g) + O(g)$$

The standard heat formations of $O_3(g)$, $O_2(g)$, and $O(g)$ are 143 kJ/mol, 0.00 kJ/mol, and 249.2 kJ/mol, respectively. What is the longest wavelength of radiation that will photodissociate an ozone molecule?

Information

A balanced chemical equation; standard heats of formation for $O_3(g)$, $O_2(g)$, and $O(g)$ of 143, 0.00, and 249.2 kJ/mol, respectively; the question of what wavelength is necessary

Connections

ΔH_{rxn} = Products – Reactants; $E = \dfrac{hc}{\lambda}$

Solution

The heat of reaction depends upon the standard heats of formation for the substances involved (elements in their standard states are exactly 0).

ΔH_{rxn} = Products – Reactants

$\quad = [(\Delta H_f° \; O_2(g)) + (\Delta H_f° \; O(g))] - [(\Delta H_f° \; O_3(g))]$

$\quad = [(0.000) + (249.2)] - [(143)] = 106.2 = 106 \; kJ$

This is the energy required (per mole). Rearrange $E = \dfrac{hc}{\lambda}$ and enter the appropriate values:

$$\text{Wavelength} = \lambda = \frac{hc}{E} = \frac{(6.63 \times 10^{-34} \; Js)\left(\dfrac{3.00 \times 10^8 \; m}{s}\right)}{\left(\dfrac{106.2 \; kJ}{mol}\right)\left(\dfrac{1,000}{k}\right)\left(\dfrac{mol}{6.022 \times 10^{23}}\right)} = 1.1278 \times 10^{-6} = \mathbf{1.13 \times 10^{-6} \; m}$$

7.102 An alpha particle (mass = 6.6×10^{-24} g) emitted by radium travels at 3.4×10^7 mi/h. What is its de Broglie wavelength (in meters)?

Solution

Enter the appropriate values and conversions into the de Broglie relationship:

$$\lambda = \frac{h}{mv} = \left[\frac{6.626 \times 10^{-34} \; Js}{(6.6 \times 10^{-24} \; g)\left(\dfrac{3.4 \times 10^7 \; mi}{h}\right)}\right]\left(\frac{\left(\dfrac{kg \; m^2}{s^2}\right)}{J}\right)\left(\frac{3,600 \; s}{h}\right)\left(\frac{1,000}{k}\right)\left(\frac{1 \; mi}{1609 \; m}\right)$$

$$= 6.6065547 \times 10^{-15} = \mathbf{6.6 \times 10^{-15} \; m}$$

CHAPTER 8

Electron Configuration

The successful completion of these problems requires the following ten (10) items.

1. The rules for assigning quantum numbers make more sense after you have worked through a few examples.

2. The number of valence electrons present on an atom is very important to the next few chapters.

3. The assignment of valence electrons does not work for the transition elements and inner transition elements.

4. Relative periodic trends are useful; however, the trends are not explanations. For example, saying that Li is smaller than Na because Li is higher on the periodic table is not a valid explanation of why Li is smaller (Li has fewer electron shells).

5. Relative periodic trends work well for the representative elements. Trends do not work well for the transition and inner transition elements.

6. Relative periodic trends ignore exceptions. If you compare actual values, these exceptions become obvious. If you are asked for the exceptions, it is important to note them; otherwise, follow the relative trends.

7. Vertical changes in relative trends are, in general, greater than horizontal changes. For example, moving down one row of the periodic table (for example, from Li to Na) will probably result in a greater change than moving over one column (for example, from Li to Be).

8. The relative difference in electronegativity is much more important than the actual electronegativity values presented in a table.

9. Fluorine, F, is the key to electronegativity. The closer an element, X, is to fluorine on the periodic table, the higher the electronegativity of X is. If two elements are the same distance from fluorine, the one higher on the periodic table has the higher electronegativity.

10. In the next few chapters, it will be important to focus on the differences in electronegativity. The further apart two elements are, the greater the electronegativity difference is.

Example Problems From the Text

Example Problem 8.1

Write the complete electron configuration for lead, Pb.

Information

The name of the element

Connections

The atomic number of lead from the periodic table (82), which tells us the number of electrons in an <u>atom</u>; figure 8.3

Solution

Beginning at the top of figure 8.3, we see that the first 2 electrons will enter the 1s orbital to give $1s^2$ and leave 80 electrons.

The next arrow in the figure indicates that the next 2 electrons should enter the 2s orbital, to give $1s^2 2s^2$ and leave 78 electrons.

The third arrow indicates that 6 electrons will enter the 2p orbitals, followed by 2 electrons in 3s. This leaves us with $1s^2 2s^2 2p^6 3s^2$ and 70 electrons.

The fourth arrow fills the 3p and the 4s orbitals, to give $1s^2 2s^2 2p^6 3s^2 3p^6 4s^2$ and leave us with 62 electrons.

The next arrow begins with the filling of the 3d orbitals, which hold a total of 10 electrons, followed by the 4p and the 5s orbitals. With this arrow, we get to $1s^2 2s^2 2p^6 3s^2 3p^6 4s^2 3d^{10} 4p^6 5s^2$, leaving 44 electrons to distribute.

The next arrow, like the previous one, fills d, p, and s subshells. This gives $1s^2 2s^2 2p^6 3s^2 3p^6 4s^2 3d^{10} 4p^6 5s^2 4d^{10} 5p^6 6s^2$, and now 26 electrons remain.

As we begin the seventh arrow, we see that 14 electrons will enter the 4f orbitals and 10 electrons will enter the 5d orbitals, giving us $1s^2 2s^2 2p^6 3s^2 3p^6 4s^2 3d^{10} 4p^6 5s^2 4d^{10} 5p^6 6s^2 4f^{14} 5d^{10}$ and leaving only 2 electrons.

The next orbitals are the 6p orbitals, which can hold a maximum of 6 electrons. However, there are only 2 electrons remaining, indicating that the 6p orbitals will fill only partially. The final electron configuration for a lead atom is $\mathbf{1s^2 2s^2 2p^6 3s^2 3p^6 4s^2 3d^{10} 4p^6 5s^2 4d^{10} 5p^6 6s^2 4f^{14} 5d^{10} 6p^2}$.

Reality Check

To check this answer, we can add all the superscripts together. A correct answer will have the same total as we started with—in this case, 82.

Follow-Up Problem 8.1a

Write the complete electron configuration for francium, Fr.

Information
The name of the element

Connections
The atomic number of francium from the periodic table (87), which tells us the number of electrons in an atom; figure 8.3

Solution
Beginning at the top of figure 8.3, put electrons into the orbitals until all 87 electrons are accounted for in the electron configuration. The result is $1s^22s^22p^63s^23p^64s^23d^{10}4p^65s^24d^{10}5p^66s^24f^{14}5d^{10}6p^67s^1$.

Reality Check
To check this answer, we can add all the superscripts together. A correct answer will have the same total as we started with—in this case, 87.

Follow-Up Problem 8.1b
Platinum, Pt, is an exception to the aufbau principle because the final electrons rearrange to form a stable d^{10} configuration. Considering this d^{10} configuration, write the complete electron configuration of platinum.

Information
The name of the element; information about the stability of a d^{10} electron configuration

Connections
The atomic number of platinum from the periodic table (78), which tells us the number of electrons in an atom; figure 8.3

Solution
Beginning at the top of figure 8.3, put electrons into the orbitals until all 78 electrons are accounted for in the electron configuration. The result is $1s^22s^22p^63s^23p^64s^23d^{10}4p^65s^24d^{10}5p^66s^24f^{14}5d^8$. However, the information given in the problem indicates that the electrons will rearrange from the expected configuration, just derived, to a more stable arrangement with a filled d subshell. The rearranged configuration moves 2 electrons from the 6s to the 5d, giving $1s^22s^22p^63s^23p^64s^23d^{10}4p^65s^24d^{10}5p^64f^{14}5d^{10}$.

Reality Check
To check this answer, we can add all the superscripts together. A correct answer will have the same total as we started with—in this case, 78.

Example Problem 8.2
How many electrons are in the valence shell of sulfur?

Information
The identity of the element, S

Connections
The periodic table on the inside front cover of this textbook

Solution

Locate sulfur on the periodic table. The element is in group 16 (6A). From its location, there are six valence electrons.

Reality Check

The electron configuration (with the valence shell in boldface) is $1s^2 2s^2 \mathbf{3s^2 3p^4}$.

There are six valence electrons (denoted as boldface superscript).

Follow-Up Problem 8.2a

How many electrons are in the valence shell of antimony?

Information

The identity of the element, Sb

Connections

The periodic table on the inside front cover of this textbook

Solution

Locate antimony on the periodic table. The element is in group 15 (5A). From its location, there are six valence electrons.

Reality Check

The electron configuration (with the valence shell in boldface) is $1s^2 2s^2 3s^2 3p^6 4s^2 3d^{10} 4p^6 \mathbf{5s^2} 4d^{10} \mathbf{5p^3}$. There are five valence electrons (boldfaced).

Follow-Up Problem 8.2b

How many electrons are in the valence shell of iron?

Information

The identity of the element, Fe

Connections

The periodic table on the inside front cover of this textbook

Solution

Locate iron on the periodic table. The element is in group 8 (8B). From its location, iron is a transition metal. It is not possible to unambiguously assign valence electrons to transition elements.

Reality Check

This method does not work for transition metals.

END-OF-CHAPTER PROBLEMS

8.1 The Pauli Principle and the Aufbau Principle

8.2 When two atoms collide and react, what parts of the atom directly interact?

Solution

The outer regions of the atoms will interact. This is where the outer electrons are.

8.5 If the value of the principal quantum number, n, is 4, what are the possible values of the l quantum number?

Solution

If n is equal to 4, then l may be 0, 1, 2, or 3 (= $n - 1$).

8.7 What are the possible values of the m_l quantum number if $l = 2$?

Solution

If l is equal to 2, then m_l may be -2, -1, 0, $+1$, or $+2$.

8.2 Writing Electron Configurations

8.10 What is the relationship between two spin-paired electrons?

Solution

The two spin-paired electrons will have opposite values of m_s. One will have m_s equal to $+1/2$, and the other will have m_s equal to $-1/2$.

8.13 What are the first 10 orbitals to fill in an atom? List these orbitals in order of increasing energy.

Solution

1s, 2s, (2p$_x$, 2p$_y$, and 2p$_z$), 3s, (3p$_x$, 3p$_y$, and 3p$_z$), 4s (All the 2p orbitals all have the same energy, as do all the 3p orbitals; therefore, the 2p orbitals may fill in any order, as may the 3p orbitals.)

8.15 What is the first element to which Hund's rule becomes applicable? Why is this true?

Solution

The element is carbon. This is the first element where there is more than one electron in a degenerate set of orbitals (the 2p set).

8.3 Interpreting the Periodic Table

8.17 Determine the maximum number of electrons allowed to have the following quantum numbers in a single atom: **(a)** $n = 4$; **(b)** $n = 3$ and $l = 2$; **(c)** $n = 6$, $l = 1$, and $m_l = 0$; **(d)** $n = 5$, $l = 0$, $m_l = 0$, and $m_s = +1/2$.

Solution

(a) This refers to the entire fourth shell, which can hold a maximum of <u>32</u> electrons. **(b)** This refers to the 3d subshell, which can hold a maximum of <u>10</u> electrons. **(c)** This refers to the 5s subshell, which can hold a maximum of <u>2</u> electrons. **(d)** There can be only <u>1</u> electron, as no two electrons can have the same set of quantum numbers and all four quantum numbers are assigned.

8.19 List all possible sets of the four quantum numbers for a 3d electron on a hydrogen atom.

Solution

The 3d subshell has $n = 3$ and $l = 2$; therefore, all choices must use these two values. This allows only m_l and m_s to vary. The accompanying table use the rules for quantum numbers. The rows may be listed in any order.

n	l	m_l	m_s
3	2	-2	$-1/2$
3	2	-1	$-1/2$
3	2	0	$-1/2$
3	2	$+1$	$-1/2$
3	2	$+2$	$-1/2$

3	2	−2	+1/2
3	2	−1	+1/2
3	2	0	+1/2
3	2	+1	+1/2
3	2	+2	+1/2

These are all excited state configurations for hydrogen.

8.21 The electron configuration of a potassium atom is $1s^2 2s^2 2p^6 3s^2 3p^6 4s^1$. **(a)** How many core electrons does a potassium atom have? **(b)** How many valence electrons does a potassium atom have?

Solution

As illustrated by the given electron configuration, a potassium atom has 19 electrons, which can be confirmed by the atomic number of potassium listed on the periodic table.

(a) Potassium has 18 core electrons (all electrons except the 4s electron are core electrons).
(b) Potassium has only 1 valence electron, it is in the 4s orbital because the fourth shell is the outermost shell.

8.24 **(a)** List in order of increasing energy the various subshells of the fourth shell. **(b)** List in order of increasing energy the orbitals in the 4p subshell.

Solution

The solution is an illustration of the aufbau principle.

(a) 4s < 4p < 4d < 4f (for a hydrogen atom, all the orbitals have the same energy)
(b) All the 4p orbitals have the same energy.

8.26 Convert each of the following excited-state electron configurations to ground-state electron configurations, and identify the element:

(a) $1s^2 2s^1 2p^6$
(b) $1s^2 2s^2 2p^6 3s^2 3p^5 4s^1$
(c) $1s^2 2s^2 2p^6 3s^2 3p^6 4s^1 3d^{10} 4p^4$
(d) $1s^2 2s^2 2p^6 3s^2 3p^6 4s^2 3d^{10} 4p^6 5s^2 4d^9 5p^2$
(e) $1s^2 2s^2 2p^6 3s^2 3p^6 4s^2 3d^{10} 4p^6 5s^2 4d^{10} 5p^6 6s^2 4f^{13} 5d^8$

Solution

Using the aufbau principle, move electrons from the outer orbitals to fill all lower energy orbitals. Count the electrons present; this gives the atomic number, which is listed for each element on the periodic table.

(a) $1s^2 2s^2 2p^5$ Fluorine
(b) $1s^2 2s^2 2p^6 3s^2 3p^6$ Argon
(c) $1s^2 2s^2 2p^6 3s^2 3p^6 4s^2 3d^{10} 4p^3$ Arsenic
(d) $1s^2 2s^2 2p^6 3s^2 3p^6 4s^2 3d^{10} 4p^6 5s^2 4d^{10} 5p^1$ Indium
(e) $1s^2 2s^2 2p^6 3s^2 3p^6 4s^2 3d^{10} 4p^6 5s^2 4d^{10} 5p^6 6s^2 4f^{14} 5d^7$ Iridium

8.28 **(a)** Define the terms *paramagnetic* and *diamagnetic*. **(b)** Give the names of two second-period elements with atoms that are paramagnetic. **(c)** Give the names of two second-period elements with atoms that are diamagnetic.

Solution

(a) A paramagnetic substance is one that has at least one unpaired electron. A diamagnetic substance has all electrons paired. **(b)** You do not need to list all the options; just list any two of the following. Lithium, boron, carbon, nitrogen, oxygen, and fluorine qualify as second-period paramagnetic elements. **(c)** Only beryllium and neon are diamagnetic second-period elements.

8.31 Which of the following atoms is the most paramagnetic? N, Ar, Mn, K, or O

Solution

Nitrogen atoms have three unpaired electrons, argon has no unpaired electrons, manganese has five unpaired electrons, potassium has one unpaired electron, and oxygen has two unpaired electrons. Since manganese has the most unpaired electrons, it is the most paramagnetic.

8.35 What distinguishes the electron configuration of helium from that of all the other noble gases?

Solution

Helium is $1s^2$ and is the only noble gas without a p^6 in the ground-state electron configuration.

8.37 Which outermost orbitals are being filled in the following types of elements? **(a)** representative elements, **(b)** transition metals, **(c)** inner transition metals

Solution

(a) The representative elements are filling the s and p orbitals. **(b)** The transition elements are filling the d orbitals. **(c)** The inner transition metals are filling the f orbitals.

8.4 Atomic Radii

8.42 Why do the atomic radii tend to increase down a column on the periodic table?

Solution

When going down a column, each period resents the addition of an additional energy level. Adding an energy level increases the size of the atom. (As always, there are exceptions.)

8.43 **(a)** Why is an argon atom smaller than a krypton atom? **(b)** Why is an argon atom smaller than a chlorine atom?

Solution

(a) In the ground state, an argon atom has fewer energy levels than a ground-state krypton atom. **(b)** An argon atom has a greater effective nuclear charge than a chlorine atom. The greater nuclear charge pulls the electrons closer to the nucleus, making the atom smaller.

8.45 Using only the periodic table, arrange the elements in each of the following groups in order of decreasing atomic radius: **(a)** C, S, Ca, Pt, and Sb; **(b)** Cr, Ga, N, Ta, and Mo; **(c)** Al, Te, He, Mg, and Cs

Solution

In general, atomic radii decrease toward the top and toward the left on the periodic table.

(a) Pt > Sb > C > S > C; **(b)** Ta > Cr > Ga > N; **(c)** Cs > Te > Mg > Al > He (This ignores exceptions, if any are present.)

8.47 Why does the effective nuclear charge increase across a period?

Solution

In general, the effective nuclear charge increases toward the right of any period.

8.5 Ionization Energy

8.52 Write balanced chemical equations illustrating the first and second ionization energies of calcium.

Solution

The first ionization energy involves removing an electron from a gaseous calcium atom to produce a $Ca^+(g)$ ion.

$$\text{First ionization energy} \qquad Ca(g) \rightarrow Ca^+(g) + e^-$$

The second ionization energy involves removing an electron from a $Ca^+(g)$ ion (from the first ionization energy) to produce a $Ca^{2+}(g)$ ion. (This will require more energy than the first ionization energy.)

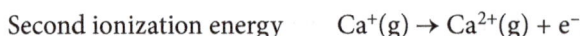

$$\text{Second ionization energy} \qquad Ca^+(g) \rightarrow Ca^{2+}(g) + e^-$$

8.54 Using only the periodic table, pick the member of each pair with the higher ionization energy: **(a)** Na and Rb; **(b)** Si and Sb; **(c)** Li and Be; **(d)** B and Al; **(e)** C and N

Solution

(a) Na, because Na is nearer the top of the periodic table. **(b)** Si, because Si is nearer the top of the periodic table. **(c)** Be, because Be is further to the right on the periodic table (also, Be has a very stable s^2 configuration). **(d)** B, because B is nearer the top of the periodic table. **(e)** N, because N is further to the right on the periodic table (also, N has a very stable p^3 configuration).

8.6 Electron Affinity

8.56 What is the definition of *electron affinity*?

Solution

The **electron affinity** is the energy change when a gaseous atom, in the ground state, accepts an electron. (The energy change may be either endothermic or exothermic.)

8.58 Why, in most cases, is it more difficult to form a dianion (–2 ion) than it is to form a –1 ion?

Solution

It is more difficult to force an anion to accept an electron than a neutral atom. The negative charge on the anion repels the electron, whereas the neutral atom does not have a negative charge to repel the incoming electron.

8.60 Write the full electron configuration of each of the following atoms or ions: O, O^{2-}, Ne

Solution

The electron configurations are

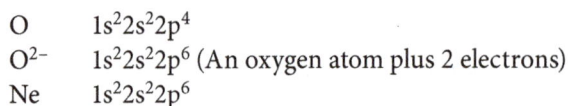

O	$1s^2 2s^2 2p^4$
O^{2-}	$1s^2 2s^2 2p^6$ (An oxygen atom plus 2 electrons)
Ne	$1s^2 2s^2 2p^6$

8.63 **(a)** Write the electron configuration of oxygen. **(b)** Write electron configurations for the anions formed as one or two electrons are added to an oxygen atom. **(c)** Why is the addition of two electrons the limit for an oxygen atom? **(d)** Based on your answer to part (c), what is the limit for a nitrogen atom?

Solution

(a) The electron configuration of oxygen is $1s^22s^22p^4$. **(b)** The electron configurations after the addition of one or two electrons are +1 e⁻ $1s^22s^22p^5$, + 2 e⁻ $1s^22s^22p^6$ (filled). **(c)** There is no more room in the outer shell. **(d)** The limit is three electrons (to go from $1s^22s^22p^3$ to $1s^22s^22p^6$).

8.65 Write the full electron configuration of each of the following atoms or ions: Co, Co^{2+}, Co^{3+}

Solution

The electron configurations are

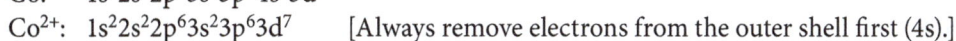

Co: $1s^22s^22p^63s^23p^64s^23d^7$
Co^{2+}: $1s^22s^22p^63s^23p^63d^7$ [Always remove electrons from the outer shell first (4s).]
Co^{3+}: $1s^22s^22p^63s^23p^63d^6$

8.69 List the atoms or ions in each group in order of decreasing radius: **(a)** Y^{3+}, Rb^+, and Sr^{2+}; **(b)** Ne, F^-, and Na^+; **(c)** P^{3-}, Cl^-, and S^{2-}; **(d)** Li^+, Ca^{2+}, and Cl^-; **(e)** Kr, Br, and Br^-

Solution

(a) These three ions are electronic; therefore, the one with the highest (positive) charge is the smallest: $Rb^+ > Sr^{2+} > Y^{3+}$
(b) The fluoride ion is isoelectronic with neon, and the negative charge makes it larger than a Ne atom. The removal of an electron from Ne to form Ne^+, which is smaller. $F^- > Ne > Ne^+$
(c) These three ions are electronic; therefore, the one with the lowest (negative) charge is the largest: $P^{3-} > S^{2-} > Cl^-$
(d) The chloride and calcium ions are isoelectronic; therefore, the anion is larger than the cation. Lithium, in the second period, is a much smaller atom, and a Li^+ ion would be even smaller. $Cl^- > Ca^{2+} > Li^+$
(e) The bromide ion has one more electron than a bromine atom, which makes it larger due to electron repulsion. Krypton has a greater effective nuclear charge than bromine; therefore, a krypton atom will be smaller. $Br^- > Br > Kr$

8.7 Electronegativity
8.70 What is *electronegativity*?

Solution

Electronegativity is the relative attraction that an atom in a compound has for electrons.

8.73 **(a)** What type of ions do atoms with high electronegativities tend to form? **(b)** What type of ions do atoms with low electronegativities tend to form?

Solution

(a) Atoms with high electronegativities tend to gain electrons and form anions because of their high attraction for electrons. **(b)** Atoms with low electronegativities tend to lose electrons and form cations due to their low attraction for electrons.

8.75 **(a)** How does the trend in electronegativities compare to the trend in ionization energies? **(b)** How does the trend in electronegativities compare to the trend in electron affinities?

Solution

(a) The general trends are similar in that elements with higher ionization energies have higher electronegativities. (b) The general trends are the same in that elements with higher electron affinities tend to have higher electronegativities. However, elements with filled s subshells and the noble gases have very little or no electron affinity, which does not correlate with their electronegativity values.

8.8 Applications and Extensions

8.77 Which element is considered the "unique" element? Why is this element unique?

Solution

Hydrogen is the "unique" element because it is the only reactive element with no electrons in the core. (Helium also has no electrons in the core, but it is a noble gas and not a reactive element.)

8.79 (a) In general, how do the properties of metals compare to the properties of nonmetals? (b) How do the properties of metalloids compare to the properties of metals and nonmetals?

Solution

(a) Metals tend to have properties that are the opposite of nonmetals. (b) The metalloids (semimetals) have properties that are intermediate between metals and nonmetals.

8.81 Arrange the following elements in order of increasing electrical conductivity: Si, K, P

Solution

The order is from nonmetal (poor conductor) to metalloid to metal (good conductor):

$$P < Si < K$$

8.84 (a) What type of compounds do nonmetal oxides tend to form when added to water? (b) What type of compounds do metal oxides tend to form when added to water?

Solution

(a) Nonmetal oxides tend to form <u>acids</u> when added to water. (b) Metal oxides tend to form <u>bases</u> when added to water.

8.86 Complete and balance the equations for each of the following: (a) calcium oxide reacts with water; (b) sulfur dioxide reacts with water; (c) manganese(II) oxide reacts with hydrochloric acid; (d) carbon dioxide reacts with an aqueous solution of sodium hydroxide; (e) calcium oxide reacts with sulfur dioxide

Solution

Use the Nomenclature Resource and the normal procedure for balancing chemical equations.

(a) calcium oxide reacts with water

$$CaO(s) + H_2O(l) \rightarrow Ca(OH)_2(aq)$$

The reaction of a metal oxide with water to produce a base

(b) sulfur dioxide reacts with water

$$SO_2(g) + H_2O(l) \rightarrow H_2SO_3(aq)$$

The reaction of a nonmetal oxide with water to produce an acid

(c) manganese(II) oxide reacts with hydrochloric acid

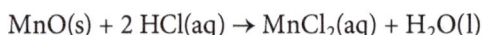

$$MnO(s) + 2\,HCl(aq) \rightarrow MnCl_2(aq) + H_2O(l)$$

The reaction of a metal oxide (basic) with an acid to produce a salt (and water)

(d) carbon dioxide reacts with an aqueous solution of sodium hydroxide

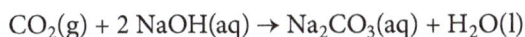

$CO_2(g) + 2\ NaOH(aq) \rightarrow Na_2CO_3(aq) + H_2O(l)$

The reaction of a nonmetal oxide (acid) with a base to produce a salt (and water)

(e) calcium oxide reacts with sulfur dioxide

$CaO(s) + SO_2(g) \rightarrow CaSO_3(s)$

The reaction of a metal oxide (base) with a nonmetal oxide (acid) to produce a salt

8.88 Complete and balance the equations for each of the following reactions: **(a)** solid selenium reacts with calcium metal; **(b)** dinitrogen oxide decomposes to the elements; **(c)** magnesium metal burns in oxygen gas; **(d)** sulfur vapor reacts with beryllium metal; **(e)** water vapor burns in fluorine gas to produce hydrogen fluoride gas and oxygen gas

Solution

Use the Nomenclature Resource and the normal procedure for balancing chemical equations.

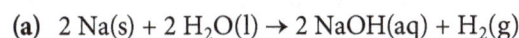

(a) $Se(s) + Ca(s) \rightarrow CaSe(s)$

The reaction of a nonmetal with a metal to produce a salt

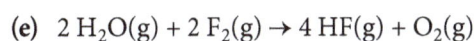

(b) $2\ N_2O(g) \rightarrow 2\ N_2(g) + O_2(g)$

As described in the problem

(c) $2\ Mg(g) + O_2(g) \rightarrow 2\ MgO(s)$

The reaction of a nonmetal with a metal to produce a salt

(d) $S(g) + Be(s) \rightarrow BeS(s)$

The reaction of a nonmetal with a metal to produce a salt

(e) $2\ H_2O(g) + 2\ F_2(g) \rightarrow 4\ HF(g) + O_2(g)$

As described in the problem

8.90 Complete and balance the equations for each of the following: **(a)** sodium is placed in a beaker of water; **(b)** calcium is placed in a beaker of water; **(c)** lithium metal reacts with liquid bromine; **(d)** hydrogen gas burns in fluorine gas; **(e)** magnesium metal reacts when heated with nitrogen gas

Solution

Use the Nomenclature Resource and the normal procedure for balancing chemical equations.

(a) $2\ Na(s) + 2\ H_2O(l) \rightarrow 2\ NaOH(aq) + H_2(g)$

The reaction of an active metal with water (see the activity series)

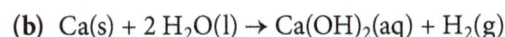

(b) $Ca(s) + 2\ H_2O(l) \rightarrow Ca(OH)_2(aq) + H_2(g)$

The reaction of an active metal with water (see the activity series)

(c) $2\ Li(s) + Br_2(l) \rightarrow 2\ LiBr(s)$

The reaction of a nonmetal with a metal to produce a salt

(d) $H_2(g) + F_2(g) \rightarrow 2\ HF(g)$

The reaction of two nonmetals to produce a molecular compound

(e) $3\,Mg(s) + N_2(g) \rightarrow Mg_3N_2(s)$

     The reaction of a nonmetal with a metal to produce a salt

8.92 Hydrogen may form two ions. Give the electron configuration of each of these ions.

Solution

The two ions and their electron configurations are $H^+\ 1s^0$ and $H^-\ 1s^2$.

8.95 The alkali metals are very reactive. Write a general chemical equation to illustrate the reaction of an alkali metal with water.

Solution

The general chemical equation is

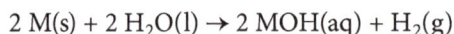

$$2\,M(s) + 2\,H_2O(l) \rightarrow 2\,MOH(aq) + H_2(g)$$

8.97 Which alkaline earth metals are among the most abundant elements in the Earth's crust?

Solution

The most abundant alkaline earth metals in the Earth's crust are magnesium and calcium.

8.100 How is aluminum hydroxide different from the alkali metal hydroxides?

Solution

Aluminum hydroxide is amphoteric (may behave as either an acid or a base), while the alkali metal hydroxides are strong bases.

8.102 Which carbon family element is the most abundant element in the Earth's crust?

Solution

Silicon is the most abundant carbon family element in the Earth's crust.

8.105 Which oxygen-containing anion is analogous to the disulfide ion?

Solution

The peroxide ion, O_2^{2-}, is analogous to the disulfide ion, S_2^{2-}.

8.107 Which elements in the oxygen family are essential to most living organisms?

Solution

Oxygen, sulfur, and selenium are essential elements for most living organisms.

8.111 **(a)** What is the formula for platinum(VI) fluoride? **(b)** Why is platinum(VI) fluoride important to the chemistry of the noble gases?

Solution

(a) PtF_6

(b) The first synthesis of a noble gas compound involved the reaction of platinum(VI) fluoride with xenon.

Putting It All Together

8.115 The most abundant isotopes of the nitrogen family elements are ^{14}N, ^{31}P, ^{75}As, ^{121}Sb, and ^{209}Bi. List the number of protons, neutrons, and electrons in an atom for each of these isotopes.

Solution

See chapter 2.

	Protons	Neutrons	Electrons
^{14}N	7	7	7
^{31}P	15	16	15
^{75}As	33	42	33
^{121}Sb	51	70	51
^{209}Bi	83	126	83

8.117 Locate the following elements on the periodic table: N, Te, Ge, Pb, and Cl. **(a)** Arrange these elements in order of decreasing electron affinity. **(b)** Arrange these elements in order of decreasing first ionization energy. **(c)** Arrange these elements in order of decreasing atomic radius.

Solution

Assuming that there are no exceptions, and following the general trends based upon the position of the elements on the periodic table:

(a) Cl > N > Ge > Te > Pb
(b) Cl > N > Ge > Te > Pb
(c) Pb > Te > Ge > Cl > N

8.121 Write complete, balanced equations for the following pairs of reactions. Compare the products of the reactions in each pair: **(a)** potassium metal reacts with iodine vapor, and hydrogen gas reacts with iodine vapor; **(b)** strontium metal reacts with chlorine gas, and strontium metal reacts with hydrogen gas

Solution

(a) $2\,K(s) + I_2(g) \rightarrow 2\,KI(s)$ and $H_2(g) + I_2(g) \rightarrow 2\,HI(g)$

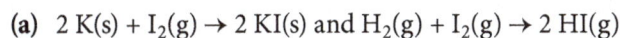

K produces an ionic solid, while H_2 produces a covalent molecule.
Both general formulas, XI, are the same, so hydrogen is like potassium.

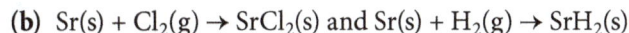

(b) $Sr(s) + Cl_2(g) \rightarrow SrCl_2(s)$ and $Sr(s) + H_2(g) \rightarrow SrH_2(s)$

Both reactions produce an ionic solid.
Both formulas, SrX_2, are the same, so hydrogen is like chlorine.

8.123 Give the full electron configuration of each of the following: **(a)** silicon, **(b)** iron, **(c)** lead

Solution

See figure 8.3.

(a) $1s^2 2s^2 2p^6 3s^2 3p^2$
(b) $1s^2 2s^2 2p^6 3s^2 3p^6 4s^2 3d^6$
(c) $1s^2 2s^2 2p^6 3s^2 3p^6 4s^2 3d^{10} 4p^6 5s^2 4d^{10} 5p^6 6s^2 4f^{14} 5d^{10} 6p^2$

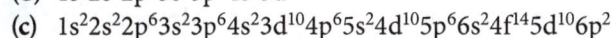

8.125 Using only the periodic table as a guide, arrange each of the following sets of elements in order of decreasing electronegativity: **(a)** Br, I, and Cl; **(b)** Mg, Al, and Cs; **(c)** C, N, and Br; **(d)** Se, B, and F; **(e)** H, C, and Na

Solution

Begin with the element nearest fluorine and move away. If two elements are the same distance from fluorine, the one higher on the periodic table is higher.

(a) Cl > Br > I; **(b)** Al > Mg > Cs; **(c)** N > Br > C; **(d)** F > Se > B; **(e)** C > H > Na

CHAPTER 9

Chemical Bonding I— Transfer of Electrons

The successful completion of these problems requires the following seven (7) items.

1. This chapter focuses on ionic bonding, while the next chapter focuses on covalent bonding. In general, these two types of bonding are treated differently. Do not mix these approaches.
2. When drawn correctly, Lewis structures for covalent bonds look different from Lewis structures for ionic bonds. Do not draw an ionic structure to represent a covalent structure or vice versa.
3. The total number of valence electrons can never change. If, for example, you start with 30 valence electrons, a correct conclusion must have 30 valence electrons.
4. The octet rule is useful, but not infallible.
5. No element in the second period can ever have more than an octet.
6. Hydrogen can either gain one electron or lose one electron; all other options are impossible.
7. "Metal plus nonmetal = ions" is only a guideline (there are exceptions).

Example Problem 9.1

Determine the most likely type of bonding in each of the following combinations: **(a)** a combination containing fluorine and sodium; **(b)** a combination containing chlorine and hydrogen; **(c)** a combination of fluorine and silicon; **(d)** a combination of zinc and copper

Information

Four sets of elements: fluorine, sodium; chlorine, hydrogen; fluorine, silicon; zinc, and copper; the question of what is the most likely type of bonding for each pair of elements

Connections

The periodic table

Solution

(a) Locate fluorine and sodium on the periodic table. The two elements are on opposite sides of the table, which suggests a large electronegativity difference. Combinations with large electronegativity differences tend to have **ionic bonds**.

(b) Locate chlorine and hydrogen on the periodic table. The two elements are on opposite sides of the table, which usually means a large difference in their electronegativities. However, hydrogen is an exception to the rule: Its electronegativity is higher than its position on the periodic table would suggest. Consequently, the difference in electronegativity is less than indicated by the positions of these elements on the periodic table. This smaller electronegativity difference predicts a polar **covalent bond**.

(c) Locate fluorine and silicon on the periodic table. These elements are nonmetals that are relatively close together on the periodic table. Their positions indicate a small electronegativity difference and thus a polar **covalent bond**.

(d) Locate zinc and copper on the periodic table. Both elements are metals. Metals interact to form **metallic bonds**.

Reality Check

Our bond predictions are reasonable. A nonmetal combined with a different nonmetal (or metalloid) normally yields a polar covalent bond. A metal combined with a nonmetal normally yields an ionic bond. Two metals give a metallic bond.

Follow-Up Problem 9.1a

Determine the most likely type of bonding in each of the following: **(a)** a combination of manganese and iron; **(b)** a combination of germanium and chlorine; **(c)** elemental nitrogen; **(d)** a combination containing iodine and calcium

Information

Four sets of elements: manganese, iron; germanium, chlorine; nitrogen; iodine, and calcium; the question of what is the most likely type of bonding for each pair of elements

Connections

The periodic table

Solution

(a) Locate manganese and iron on the periodic table. Both elements are metals. Metals interact to form **metallic bonds**.

(b) Locate germanium and chlorine on the periodic table. These two elements are relatively close together on the periodic table; therefore, the electronegativity difference will be small. A small electronegativity difference means there will be a **polar covalent bond**.

(c) Locate nitrogen on the periodic table. Nonmetal atoms bonded to themselves have no difference in electronegativity, which means the bond is a **covalent bond** (nonpolar).

(d) Locate iodine and calcium on the periodic table. The two elements are on opposite sides of the table, which suggests a large electronegativity difference. Combinations with large electronegativity differences tend to have **ionic bonds**.

Reality Check

Our bond predictions are reasonable. A nonmetal with a different nonmetal (or metalloid) normally yields a polar covalent bond. A metal and a nonmetal normally yield an ionic bond. Two metals give a metallic bond.

Follow-Up Problem 9.1b

Determine the most likely type of bonding in each of the following: **(a)** a combination of sodium and hydrogen; **(b)** a combination of phosphorus and chlorine; **(c)** a combination of xenon and neon; **(d)** a combination of aluminum and fluorine

Information

Four sets of elements: sodium and hydrogen, phosphorus and chlorine, xenon and neon, aluminum and fluorine; the question of what is the most likely type of bonding for each pair of elements

Connections

The periodic table

Solution

(a) Locate sodium and hydrogen on the periodic table. Even though these two elements are close, hydrogen is an exception as its electronegativity is unusually high. Since the electronegativity of hydrogen is unusually high, the difference between sodium and hydrogen is high enough to yield an **ionic bond**.

(b) Locate phosphorus and chlorine on the periodic table. These two elements are relatively close together on the periodic table; therefore, the electronegativity difference will be small. A small electronegativity difference means there will be a **polar covalent bond**.

(c) Locate xenon and neon on the periodic table. These two elements are noble gases, which do not readily form compounds—and, when they do, it is never with another noble gas. There will be no bond forms.

(d) Locate aluminum and fluorine on the periodic table. Even though both elements are on the right side of the periodic table, the difference between the electronegativity of a metal and the electronegativity of a nonmetal is usually sufficient to result in an **ionic bond**.

Reality Check

Our bond predictions are reasonable. A nonmetal combined with a different nonmetal (or metalloid) normally yields a polar covalent bond. A metal combined with a nonmetal normally yields an ionic bond.

Example Problem 9.2

How many valence electrons does arsenic, As, have?

Information

Element name and symbol—arsenic, As; the question of how many valence electrons are present

Connections

The periodic table

Solution

Locate arsenic on the periodic table, where it is in group 15 (5A). Elements in this column have **five** valence electrons.

Reality Check

The electron configuration of arsenic is $1s^2 2s^2 2p^6 3s^2 3p^6 4s^2 3d^{10} 4p^3$. The outer shell ($4s^2 4p^3$) is the valence shell, which has $2 + 3 = 5$ electrons.

Follow-Up Problem 9.2a

How many valence electrons does tin, Sn, have?

Information

Element name and symbol—tin, Sn; the question of how many valence electrons are present

Connections

The periodic table

Solution

Locate tin on the periodic table, where it is in group 14 (4A). Elements in this column have **four** valence electrons.

Reality Check

The electron configuration of tin is $1s^2 2s^2 2p^6 3s^2 3p^6 4s^2 3d^{10} 4p^6 5s^2 4d^{10} 5p^2$. The outer shell ($5s^2 5p^2$) is the valence shell, which has $2 + 2 = 4$ electrons.

Follow-Up Problem 9.2b

How many valence electrons does cadmium, Cd, have?

Information

Element name and symbol—cadmium, Cd; the question of how many valence electrons are present

Connections

The periodic table

Solution

Locate cadmium on the periodic table, where it is in group 12 (2B). Elements in this column have **two** valence electrons.

Reality Check

The electron configuration of cadmium is $1s^2 2s^2 2p^6 3s^2 3p^6 4s^2 3d^{10}$. The outer shell ($4s^2$) is the valence shell, which has $2 + 0 = 2$ electrons. Note, that while cadmium is technically a transition element, the filled d-subshell makes it an exception to the rule considering transition metals.

Example Problem 9.3

Predict the formula of an ionic compound containing aluminum and fluorine.

Information

Elements in ionic compound—aluminum and fluorine; the question of what is the ionic formula

Connections
The periodic table

Solution
Locate the elements on the periodic table. Aluminum is in column 13 (3A), and fluorine is in column 17 (7A), indicating that aluminum has three valence electrons and fluorine has seven. Their relative positions suggest that aluminum is less electronegative than fluorine, so aluminum will lose electrons and fluorine will gain electrons. Aluminum has three electrons to lose, and fluorine can gain one, so three fluorine atoms would be required to accommodate the three electrons lost by aluminum: a ratio of three fluorine atoms for every aluminum atom. Aluminum, the cation, goes first in the formula, which is therefore **AlF_3**.

Reality Check
The Nomenclature Resource confirms that aluminum should form Al^{3+} and fluorine should form F^-. The combination of a +3 ion with a –1 ion gives AlF_3.

Follow-Up Problem 9.3a
Predict the formula of an ionic compound containing calcium and nitrogen.

Information
Elements in ionic compound—calcium and nitrogen; the question of what is the ionic formula

Connections
The periodic table

Solution
Locate the elements on the periodic table. Calcium is in column 2 (2A) and nitrogen is in column 15 (5A), indicating that calcium has two valence electrons and nitrogen has three. Their relative positions suggest that calcium is less electronegative than nitrogen, so calcium will lose electrons and nitrogen will gain electrons. Calcium has two electrons to lose, and nitrogen can gain three. The lowest common multiple of two and three is six. Three calcium atoms donate six electrons and two nitrogen atoms accept six electrons. This gives ratio of three calcium atoms for every two nitrogen atoms. Calcium, the cation, goes first in the formula, which is therefore **Ca_3N_2**.

Reality Check
The Nomenclature Resource confirms that calcium should form Ca^{2+} and nitrogen should form N^{3-}. The combination of a +2 ion with a –3 ion gives Ca_3N_2.

Follow-Up Problem 9.3b
Predict the formula of an ionic compound containing magnesium and hydrogen.

Information
Elements in ionic compound—magnesium and hydrogen; the question of what is the ionic formula

Connections
The periodic table

Solution
Locate the elements on the periodic table. Magnesium is in column 2 (2A) and hydrogen is in column 1 (1A), indicating that magnesium has two valence electrons and hydrogen has one. Their relative positions suggest that magnesium is less electronegative than hydrogen (an exception), so

magnesium will lose electrons and hydrogen will gain electrons. Magnesium has two electrons to lose, and hydrogen can gain one. The lowest common multiple of two and one is two. One magnesium atom donates two electrons and two hydrogen atom accepts two electrons. This gives a ratio of one magnesium atoms for every two hydrogen atoms. Magnesium, the cation, goes first in the formula, which is therefore **MgH$_2$**.

Reality Check

The Nomenclature Resource confirms that magnesium should form Mg^{2+}; however, hydrogen can form H^+ and H^-. Since two cations cannot combine (Mg^{2+} and H^+), the combination of the +2 ion must be the −1 ion to give MgH$_2$.

Example Problem 9.4

Determine the lattice energy for sodium iodide from the following information: heat of formation of sodium iodide, −287.78 kJ/mol; first ionization energy of sodium, 494 kJ/mol; electron affinity of iodine, 295 kJ/mol; sublimation energy of sodium, 107.32 kJ/mol; bond energy of iodine, 151.0 kJ/mol; sublimation energy of iodine, 62.44 kJ/mol

Information

$\Delta H_f^\circ(\text{NaI}) = -287.78$ kJ/mol, $IE_1(\text{Na}) = 494$ kJ/mol, $EA(\text{I}) = 295$ kJ/mol, $\Delta H_{subl}(\text{Na}) = 107.32$ kJ/mol, $\Delta H_{subl}(\text{I}_2) = 62.44$ kJ/mol, $\Delta H_{BE}(\text{I}_2) = 151.0$ kJ/mol; the question of what is the lattice energy

Connections

The Born–Haber cycle

Solution

We will begin by constructing a Born–Haber cycle:

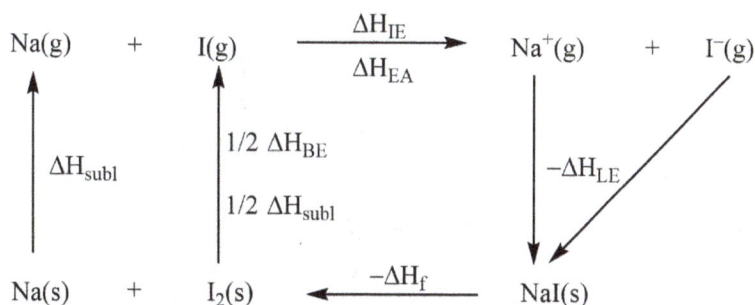

Since both sodium and iodine are solids, we need a separate sublimation energy for each.

The sum of energy changes for the reactions that make up this loop must be zero. We can start recording them at any point:

$$\Delta H_{subl}(\text{Na}) + 1/2\,\Delta H_{subl}(\text{I}_2) + 1/2\,\Delta H_{BE} + \Delta H_{IE} + \Delta H_{EA} - \Delta H_{LE} - \Delta H_f = 0$$

Rearranging to isolate the lattice energy gives

$$\Delta H_{subl}(\text{Na}) + 1/2\,\Delta H_{subl}(\text{I}_2) + 1/2\,\Delta H_{BE} + \Delta H_{IE} + \Delta H_{EA} - \Delta H_f = \Delta H_{LE}$$

Entering the appropriate values gives

$$107.32 \text{ kJ/mol} + 1/2\,(62.44 \text{ kJ/mol}) + 1/2\,(151.0 \text{ kJ/mol}) + 494 \text{ kJ/mol} + 295 \text{ kJ/mol}$$

$$-(-287.78 \text{ kJ/mol}) = \Delta H_{LE}$$

$$\Delta H_{LE} = 1,290.82 = \textbf{1,291 kJ/mol}$$

Reality Check

The magnitude of the answer seems reasonable. The significant figures and units are correct.

Follow-Up Problem 9.4a

Determine the lattice energy for zinc oxide, using the following information:

- heat of formation of zinc oxide, −348 kJ/mol
- first ionization energy of zinc, 0.906 MJ/mol
- second ionization energy of zinc, 1.733 MJ/mol
- first electron affinity of oxygen, −141 kJ/mol
- second electron affinity of oxygen, 744 kJ/mol
- sublimation energy of zinc, 130.3 kJ/mol
- bond energy of oxygen, 498.7 kJ/mol

Information

$\Delta H_f^\circ(ZnO) = -348$ kJ/mol, $IE_1(Zn) = 0.906$ MJ/mol, $IE_2(Zn) = 1.733$ MJ/mol, $EA_1(O) = -141$ kJ/mol, $EA_2(O) = 744$ kJ/mol, $\Delta H_{subl}(Zn) = 130.3$ kJ/mol, $\Delta H_{BE}(O_2) = 498.7$ kJ/mol; the question of what is the lattice energy

Connections

The Born–Haber cycle

Solution

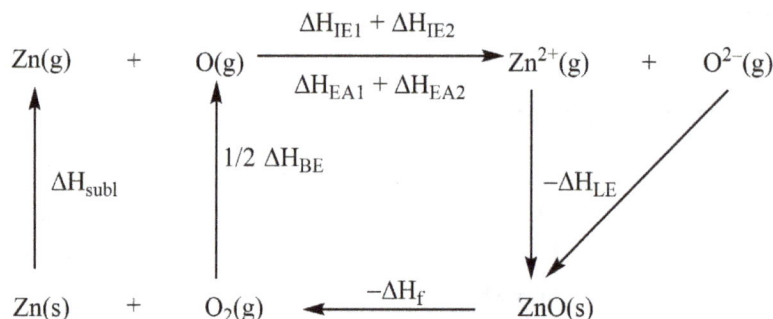

The sum of energy changes for the reactions that make up this loop must be zero. We can start recording them at any point.

To change a zinc atom to a zinc ion requires both the first and second ionization energy.

To change an oxygen atom to an oxide ion requires both the first and second electron affinity:

$$\Delta H_{subl}(Zn) + 1/2\ \Delta H_{BE}(O_2) + \Delta H_{IE1}(Zn) + \Delta H_{IE2}(Zn) + \Delta H_{EA1}(O) + \Delta H_{EA2}(O)$$
$$-\Delta H_{LE} - \Delta H_f = 0$$

Rearranging to isolate the lattice energy gives

$$\Delta H_{subl}(Zn) + 1/2\ \Delta H_{BE} + \Delta H_{IE1}(Zn) + \Delta H_{IE2}(Zn) + \Delta H_{EA1}(O) + \Delta H_{EA2}(O) - \Delta H_f = \Delta H_{LE}$$

Entering the appropriate values gives

$$130.3\ \text{kJ/mol} + 1/2\ (498.7\ \text{kJ/mol}) + (0.906 + 1.733)\ \text{MJ/mol}\left(\frac{10^6}{M}\right)\left(\frac{k}{10^3}\right)$$

$$+\ (-141 + 744)\ \text{kJ/mol} - (-348\ \text{kJ/mol}) = \Delta H_{LE}$$

$$\Delta H_{LE} = 396.65 = \textbf{3,970. kJ/mol}$$

Reality Check

The magnitude of the answer seems reasonable. The significant figures and units are correct.

Follow-Up Problem 9.4b

Determine the electron affinity for fluorine, using the following information:

- lattice energy for sodium fluoride, NaF, 914 kJ/mol
- heat of formation of sodium fluoride, −577 kJ/mol
- ionization energy of sodium, 494 kJ/mol;
- sublimation energy of sodium, 107.32 kJ/mol
- bond energy of fluorine, 150.6 kJ/mol

Information

$\Delta H_{LE}(NaF) = 914$ kJ/mol, $\Delta H_f^\circ(NaF) = -577$ kJ/mol, $IE_1(Na) = 494$ kJ/mol, $\Delta H_{subl}(Na) = 107.32$ kJ/mol, $\Delta H_{BE}(F_2) = 150.6$ kJ/mol; the question of what is the electron affinity for fluorine

Connections

The Born–Haber cycle

Solution

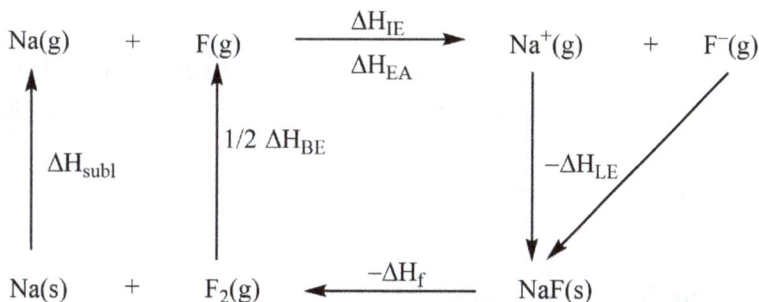

The sum of energy changes for the reactions that make up this loop must be zero. We can start recording them at any point.

$$\Delta H_{subl}(Na) + 1/2\ \Delta H_{BE}(F_2) + \Delta H_{IE}(Na) + \Delta H_{EA}(F) - \Delta H_{LE}(NaF) - \Delta H_f(NaF) = 0$$

Rearranging to isolate the electron affinity gives

$$-\Delta H_{subl}(Na) - 1/2\ \Delta H_{BE}(F_2) - \Delta H_{IE}(Na) + \Delta H_{LE}(NaF) + \Delta H_f(NaF) = \Delta H_{EA}(F)$$

Entering the appropriate values gives

$$\Delta H_f^\circ(NaF) = -577 \text{ kJ/mol, } IE_1(Na) = 494 \text{ kJ/mol}$$

$$-107.32 \text{ kJ/mol} - 1/2\ (150.6 \text{ kJ/mol}) - 494 \text{ kJ/mol} + 914 \text{ kJ/mol} + (-577 \text{ kJ/mol}) = \Delta H_{EA}(F)$$

$$\Delta H_{EA}(F) = -339.62 = \textbf{−340. kJ/mol}$$

Reality Check

The magnitude of the answer seems reasonable. The significant figures and units are correct.

END-OF-CHAPTER PROBLEMS

9.1 Basic Bonding Types

9.1 Which electrons are the key to the chemistry of atoms?

Solution

The valence electrons are the key to the chemistry of atoms.

9.3 If zinc were treated as a representative element, how many valence electrons would it have?

Solution

Zinc has the electron configuration $[Ar]4s^23d^{10}$, which would indicate <u>two valence electrons</u>. These are the $4s^2$ electrons, the only electrons in the outside shell.

9.4 How many valence electrons does each of the following atoms possess? **(a)** Na, **(b)** Al, **(c)** As, **(d)** Se, **(e)** F

Solution

While it is possible to write the full electron configuration for these elements, it is easier to simply locate each of the elements on the periodic table and note which column they are located in. (Notice that the old method of identifying columns with a number and a letter is more useful.)

(a) one valence electron [column 1 (1A)]; **(b) three** valence electrons [column 13 (3A)]; **(c) five** valence electrons [column 15 (5A)]; **(d) six** valence electrons [column 16 (6A)]; **(e) seven** valence electrons [column 17 (7A)]

9.5 What are the three bonding types?

Solution

The three types of bonds are ionic, covalent, and metallic.

9.7 In which of the following substances is the bonding like that found in water, H_2O? **(a)** gasoline, **(b)** chalk, **(c)** brass, **(d)** vegetable oil, **(e)** sugar

Solution

Water has covalent bonding like gasoline, vegetable oil, and sugar. Brass, an alloy of Cu and Zn, has metallic bonding, and chalk, $CaCO_3$, has ionic bonding.

9.11 **(a)** If a compound is ionic, what is the minimum electronegativity difference between the atoms? **(b)** If a compound is covalent, what is the minimum electronegativity difference between the atoms?

Solution

(a) The minimum difference for ionic bonding is 1.7 (in this textbook). **(b)** The minimum difference for covalent bonding is 0.

9.14 Arrange the following compounds in order of increasing ionic bonding character: **(a)** $MgCl_2$, **(b)** $SiCl_4$, **(c)** NaCl, **(d)** $AlCl_3$, **(e)** PCl_5

Solution

All these compounds contain chlorine, Cl. Locate chlorine on the periodic table. The further another element is from chlorine, the more ionic the bond will be. This gives the following sequence: **PCl_5 < $SiCl_4$ < $AlCl_3$ < $MgCl_2$ < NaCl** (most ionic).

9.2 Lewis Structures of Atoms and Ions

9.16 Show four different ways to draw the Lewis symbol of a hydrogen atom.

Solution

There are numerous ways besides the ones shown here. For hydrogen, every correct Lewis symbol must have the symbol for hydrogen, H, and some indication of the one valence electron present in a hydrogen atom.

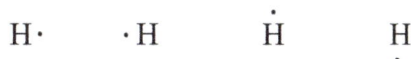

$$H \cdot \qquad \cdot H \qquad \overset{\cdot}{H} \qquad \underset{\cdot}{H}$$

9.20 Draw a Lewis symbol for each of the following: **(a)** Li, **(b)** Se, **(c)** Pb, **(d)** Al^{3+}, **(e)** P^{3-}

Solution

The Lewis symbol must show the chemical symbol for the element plus some indication of the valence electrons present in an atom of that element. Anions have additional electrons equal to the negative charge. Cations lose electrons from the Lewis symbol of the atoms; the number of electrons lost equals the positive charge.

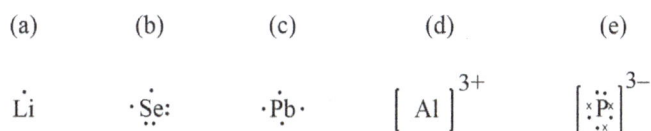

(a)	(b)	(c)	(d)	(e)
$\overset{\cdot}{Li}$	$\cdot \overset{\cdot}{\underset{\cdot\cdot}{Se}}:$	$\cdot \overset{\cdot}{\underset{\cdot}{Pb}} \cdot$	$\left[Al \right]^{3+}$	$\left[{}_{x}^{\cdot\cdot}\overset{\cdot\cdot}{\underset{\cdot x}{P}}{}_{x} \right]^{3-}$

The positions and symbols of the electrons may vary. For each symbol, dots are used for original electrons and x's are used for the electrons added when forming an anion.

9.3 Ionic Bonding

9.21 **(a)** Which elements are most likely to form anions? **(b)** Which elements are most likely to form cations? **(c)** Locate these groups on the periodic table.

Solution

(a) Nonmetals are more likely to form anions. **(b)** Metals are more likely to form cations. **(c)** Nonmetals are to the (upper) right and metals are to the left of the periodic table. (Hydrogen, as usual, is an exception, as it is a nonmetal in the metal region of the periodic table.)

9.24 The electron configuration for sulfur is $1s^2 2s^2 2p^6 3s^2 3p^4$. **(a)** How many valence electrons does sulfur have? **(b)** What is the relationship between sulfur's valence electrons and its position on the periodic table? **(c)** Which of the electrons on sulfur are the valence electrons? **(d)** How many electrons would sulfur be expected to gain when forming an anion? **(e)** Write the electron configuration for the anion sulfur is expected to form.

Solution

(a) Sulfur has <u>six</u> valence electrons. **(b)** It is in column 16 (6A), and all elements in this column have six valence electrons. **(c)** The valence electrons are $3s^2$ and $3p^4$. **(d)** Sulfur would be expected to add <u>two</u> electrons (to complete an octet). **(e)** The electron configuration of S^{2-} is $1s^2 2s^2 2p^6 3s^2 3p^6$.

9.27 Give Lewis structures for the following compounds, and identify any ions that do not obey the octet rule: **(a)** calcium fluoride, **(b)** lithium phosphide, **(c)** tin(II) oxide, **(d)** sodium sulfide, **(e)** magnesium nitride

Solution

(a) Both ions obey the octet rule. (b) Li^+ does not obey the octet rule but P^{3-} does. (c) Sn^{2+} does not obey the octet rule but O^{2-} does. (d) Both ions obey the octet rule. (e) Both ions obey the octet rule.

You may have a different arrangement of the electrons. For each symbol, dots are used for original electrons on the nonmetals and x's are used for the electrons originally on the metal atom.

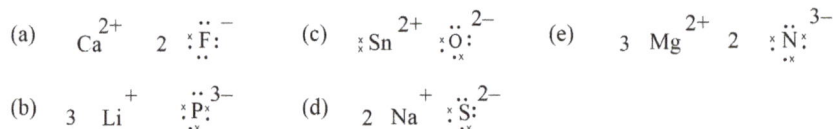

(a) Ca^{2+} 2 $\colon\overset{\cdot\cdot}{\underset{\cdot\cdot}{F}}\colon^{-}$ (c) $_x Sn^{2+}$ $\colon\overset{\cdot\cdot}{\underset{\cdot x}{O}}\colon^{2-}$ (e) 3 Mg^{2+} 2 $_x\overset{\cdot\cdot}{\underset{\cdot x}{N}}\colon^{3-}$

(b) 3 Li^{+} $_x\overset{\cdot\cdot}{\underset{\cdot x}{P}}\colon^{3-}$ (d) 2 Na^{+} $_x\overset{\cdot\cdot}{\underset{\cdot x}{S}}\colon^{2-}$

Reality Check

To prove which ions obey the octet rule, just write their electron configurations. The electron configurations of the ions obeying the octet rule are $Ca^{2+} = P^{3-} = S^{2-} = 1s^2 2s^2 2p^6 \mathbf{3s^2 3p^6}$ and $F^- = O^{2-} = N^{3-} = Na^+ = 1s^2 \mathbf{2s^2 2p^6}$. The octets are in boldface.

9.29 (a) Is the formation of a cation oxidation, or is it reduction? (b) Is the formation of an anion oxidation, or is it reduction?

Solution

(a) The formation of a cation is an oxidation. (b) The formation of an anion is a reduction.

9.31 (a) Draw the Lewis symbols of a nitrogen atom, an oxygen atom, and a fluorine atom. (b) On your Lewis symbols, indicate where the atom will gain electrons to form an anion.

Solution

The positioning of the arrows depends upon how you arranged your electrons. Your answers should have the same number of arrows.

9.33 Use Lewis symbols to diagram the reaction of potassium atoms with bromine atoms to form a compound.

Solution

The reaction asked for is $K + Br \rightarrow KBr$. In the following, the Lewis symbol for the K atom is the chemical symbol for potassium plus a circle to indicate the one valence electron. The Lewis symbol for the Br is the chemical symbol for bromine plus a dot for each of the seven valence electrons. The K loses its one valence electron to become K^+, while the Br gains the electron lost by the K to form Br^-. Using different symbols for the electrons on the two atoms involved makes it easier to see how the electron was transferred during the reaction.

$$K° + \cdot\overset{\cdot\cdot}{\underset{\cdot\cdot}{Br}}\colon \longrightarrow K^+ + \overset{\cdot\cdot}{\underset{\cdot\cdot}{_\circ Br}}\colon^{-}$$

Note that this problem says to begin with atoms. Therefore, there is no Br_2 present. The small circle is the electron transferred from the K to the Br.

9.35 Each of the following pairs of elements will form an ionic compound. In each case, predict the formula for the compound: (a) Li and I; (b) Ba and Cl; (c) Na and P; (d) Ca and S; (e) Al and Se

Solution

You may wish to refer to the Nomenclature Resource. The ions that will form and the formulas are as follows:

(a) Li^+ and I^- form and combine to give **LiI**.

(b) Ba^{2+} and Cl^- form and combine to give **$BaCl_2$**.

(c) Na^+ and P^{3-} form and combine to give **Na_3P**.

(d) Ca^{2+} and S^{2-} form and combine to give **CaS**.

(e) Al^{3+} and Se^{2-} form and combine to give **Al_2Se_3**.

Reality Check

As always, the total charge of the ions for any compound must be 0.

9.37 What is the name or the formula of each of the following ionic compounds: **(a)** $FeCl_3$; **(b)** $CdCl_2$; **(c)** $MnCl_3$; **(d)** $CoSO_4$; **(e)** ZnF_2; **(f)** manganese(IV) oxide; **(g)** lead(II) fluoride; **(h)** iron(III) oxide; **(i)** silver(II) fluoride; **(j)** nickel(II) thiosulfate

Solution

You may wish to refer to the Nomenclature Resource.

(a) $FeCl_3$		iron(III) chloride
(b) $CdCl_2$		cadmium chloride
(c) $MnCl_3$		manganese(III) chloride
(d) $CoSO_4$		cobalt(II) sulfate
(e) ZnF_2		zinc fluoride
(f) manganese(IV) oxide		MnO_2
(g) lead(II) fluoride		PbF_2
(h) iron(III) oxide		Fe_2O_3
(i) silver(II) fluoride		AgF_2
(j) nickel(II) thiosulfate		NiS_2O_3

9.4 The Octet Rule

9.41 Using electron configurations, show why each of the following obeys the octet rule: **(a)** O^{2-}; **(b)** K^+; **(c)** Xe; **(d)** As^{3-}; **(e)** Ra^{2+}

Solution

The bold electrons make the octet.

(a) $1s^2\mathbf{2s^2 2p^6}$

(b) $1s^2 2s^2 2p^6 \mathbf{3s^2 3p^6}$

(c) $1s^2 2s^2 2p^6 3s^2 3p^6 4s^2 3d^{10} 4p^6 \mathbf{5s^2} 4d^{10} \mathbf{5p^6}$

(d) $1s^2 2s^2 2p^6 3s^2 3p^6 \mathbf{4s^2} 3d^{10} \mathbf{4p^6}$

(e) $1s^2 2s^2 2p^6 3s^2 3p^6 4s^2 3d^{10} 4p^6 5s^2 4d^{10} 5p^6 \mathbf{6s^2} 4f^{14} 5d^{10} \mathbf{6p^6}$

9.43 Assign the most likely charge to the ions formed by the second-period elements. Which of these ions do obey the octet rule and which do not?

Solution

The most likely ions to form are Li^+, Be^{2+}, B^{3+}, C^{4+} or C^{4-}, N^{3-}, O^{2-}, F^-, and no ion for Ne; however, neither carbon ion really occurs in compounds.

Octets occur for C^{4-}, N^{3-}, O^{2-}, F^-, and Ne; all are isoelectronic: $1s^2\mathbf{2s^22p^6}$

9.45 Write a chemical equation illustrating the reaction of a chlorine atom to produce an ion obeying the octet rule. What is the name of this energy change?

Solution

The process is: $Cl + e^- \rightarrow Cl^-$. During this reaction the chlorine goes from $1s^22s^22p^63s^23p^5$ to $1s^22s^22p^6\mathbf{3s^23p^6}$ (octet in bold).

The energy change is the **electron affinity**.

9.47 Which noble gas does not obey the octet rule?

Solution

Helium only has two electrons ($1s^2$); therefore, it cannot obey the octet rule.

9.5 The Born–Haber Cycle

9.50 The Born–Haber cycle requires the following information: (a) *the standard heat of formation*, (b) *the ionization energy*, (c) *the electron affinity*, (d) *the sublimation energy*, and (e) *the bond energy*. Define each of these terms.

Solution

(a) The **standard heat of formation** is the energy change when one mole of a substance is produced from the elements under standard conditions.

(b) The **ionization energy** is the energy required to remove an electron from a gaseous atom it the ground state.

(c) The **electron affinity** is the energy change when an electron is added to a gaseous atom in the ground state.

(d) The **sublimation energy** is the energy required to convert a solid directly to a gas.

(e) The **bond energy** is the energy required to break a covalent bond.

9.53 Which member of each of the following pairs has the higher lattice energy? Explain your answer in each case. (a) NaCl and KCl; (b) $BaCl_2$ and $MgCl_2$; (c) NaF and CaO

Solution

(a) **NaCl** has a higher lattice energy, because Na^+ is smaller than K^+ with everything else being the same. (b) $\mathbf{MgCl_2}$ has a higher lattice energy, because Mg^{2+} is smaller than Ba^{2+} with everything else being the same. (c) **CaO** has a higher lattice energy, because the charges of the ions are higher in CaO (+2 and –2) than in NaF (+1 and –1).

9.55 Determine the lattice energy for potassium fluoride. Use the following information: heat of formation of potassium fluoride, –568.6 kJ/mol; ionization energy of potassium, 419 kJ/mol; electron affinity of fluorine, –328 kJ/mol; sublimation energy of potassium, 89.2 kJ/mol; bond energy of fluorine, 150.6 kJ/mol.

Information

$\Delta H_f^{\circ}(KF) = -348$ kJ/mol, $IE_1(K) = 419$ kJ/mol, $EA_1(F) = -328$ kJ/mol, $\Delta H_{subl}(K) = 89.2$ kJ/mol, $\Delta H_{BE}(F_2) = 150.6$ kJ/mol; the question of what is the lattice energy

Connections

The Born–Haber cycle

Solution

For this compound, the Born–Haber cycle is

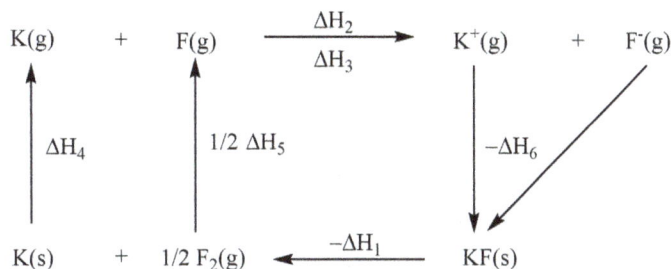

$\Delta H_1 = -568.6$ kJ/mole, $\Delta H_2 = 419$ kJ/mole, $\Delta H_3 = -328$ kJ/mole, $\Delta H_4 = 89.2$ kJ/mole, $\Delta H_5 = 150.6$ kJ/ mole, $\Delta H_6 = ?$

$$\Delta H_4 + (1/2)\, \Delta H_5 + \Delta H_2 + \Delta H_3 - \Delta H_6 - \Delta H_1 = 0$$

$$\Delta H_4 + (1/2)\, \Delta H_5 + \Delta H_2 + \Delta H_3 - \Delta H_1 = \Delta H_6$$

(89.2 kJ/mole) + (1/2)(150.6 kJ/mole) + (419 kJ/mole) +(−328 kJ/mole) − (−568.6 kJ/mole)
= 824.1 = **824 kJ/mol**

9.57 Determine the ionization energy for cesium. Use the following information: lattice energy for cesium fluoride, CsF, 743.9 kJ/mol; heat of formation of cesium fluoride, −554.7 kJ/mol; electron affinity of fluorine, −328 kJ/mol; sublimation energy of cesium, 76.7 kJ/mol; bond energy of fluorine, 150.6 kJ/mol.

Information

$\Delta H_{LE}(CsF) = 743.9$ kJ/mol, $\Delta H_f^{\circ}(CsF) = -554.7$ kJ/mol, $EA_1(F) = -328$ kJ/mol, $\Delta H_{subl}(Cs) = 76.7$ kJ/mol, $\Delta H_{BE}(F_2) = 150.6$ kJ/mol; the question of what is the ionization energy of cesium

Connections

The Born–Haber cycle

Solution

For this compound, the Born–Haber cycle is

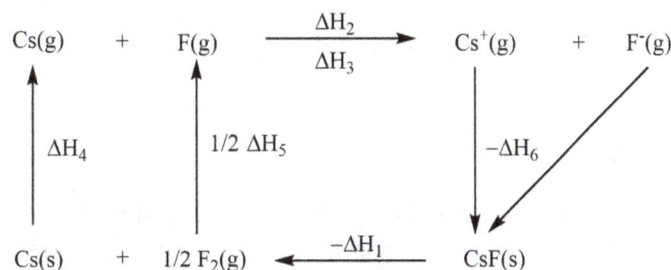

$\Delta H_1 = -554.7$ kJ/mole, $\Delta H_2 = \underline{?}$, $\Delta H_3 = -328$ kJ/mole, $\Delta H_4 = 76.7$ kJ/mole, $\Delta H_5 = 150.6$ kJ/mole, $\Delta H_6 = 743.9$ kJ/mole

$$\Delta H_4 + (1/2)\,\Delta H_5 + \Delta H_2 + \Delta H_3 - \Delta H_6 - \Delta H_1 = 0$$

$$-\Delta H_4 - (1/2)\,\Delta H_5 - \Delta H_3 + \Delta H_1 + \Delta H_6 = \Delta H_2$$

$-(76.7$ kJ/mole$) - (1/2)(150.6$ kJ/mole$) - (-328$ kJ/ mole$) + (-554.7$ kJ/mole$) + (743.9$ kJ/mole$)$
$= 365.2 = $ **365 kJ/mol**

9.6 Applications and Extensions

9.60 **(a)** List five important cations present in blood. **(b)** List three important anions present in blood.

Solution

See table 9.3.

(a) Five important cations in the blood are Ca^{2+}, Fe^{2+}/Fe^{3+}, Mg^{2+}, K^+, and Na^+.

(b) Three important anions in the blood are Cl^-, HCO_3^-, and PO_4^{3-}.

9.62 What ion is typically present in the highest concentration in blood plasma?

Solution

The ion that typically has the highest concentration in blood is Na^+ (135–146 mmol/L).

9.66 If a person has an iron level of 0.02 mmol/L, how many milligrams of iron(II) sulfate, $FeSO_4$, are needed to raise this level to 180 mg/kg of body weight? Assume that there are 4.7 L of blood plasma present in the person's body and that the person weighs 73 kg.

Information

The initial iron level of 0.02 mmol/L and the desired iron level of 180 mg/kg; 4.7 L of blood plasma; the person's weight of 73 kg; the question of how many milligrams of $FeSO_4$ are needed to raise the level

Solution

$$\text{Mass of iron necessary} = (73 \text{ kg})\left(\frac{180 \text{ mg Fe}}{\text{kg}}\right) = 1{,}3140 = 1.3 \times 10^4 \text{ mg Fe}$$

$$\text{Mass of iron present} = (4.7 \text{ L})\left(\frac{0.02 \text{ mmol Fe}}{\text{L}}\right)\left(\frac{55.845 \text{ mg Fe}}{1 \text{ mmol Fe}}\right) = 5.24943 = 5 \text{ mg Fe}$$

Mass of iron needed to increase the concentration $= (1{,}3140 - 5.24943)$ mg $\approx 1{,}3135$ mg Fe

$$\text{Mass of } FeSO_4 \text{ needed} = (13{,}135 \text{ mg Fe})\left(\frac{1 \text{ mmol Fe}}{55.845 \text{ mg Fe}}\right)\left(\frac{1 \text{ mmole } FeSO_4}{1 \text{ mmole Fe}}\right)\left(\frac{151.905 \text{ mg } FeSO_4}{1 \text{ mmole } FeSO_4}\right)$$

$$= 35{,}728.75 = \mathbf{3.6 \times 10^4 \text{ mg } FeSO_4}$$

9.67 List the three Solubility Rules.

Solution

1. Compounds containing ions with a +1 or –1 charge are normally soluble.
2. Compounds containing ions with a ±3 or greater charge are normally not soluble.
3. Compounds containing ions with a –2 charge are normally not soluble.

9.71 What effect does the size of an ion have on the solubility of compounds containing the ion?

Solution

Compounds with larger ions tend to have lower lattice energies and, for this reason, they tend to be more soluble.

9.74 Write net ionic equations for each of the following reactions: **(a)** An aqueous solution of ammonium iodide, NH_4I, reacts with an aqueous solution of lead(II) nitrate, $Pb(NO_3)_2$. **(b)** An aqueous solution of potassium sulfide, K_2S, reacts with an aqueous solution of cobalt(II) sulfate, $CoSO_4$. **(c)** An aqueous solution of ammonium arsenate, $(NH_4)_3AsO_4$, reacts with an aqueous solution of magnesium chlorate, $Mg(ClO_3)_2$. **(d)** An aqueous solution of barium nitrite, $Ba(NO_2)_2$, reacts with an aqueous solution of lithium sulfate, Li_2SO_4. **(e)** An aqueous solution of lead(II) acetate, $Pb(C_2H_3O_2)_2$, reacts with an aqueous solution of cesium bromide, CsBr.

Solution

In each case, begin with the balanced molecular equation, then separate the ions for all strong electrolytes. Finally, cancel the spectator ions. As a simplification, since all the reactants are in aqueous solution, the ionic reactants must be strong electrolytes.

(a)
$$2\ NH_4I(aq) + Pb(NO_3)_2(aq) \rightarrow PbI_2(s) + 2\ NH_4NO_3(aq)$$

$$2\ NH_4^+(aq) + 2\ I^-(aq) + Pb^{2+}(aq) + 2\ NO_3^-(aq) \rightarrow PbI_2(s) + 2\ NH_4^+(aq) + 2\ NO_3^-(aq)$$

$$\mathbf{2\ I^-(aq) + Pb^{2+}(aq) \rightarrow PbI_2(s)}$$

(b)
$$K_2S(aq) + CoSO_4(aq) \rightarrow CoS(s) + K_2SO_4(aq)$$

$$2\ K^+(aq) + S^{2-}(aq) + Co^{2+}(aq) + SO_4^{2-}(aq) \rightarrow CoS(s) + 2\ K^+(aq) + SO_4^{2-}(aq)$$

$$\mathbf{S^{2-}(aq) + Co^{2+}(aq) \rightarrow CoS(s)}$$

(c)
$$2\ (NH_4)_3AsO_4(aq) + 3\ Mg(ClO_3)_2(aq) \rightarrow Mg_3(AsO_4)_2(s) + 6\ NH_4ClO_3(aq)$$

$$6\ NH_4^+(aq) + 2\ AsO_4^{3-}(aq) + 3\ Mg^{2+}(aq) + 6\ ClO_3^-(aq) \rightarrow Mg_3(AsO_4)_2(s) + 6\ NH_4^+(aq) + 6\ ClO_3^-(aq)$$

$$\mathbf{2\ AsO_4^{3-}(aq) + 3\ Mg^{2+}(aq) \rightarrow Mg_3(AsO_4)_2(s)}$$

(d)
$$Ba(NO_2)_2(aq) + Li_2SO_4(aq) \rightarrow BaSO_4(s) + 2\ LiNO_2(aq)$$

$$Ba^{2+}(aq) + 2\ NO_2^-(aq) + 2\ Li^+(aq) + SO_4^{2-}(aq) \rightarrow BaSO_4(s) + 2\ NO_2^-(aq) + 2\ Li^+(aq)$$

$$\mathbf{Ba^{2+}(aq) + SO_4^{2-}(aq) \rightarrow BaSO_4(s)}$$

(e)
$$Pb(C_2H_3O_2)_2(aq) + 2\ CsBr(aq) \rightarrow PbBr_2(s) + 2\ CsC_2H_3O_2(aq)$$

$$Pb^{2+}(aq) + 2\ C_2H_3O_2^-(aq) + 2\ Cs^+(aq) + 2\ Br^-(aq) \rightarrow PbBr_2(s) + 2\ C_2H_3O_2^-(aq) + 2\ Cs^+(aq)$$

$$\mathbf{2\ Br^-(aq) + Pb^{2+}(aq) \rightarrow PbBr_2(s)}$$

Putting it All Together

9.77 For the representative elements, how does the number of valence electrons relate to the position of the element on the periodic table?

Solution

For the representative elements (the A columns) the number of valence electrons equals the number in front of the A (except for He).

In the newer system (no A's or B's), the number of valence electrons equals the column number for the first two columns and equals the column number minus 10 for the last 6 columns (except for He)

9.79 Use arrows to indicate the direction the electrons will shift in each of the following polar bonds (The arrows should go from the less electronegative atom to the more electronegative atom.): **(a)** O–As; **(b)** Cl–F; **(c)** O–C; **(d)** S–Al; **(e)** C–H

Solution

The arrow must point toward the more electronegative element (closer to F on the periodic table). As expected, hydrogen is an exception.

(a) O←As

(b) Cl→F

(c) O←C

(d) S←Al

(e) C←H

9.81 What type of bonding is expected to occur in each of the following compounds?
(a) Mg_3N_2; **(b)** CuZn; **(c)** ClF_3

Solution

(a) A metal plus a nonmetal combined is usually **ionic**. **(b)** Two metals combined is usually **metallic**. **(c)** Two nonmetals combined are usually **covalent**.

9.84 Name or give the formula for each of the following ionic compounds: **(a)** potassium phosphate; **(b)** calcium nitrite; **(c)** aluminum chloride; **(d)** barium carbonate; **(e)** cadmium acetate; **(f)** KO_2; **(g)** Mg_3N_2; **(h)** SrS; **(i)** $(NH_4)H_2PO_4$; **(j)** $Mg(HCO_3)_2$

Solution

See the Nomenclature Resource.

(a)	potassium phosphate	K_3PO_4
(b)	calcium nitrite	$Ca(NO_2)_2$
(c)	aluminum chloride	$AlCl_3$
(d)	barium carbonate	$Ba(HCO_3)_2$
(e)	cadmium acetate	$Cd(C_2H_3O_2)_2$
(f)	KO_2	**potassium superoxide**
(g)	Mg_3N_2	**magnesium nitride**
(h)	SrS	**strontium sulfide**
(i)	$(NH_4)H_2PO_4$	**ammonium dihydrogen phosphate**
(j)	$Mg(HCO_3)_2$	**magnesium bicarbonate or magnesium hydrogen carbonate**

9.86 **(a)** Write the electron configuration of phosphorus. **(b)** Indicate the valence electrons in your electron configuration of phosphorus. **(c)** How many electrons does phosphorus need to gain to achieve an octet?

Solution

(a) The electron configuration of P is **$1s^2 2s^2 2p^3 3s^2 3p^3$**. **(b)** The valence electrons are the **$3s^2 3p^3$** electrons. **(c)** Phosphorus has five valence electrons, and it needs $(8 - 5) = 3$ electrons to complete an octet.

9.89

(a) A 0.500-g sample of sodium metal was placed in a bomb calorimeter and reacted with an excess of fluorine gas. The temperature of the calorimeter rose from 23.25°C to 28.25°C. The heat capacity of the calorimeter was 3.97 kJ/°C. Determine the heat of formation of sodium fluoride.

(b) Determine the lattice energy for sodium fluoride. Use the following information: ionization energy of sodium, 496 kJ/mol; electron affinity of fluorine, –328 kJ/mol; sublimation energy of sodium, 107.76 kJ/mol; bond energy of fluorine, 150.6 kJ/mol

Information

(a) The mass of a sample of Na (0.500 g); a temperature change (23.25°C to 28.25°C); the heat capacity of the calorimeter (3.97 kJ/°C); the question of what is the heat of formation of sodium fluoride

(b) $\Delta H_f^\circ(\text{NaF})$ = from (a); $IE_1(\text{Na})$ = 496 kJ/mol; $EA_1(\text{F})$ = –328 kJ/mol; $\Delta H_{subl}(\text{Na})$ = 107.76 kJ/mol; $\Delta H_{BE}(\text{F}_2)$ = 150.6 kJ/mol; the question of what is the lattice energy of NaF

Connections

As always, moles are the key.

Solution

(a) Na(s) + 1/2 F$_2$(g) → NaF(s)

$$\text{Heat of formation of NaF} = \frac{\left(\frac{3.97 \text{ kJ}}{°C}\right)(28.25 - 23.25)°C}{(0.500 \text{ g Na})\frac{1 \text{ mol Na}}{22.9898 \text{ g Na}}\left(\frac{1 \text{ mol NaF}}{1 \text{ mol Na}}\right)} = -912.69506$$

$$= \mathbf{-913 \text{ kJ/mol}}$$

(b) For this compound, the Born–Haber cycle is

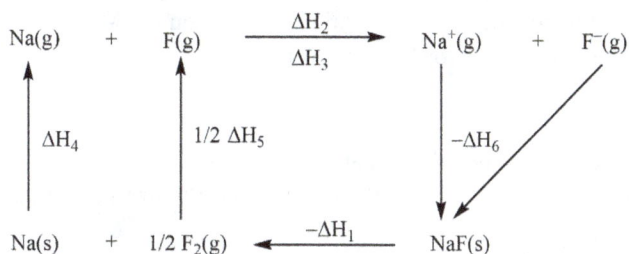

ΔH_1 = –912.69506 kJ/mole, ΔH_2 = 496 kJ/mole, ΔH_3 = –328 kJ/mole, ΔH_4 = 107.76 kJ/mole, ΔH_5 = 150.6 kJ/mole, ΔH_6 = ?

$$\Delta H_4 + (1/2)\,\Delta H_5 + \Delta H_2 + \Delta H_3 - \Delta H_6 - \Delta H_1 = 0$$

$$\Delta H_4 + (1/2)\,\Delta H_5 + \Delta H_2 + \Delta H_3 - \Delta H_1 = \Delta H_6$$

(107.76 kJ/mole) − (1/2) (150.6 kJ/mole) + (496 kJ/mole) + (−328 kJ/mole) − (−912.69506/mole) = 1,113.155 = **1,113 kJ/mol**

9.92 **(a)** What volume, in milliliters, of hydrogen chloride gas at 745 mmHg and 27°C is needed to precipitate all the lead ions from 150.0 mL of a 0.15 M lead(II) nitrate? **(b)** What is the percent yield if only 975 mL formed?

Information
(a) A HCl sample has a pressure of 745 mmHg at 27°C reacting with 150.0 mL of a 0.15 M $Pb(NO_3)_2$; the question of what is the volume of HCl (mL); **(b)** If there are only 975 mL HCl, the question of what is the percent yield

Connections
Moles are the key. $PV = nRT$; the definition of *percent yield*

$$(\text{Percent yield} = \frac{\text{Actual yield}}{\text{Theoretical yield}} \times 100\%)$$

Solution
(a) We need to begin with a balanced chemical equation:

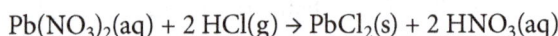

$$Pb(NO_3)_2(aq) + 2\ HCl(g) \rightarrow PbCl_2(s) + 2\ HNO_3(aq)$$

Rearrange $PV = nRT$ and enter the appropriate values. (The calculation in the numerator enclosed in [ ] is the determine in the moles, *n*.)

$$V = \frac{nRT}{P}$$

$$= \frac{\left[\left[\left(\dfrac{0.15\ \text{mol}\ Pb(NO_3)_3}{1,000\ \text{mL}}\right)(150.0\ \text{mL})\left(\dfrac{2\ \text{mol}\ HCl}{1\ \text{mol}\ Pb(NO_3)_3}\right)\right]\left(0.08206\ \dfrac{\text{L}\cdot\text{atm}}{\text{mol}\cdot\text{K}}\right)(300.\text{K})\right]}{(745\ \text{mmHg})\left(\dfrac{1\ \text{atm}}{760\ \text{mmHg}}\right)}\left(\dfrac{\text{m}}{0.001}\right)$$

$$= 1,130.11 = \mathbf{1.1 \times 10^3\ mL\ HCl} \quad \text{(Theoretical yield)}$$

(b) Percent yield $= \dfrac{\textit{Actual yield}}{\textit{Theoretical yield}} \times 100\% = \dfrac{975\ \text{mL}}{1130.11\ \text{mL}} \times 100\% = 86.27 = \mathbf{86\%}$

9.94 A 0.500-g sample of a compound containing aluminum and oxygen was decomposed to the elements. After the decomposition, 178.6 mL of oxygen gas at 765 torr and 25°C was isolated. Write the Lewis structure for the compound.

Information
A sample (0.500 g) of a compound Al_xO_y that was decomposed to release 178.6 mL of O_2 at 765 torr and 25°C; the question of what is the Lewis structure of this compound

Connections
Moles are the key. $PV = nRT$

Solution

First, determine the moles of O:

$$n = \frac{PV}{RT} = \frac{(765 \text{ torr})(178.6 \text{ mL})}{\left(0.08206 \frac{\text{L atm}}{\text{mol K}}\right)(298 \text{ K})} \left(\frac{0.001}{\text{m}}\right)\left(\frac{1 \text{ atm}}{760 \text{ torr}}\right)\left(\frac{2 \text{ mole O}}{1 \text{ mole O}_2}\right) = \frac{1.4703 \times 10^{-2} \text{ mole O}}{9.8134 \times 10^{-3} \text{ mole Al}}$$

$$= 1.498$$

Next, determine the mass and then the moles of Al. Diving by the smaller number of moles leads to the formula.

$$\text{Mass Al} = 0.500\text{-g sample} - [1.4703 \times 10^{-2} \text{ mol O } (15.999 \text{ g O / mol O})] = 0.2647667 \text{ g Al}$$

$$(0.2647667 \text{ g Al})\left(\frac{1 \text{ mole Al}}{26.98 \text{ g Al}}\right) = \frac{9.8134 \times 10^{-3} \text{ mole Al}}{9.8134 \times 10^{-3} \text{ mole Al}} = 1$$

We need to multiply both results by 2 to get whole number answers:

$$\text{O: } 1.498 \times 2 = 3$$
$$\text{Al: } 1 \times 2 = 2$$

This gives **Al_2O_3**

$$2 \quad Al^{3+} \quad + \quad 3 \quad :\overset{..}{\underset{.x}{O}}\overset{x}{:}^{2-}$$

The electrons on the oxide ion are dots for the original six electrons and the x's for the electrons transferred from the aluminum.

Reality Check

The compound of aluminum and oxygen is expected to be ionic as shown in the Lewis structure. The empirical formula of an ionic compound is the same as its chemical formula.

9.96 The most stable ions of the first-row transition elements are Sc^{3+}, Ti^{4+}, V^{5+}, Cr^{3+}, Mn^{2+}, Fe^{3+}, Co^{2+}, Ni^{2+}, Cu^{2+}, and Zn^{2+}. **(a)** Write electron configurations for each of these ions. **(b)** Which of the most stable ions of the first-row transition elements obey the octet rule?

Solution

	(a)	(b)
Sc^{3+}	**[Ar]**	**Octet**
Ti^{4+}	**[Ar]**	**Octet**
V^{5+}	**[Ar]**	**Octet**
Cr^{3+}	**[Ar]3d³**	**No octet**
Mn^{2+}	**[Ar]3d⁵**	**No octet**
Fe^{3+}	**[Ar]3d⁵**	**No octet**
Co^{2+}	**[Ar]3d⁷**	**No octet**
Ni^{2+}	**[Ar]3d⁸**	**No octet** (the octet rule refers to s²p⁶, not d⁸)
Cu^{2+}	**[Ar]3d⁹**	**No octet**
Zn^{2+}	**[Ar]3d¹⁰**	**No octet**

9.99 Using Lewis symbols write a balanced chemical equation for the reaction of aluminum atoms with oxygen atoms to form a compound.

Solution

Each Al needs to lose three electrons and each oxygen needs to gain two electrons. The lowest common multiple of two and three is six. Two aluminum atoms must lose $2 \times 3 = 6$ electrons (x's) and three oxygen atoms must gain $3 \times 2 = 6$ electrons. Electrons lost = Electrons gained. The original oxygen electrons are indicated by dots.

$$2 \, \overset{x}{\underset{x}{Al}} \; + \; 3 \; \overset{\cdot\cdot}{\underset{\cdot}{O}} \colon \; \longrightarrow \; 2 \; Al^{3+} \; + \; 3 \; \overset{\cdot\cdot}{\underset{\cdot x}{\colon O}} \colon^{2-}$$

9.102 The assumption that metals combine with nonmetals to form ionic compounds is a useful guideline. As with all assumptions, however, there are exceptions. Determine the electronegativity difference in each of the following known compounds, and predict the type of bonding (assume that an electronegativity difference greater than 1.7 is ionic): (a) BeI_2; (b) ZnSe; (c) CsAu

Solution

Begin by determining the electronegativity values from figure 8.9.

Be = 1.57

I = 2.66

Zn = 1.65

Se = 2.55

Cs = 0.79

Au = 2.54

The electronegativity differences are

BeI_2: $(2.66 - 1.57) = 1.09$

ZnSe: $(2.55 - 1.65) = 0.90$

CsAu: $(2.54 - 0.79) = 1.75$

The first two compounds (BeI_2 and ZnSe) are **covalent**, not ionic, even though each is the combination of a metal with a nonmetal.

The last compound, CsAu, is **ionic**. CsAu is unusual in that it is a combination of two metals that has ionic bonding instead of metallic bonding.

CHAPTER 10

Chemical Bonding II— Sharing Electrons

The successful completion of these problems requires the following ten (10) items.

1. This chapter focuses on covalent bonding, while the last chapter focused on ionic bonding. In general, these two types of bonding are treated differently.
2. Lewis structures for covalent and ionic bonds appear different. Do not draw an ionic structure to represent a covalent structure, or vice versa.
3. The only choices for the representative elements are single, double, and triple bonds. There will never be more than six electrons being shared between two representative element atoms.
4. Hydrogen will never be a central atom.
5. The octet rule is a suggestion, not an absolute rule.
6. Elements in the first two periods on the periodic table will never ever exceed an octet of electrons. However, they may have less than an octet.
7. More than an octet becomes an option beginning with the third-period elements.
8. Other than the elements in groups 11 and 12 (1A and 2A), Lewis structures do not work well for transition elements.
9. Even though there is only a small difference in electronegativity, representative metals do not form covalent bonds with other metals.
10. Formal charges can be very important when we are predicting the stability of a Lewis structure.

Example Problem 10.1

Draw the Lewis structure for hydrogen chloride, HCl.

Information

The formula for the compound; the question of what is the Lewis structure

Connections

The number of valence electrons for each atom (H = 1, Cl = 7), from the periodic table or the electron configurations

Solution

Hydrogen, in column 1 on the periodic table, has one valence electron, while chlorine, in column 17 (7A), has seven valence electrons. The total number of electrons in the Lewis structure must be 1 + 7 = 8. Since there are only two atoms, they must be adjacent. We will examine the atoms in the order found in the formula, although since there are only two atoms, we may use any order (the best approach for a more complex molecule will be discussed below). Hydrogen has one valence electron (indicated by an ×) and needs one more electron to fill its outer shell. Placing the hydrogen valence electron between the two atoms gives

$$\text{H} \overset{\times}{} \text{Cl}$$

We can use one electron from the chlorine (indicated by a dot) to form a pair with the hydrogen electron. This satisfies the hydrogen requirement of one electron, and it yields a hydrogen-to-chlorine bond. The structure becomes

$$\text{H} \overset{.}{\times} \text{Cl}$$

We have now finished the hydrogen end of the molecule—we used its one electron and added the one electron needed to pair with it (optionally, this shared paired may be replaced by a line). We will now turn to the chlorine atom. Originally, the chlorine had seven electrons and needed one, but by placing the hydrogen electron between the two atoms, we have given the chlorine the one electron it required; therefore, it needs no more electrons. We also placed one of the seven valence electrons from the chlorine atom between the two atoms, and now we need to distribute the remaining six electrons (represented by dots). Adding these six electrons, as three pairs about the chlorine atom, gives the final Lewis structure:

$$\text{H} \overset{..}{\underset{..}{\times}} \overset{..}{\underset{..}{\text{Cl}}} \colon \quad \text{or} \quad \text{H} - \overset{..}{\underset{..}{\text{Cl}}} \colon$$

Reality Check

We should now check the result, making sure that all eight valence electrons are present. Hydrogen has its full complement of two electrons, and chlorine has its octet. Note: Instead of using different symbols for the electrons from different atoms, we could use different colors.

Follow-Up Problem 10.1a

Draw the Lewis structure for hydrogen selenide, H_2Se.

Information

The formula for the compound; the question of what is the Lewis structure

Connections

The number of valence electrons for each atom (H = 1, Se = 6), from the periodic table or the electron configurations

Solution

Hydrogen, in column 1 on the periodic table, has one valence electron (×), while selenium, in column 16 (6A), has six valence electrons (dots). The total number of electrons in the Lewis structure must be 2(1) + 6 = 8. Since there are three atoms, the selenium must be central to keep the hydrogen atoms separated (though the exact positioning is unimportant). Each hydrogen has one valence electron and needs one more electron to fill its outer shell. Each hydrogen will complete its pair by sharing one of the selenium electrons. The selenium atom began with six electrons and shares one electron from each of the hydrogen atoms to complete its octet. The resultant Lewis structure could be any of the following:

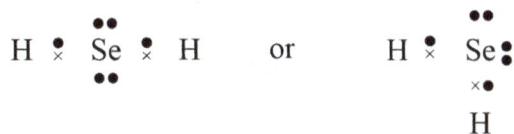

$$H \overset{\bullet\bullet}{\underset{\bullet\bullet}{\overset{\times}{:}}} Se \overset{\times}{:} H \qquad \text{or} \qquad H \overset{\bullet\bullet}{\underset{\times\bullet}{\overset{\times}{:}}} Se \overset{\bullet\bullet}{:}$$
$$\qquad\qquad\qquad\qquad\qquad\qquad\qquad\qquad H$$

Alternate representations could be

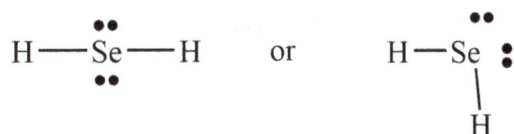

$$H \overset{\bullet\bullet}{\underset{\bullet\bullet}{—Se—}} H \qquad \text{or} \qquad H—\overset{\bullet\bullet}{Se} :$$
$$\qquad\qquad\qquad\qquad\qquad\qquad\qquad | $$
$$\qquad\qquad\qquad\qquad\qquad\qquad\qquad H$$

Reality Check

We should now check the result, making sure that all eight valence electrons are present. Hydrogen has its full complement of two electrons, and selenium has its octet. Note: No matter what arrangement is used, each hydrogen atom forms one bond to the selenium atom, and the selenium atom has two electron pairs that are not used in bonding.

Follow-Up Problem 10.1b

Draw the Lewis structure for carbon tetrachloride, CCl_4.

Information

The formula for the compound; the question of what is the Lewis structure

Connections

The number of valence electrons for each atom (C = 4, Cl = 7), from the periodic table or the electron configurations

Solution

Carbon, in column 14 (4A) on the periodic table, has four valence electrons, while chlorine, in column 17 (7A), has seven valence electrons. The total number of electrons in the Lewis structure must be 4(7) + 4 = 32. The carbon, which needs the most electrons to complete its octet, must be the central atom. This keeps the chlorine atoms separated from each other. Each chlorine has seven valence electrons and needs one more electron to complete an octet. Each chlorine will complete its octet by sharing one of the carbon electrons. The carbon atom began with four electrons, and it shares one electron from each of the chlorine atoms to complete its octet. The result is

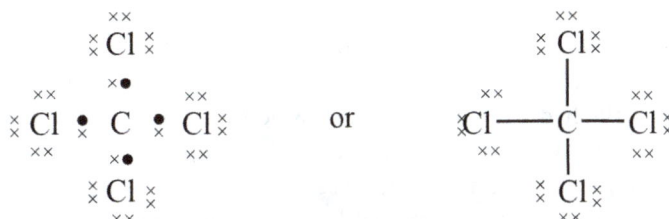

Reality Check

We should now check the result, making sure that all 32 valence electrons are present. All atoms have an octet.

Example Problem 10.2

Draw the Lewis structure for sulfuric acid, H_2SO_4.

Information

The formula for the compound; the question of what is the Lewis structure

Connections

The number of valence electrons for each atom (H = 1, O = 6, S = 6), from the periodic table or the electron configuration

Solution

Each hydrogen atom has one valence electron, the sulfur atom has six valence electrons, and each oxygen atom has six valence electrons, for a total of thirty-two valence electrons in a sulfuric acid molecule. Both sulfur and oxygen need two electrons each to complete an octet; one of these should be the central atom. The larger, sulfur, atom is the more likely candidate; as mentioned earlier, oxygen is seldom the central atom. Acidic hydrogen atoms attach to oxygen atoms. There are two acidic hydrogen atoms in sulfuric acid, so two oxygen atoms will have acidic hydrogen atoms attached. It does not matter which two of the four oxygen atoms are chosen. (There are numerous equivalent arrangements, all of which will yield a correct Lewis structure.) We will begin with the following arrangement:

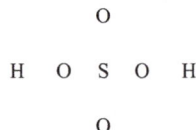

$$O$$
$$H \quad O \quad S \quad O \quad H$$
$$O$$

We can now start placing the electrons, beginning with any atom. Since there are two hydrogen atoms, let's treat them simultaneously: each of them has one electron and needs one electron. Inserting the hydrogen electrons (dots) between the hydrogen and oxygen atoms gives

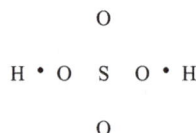

$$O$$
$$H \bullet O \quad S \quad O \bullet H$$
$$O$$

To complete the bonds and give each hydrogen atom its needed electron, an electron from the adjacent oxygen atom (×) must pair with each hydrogen electron. This gives

$$O$$
$$H \, \vdots \, O \quad S \quad O \, \vdots \, H$$
$$O$$

Having taken care of the hydrogen atoms, let's now go to the oxygen atoms adjacent to them. Each of these oxygen atoms began with six valence electrons and needed two more electrons. Beginning with the oxygen atom on the left, we see that it has already gained one of the needed electrons from the hydrogen atom adjacent to it. The second needed electron must come from the only other atom adjacent to that oxygen—the sulfur atom. If we place one of the sulfur electrons next to the oxygen atom, this oxygen atom has now gained the two electrons necessary. We do the same for the other oxygen atom adjacent to the other acidic hydrogen. The structure is now

$$O$$
$$H \overset{.}{:} O \overset{x}{_x} S \overset{x}{_x} O \overset{.}{:} H$$
$$O$$

Inserting an oxygen electron to form a pair with each lone sulfur electron completes a sulfur–oxygen bond on either side:

$$O$$
$$H \overset{.}{:} O \overset{.}{:} S \overset{.}{:} O \overset{.}{:} H$$
$$O$$

The oxygen atoms with the acidic hydrogen atoms have each used two of their six valence electrons, and each has four remaining. These four remaining valence electrons will appear as two pairs on each of those oxygen atoms, giving

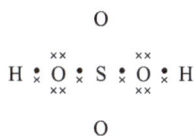

$$O$$
$$H \overset{.}{:} \overset{xx}{\underset{xx}{O}} \overset{.}{:} S \overset{.}{:} \overset{xx}{\underset{xx}{O}} \overset{.}{:} H$$
$$O$$

We are now finished with those two oxygen atoms. Let's go to the remaining oxygen atoms, each of which needs to gain two electrons. The source of these electrons must be the only atom adjacent to the oxygen atoms—the sulfur atom. Positioning two of the sulfur valence electrons adjacent to the remaining oxygen atoms will complete the electron requirement of each of the oxygen atoms and will place all six sulfur valence electrons in our Lewis structure:

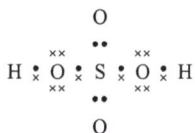

$$O$$
$$H \overset{.}{:} \overset{xx}{\underset{xx}{O}} \overset{.}{:} \overset{\bullet\bullet}{\underset{\bullet\bullet}{S}} \overset{.}{:} \overset{xx}{\underset{xx}{O}} \overset{.}{:} H$$
$$O$$

The sulfur has gained the two electrons it originally needed, and now it needs no more. We complete the Lewis structure by giving each of the top and bottom oxygen atoms their six valence electrons.

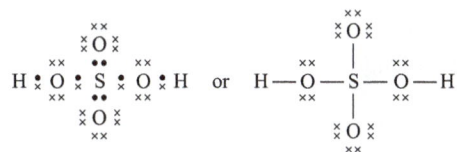

$$H \overset{.}{:} O \overset{.}{:} S \overset{.}{:} O \overset{.}{:} H \quad \text{or} \quad H-O-S-O-H$$

Reality Check

Whenever you build a Lewis structure, you should check the results to make sure all the valence electrons (in this case, 32) are present. Then check that each atom has an appropriate compliment of electrons—that is, that the sulfur atoms and the four oxygen atoms each have an octet of electrons, while each of the hydrogen atoms has a stable pair of electrons.

Later you will find that a further modification in this structure may be necessary, to accommodate a concept known as formal charge, which is discussed later in this chapter.

Follow-Up Problem 10.2a
Draw the Lewis structure for ethane, C_2H_6.

Information

The formula for the compound; the question of what is the Lewis structure

Connections

The number of valence electrons for each atom (H = 1, C = 4), from the periodic table or the electron configurations

Solution

Hydrogen, in column 1 on the periodic table, has one valence electron, while carbon, in column 14 (4A), has two valence electrons. The total number of electrons in the Lewis structure must be 6(1) + 2(4) = 14. The hydrogen cannot be the central atom, so the carbon is required to be central. There is no option other than to bond the carbon atoms together.

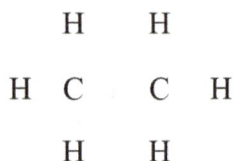

$$
\begin{array}{ccc}
\text{H} & & \text{H} \\
\text{H} & \text{C} & \text{C} \quad \text{H} \\
\text{H} & & \text{H}
\end{array}
$$

Each hydrogen has one valence electron and needs one more electron to fill its outer shell. Each hydrogen will complete its pair by sharing one of the carbon electrons. The carbon atom began with four electrons and shares one electron from each of the adjacent hydrogen atoms and one electron from the other carbon atom to complete its octet. The result is

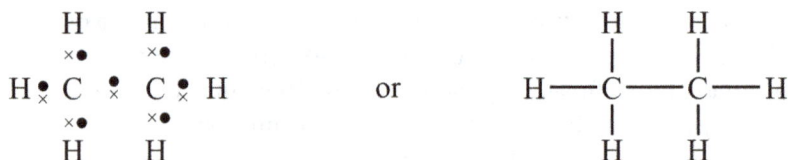

Reality Check

Whenever you build a Lewis structure, you should check the results to make sure all the valence electrons (in this case, 16) are present. Then check that each atom has an appropriate compliment of electrons—that is, the carbon has an octet of electrons, while each of the hydrogen atoms has a stable pair of electrons.

Follow-Up Problem 10.2b

Draw the Lewis structure for nitrogen dioxide, NO_2.

Information

The formula for the compound; the question of what is the Lewis structure

Connections

The number of valence electrons for each atom (N = 5, O = 6), from the periodic table or the electron configurations

Solution

Nitrogen, in column 15 (5A) on the periodic table, has five valence electrons, while oxygen, in column 16 (6A), has six valence electrons. The total number of electrons in the Lewis structure must be 2(6) + 5 = 17. Since this is an odd number, not all atoms will complete their octets. Oxygen is the more electronegative element; therefore, it is the more likely element to complete its octet. The nitrogen, which needs the most electrons to complete its octet, must be the central atom. This keeps the oxygen atoms separated from each other. Each oxygen has six valence electrons and needs two more electrons to complete an octet. Each oxygen will complete its octet by sharing two of the nitrogen electrons. The nitrogen atom began with five electrons and can get closer to an octet by sharing two electrons from one of the oxygen atoms. Sharing two electrons from each oxygen atom would give nitrogen more than an octet, which is impossible for a second-period element. The result is

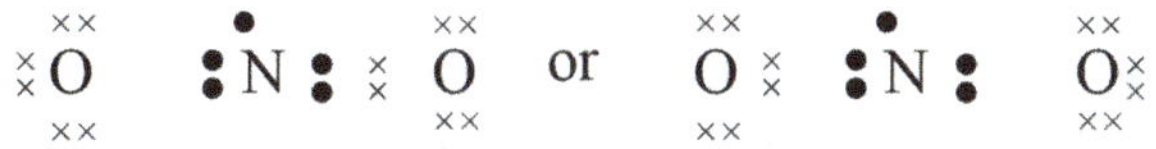

Alternatively,

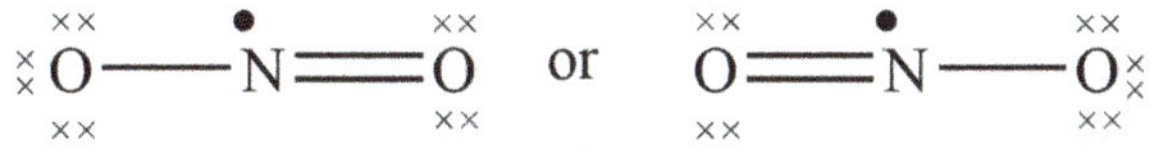

Reality Check

Whenever you build a Lewis structure, you should check the results to make sure all the valence electrons (in this case, 17) are present. Then check that each atom has an appropriate compliment of electrons—that is, that the two oxygen atoms each have an octet of electrons, while the nitrogen atom has seven electrons (an octet would be better; however, there are not enough electrons). In any case, the more electronegative atoms (O) have octets.

Example Problem 10.3

Draw the Lewis structure for sulfur hexafluoride, SF_6.

Information

The formula for the compound; the question of what is the Lewis structure

Connections

The number of valence electrons for each atom (F = 7, S = 6), from the periodic table or the electron configuration

Solution

The sulfur will be the central atom, with the six fluorine atoms distributed about it (sometimes, as shown here, it helps to make the symbol for the crowded central atom larger than the symbols for the other atoms). This Lewis structure can become very crowded, so we will need to be careful with our placement. We can begin with any atom, so let's pick one of the fluorine atoms. This atom has seven valence electrons and needs one more electron to complete its octet. We can begin by placing one of the sulfur electrons next to this fluorine and pair the electron with one of the fluorine electrons to complete the bond. We next place the six remaining fluorine electrons in three pairs about the fluorine atom. This fluorine atom now has an octet:

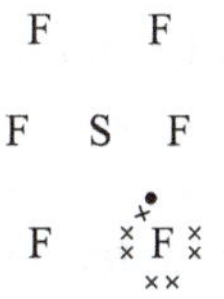

We can repeat the procedure for the remaining five fluorine atoms:

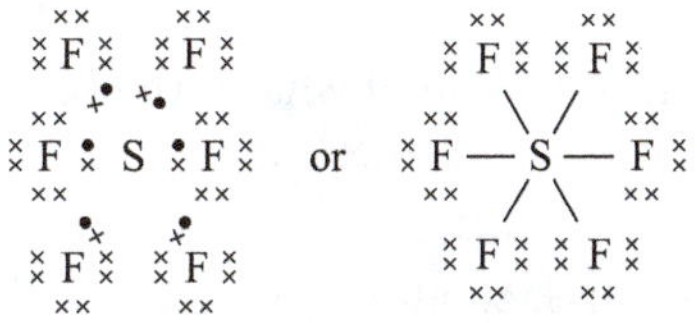

At this point, all the fluorine atoms have octets. In addition, we have accounted for all the sulfur electrons (by sharing one electron with each of the fluorine atoms.) The sulfur now has 12 total electrons surrounding it. This is acceptable, because the sulfur atom is large enough to exceed an octet.

Reality Check

The fluorine atoms, more electronegative than sulfur, each achieve a stable octet of electrons. The sulfur atom has 12 electrons around it, which is possible only because sulfur is located below the second period (i.e., farther down the column) on the periodic table.

Follow-Up Problem 10.3a

Draw the Lewis structure for sulfur tetrafluoride, SF_4.

Information

The formula for the compound; the question of what is the Lewis structure

Connections

The number of valence electrons for each atom (S = 6, F = 7), from the periodic table or the electron configurations

Solution

The sulfur will be the central atom, with the four fluorine atoms distributed about it. This Lewis structure can become very crowded, so we will need to be careful with our placement. We can begin with any atom, so we'll start with one of the fluorine atoms. This atom has seven valence electrons and needs one more electron to complete its octet. We can begin by placing one of the sulfur electrons next to this fluorine and pair the electron with one of the fluorine electrons to complete the bond. Next, we place the six remaining fluorine electrons in three pairs about the fluorine atom. This fluorine atom now has an octet. Repeat this procedure for each of the other fluorine atoms. At this point, four of the sulfur electrons have been used. The remaining two form a pair on the sulfur. This gives

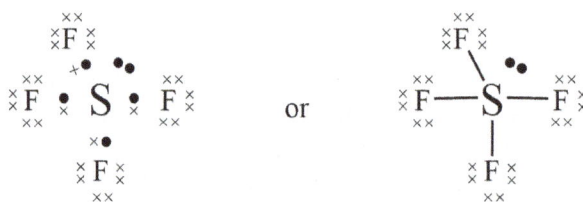

Reality Check

The fluorine atoms, more electronegative than sulfur, each achieve a stable octet of electrons. The sulfur atom has ten electrons around it, which is possible only because sulfur is located below the second period (i.e., farther down the column) on the periodic table.

Follow-Up Problem 10.3b

Draw the Lewis structure for beryllium iodide, BeI_2. This is one of the few metal–nonmetal compounds to exhibit covalent bonding.

Information

The formula for the compound; the question of what is the Lewis structure

Connections

The number of valence electrons for each atom (Be = 2, I = 7), from the periodic table or the electron configurations

Solution

Beryllium has a high electronegativity for a metal and iodine has a low electronegativity for a nonmetal, which means the electronegativity difference is small enough for the bond to be covalent. (You may wish to prove this by calculating the electronegativity difference using the table of electronegativities in chapter 8, "Electron Configuration.") The beryllium will be the central atom, with the two iodine atoms distributed about it. As always, we can begin with any atom, so we'll start with one of the iodine atoms. This atom has seven valence electrons and needs one more electron to complete its octet. We can begin by placing one of the beryllium electrons next to this iodine and then pair the electron with one of the iodine electrons to complete the bond. Next we place the six remaining iodine electrons in three pairs about the iodine atom. This iodine atom now has an octet. Repeat this procedure for each of the other iodine atom. At this point, all the beryllium electrons have been used. The beryllium is not sufficiently electronegative to "force" the iodine to donate more electrons to produce a double bond. The result is

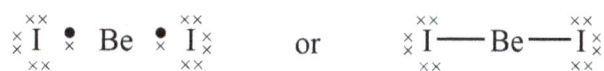

$$\overset{\times\times}{\underset{\times\times}{\times}}\text{I} \bullet \text{ Be } \bullet \overset{\times\times}{\underset{\times\times}{\text{I}}}_{\times} \qquad \text{or} \qquad \overset{\times\times}{\underset{\times\times}{\times}}\text{I} \text{---} \text{Be} \text{---} \overset{\times\times}{\underset{\times\times}{\text{I}}}_{\times}$$

Reality Check

The iodine atoms, more electronegative than beryllium, each achieve a stable octet of electrons. The beryllium atom has four electrons around it, which is possible only because beryllium began with fewer than four valence electrons.

Example Problem 10.4

Draw resonance structures for the fulminate ion, CNO⁻. The atoms are connected in the order given in the formula.

Information

The formula for the ion; the question of what are the Lewis structures of the resonance forms

Connections

The number of valence electrons for each atom (C = 4, N = 5, O = 6), from the periodic table or the electron configuration; an additional electron from the charge (16 electrons total)

Solution

We do not know how many resonance structures there will be. All we know is that if there is resonance, there must be more than one favorable structure. We have been told the three atoms are connected in the order given by the formula:

$$\text{C} \quad \text{N} \quad \text{O}$$

The construction of the first resonance structure begins in the same manner as the construction of any Lewis structure (remember, there will be additional answers). There are sixteen electrons available. We can begin assigning electrons to any of the three atoms. In this example, we will begin with the oxygen atom. This atom has six valence electrons and needs two to complete its octet. One or both electrons could come from the adjacent atom, nitrogen. If the nitrogen supplies one electron, the oxygen will still need to gain one electron. This could be the extra electron that gives the compound its ionic charge. Placing one nitrogen electron (×) on the side of the nitrogen atom nearest the oxygen atom and placing the charge electron (o) next to the oxygen atom gives

$$\text{C} \quad \text{N}^{\times}\underset{\circ}{\text{O}}$$

(Note the charge electron can go anywhere next to the oxygen, or even elsewhere in the molecule.) We can now add the six valence electrons from oxygen. (Oxygen will probably behave differently in the other resonance structures.) One of these valence electrons will complete a nitrogen–oxygen single bond, and one will pair with the charge electron. The remaining four electrons will form two pairs:

$$C \quad N \, {\overset{\bullet}{\underset{\circ}{\vphantom{|}}}} \, \overset{\bullet\bullet}{\underset{\circ\bullet}{O}} \, {\overset{\bullet}{\underset{\bullet}{\vphantom{|}}}}$$

We now move to the nitrogen atom. (Nitrogen will probably behave differently in the other resonance structures.) A nitrogen atom has five valence electrons and needs three more to complete its octet. We have already used one of the nitrogen electrons to form the bond to the oxygen (pairing that electron with an electron belonging to oxygen), and as a result, the oxygen is supplying one of the three electrons needed by nitrogen. The nitrogen still needs two more electrons. Since the charge electron and the oxygen electrons have been accounted for, the only source of these two electrons is the carbon atom. For this reason, we will place two of the carbon electrons (we can use dots since the carbon is not adjacent to the oxygen) on the side of the carbon atom nearest the nitrogen atom:

$$C \, {\overset{\bullet}{\underset{\bullet}{\vphantom{|}}}} \, N \, {\overset{\bullet}{\underset{\circ}{\vphantom{|}}}} \, \overset{\bullet\bullet}{\underset{\circ\bullet}{O}} \, {\overset{\bullet}{\underset{\bullet}{\vphantom{|}}}}$$

The carbon atom needs four electrons to complete its octet. (Carbon will probably behave differently in the other resonance structures.) The only possible source for these electrons is the nitrogen atom. We must therefore place the four remaining nitrogen electrons between the nitrogen and the carbon atom to form a triple bond:

$$C \, {\overset{\bullet\bullet}{\underset{\times\times}{\vphantom{|}}}} \, N \, {\overset{\bullet}{\underset{\circ}{\vphantom{|}}}} \, \overset{\bullet\bullet}{\underset{\circ\bullet}{O}} \, {\overset{\bullet}{\underset{\bullet}{\vphantom{|}}}}$$

We still have two carbon valence electrons remaining. These two electrons form a pair on the carbon atom.

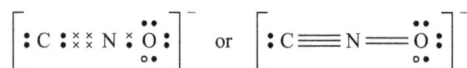

$$\left[{\overset{\bullet}{\underset{\bullet}{\vphantom{|}}}} C \, {\overset{\bullet\bullet}{\underset{\times\times}{\vphantom{|}}}} \, N \, {\overset{\bullet}{\underset{\circ}{\vphantom{|}}}} \, \overset{\bullet\bullet}{\underset{\circ\bullet}{O}} \, {\overset{\bullet}{\underset{\bullet}{\vphantom{|}}}} \right]^{-} \quad \text{or} \quad \left[{\overset{\bullet}{\underset{\bullet}{\vphantom{|}}}} C \equiv N = \overset{\bullet\bullet}{\underset{\circ\bullet}{O}} \, {\overset{\bullet}{\underset{\bullet}{\vphantom{|}}}} \right]^{-}$$

All the electrons are now accounted for, and each of the atoms has an octet.

We know that there must be at least one more structure. To find another resonance structure, we need to use a different approach. For example, we can try having the nitrogen share two electrons with the oxygen instead of one. The oxygen can then contribute two of its electrons to form a double bond.

The choices are (in any order)

$$C \quad N \, {\overset{\times}{\underset{\times}{\vphantom{|}}}} \, {\overset{\bullet}{\underset{\bullet}{\vphantom{|}}}} \, O$$

The remaining four valence electrons of the oxygen form two pairs about the oxygen atom:

$$C \quad N \, {\overset{\times}{\underset{\times}{\vphantom{|}}}} \, {\overset{\bullet}{\underset{\bullet}{\vphantom{|}}}} \, \overset{\bullet\bullet}{\underset{\bullet\bullet}{O}}$$

The nitrogen atom originally needed three electrons to complete its octet. The nitrogen received two of these electrons from the oxygen, so it needs only one additional electron. We will give it one of the carbon electrons, and we will place the three unused nitrogen electrons between the nitrogen atom and the carbon atom. There is now a double bond between the carbon and the nitrogen:

$$C \, {\overset{\bullet}{\underset{\times}{\vphantom{|}}}} \, {\overset{\times}{\underset{\bullet}{\vphantom{|}}}} \, N \, {\overset{\times}{\underset{\times}{\vphantom{|}}}} \, {\overset{\bullet}{\underset{\bullet}{\vphantom{|}}}} \, \overset{\bullet\bullet}{\underset{\bullet\bullet}{O}}$$

The carbon used one of its four valence electrons to bond to the nitrogen and received three of the four electrons it needed from the nitrogen. The three remaining carbon valence electrons plus the charge electron form two nonbonding pairs about the carbon:

$$\left[\ddot{\underset{\circ\circ}{C}} \; _\times^\times \; N \; _\times^\times \; \ddot{\underset{\bullet\bullet}{O}}\right]^- \quad \text{or} \quad \left[\ddot{\underset{\circ\bullet}{C}} = N = \ddot{\underset{\bullet\bullet}{O}}\right]^-$$

This accounts for all the electrons, and each of the atoms has an octet. (For practice, show how you can get this same bonding structure by using the charge electron instead of the carbon electron to provide the one electron needed by nitrogen after the formation of the nitrogen-oxygen double bond.)

There is another possibility, and that is to have the oxygen atom donate three electrons to the nitrogen atom and again put the charge on the oxygen atom.

$$C \quad N \quad \overset{\circ\circ}{\underset{\bullet\bullet}{\bullet\; O}}$$

Next, distribute the nitrogen electrons. The nitrogen atom can donate one electron to the oxygen atom to complete the octet on the oxygen atom. At the same time, the nitrogen atom can donate four electrons to the carbon atom, to complete the octet on the carbon atom.

$$\left[\ddot{\bullet\; C} \; _\times^\times \; N \; _\times^\times \; \overset{\circ\circ}{\ddot{O}}\bullet\right]^-$$

Even though the structure was derived differently, it is identical to the preceding structure (not a new resonance structure) because there are two double bonds present, one on each side of the nitrogen atom. It is important to realize that there is more than one way to arrive at a structure. The difference in appearance is artificial, because of the artificial device of using different symbols for different electrons. In reality, all electrons "look" the same.

We will attempt one more structure. In this case, we will begin with a triple bond between the nitrogen and oxygen. This bond will consist of four electrons from the oxygen and two electrons from the nitrogen:

$$\left[\ddot{\underset{\times\circ}{C}} \; _\times \; N \; _\times^\times \; \bullet\bullet \; O\bullet\right]^- \quad \text{or} \quad \left[\ddot{\underset{\times\circ}{C}} - N \equiv O\bullet\right]^-$$

In this structure, all atoms have an octet; however, it was necessary to move one of the nitrogen electrons onto the carbon atom. This is unfavorable. The unfavorable nature of this structure would be missed if all the electrons were given the same symbol or if lines were used for the bonds.

We can try to construct other resonance structures by beginning at the carbon end of the molecule. We have already seen that the carbon will need to gain either three or four electrons from the nitrogen atom, so this approach fails to lead us to a different structure. Similarly, starting with the nitrogen fails to produce anything new. (Of course, if we ignored the octet rule, we could get structures, but this should not be done if structures are available that do obey the octet rule.) In addition, these elements are in the second period; therefore, none can ever exceed an octet.

Reality Check

In each of the structures we have produced, each atom has a stable octet of electrons. A better understanding of the stability of these structures, and others, will depend on the determination of formal charges later in this chapter.

Follow-Up Problem 10.4a

Draw resonance structures for the carbonate ion, CO_3^{2-}.

Information

The formula for the ion; the question of what are the Lewis structures of the resonance forms

Connections

The number of valence electrons for each atom (C = 4, O = 6), from the periodic table or the electron configuration; two additional electrons from the charge

Solution

Each oxygen atom needs two electrons to complete their octets. There are several ways to do this. One way is to donate two of the carbon electrons to each of two oxygen atoms, and these use the two additional electrons from the charge to complete the octet on the third oxygen atom. The carbon atom needs four electrons to achieve an octet. It could gain two electrons from the charge and two electrons from one of the oxygen atoms. The different forms depend on which oxygen atom donates the pair of electrons:

or

Reality Check

In each of the structures we have produced, each atom has a stable octet of electrons. A better understanding of the stability of these structures, and others, will depend on the determination of formal charges later in this chapter.

Follow-Up Problem 10.4b

Draw resonance structures for sulfur dioxide, SO_2.

Information

The formula for the ion; the question of what are the Lewis structures of the resonance forms

Connections

The number of valence electrons for each atom (S = 6, O = 6), from the periodic table or the electron configuration

Solution

Each oxygen atom needs a pair of electrons to complete its octet. In each case, this pair of electrons can come from the sulfur. The remaining two sulfur electrons form a lone pair on the sulfur. The sulfur atom needs two electrons to complete an octet. The resonance forms depend on which oxygen atom donates this pair of electrons:

or

Reality Check

In each of the structures we have produced, each atom has a stable octet of electrons. A better understanding of the stability of these structures, and others, will depend on the determination of formal charges later in this chapter.

Example Problem 10.5

Using bond energies, calculate the heat of reaction for the reaction of carbon monoxide, CO, with chlorine, Cl_2, to form phosgene, $COCl_2$.

Information

Formulas of the reactants (CO, Cl_2) and product ($COCl_2$); the question of what is the heat of reaction

Connections

The Lewis structures; the table of bond energies (table 10.1)

Solution

The first step is to write a balanced chemical equation for the reaction. In this case, the equation is straightforward:

$$CO(g) + Cl_2(g) \rightarrow COCl_2(g)$$

We now need the Lewis structures of each reactant and product. If resonance is present, only one of the resonance structures is necessary.

Table 10.1 lists the bond energies. The carbon–oxygen triple bond has a bond energy of 1072 kJ/mol. The chlorine–chlorine bond energy is 242.7 kJ/mol. The carbon–oxygen double bond has a bond energy of 781 kJ/mol. Finally, each carbon–chlorine bond requires 331 kJ/mol. It is now possible to calculate the heat of reaction from

$$\Delta H = \Sigma \text{ bonds broken} - \Sigma \text{ bonds formed}$$

Entering the bond energies from the table gives

$$\Delta H = (1{,}072 + 242.7) \text{ kJ} - [781 + 2(331)] \text{ kJ} = -128.3 = \mathbf{-128 \text{ kJ}}$$

The term *2(331)* indicates that there are two carbon–chlorine bonds present in $COCl_2$.

Reality Check

The sign and the magnitude of the answer are reasonable. The number of significant figures is correct.

Follow-Up Problem 10.5a

Using bond energies, calculate the heat of reaction for the reaction of methane (CH_4) with chlorine, Cl_2, to form carbon tetrachloride, CCl_4, and hydrogen chloride, HCl.

Information

Formulas of the reactants (CH_4, Cl_2) and products (CCl_4, HCl); the question of what is the heat of reaction

Connections

The Lewis structures and the table of bond energies

Solution

The first step is to write a balanced chemical equation for the reaction. In this case, the equation is straightforward:

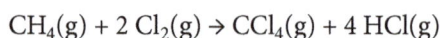

$$CH_4(g) + 2\,Cl_2(g) \rightarrow CCl_4(g) + 4\,HCl(g)$$

We now need the Lewis structures of each reactant and product. If resonance is present, only one of the resonance structures is necessary.

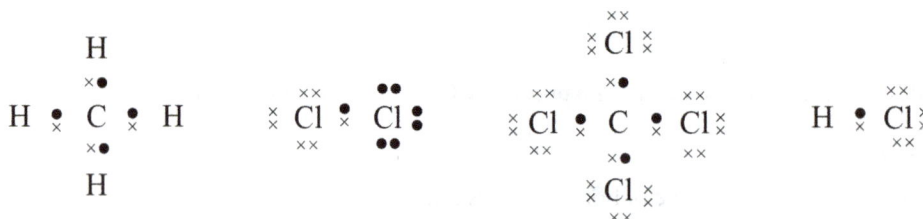

Table 10.1 lists the bond energies. The carbon-hydrogen bond has a bond energy of 414 kJ/mol. The chlorine-chlorine bond energy is 242.7 kJ/mol. The hydrogen-chlorine bond has a bond energy of 431.9 kJ/mol. Finally, each carbon-chlorine bond requires 331 kJ/mol. It is now possible to calculate the heat of reaction from

$$\Delta H = \Sigma \text{ bonds broken} - \Sigma \text{ bonds formed}$$

Entering the bond energies from the table gives

$$\Delta H = [4(414) + 2(242.7)]\text{ kJ} - [4(331) + 4(431.9)]\text{ kJ} = -910.2 = \mathbf{-910\ kJ}$$

The 4(414) and the 4(331) are because there are four bonds present in CH_4 and CCl_4, respectively. There are two Cl_2 in the balanced chemical equation, to give 2(242.7). There are four HCl in the equation, so the calculation has 4(431.9).

Reality Check

The sign and the magnitude of the answer are reasonable. The number of significant figures is correct.

Follow-Up Problem 10.5b

Using bond energies, calculate the heat of reaction for the decomposition of dinitrogen oxide, N_2O, to the elements.

Information

Formula of the reactant (N_2O); names of the products; the question of what is the heat of reaction

Connections

From the Nomenclature Resource, the formulas of the products N_2 and O_2, the Lewis structures and the table of bond energies

Solution

The first step is to write a balanced chemical equation for the reaction. In this case, the equation is straightforward:

$$2\,N_2O(g) \rightarrow 2\,N_2(g) + O_2(g)$$

We now need the Lewis structures of each reactant and product. Even though resonance is present, only one of the resonance structures is necessary.

$$\ddot{\times}\!\overset{\times\times}{\underset{\times\times}{O}}\;\; :N\overset{\bullet}{\underset{\bullet}{\vdots}}\overset{\times}{\underset{\times}{}}N\overset{\times}{\underset{\times}{}} \longleftrightarrow \overset{\times\times}{\underset{\times\times}{O}}\overset{\times}{}\;\;:N\overset{\bullet}{\underset{\bullet}{\vdots}}\overset{\times\times}{}N\qquad \overset{\times}{}N\overset{\times}{\underset{\times}{\vdots}}N\overset{\times}{}: \qquad O\overset{\times}{\underset{\times}{}}:\overset{\bullet\bullet}{\underset{\times\times}{O}}:$$

Table 10.1 lists the bond energies. We can use either of the dinitrogen oxide resonance forms. In this example, we'll use the left structure. The nitrogen–oxygen bond has a bond energy of 176 kJ/mol. The nitrogen–nitrogen triple bond energy is 941.4 kJ/mol. Finally, the oxygen–oxygen double bond requires 498.7 kJ/mol. It is now possible to calculate the heat of reaction from

$$\Delta H = \Sigma \text{ bonds broken} - \Sigma \text{ bonds formed}$$

Entering the bond energies from the table gives

$$\Delta H = [2(176) + 2(941.4)]\text{ kJ} - [2(941.4) + (498.7)]\text{ kJ} = -146.7 = \mathbf{-147\ kJ}$$

The answer would be **–332 kJ** if the other resonance structure of N_2O were used.

Reality Check

The sign and the magnitude of the answer are reasonable. The number of significant figures is correct.

Example Problem 10.6

Label the Lewis acid and Lewis base in each of the following reactions:

(a) $Be^{2+} + 4\,F^- \rightarrow BeF_4{}^{2-}$

(b) $4\,NH_3 + Cu^{2+} \rightarrow [Cu(NH_3)_4]^{2+}$

(c) $CO_2 + H_2O \rightarrow H_2CO_3$

Information

The formulas for the reacting species and their products; the question of which are Lewis acids, and which are Lewis bases

Connections

The definitions of *Lewis acid* and *Lewis base*

Solution

In each case, one of the reactants is the Lewis acid and the other reactant in the Lewis base. The product may provide a hint in a few cases, but in general, the product can be ignored.

(a) $Be^{2+} + 4 F^- \rightarrow BeF_4^{2-}$

In general, we need to examine only the Lewis symbol or Lewis structure of one of the reactants to identify it as the Lewis acid or the Lewis base. Once we label one reactant, the other must be the opposite. If we draw the Lewis symbol of the beryllium ion, we see that it has no electron pairs to donate; thus, it cannot possibly be a Lewis base. Therefore, the beryllium ion must be the Lewis acid, and the fluoride ion must be the Lewis base.

If we were to start with the Lewis symbol for the fluoride ion, we would see an ion with an octet of electrons (four pairs). Since the fluoride ion already has an octet, it is not likely to accept any more electrons. This means the fluoride ion is unlikely to be a Lewis acid. However, the fluoride ion does have electron pairs ready to donate, so it can be a Lewis base. If the Lewis base is the fluoride ion, then the beryllium ion is the Lewis acid.

In short, we can reach the same conclusion by starting with either reactant.

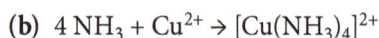

(b) $4 NH_3 + Cu^{2+} \rightarrow [Cu(NH_3)_4]^{2+}$

When cations are present, especially metal cations, the task of identifying the Lewis acid and base is often simplified. The loss of electrons to form a cation results in an attraction for new electrons. Thus, the copper ion will tend to accept electrons. The positive charge on the copper ion indicates that it will probably not be able to donate any of its remaining electrons. The copper ion is therefore the Lewis acid; in this case, then, the ammonia molecule must be the Lewis base. We can check the suitability of ammonia as a potential Lewis base by drawing the Lewis structure of ammonia, which shows that the nitrogen has a lone pair it can donate.

(c) $CO_2 + H_2O \rightarrow H_2CO_3$

If we begin by drawing the Lewis structure of carbon dioxide, we see the following:

$$\overset{\times\times}{\underset{\times\times}{O}} \overset{\times}{\underset{\times}{}} \colon C \colon \overset{\times}{\underset{\times}{}} \overset{\times\times}{\underset{\times\times}{O}}$$

If the classification of carbon dioxide is not clear from this Lewis structure, then we should draw the Lewis structure of water:

$$H \colon \overset{\bullet\bullet}{\underset{\times\bullet}{O}} \colon$$
$$H$$

If the classification of water is not clear from this Lewis structure, then we can look at the Lewis structure of the product, carbonic acid, for further clues:

$$H \colon \overset{\times\times}{\underset{\times\times}{O}} \colon C \colon \overset{\times\times}{\underset{\times\times}{O}}$$
$$\overset{\times}{\underset{\times\bullet}{O}}$$
$$H$$

Comparing the structures of reactants and products can provide useful clues. For example, the Lewis structure of carbonic acid shows that a third oxygen atom attaches to the carbon, and yet the Lewis structure of carbon dioxide shows no electron pair on the carbon for donation. Thus, the attachment of the third oxygen cannot involve the donation of an electron pair from the carbon. The third oxygen must attach through the donation of one of the electron pairs on the oxygen in the water molecule. Since water is donating an electron pair, water is the Lewis base. If water is the Lewis base, then carbon dioxide is the Lewis acid.

Reality Check

Each answer identifies a Lewis acid and a Lewis base that react to produce the product.

Follow-Up Problem 10.6a

Label the Lewis acid and Lewis base in each of the following reactions:

(a) $SiF_4 + 2\ F^- \rightarrow SiF_6{}^{2-}$

(b) $6\ H_2O + Zn^{2+} \rightarrow [Zn(H_2O)_6]^{2+}$

(c) $SO_3 + H_2O \rightarrow H_2SO_4$

Information

The formulas for the reacting species and their products; the question of which are Lewis acids, and which are Lewis bases

Connections

The definitions of *Lewis acid* and *Lewis base*

Solution

(a) $SiF_4 + 2\ F^- \rightarrow SiF_6{}^{2-}$

The fluoride ion has an octet of electrons, and as a second-period element it cannot exceed an octet; therefore, the fluoride ion cannot be a Lewis acid, so it must be the Lewis base. If F^- is the Lewis base, SiF_4 must be the Lewis acid.

(b) $6\ H_2O + Zn^{2+} \rightarrow [Zn(H_2O)_6]^{2+}$

The zinc ion is missing two electrons (2+ charge); therefore, it is probably the Lewis acid. This means that water is the Lewis base.

(c) $SO_3 + H_2O \rightarrow H_2SO_4$

Using Lewis structures, we can show the reaction beginning as

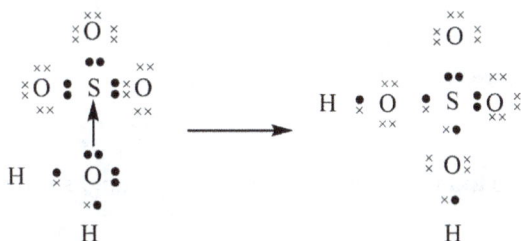

The arrow between the water and the SO_3 indicates the electron pair transfer, which indicates that water is the Lewis base and SO_3 is the Lewis acid. There will be additional rearrangement of the electrons to get the final product.

Reality Check

Each answer identifies a Lewis acid and a Lewis base that react to produce the product.

Follow-Up Problem 10.6b

Label the Lewis acid and Lewis base in each of the following reactions:

(a) $H^+ + OH^- \rightarrow H_2O$

(b) $Fe^{3+} + 4\ CN^- \rightarrow [Fe(CN)_6]^{3+}$

(c) $Al(OH)_3 + OH^- \rightarrow [Al(OH)_4]^-$

Information

The formulas for the reacting species and their products; the question of which are Lewis acids, and which are Lewis bases

Connections

The definitions of *Lewis acid* and *Lewis base*

Solution

(a) $H^+ + OH^- \rightarrow H_2O$

The hydrogen ion, H^+, has no electrons; therefore, it cannot possibly be the Lewis base. This means that H^+ is the Lewis acid and OH^- is the Lewis base.

(b) $Fe^{3+} + 4\ CN^- \rightarrow [Fe(CN)_6]^{3+}$

The iron ion is missing three electrons (3+ charge); therefore, it is probably the Lewis acid. This means that the cyanide ion is the Lewis base.

(c) $Al(OH)_3 + OH^- \rightarrow [Al(OH)_4]^-$

The oxygen atom in the hydroxide ion has a complete octet, and since oxygen is a second-period element, it cannot exceed an octet. Therefore, the hydroxide ion is the Lewis base, which means that the aluminum hydroxide is the Lewis acid.

Reality Check

Each answer identifies a Lewis acid and a Lewis base that react to produce the product.

Example Problem 10.7

If an average lightning strike produces 418 pounds of ozone, how many moles of oxygen undergo reaction?

Information

The mass of ozone (418 pounds); the question of how many moles of oxygen reacted

Connections

The balanced chemical equation; the periodic table; table of English-to-metric conversions

Solution

As with any stoichiometry problem, we need to begin with a balanced chemical equation:

$$3\ O_2(g) \rightarrow 2\ O_3(g)$$

We now need to convert 418 pounds of ozone to grams:

$$(418\ \text{lb}\ O_3)\left(\frac{453.59\ \text{g}}{1\ \text{lb}}\right)$$

We can now find the moles of ozone by using the molecular weight of ozone:

$$(418\ \text{lb}\ O_3)\left(\frac{453.59\ \text{g}}{1\ \text{lb}}\right)\left(\frac{1\ \text{mol}\ O_3}{48.0\ \text{g}\ O_3}\right)$$

Finally, using the mole ratio for the balanced chemical equation, we determine the moles of oxygen:

$$(418\ \text{lb}\ O_3)\left(\frac{453.59\ \text{g}}{1\ \text{lb}}\right)\left(\frac{1\ \text{mol}\ O_3}{48.0\ \text{g}\ O_3}\right)\left(\frac{3\ \text{mol}\ O_2}{2\ \text{mol}\ O_3}\right) = 5925.0 = \mathbf{5.92 \times 10^3\ mol\ O_2}$$

Reality Check

The answer is reasonable in magnitude. The units and significant figures are correct.

Follow-Up Problem 10.7a

What is the volume, in liters, of 418 pounds of ozone at a pressure of 755 torr and a temperature of 25°C?

Information

The weight of the ozone (418 pounds); its pressure (755 torr) and temperature (25°C or 298 K); the question of what is the volumes in liters

Connections

The equation $PV = nRT$; a table of English-to-metric conversions

Solution

Rearrange the ideal gas equation to $V = nRT/P$ and enter the appropriate values:

$$V = \frac{\left[(418\ \text{lb})\left(\dfrac{453.59\ \text{g}}{\text{lb}}\right)\left(\dfrac{1\ \text{mole O}_3}{47.997\ \text{g O}_3}\right)\right]\left(\dfrac{0.08206\ \text{L}\cdot\text{atm}}{\text{mol}\cdot\text{K}}\right)(298\ \text{K})}{\left[(755\ \text{torr})\left(\dfrac{1\ \text{atm}}{760\ \text{torr}}\right)\right]} = 97238.9 = \mathbf{9.72 \times 10^4\ L}$$

Reality Check

The answer is reasonable in magnitude. The units and significant figures are correct.

Follow-Up Problem 10.7b

How many oxygen molecules are needed to produce 418 pounds of ozone?

Information

The weight of the ozone (418 pounds); the question of how many molecules are present

Connections

Avogadro's number; a table of English-to-metric conversions

Solution

First, a balanced chemical equation is necessary:

$$3\ O_2(g) \rightarrow 2\ O_3(g)$$

To convert the weight to moles, use the mole ratio from the balanced chemical equation, and then use Avogadro's number to determine the number of molecules:

$$\text{Molecules} = (418\ \text{lb})\left(\frac{453.59\ \text{g}}{\text{lb}}\right)\left(\frac{1\ \text{mole O}_3}{47.997\ \text{g O}_3}\right)\left(\frac{3\ \text{mol O}_2}{2\ \text{mol O}_3}\right)\left(\frac{6.022 \times 10^{23}\ O_2}{1\ \text{mol O}_2}\right)$$

$$= 3.568 \times 10^{27} = \mathbf{3.57 \times 10^{27}\ O_2\ molecules}$$

Reality Check

The answer is reasonable in magnitude. The units and significant figures are correct.

END-OF-CHAPTER PROBLEMS

10.1 The Octet Rule Revisited and Covalent Bonding

10.1 (a) What are the three distinct types of bonding? (b) What role does electronegativity play in these bonding types?

Solution

(a) The three distinct types of bonding are ionic bonding, covalent bonding, and metallic bonding. (b) A large electronegativity difference leads to ionic bonding. Both covalent bonding and metallic bonding have smaller (or zero) electronegativity differences.

10.3 How is the Lewis structure of a molecule related to the Lewis structures of atoms?

Solution

The Lewis structure of a molecule is the "sum" of the Lewis structures of the atoms.

10.5 What theory applies quantum mechanics to molecules?

Solution

Molecular orbital theory applies quantum mechanics to molecules.

10.7 What electronegativity difference separates ionic bonding from covalent bonding?

Solution

If the difference is greater than 1.7, the bonding is ionic. If the difference is less than 1.7, the bonding is covalent (or polar covalent).

10.9 (a) Which elements, commonly considered transition metals, may be treated as representative elements when it comes to Lewis structures? (b) Write the electron configurations of these elements.

Solution

(a) Zinc, cadmium, and mercury are commonly considered to be transition metals, but they may be treated as representative elements. (b) The electron configurations of these elements are

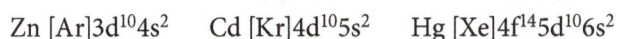

$$\text{Zn [Ar]}3d^{10}4s^2 \qquad \text{Cd [Kr]}4d^{10}5s^2 \qquad \text{Hg [Xe]}4f^{14}5d^{10}6s^2$$

10.11 What is the difference between a bonding pair of electrons and a lone pair of electrons?

Solution

A bonding pair is being shared by two atoms. A lone pair is only associated with one atom (unshared).

10.13 What is the maximum number of bonds that may be present between two representative element atoms?

Solution

The maximum number of bonds between two representative element atoms is <u>three</u>.

10.17 Using Lewis symbols diagram the reaction of silicon atoms with fluorine atoms.

Information

The names of two elements whose atoms are to combine to form a compound; the question of using Lewis symbols to diagram the reaction

Connections

The number of valence electrons for each atom, from either the periodic table or the electron configurations

Solution

The question says to begin with atoms, so the reaction must begin with the appropriate atoms (even though fluorine normally occurs as diatomic molecules):

$$Si + F \rightarrow$$

We need to convert these to Lewis symbols:

A fluorine atom needs one electron to complete its octet. Since the silicon atom has four electrons available, the silicon atom can complete the octet of four fluorine atoms. If the silicon shares one electron with each of the fluorine atoms, the silicon will also have a complete octet. This gives

10.20 Even in Lewis structures that are exceptions to the octet rule, there is always one type of atom that will obtain its octet if possible. What type of atom will achieve its octet in these structures?

Solution

The more electronegative element will achieve its octet if possible.

10.22 Which of the following elements can exceed an octet in at least some of their compounds? **(a)** Xe, **(b)** C, **(c)** N, **(d)** S, **(e)** B, **(f)** Li, **(g)** As, **(h)** Si, **(i)** O, **(j)** I

Solution

The elements than can exceed an octet (third period or below) are Xe, S, As, Si, and I.

10.24 Write a Lewis structure for each of the following, and identify any atom not obeying the octet rule: **(a)** beryllium chloride, $BeCl_2$; **(b)** krypton difluoride, KrF_2; **(c)** bromine dioxide, BrO_2; **(d)** tellurium tetrafluoride, TeF_4; **(e)** aluminum fluoride, AlF_3

Information

The formulas for five compounds or ions (plus some additional structural information); the question of what are the Lewis structures

Connections

The number of valence electrons for each atom, from either the periodic table or the electron configurations

Solution

None of the second-period elements present (F and O) can exceed an octet. In each case, the more electronegative elements present (Cl, O, and F) will probably achieve an octet.

(a) Beryllium has an unusually high electronegativity for a metal, so the electronegativity difference is small enough for this to be covalent and not ionic. Each chlorine shares one electron from the beryllium and shares one back to the beryllium. The beryllium began with two electrons and gained two additional electrons from the chlorine atoms, which gives the beryllium four electrons. The element Be does not obey the octet rule, because it has fewer than eight electrons.

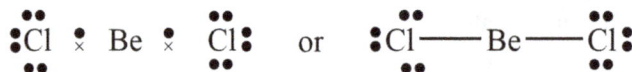

$$:\overset{\cdot\cdot}{\underset{\cdot\cdot}{Cl}} \overset{\times}{} Be \overset{\times}{} \overset{\cdot\cdot}{\underset{\cdot\cdot}{Cl}}: \quad \text{or} \quad :\overset{\cdot\cdot}{\underset{\cdot\cdot}{Cl}} \!\!-\!\! Be \!\!-\!\! \overset{\cdot\cdot}{\underset{\cdot\cdot}{Cl}}:$$

(b) Each fluorine shares one electron from the krypton and shares one back to the krypton. The krypton began with eight electrons and gained two additional electrons from the fluorine atoms, which gives the krypton ten electrons. The element Kr does not obey the octet rule, because it has more than eight electrons.

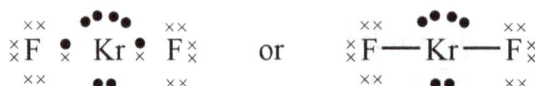

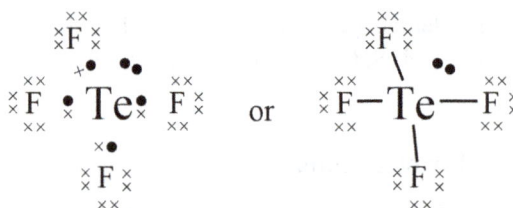

$$\overset{\times\times}{\underset{\times\times}{\times F}} \overset{\cdot\cdot\cdot\cdot}{\underset{\cdot\cdot}{ Kr }} \overset{\times\times}{\underset{\times\times}{F \times}} \quad \text{or} \quad \overset{\times\times}{\underset{\times\times}{\times F}} \!\!-\!\! \overset{\cdot\cdot\cdot\cdot}{\underset{\cdot\cdot}{Kr}} \!\!-\!\! \overset{\times\times}{\underset{\times\times}{F \times}}$$

(c) There are an odd number of electrons (19); therefore, there must be an exception. Oxygen is more electronegative, so it gets its octet. The bromine atom ends with seven electrons. The element Br does not obey the octet rule, because it has less than eight electrons.

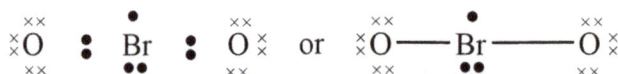

$$\overset{\times\times}{\underset{\times\times}{\times O}} \overset{\cdot}{\underset{\cdot\cdot}{ Br }} \overset{\times\times}{\underset{\times\times}{O \times}} \quad \text{or} \quad \overset{\times\times}{\underset{\times\times}{\times O}} \!\!-\!\! \overset{\cdot}{\underset{\cdot\cdot}{Br}} \!\!-\!\! \overset{\times\times}{\underset{\times\times}{O \times}}$$

(d) Each fluorine shares one electron from the tellurium and shares one back to the tellurium. The tellurium began with six electrons and gained four additional electrons from the fluorine atoms, which gives the tellurium ten electrons. **Te** does not obey the octet rule, because it has more than eight electrons.

(e) This is a typical metal–nonmetal compound; therefore, the expected bonding is ionic. Each fluorine gains one of the aluminum electrons to achieve a complete octet. It is not obvious from the Lewis structure that the aluminum ion has an octet. However, the electron configuration of the aluminum ion shows the octet (highlighted) $1s^2 2s^2 2p^6$. Both ions obey.

$$Al^{3+} \quad + \quad 3 \quad \overset{\cdot\cdot}{\underset{\cdot\cdot}{\times F}}^{-}$$

Reality Check
There are alternative ways to derive the correct Lewis structures.

10.2 Formal Charge
10.27 Write the equation for determining the formal charge on an atom.

Solution

The formal charge for an atom is calculated using the following formula:

Formal charge = *Number of valence electrons – Number of nonbonding electrons*
– 1/2 Number of bonding electrons

10.29   Draw the Lewis structure for each of the following, and predict the formal charge on each atom: **(a)** nitrite ion, NO_2^-; **(b)** sulfuric acid, H_2SO_4; **(c)** ozone, O_3; **(d)** hydrogen phosphate ion, HPO_4^{2-}; **(e)** hydrogen carbonate ion, HCO_3^-

Information

The formulas for five compounds or ions (plus some additional structural information); the question of what are the Lewis structures

Connections

The number of valence electrons for each atom, from either the periodic table or the electron configurations

Solution

All calculations are

Formal charge = *Number of valence electrons – Number of nonbonding electrons*
– 1/2 Number of bonding electrons

There are no duplicate calculations for identical atoms.

There are subscripts, where necessary, to distinguish different atoms of the same element.

(a)   First, draw the Lewis structure for the nitrite ion. You do not need to worry about the other resonance structure.

$$N = 5 - 2 - (1/2)\,(6) = 0$$
$$O_a = 6 - 4 - (1/2)\,(4) = 0$$
$$O_b = 6 - 6 - (1/2)\,(2) = -1$$

(b)   First, draw the Lewis structure for sulfuric acid. (There are other structures beside the one shown.) Both O_a atoms are identical to each other, as are both O_b atoms.

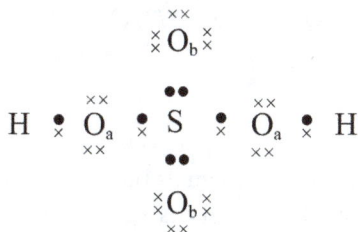

$$S = 6 - 0 - (1/2)\,(8) = 2$$
$$H = 1 - 0 - (1/2)\,(2) = 0$$
$$O_a = 6 - 4 - (1/2)\,(4) = 0$$
$$O_b = 6 - 6 - (1/2)\,(2) = -1$$

(c) First, draw the Lewis structure for ozone. You do not need to worry about the other resonance structure.

$$O_a = 6 - 6 - (1/2) (2) = -1$$
$$O_b = 6 - 2 - (1/2) (6) = 1$$
$$O_c = 6 - 4 - (1/2) (4) = 0$$

(d) First, draw the Lewis structure for the hydrogen phosphate ion. The lone hydrogen may be attached to any of the oxygen atoms. All oxygen atoms without a hydrogen atom attached are identical to each other.

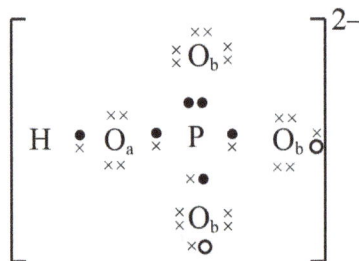

$$P = 5 - 0 - (1/2) (8) = 1$$
$$H = 1 - 0 - (1/2) (2) = 0$$
$$O_a = 6 - 4 - (1/2) (4) = 0$$
$$O_b = 6 - 6 - (1/2) (2) = -1$$

(e) First, draw the Lewis structure for the bicarbonate ion. You do not need to worry about the other resonance structure.

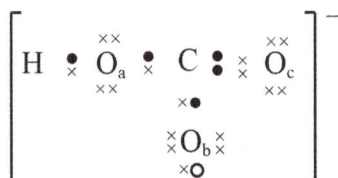

$$C = 4 - 0 - (1/2) (8) = 0$$
$$H = 1 - 0 - (1/2) (2) = 0$$
$$O_a = 6 - 4 - (1/2) (4) = 0$$
$$O_b = 6 - 6 - (1/2) (2) = -1$$
$$O_c = 6 - 4 - (1/2) (4) = 0$$

Reality Check

In each case, the sum of the formal charges equals the charge on the species—either 0 for molecules or the charge on an ion. The formal charge of 2 on the sulfur in H_2SO_4 indicates that there may be a better structure with a 0 or ±1 charge on the sulfur.

10.3 Resonance

10.31 What term describes a molecule or an ion that has more than one favorable Lewis structure?

Solution

When a species has more than one favorable Lewis structure, the molecule has **resonance**.

10.33 What is the difference between a resonance structure and a resonance hybrid?

Solution

A resonance structure is one of several possible structures, and a resonance hybrid is an average of all resonance structures.

10.4 Bond Energy and Bond Length

10.36 **(a)** Define *bond energy*. **(b)** Are bond energy values endothermic, or are they exothermic?

Solution

(a) The **bond energy** is the energy required to break a bond. **(b)** It requires energy to break a bond; therefore, the bond energy is endothermic.

10.38 What is the relationship between bond length and bond energy?

Solution

A shorter bond tends to have a higher bond energy.

10.41 Nitrogen forms compounds with hydrogen in addition to ammonia, NH_3. One of these compounds is hydrazine, N_2H_4. The other nitrogen–hydrogen compounds are thermally unstable and include diazene, N_2H_2, triazene, $HNNNH_2$, and tetrazene, H_2NNNNH_2. **(a)** Draw Lewis structures for nitrogen gas, N_2, and each of the five nitrogen–hydrogen compounds listed. **(b)** Rank the five structures with nitrogen–nitrogen bonds in order of decreasing bond length. **(c)** Rank the five structures with nitrogen–nitrogen bonds in order of increasing bond strength.

Information

The formulas for five compounds or ions (plus some additional structural information); the question of what are the Lewis structures

Connections

The number of valence electrons for each atom, from either the periodic table or the electron configurations

Solution

We need to draw a Lewis structure for each of the molecules or ions. We do not need to draw all resonance forms.

In all cases, every atom except hydrogen obeys the octet rule.

There is no nitrogen–nitrogen bond in NH_3; therefore, ammonia is not included in parts (b) and (c).

The bond length and bond strength depend on the average number of bonds between the nitrogen atoms.

Where other options are available, the way the formulas are written gives an indication of the structure. For example, $HNNNH_2$ has one hydrogen atom attached to the first nitrogen atom, followed by the second nitrogen atom, and then the third nitrogen atom with two hydrogen atoms attached.

(a)

$$: \ddot{N} : : N : \quad H : \ddot{N} : H \quad H : \ddot{N} : \ddot{N} : H$$
$$H \qquad\qquad H \quad H$$

$$H : \ddot{N} : : \ddot{N} : H \qquad H : \ddot{N} : \ddot{N} : : \ddot{N} : H$$
$$H$$

$$H : \ddot{N} : \ddot{N} : : \ddot{N} : \ddot{N} : H$$
$$H \qquad\qquad\qquad H$$

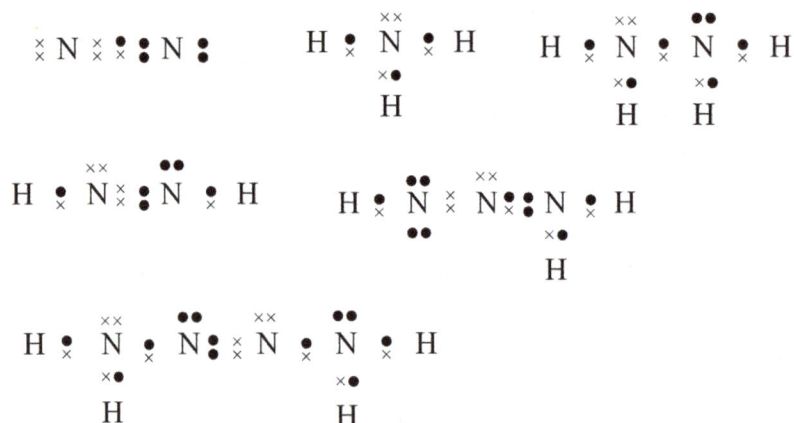

The nitrogen-nitrogen bonds are

N_2	3 bonds
NH_2NH_2	1 bond
HNNH	2 bonds
$HNNNH_2$	1.5 bonds (average)
NH_2NNNH_2	1.33 bonds (average)

Listing these five species in order of increasing number of nitrogen–nitrogen bonds gives

$$NH_2NH_2 > NH_2NNNH_2 > HNNNH_2 > HNNH > N_2$$

(b) The greater the number of bonds, the shorter the bond length; therefore, the order is

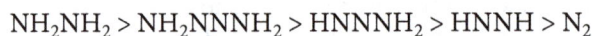

$$NH_2NH_2 > NH_2NNNH_2 > HNNNH_2 > HNNH > N_2$$

(c) The greater the number of bonds, the greater the bond strength; therefore, the order is

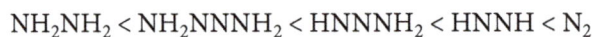

$$NH_2NH_2 < NH_2NNNH_2 < HNNNH_2 < HNNH < N_2$$

10.43 Estimate the enthalpy change for each of the following reactions based on bond energies.

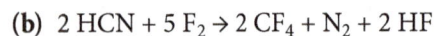

(a) $2\,CO + O_2 \rightarrow 2\,CO_2$

(b) $2\,HCN + 5\,F_2 \rightarrow 2\,CF_4 + N_2 + 2\,HF$

Information
Two balanced chemical equations; in each case, the question of what is the enthalpy change based on the bond energies

Connections
The table of bond energies in this chapter

Solution
We need to determine the number and type of bonds present. We can do this by using Lewis structures.

(a) $2 \text{ C}\equiv\text{O} + \text{O}=\text{O} \rightarrow 2 \text{ O}=\text{C}=\text{O}$

$\Delta H = [2 \text{ (C}\equiv\text{O)} + \text{(O}=\text{O)}] - [2 \text{ (2 (C}=\text{O))}] = [2 \text{ (1,072)} + \text{(498.7)}] - [2 \text{ (2 (799))}] = -553.3$
$$= -553 \text{ kJ}$$

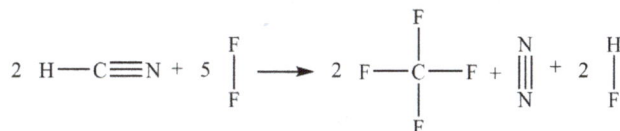

(b) $2 \text{ HCN} + 5 \text{ F}_2 \rightarrow 2 \text{ CF}_4 + \text{N}_2 + 2 \text{ HF}$

$\Delta H = [2 \text{ (C–H)} + 2 \text{ (C}\equiv\text{N)} + 5 \text{ (F–F)}] - [2 \text{ (4 (C–F))} + \text{(N}\equiv\text{N)} + 2 \text{ (F–H)}]$
$= [2 \text{ (414)} + 2 \text{ (891)} + 5 \text{ (150.6)}] - [2 \text{ (4 (439))} + \text{(941.4)} + 2 \text{ (568.2)}]$
$= -2,226.8 = \mathbf{-2,227 \text{ kJ}}$

Reality Check

It is possible to use the standard heats of formation to calculate the enthalpy changes. The values should be close to the answers determined in this problem.

10.5 Orbital Overlap

10.49 What type of bond restricts rotation about a bond in a molecule? Why?

Solution

A π bond restricts rotation about the bond in a molecule. It is necessary to break the π bond to rotate one end of the bond relative to the other end.

10.6 Lewis Acids and Bases

10.52 **(a)** What is a *Lewis acid*? **(b)** What is a *Lewis base*?

Solution

(a) A *Lewis acid* is a species that accepts a pair of electrons. **(b)** A *Lewis base* is a species that donates a pair of electrons.

10.55 Explain why a molecule with no lone pairs cannot serve as a Lewis base.

Solution

A Lewis base must be able to donate a pair of electrons; so if there are no lone pairs, there is nothing to donate. If there is nothing to donate, the substance cannot be a Lewis base.

10.57 In each of the following reactions, which of the reactants is the Lewis acid and which of the reactants is the Lewis base?

(a) $\text{FeCl}_3(s) + \text{Cl}^-(aq) \rightarrow \text{FeCl}_4^-(aq)$

(b) $\text{H}_2\text{O}(l) + \text{NO}_2^-(aq) \rightarrow \text{HNO}_2(aq) + \text{OH}^-(aq)$

(c) $\text{NH}_3(g) + \text{BF}_3(g) \rightarrow \text{H}_3\text{NBF}_3(s)$

(d) $\text{BrF}_3(l) + \text{HF}(l) \rightarrow \text{H}^+(sol) + \text{BrF}_4^-(sol)$ (sol = solvated)

(e) $\text{CaO}(s) + \text{H}_2\text{O}(l) \rightarrow \text{Ca(OH)}_2(s)$

Solution

In all cases, one or more Lewis structures may help. The products may give hints; however, the Lewis acid and the Lewis base are always reactants.

(a) The compound $FeCl_3$ contains Fe^{3+} and metal cations are often Lewis acids, which means the chloride ion with its octet of four electron pairs is a Lewis base:

Lewis acid = $FeCl_3(s)$ 　　　　　　Lewis base = $Cl^-(aq)$

(b) This is better illustrated using Lewis structures:

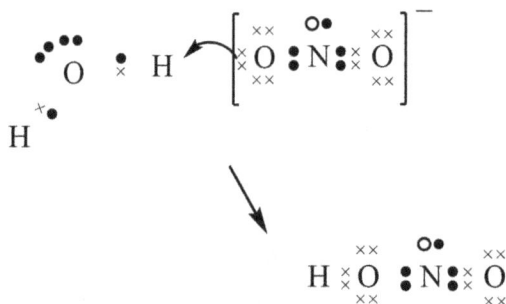

The curved arrow shows the nitrite ion donating an electron pair (Lewis base) to one of the hydrogen atoms in the water molecule (Lewis acid).

Lewis acid = $H_2O(l)$ 　　　　　　Lewis base = $NO_2^-(aq)$

(c) The boron in BF_3 only has six electrons; therefore, it needs a pair of electrons to complete an octet. Since BF_3 needs to accept two electrons, BF_3 must be the Lewis acid. The nitrogen in the ammonia has a lone pair to donate, which makes NH_3 the Lewis base.

Lewis acid = $BF_3(g)$ 　　　　　　Lewis base = $NH_3(g)$

(d) This is better illustrated using Lewis structures:

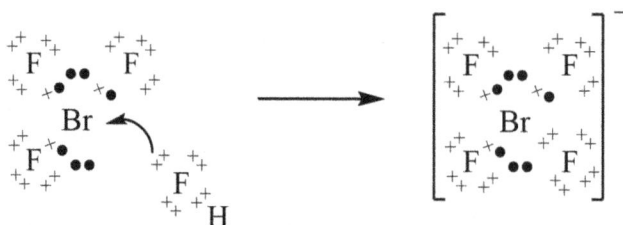

The curved arrow shows the HF donating an electron pair (Lewis base) to the Br in the BrF_3 molecule (Lewis acid).

Lewis acid = $BrF_3(l)$ 　　　　　　Lewis base = $HF(l)$

(e) This is better illustrated using Lewis structures:

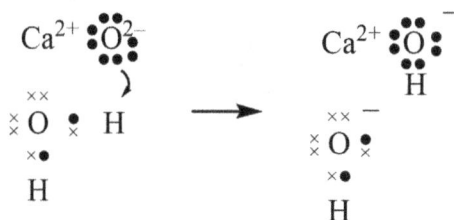

The curved arrow shows the oxygen, in the CaO, donating an electron pair (Lewis base) to one of the hydrogen atoms in the water molecule (Lewis acid).

Lewis acid = $H_2O(l)$ 　　　　　　Lewis base = $CaO(s)$

10.7 Molecular Orbitals

10.59 Which of the following guidelines, introduced in the chapters on atomic orbitals, apply to molecular orbitals? **(a)** Hund's rule; **(b)** the aufbau principle; **(c)** the Pauli Exclusion Principle

Solution

(a), **(b)**, and **(c)** All three guidelines apply to both atomic orbitals and molecular orbitals.

10.61 When two atoms come together, molecular orbitals form. **(a)** Describe the similarities and differences between the atomic orbitals and the molecular orbitals. **(b)** Compare the bonding molecular orbitals to the antibonding molecular orbitals.

Solution

(a) The number of molecular orbitals formed is equal to the number of atomic orbitals combined. The Pauli Exclusion Principle, aufbau principle, and Hund's rule apply to both atomic and molecular orbitals. Atomic orbitals hold electrons around an atom, while molecular orbitals involve all the atoms in a molecule. **(b)** Bonding molecular orbitals are lower-energy and involve overlap to allow the atoms to share electrons. Antibonding molecular orbitals are higher-energy and there is a node (no overlap) between the atoms that eliminates the sharing of electrons.

10.64 **(a)** How do electrons in bonding molecular orbitals affect the stability of a molecule or an ion? **(b)** How do electrons in antibonding molecular orbitals affect the stability of a molecule or an ion?

Solution

(a) Electrons in bonding molecular orbitals make a molecule or an ion more stable. **(b)** Electrons in antibonding molecular orbitals make a molecule or an ion less stable.

10.65 What is the equation for calculating bond order?

Solution

The equation for determining the bond order is

$$\text{Bond order} = \frac{\textit{Number of bonding electrons} - \textit{Number of antibonding electrons}}{2}$$

10.67 What does a bond order of 0 (zero) tell you about the stability of a molecule?

Solution

If the bond order is zero, the molecule is not stable.

10.69 **(a)** Which diatomic molecules of the second-period elements are paramagnetic? **(b)** Which diatomic molecules of the second-period elements are diamagnetic?

Solution

(a) The paramagnetic diatomic molecules are B_2 and O_2. **(b)** The diamagnetic diatomic molecules are Li_2, C_2, N_2, and F_2. The molecules Be_2 and Ne_2 would be diamagnetic if they existed. (You might need to confirm these by drawing the appropriate molecular orbital energy level diagram.)

10.73 What is the maximum number of electrons that may be accommodated by each of the following? **(a)** a σ bonding molecular orbital; **(b)** a π antibonding molecular orbital

Solution

(a) There can be a maximum of two electrons. **(b)** There can be a maximum of two electrons.

10.8 Metallic Bonding

10.75 What is a conduction band?

Solution

A conduction band is a partially filled band, which allows electrical conductivity.

10.9 Applications and Extensions

10.77 Define *valence band* and *band gap*.

Solution

The valence band is the lower portion of the band diagram, with the bonding molecular orbitals. The *band gap* is the separation between the conduction band and the valence band in the band diagram.

10.81 Describe how p-type and n-type semiconductors differ from a pure metalloid such as silicon.

Solution

In silicon, the valence band in full and the conduction band is empty; however, since the band gap is small, a few electrons may move from the valence band to the conduction band, which leads to electrical conductivity. In a p-type semiconductor, the valence band is no longer full so it may conduct electricity. In an n-type semiconductor, there are additional orbitals, with electrons, just below the conduction band, which are easier to move to the conduction band than are the electrons in the valence band.

10.83 The density of ozone gas is 2.144 g/L. What is the density of ozone in pounds per cubic foot?

Information

The density of ozone in one set of units (2.144 g/L); the question of what is the density in pounds per cubic foot

Connections

Several unit conversions

Solution

This problem requires several unit conversions. The following uses one set of unit conversions; however, other sets of conversions will work equally well. As always, the conversions may be in any order.

$$\text{Density} = \left(\frac{2.144 \text{ g}}{\text{L}}\right)\left(\frac{1 \text{ lb}}{453.59 \text{ g}}\right)\left(\frac{1 \text{ L}}{1 \text{ dm}^3}\right)\left(\frac{d}{0.1}\right)^3\left(\frac{0.01}{c}\right)^3\left(\frac{2.54 \text{ cm}}{1 \text{ in}}\right)^3\left(\frac{12 \text{ in}}{1 \text{ ft}}\right)^3$$

$$= 0.133846 = \mathbf{0.1338 \text{ lb/ft}^3}$$

10.85 Ozone absorbs ultraviolet radiation in the 200-nm to 310-nm region. **(a)** What is the frequency of a 275-nm wave of ultraviolet light? **(b)** What is the energy, in joules, of an ultraviolet photon with a wavelength of 285 nm? **(c)** How many kilojoules will your skin receive if it absorbs 1.00×10^{-3} moles of photons from 200.0-nm ultraviolet light?

Information

The ultraviolet light absorbed by ozone; the three questions of what is the frequency of 275-nm light, how many joules are in a photon of 285-nm light, and how many kilojoules are in 1.00×10^{-3} moles of 200.0-nm photons

Connections

Two of the following three equations: $E = h\nu$, $c = \lambda\nu$, $E = hc/\lambda$; Avogadro's number

Solution

Rearrange the given equations (when necessary), then enter the appropriate values and conversions.

(a) Frequency $= \nu = \dfrac{c}{\lambda} = \dfrac{2.9979 \times 10^8 \text{ m/s}}{275 \text{ nm}}\left(\dfrac{n}{10^{-9}}\right) = 1.090145 \times 10^{15} = \mathbf{1.09 \times 10^{15} \text{ s}^{-1}}$

(b) Energy $= E = \dfrac{hc}{\lambda} = \left(\dfrac{(6.626 \times 10^{-34} \text{ J}\cdot\text{s})(2.9979 \times 10^8 \text{ m/s})}{285 \text{ nm}}\right)\left(\dfrac{n}{10^{-9}}\right) = 6.9698545 \times 10^{-19}$

$$= \mathbf{6.97 \times 10^{-19} \text{ J}}$$

(c) Energy $= E = \dfrac{hc}{\lambda} = \left(\dfrac{(6.626 \times 10^{-34} \text{ J}\cdot\text{s})(2.9979 \times 10^8 \text{ m/s})}{200.0 \text{ nm}}\right)\left(\dfrac{n}{10^{-9}}\right)\left(\dfrac{k}{1{,}000}\right)\left(\dfrac{6.022 \times 10^{23}}{1 \text{ mol}}\right)$

$$\times\,(1.00 \times 10^{-3} \text{ mol}) = 0.5981076 = \mathbf{0.5981 \text{ kJ}}$$

10.87 It is possible to produce ozone by the reaction of oxygen gas with oxygen atoms:

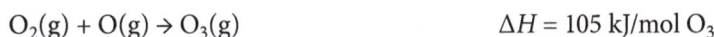

$$O_2(g) + O(g) \rightarrow O_3(g) \qquad\qquad \Delta H = 105 \text{ kJ/mol } O_3$$

(a) Use bond energies to estimate the standard enthalpy for this reaction. **(b)** The difference between the standard enthalpy of formation of ozone and the estimated value from part (a) is primarily due to resonance. Calculate the extent to which resonance contributes to the stability of ozone.

Information

The standard enthalpy change form a reaction producing ozone (105 kJ/mol); using bond energies, the two questions of what is the enthalpy change for this reaction, and how much energy does resonance contribute

Connections

Table 10.1, which gives bond energies

Solution

(a) The Lewis structures of the species in formation reaction are

$$\Delta H = [O{=}O + 0] - [O{=}O + O{-}O]$$
$$[498.7 + 0] - [498.7 + 142] = \mathbf{-142 \text{ kJ}}$$

The oxygen atom is shown as 0 because there is no bond.

(b) The enthalpy change due to resonance is the difference between the answer in part (a) and the given enthalpy of formation (105 kJ/mol):

$$\Delta H_{\text{resonance}} = (-142 - 105) \text{ kJ} = \mathbf{-247 \text{ kJ}}$$

Putting It All Together

10.91 Rank the following bonds in order of increasing polarity: N–P, N–N, N–O, N–F

Solution

All the bonds have nitrogen in common, so the further an element is from nitrogen, the greater the electronegativity difference and the greater the polarity. N–N < N–P < N–O < N–F

10.94 Draw Lewis structures for each of the following: **(a)** carbon monoxide, CO; **(b)** methane, CH_4; **(c)** dimethylberyllium, $Be(CH_3)_2$; **(d)** xenon tetraoxide, XeO_4; **(e)** paraperiodic acid, H_5IO_6

Information

The formulas for five compounds or ions (plus some additional structural information); the question of what are the Lewis structures

Connections

The number of valence electrons for each atom, from either the periodic table or the electron configurations

Solution

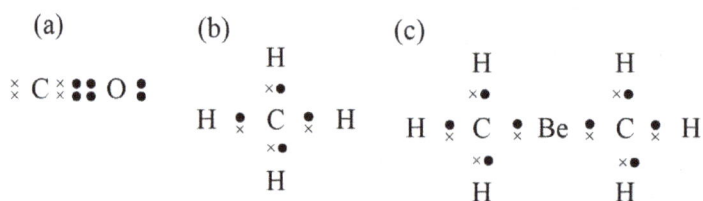

OR

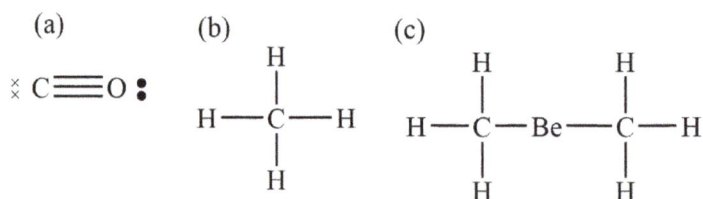

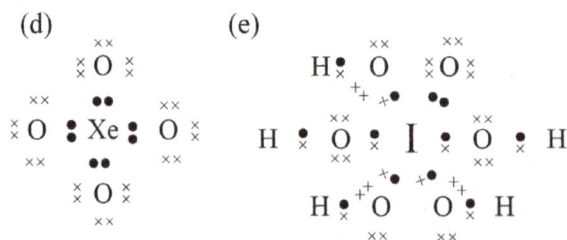

OR

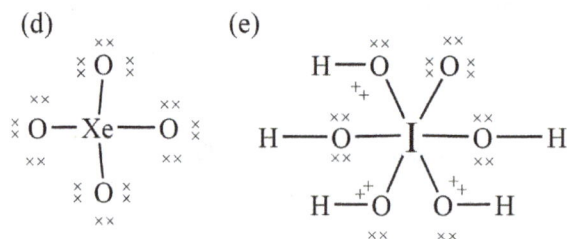

10.96 A gas with a formula weight of about 166 g/mol is found to be 14.49% carbon and 85.51% chlorine. Draw the Lewis structure of the molecule.

Information

The molar mass (166 g/mol) and composition (14.49% C and 85.51% Cl) of a substance; the question of what is the Lewis structure

Connections

The number of valence electrons for each atom, from either the periodic table or the electron configurations

Solution

To draw the Lewis structure of a molecule, we need to determine the molecular formula. To determine the molecular formula, we first need to determine the empirical formula.

Start by determining the empirical formula, assuming 100 g of sample:

$$\text{Mole C} = (14.49 \text{ g C})\left(\frac{1 \text{ mol C}}{12.011 \text{ g C}}\right) = \left(\frac{1.206 \text{ mol C}}{1.206 \text{ mol C}}\right) = 1$$

$$\text{Mole Cl} = (85.51 \text{ g Cl})\left(\frac{1 \text{ mol Cl}}{35.453 \text{ g Cl}}\right) = \left(\frac{2.412 \text{ mol Cl}}{1.206 \text{ mol C}}\right) = 2$$

This gives CCl_2 as the empirical formula (83 g/mol).

To convert the empirical formula to the molecular formula, we need to compare their molar masses.

Empirical formula	→	**Molecular formula**
CCl_2		?
83 g/mole	→	166 g/mole
83 × 2 = 166	and	$CCl_2 × 2 = C_2Cl_4$

From the molecular formula, C_2Cl_4, finish the problem by drawing the Lewis structure of C_2Cl_4.

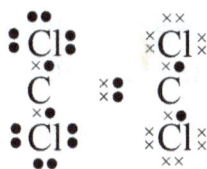

10.98 The Haber process is used industrially to synthesize ammonia from the elements. The reaction is

$$N_2(g) + 3\, H_2(g) \rightarrow 2\, NH_3(g)$$

(a) Calculate the heat of reaction using $\Delta H_f°$ values from appendix C. **(b)** Calculate the heat of reaction using bond energies. **(c)** Account for any discrepancies between your answers for (a) and (b).

Information

A balanced chemical equation; the three questions of what is the heat of reaction based on standard heats of formation, what is the heat of reaction based on bond energies, and—if there are discrepancies—why is there a difference.

Connections

Standard heats of formation from appendix C; bond energies given in table 10.1

Solution

(a) Find the standard heat of formation of NH_3 in appendix C. (The elements, N_2 and H_2, have a standard heat of formation of exactly 0.)

$$[2(-46.1 \text{ kJ})] - [(0 \text{ kJ}) + 3(0 \text{ kJ})] = \textbf{-92.2 kJ}$$

(b) Draw the Lewis structures and then use table 10.1 to determine the bond energies.

$$\text{:N} \vdots \text{N} \quad\quad \text{H} \cdot \text{H} \quad\quad \text{H} \cdot \text{N} \cdot \text{H} \atop \text{H}$$

$$[N\equiv N + 3 \text{ (H–H)}] - [2(3(N–H))] = [941.4 \text{ kJ} + 3 \text{ (436.4 kJ)}] - [2(3(393 \text{ kJ}))]$$
$$= -107.4 = \textbf{-107 kJ}$$

(c) The values for part b are average values. The value for a specific compound, NH_3, may deviate from the average as it appears to do in this case.

10.101 Name or give the formula for each of the following compounds: (a) potassium peroxide; (b) calcium phosphate; (c) aluminum sulfide; (d) barium chloride; (e) cadmium arsenate; (f) PbO_2; (g) $Mg(NO_2)_2$; (h) $SrSO_4$; (i) $(NH_4)_2HPO_4$; (j) $Mg(HSO_3)_2$

Solution

Use the Nomenclature Resource.

(a)	potassium peroxide	K_2O_2
(b)	calcium phosphate	$Ca_3(PO_4)_2$
(c)	aluminum sulfide	Al_2S_3
(d)	barium chloride	$BaCl_2$
(e)	cadmium arsenate	$Cd_3(AsO_4)_2$
(f)	PbO_2	**lead(IV) oxide**
(g)	$Mg(NO_2)_2$	**magnesium nitrite**
(h)	$SrSO_4$	**strontium sulfate**
(i)	$(NH_4)_2HPO_4$	**ammonium hydrogen phosphate**
(j)	$Mg(HSO_3)_2$	**magnesium bisulfite or magnesium hydrogen sulfite**

10.104 What is the name or the formula of each of the following compounds: (a) molybdenum(VI) oxide; (b) $V(ClO_4)_3$; (c) Cu_2S; (d) iron(II) chlorite; (e) $Pb(BrO)_2$; (f) titanium(III) thiosulfate; (g) CrO_3; (h) iron(III) arsenate; (i) tungsten(IV) oxide; (j) MnO_2

Solution

Use the Nomenclature Resource.

(a)	molybdenum(VI) oxide	MoO_3
(b)	$V(ClO_4)_3$	**vanadium(IV) perchlorate**
(c)	Cu_2S	**copper(I) sulfide**
(d)	iron(II) chlorite	$Fe(ClO_2)_2$
(e)	$Pb(BrO)_2$	**lead(II) hypobromite**

(f) titanium(III) thiosulfate $Ti_2(S_2O_3)_3$

(g) CrO_3 **chromium(VI) oxide**

(h) iron(III) arsenate $FeAsO_4$

(i) tungsten(IV) oxide WO_2

(j) MnO_2 **manganese(IV) oxide**

10.106 A sample of a xenon fluoride partially reacts with water to produce a compound containing xenon, oxygen, and fluorine. Analysis of the compound showed it to have a molar mass of 220 g/mole and to contain 58.8% Xe, 7.2% O, and 34.0% F, by mass. Draw the Lewis structure of the compound.

Information

The molar mass (220 g/mol) and composition (58.8% Xe, 7.2% O, and 34.0% F) of a substance; the question of what is the Lewis structure

Connections

The number of valence electrons for each atom, from either the periodic table or the electron configurations

Solution

To draw the Lewis structure of a molecule, we need to determine the molecular formula. To determine the molecular formula, we first need to determine the empirical formula.

Determine the empirical formula. assuming 100 g of sample:

$$Xe = (58.8 \text{ g Xe})\left(\frac{1 \text{ mol Xe}}{131.293 \text{ g Xe}}\right) = \frac{0.447853 \text{ mol Xe}}{0.447853} = 1$$

$$O = (7.2 \text{ g O})\left(\frac{1 \text{ mol O}}{15.9994 \text{ g O}}\right) = \frac{0.450017 \text{ mol O}}{0.447853} = 1$$

$$F = (34.0 \text{ g F})\left(\frac{1 \text{ mol F}}{18.9984 \text{ g F}}\right) = \frac{1.78962 \text{ mol F}}{0.447853} = 4$$

This gives $XeOF_4$ for the empirical formula (223 g/mol).

To convert the empirical formula to the molecular formula, we need to compare the molar masses:

$XeOF_4$ (Molar mass = 223 g/mol, so the empirical formula is the same as the molecular formula.)

Finish the problem by drawing the Lewis structure of $XeOF_4$. The large Xe atom will be the central atom. The very electronegative O and F atoms will obtain an octet.

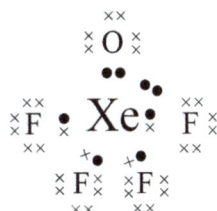

10.109 Arsenic, for semiconductors, occurs naturally as the mineral realgar, AsS. If realgar is heated in air, atmospheric oxygen reacts to produce sulfur dioxide gas and solid arsenic(III) oxide. The arsenic(III) oxide is mixed with carbon and heated to produce solid elemental and gaseous carbon monoxide. Write balanced chemical equations for these reactions.

Solution

Use the Nomenclature Resource to derive the formulas not given and use the normal procedures for balancing equations.

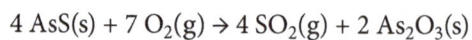

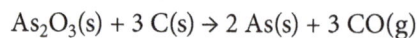

$$4\ AsS(s) + 7\ O_2(g) \rightarrow 4\ SO_2(g) + 2\ As_2O_3(s)$$

$$As_2O_3(s) + 3\ C(s) \rightarrow 2\ As(s) + 3\ CO(g)$$

CHAPTER 11

Molecular Geometry— Shapes of Molecules

The successful completion of these problems requires the following eight (8) items.

1. This chapter combines many ideas from the preceding three chapters (you may wish to review this initial table for those chapters in addition to this table).
2. The octet rule is still important.
3. Ionic and covalent bonds are still drawn differently.
4. Both ionic bonds and covalent bonds may occur in the same compound.
5. Understanding table 11.1 in the Chapter Summary section is the key.
6. Resonance does not change the molecular geometry, so we usually do not need to draw all resonance forms.
7. The way a Lewis structure is drawn does not alter the true shape of a molecule or an ion.
8. The polar or nonpolar nature of a molecule is important for understanding the concept of intermolecular forces in the next two chapters of this textbook (chapter 12, "Liquids and Solids," and chapter 13, "Mixtures—Solutions and Colloids").

Example Problem 11.1

Draw the Lewis structure of ethane, C_2H_6, and predict the molecular geometry and hybridization of each carbon atom.

Information

The molecular formula, C_2H_6; the question of what is the compound's Lewis structure and the molecular geometry and hybridization of each carbon

Connections
The number of valence electrons for each atom (from the periodic table or from the electron configuration); the rules for constructing Lewis structures

Solution
Begin by trying different arrangements of the atoms described in the formula, using what you know of their valence electrons. Carbon has four valence electrons and needs four more to complete its octet. Hydrogen has one valence electron and needs one more electron. Since carbon needs to acquire more electrons than hydrogen does, the carbon atoms are likely candidates to be central atoms, while hydrogen, which needs to acquire only one electron, is an unlikely candidate (besides, hydrogen is never a central atom). We need to place the carbon atoms adjacent to each other, because the hydrogen atoms cannot be between carbon atoms and bond to both carbon atoms. Each carbon atom has three hydrogen atoms arranged around it.

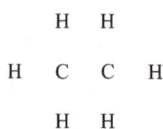

```
    H   H
H   C   C   H
    H   H
```

There are several correct ways to proceed from this point. For example, we can place the valence electrons from each of the hydrogen atoms between the hydrogen and the adjacent carbon atom:

```
    H  H
    •  ×
H • C   C × H
    •  ×
    H  H
```

Notice that, in order to keep track of the hydrogen valence electrons, we used dots around one carbon and ×'s around the other. (As an alternative to using different symbols for the electrons, it is acceptable to use different colors.) This accounts for three of the four electrons that each carbon atom needs.

We can now add valence electrons (either · or ×) from each carbon atom to complete the bonds to hydrogen. This uses three of each carbon's four valence electrons:

```
    H  H
   •× •×
H ×C  C ×H
   •× •×
    H  H
```

Each carbon atom still has one valence electron, and each still needs one more electron to complete its octet. The remaining valence electrons from the carbon atoms form a bond between the two atoms. (If desired, it is possible to convert the bonding pairs to a line indicating a bond.)

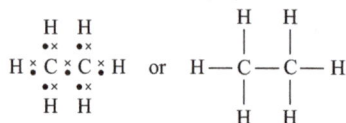

```
    H  H                 H   H
   •× •×                 |   |
H ×C×C×H   or     H — C — C — H
   •× •×                 |   |
    H  H                 H   H
```

This completes the Lewis structure. Each carbon atom is a central atom surrounded by four electron groups and no lone pairs. (The other answers will therefore be the same for each carbon atom.) The maximum separation of four groups occurs in a tetrahedral orbital geometry, and since there are no lone pairs, this is also the molecular geometry. The presence of four electron groups and no lone pairs or multiple bonds around an atom means the hybridization is sp³. (Note: It is easy for the ends of the molecule to rotate about the carbon–carbon (single) bond. The ability to rotate leads to greater flexibility. Details like this are important in biochemistry.)

Reality Check

The proposed Lewis structure gives each carbon atom an octet, and each hydrogen atom has its stable set of two electrons.

Follow-up Problem 11.1a

Draw the Lewis structure of ethene, C_2H_4, and predict the molecular geometry and hybridization of each carbon atom.

Information

The molecular formula, C_2H_4; the questions of what is the compound's Lewis structure and what are the molecular geometry and hybridization of each carbon

Connections

The number of valence electrons for each atom (from the periodic table or from the electron configuration); the rules for constructing Lewis structures

Solution

Begin by trying different arrangements of the atoms described in the formula, using what you know about their valence electrons. Carbon has four valence electrons and needs four more to complete its octet. Hydrogen has one valence electron and needs one more electron. Since carbon needs to acquire more electrons than hydrogen does, the carbon atoms are likely candidates to be central atoms, while hydrogen, which needs to acquire only one electron, is an unlikely candidate (besides, hydrogen is never a central atom). We need to place the carbon atoms adjacent to each other, because the hydrogen atoms cannot be between carbon atoms and bond to both carbon atoms. Each carbon atom has two hydrogen atoms arranged around it (the exact placement of these hydrogen atoms is unimportant).

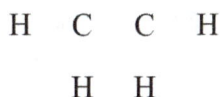

$$H \quad C \quad C \quad H$$
$$\qquad H \quad H$$

Now add the one valence electron from each hydrogen atom to the diagram.

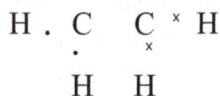

$$H \cdot C \quad \overset{\times}{\underset{\times}{C}} \times H$$
$$\qquad H \quad H$$

Notice that to keep track of the hydrogen valence electrons, we used dots around one carbon and ×'s around the other (to avoid using the same symbols on adjacent atoms). This accounts for two of the four electrons each carbon needs.

We can now add valence electrons (either · or ×) from each carbon atom to complete the bonds to hydrogen. This uses two of each carbon's four valence electrons.

$$H \overset{\times}{\underset{\cdot \times}{C}} \quad \overset{\times}{\underset{\cdot \times}{C}} H$$
$$\qquad H \quad H$$

Each carbon atom still has two valence electrons remaining, and each still needs two more electrons to complete its octet. The remaining valence electrons from the carbon atoms form a double bond between the two atoms. (It is now optional to convert each of the bonding pairs into a line to indicate the bond.)

$$H \overset{\times}{\underset{\cdot\times}{:}} C \overset{\times}{\underset{\cdot\times}{:}} C \overset{\times}{:} H$$
$$\quad\quad H \quad H$$

or

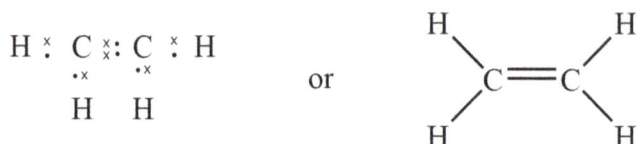

This completes the Lewis structure. Each carbon atom is a central atom surrounded by three electron groups and no lone pairs. (The remaining answers will therefore be the same for each carbon atom.) The maximum separation of three groups occurs in a trigonal planar orbital geometry, and, since there are no lone pairs, this is also the molecular geometry. The presence of three electron groups means the hybridization is sp^2. (Note: The double bond restricts rotation about the bond. This restricted rotation is significant to the behavior of many organic and biochemical molecules. One consequence of restricted rotation is the nutritional concerns about trans fats.)

Reality Check
The proposed Lewis structure gives each carbon atom an octet, and each hydrogen atom has its stable set of two electrons.

Follow-up Problem 11.1b
Draw the Lewis structure of ethyne, C_2H_2, and predict the molecular geometry and hybridization of each carbon atom.

Information
The molecular formula, C_2H_2; the questions of what is the compound's Lewis structure and what is the molecular geometry and hybridization of each carbon

Connections
The number of valence electrons for each atom (from the periodic table or from the electron configuration); the rules for constructing Lewis structures

Solution
Begin by trying different arrangements of the atoms described in the formula, using what you know about their valence electrons. Carbon has four valence electrons and needs four more to complete its octet. Hydrogen has one valence electron and needs one more electron. Since carbon needs to acquire more electrons than hydrogen does, the carbon atoms are likely candidates to be central atoms, while hydrogen, which needs to acquire only one electron, is an unlikely candidate (besides, hydrogen is never a central atom). We need to place the carbon atoms adjacent to each other, because the hydrogen atoms cannot be between carbon atoms and bond to both carbon atoms. Each carbon atom has one hydrogen atom arranged around it (the exact placement of these hydrogen atoms is unimportant).

$$H \quad C \quad C \quad H$$

Now add the one valence electron from each hydrogen atom.

$$H \cdot C \quad C \overset{\times}{\,} H$$

Notice that to keep track of the hydrogen valence electrons, we used dots around one carbon and ×'s around the other (to avoid using the same symbol on adjacent atoms). This accounts for one of the four electrons that each carbon needs.

We can now add valence electrons (either · or ×) from each carbon atom to complete the bonds to hydrogen. This uses one of each carbon's four valence electrons.

$$\text{H} \overset{\times}{:} \text{C} \quad \text{C} \overset{\times}{:} \text{H}$$

Each carbon atom still has three valence electrons remaining, and each still needs three more electrons to complete its octet. The remaining valence electrons from the carbon atoms form a triple bond between the two atoms.

$$\text{H} \overset{\times}{:} \text{C} \overset{\times}{\underset{\times}{:}} \text{C} \overset{\times}{:} \text{H} \qquad \text{or} \qquad \text{H} - \text{C} \equiv \text{C} - \text{H}$$

This completes the Lewis structure. Each carbon atom is a central atom surrounded by two electron groups and no lone pairs. (The remaining answers will therefore be the same for each carbon atom.) The maximum separation of two groups occurs in a linear orbital geometry, and, since there are no lone pairs, this is also the molecular geometry. The presence of two electron groups means the hybridization is sp.

Reality Check

The proposed Lewis structure gives each carbon atom an octet, and each hydrogen atom has its stable set of two electrons.

END-OF-CHAPTER PROBLEMS

11.1 Molecular Polarity

11.2 What key information does the VSEPR approach rely on?

Solution

VSEPR relies upon the minimization of the repulsion between the electron pairs surrounding an atom.

11.4 What behavior characterizes the interaction of polar molecules?

Solution

The partial positive charges attract the partial negative charges, so polar molecules attract other polar molecules. (Opposite charges attract.)

11.2 Determining Molecular Geometry

11.6 Consider the molecules H_2 and ClF. **(a)** Which has a polar covalent bond? **(b)** Which is a polar molecule?

Solution

(a) The bond in ClF is polar covalent because the electronegativity of the two atoms differ significantly. (There is no need to calculate the actual difference; just locate the elements on the periodic table.) The bond in H_2 is nonpolar as both atoms have the same electronegativity, which means that the electronegativity difference is 0. **(b)** ClF is a polar molecule, because of the polar covalent bond between the two atoms.

11.8 The molecule IF is polar. Show two methods of illustrating that it is polar.

Solution

Draw the Lewis structure. Fluorine is more electronegative than iodine; therefore, the electrons shift toward the fluorine making the fluorine end of the molecule partially negative (and the iodine end partially positive). One way to indicate the polarity is to use an arrow (with a cross at the end nearest the less-electronegative atom). The second method is to use the symbols $\delta+$ and $\delta-$ to indicate the partially positive (lower-electronegativity element) and the partially negative (higher-electronegativity element) ends of the bond.

11.10 What effect does the polarity of water have on the boiling point of water?

Solution

The polarity of water increases the strength of the intermolecular forces present, which, in turn, increases the boiling point.

11.13 What two terms may be used to describe the positions of electron groups about the central atom?

Solution

The electron pairs may be *bonding pairs* (groups) or *lone* (nonbonding) *pairs* (groups). Bonding pairs are shared by atoms and lone pairs are not shared by atoms.

11.15 Which type of repulsion does the VSEPR model try hardest to reduce?

Solution

The VSEPR model tries hardest to avoid lone pair–lone pair repulsions.

11.3 Geometries of Representative Molecules

11.17 If an atom hybridizes five atomic orbitals, how many hybrid orbitals will form?

Solution

The number of hybridized orbitals always equals the number of atomic orbitals; therefore, five atomic orbitals will give five hybridized orbitals.

Two Electron Groups

11.19 **(a)** What orbital geometry results when the central atom has two electron groups? **(b)** What molecular geometry results when the central atom has two electron groups and no lone pairs?

Solution

(a) The orbital geometry is linear (180° apart). **(b)** The molecular geometry is linear.

11.22 The compound cadmium iodide, CdI_2, may be treated as covalent. **(a)** Write the electron configuration for cadmium. **(b)** Draw a Lewis structure for cadmium iodide. **(c)** What is the orbital geometry about the cadmium in the compound? **(d)** What is the molecular geometry of cadmium iodide? **(e)** What is the hybridization of cadmium in cadmium iodide? **(f)** Is cadmium iodide polar, or is it nonpolar?

Solution

(a) The electron configuration is $1s^22s^22p^63s^23p^64s^23d^{10}4p^65s^24d^{10}$ or $[Kr]4s^24d^{10.}$

(b) The cadmium will be the central atom (to prevent identical atoms from being adjacent). Each iodine atom (more electronegative) needs one electron to complete an octet.

$$: \overset{..}{\underset{..}{I}} \quad \overset{.}{\times} \quad Cd \quad \overset{.}{\times} \quad \overset{..}{\underset{..}{I}} :$$

(c) There are two electron groups around the central atom (Cd), so the orbital geometry is **linear**.

(d) There are two electron groups around the central atom (Cd), so the molecular geometry is **linear**.

(e) There are two electron groups around the central atom (Cd), so the hybridization is **sp**.

(f) The two polar covalent bonds are arranged so that their polarities cancel, which means the molecule is **nonpolar**.

Three Electron Groups

11.24 **(a)** What is the bond angle when a central atom has three electron groups? **(b)** How does the bond angle change if one of the pairs is a lone pair?

Solution

(a) The bond angle is **120°** if there are no lone pairs present. **(b)** The bond angle will decrease slightly if there is a lone pair present.

11.27 The compound B_2Cl_4 is unusual in that the boron atoms are bonded to each other. Identify the orbital geometry and molecular geometry around each boron atom.

Solution

The geometry around each boron atom is trigonal planar.

Four Electron Groups

11.30 **(a)** What bond angle occurs in a molecule when the central atom has four electron groups? **(b)** How does the bond angle change if one of the pairs is a lone pair? **(c)** How does the bond angle change if two of the pairs are lone pairs?

Solution

(a) The ideal bond angle is **109.5°**. **(b)** The bond angle **decreases**. **(c)** The bond angle will decrease more than if there were only one lone pair.

11.32 Carbon is the only element that readily forms bonds with itself. The ability of an unlimited number of carbon atoms to bond together is very important to organic chemistry and biochemistry. Predict the orbital geometry, molecular geometry, and hybridization about the carbon atoms in each of the following compounds, all of which contain carbon atoms bonded to each other: **(a)** ethane, C_2H_6; **(b)** ethene, C_2H_4; **(c)** ethyne, C_2H_2

Solution

In each compound, the hydrogen atoms cannot be central atoms, so the carbon atoms must be adjacent. Each hydrogen atom has one valence electron and must gain one electron. The carbon atoms each have four valence electrons and need to gain four electrons. The results are the following Lewis structures.

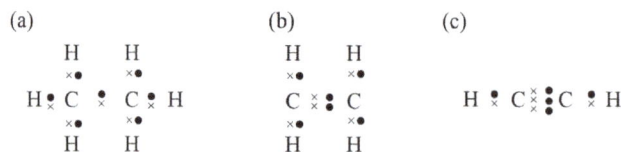

(a) Both carbon atoms have four electron groups and have **tetrahedral** orbital and molecular geometry. The hybridization of both carbon atoms is sp^3.

(b) Both carbon atoms have three electron groups and have **trigonal planar** orbital and molecular geometry. The hybridization of both carbon atoms is sp^2.

(c) Both carbon atoms have two electron groups and have **linear** orbital and molecular geometry. The hybridization of both carbon atoms is **sp**.

11.35 Dichloroethene, with the general formula $C_2H_2Cl_2$, has three isomers (different compounds with the same formula). Draw the structures of the three isomers of dichloroethene and predict which are polar.

Solution

Begin by drawing the Lewis structures. Carbon, needing the most electrons, will be the central atom with the other four atoms distributed around it. All the structures are the same except for the relative placement of the H and Cl atoms.

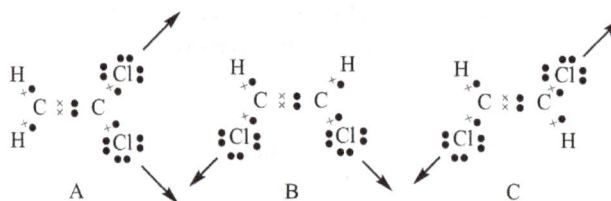

The chlorine atoms are the most electronegative atoms; therefore, the polarity of the C–Cl bonds (indicated by the arrows) is the key.

In structure A, both arrows point to the right (not canceling); therefore, the molecule is polar.

In structure B, both arrows point down (not canceling); therefore, the molecule is polar.

In structure C, the arrows point in opposite directions, so they cancel; therefore, the molecule is nonpolar.

11.38 The bond angle in methane is the ideal tetrahedral angle of 109.5°. Why are bond angles in other compounds with tetrahedral orbital geometries not always ideal?

Solution

The ideal bond angles occur when all electron groups are equivalent. The presence of lone pairs and bonding pairs leads to all pairs not being equivalent. Lone pairs repel bonding pairs more than bonding pairs repel other pairs. For this reason, the angles to the lone pairs increase and the other angles decrease.

11.40 The structure of ethyl acetate is

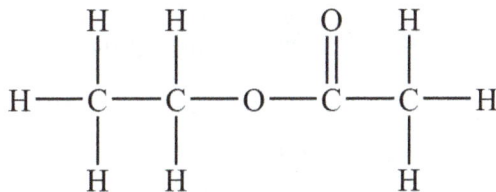

Each carbon and the oxygen bonded to two different carbons may be treated as a central atom. (a) Give the hybridization of each central atom. (b) Give the approximate bond angles about each central atom. (c) What is the total number of σ bonds present? (d) What is the total number of π bonds present?

Solution
Remember, even though they do not appear in the structure shown, oxygen atoms each have two lone pairs (to complete their octets).

(a) The three carbon atoms with hydrogen atoms attached are sp³-hybridized (four electron groups) and the remaining carbon atom is sp²-hybridized (three electron groups). (b) The angles about the sp³-hybridized atoms are 109.5° for C, and slightly less for the central O. The angles about the sp²-hybridized carbon atom are 120°. (c) There are thirteen σ bonds (all single bonds plus one of the two bonds in the double bond). (d) There is one π bond (one of the two bonds in the double bond).

11.44 The structure of diazepam (Valium) is

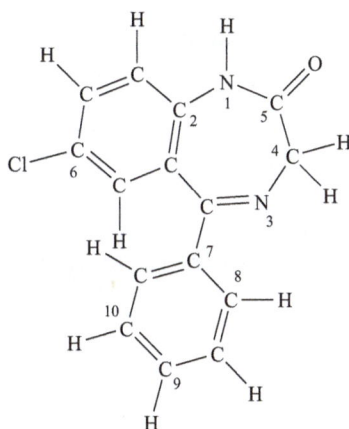

(a) What is the orbital geometry around each numbered atom? (b) What is the molecular geometry around each numbered atom? (c) What is the hybridization around each numbered atom? (d) How many σ bonds are present? (e) How many π bonds are present?

Solution
This structure, like many similar structures, does not show the lone pairs. In this example, the nitrogen atom has a lone pair, chlorine has three lone pairs, and each oxygen atom has two lone pairs. These pairs are necessary to give each atom an octet. You may wish to add these lone pairs to the structure shown and/or show the separate bonds to the H atoms.

(a) (1) four groups = **tetrahedral**; (2) three groups = **trigonal planar**; (3) three groups = **trigonal planar**; (4) four groups = **tetrahedral**; (5) three groups = **trigonal planar**; (6) three groups = **trigonal planar**; (7) three groups = **trigonal planar**; (8) three groups = **trigonal planar**; (9) three groups = **trigonal planar**; (10) three groups = **trigonal planar**

(b) (1) three groups and 1 lone pair = **trigonal pyramidal**; (2) three groups and zero lone pair = **trigonal planar**; (3) three groups and one lone pair = **bent**; (4) four groups and zero lone pair = **tetrahedral**; (5) three groups and zero lone pair = **trigonal planar**; (6) three groups and zero lone pair = **trigonal planar**; (7) three groups and zero lone pair = **trigonal planar**; (8) three groups and zero lone pair = **trigonal planar**; (9) three groups and zero lone pair = **trigonal planar**; (10) three groups and zero lone pair = **trigonal planar**

(c) (1) four groups = sp^3; (2) three groups = sp^2; (3) three groups = sp^2; (4) four groups = sp^3; (5) three groups = sp^2; (6) three groups = sp^2; (7) three groups = sp^2; (8) three groups = sp^2; (9) three groups = sp^2; (10) three groups = sp^2

(d) All single bonds and one of each double or triple bond in a σ bond; the total is **32**.

(e) One from each double bond and two from each tripe bond in a π bond; the total is **8**.

Five Electron Groups

11.46 **(a)** What is the orbital geometry for a molecule where the central atom has five electron groups and no lone pairs? **(b)** Would the orbital geometry be the same if one or more of the five pairs were a lone pair? **(c)** What is the molecular geometry for a molecule where the central atom has five electron groups and no lone pairs? **(d)** Would the molecular geometry be the same if one or more of the five pairs were a lone pair?

Solution

(a) The orbital geometry is **trigonal bipyramid**. **(b)** Yes, because orbital geometry only depends upon the electron groups present. **(c)** The molecular geometry is **trigonal bipyramidal**. **(d)** No, the molecular geometry would be changed with the number of lone pairs.

11.49 Determine which of the following are polar: **(a)** hydrogen chloride, HCl; **(b)** nitrogen dioxide, NO_2; **(c)** krypton difluoride, KrF_2; **(d)** ammonia, NH_3; **(e)** boron trifluoride, BF_3

Solution

Begin by drawing the Lewis structure for each molecule or ion.

(a) There are two different atoms present, so **polar**. (A Lewis structure is not necessary if there are only two atoms present.)

$$\text{H} \overset{\times\times}{\underset{\times\times}{\overset{\bullet}{\times}} \text{Cl}^{\times}_{\times}}$$

(b) Three electron groups and one lone "pair," so **polar**. There is a lone electron on the nitrogen because this is an odd electron molecule (17 electrons) and the less electronegative atom does not achieve an octet. The lone electron assumes the position of a lone pair; however, one electron does not repel as strongly as two electrons. The oxygen atoms achieve octets because they are more electronegative than nitrogen.

$$\overset{\times\times}{\underset{\times\times}{\overset{\bullet}{\times}\text{O}}} \quad \overset{\bullet}{\underset{\times}{:\text{N}:}} \overset{\times\times}{\underset{\times\times}{\text{O}^{\times}_{\times}}} \longleftrightarrow \overset{\times\times}{\underset{\times\times}{\text{O}^{\times}_{\times}}} \quad \overset{\bullet}{:\text{N}:} \overset{\times\times}{\underset{\times\times}{\text{O}^{\times}_{\times}}}$$

(c) Five electron groups and three lone pairs, so **nonpolar**. Based on its position on the periodic table, krypton can exceed an octet. The fluorine atoms have octets.

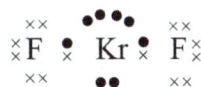

$$ \overset{\times\times}{\underset{\times\times}{\times}F}\;\bullet\;\overset{\bullet\bullet\bullet\bullet}{\underset{\bullet\bullet}{Kr}}\;\bullet\;\overset{\times\times}{\underset{\times\times}{F}\times} $$

(d) Four electron groups and one lone pair, so **polar**. The nitrogen atom has an octet.

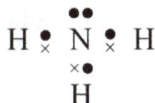

$$ H\;\overset{\bullet\bullet}{\underset{\times\bullet}{\times}N}\;H $$
$$ H $$

(e) Three electron groups and no lone pairs, so **nonpolar**. The fluorine atoms have octets, while the boron atom only has six electrons.

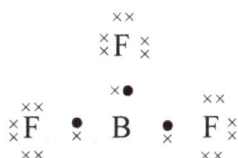

$$ \overset{\times\times}{\underset{}{\times}F}\times $$
$$ \overset{\times\bullet}{} $$
$$ \overset{\times\times}{\underset{\times\times}{\times}F}\;\bullet\;\overset{}{\underset{\times}{}}B\;\bullet\;\overset{\times\times}{\underset{\times\times}{F}\times} $$

Six Electron Groups

11.52 (a) What orbital geometry results when a central atom has six electron groups? **(b)** What is the molecular geometry when the central atom has six electron groups and no lone pairs? **(c)** What is the molecular geometry when the central atom has six electron groups and one is a lone pair? **(d)** What is the molecular geometry when the central atom has six electron groups and two are lone pairs?

Solution

(a) The orbital geometry for six electron groups is octahedral. **(b)** The molecular geometry is octahedral. **(c)** The molecular geometry is square pyramidal. **(d)** The molecular geometry is square planar.

11.54 What is the hybridization about the central atom if there are six electrons groups about it?

Solution

The hybridization for six electron groups is **sp^3d^2**.

11.57 Several species have the general molecular formula XF_4. Among these are carbon tetrafluoride, CF_4; sulfur tetrafluoride, SF_4; and xenon tetrafluoride, XeF_4. Determine the molecular geometry for each and explain why they have the same general formula but differing geometries.

Solution

Begin by drawing the Lewis structure for each molecule or ion. In all cases, the very electro-negative fluorine will achieve an octet.

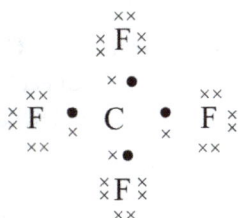

$$ \overset{\times\times}{\underset{}{\times}F\times} $$
$$ \times\;\bullet $$
$$ \overset{\times\times}{\underset{\times\times}{\times}F}\;\bullet\;C\;\bullet\;\overset{\times\times}{\underset{\times\times}{F}\times} $$
$$ \times\;\bullet $$
$$ \overset{}{\underset{\times\times}{\times}F\times} $$

Four electron groups and no lone pairs means **tetrahedral**.

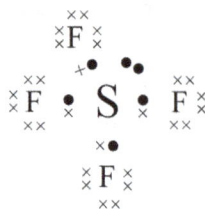

$$\underset{\times\times}{\underset{\times}{\overset{\times\times}{\overset{\times}{\text{F}}}}} \bullet \text{S} \bullet \underset{\times\times}{\underset{\times}{\overset{\times\times}{\overset{\times}{\text{F}}}}}$$

Five electron groups and one lone pair means **irregular tetrahedron**.

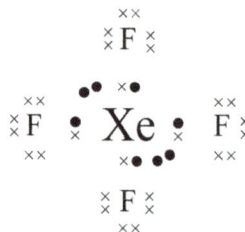

$$\text{F} \bullet \text{Xe} \bullet \text{F}$$

Six electron groups and two lone pairs mean **square planar**.

Since the number of electron groups and the number of lone pairs vary, so will the geometry.

11.4 Applications and Extensions

Putting It All Together

11.60 (a) Draw Lewis structures for carbon monoxide, CO, and hydrogen chloride, HCl. **(b)** What is the molecular geometry of each of these molecules? **(c)** Why is it unnecessary to have a line in the geometry table to accommodate these electron pair combinations?

Solution

(a) The Lewis structures are as shown. All atoms except H have an octet.

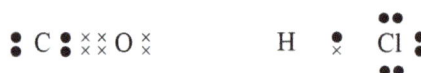

$$\text{C} \vdots \text{O} \qquad\qquad \text{H} \bullet \text{Cl}$$

(b) Both molecules are linear.

(c) Two atoms always result in a linear molecule.

11.62 How many electron groups must surround the central atom to yield the following angles between the pairs: **(a)** 180°, **(b)** 120°, **(c)** 109.5°, **(d)** 90°. Some of these angles may have more than one answer.

Solution

(a) two (linear); **(b) three** (trigonal planar) or **five** (trigonal bipyramid); **(c) four** (tetrahedral); **(d) five** (trigonal bipyramid) or **six** (octahedral)

11.65 (a) Draw resonance structures for the oxalate ion, $C_2O_4^{2-}$. The two carbon atoms are connected. **(b)** What is the molecular geometry about each carbon atom? **(c)** Determine the hybridization of each carbon atom. **(d)** Is the π bond delocalized?

Solution

(a) These are the resonance structures of the oxalate ion:

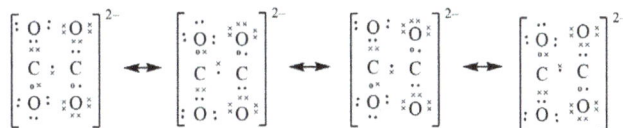

(b) The molecular geometry about each carbon atom (three electron groups and no lone pairs) is **trigonal planar**. (c) Each carbon atom (three electron groups and no lone pairs) has sp^2 hybridization. (d) **Yes**, the π bonds are delocalized.

11.68 Determine the hybridization around the central atom in each of the following:

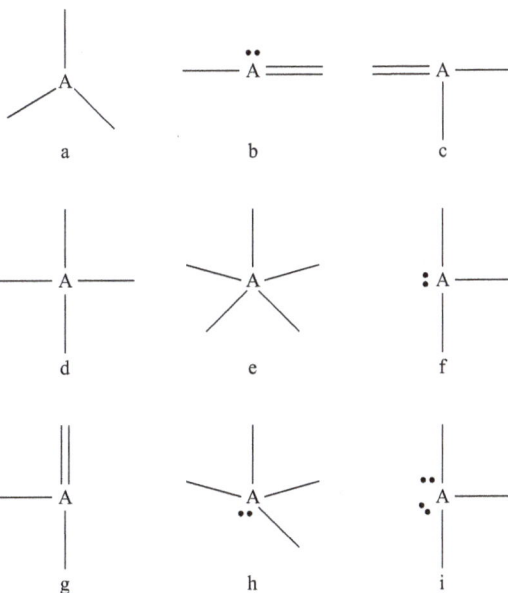

Solution

Each line or double line counts as one electron group. Take the electron groups from the lines and add the number of electron pairs shown to get the total number of electron groups.

(a) sp^2 (three electron groups); (b) sp^2 (three electron groups); (c) sp^2 (three electron groups); (d) sp^3 (four electron groups); (e) sp^3d (five electron groups); (f) sp^3 (four electron groups); (g) sp^2 (three electron groups); (h) sp^3d (five electron groups); (i) sp^3d (five electron groups)

11.70 Give the hybridization and the number of surrounding electron groups for the central atom in each of the following orbital geometries: (a) octahedral, (b) trigonal bipyramidal, (c) tetrahedral, (d) trigonal planar, (e) linear

Solution

(a) sp^3d^2 with six electron groups; (b) sp^3d with five electron groups; (c) sp^3 with four electron groups; (d) sp^2 with three electron groups; (e) sp with two electron groups, or sp^3d with five electron groups (three lone pairs)

11.73 What is the name or the formula of each of the following compounds: (a) $MnCl_2$; (b) $MnCl_3$; (c) $FeCl_3$; (d) $CrSO_4$; (e) $CuCl_2$; (f) lead(II) oxide; (g) tin(IV) fluoride; (h) chromium(III) oxide; (i) gold(I) chloride; (j) nickel(II) sulfite

Solution

See the Nomenclature Resource.

(a)	$MnCl_2$	**manganese(II) chloride**
(b)	$MnCl_3$	**manganese(III) chloride**
(c)	$FeCl_3$	**iron(III) chloride**
(d)	$CrSO_4$	**chromium(II) sulfate**
(e)	$CuCl_2$	**copper(II) chloride**
(f)	lead(II) oxide	**PbO**
(g)	tin(IV) fluoride	**SnF_4**
(h)	chromium(III) oxide	**Cr_2O_3**
(i)	gold(I) chloride	**AuCl**
(j)	nickel(II) sulfite	**$NiSO_3$**

11.77 Boron trichloride is a Lewis acid that will react with ammonia and other Lewis bases. **(a)** Write a balanced chemical equation for the reaction of gaseous boron trichloride with ammonia gas to produce solid BCl_3NH_3. **(b)** Draw Lewis structures for all reactants and products in this reaction. **(c)** Which atom(s) change molecular geometry during the reaction?

Solution

(a) The reaction is

$$BCl_3(g) + NH_3(g) \rightarrow BCl_3NH_3(s)$$

(b) Rewriting the balanced chemical equation using Lewis structures gives

(c) The molecular geometry of the boron changes from trigonal planar to tetrahedral. The molecular geometry of nitrogen changes from trigonal pyramidal to tetrahedral.

11.79 The liquid compound benzene, C_6H_6, will burn in oxygen gas to form carbon dioxide gas and water vapor. **(a)** Write a balanced chemical equation for this reaction. **(b)** What are the molecular geometries of the products? **(c)** Using standard heats of formation, calculate the heat of reaction. **(d)** Calculate the heat of reaction using bond energies. **(e)** What might be the major source of the discrepancy between your answers in parts (c) and (d)?

Solution

(a) The balanced chemical equation is

$$2\ C_6H_6(l) + 15\ O_2(g) \rightarrow 12\ CO_2(g) + 6\ H_2O(g)$$

(b) Carbon dioxide is linear, and water is bent (see the structures in part d).

(c) The standard heats of formation are in appendix C. The heat of reaction is the sum of the heats of reaction for the products minus the sum of the heats of reaction for the reactants.

$$\Delta H°(\text{rxn}) = [12 \ \Delta H_f°(CO_2(g)) + 6 \ \Delta H_f°(H_2O(g))] - [2 \ \Delta H_f°(C_6H_6(l)) + 15 \ \Delta H_f°(O_2(g))]$$

$$\Delta H°(\text{rxn}) = [12 \ (-393.5 \ \text{kJ}) + 6 \ (-241.8 \ \text{kJ})] - [2 \ (49.0 \ \text{kJ}) + 15 \ (0.0 \ \text{kJ})]$$

$$= -6270.8 \ \textbf{kJ/mol}$$

(d) First, we need to determine the number and types of bonds present (Lewis structures).

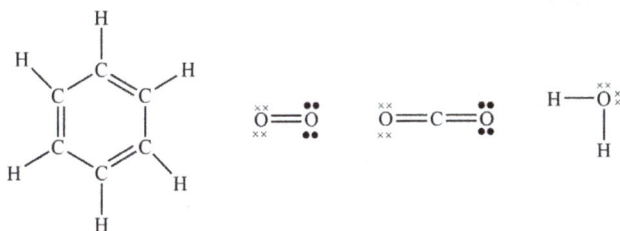

The average bond energies are provided in **table 10.1**. The sum of the bond energies for the reactants minus the sum of the bond energies for the products gives the heat of reaction.

$$\Delta H_{\text{rxn}} = \{2[3(C–C) + 3(C=C) + 6(C–H)] + 15 \ (O=O)\} - [12(2(C=O)) + 6(2(O–H))] = -6091.5$$

$$= \{2[3(347) + 3(615) + 6(414)] + 15 \ (498.7)\} - [12(2(781)) + 6(2(464))] = -6091.5$$

$$= \textbf{–6092 kJ}$$

(e) The difference is due to the presence of resonance (in benzene). The resonance leads to additional stability.

11.81 The analysis of a compound containing carbon, hydrogen, and oxygen found 52.1% C, 13.1% H, and 34.7% O. The molar mass of the compound is about 45 g/mol. There are two compounds with this molecular formula. Draw the Lewis structures for each of these two compounds.

Information
The composition (52.1% C, 13.1% H, and 34.7% O) and molar mass ($\approx$45 g/mol) of a compound, the question of what are the Lewis structures of two compounds with this formula.

Connections
Moles are the key.

Solution
It is necessary to determine the molecular formula to draw the Lewis structures. However, it is necessary to determine the empirical formula first.

Assume 100 grams of sample, which makes the percentages numerically the same as the number of grams.

$$(52.1 \ \text{g C}) \left(\frac{1 \ \text{mol C}}{12.011 \ \text{g C}} \right) = \frac{4.337690 \ \text{mol C}}{2.16888} = 2$$

$$(13.1 \ \text{g H}) \left(\frac{1 \ \text{mol H}}{1.0079 \ \text{g H}} \right) = \frac{12.99732 \ \text{mol H}}{2.16888} = 6$$

$$(34.7 \ \text{g O}) \left(\frac{1 \ \text{mol O}}{15.999 \ \text{g O}} \right) = \frac{2.16888 \ \text{mol O}}{2.16888} = 1$$

Empirical formula = C_2H_6O

Empirical formula mass ≈ 2 (12) + 6 (1) + 1 (16) = 46 amu

The empirical formula mass is close to the molecular mass given; therefore, the empirical formula and the molecular formula are the same.

Molecular formula = C_2H_6O

As indicated in the problem, there are two different bonding schemes (not resonance forms). In one structure there is only one C–O bond, while in the other structure, there are two C–O bonds.

11.83

(a) Using

$$N_2H_4(l) + O_2(g) \rightarrow N_2(g) + 2\ H_2O(l) \qquad \Delta H = -622.2\ kJ$$

and

$$2\ H_2(g) + O_2(g) \rightarrow 2\ H_2O(l) \qquad \Delta H = -571.6\ kJ$$

determine ΔH for the following reaction:

$$N_2(g) + 2\ H_2(g) \rightarrow N_2H_4(l)$$

(b) Using bond energies, determine the value of ΔH for the following reaction:

$$N_2(g) + 2\ H_2(g) \rightarrow N_2H_4(g)$$

(c) Determine the hybridization of the nitrogen atoms in N_2H_4.

Solution

(a) We need to use Hess's law to determine the enthalpy change.

Reverse the first reaction and add it to the second reaction. Cancel formulas appearing on both sides and add energies.

$$N_2(g) + \cancel{2\ H_2O(l)} \rightarrow N_2H_4(l) + \cancel{O_2(g)} \qquad \Delta H = +622.2\ kJ$$
$$2\ H_2(g) + \cancel{O_2(g)} \rightarrow \cancel{2\ H_2O(l)} \qquad \Delta H = -571.6\ kJ$$
$$\text{Total} \quad N_2(g) + 2\ H_2(g) \rightarrow N_2H_4(l) \qquad \mathbf{\Delta H = +50.6\ kJ}$$

(b) We need to draw the Lewis structures to determine the number and type of bonds present.

The bond energies are in provided in **table 10.1**. The heat of reaction is the sum of the bond energies for the reactants minus the sum of the bond energies for the products.

$$\Delta H = [(N \quad N) + 2(H-H)] - [(N-N) + 4(N-H)]$$

$$= [(941.4) + 2(436.4)] - [(159) + 4(393)] = 83.2 = \textbf{83 kJ}$$

(c) Both nitrogen atoms are **sp³**-hybridized in N_2H_4.

11.86 (a) Draw resonance structures for the thiocyanate ion. **(b)** What is the hybridization of the central atom in each of the resonance structures?

Solution

(a) These are the resonance structures (they may appear in any order); however, changing the order of the atoms is unacceptable. Remember, carbon is the more likely to be the central atom, because it needs more electrons than the other two atoms.

(b) The central atom is **sp**-hybridized.

11.89 Determine the hybridization about each carbon atom in each of the following:
(a) methanol, CH_3OH; (b) sodium acetate, $NaC_2H_3O_2$; (c) potassium cyanate, KOCN;
(d) calcium carbonate, $CaCO_3$; (e) oxalic acid, $H_2C_2O_4$

Solution

(a) methanol, CH_3OH

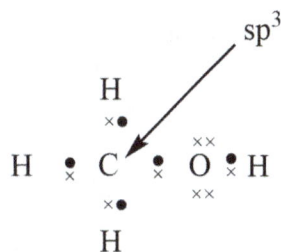

(b) sodium acetate, $NaC_2H_3O_2$ (there is an ionic bond between the Na^+ and the $C_2H_3O_2{}^-$)

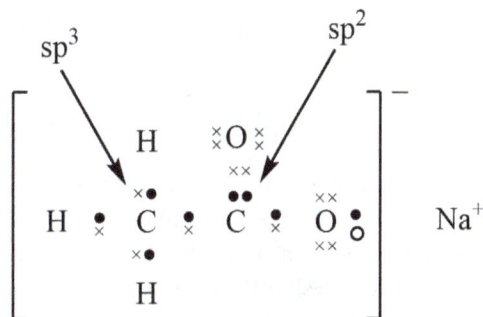

(c) potassium cyanate, KOCN (the cyanate ion undergoes resonance) (there is an ionic bond between the K⁺ and the OCN⁻)

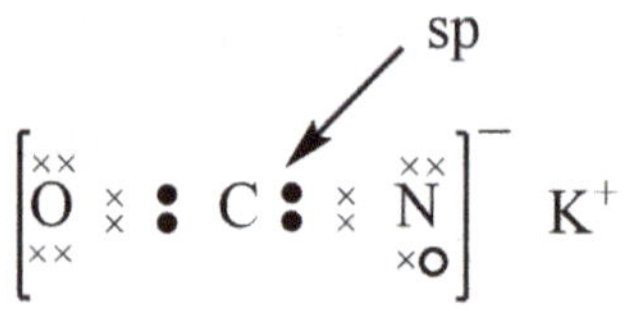

$$\left[O : C : N \right]^- \quad K^+$$

sp

(d) calcium carbonate, CaCO₃ (the carbonate ion undergoes resonance) (there is an ionic bond between the Ca²⁺ and the CO₃²⁻)

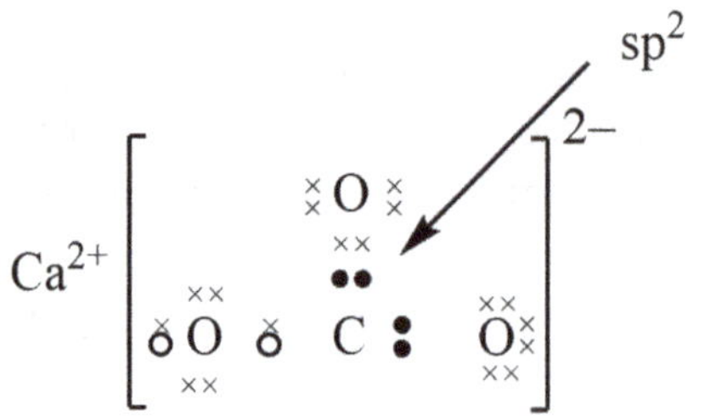

$$Ca^{2+} \left[O \quad C \quad O \right]^{2-}$$

sp²

(e) oxalic acid, H₂C₂O₄

sp²   sp²

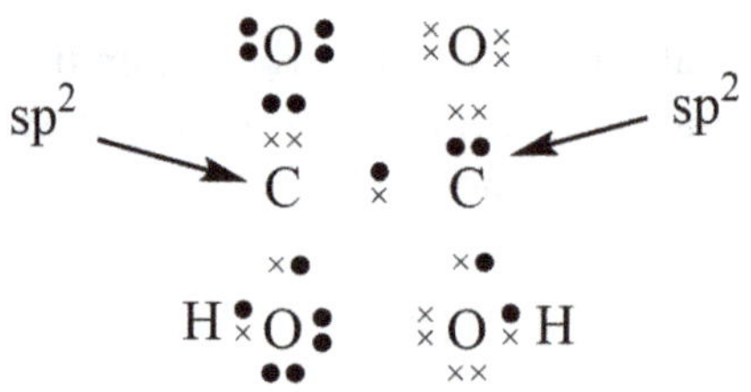

11.92 The amide ion, NH₂⁻, and the ammonium ion, NH₄⁺, are like ammonia, NH₃. Draw Lewis structures for all three and match each Lewis structure with one of the following observed bond angles—109.5°, 107°, and 105°.

Solution
Begin by drawing Lewis structures.

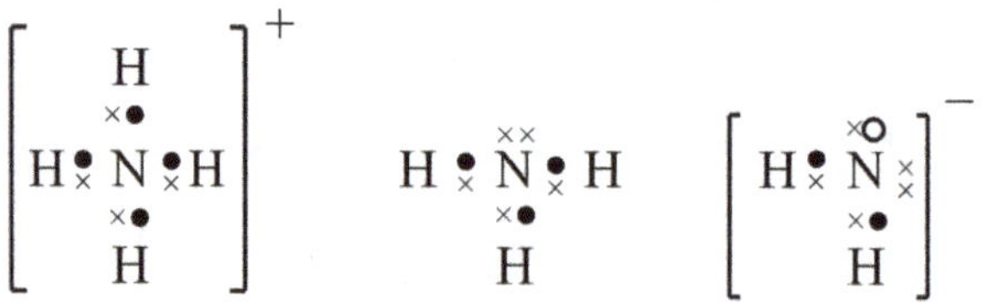

109.5°   107°   105°

In all three cases, there are four electron groups around the central nitrogen atom. The ideal angle between four electron pairs is 109.5°. The ammonium ion, with no lone pairs, should have the ideal angle. Ammonia, with one lone pair, should be slightly less than ideal (107°). The amide ion, with two lone pairs, should be slightly less than ideal with only one lone pair (105°).

11.94 How many unhybridized p orbitals are present in the central atom in each of the following? **(a)** carbon dioxide, **(b)** hydrocyanic acid, **(c)** methane, **(d)** boron trifluoride, **(e)** nitrogen dioxide

Solution

First, draw the Lewis structures, and then determine the hybridization on the central atom. Initially, the central atom has three p orbitals. The number of unhybridized p orbitals is three minus the p orbital used in the hybridization.

(a) two (C is sp); **(b) two** (C is sp); **(c) zero** (C is sp^3); **(d) one** (B is sp^2); **(e) one** (N is sp^2)

11.97 The molecule N_2F_2 exists in two forms. In each form, the nitrogen atoms are connected, and each nitrogen atom has a fluorine atom attached. One of the forms is polar and the other is nonpolar. Draw the structures for the two forms, and label each as polar or as nonpolar.

Solution

Begin by drawing Lewis structures.

When the fluorine atoms point "away" from each other, the polarity of the bonds cancels to leave a nonpolar molecule. When the fluorine atoms are on the same side, the polarity of the bonds does not cancel, so the molecule is polar. (The arrows point in the direction of the bond polarity.)

11.100 Cyclopropane, C_3H_6, is an unstable hydrocarbon, with the three carbon atoms forming an equilateral triangle. Each carbon atom is attached to two hydrogen atoms. **(a)** Draw a Lewis structure for cyclopropane. **(b)** Predict the bond angle between the carbon atoms. **(c)** Why does your prediction in part (b) help explain why cyclopropane is unstable?

Solution

(a) The Lewis structure is

(b) The angles for an equilateral triangle are 60°.

(c) An angle of 60° is much less than the ideal angle of 109.5° (carbon with four groups). This results in a significant amount of strain, which makes the molecule unstable.

11.102 There are three organic compounds with the formula C_3H_4. **(a)** Draw structures for each of these compounds. **(b)** What is the hybridization of each carbon atom in each of your answers to part (a)?

Solution

(a) The Lewis structures are

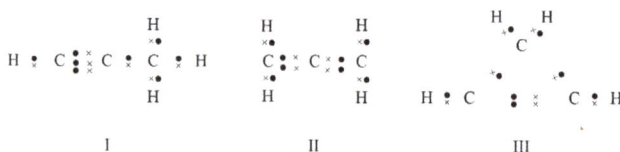

It does not matter what order or orientation you use, which is why the structures are labeled.

(b) In I, the left and center carbon atoms are sp-hybridized. Right carbon atom is **sp³**-hybridized.

In II, the end carbon atoms are **sp²**-hybridized, and the center carbon atom is sp-hybridized.

In III, the top carbon atom is **sp³**-hybridized and the bottom two carbon atoms are **sp²**-hybridized.

CHAPTER 12

Liquids and Solids

The successful completion of these problems requires the following six (6) items.

1. When using the Clausius–Clapeyron equation, $(\ln\dfrac{P_1}{P_2} = \dfrac{\Delta H_{vap}}{R}\left[\dfrac{1}{T_2} - \dfrac{1}{T_1}\right])$, be very careful about rounding. What may seem like a little rounding may lead to a very different answer.

2. Intermolecular forces are the key to the answers to many of the problems in this chapter.

3. The strength of an intermolecular force does not vary significantly with temperature; however, the kinetic energy does. Thus, the hydrogen bonds in ice are no stronger than the hydrogen bonds in liquid or gaseous water.

4. Many of the calculations are unit conversion problems similar in style to those in chapter 1, "The Tools of Chemistry."

5. Know how to determine the contents of a unit cell.

6. Most one-component phase diagrams look very similar.

Example Problem 12.1

Answer the following questions by consulting figure 12.2. **(a)** A sample of water, initially at 50°C and 0.1 atm, is compressed at constant temperature to a pressure of 100 atm. What phase changes, if any, occur? **(b)** Another sample of water, initially at –10°C and 1.0 atm, is heated at constant pressure to 125°C. What phase changes, if any, occur? **(c)** A third sample of water, initially at –5°C and 1.0 atm, is compressed at constant temperature to 150 atm. What phase changes, if any, occur?

Information

The phase diagram of water (figure 12.2); three changes: **(a)** 50°C and 0.1 atm to 50°C and 100 atm, **(b)** −10°C and 1.0 atm to 125°C and 1.0 atm, **(c)** −5°C and 1.0 atm to −5°C and 150 atm

Connections

The phase diagram; various definitions

Solution

Begin with figure 12.2 and add arrows representing the changes. The arrows should point in the direction of the change. This is a sketch, so the positions do not need to be perfect.

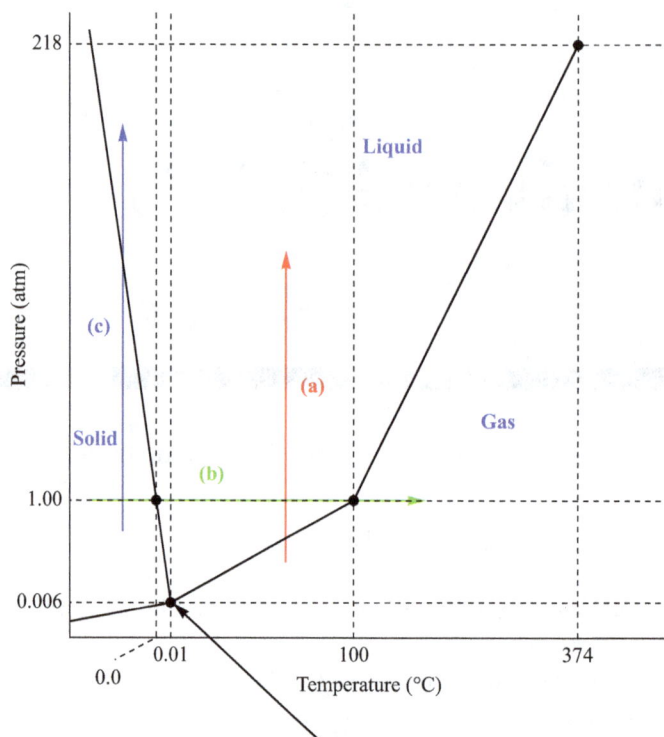

(a) Moving in the direction indicated by the arrow, nothing happens until the liquid–gas line is reached, where the gas condenses. After all the gas has condensed, the water continues along the arrow with no further phase changes. The only phase change is **condensation**.

(b) Moving in the direction indicated by the arrow, nothing happens until the solid–liquid line is reached, where the solid melts. After all the solid has melted, the water continues along the arrow until the liquid–gas line is reached, where the liquid vaporizes. After all the water has vaporized, the water continues along the arrow with no further phase changes. The phase changes, in order, are **fusion** and **vaporization**.

(c) Moving in the direction indicated by the arrow, nothing happens until the solid–liquid line is reached, where the solid melts. After all the solid has melted the water continues along the arrow with no further phase changes. The only phase change is **fusion**.

Reality Check

The phase lines crossed indicate the phase change taking place. The direction is important. For example, part (a) changes a gas to a liquid, which is condensation; however, if the arrow were reversed, the change would be liquid to gas, which is vaporization.

Follow-Up Problem 12.1a

Answer the following questions by consulting figure 12.4. **(a)** A sample of carbon dioxide, initially at −56°C and 70 atm, is compressed at constant temperature to a pressure of 4 atm. What phase changes, if any, occur? **(b)** Another sample of carbon dioxide, initially at 25°C and 10 atm, is heated at constant pressure to −80°C. What phase changes, if any, occur? **(c)** A third sample of carbon dioxide, initially at 25°C and 4.0 atm, is heated at constant pressure to −100°C. What phase changes, if any, occur?

Information

The phase diagram of carbon dioxide (figure 12.4); three changes: **(a)** 50°C and 0.1 atm to 50°C and 100 atm, **(b)** −10°C and 1.0 atm to 125°C and 1.0 atm, **(c)** −5°C and 1.0 atm to −5°C and 150 atm

Connections

The phase diagram; various definitions

Solution

Begin with figure 12.4 and add arrows representing the changes. The arrows should point in the direction of the change. This is a sketch; therefore, the positions do not need to be perfect.

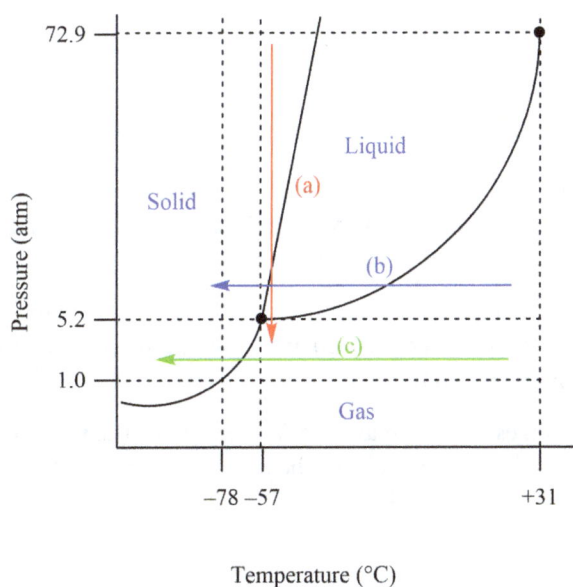

(a) Moving in the direction indicated by the arrow, nothing happens until the solid-liquid line is reached, where the solid melts. After all the solid has melted, the liquid continues along the arrow until the liquid–gas line is reached, where the liquid vaporizes. After all the liquid has vaporized, the gas continues along the arrow with no further phase changes. The phase changes, in order, are **fusion** and **vaporization**.

(b) Moving in the direction indicated by the arrow, nothing happens until the liquid–gas line is reached, where the gas condenses. After all the gas has condensed, the liquid continues along the arrow until the solid–liquid line is reached, where the liquid freezes. After all the liquid has frozen, the solid continues along the arrow with no further phase changes. The phase changes, in order, are **condensation** and **solidification**.

(c) Moving in the direction indicated by the arrow, nothing happens until the solid–gas line is reached, where the gas undergoes deposition. After all the gas has deposited, the solid continues along the arrow with no further phase changes. The only phase change is **deposition**.

Reality Check

The phase lines crossed indicate the phase change taking place. The direction is important. For example, part (c) changes a gas to a solid, which is deposition; however, if the arrow were reversed, the change would be from solid to gas, which is sublimation.

Follow-Up Problem 12.1b

Answer the following questions by consulting figure 12.2 and figure 12.4. **(a)** A sample of water, initially at a pressure just to the left of the triple point in figure 12.2, is compressed at constant temperature to a pressure of 100 atm. What phase changes, if any, occur? **(b)** A sample of carbon dioxide, initially at a pressure just to the left of the triple point in figure 12.4 is heated at constant pressure to 40°C, is compressed at constant temperature to a pressure of 100 atm. What phase changes, if any, occur? **(c)** Compare your answers to parts (a) and (b).

Information

The two different phase diagrams (figure 12.2 and figure 12.4); two descriptions of changes; the question of a comparison of the two changes

Connections

The phase diagrams and definitions

Solution

(a) Examining the phase in figure 12.2, we find that the described change is a vertical change. The initial phase is a solid, which changes to a liquid when the solid–liquid line in encountered. Therefore, the phase change is **fusion**.

(b) Examining the phase in figure 12.4, we find that the described change is a vertical change. The initial phase is a solid. As the pressure increases, no phase lines are encountered. Therefore, there is **no phase change**.

(c) Even though the changes described are similar (except for the variations in the numbers), there are different results. Water is one of the few exceptions, in that an increase in pressure leads to fusion.

Reality Check

While most one-component phase diagrams are similar, there are subtle differences. In this case, and in many others, water behaves differently than do most other substances.

Example Problem 12.2

In which of the following compounds is hydrogen bonding the strongest intermolecular force present? **(a)** sodium hydroxide, $NaOH$; **(b)** difluoromethane, CH_2F_2; **(c)** silicic acid, H_4SiO_4

Information

The formula of the compounds; the question of which compound has hydrogen bonding as the strongest intermolecular force

Connections

The definitions and characteristics of the various types of intermolecular forces

Solution

It may help to draw the structures of the compounds. If needed, the structures are

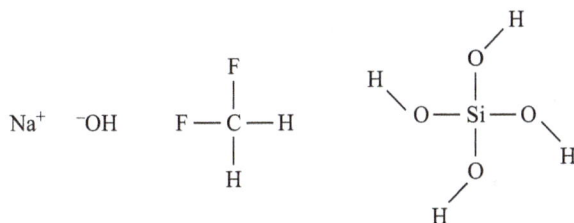

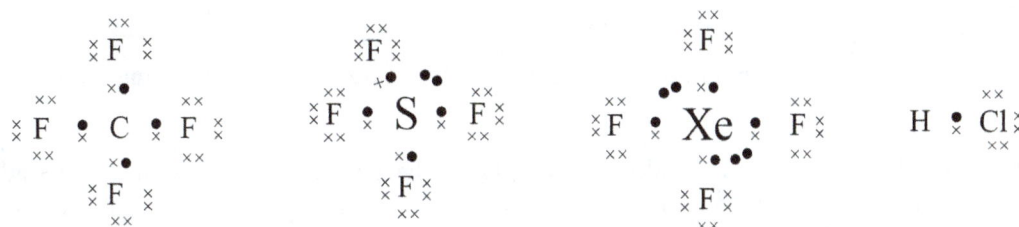

$$Na^+ \quad {}^-OH \qquad F-\underset{\underset{H}{|}}{\overset{\overset{F}{|}}{C}}-H$$

(a) Sodium hydroxide is an ionic compound; hydrogen bonding is not stronger than ionic bonds.

(b) Even though this compound contains both hydrogen and fluorine; there will be no hydrogen bonding because the hydrogen is bonded to the carbon and not the fluorine. The strongest intermolecular force present in this compound is dipole–dipole forces, which are weaker than hydrogen bonds.

(c) This is an oxyacid, so the acidic hydrogen atoms (all the hydrogen atoms in this case) are attached to an oxygen atom. Whenever hydrogen is attached to an oxygen atom, hydrogen bonding will occur.

The only compound in which hydrogen bonding is the strongest intermolecular force is **silicic acid**.

Reality Check

All the conclusions agree with what constitutes the different intermolecular forces.

Follow-Up Problem 12.2a

What is the strongest type of intermolecular force in each of the following? (a) carbon tetrafluoride, CF_4; (b) sulfur tetrafluoride, SF_4; (c) xenon tetrafluoride, XeF_4; (d) hydrochloric acid, HCl

Information

The formula of the compounds; the question of what is the strongest intermolecular force in each

Connections

The definitions and characteristics of the various types of intermolecular forces

Solution

It may help to draw the structures of the compounds. If needed, the structures are

(a) The central carbon atom has four electron groups and no lone pairs; therefore, it is nonpolar. The strongest intermolecular force for a nonpolar molecule is London dispersion forces.

(b) The central sulfur atom has five electron groups and one lone pair; therefore, it is polar. The strongest intermolecular force for a polar molecule is dipole–dipole forces.

(c) The central xenon atom has six electron groups and two lone pairs; therefore, it is nonpolar. The strongest intermolecular force for a nonpolar molecule is London dispersion forces.

(d) A diatomic molecule containing two different atoms is polar. The strongest intermolecular force for a polar molecule is dipole–dipole forces.

Reality Check
All the predictions agree with information from both this chapter and the preceding chapter.

Follow-Up Problem 12.2b
What is the strongest type of intermolecular force in each of the following? **(a)** arsenic pentafluoride, AsF_5; **(b)** iodine pentafluoride, IF_5; **(c)** hypochlorous acid, $HOCl$

Information
The formula of the compounds; the question of what is the strongest intermolecular force in each compound

Connections
The definitions and characteristics of the various types of intermolecular forces

Solution
It may help to draw the structures of the compounds. If needed, the structures are

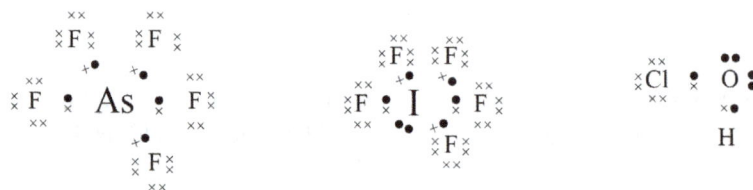

(a) The central arsenic atom has five electron groups and no lone pairs; therefore, it is nonpolar. The strongest intermolecular force for a nonpolar molecule is London dispersion forces.

(b) The central iodine atom has six electron groups and one lone pair; therefore, it is polar. The strongest intermolecular force in for a polar molecule is dipole–dipole forces.

(c) The central oxygen atom has a hydrogen atom attached, which means the strongest intermolecular force for the molecule is hydrogen bonding.

Reality Check
All the predictions agree with information from both this chapter and the preceding chapter.

Example Problem 12.3
The normal boiling point of ethyl alcohol is 78.4°C. The heat of vaporization of this compound is 40.5 kJ/mol. Calculate the vapor pressure, in atmospheres, of ethyl alcohol at a temperature of 55.0°C.

Information
The normal boiling point of ethyl alcohol, 78.4°C; the heat of vaporization of ethyl alcohol, $\Delta H_{vap} = 40.5$ kJ/mol; the question of what is the vapor pressure in atm at $T = 55.0$°C

Connections

The Clausius–Clapeyron equation, relating temperature, vapor pressure, and heat of vaporization:

$$\ln\frac{P_1}{P_2} = \frac{\Delta H_{vap}}{R}\left[\frac{1}{T_2} - \frac{1}{T_1}\right]$$

Solution

$$78.4°C + 273.2 = 351.6 \text{ K}$$
$$55.0°C + 273.2 = 328.2 \text{ K}$$

Either of these two temperatures could be T_1, and the other would be T_2. We will assume $T_1 = 328.2$ K. This means we are looking to find P_1. Since T_2 is the normal boiling point, P_2 is 1.00 atm. The value of P_2 comes from the definition of *normal boiling point*. We need to use $R = 8.314$ J/mol · K because the heat of vaporization contains energy units (J).
We now enter the known values into the equation:

▶ The value $R = 0.0821$ L · atm/mol · K is useful in calculations where energy is not included; however, if energy (joules) is involved, 8.314 J/mol · K is more likely needed.

$$\ln\frac{P_1}{1.00 \text{ atm}} = \frac{40.5 \text{ }^{kJ}/_{mol}}{8.314 \text{ }^{J}/_{mol \cdot K}}\left[\frac{1}{351.6 \text{ K}} - \frac{1}{328.2 \text{ K}}\right]$$

We also need to convert the kilojoules to joules:

$$\ln\frac{P_1}{1.00 \text{ atm}} = \frac{40.5 \text{ }^{kJ}/_{mol}}{8.314 \text{ }^{J}/_{mol \cdot K}}\left[\frac{1}{351.6 \text{ K}} - \frac{1}{328.2 \text{ K}}\right]\left(\frac{10^3}{k}\right)$$

Solving this equation gives

$$\ln\frac{P_1}{1.00 \text{ atm}} = \frac{40.5 \text{ }^{kJ}/_{mol}}{8.314 \text{ }^{J}/_{mol \cdot K}}[-0.000202781]\left(\frac{10^3}{k}\right)$$

$$\ln\frac{P_1}{1.00 \text{ atm}} = -0.987809997 \qquad \text{(unrounded)}$$

$$\frac{P_1}{1.00 \text{ atm}} = 0.3723913$$

$$P_1 = \textbf{0.372 atm}$$

Reality Check

This answer is consistent with the fact that gas pressures decrease with temperature. Furthermore, the magnitude is reasonable, and the units and significant figures are correct.

Follow-Up Problem 12.3a

At 25.0°C, diethyl ether, $(C_2H_5)_2O$, has a vapor pressure of 534 torr. The heat of vaporization of this compound is 29.1 kJ/mol. Calculate the vapor pressure, in torr, of diethyl ether at a temperature of 45.0°C.

Information

The vapor pressure of ethyl ether at 25.0°C is 534 torr; the heat of vaporization of ethyl ether is $\Delta H_{vap} = 29.1$ kJ/mol; the question of what is the vapor pressure in torr at $T = 45.0°C$

Connections

The Clausius–Clapeyron equation, relating temperature, vapor pressure, and heat of vaporization:

$$\ln\frac{P_1}{P_2} = \frac{\Delta H_{vap}}{R}\left[\frac{1}{T_2} - \frac{1}{T_1}\right]$$

Solution

The two temperatures must be expressed in Kelvin units:

$$25.0°C + 273.2 = 298.2 \text{ K}$$
$$45.0°C + 273.2 = 318.2 \text{ K}$$

Either of these two temperatures could be T_1, in which case the other would be T_2. We will assume that $T_1 = 318.2$ K. This means we are looking to find P_1. The value of P_2 is 534 torr. We need to use $R = 8.314$ J/mol · K, because the heat of vaporization contains energy units (J). We now enter the known values into the equation:

$$\ln\frac{P_1}{534 \text{ torr}} = \frac{29.1 \text{ kJ}/\text{mol}}{8.314 \text{ J}/\text{mol}\cdot\text{K}}\left[\frac{1}{298.2 \text{ K}} - \frac{1}{318.2 \text{ K}}\right]$$

We also need to convert the kilojoules to joules:

$$\ln\frac{P_1}{534 \text{ torr}} = \frac{29.1 \text{ kJ}/\text{mol}}{8.314 \text{ J}/\text{mol}\cdot\text{K}}\left[\frac{1}{298.2 \text{ K}} - \frac{1}{318.2 \text{ K}}\right]\left(\frac{10^3}{\text{k}}\right)$$

Solving this equation gives

$$\ln\frac{P_1}{534 \text{ torr}} = \frac{29.1 \text{ kJ}/\text{mol}}{8.314 \text{ J}/\text{mol}\cdot\text{K}}[0.000210776496]\left(\frac{10^3}{\text{k}}\right)$$

$$\ln\frac{P_1}{534 \text{ torr}} = 0.737743089 \quad \text{(unrounded)}$$

$$\frac{P_1}{534 \text{ torr}} = 2.0912$$

$$P_1 = 1116.7 = \mathbf{1.12 \times 10^3 \text{ torr}}$$

Reality Check

This answer is consistent with the fact that gas pressures increase with temperature. Furthermore, the magnitude is reasonable, and the units and significant figures are correct.

Follow-Up Problem 12.3b

At –164.0°C, methane, CH_4, has a vapor pressure of 760.0 torr. At –100.0°C, methane has a vapor pressure of 3.25×10^4 torr. Calculate the heat of vaporization of methane in kilojoules per mole.

Information

The vapor pressure of methane at –164.0°C is 760.0 torr; the heat of vapor pressure is 3.25×10^4 torr at –100.0°C; the question of what is the heat of vaporization of methane in kJ/mol

Connections

The Clausius–Clapeyron equation, relating temperature, vapor pressure, and heat of vaporization:

$$\ln \frac{P_1}{P_2} = \frac{\Delta H_{vap}}{R} \left[\frac{1}{T_2} - \frac{1}{T_1} \right]$$

Solution

The two temperatures must be expressed in Kelvin units:

$$-164.0°C + 273.2 = 109.2 \text{ K}$$
$$-100.0°C + 273.2 = 173.2 \text{ K}$$

Either of these two temperatures could be T_1, in which case the other would be T_2. We will assume that $T_1 = 173.2$ K. The pressures are $P_1 = 3.25 \times 10^4$ torr and $P_2 = 760.0$ torr. We need to use $R = 8.314$ J/mol · K, because the heat of vaporization contains energy units (J).
We need to rearrange the Clausius–Clapeyron equation to

$$\Delta H_{vap} = \frac{(R) \left(\ln \dfrac{P_1}{P_2} \right)}{\left[\dfrac{1}{T_2} - \dfrac{1}{T_1} \right]}$$

We now enter the known values into the equation:

$$\Delta H_{vap} = \frac{\left(8.314 \dfrac{J}{mol \cdot K} \right) \left(\ln \dfrac{3.25 \times 10^4 \text{ torr}}{760.0 \text{ torr}} \right)}{\left[\dfrac{1}{109.2 \text{ K}} - \dfrac{1}{173.2 \text{ K}} \right]}$$

We also need to convert the joules to kilojoules:

$$\Delta H_{vap} = \frac{\left(8.314 \dfrac{J}{mol \cdot K} \right) \left(\ln \dfrac{3.25 \times 10^4 \text{ torr}}{760.0 \text{ torr}} \right)}{\left[\dfrac{1}{109.2 \text{ K}} - \dfrac{1}{173.2 \text{ K}} \right]} \left(\frac{k}{1,000} \right)$$

Solving this equation gives

$$\Delta H_{vap} = \frac{\left(8.314 \dfrac{J}{mol \cdot K} \right) (\ln 42.76315789)}{[0.003383837]} \left(\frac{k}{1,000} \right)$$

$$\Delta H_{vap} = \frac{\left(8.314 \dfrac{J}{mol \cdot K} \right) (3.7556769)}{[0.003383837]} \left(\frac{k}{1,000} \right)$$

$$\Delta H_{vap} = \frac{\left(8.314 \dfrac{J}{mol \cdot K} \right) (3.7556769)}{[0.003383837]} \left(\frac{k}{1,000} \right)$$

$$\Delta H_{vap} = 9.227601 = \textbf{9.23 kJ/mol}$$

Reality Check

This answer is consistent with the fact that a small nonpolar gas should have a small heat of vaporization. Furthermore, the magnitude is reasonable, and the units and significant figures are correct.

Example Problem 12.4

Using figure 12.17, show how to determine the number of cesium chloride formula units in a unit cell. Then predict whether the unit cell is primitive, body-centered, or face-centered cubic.

Information

Figure 12.17 (showing the CsCl structure); the question of what type of unit cell is present

Connections

The procedure for determining the contents of a unit cell; the structures of primitive, body-centered, or face-centered cubic unit cells

Solution

There is one cesium ion in the center of the unit cell.

There are chloride ions in all eight corners; each corner contributes one-eighth of a chloride ion to the contents. Thus, there is $8 \times 1/8 = 1$ chloride ion.

$$1 \text{ Cs} + 1 \text{ Cl in the unit cell} = 1 \text{ CsCl formula unit}$$

One formula unit in the unit cell means that the unit cell is **primitive cubic**.

Reality Check

When you first look at the cesium chloride unit cell, it may appear to you to be body-centered cubic. This would not be the correct answer, however, because if the unit cell were body-centered cubic, the ion in the center would be identical to the corner ions. A cesium ion is clearly not identical to a chloride ion.

Follow-Up Problem 12.4a

Using figure 12.16, show how to determine the number of sodium chloride formula units in a unit cell. Then predict whether the unit cell is primitive, body-centered, or face-centered cubic.

Information

Figure 12.16 (showing the NaCl structure); the question of what type of unit cell is present

Connections

The procedure for determining the contents of a unit cell and the structures of primitive, body-centered, or face-centered cubic unit cells

Solution

There is 1 sodium ion in the center of the unit cell, and there are additional sodium ions at the center of each edge. Edge atoms contribute one fourth of an atom to the cell contents. Thus, there are $1 + (12 \times 1/4) = 4$ sodium ions.

There are chloride ions in all eight corners; each corner contributes one-eighth of a chloride ion to the contents. In addition, there are chloride ions in the center of each face; each face contributes one-half to the cell contents. Thus, there are $(8 \times 1/8) + (6 \times 1/2) = 4$ chloride ions:

$$4 \text{ Na} + 4 \text{ Cl in the unit cell} = 4 \text{ NaCl formula units}$$

Four formula units in the unit cell indicates that the unit cell is **face-centered cubic**.

Reality Check

If the sodium ions and chloride ions are reversed, the answer remains the same.

Follow-Up Problem 12.4b

Using figure 12.18, show how to determine the number of calcium fluoride formula units in a unit cell. Then predict if the calcium fluoride unit cell is primitive, body-centered, or face-centered cubic.

Information

Figure 12.18 (showing the CaF_2 structure); the question of what type of unit cell is present

Connections

The procedure for determining the contents of a unit cell; the structures of primitive, body-centered, or face-centered cubic unit cells

Solution

There are eight fluoride ions entirely within the cell; therefore, each ion counts as one.

There are calcium ions in all eight corners; each corner contributes one-eighth of a calcium ion to the contents. In addition, there are calcium ions in the center of each face; each face contributes one-half to the cell contents. Thus, there are $(8 \times 1/8) + (6 \times 1/2) = 4$ calcium ions:

$$4 \text{ Ca} + 8 \text{ F in the unit cell} = 4 \text{ } CaF_2 \text{ formula units}$$

Four formula units in the unit cell indicates that the unit cell is **face-centered cubic**.

Reality Check

This cell is more difficult to visualize than the CsCl and NaCl structures.

Example Problem 12.5

Calculate the density of chromium, in grams per cubic centimeter, if it forms in a body-centered cubic lattice with a cell edge of 2.8846 Å.

Information

The unit cell edge of chromium metal, 2.8846 Å; the body-centered cubic lattice type; the question of what is the density (? g/cm^3)

Connections

The definition of *density* (chapter 1, "The Tools of Chemistry"); the atomic mass of chromium; the unit conversion method for converting angstroms to cubic centimeters and amu to grams

Solution

The definition of *density* is mass/volume. To determine the density of chromium, we need to determine the volume and the mass of a unit cell. A body-centered cubic unit cell contains two chromium atoms (51.996 amu each) in a volume of $(2.8846 \text{ Å})^3$. This gives

$$\text{Density} = \left(\frac{2 \text{ (51.996 amu)}}{(2.8846 \text{ Å})^3} \right)$$

Now we need to convert the mass from amu to grams and the volume from Å^3 to cubic centimeters. We can do these conversions in either order. Doing the mass conversion first gives

$$\text{Density} = \left(\frac{2 \text{ (51.996 amu)}}{(2.8846 \text{ Å})^3} \right)\left(\frac{1 \text{ g}}{6.02214 \times 10^{23} \text{ amu}} \right)$$

Next would come the volume (length^3) conversion:

$$\text{Density} = \left(\frac{2\,(51.996\text{ amu})}{(2.8846\text{ Å})^3}\right)\left(\frac{1\text{ g}}{6.02214\times10^{23}\text{ amu}}\right)\left(\frac{1\text{ Å}}{10^{-10}\text{ m}}\right)^3$$

Additional digits are necessary for Avogadro's number because of the precision of the data supplied in the problem. Finally, we need to convert cubic meters to cubic centimeters:

$$\text{Density} = \left(\frac{2\,(51.996\text{ amu})}{(2.8846\text{ Å})^3}\right)\left(\frac{1\text{ g}}{6.02214\times10^{23}\text{ amu}}\right)\left(\frac{1\text{ Å}}{10^{-10}\text{ m}}\right)^3\left(\frac{0.01}{c}\right)^3$$

$$= 7.194361986 = \mathbf{7.1944\ g/cm^3}$$

Reality Check
The magnitude is reasonable. The units and the significant figures are correct.

Follow-Up Problem 12.5a
Determine the density of lithium, Li, in grams per cubic centimeter if it forms in a body-centered cubic lattice with a cell edge of 3.51 Å.

Information
The unit cell edge of lithium metal is 3.51 Å; the lattice type is body-centered cubic; the question of what is the density (? g/cm^3)

Connections
The definition of *density* (chapter 1, "The Tools of Chemistry"); the atomic mass of lithium, unit conversion factors for converting angstroms to cubic centimeters and amu to grams

Solution
The definition of *density* is mass/volume. To determine the density of lithium, we need to determine the volume and the mass of a unit cell. A body-centered cubic unit cell contains two chromium atoms (6.941 amu each) in a volume of (3.51 Å)^3. This gives

$$\text{Density} = \left(\frac{2\,(6.941\text{ amu})}{(3.51\text{ Å})^3}\right)$$

Now we need to convert the mass from amu to grams and the volume from Å^3 to cubic centimeters. It is possible to do these conversions in either order. Doing the mass conversion first gives

$$\text{Density} = \left(\frac{2\,(6.941\text{ amu})}{(3.51\text{ Å})^3}\right)\left(\frac{1\text{ g}}{6.02214\times10^{23}\text{ amu}}\right)$$

Next would come the volume (length^3) conversion:

$$\text{Density} = \left(\frac{2\,(6.941\text{ amu})}{(3.51\text{ Å})^3}\right)\left(\frac{1\text{ g}}{6.02214\times10^{23}\text{ amu}}\right)\left(\frac{1\text{ Å}}{10^{-10}\text{ m}}\right)^3$$

Additional digits are needed for Avogadro's number because of the precision of the data supplied in the problem. Finally, we need to convert cubic meters to cubic centimeters:

$$\text{Density} = \left(\frac{2\,(6.941\text{ amu})}{(3.51\text{ Å})^3}\right)\left(\frac{1\text{ g}}{6.02214\times10^{23}\text{ amu}}\right)\left(\frac{1\text{ Å}}{10^{-10}\text{ m}}\right)^3\left(\frac{0.01}{c}\right)^3$$

$$= 0.5330646 = \mathbf{0.533\ g/cm^3}$$

Reality Check

The magnitude is reasonable. The units and the significant figures are correct.

Follow-Up Problem 12.5b

The density of europium, Eu, metal is 5.245 g/cm^3. The unit cell of europium is body-centered cubic. What is the length of the unit cell edge in picometers?

Information

The density of europium metal is 5.245 g/cm^3; the lattice type is body-centered cubic; the question of what is the unit cell edge in pm

Connections

The definition of *density* (chapter 1, "The Tools of Chemistry"); the atomic mass of europium; unit conversion factors for converting angstroms to cubic centimeters and amu to grams

Solution

First, we need to determine the volume of the unit cell; since the unit cell is a cube, the cube root of the volume will be the unit cell edge.

To determine the volume of the europium unit cell, we need to use the definition of *density*. A body-centered cubic unit cell contains two europium atoms (151.964 amu each). This gives

$$\text{Edge} = \sqrt[3]{V} = \sqrt[3]{\left(\frac{\text{cm}^3}{5.245 \text{ g}}\right)}$$

We need to convert the grams to amu:

$$\text{Edge} = \sqrt[3]{\left(\frac{\text{cm}^3}{5.245 \text{ g}}\right)\left(\frac{1 \text{ g}}{6.02214 \times 10^{23} \text{ amu}}\right)}$$

Now we can use the mass of the two europium atoms in the unit cell:

$$\text{Edge} = \sqrt[3]{\left(\frac{\text{cm}^3}{5.245 \text{ g}}\right)\left(\frac{1 \text{ g}}{6.02214 \times 10^{23} \text{ amu}}\right)[2(151.964 \text{ amu})]}$$

Finally, we convert cm to pm:

$$\text{Edge} = \sqrt[3]{\left(\frac{\text{cm}^3}{5.245 \text{ g}}\right)\left(\frac{1 \text{ g}}{6.02214 \times 10^{23} \text{ amu}}\right)[2(151.964 \text{ amu})]\left[\left(\frac{.01}{\text{c}}\right)^3\left(\frac{\text{p}}{10^{-12}}\right)^3\right]}$$

$$= 458.238 = \textbf{458.2 pm}$$

Reality Check

The magnitude is reasonable. The units and the significant figures are correct.

Example Problem 12.6

Platinum metal has a face-centered cubic unit cell. The density of platinum is 21.45 g/cm^3. Determine the atomic radius of platinum atoms in picometers.

Information

For platinum, the face-centered cubic lattice type and the density of 21.45 g/cm^3; the question of what is the radius (pm)

Connections

Structure of the unit cell; unit conversion factors; the Pythagorean theorem

Solution

The close packing of same-size atoms allows us to calculate their radius, but first we must determine the length of the edge of the unit cell. For convenience, we will do it in picometers. Recall that the length of the edge of a cube is simply the cube root of the volume, and we can determine the volume of this "cube" of platinum from the density we have been given, along with conversion factors consisting of the molar mass of platinum (195.1 g/mol), Avogadro's number, and the contents of a face-centered cubic unit cell (four atoms):

$$\text{Volume} = \left(\frac{\text{cm}^3}{21.45\ \text{g}}\right)\left(\frac{195.1\ \text{g}}{\text{mol}}\right)\left(\frac{1\ \text{mol}}{6.022 \times 10^{23}\ \text{atoms}}\right)(4\ \text{atoms})$$

Into this expression, we insert factors converting cubic centimeters to cubic picometers:

$$\text{Volume} = \left(\frac{\text{cm}^3}{21.45\ \text{g}}\right)\left(\frac{195.1\ \text{g}}{\text{mol}}\right)\left(\frac{1\ \text{mol}}{6.022 \times 10^{23}\ \text{atoms}}\right)(4\ \text{atoms})\left(\frac{0.01}{\text{c}}\right)^3\left(\frac{\text{p}}{10^{-12}}\right)^3$$

$$= 60415616.7\ \text{pm}^3$$

Taking the cube root of the volume gives 392.38862 = 392.4 pm.

The face of a face-centered cubic unit cell can be depicted as

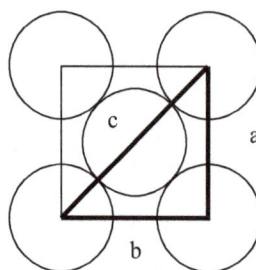

This diagram emphasizes the presence of a right triangle on the face of the unit cell. For any right triangle, the Pythagorean theorem applies: $a^2 + b^2 = c^2$. In this case, $a = b = 392.38862$ pm, and $c = 4$ times the radius of a platinum atom. (The face diagonal c is two radii plus one diameter long.) By these relationships,

$$a^2 + b^2 = a^2 + a^2 = 2\,a^2 = c^2$$

$$c = \sqrt{2\,(392.38862)^2} = \sqrt{2}\ (392.38862\ \text{pm}) = 554.9213\ \text{pm}$$

$$\text{Radius} = c/4 = 138.730327 = \mathbf{138.7\ pm}$$

Reality Check

The magnitude of the answer seems reasonable. The units and the significant figures are correct.

Follow-Up Problem 12.6a

The noble gas krypton freezes at 116 K. Solid krypton has a face-centered cubic unit cell. At 88 K, the density of krypton is 3.021 g/cm³. Determine the atomic radius of krypton atoms in picometers at this temperature.

Information

Solid krypton; the lattice type face-centered cubic; the density 3.021 g/cm³; the question of what is the radius (pm)

Connections

Structure of the unit cell; unit conversion factors; the Pythagorean theorem

Solution

The close packing of same-size atoms allows us to calculate their radius, but first we must determine the length of the edge of the unit cell. For convenience, we will do it in picometers. Recall that the length of the edge of a cube is simply the cube root of the volume, and we can determine the volume of this "cube" of krypton from the density we have been given, along with conversion factors consisting of the molar mass of krypton (83.798 g/mol), Avogadro's number, and the contents of a face-centered cubic unit cell (4 atoms):

$$\text{Volume} = \left(\frac{cm^3}{3.021\ g}\right)\left(\frac{83.798\ g}{mol}\right)\left(\frac{1\ mol}{6.022 \times 10^{23}\ atoms}\right)(4\ atoms)$$

Into this expression, we insert factors converting cubic centimeters to cubic picometers:

$$\text{Volume} = \left(\frac{cm^3}{3.021\ g}\right)\left(\frac{83.798\ g}{mol}\right)\left(\frac{1\ mol}{6.022 \times 10^{23}\ atoms}\right)(4\ atoms)\left(\frac{0.01}{c}\right)^3\left(\frac{p}{10^{-12}}\right)^3$$

$$= 1{,}842{,}477{,}739.5\ pm^3$$

Taking the cube root of the volume gives 569.0285 = 569.0 pm.

The face of a face-centered cubic unit cell can be depicted as

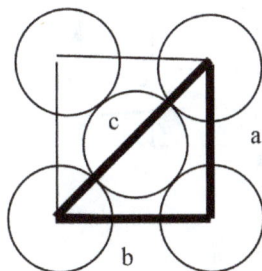

This diagram emphasizes the presence of a right triangle on the face of the unit cell. For any right triangle, the Pythagorean theorem applies: $a^2 + b^2 = c^2$. In this case, $a = b = 392.38862$ pm, and $c = 4$ times the radius of a platinum atom. (The face diagonal c is two radii plus one diameter long.) By these relationships,

$$a^2 + b^2 = a^2 + a^2 = 2\,a^2 = c^2$$

$$c = \sqrt{2\,(569.0285)^2} = \sqrt{2}\ (569.0285\ pm) = 804.72789\ pm$$

$$\text{Radius} = c/4 = 201.18197 = \textbf{201.2 pm}$$

Reality Check

The magnitude of the answer seems reasonable. The units and the significant figures are correct.

Follow-Up Problem 12.6b

Europium metal has a body-centered cubic unit cell with a unit cell edge of 458.2 pm. The europium atoms touch each other along the body diagonal of the unit cell. Determine the atomic radius of europium atoms in picometers.

Information

Solid europium; the lattice type body-centered cubic; a unit cell edge of 458.2 pm; the atoms touching along the body diagonal; the question of what is the radius (pm)

Connections

Structure of the unit cell; unit conversion factors; the Pythagorean theorem

Solution

The atoms touch along the body diagonal of the cell; this means that the body diagonal is four times the radius of a europium atom. The body diagonal is also the hypotenuse of the large heavy-black right triangle in the figure below. The sides of the large triangle are A, B, and C. Side A is the unit cell edge, and side B is the face diagonal.

There is a second, red triangle shown in the figure. The sides of the red triangle are a, b, and c. Both a and b are sides of the unit cell, and the hypotenuse, c, is the same as the B on the first triangle.

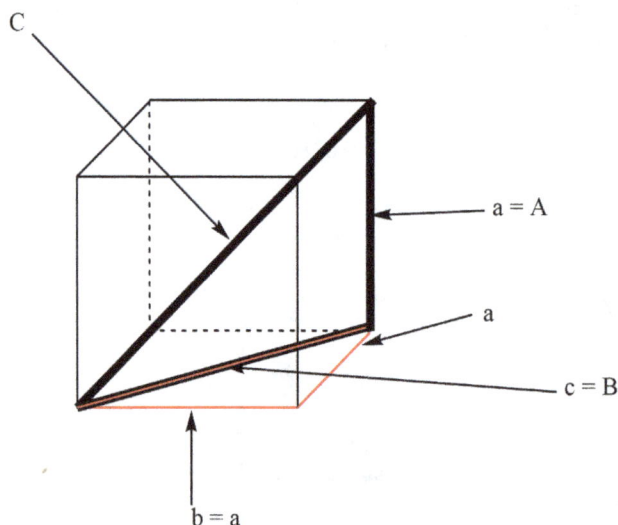

Applying the Pythagorean theorem to the small triangle (red) gives

$$a^2 + b^2 = c^2$$

Since $a = b$, this makes $2\,a^2 = c^2$.

Applying the Pythagorean theorem to the large triangle (dark) gives

$$A^2 + B^2 = C^2$$

since $A^2 = a^2$ and $B^2 = c^2 = 2\,a^2$.

Combining the information from the two triangles gives

$$C^2 = 3\,a^2$$

$$C = \sqrt{3\,a^2} = \sqrt{3\,(458.2\ \text{pm})^2} = 793.62568 = 793.6\ \text{pm}$$

Recall that C is four times the radius of a europium atom; therefore, the radius is

$$C/4 = (793.62568 \text{ pm})/4 = 198.40642 = \textbf{198.4 pm}$$

Reality Check

The magnitude of the answer seems reasonable. The units and the significant figures are correct.

END-OF-CHAPTER PROBLEMS

12.1 Phase Diagrams

12.2 What is the name associated with each of the following phase changes? **(a)** solid to liquid; **(b)** liquid to gas; **(c)** solid to gas; **(d)** liquid to solid; **(e)** gas to liquid; **(f)** gas to solid

Solution

In each case, both the phases involved, and the direction are important.

(a) solid to liquid = **melting** (fusion)

(b) liquid to gas = **boiling** (vaporization or evaporation)

(c) solid to gas = **sublimation**

(d) liquid to solid = **freezing** (crystallization)

(e) gas to liquid = **condensation**

(f) gas to solid = **deposition**

12.4 Compare solids to liquids to gases with respect to internal order and distance between particles.

Solution

In a solid, there is internal order; in a liquid or a gas, there is no internal order. The distances between the particles are about the same in a solid and a liquid as the particles are in contact, while the particles in a gas are widely separated.

12.6 (a) Why do the densities of gases tend to be much less than those of liquids and solids? **(b)** Why would you expect the densities of a substance to be similar in the liquid state and the solid state?

Solution

(a) There is a great deal of empty space between the particles in a gas and very little space between the particles in a liquid or a solid. The empty space lowers the density of a gas. **(b)** The distances between the particles in solids and liquids are about the same; therefore, the densities are about the same.

12.8 What is the *triple point* on a phase diagram?

Solution

The *triple point* is a fixed point on a phase diagram where there are three phases in equilibrium.

12.11 Explain why the liquid–gas line on a phase diagram ends at the critical point.

Solution

In both the liquid and gas states, the particles present are the same (disordered). The difference between the liquid and gas phases is the distance between the particles. In the liquid state, the particles are in contact, while in the gaseous state, the particles are widely separated. As the pressure increases, the particles in the gas phase move closer together. At the critical pressure, the gas particles come into contact. When the gas particles come into contact, there is no longer any difference between the gas and liquid phases.

12.14 Answer the following questions by consulting figure 12.4. **(a)** A sample of carbon dioxide, initially at –56°C and 4.0 atm, is compressed at constant temperature to a pressure of 100 atm. What phase changes, if any, occur? **(b)** Another sample of carbon dioxide, initially at –80°C and 10 atm, is heated at constant pressure to 40°C. What phase changes, if any, occur? **(c)** A third sample of carbon dioxide, initially at –100°C and 4.0 atm, is heated at constant pressure to 25°C. What phase changes, if any, occur?

Information

The phase diagram of carbon dioxide (figure 12.4); three changes: **(a)** –56°C and 4.0 atm to –56°C and 100 atm, **(b)** –80°C and 10 atm to 40°C and 10 atm, and **(c)** –100°C and 4.0 atm to 25°C and 4.0 atm; for each, the question of what phase change, if any, occurs

Solution

Begin with figure 12.4 and add arrows representing the changes. The arrows should point in the direction of the change. This is a sketch; therefore, the positions do not need to be perfect.

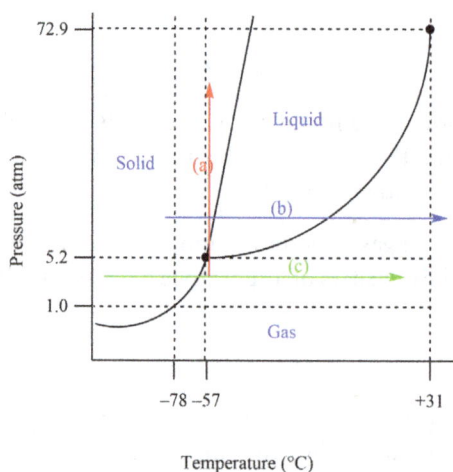

(a) Moving in the direction indicated by the arrow, nothing happens until the liquid–gas line is reached, where the gas condenses. After all the gas has condensed the liquid continues along the arrow until the solid–liquid line is reached, where the liquid freezes. After all the liquid has frozen, the solid continues along the arrow with no further phase changes. The phase changes, in order, are **condensation** and **solidification**.

(b) Moving in the direction indicated by the arrow, nothing happens until the solid–liquid line is reached, where the solid melts. After all the solid has fused, the liquid continues along the arrow until the liquid–gas line is reached, where the liquid vaporizes. After all the liquid has frozen, the solid continues along the arrow with no further phase changes. The phase changes, in order, are **fusion** and **vaporization**.

(c) Moving in the direction indicated by the arrow, nothing happens until the solid–gas line is reached, where the solid undergoes sublimation. After all the solid has sublimed, the gas continues along the arrow with no further phase changes. The only phase change is **sublimation**.

12.17 Two pans of water are placed on a stove and the heat is turned up to high. One pan contains 1 L of water, and the other contains 2 L of water. **(a)** If both pans are heated at the same rate, which will boil first? **(b)** If the water in the pan with less water is boiling at 100°C, what is the temperature of boiling water in the other pan? **(c)** Once both pans begin to boil, the heat is turned down on one pan so that it is barely boiling, while the other is left on high and boils vigorously. How do the temperatures of the water in the two pans compare?

Solution

This ties to relationships first developed in chapter 6, "Thermochemistry—The Study of Energy Change."

(a) The one with less water will boil first.

(b) 100°C, because the boiling point does not depend upon the quantity of water

(c) The two pans are at the same temperature, because the rate of boiling depend on the temperature.

12.2 Types of Intermolecular Forces

12.19 What are *London dispersion forces*?

Solution

London dispersion forces are the intermolecular forces due to instantaneous (temporary) dipoles. London dispersion forces are present in any substance that contains electrons.

12.21 (a) What is the strongest type of intermolecular force that may be present between two nonpolar molecules of a substance? **(b)** What is the strongest type of intermolecular force that may be present between two polar molecules of a substance?

Solution

(a) London dispersion forces are the strongest intermolecular forces that may be present between nonpolar molecules. **(b)** Hydrogen bonding is the strongest intermolecular forces that may be present. However, a more general answer would be dipole–dipole forces. Weak London dispersion forces are also present (they are always present).

12.24 (a) What *is hydrogen bonding*? **(b)** What are the requirements for a hydrogen bond to be present?

Solution

(a) Hydrogen bonding is an especially strong type of dipole–dipole force. **(b)** For hydrogen bonding to occur between molecules, there must be a hydrogen atom directly bonded to one of three highly electronegative elements: nitrogen, oxygen, or fluorine.

12.26 List the different types of van der Waals forces in order from weakest to strongest.

Solution

The sequence is London dispersion forces (weakest), dipole-induced dipole forces, dipole–dipole forces, hydrogen bonding, ion–dipole forces (strongest). (A substance may be an exception to this order.)

12.28 (a) In what type of material is ionic bonding the strongest intermolecular force? **(b)** In what type of material is covalent bonding the strongest intermolecular force? **(c)** In what type of material is metallic bonding the strongest intermolecular force?

Solution

In each case, consider what interactions are present. Bonds such as these are not "true" intermolecular forces, but they may be treated as such.

(a) ionic solids; **(b)** covalent (network) solids; **(c)** metallic solids

12.30 List the type of intermolecular force that must be overcome in each of the following cases: **(a)** boiling liquid bromine, Br_2; **(b)** melting iron, Fe; **(c)** melting solid sulfur dioxide, SO_2; **(d)** vaporizing graphite, C; **(e)** subliming ice, H_2O

Solution

(a) London dispersion forces, because Br_2 contains nonpolar molecules; **(b)** metallic bonding, because iron is a metal; **(c)** dipole–dipole forces, because SO_2 contains polar molecules; **(d)** covalent bonding, because graphite is a network solid; **(e)** hydrogen bonding, because H_2O contains hydrogen atoms bonded to very electronegative oxygen atoms

12.3 Properties of Liquids

12.32 (a) What is *surface tension*? **(b)** What happens to the surface tension if the intermolecular forces increase in strength?

Solution

(a) The **surface tension** is the result of the attractive forces within a liquid tightly holding molecules on the surface of the liquid. **(b)** The surface tension will increase as the intermolecular forces increase, because the molecules are more strongly held together.

12.33 (a) What is *viscosity*? **(b)** What happens to the viscosity if the intermolecular forces increase in strength?

Solution

(a) **Viscosity** is the resistance to flow. **(b)** The viscosity increases as the intermolecular forces increase, because stronger intermolecular forces inhibit the movement of the molecules.

12.36 How does the viscosity of a liquid vary with temperature?

Solution

The viscosity is inversely proportional to the temperature, because at the higher temperature the molecules have more kinetic energy (energy of motion).

12.38 What is one way of differentiating between a true solid and an amorphous solid?

Solution

True solids melt at a specific temperature, while an amorphous solid softens (decreasing viscosity) upon heating. In a true solid, there is a definite arrangement of the particles. In an amorphous solid, the particles are disordered (the same as in a liquid).

12.40 What is a *dynamic equilibrium*?

Solution

A **dynamic equilibrium** is present any time the forward process and the reverse process are taking place at equal rates.

12.41 State *Le Châtelier's principle.*

Solution

Under *Le Châtelier's principle*, if stress is applied to a system in equilibrium, the system will respond to counter the stress and go to a new equilibrium.

12.45 Explain how an increase in the intermolecular forces would affect each of the following properties: **(a)** surface tension; **(b)** melting point; **(c)** viscosity; **(d)** heat of condensation; **(e)** vapor pressure

Solution

(a), (b), (c), and **(d)** All but vapor pressure increases as the intermolecular forces increase, because it is more difficult to move (separate) the particles if the forces are greater. **(e)** The vapor pressure decreases, because it becomes more difficult for the particles to escape in the gas phase.

12.46 Atmospheric pressure at the top of Mount Everest is about 240 mmHg. Use figure 12.7 to estimate the boiling point of water at the top of Mount Everest.

Solution

The boiling point is about 70°C (this is an estimate from the figure).

12.48 Lead melts at 327°C and boils at 1741°C. The enthalpy of fusion of lead is 5.121 kJ/mol, and its enthalpy of vaporization is 177.8 kJ/mol. The specific heats of solid, liquid, and gaseous lead are 0.129 J/g · K, 0.154 J/g · K, and 0.100 J/g · K, respectively. How much heat is required to convert 1,500.0 g of lead at 127°C to the vapor phase at 1,855°C?

Information

The properties of lead: melting point = 327°C, boiling point = 1,741°C, enthalpy of fusion = 5.121 kJ/mol, enthalpy of vaporization = 177.8 kJ/mol; specific heats of solid, liquid, and gaseous lead are 0.129 J/g · K, 0.154 J/g · K, and 0.100 J/g · K, respectively; the question of how much heat is required to heat 1,500.0 g of Pb from 127°C to 1,855°C

Connections

$\Delta T = T_{\text{final}} - T_{\text{initial}}$; substitute °C for K

Solution

The total energy is the sum of the different processes.

Below, significant figures in the preliminary answers are underlined to help you keep track of the significant figures when shifting from the multiplication rule (individual values) to the addition-subtraction rule (obtaining the final answer).

Heating the solid:

$$\text{Solid} = \left(\frac{0.129\,\text{J}}{\text{g°C}}\right)\left(\frac{\text{k}}{1{,}000}\right)(1{,}500.0\,\text{g})(327 - 127)°\text{C} = \underline{38.7}\,\text{kJ}$$

Melting the solid:

$$\text{Melt} = \left(\frac{5.121\,\text{kJ}}{\text{mol}}\right)(1{,}500.0\,\text{g})\left(\frac{1\,\text{mol}}{207.2\,\text{g}}\right) = \underline{37.0}72876\,\text{kJ}$$

Heating the liquid:

$$\text{Liquid} = \left(\frac{0.154 \text{ J}}{\text{g}°\text{C}}\right)\left(\frac{\text{k}}{1,000}\right)(1500.0 \text{ g})(1{,}741 - 327)°\text{C} = \underline{326}.634 \text{ kJ}$$

Vaporizing the liquid:

$$\text{Boil} = \left(\frac{177.8 \text{ kJ}}{\text{mol}}\right)(1{,}500.0 \text{ g})\left(\frac{1 \text{ mol}}{207.2 \text{ g}}\right) = \underline{1{,}287}.162 \text{ kJ}$$

Heating the vapor:

$$\text{Vapor} = \left(\frac{0.100 \text{ J}}{\text{g}°\text{C}}\right)\left(\frac{\text{k}}{1,000}\right)(1{,}500.0 \text{ g})(1{,}855 - 1{,}741)°\text{C} = \underline{17.1} \text{ kJ}$$

$$\text{Total} = (\underline{38.7} + \underline{37.0}72876 + \underline{326}.634 + \underline{1{,}287}.162 + \underline{17.1}) \text{ kJ} = 1{,}706.668876 = \mathbf{1{,}707 \text{ kJ}}$$

12.4 Structures of Solids

12.50 **(a)** What is a *unit cell*? **(b)** How does a unit cell relate to a lattice?

Solution

(a) The *unit cell* is the smallest repeating portion of a lattice. **(b)** It is possible to reconstruct the entire lattice by stacking identical copies of the unit cell.

12.54 **(a)** What is a *closest packed structure*? **(b)** What is the difference between a cubic closest packed structure and a hexagonal closest packed structure? **(c)** What is the coordination number of each atom in a closest packed structure?

Solution

(a) A **closest packed structure** is the most efficient way of packing equal spheres together.

(b) The difference is the arrangement of the layers. Every other layer is the same in hexagonal closest packed, while there is a three-layer sequence in cubic closest packed.

(c) The coordination number of each atom is 12 for all closest packed structures.

12.58 The platinum(II) sulfide structure is shown below. The approximate geometry around the platinum atoms is square planar, as indicated by the dashed lines. The geometry about the sulfur atoms is tetrahedral. The cell is tetragonal with a height of 12.220 Å, and the other two dimensions are 3.470 Å.

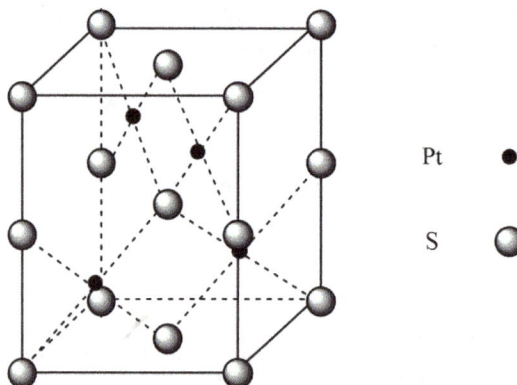

(a) How many PtS formula units are present in the unit cell? **(b)** Determine the density of platinum(II) sulfide in g/cm^3.

Information

A figure and description of the PtS structure (tetragonal with 12.220 Å × 3.470 Å × 3.470 Å); the two questions of how many formula units are present and what is the density in g/cm^3

Connections

How to calculate the contribution from an atom to the contents of a unit cell; the definition of *density*; various unit conversions

Solution

(a) All four of the platinum atoms are within the body; thus, there are four Pt atoms. There are sulfur atoms at all corners [(8 corners) (1/8 atom/corner) = 1 S atom], plus sulfur atoms on four edges [(4 edges) (1/4 atom/edge) = 2 S atoms], plus one atom in the top and in the bottom face [(2 faces) (1/2 atom/face) = 1 S atom]; thus, there are four S atoms. The result: 4 Pt + 4 S = **4 PtS**

(b) The definition of *density* is mass/volume. The mass is the mass of the 4 PtS units determined in part (a), and the volume is the length × width × height of the unit cell:

$$\text{Density} = \left(\frac{4\ \text{PtS}}{(12.220 \times 3.470 \times 3.470)\ \text{Å}^3}\right)$$

Next, we need to add the appropriate conversions:

$$\text{Density} = \left(\frac{4\ \text{PtS}}{(12.220 \times 3.470 \times 3.470)\text{Å}^3}\right)\left(\frac{1\ \text{Å}}{10^{-10}\ \text{m}}\right)^3\left(\frac{0.01}{\text{c}}\right)^3\left(\frac{1\ \text{mol PtS}}{6.022 \times 10^{23}\ \text{PtS}}\right)\left(\frac{227.143\ \text{g PtS}}{1\ \text{mol PtS}}\right)$$

$$= 10.25388 = \textbf{10.25 g/cm}^3$$

12.60 Barium oxide, BaO, like many compounds, adopts the sodium chloride structure (see figure 12.16). The unit cell edge is 3.90 Å. What is the density of barium oxide in g/cm^3?

Information

Barium adopts the NaCl structure; a unit cell edge of 3.90 Å; the question of what is the density in g/cm^3

Connections

How to calculate the contribution from an atom to the contents of a unit cell; the definition of *density*; various unit conversions

Solution

There are four formula units in the NaCl structure.

The definition of *density* is mass/volume. The mass is the mass of the four BaO, and the volume is the length × width × height of the unit cell (since the cell is cubic $V = a^3$):

$$\text{Density} = \left(\frac{4\ \text{BaO}}{(3.90\ \text{Å})^3}\right)$$

Next, we need to add the appropriate conversions:

$$\text{Density} = \left(\frac{4\ \text{BaO}}{(3.90\ \text{Å})^3}\right)\left(\frac{1\ \text{Å}}{10^{-10}\ \text{m}}\right)^3\left(\frac{0.01}{\text{c}}\right)^3\left(\frac{1\ \text{mol BaO}}{6.022 \times 10^{23}\ \text{BaO}}\right)\left(\frac{153.326\ \text{g BaO}}{1\ \text{mol BaO}}\right)$$

$$= 17.16885 = \textbf{17.2 g/cm}^3$$

12.62 Ultrapure silicon may be used to calculate very accurate values of Avogadro's number. Silicon is cubic, with a unit cell edge of 5.430940 Å. The unit cell contains eight silicon atoms, with an atomic mass of 28.0855 amu. The density of silicon is 2.329143 g/cm^3. Determine the value of Avogadro's number.

Information

Silicon is cubic with eight atoms per unit cell; its unit cell edge is 5.430940 Å; its atomic mass is 28.0855 amu; its density is 2.329143 g/cm^3; the question of what is the value of Avogadro's number

Connections

The definition of *density*; various unit conversions

Solution

To find the number of silicon atoms in a mole (Avogadro's number), we need to begin with the number of silicon atoms (eight) in a unit cell (edge^3) and apply the appropriate conversions:

$$\text{Avogadro's number} = \left(\frac{8\ \text{Si}}{(5.430940\ \text{Å})^3}\right)\left(\frac{1\ \text{Å}}{10^{-10}\ \text{m}}\right)^3\left(\frac{0.01}{\text{c}}\right)^3\left(\frac{\text{cm}^3}{2.329143\ \text{g Si}}\right)\left(\frac{28.0855\ \text{g}}{\text{mole Si}}\right)$$

$$= 6.0222141825 \times 10^{23} = \textbf{6.02221} \times \textbf{10}^{23}\ \textbf{Si atoms/mol}$$

Reality Check

The final answer is close to Avogadro's number. It is important to resist the temptation of including Avogadro's number in the calculation, because you are looking to calculate the value.

12.65 Iron has a density of 7.8752 g/cm^3. The edge of a body-centered cubic iron unit cell is 2.8664 Å. Using this information, calculate Avogadro's number.

Information

Iron is body-centered cubic; its unit cell edge is 2.8664 Å; its density is 7.8752 g/cm^3; the question of what is the value of Avogadro's number

Connections

How to calculate the contribution from an atom to the contents of a unit cell; the definition of *density*; various unit conversions

Solution

To find the number of iron atoms in a mole (Avogadro's number), we need to begin with the number of iron atoms (two, because the cell is body-centered cubic) in a unit cell (edge^3) and apply the appropriate conversions:

$$\text{Avogadro's number} = \left(\frac{2\ \text{Fe}}{(2.8664\ \text{Å})^3}\right)\left(\frac{1\ \text{Å}}{10^{-10}\ \text{m}}\right)^3\left(\frac{0.01}{\text{c}}\right)^3\left(\frac{\text{cm}^3}{7.8752\ \text{g Fe}}\right)\left(\frac{55.845\ \text{g Fe}}{\text{mol Fe}}\right)$$

$$= 6.02202 \times 10^{23} = \textbf{6.02} \times \textbf{10}^{23}\ \textbf{Fe atoms/mol}$$

Reality Check

The final answer is close to Avogadro's number. It is important to resist the temptation of including Avogadro's number in the calculation.

12.68 A metal with a density of 0.966 g/cm³ adopts a body-centered cubic lattice. The cell edge is 4.2908 Å. Determine the atomic mass of the metal.

Information

A metal is body-centered cubic; its density is 0.966 g/cm³; it has a cell edge of 4.2908 Å; the question of what is the atomic mass of the metal

Connections

How to calculate the contribution from an atom to the contents of a unit cell, the definition of density; various unit conversions; the atomic mass may be expressed either as amu/atom or as g/mole

Solution

This is mostly a unit conversion problem. In this example, the conversion will be in g/mole. The simplest way to begin is with either grams or moles. The density has grams (0.966 g/cm³), so that's a good place to start. We begin the conversions by changing cm³ to Å³. A body-centered cubic unit cell has a volume in Å³ (since the cell is cubic $V = a^3$), and it contains two atoms. The final step is to use Avogadro's number to convert the two atoms to moles:

$$\text{Atomic mass} = \left(\frac{0.966 \text{ g}}{\text{cm}^3}\right)\left(\frac{c}{0.01}\right)^3\left(\frac{10^{-10} \text{ m}}{\text{Å}}\right)^3\left(\frac{(4.2908 \text{ Å})^3}{2 \text{ atoms}}\right)\left(\frac{6.022 \times 10^{23} \text{ atoms}}{\text{mol}}\right)$$

$$= 22.9774959 = \textbf{23.0 g/mol}$$

The element with the atomic mass closest to this value is sodium, Na.

12.70 Tungsten metal has a body-centered cubic unit cell. The density of tungsten is 19.3 g/cm³. The tungsten atoms touch each other along the body diagonal of the unit cell. Determine the atomic radius of tungsten atoms in pm.

Information

Tungsten is body-centered cubic; its density is 19.3 g/cm³; the question of what is the radius (pm) of a W atom

Connections

Structure of the unit cell; unit conversion factors; the Pythagorean theorem

Solution

The first step is to determine the unit cell edge. The unit cell is cubic; therefore, the edge is the cube root of the cell volume. It is possible to determine the cell volume from the reciprocal of the density and a series of conversions ending with two W atoms in a body-centered unit cell:

$$\text{Cell edge} = \sqrt[3]{\left(\frac{\text{cm}^3}{19.3 \text{ g W}}\right)\left(\frac{183.84 \text{ g W}}{\text{mol W}}\right)\left(\frac{\text{mol W}}{6.022 \times 10^{23} \text{ W}}\right)(2 \text{ W atoms})}$$

$$= 3.1627 \times 10^{-8} = 3.16 \times 10^{-8} \text{ cm}$$

Since the answer is to be in picometers, we need to convert the cell edge to pm:

$$\text{Unit cell edge} = (3.1627 \times 10^{-8} \text{ cm})\left(\frac{0.01}{c}\right)\left(\frac{p}{10^{-12}}\right) = 316.27 \text{ pm} = \mathbf{316 \text{ pm}}$$

Once the cell edge is known, it is possible to determine the atomic radius of a tungsten atom.

The atoms are touching along the body diagonal, which means the body diagonal is four times the atomic radius. The body diagonal is also the hypotenuse (C) of the large (black) triangle in the accompanying figure. The other sides of this black triangle are the face diagonal (B) of the unit cell and one of the edges (A) of the unit cell.

To determine B, we need to use a second right triangle (red). The hypotenuse (c) of this triangle is the face diagonal. The other two sides of the small triangle are sides (a and b) of the unit cell.

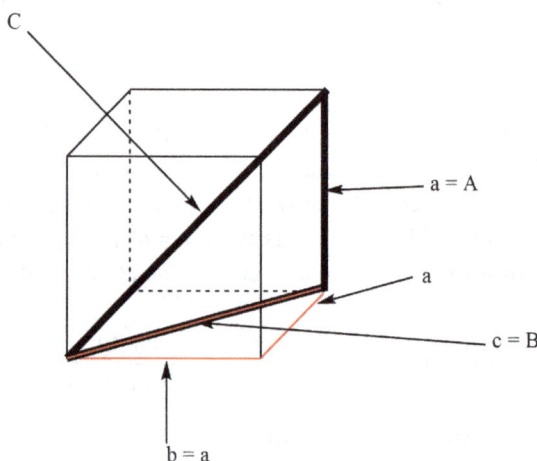

$A = a = 316.27$ pm, the unit cell edge   (unrounded)

For the small (red) triangle, according to the Pythagorean theorem,

$$a^2 + b^2 = c^2$$

Since this is a cubic unit cell, $a = b$ so $2\,a^2 = c^2$.

For the large (black) triangle, according to the Pythagorean theorem,

$$A^2 + B^2 = C^2$$

Since $A^2 = a^2$ and $B^2 = c^2 = 2\,a^2$, $C^2 = 3\,a^2$:

$$C = \sqrt{3\,a^2} = \sqrt{3\,(316.27 \text{ pm})^2} = 547.7957 = 5.47 \times 10^2 \text{ pm}$$

C is four times the radius of a tungsten atom; therefore, the radius is

$$C/4 = (547.7957 \text{ pm})/4$$
$$= 136.9489 = \mathbf{137 \text{ pm}}$$

12.74 A metal with a density of 21.472 g/cm^3 adopts a face-centered cubic lattice. The lattice edge is 3.9231 Å. Determine the atomic mass of the metal.

Information

The metal is face-centered cubic; its density is 21.472 g/cm^3; its cell edge is 3.9231 Å; the question of what is the atomic mass of the metal

Connections

How to calculate the contribution from an atom to the contents of a unit cell; the definition of *density*; various unit conversions; the atomic mass may be expressed either as amu/atom or as g/mole

Solution

This is mostly a unit conversion problem. In this example, the conversion will be in g/mole. The simplest way to begin is with either grams or moles. The density has grams (21.472 g/cm³), so that's a good place to start. We begin the conversions by changing cm³ to Å³. A body-centered cubic unit cell has a volume in Å³ and contains two atoms. The final step is to use Avogadro's number to convert the two atoms to moles:

$$\text{Atomic mass} = \left(\frac{21.472 \text{ g}}{\text{cm}^3}\right)\left(\frac{\text{c}}{0.01}\right)^3\left(\frac{10^{-10} \text{ m}}{1 \text{ Å}}\right)^3\left(\frac{(3.9231 \text{ Å})^3}{4 \text{ atoms}}\right)\left(\frac{6.02214 \times 10^{23} \text{ atoms}}{\text{mol}}\right)$$

$$= 195.1827325 = \textbf{195.18 g/mol}$$

Reality Check

The answer is reasonable because it is close to the value of a real element (Pt).

12.5 Properties of Solids

12.76 What are the four categories of solids?

Solution

The four categories of solids are ionic solids, covalent (network) solids, metallic solids, and molecular solids.

12.79 Summarize the general properties of a metallic solid.

Solution

Metallic solids have variable hardness and have high melting and boiling points. They are usually not soluble in either polar or nonpolar solvents. The solids are excellent conductors of heat and electricity.

12.81 Why may a network solid also be called a covalent solid?

Solution

The network holding the solid together consists of covalent bonds; therefore, a network solid is also a covalent solid.

12.83 Predict the type of crystal that each of the following substances is expected to form: **(a)** water, H_2O; **(b)** silicon dioxide, SiO_2; **(c)** uranium, U; **(d)** carbon dioxide, CO_2; **(e)** ammonium nitrate, NH_4NO_3

Solution

(a) Water consists of small molecules, so ice is a **molecular solid**. **(b)** Silicon dioxide is one of the few **network solids** discussed in the chapter. **(c)** Uranium is a metal, so it is a **metallic solid**. **(d)** Carbon dioxide consists of small molecules, so dry ice is a **molecular solid**. **(e)** Ammonium nitrate contains ammonium ions and nitrate ions. The presence of ions makes the compound an **ionic solid**.

12.86 A bright yellow solid melts at 968°C. The solid does not conduct electricity, but an aqueous solution of the solid will conduct electricity. This material is most likely to be which type of solid?

Solution

The high melting point and the fact that an aqueous solution, but not the solid, will conduct electricity indicate that the material is probably an ionic solid.

12.6 Applications and Extensions

12.88 How do the high specific heat of water and the high vaporization energy of water mediate the weather on Earth?

Solution

The high specific heat and vaporization energy mean that water can absorb a large amount of energy with only a small temperature change. These factors enable water to minimize temperature changes, which in turn mediates weather changes.

12.89 At what temperature is the density of water the greatest?

Solution

The maximum density of water (1.0 g/cm^3) occurs at 4°C.

12.92 What is the environmental impact of the density of ice being less than the density of liquid water?

Solution

When water freezes, it expands. This expansion can cause rocks to break if there is freezing water in the cracks in the rock. In addition, ice floats on water, forming an insulating blanket.

12.95 What is the advantage of a superconductor over a normal electrical conductor?

Solution

Resistance leads to an energy loss for electrical currents. A superconductor has zero resistance, so there is no energy loss.

12.99 What is the cost advantage of "high-temperature" superconductors?

Solution

No energy is lost to resistance as in other conductors, and it is not necessary to use expensive liquid helium to maintain the low temperatures.

Putting It All Together

12.101 Rank the following compounds in order of decreasing vapor pressure:
(a) $CH_3CH_2CH_2CH_3$; **(b)** $CH_3CH_2CH_2OH$; **(c)** $CH_3OCH_2CH_3$; **(d)** $HOCH_2CH_2OH$

Solution

The weaker the intermolecular force, the higher the vapor pressure.

The CH portions of the molecules are nonpolar, which means London dispersion forces. The presence of oxygen leads to a dipole–dipole contribution to the intermolecular forces. In addition, if an OH is present, very strong hydrogen bonding occurs.

The compound $CH_3CH_2CH_2CH_3$ is nonpolar with London dispersion forces (weakest intermolecular force).

The compound $CH_3OCH_2CH_3$ is polar, which is stronger than London dispersion forces.

The other two molecules—$CH_3CH_2CH_2OH$ and $HOCH_2CH_2OH$—both have hydrogen bonding (strongest intermolecular force in these compounds); however, $CH_3CH_2CH_2OH$ can form only one hydrogen bond, while $HOCH_2CH_2OH$ can form two hydrogen bonds.

Therefore, the order is

(a) $CH_3CH_2CH_2CH_3$ > (c) $CH_3OCH_2CH_3$ > (b) $CH_3CH_2CH_2OH$ > (d) $HOCH_2CH_2OH$

12.104 Molybdenum metal has a body-centered cubic unit cell. The density of molybdenum is 10.2 g/cm^3. **(a)** Determine the edge of a unit cell of molybdenum. **(b)** The molybdenum atoms touch each other along the body diagonal of the unit cell. Determine the atomic radius of molybdenum atoms.

Information

Molybdenum is body-centered cubic; its density is 10.2 g/cm^3; the questions of what is the unit cell edge and what is the radius of a Mo atom

Connections

How to calculate the contribution from an atom to the contents of a unit cell; the definition of *density*; various unit conversions

Solution

(a) The first step is to determine the unit cell edge. The unit cell is cubic; therefore, the edge is the cube root of the cell volume. It is possible to determine the cell volume from the reciprocal of the density and a series of conversions ending with 2 Mo atoms in a body-centered unit cell:

$$\text{Cell edge} = \sqrt[3]{\left(\frac{cm^3}{10.2 \text{ g Mo}}\right)\left(\frac{95.94 \text{ g Mo}}{\text{mol Mo}}\right)\left(\frac{\text{mol Mo}}{6.022 \times 10^{23} \text{ Mo}}\right)(2 \text{ Mo atoms})}$$

$$= 3.14941 \times 10^{-8} = \mathbf{3.15 \times 10^{-8} \text{ cm}}$$

(b) Once the cell edge is known, we can determine the atomic radius of a molybdenum atom.

The atoms are touching along the body diagonal, which means the body diagonal is four time the atomic radius. The body diagonal is also the hypotenuse (C) of the large (black) triangle in the accompanying figure. The other sides of this black triangle are the face diagonal (B) of the unit cell and one of the edges (A) of the unit cell.

To determine B, we need to use a second right triangle (red). The hypotenuse (c) of this triangle is the face diagonal. The other two sides of the small triangle are sides (a and b) of the unit cell.

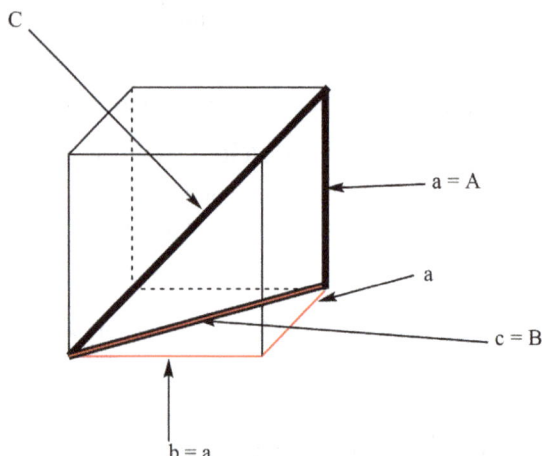

$A = a = 614.74189$ pm, the unit cell edge (unrounded)

For the small (red) triangle, according to the Pythagorean theorem, $a^2 + b^2 = c^2$.

Since this is a cubic unit cell, $a = b$ so $2 a^2 = c^2$.

For the large (black) triangle, according to the Pythagorean theorem, $A^2 + B^2 = C^2$.

Since $A^2 = a^2$ and $B^2 = c^2 = 2 a^2$, $C^2 = 3 a^2$:

$$C = \sqrt{3\, a^2} = \sqrt{3\,(3.14941 \times 10^{-8}\ \text{cm})^2} = 5.45494 \times 10^{-8} = 5.45 \times 10^{-8}\ \text{cm}$$

C is four times the radius of a molybdenum atom; therefore, the radius is

$$C/4 = (5.45494 \times 10^{-8}\ \text{cm})/4$$

$$= 1.3637 \times 10^{-8} = \mathbf{1.36 \times 10^{-8}\ cm}$$

12.106 It is possible to cool water by evaporation; this is especially effective in the desert. The evaporation of water from the outside surface of a closed container will cool the water inside the container. What volume of water, in milliliters, can the evaporation of 25.0 g of water cool from 45.0°C to 20.0°C? The heat of vaporization of water is 40.7 kJ/mol, the specific heat of water is 4.18 J/g °C, and the density of water is 1.00 g/mL.

Information

The properties of water (heat of vaporization = 40.7 kJ/mol, specific heat = 4.18 J/g °C, and density = 1.00 g/mL); a 25.0-g sample evaporates and a second sample cools from 45.0°C to 20.0°C; the question of how many milliliters of water were cooled

Connections

Heat lost = Heat gained (law of conservation of energy); various unit conversions

Solution

We need to determine the heat lost and the heat gained and set the two values equal.

The heat lost (negative) is on the left of the equal sign, and the heat gained (positive) is on the right:

$$-\left(\frac{4.18\ \text{J}}{\text{g} °\text{C}}\right)\left(\frac{1.00\ \text{g}}{\text{mL}}\right)(?\,\text{mL})(20.0 - 45.0)°\text{C} = \left(\frac{40.7\ \text{kJ}}{\text{mol}}\right)\left(\frac{1\ \text{mol}\ \text{H}_2\text{O}}{18.015\ \text{g}\ \text{H}_2\text{O}}\right)(25.0\ \text{g}\ \text{H}_2\text{O})\left(\frac{1{,}000}{\text{K}}\right)$$

Cancelling units and combining terms gives

$$-(4.18 \text{ J})(?)(-25.0)= (40.7 \text{ J})\left(\frac{25.0 \times 1,000}{18.015}\right)$$

Further combination of terms gives

$$(104.5 \text{ J})(?)= (56480.7 \text{ J})$$

Finally, we solve for the unknown value (volume of water cooled):

$$? \text{ mL} = \frac{56480.7 \text{ J}}{104.5 \text{ J}} = 540.485 = \textbf{5.40} \times \textbf{10}^2 \textbf{ mL}$$

12.109 The vapor pressure of diethyl ether at 25.0°C is 545 torr. The heat of vaporization of this compound is 26.5 kJ/mol. Calculate the normal boiling point, in degrees Celsius, of diethyl ether.

Information
The vapor pressure of diethyl ether at 25.0°C, is 545 torr; the heat of vaporization of diethyl ether is ΔH_{vap} = 26.5 kJ/mol; the question of what is the normal boiling point (in °C)

Connections
The Clausius–Clapeyron equation, relating temperature, vapor pressure, and heat of vaporization:

$$\ln\frac{P_1}{P_2} = \frac{\Delta H_{vap}}{R}\left[\frac{1}{T_2} - \frac{1}{T_1}\right]$$

Solution
The variables can be assigned as follows:

P_1 = 545 torr　　T_1 = 25.0°C = 298.2 K

P_2 = 760 torr　　T_2 = ?

Entering the given values into the Clausius–Clapeyron equation gives

$$\ln\left(\frac{545 \text{ torr}}{760 \text{ torr}}\right) = \frac{26.5 \text{ kJ/mol}}{8.314 \text{ J/molK}}\left[\frac{1}{T_2} - \frac{1}{298.2 \text{ K}}\right]\left(\frac{1,000}{k}\right)$$

Solving for T_2 gives

$$T_2 = 307.775 - 273.15 = 34.625 = \textbf{35°C}$$

12.111 The analysis of a green mineral sample showed it to contain beryllium, aluminum, silicon, oxygen, and a trace amount of chromium. The mass percentages of Be, Al, and Si are 5.030% Be, 10.030% Al, and 31.351% Si. The remainder of the sample was assumed to be oxygen. Determine the empirical formula of the mineral.

Information
The composition of the sample (5.030 % Be, 10.030 % Si, 31.351 % Si); the question of what is the empirical formula of this mineral

Connections
Moles are the key.

Solution

Assume the trace amount of chromium does not significantly affect the formula.

First, we need to determine the percent oxygen by subtracting the percentages of the other elements from 100%:

$$\text{Percent O} = 100.000\% - (5.030 + 10.030 + 31.351\%)\% = 53.589\% \text{ O}$$

Assume we have 100 grams of the sample, which makes the percentages numerically the same as the number of grams.

Convert the masses to moles by dividing each mass by the appropriate atomic mass, and then divide each of the answers by the smallest of the four mole values:

$$(5.030 \text{ g Be})\left(\frac{1 \text{ mol Be}}{9.01218 \text{ g Be}}\right) = \frac{0.5581335 \text{ mol Be}}{0.371736} = 1.501$$

$$(10.030 \text{ g Al})\left(\frac{1 \text{ mol Al}}{26.9815 \text{ g Al}}\right) = \frac{0.371736 \text{ mol Al}}{0.371736} = 1$$

$$(31.351 \text{ g Si})\left(\frac{1 \text{ mol Si}}{28.0855 \text{ g Si}}\right) = \frac{1.086501 \text{ mol Si}}{0.371736} = 2.9227 \approx 3$$

$$(53.589 \text{ g O})\left(\frac{1 \text{ mol O}}{15.9994 \text{ g O}}\right) = \frac{3.349438 \text{ mol O}}{0.371736} = 9.0102 \approx 9$$

All of the values except the beryllium are either a whole number or close enough to a whole number to round to a whole number. The conversion of the beryllium requires multiplication by 2, which means that all the values are to be multiplied by 2. This gives Be = 3, Al = 2, Si = 6, and O = 18.

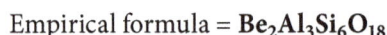

$$\text{Empirical formula} = \mathbf{Be_2Al_3Si_6O_{18}}$$

Reality Check

The formula is that of the mineral beryl. The trace amount of chromium means this could be the variety of beryl known as emerald.

CHAPTER 13

Mixtures—Solutions and Colloids

The successful completion of these problems requires the following six (6) items.

1. This chapter builds upon chapter 4, "Aqueous Solutions and Their Chemical Reactions," so it might be useful to review chapter 4.
2. The definitions of the concentration units greatly simplify unit conversions.
3. This is another chapter where moles are the key.
4. When considering colligative properties, it is necessary to use a van't Hoff factor for all solutions that contain electrolytes.
5. The difference between a strong electrolyte, a weak electrolyte, and a nonelectrolyte affects many of the calculations.
6. Many people are rusty on conversions when they reach this chapter; therefore, they may need to review conversions.

Example Problem 13.1

At room temperature, 13.20 g of ammonia will dissolve in 100.0 mL of ethyl alcohol (C_2H_5OH). Calculate the mass percent, molarity (m), and mole fraction (X) of ammonia in the resulting solution. (The density of ethyl alcohol is 0.7893 g/cm^3.)

Information

Mass of ammonia (13.20 g); volume of ethyl alcohol (100.0 mL); density of ethyl alcohol (0.7893 g/cm^3), the questions of what are the mass percent, molarity, and X of the ammonia solution

Connections

The definitions of concentration units in table 13.1

Solution

It is possible to calculate the different expressions of concentration in any order. A few preliminary calculations will provide us with the values we need to use the definitions in the table. These, with results unrounded, are

Mass of ethyl alcohol

$$= (100.0 \text{ mL } C_2H_5OH) (0.7893 \text{ g/cm}^3) (1 \text{ mL/1 cm}^3)$$
$$= 78.93 \text{ g ethyl alcohol}$$

Moles of ammonia

$$= (13.20 \text{ g NH}_3) (1 \text{ mole NH}_3/17.031 \text{ g NH}_3)$$
$$= 0.775077 \text{ mole NH}_3$$

Moles of ethyl alcohol

$$= (78.93 \text{ g } C_2H_5OH) (1 \text{ mole } C_2H_5OH/46.069 \text{ g } C_2H_5OH)$$
$$= 1.7133 \text{ mole } C_2H_5OH$$

Mass percent

$$\left(\frac{13.20 \text{ g NH}_3}{(13.20 + 78.93) \text{ g}} \right)(100\%) = 14.32758 = \mathbf{14.33\%}$$

Molality

$$\left(\frac{0.775077 \text{ mol NH}_3}{78.93 \text{ g } C_2H_5OH} \right)\left(\frac{10^3}{k} \right) = 9.819802 = \mathbf{9.820 \; m \; NH_3}$$

Mole fraction

$$\frac{0.775077 \text{ mol NH}_3}{(0.775077 + 1.7133) \text{ mol}} = 0.3114789 = \mathbf{0.3115}$$

Reality Check

The magnitudes of the answers are reasonable. The units and significant figures are correct.

Follow-Up Problem 13.1a

An aqueous ammonia solution contains 25.0 g of ammonia in 75.0 g of water. Calculate the mass percent, molality, and mole fraction of ammonia.

Information

Mass of ammonia (25.0 g); mass of water (75.0 g); the questions of what are the mass percent, molarity, and X of the ammonia solution

Connections

The definitions of concentration units in table 13.1

Solution

We can calculate the different expressions of concentration in any order. A few preliminary calculations will provide us with the values we need to use the definitions in the table. These, with results unrounded, are

$$\text{Moles of ammonia} = (25.0 \text{ g NH}_3) (1 \text{ mole NH}_3/17.031 \text{ g NH}_3) = 1.46791 \text{ mole NH}_3$$
$$\text{Moles of water} = (75.0 \text{ g } H_2O) (1 \text{ mole } H_2O /18.015 \text{ g } H_2O) = 4.163197 \text{ mole } H_2O$$

Mass percent

$$\left(\frac{25.0 \text{ g NH}_3}{(25.0 + 75.0) \text{ g}}\right)(100\%) = \textbf{25.0\%}$$

Molality

$$\left(\frac{1.46791 \text{ mol NH}_3}{75.0 \text{ g H}_2\text{O}}\right)\left(\frac{10^3}{\text{k}}\right) = 19.57213 = \textbf{19.6 m NH}_3$$

Mole fraction

$$\frac{1.46791 \text{ mol NH}_3}{(1.46791 + 4.163197) \text{ mol}} = 0.26067876 = \textbf{0.261}$$

Reality Check

The magnitudes of the answers are reasonable. The units and significant figures are correct.

Follow-Up Problem 13.1b

A hydrochloric acid solution has a density of 1.0878 g/mL. The solution contains 19.6 g of HCl in 100.0 mL of solution. Calculate the mass percent, molality, and mole fraction of hydrochloric acid.

Information

Mass of HCl (19.6 g); volume of solution (100.0 mL); density of the solution (1.0878 g/mL); the questions of what are the mass percent, molality, and X of hydrochloric acid

Connections

The definitions of concentration units given in table 13.1. The solution is hydrochloric acid; therefore, it consists of HCl dissolved in water.

Solution

We can calculate the different expressions of concentration in any order. A few preliminary calculations will provide us with the values we need to use the definitions in the table. These, with results unrounded, are

Mass of solution = (100.0 mL solution) (1.0878 g/mL) = 108.78 g
Mass of water = 108.78 g – 19.6 g HCl = 89.18 g H_2O
Moles of HCl = (19.6 g HCl) (1 mole HCl/36.461 g HCl) = 0.53756 mole HCl
Moles of water = (89.18 g H_2O) (1 mole H_2O /18.015 g H_2O) = 4.9503 mole H_2O

Mass percent

$$\left(\frac{19.6 \text{ g HCl}}{(108.78) \text{ g}}\right)(100\%) = 18.0180 = \textbf{18.0\%}$$

Molality

$$\left(\frac{0.53756 \text{ mol HCl}}{89.18 \text{ g H}_2\text{O}}\right)\left(\frac{10^3}{\text{k}}\right) = 6.0278 = \textbf{6.03 m HCl}$$

Mole fraction

$$\frac{0.53756 \text{ mol HCl}}{(0.53756 + 4.9503) \text{ mol}} = 0.097954 = \textbf{0.0980}$$

Reality Check

The magnitudes of the answers are reasonable. The units and significant figures are correct.

Example Problem 13.2

What is the vapor pressure of a solution made by mixing 80.0 g of chloroform, $CHCl_3$, in 800.0 g of carbon tetrachloride, CCl_4? The vapor pressure of chloroform is 197 torr, and the vapor pressure of carbon tetrachloride is 114 torr (all vapor pressures are determined at 25°C).

Information

Mass of $CHCl_3$ (80.0 g); vapor pressure of $CHCl_3$ (197 torr); mass of CCl_4 (800.0 g); vapor pressure of CCl_4 (114 torr); the question of what is the vapor pressure of the solution (all vapor pressures are determined at 25°C)

Connections

$$P_{solution} = X_{solvent}\, P°_{solvent} + X_{solute}\, P°_{solute} \qquad \text{(Raoult's law)}$$

Solution

This problem requires the use of Raoult's law, for which we need the mole fractions and their vapor pressures. We are given the vapor pressures. To calculate the mole fractions, we first calculate the moles of each constituent of the solution:

Moles chloroform

$$= (80.0 \text{ g CHCl}_3)\,(1 \text{ mole CHCl}_3/119.378 \text{ g CHCl}_3)$$
$$= 0.6701402 \text{ mole CHCl}_3 \qquad \text{(unrounded)}$$

Moles carbon tetrachloride

$$= (800.0 \text{ g CCl}_4)\,(1 \text{ mole CCl}_4/153.823 \text{ g CCl}_4)$$
$$= 5.2007827 \text{ mole CCl}_4 \qquad \text{(unrounded)}$$

The mole fraction of chloroform (the solute) is

$$X_{solute} = \frac{0.6701402 \text{ mol CHCl}_3}{(0.6701402 + 5.2007827) \text{ mol}} = 0.1141456 \qquad \text{(unrounded)}$$

We could calculate the mole fraction of carbon tetrachloride (the solvent) in a similar manner. However, for a two-component system, the sum of the two mole fractions must equal 1. Therefore, simply subtracting the mole fraction of chloroform from 1 will give us the needed value:

$$X_{solvent} = 1 - 0.1141456 = 0.8858544$$

Using Raoult's law gives

$$P_{solution} = (0.8858544)\,(114 \text{ torr}) + (0.1141456)\,(197 \text{ torr})$$
$$= 123.47408 = \textbf{123 torr}$$

Reality Check

The magnitude of the answer is reasonable. The units and significant figures are correct.

Follow-Up Problem 13.2a

What is the vapor pressure of a solution made by mixing 180.0 g of acetone, C_3H_6O, in 520.0 g of cyclohexanone, $C_6H_{10}O$? The vapor pressure of acetone is 231 torr, and the vapor pressure of cyclohexanone is 3.98 torr (all vapor pressures are determined at 25°C).

Information

Mass of C_3H_6O (180.0 g); vapor pressure of C_3H_6O (231 torr); mass of $C_6H_{10}O$ (520.0 g); vapor pressure of $C_6H_{10}O$ (3.98 torr); the question of what is the vapor pressure of the solution (all vapor pressures are determined at 25°C)

Connections

$$P_{solution} = X_{solvent} P°_{solvent} + X_{solute} P°_{solute} \qquad \text{(Raoult's law)}$$

Solution

This problem requires the use of Raoult's law, for which we need the mole fractions and their vapor pressures. We are given the vapor pressures. To calculate the mole fractions, we first calculate the moles of each constituent of the solution:

$$\text{Moles } C_3H_6O = (180.0 \text{ g } C_3H_6O) (1 \text{ mole } C_3H_6O/58.080 \text{ g } C_3H_6O)$$
$$= 3.09917 \text{ mole } C_3H_6O \qquad \text{(unrounded)}$$
$$\text{Moles } C_6H_{10}O = (520.0 \text{ g } C_6H_{10}O) (1 \text{ mole } C_6H_{10}O/98.145 \text{ g } C_6H_{10}O)$$
$$= 5.298283 \text{ mole } C_6H_{10}O \qquad \text{(unrounded)}$$

The mole fraction of C_3H_6O (the solute) is

$$X_{solute} = \frac{3.09917 \text{ mol } C_3H_6O}{(3.09917 + 5.298283) \text{ mol}} = 0.3690607 \qquad \text{(unrounded)}$$

We could calculate the mole fraction of $C_6H_{10}O$ (the solvent) in a similar manner. However, for a two-component system, the sum of the two mole fractions must equal 1. Therefore, simply subtracting the mole fraction of C_3H_6O from 1 will give the needed value:

$$X_{solvent} = 1 - 0.3690607 = 0.630939$$

Using Raoult's law gives

$$P_{solution} = (0.630939) (3.98 \text{ torr}) + (0.3690607) (231 \text{ torr})$$
$$= 87.764 = \textbf{87.8 torr}$$

Reality Check

The magnitude of the answer is reasonable. The units and significant figures are correct.

Follow-Up Problem 13.2b

A solution made by mixing 275.0 g of benzene, C_6H_6, in 525.0 g of benzaldehyde, C_7H_6O, has a vapor pressure of 38.2 torr. The vapor pressure of benzene is 95.3 torr, and the vapor pressure of benzaldehyde is 1.28 torr (all vapor pressures are determined at 25°C). Is the solution ideal?

Information

Mass of C_6H_6 (275.0 g); vapor pressure of C_6H_6 (93.5 torr); mass of C_7H_6O (525.0 g); vapor pressure of C_7H_6O (1.28 torr); the vapor pressure of the solution (38.2 torr); the question of whether the solution is ideal (all vapor pressures are determined at 25°C)

Connections

$$P_{solution} = X_{solvent} P°_{solvent} + X_{solute} P°_{solute} \qquad \text{(Raoult's law)}$$

Solution

This problem requires the use of Raoult's law, for which we need the mole fractions and their vapor pressures. We are given the vapor pressures. To calculate the mole fractions, we first calculate the moles of each constituent of the solution:

$$\text{Moles } C_6H_6 = (275.0 \text{ g } C_6H_6) (1 \text{ mole } C_6H_6/78.114 \text{ g } C_6H_6)$$
$$= 3.5204957 \text{ mole } C_6H_6 \qquad \text{(unrounded)}$$
$$\text{Moles } C_7H_6O = (525.0 \text{ g } C_7H_6O) (1 \text{ mole } C_7H_6O/106.124 \text{ g } C_7H_6O)$$
$$= 4.947043 \text{ mole } C_7H_6O \qquad \text{(unrounded)}$$

The mole fraction of C_6H_6 (the solute) is

$$X_{solute} = \frac{3.5204957 \text{ mol } C_6H_6}{(3.5204957 + 4.947043) \text{ mol}} = 0.4157638 \qquad \text{(unrounded)}$$

We could calculate the mole fraction of carbon tetrachloride (the solvent) in a similar manner. However, for a two-component system, the sum of the two mole fractions must equal 1. Therefore, simply subtracting the mole fraction of C_6H_6 from 1 will give the needed value:

$$X_{solvent} = 1 - 0.4157638 = 0.5842362$$

Using Raoult's law gives

$$P_{solution} = (0.4157638)(93.5 \text{ torr}) + (0.5842362)(1.28 \text{ torr})$$
$$= 39.6217 = \textbf{39.6 torr}$$

The observed vapor pressure (38.2 torr) is lower than the calculated value; therefore, the solution is **not ideal**, because it shows a negative deviation.

Reality Check

The magnitude of the answer is reasonable, and the comparison to Raoult's law is correct. The units and significant figures are correct.

Example Problem 13.3

A 10.0-g sample of lauryl alcohol, extracted from coconut oil, was dissolved in 225.0 g of benzene, C_6H_6. The freezing point depression of the benzene solution was 1.22°C. Determine the molar mass of lauryl alcohol. The value of K_f for benzene is 5.12°C/m.

Information

Mass of lauryl alcohol (10.0 g); mass of C_6H_6 (225.0 g); freezing point depression for C_6H_6 (1.22°C); freezing point depression constant for C_6H_6 (5.12°C/m); the question of what is the molar mass of lauryl alcohol

Connections

$\Delta T_f = K_f m$

Solution

As this is a freezing point depression problem, we can use the equation $\Delta T_f = K_f m$. Rearranging this equation and plugging in the values gives the molality:

$$m = \Delta T/K_f = (1.22°C)/(5.12°C/m) = 0.2383 \text{ } m \qquad \text{(unrounded)}$$

We can now find the moles of lauryl alcohol:

$$\text{Moles lauryl alcohol} = \left(\frac{0.2383 \text{ mol}}{\text{kg}}\right)\left(\frac{k}{10^3}\right)(225.0 \text{ g}) = 0.05361 \text{ mol} \qquad \text{(unrounded)}$$

The molar mass is the grams of lauryl alcohol divided by the moles of lauryl alcohol:

$$\text{Molar mass} = (10.0 \text{ g})/(0.05361 \text{ mole}) = 186.532 = \textbf{187 g/mole}$$

Reality Check

The magnitude of the answer seems reasonable. The units and significant figures are correct.

Follow-Up Problem 13.3a

A 12.5-g sample of an amino acid was dissolved in 275.0 g of carbon disulfide, CS_2. The freezing point depression of the carbon disulfide solution was 0.853°C. Determine the molar mass of the amino acid. The value of K_f for carbon disulfide is 3.83°C/m.

Information

Mass of an amino acid (12.5 g); mass of CS_2 (275.0 g); freezing point depression for benzene, (0.853°C); freezing point depression constant for CS_2 (3.83°C/m); the questions of what is the molar mass of the amino acid

Connections

$\Delta T_f = K_f m$

Solution

As this is a freezing point depression problem, we can use the equation $\Delta T_f = K_f m$. Rearranging this equation and plugging in the values gives the molality:

$$m = \Delta T / K_f = (0.853°C)/(3.83°C/m) = 0.222715 \ m \qquad \text{(unrounded)}$$

We can now find the moles of lauryl alcohol:

$$\text{Moles amino acid} = \left(\frac{0.222715 \ \text{mol}}{\text{kg}}\right)\left(\frac{k}{10^3}\right)(275.0 \ \text{g}) = 0.0612467 \ \text{mole} \qquad \text{(unrounded)}$$

The molar mass is the grams of the amino acid divided by the moles of amino acid:

$$\text{Molar mass} = (12.5 \ \text{g})/(0.0612467 \ \text{mole}) = 204.0925 = \textbf{204 g/mole}$$

Reality Check

The magnitude of the answer seems reasonable. The units and significant figures are correct.

Follow-Up Problem 13.3b

A 13.0-g sample of an unknown compound was dissolved in 325.0 g of benzene, C_6H_6. The boiling point elevation of the benzene solution was 0.514°C. Determine the molar mass of the unknown compound. The value of K_b for benzene is 2.34°C/m.

Information

Mass of an unknown compound (13.0 g); mass of C_6H_6 (325.0 g); elevation of boiling point for benzene, (0.514°C); boiling point elevation constant for C_6H_6 (2.34°C/m); the questions of what is the molar mass of the unknown compound

Connections

$\Delta T_b = K_b m$

Solution

As this is a boiling point elevation problem, we can use the equation $\Delta T_b = K_b m$. Rearranging this equation and plugging in the values gives the molality:

$$m = \Delta T_b / K_b = (0.514°C)/(2.34°C/m) = 0.219658 \ m \qquad \text{(unrounded)}$$

We can now find the moles of unknown compound:

$$\text{Moles unknown compound} = \left(\frac{0.219658 \text{ mol}}{\text{kg}}\right)\left(\frac{k}{10^3}\right)(325.0 \text{ g})$$

$$= 0.0713889 \text{ mole} \quad \text{(unrounded)}$$

The molar mass is the grams of unknown compound divided by the moles of unknown compound:

$$\text{Molar mass} = (13.0 \text{ g})/(0.0713889 \text{ mole}) = 182.101 = \textbf{182 g/mole}$$

Reality Check
The magnitude of the answer seems reasonable. The units and significant figures are correct.

Example Problem 13.4
A solution made by dissolving 0.1232 g of an unknown solid in 100.00 mL of cyclohexane gives an osmotic pressure of 159.4 mmHg at 27°C. Calculate the molar mass of the unknown solid.

Information
Mass of unknown (0.1232 g); volume of solution (100.00 mL); osmotic pressure (159.4 mmHg); temperature (27°C); the question of what is the molar mass of the solute

Connections
$\Pi V = nRT$

Solution
The mention of osmotic pressure leads us to the equation $\Pi V = nRT$. We can rearrange this equation to find the number of moles present:

$$\text{Moles} = n = \Pi V/RT = \left(\frac{(159.4 \text{ mmHg})(100.00 \text{ mL})}{\left(0.08206 \frac{\text{L} \cdot \text{atm}}{\text{mol} \cdot \text{K}}\right)(300 \text{ K})}\right)\left(\frac{1 \text{ atm}}{760 \text{ mmHg}}\right)\left(\frac{10^{-3}}{m}\right)$$

$$= 8.5196539 \times 10^{-4} \text{ mole} \quad \text{(unrounded)}$$

The molar mass is the grams of the unknown solid divided by the moles of the unknown solid:

$$\text{Molar mass} = (0.1232 \text{ g})/(8.5196539 \times 10^{-4} \text{ mole}) = 144.607 = \textbf{145 g/mole}$$

Reality Check
The magnitude seems reasonable. The units and the significant figures are correct.

Follow-Up Problem 13.4a
A solution made by dissolving 1.500 g of protein in 500.0 mL of water has an osmotic pressure of 9.72 torr at 25°C. Calculate the molar mass of the protein.

Information
Mass of protein (1.500 g); volume of water (500.00 mL); osmotic pressure (9.72 torr); temperature (25°C); the question of what is the molar mass of the protein

Connections
$\Pi V = nRT$

Solution

The mention of osmotic pressure leads us to the equation $\Pi V = nRT$. We can rearrange this equation to find the number of moles present:

$$\text{Moles} = n = \Pi V/RT = \left| \frac{(9.72 \text{ torr})(500.00 \text{ mL})}{\left(0.08206 \, \dfrac{\text{L} \cdot \text{atm}}{\text{mol} \cdot \text{K}}\right)(298 \text{ K})} \right| \left(\frac{1 \text{ atm}}{760 \text{ mmHg}}\right)\left(\frac{10^{-3}}{m}\right)$$

$$= 2.615019 \times 10^{-4} \text{ mole} \qquad \text{(unrounded)}$$

The molar mass is the grams of the protein divided by the moles of protein:

$$\text{Molar mass} = (1.500 \text{ g})/(2.615019 \times 10^{-4} \text{ mole}) = 5736.095 = \mathbf{5.74 \times 10^3 \text{ g/mol}}$$

Reality Check

The magnitude seems reasonable. The units and the significant figures are correct.

Follow-Up Problem 13.4b

Determine the molar mass of an unknown strong electrolyte that dissociates to yield two ions, if a solution, prepared by dissolving 3.640 g of unknown in enough water to make 350.0 mL of solution, has an osmotic pressure of 10.44 mmHg at 25°C.

Information

Mass of an unknown strong electrolyte (3.640 g); the van't Hoff factor (2); volume of solution (350.0 mL); osmotic pressure (10.44 mmHg); temperature (25°C); the question of what is the molar mass of the solute

Connections

$\Pi V = inRT$

Solution

The mention of osmotic pressure leads us to the equation $\Pi V = inRT$. We can rearrange this equation to find the number of moles present.

$$\text{Moles} = n = i\Pi V/RT = \left| \frac{2\,(10.44 \text{ mmHg})(350.0 \text{ mL})}{\left(0.08206 \, \dfrac{\text{L} \cdot \text{atm}}{\text{mol} \cdot \text{K}}\right)(298 \text{ K})} \right| \left(\frac{1 \text{ atm}}{760 \text{ mmHg}}\right)\left(\frac{10^{-3}}{m}\right)$$

$$= 3.932214 \times 10^{-4} \text{ mole} \qquad \text{(unrounded)}$$

The molar mass is the grams of the unknown solid divided by the moles of unknown solid:

$$\text{Molar mass} = (3.640 \text{ g})/(3.932214 \times 10^{-4} \text{ mole}) = 9256.871 = \mathbf{9.26 \times 10^3 \text{ g/mol}}$$

Reality Check

The magnitude seems reasonable. The units and the significant figures are correct.

END-OF-CHAPTER PROBLEMS

13.1 The Solution Process

13.2 **(a)** List the general characteristics of a homogeneous mixture. **(b)** List the general characteristics of a heterogeneous mixture.

Solution

As seen in chapter 1, "The Tools of Chemistry," where homogeneous and heterogeneous mixtures were first introduced:

(a) The properties of a homogeneous mixture are uniform throughout.

(b) The properties of a homogeneous mixture are not uniform throughout.

13.4 What does the phrase "like dissolves like" mean?

Solution

A solvent will dissolve a solute if both have similar (like) intermolecular forces.

13.6 Why is a nonpolar substance like oxygen capable of dissolving in a very polar solvent like water?

Solution

No matter what the strength (or weakness) of the interactions in the mixture, a solution will tend to form between a gas and a solvent. (This is necessary to, for example, keep fish alive in water.)

13.8 Sodium chloride will dissolve in water. What would be the general characteristics of another solvent that might dissolve sodium chloride?

Solution

The other solvent must be able to form strong ion–dipole forces. For this reason, the other solvent must be very polar.

13.10 Which of the following solvents are polar, and which are nonpolar? **(a)** methanol, CH_3OH; **(b)** carbon tetrachloride, CCl_4; **(c)** ammonia, NH_3; **(d)** bromine trifluoride, BrF_3; **(e)** ethane, C_2H_6

Solution

It may help to draw the structures of the molecules listed. In some cases, VSEPR may be helpful.

(a) polar; **(b)** nonpolar; **(c)** polar; **(d)** polar; **(e)** nonpolar

13.13 Define *heat of solution* and tell what factors influence its value.

Solution

The **heat of solution** is the energy change that takes place when the solution forms. The strengths of the various intermolecular forces present influence the heat of solution.

13.2 Solubility

13.16 **(a)** How does a change in temperature affect the solubility of most solids? **(b)** How does a change in temperature affect the solubility of gases?

Solution

(a) The solubility of most solids increases with increasing temperature.

(b) The solubility of gases decreases with increasing temperature.

13.17 **(a)** How does a change in pressure affect the solubility of most solids? **(b)** How does a change in pressure affect the solubility of gases?

Solution

(a) Changes in pressure have negligible effect upon the solubility of solids.

(b) Gases are more soluble at higher pressures.

13.3 Concentration Units

13.20 Define the following concentration units: **(a)** *molarity*, **(b)** *mole fraction*, **(c)** *mass (weight) percent*, **(d)** *volume percent*, **(e)** *molality*

Solution

(a) **Molarity** is the moles of solute divided by the liters of solution.

(b) **Mole fraction** is the moles of a substance divided by the total moles present.

(c) **Mass (weight) percent** is the mass of the solute divided by the mass of the solution, with the result multiplied by 100%.

(d) **Volume percent** is the volume of solute divided by the volume of solution, with the result multiplied by 100%.

(e) **Molality** is the moles of solute divided by the kilograms of solvent.

13.23 Calculate the mass percent of solute in each of the following solutions. **(a)** 25.0 g of sodium chloride, NaCl, in 1000.0 g of water; **(b)** 0.25 mole of nitric acid, HNO_3, in 100.0 g of water

Information

(a) the mass of the solute (25.0 g NaCl) and the mass of the solvent (1000.0 g H_2O); **(b)** the moles of the solute (0.25 mole HNO_3) and the mass of the solvent (100.0 g H_2O); in both cases, the question of what is the mass percent of the solute

Connections

The definition of *mass percent*

Solution

In each case, we need to use the definition of *mass percent*:

$$Mass\ percent = \left(\frac{Mass\ of\ solute}{Mass\ of\ solution} \right) \times 100\%$$

(a) We need to enter the mass of the solute and the mass of the solution (solute + solvent).

$$Mass\ percent = \left(\frac{25.0\ g}{(1000.0 + 25.0)\ g} \right) \times 100\% = 2.43902 = \mathbf{2.44\%}$$

(b) We need to first determine the mass of the solute, using the moles and the molar mass:

$$Mass\ HNO_3 = (0.25\ mol\ HNO_3) \left(\frac{63.012\ g\ HNO_3}{1\ mol\ HNO_3} \right) = 15.753 = 16\ g$$

Then we need to enter the mass of the solute and the mass of the solution (solute + solvent).

$$Mass\ percent = \left(\frac{15.753\ g}{(100.0 + 15.753)\ g}\right) \times 100\% = 13.60915 = \textbf{14\%}$$

13.25 Calculate the mole fraction of solute in each of the following solutions: **(a)** 1.2 mol of ethanol, CH_3CH_2OH, in 5.2 mole of water; **(b)** 0.55 mole of acetone, CH_3COCH_3, in 250.0 g of water; **(c)** 15.5 g of iodine, I_2, dissolved in 275 g of carbon tetrachloride, CCl_4

Information
(a) the moles of solute (1.2 mole) and the moles of solvent (5.2 mole); **(b)** the moles of solute (0.55 mole) and the mass of solvent (250.0 g H_2O); **(c)** the mass of solute (15.5 g I_2) and the mass of solvent (275 g CCl_4); in all cases, the question of how to calculate the mole fraction of the solute

Connections
The definition of *mole fraction*

Solution
The definition of *mole fraction* requires the amounts of all substances be in units of moles (either given or determined using the molar mass).

(a) The quantities are already in moles; therefore, no further conversions are necessary. Now we only need to enter the moles of solute and total moles into the definition of mole fraction:

$$\frac{1.2\ mol}{(1.2 + 5.2)\ mol} = 0.1875 = \textbf{0.19}$$

(b) The mass of water needs to be changed to moles:

$$(250.0g\ H_2O)\left(\frac{1\ mol\ H_2O}{18.015\ g\ H_2O}\right) = 13.87732\ mole\ H_2O$$

Now we only need to enter the moles of solute and total moles into the definition of *mole fraction*:

$$\frac{0.55\ mol}{(0.55 + 13.87732)\ mol} = 0.0381221 = \textbf{0.038}$$

(c) The masses of all substances need to be converted to moles. These conversions are

$$(15.5g\ I_2)\left(\frac{1\ mol\ I_2}{253.80\ g\ I_2}\right) = 0.0610717\ mole\ I_2$$

$$(275\ g\ CCl_4)\left(\frac{1\ mol\ CCl_4}{153.823\ g\ CCl_4}\right) = 1.787769\ mole\ CCl_4$$

Now we only need to enter the moles of solute and total moles into the definition of *mole fraction*:

$$\frac{0.0610717\ mol}{(0.0610717 + 1.787769)\ mol} = 0.0330324 = \textbf{0.0330}$$

13.27 Calculate the molarity of each type of ion in each of the following solutions:
(a) 0.75 mole of sodium sulfate, Na_2SO_4, dissolved in 0.650 L of solution; **(b)** 14.3 g of

potassium phosphate, K_3PO_4, dissolved in 2.50 L of solution; **(c)** 2.53 g of iron(III) bromide hexahydrate, $FeBr_3 \cdot 6H_2O$, in 875 mL of solution

Information

(a) the moles of the solute (0.75 mole Na_2SO_4) and the volume of the solution (0.650 L); **(b)** the mass of the solute (14.3 g K_3PO_4) and the volume of the solution (2.50 L); **(c)** the mass of the solute (2.53 g $FeBr_3 \cdot 6H_2O$) and the volume of the solution (875 mL); in each case, the question of what is the molarity of each type of ion in the solution

Connections

The definition of *molarity*

Solution

The definition of *molarity* requires the moles of solute and the volume of the solution in liters (or dm^3). All the solutes are strong electrolytes, which means they undergo complete dissociation in solution.

(a) The initial units are the correct ones to find molarity. The formula gives the appropriate mole ratios:

$$\frac{0.75 \text{ mol Na}_2\text{SO}_4}{0.650 \text{ L}} = 1.153846 = 1.2 \text{ M Na}_2\text{SO}_4$$

$$\left(\frac{1.153846 \text{ mol Na}_2\text{SO}_4}{\text{L}}\right)\left(\frac{2 \text{ mol Na}^+}{1 \text{ mol Na}_2\text{SO}_4}\right) = 2.307692 = \mathbf{2.3 \text{ M Na}^+}$$

$$\left(\frac{1.153846 \text{ mol Na}_2\text{SO}_4}{\text{L}}\right)\left(\frac{1 \text{ mol SO}_4^{2-}}{1 \text{ mol Na}_2\text{SO}_4}\right) = 1.153846 = \mathbf{1.2 \text{ M SO}_4{}^{2-}}$$

(b) Unlike in part (a), here we need to add a step to convert the mass of solute to moles. The formula gives the appropriate mole ratios:

$$\left(\frac{14.3 \text{ g K}_3\text{PO}_4}{2.50 \text{ L}}\right)\left(\frac{1 \text{ mol K}_3\text{PO}_4}{212.264 \text{ g K}_3\text{PO}_4}\right) = 0.0269476 = 0.0269 \text{ M K}_3\text{PO}_4$$

$$\left(\frac{0.0269476 \text{ mol K}_3\text{PO}_4}{\text{L}}\right)\left(\frac{3 \text{ mol K}^+}{1 \text{ mol K}_3\text{PO}_4}\right) = 0.0808428 = \mathbf{0.0808 \text{ M K}^+}$$

$$\left(\frac{0.0269476 \text{ mol K}_3\text{PO}_4}{\text{L}}\right)\left(\frac{1 \text{ mol PO}_4^{3-}}{1 \text{ mol K}_3\text{PO}_4}\right) = 0.0269476 = \mathbf{0.0269 \text{ M PO}_4{}^{3-}}$$

(c) We need to convert the grams of solute to moles, and we also need to convert the milliliters to liters. The formula gives the appropriate mole ratios:

$$\left(\frac{2.53 \text{ g FeBr}_3 \cdot 6H_2O}{875 \text{ mL}}\right)\left(\frac{1 \text{ mol FeBr}_3 \cdot 6H_2O}{403.647 \text{ g FeBr}_3 \cdot 6H_2O}\right)\left(\frac{m}{0.001}\right) = 0.00716326 = 0.00716 \text{ M FeBr}_3 \bullet 6 \text{ H}_2O$$

$$\left(\frac{0.00716326 \text{ mol FeBr}_3 \cdot 6H_2O}{\text{L}}\right)\left(\frac{1 \text{ mol Fe}^{3+}}{1 \text{ mol FeBr}_3 \cdot 6H_2O}\right) = 0.00716326 = \mathbf{0.00716 \text{ M Fe}^{3+}}$$

$$\left(\frac{0.00716326 \text{ mol FeBr}_3 \cdot 6H_2O}{\text{L}}\right)\left(\frac{3 \text{ mol Br}^-}{1 \text{ mol FeBr}_3 \cdot 6H_2O}\right) = 0.02148978 = \mathbf{0.0215 \text{ M Br}^-}$$

Reality Check
In general, if the mole ratio is 1:1, the calculation may be omitted.

13.29 A phosphoric acid, H_3PO_4, solution was prepared by dissolving 935 g of phosphoric acid in sufficient water to prepare 1.00 L of solution. The density of this solution is 1.461 g/cm^3. **(a)** What is the mass percentage of phosphoric acid in the solution? **(b)** What is the mole fraction of phosphoric acid in the solution? **(c)** Determine the molality of the phosphoric acid. **(d)** Calculate the molarity of the phosphoric acid.

Information
A 1.00-L solution containing 935 g of H_3PO_4 has a density of 1.463 g/cm^3; the questions of **(a)** what is the mass percentage of H_3PO_4; **(b)** what is the mole fraction of H_3PO_4; **(c)** what is the molality of H_3PO_4; **(d)** what is the molarity of H_3PO_4

Connections
The definitions of *mass percent*, *mole fraction*, *molality*, and *molarity*

Solution
Preliminary calculations needed to determine the mass of the solution, the mass of water, and the moles of both solute and solvent.

$$\text{Mass of solution} = \left(\frac{1.460 \text{ g soln}}{cm^3}\right)\left(\frac{cm^3}{mL}\right)\left(\frac{m}{0.001}\right)(1.00 \text{ L}) = 1461 = 1.46 \times 10^3 \text{ g solution}$$

$$\text{Mass } H_2O = 1{,}461 \text{ g (solvent + solute)} - 935 \text{ g solute} = 526 = 5.3 \times 10^2 \text{ g solute } (H_2O)$$

$$\text{Moles } H_2O = (526 \text{ g } H_2O)\left(\frac{1 \text{ mol } H_2O}{18.015 \text{ g } H_2O}\right) = 29.19789 = 29 \text{ mole } H_2O$$

$$\text{Moles } H_3PO_4 = (935 \text{ g } H_3PO_4)\left(\frac{1 \text{ mol } H_3PO_4}{97.994 \text{ g } H_3PO_4}\right) = 9.54140 = 9.54 \text{ mole } H_3PO_4$$

(a) Entering the masses of solute and solution into the definition of *mass percent* gives

$$\text{Mass percent} = \left(\frac{935 \text{ g}}{1461 \text{ g}}\right) \times 100\% = 63.99726 = \textbf{64.0\% } H_3PO_4$$

(b) Entering the moles of solute and solution into the definition of *mole fraction* gives

$$\text{Mole fraction} = \frac{9.54140 \text{ mol}}{(9.54140 + 29.19789) \text{ mol}} = 0.24629775 = \textbf{0.246 } H_3PO_4$$

(c) We need to convert the mass of solvent to kilograms:

$$\text{Molality} = \left(\frac{9.54140 \text{ mol } H_3PO_4}{526 \text{ g } H_2O}\right)\left(\frac{1{,}000}{k}\right) = 18.13954 = \textbf{18.1 } m \text{ } H_3PO_4$$

(d) Entering the moles of solute and volume of solution into the definition of *molarity* gives

$$\text{Molarity} = \left(\frac{9.54140 \text{ mol } H_3PO_4}{1.00 \text{ L}}\right) = 9.54140 = \textbf{9.54 M } H_3PO_4$$

13.31 Concentrated nitric acid has 68.0 mass percent acid in an aqueous solution. The density of the solution is 1.41 g/cm^3. **(a)** Calculate the molarity of nitric acid in the solution. **(b)** What is the molality of this solution?

Information

A concentrated HNO_3 solution with 68.0 mass percent HNO_3 and a density of 1.41 g/cm³; the questions of (a) what is the molarity of HNO_3 and (b) what is the molality of HNO_3

Connections

The definitions of *molarity* and *molality*

Solution

The key to this problem is to understand the definition of *mass percent*. So, "68.0% by mass" means 68.0 grams of HNO_3 in 100.0 grams of solution.

(a) We need to convert the mass of HNO_3 into moles. To determine the volume of the solution, it is necessary to use the density:

$$\left(\frac{68.0 \text{ g } HNO_3}{100.0 \text{ g solution}}\right)\left(\frac{1 \text{ mol } HNO_3}{63.012 \text{ g } HNO_3}\right)\left(\frac{1.41 \text{ g solution}}{cm^3}\right)\left(\frac{cm^3}{mL}\right)\left(\frac{m}{0.001}\right) = 15.216149 = \textbf{15.2 M } HNO_3$$

(b) We need to convert the mass of HNO_3 into moles. The mass of the solvent is the mass of the solution minus the mass of the solute. It is also necessary to convert the mass of the solvent to kilograms:

$$\left(\frac{68.0 \text{ g } HNO_3}{(100.0 - 68.0) \text{ g } H_2O}\right)\left(\frac{1 \text{ mol } HNO_3}{63.012 \text{ g } HNO_3}\right)\left(\frac{1,000}{k}\right) = 33.7237 = \textbf{33.7 } \textit{m } HNO_3$$

13.34 Oxalic acid, $H_2C_2O_4$, and its salts are present in plants such as spinach and rhubarb. A 0.580-*m* oxalic acid aqueous solution has a density of 1.022 g/mL. (a) What is the molarity of this solution? (b) What is the mass percent of oxalic acid in this solution?

Information

A 0.580 m $H_2C_2O_4$(aq) solution has a density of 1.022 g/mL; the questions of what is the molarity of this solution and what is the mass percent of $H_2C_2O_4$

Connections

The definitions of *molality* and *mass percent*

Solution

(a) To determine the molarity of the solution, we need to know the volume of the solution and the moles of $H_2C_2O_4$.

Assume exactly 1 kg (1,000 g) of water (solvent), which means there are 0.580 moles of oxalic acid.

$$\text{Volume of solution} = \left(\frac{mL \text{ soln}}{1.022 \text{ g soln}}\right)[(1,000 + 52.21972)\text{g soln}]\left(\frac{0.001}{m}\right) = 1.029569 = 1.030 \text{ L}$$

$$\text{Molarity} = \frac{0.580 \text{ mol } H_2C_2O_4}{1.029569 \text{ L}} = 0.5633424 = \textbf{0.563 M}$$

(b) To determine the mass percent, we need to know the mass of the components. The mass of the solvent was assumed to be exactly 1,000 g in part (a); therefore, it is necessary to determine only the mass of 0.580 moles of $H_2C_2O_4$—also from part (a).

$$\text{Mass oxalic acid} = (0.580 \text{ mol } H_2C_2O_4)\left(\frac{90.034 \text{ g } H_2C_2O_4}{1 \text{ mol } H_2C_2O_4}\right) = 52.21972 = 52.2 \text{ g } H_2C_2O_4$$

$$\text{Mass percent} = \frac{52.21972 \text{ g } H_2C_2O_4}{(1,000 + 52.21972) \text{ g}} \times 100\% = 4.962815 = \textbf{4.96\%}$$

13.4 Colligative Properties

13.36 What are *colligative properties?*

Solution

Colligative properties are properties that depend only upon the number of solute particles present in a solution.

13.38 What is an *ideal solution?*

Solution

Any solution that follows Raoult's law exactly is an *ideal solution.*

13.42 What is the vapor pressure of a solution that was made by adding 25.0 g of glucose, $C_6H_{12}O_6$, to 375 g of water at 80°C? Glucose is not volatile, and the vapor pressure of water at 80°C is 355 torr.

Information

A solution contains 25.0 g of nonvolatile $C_6H_{12}O_6$ in 375 g of H_2O; a vapor pressure of water of 355 torr, at 80°C; the question of what is the vapor pressure of the solution

Connections

Raoult's law

Solution

To use Raoult's law, we need to determine the moles of each component:

$$\text{Moles glucose} = (25.0 \text{ g glucose})\left(\frac{1 \text{ mole glucose}}{180.156 \text{ g glucose}}\right) = 0.1387686 = 0.139 \text{ mole glucose}$$

$$\text{Moles water} = (375 \text{ g water})\left(\frac{1 \text{ mole water}}{18.015 \text{ g water}}\right) = 20.815987 = 20.8 \text{ mole water}$$

From the moles of each component, we can now determine the mole fraction of water. (It is not necessary to determine the mole fraction of $C_6H_{12}O_6$, because glucose not volatile.)

$$\text{Mole fraction water} = \frac{20.815987 \text{ mol}}{(0.1387686 + 20.815987)\text{mol}} = 0.9933777 = 0.993$$

The mole fraction of water times the vapor pressure of pure water gives the vapor pressure of the solution:

$$\text{Vapor pressure of solution} = P = XP° = (0.9933777)(355 \text{ torr}) = 352.649 = \textbf{353 torr}$$

13.45 A solution of 96.6 g of an unknown substance in 800.0 g of carbon tetrachloride has a vapor pressure of 143 mmHg. The vapor pressure of the pure unknown is 85 torr, and the vapor pressure of pure carbon tetrachloride is 157 mmHg (all vapor pressures are determined at 30°C). Determine the molar mass of the unknown substance.

Information

At 30°C, a solution contains 96.6 g of an unknown substance in 800.0 g CCl_4 and has a vapor pressure of 143 mmHg; the vapor pressures of the unknown and CCl_4 are 85 torr ($P°_{unk}$) and 157 mmHg ($P°_{CCl_4}$), respectively; the question of what is the molar mass of the unknown substance

Connections

Raoult's law; 1 mmHg = 1 torr

Solution

The mole fraction of the solvent is X_{CCl_4}. We can determine the mole fraction of the unknown (X_{unk}) as follows. (It is also possible to solve this problem by determining the mole fraction of the solvent, as was shown in Problem 13.44.)

$$X_{CCl_4} + X_{unk} = 1 \quad \text{or} \quad 1 - X_{unk} = X_{CCl_4}$$

Using Raoult's law and the vapor pressure of the solution,

$$143 \text{ mmHg} = X_{CCl_4}P^\circ{}_{CCl_4} + X_{unk}P^\circ{}_{unk}$$

Substituting for the mole fraction of the solvent gives

$$143 \text{ mmHg} = (1 - X_{unk})P^\circ{}_{CCl_4} + X_{unk}P^\circ{}_{unk}$$
$$143 \text{ mmHg} = (1 - X_{unk})(157 \text{ mmHg}) + X_{unk}(85 \text{ torr})$$
$$143 \text{ mmHg} = 157 \text{ mmHg} - X_{unk}157 \text{ mmHg} + X_{unk}(85 \text{ torr})$$
$$143 \text{ mmHg} - 157 \text{ mmHg} = X_{unk}(85 - 157) \text{ mmHg}$$
$$X_{unk} = \frac{(143 - 157) \text{ mmHg}}{(85 - 157) \text{ mmHg}} = 0.194444 = 0.19$$

To isolate the moles of unknown, we need to determine the moles of CCl_4:

$$\text{Moles } CCl_4 = (800.0 \text{ g})(1 \text{ mole } CCl_4/153.823 \text{ g } CCl_4) = 5.2007827 = 5.201 \text{ mole } CCl_4$$

The moles of the unknown (n_{unk}) can be determined from the definition of *mole fraction* and the moles of CCl_4:

$$X_{unk} = \frac{n_{unk}}{n_{total}} = \frac{n_{unk}}{5.2007827 \text{ mol } CCl_4 + n_{unk}} = 0.194444$$

$$n_{unk} = (0.194444)(5.2007827 \text{ mol } CCl_4 + n_{unk}$$

$$n_{unk} = (1.0112040 + 0.194444 \, n_{unk}$$

$$1.0112040 = (1 - 0.194444) \, n_{unk}$$

$$\frac{1.0112040}{(1 - 0.194444)} = 1.2533 = 1.2 = n_{unk}$$

The *molar mass* is defined as the grams of a substance divided by the moles present, so

$$\text{Molar mass} = \frac{96.6 \text{ g}}{1.2533 \text{ mol}} = 76.95 = \textbf{77 g/mole}$$

13.5 Additional Colligative Properties

13.48 Rank the following 0.100-m solutions in order of decreasing freezing point: **(a)** sodium chloride, NaCl; **(b)** sucrose (table sugar), $C_{12}H_{22}O_{11}$; **(c)** aluminum nitrate, $Al(NO_3)_3$; **(d)** barium chloride, $BaCl_2$

Solution

Except for sucrose, which is a nonelectrolyte, all of the compounds are strong electrolytes. For the strong electrolytes, it is necessary to multiply the concentration by the appropriate van't Hoff factor. The van't Hoff factors are 2 for NaCl, 4 for $Al(NO_3)_3$, and 3 for $BaCl_2$. The greater the concentration, or the concentration times the van't Hoff factor, the lower the freezing point. The order for the above compounds is

$$\textbf{(b) > (a) > (d) > (c)}$$

13.51 Define *osmosis* and *osmotic pressure*.

Solution

The process responsible for the movement across the membrane is **osmosis**, the diffusion of a solvent through a semipermeable membrane into a more concentrated solution. The pressure exerted by this column when osmosis appears to stop is called the **osmotic pressure**; it is the pressure due to osmosis.

13.54 Use the data in the table below to determine the boiling and freezing points of the following solutions: **(a)** 0.75 *m* of iodine, I_2, in benzene, C_6H_6; **(b)** 5.3 g of white phosphorus, P_4, in 175 g of carbon disulfide, CS_2; **(c)** 3.5 g of ammonium sulfate, $(NH_4)_2SO_4$, in 175 mL of water. The density of water is 1.00 g/mL.

Solvent	Melting Point (°C)	Boiling Point (°C)	K_f (°C/m)	K_b (°C/m)
Water	0.00	100.00	1.858	0.512
Benzene	5.5	80.1	4.90	2.53
Carbon disulfide	-111.5	46.2	3.83	2.34

Information

The information in the table; **(a)** 0.75 *m* I_2 in C_6H_6; **(b)** 5.3 g P_4 in 175 g CS_2; **(c)** 3.5 g $(NH_4)_2SO_4$ in 175 mL of H_2O (density = 1.00 g/mL); in each of the three parts, the questions of what are the boiling points and freezing points of the solutions

Connections

The table given in the problem; the definition of *molality*; the van't Hoff factor; the equations for freezing point depression ($\Delta T_f = K_f m$) and boiling point elevation ($\Delta T_b = K_b m$)

Solution

(a) 0.75 m I_2

Iodine is a nonelectrolyte; therefore, we simply enter the values into the appropriate equation:

$$\Delta T_f = K_f m = (0.75\ m)\ (4.90°C/m) = 3.675 = 3.7°C$$

The normal freezing point minus the depression gives the freezing point of the solution:

$$T_f = (5.5 - 3.675)°C = 1.825 = \textbf{1.8°C}$$

Similarly, for the boiling point,

$$\Delta T_b = K_b m = (0.75\ m)\ (2.53°C/m) = 1.8975 = 1.9°C$$

The normal boiling point plus the elevation gives the boiling point of the solution:

$$T_b = (80.1 + 1.8975)°C = 81.9975 = \textbf{82.0°C}$$

(b) First, we need to determine the molality of the nonelectrolyte P_4:

$$\left(\frac{5.3\text{ g }P_4}{175\text{ g }CS_2}\right)\left(\frac{1\text{ mol }P_4}{123.896\text{ g }P_4}\right)\left(\frac{1{,}000}{k}\right) = 0.2444446 = 0.24\ m\ P_4$$

Since P_4 is a nonelectrolyte, we simply enter the values into the appropriate equation:

$$\Delta T_f = K_f m = (0.2444446\ m)\ (3.83°C/m) = 0.9362228 = 0.94°C$$

The normal freezing point minus the depression gives the freezing point of the solution:

$$T_f = (-111.5 - 0.9362228)°C = -112.4362228 = \textbf{-112.4°C}$$

Similarly, for the boiling point,

$$\Delta T_b = K_b m = (0.2444446\ m)\ (2.34°C/m) = 0.57200 = 0.57°C$$

The normal boiling point plus the elevation gives the boiling point of the solution:

$$T_b = (46.2 + 0.57200)°C = 46.77200 = \textbf{46.8°C}$$

(c) It is necessary to first determine the molality of the strong electrolyte $(NH_4)_2SO_4$:

$$\left(\frac{3.5\ g\ (NH_4)_4SO_4}{175\ mL\ H_2O}\right)\left(\frac{1\ mol\ (NH_4)_4SO_4}{132.139\ g\ (NH_4)_4SO_4}\right)\left(\frac{mL}{1.00\ g\ H_2O}\right)\left(\frac{1,000}{k}\right) = 0.15135769$$

$$= 0.15\ m\ (NH_4)_2SO_4$$

We need to include a van't Hoff factor in the calculation because $(NH_4)_2SO_4$ is an electrolyte. Ammonium sulfate generates two ammonium ions and one sulfate ion, which means that $i = 3$. It is now possible to enter the values into the appropriate equation:

$$\Delta T_f = iK_f m = 3(0.15135769\ m)\ (1.858°C/m) = 0.84366776 = 0.84°C$$

The normal freezing point minus the depression gives the freezing point of the solution:

$$T_f = (0.000 - 0.84366776)°C = -0.84366776 = \textbf{-0.84°C}$$

Similarly, for the boiling point,

$$\Delta T_b = iK_b m = 3(0.15135769\ m)\ (0.512°C/m) = 0.2324854 = 0.23°C$$

The normal boiling point plus the elevation gives the boiling point of the solution:

$$T_b = (100.000 + 0.2324854)°C = 100.2324854 = \textbf{100.23°C}$$

13.57 A solution that is made by dissolving 0.100 g of a polymer (a very large molecule) in 1.50 g of carbon tetrachloride has a freezing point depression of 0.61°C. If the freezing point depression constant of carbon tetrachloride is 29.8°C/m, what is the molar mass of the polymer?

Information

A solution containing 0.100 g of a polymer in 1.50 g CCl_4 has a freezing point depression of 0.61°C; the freezing point depression constant of CCl_4 is 29.8°C/m; the question of what is the molar mass of the polymer

Connections

The definition of *molality*; the equation for freezing point depression

Solution

The first step is to determine the molality from the freezing point depression equation:

$$\text{Molality of solution} = m = \frac{\Delta T}{K_f} = \frac{0.61°C}{29.8°C/m} = 0.0204698 = 0.020\ m$$

We can now determine the moles of solute from the definition of *molality* and the mass of the solvent:

$$\text{Moles solute} = \left(\frac{0.0204698\ mol}{kg}\right)(1.50\ g)\left(\frac{k}{1,000}\right) = 3.07047 \times 10^{-5} = 3.1 \times 10^{-5}\ \text{moles}$$

The *molar mass* is defined as the grams of a substance divided by the moles present. In this case,

$$\text{Molar mass} = \frac{0.100 \text{ g}}{3.07047 \times 10^{-5} \text{ mol}} = 3256.83 = \mathbf{3.2 \times 10^3 \text{ g/mol}}$$

Reality Check

The molar mass must be greater than or equal to that of the smallest known molecule (H_2 = 2 g/mole).

3.60 You are given three aqueous solutions: 0.80 *m* sodium chloride, NaCl; 0.80 *m* methanol, CH_3OH; and 0.60 *m* calcium nitrate, $Ca(NO_3)_2$. Rank the solutions in order of increasing freezing point depression.

Solution

In each case, the concentration of the particles is the molality times the van't Hoff factor:

NaCl = 0.80 *m* × 2 = 1.6 *m*   NaCl is a strong electrolyte, producing two ions (= *i*).
CH_3OH = 0.80 *m* × 1 = 0.80 *m* CH_3OH is a nonelectrolyte (*i* = 1).
$Ca(NO_3)_2$ = 0.60 *m* × 3 = 1.8 *m* $Ca(NO_3)_2$ is a strong electrolyte, producing three ions (= *i*).

The freezing point depression increases with increasing molality of particles.

$$\mathbf{CH_3OH < NaCl < Ca(NO_3)_2}$$

13.62 What is the boiling point of an aqueous solution with a freezing point of –7.35°C?

Information

An aqueous solution with a freezing point of –7.35°C; the question of what is the boiling point of this solution

Connections

The definition of *molality*; the equations for freezing point depression and boiling point elevation

Solution

The value of the molality (or van't Hoff factor × molality) will be the same for both the freezing point and the boiling point. Finding the solution begins with determining ΔT:

$$\Delta T = [0.00 - (-7.35)]°C = 7.35°C$$

The ΔT value is for the freezing point, so we can now calculate the molality (of *i* × *m*) of the solution. K_f = 1.858°C/*m* (table 13.2):

$$\text{Molality of solution} = m = \frac{\Delta T}{K_f} = \frac{7.35°C}{1.858°C \text{ / } m} = 3.955866 = 3.96 \text{ } m$$

Using the molality and the boiling point elevation equation yields ΔT for the boiling point elevation:

Boiling point K_b = 0.512°C/*m* (table 13.2)
$$\Delta T = (0.512°C/m) (3.955866 \text{ } m) = 2.02540°C$$

The boiling point is the normal boiling point plus the elevation:

$$T = (100.00 + 2.02540)°C = \mathbf{102.02°C}$$

13.65 Determine the freezing point of a solution containing 101.50 g of magnesium bromide in 200.0 g of water.

Information

A solution contains 101.50 g $MgBr_2$ and 200.0 g H_2O; the question of what is the freezing point of this solution

Connections

The definition of *molality*, the van't Hoff factor, and the equation for freezing point depression.

Solution

Magnesium bromide is a strong electrolyte (see chapter 4, "Aqueous Solutions and Their Chemical Reactions"), which means it is necessary to use a van't Hoff factor. In this case, i is 3.

We can calculate the molality of the solution from the definition of *molality* and the appropriate conversions:

$$\text{Molality of } MgBr_2 = m = \left(\frac{101.50 \text{ g } MgBr_2}{200.0 \text{ g } H_2O}\right)\left(\frac{1 \text{ mol } MgBr_2}{184.113 \text{ g } MgBr_2}\right)\left(\frac{1{,}000}{k}\right) = 2.7564593$$

$$= 2.756 \text{ m } MgBr_2$$

Entering the appropriate values into the freezing point depression equation gives the depression:

$$\text{Freezing point} \qquad K_f = 1.858°C/m \text{ (table 13.2)} \qquad \text{van't Hoff factor} = i = 3$$
$$\Delta T = (3)(1.858°C/m)(2.7564593 \text{ m}) = 15.36450°C$$

The normal freezing point minus the depression gives the freezing point of the solution:

$$T = (0.00 - 15.36450)°C = \textbf{-15.4°C}$$

13.68 A solution prepared by dissolving 6.850 g of a carbohydrate in 100.0 g of water has a density of 1.024 g/mL, and at 20.0°C the osmotic pressure is 4.61 atm. Calculate the molar mass of the carbohydrate.

Information

A solution containing 6.850 g of a carbohydrate in 100.0 g H_2O; a density of 1.024 g/mL; an osmotic pressure of 4.61 torr at 20.0°C; the question of what is the molar mass of the carbohydrate

Connections

$\Pi V = nRT$

Solution

The *molar mass* of the substance is the mass of the carbohydrate, in grams, divided by the number of moles present. The mass given in the problem is 6.850 g; therefore, we need to calculate the moles. It is possible to determine the moles present by rearranging the osmotic pressure equation to $n = \Pi V/RT$. The calculation now consists of the mass of the carbohydrate divided by the rearranged form of the osmotic pressure equation (plus appropriate conversions):

$$\text{Molar mass} = \frac{\text{Mass}}{\left[\frac{\Pi V}{RT}\right]} = \frac{6.850 \text{ g carbohydrate}}{\left[\frac{(4.61 \text{ atm})(100.0 \text{ g})}{(0.08206 \text{ L atm/mol K})(293.2 \text{ K})}\left(\frac{mL}{1.024 \text{ g}}\right)\left(\frac{0.001}{m}\right)\right]} = 366.088$$

$$= \textbf{366 g/mol}$$

Reality Check

The molar mass must be greater than or equal to that of the smallest known molecule (H_2 = 2 g/mole).

13.72 Determine the molar mass of a protein if a solution, prepared by dissolving 3.320 g of protein in enough water to make 340.0 mL of solution, has an osmotic pressure of 10.40 mmHg at 25.0°C.

Information

A solution containing 3.320 g of a protein in 340.0 mL of solution; an osmotic pressure of 10.40 mmHg at 25.0°C; the question of what is the molar mass of the protein

Connections

$\Pi V = nRT$

Solution

The *molar mass* of the substance is the mass of the substance, in grams, divided by the number of moles present. The mass is given in the problem is 3.320 g; therefore, we need to calculate the moles. It is possible to determine the moles present by rearranging the osmotic pressure equation to $n = \Pi V/RT$. The calculation now consists of the mass of the protein divided by the rearranged form of the osmotic pressure equation (plus appropriate conversions):

$$\text{Molar mass} = \frac{\text{Mass}}{\left[\dfrac{\Pi V}{RT}\right]} = \frac{3.320 \text{ g protein}}{\dfrac{(10.44 \text{ mmHg})(340.0 \text{ mL})}{(0.08206 \text{ L} \cdot \text{atm/mol} \cdot \text{K})(298.2 \text{ K})}\left(\dfrac{1 \text{ atm}}{760 \text{ mmHg}}\right)\left(\dfrac{0.001}{\text{m}}\right)} = 17{,}394.478$$

$$= \mathbf{1.739 \times 10^4 \text{ g/mol}}$$

Reality Check

The molar mass must be greater than or equal to that of the smallest known molecule (H_2 = 2 g/mole).

13.75 A solution of a polymer contains 0.400 g of material in 1.00 L of water. This solution has an osmotic pressure of 2.14 torr at 27°C. Calculate the molar mass of the polymer.

Information

A solution containing 0.400 g of a polymer in 1.00 L of water; an osmotic pressure of 2.14 torr at 27°C; the question of what is the molar mass of the polymer

Connections

$\Pi V = nRT$

Solution

The *molar mass* of the substance is the mass of the substance, in grams, divided by the number of moles present. The mass given in the problem is 0.400 g; therefore, we need to calculate the moles. It is possible to determine the moles present by rearranging the osmotic pressure equation to $n = \Pi V/RT$. The calculation now consists of the mass of the polymer divided by the rearranged form of the osmotic pressure equation (plus appropriate conversions):

$$\text{Molar mass} = \frac{\text{Mass}}{\left[\dfrac{\Pi V}{RT}\right]} = \frac{0.400 \text{ g polymer}}{\dfrac{(2.14 \text{ torr})(1.00 \text{ L})}{(0.08206 \text{ L} \cdot \text{atm/mol} \cdot \text{K})(300. \text{ K})}\left(\dfrac{1 \text{ atm}}{760 \text{ torr}}\right)} = 3{,}497.136$$

$$= \mathbf{3.50 \times 10^3 \text{ g/mol}}$$

Reality Check

The molar mass must be greater than or equal to that of the smallest known molecule ($H_2 =$ 2 g/mole).

13.77 Pepsin, an enzyme found in the stomach, is a protein that aids in digestion. A solution made by dissolving 0.600 g of pepsin in 1,000.0 mL of water has an osmotic pressure of 0.324 torr at 25°C. Calculate the molar mass of pepsin.

Information

A solution containing 0.600 g of pepsin in 1,000.0 mL of H_2O; an osmotic pressure of 0.324 mmHg at 25°C; the question of what is the molar mass

Connections

$\Pi V = nRT$

Solution

The molar mass of the substance is the mass of the substance, in grams, divided by the number of moles present. The mass given in the problem is 0.600 g; therefore, we need to calculate the moles. It is possible to determine the moles present by rearranging the osmotic pressure equation to $n = \Pi V/RT$. The calculation now consists of the mass of the pepsin divided by the rearranged form of the osmotic pressure equation (plus appropriate conversions):

$$\text{Molar mass} = \frac{\text{Mass}}{\left[\frac{\Pi V}{RT}\right]} = \frac{0.600 \text{ g pepsin}}{\left[\frac{(0.324 \text{ torr})(1000.0 \text{ mL})}{(0.08206 \text{ L} \cdot \text{atm/mol} \cdot \text{K})(298 \text{ K})}\left(\frac{1 \text{ atm}}{760 \text{ torr}}\right)\left(\frac{0.001}{\text{m}}\right)\right]} = 34,416.57$$

$$= 3.44 \times 10^4 \text{ g/mol}$$

Reality Check

The molar mass must be greater than or equal to that of the smallest known molecule ($H_2 =$ 2 g/mole).

13.6 Colloids

13.80 (a) How are a suspension and a colloid similar? (b) How are a solution and a colloid similar?

Solution

(a) It is possible to see the particles present in both a suspension and a colloid.

(b) The particles in both a solution and a colloid do not readily separate from the solvent.

13.7 Water Pollution

13.84 List the common water pollutants.

Solution

Agricultural agents including pesticides, heavy metals such as lead, infectious agents, acid rain, leaking storage tanks, decomposing organic matter, and thermal pollution are some of the common examples. (Your list may include others.)

13.86 Sulfur and nitrogen oxides lead to acid rain. However, rain is acidic even in the absence of pollutants. Why is rainwater naturally acidic?

Solution

Carbon dioxide in the air (from respiration of animals and volcanoes) and nitrogen oxides (produced by lightning) dissolve in rainwater to make the rainwater acidic (carbonic acid, nitrous acid, and nitric acid may form).

13.88 Sodium stearate, $NaC_{18}H_{35}O_2$, is a common constituent of many types of soap. This compound undergoes aerobic decomposition. **(a)** Write a balanced chemical equation for the reaction of this compound with oxygen, O_2, to yield carbon dioxide, CO_2, water, H_2O, and sodium ions, Na^+; assume the solution is acidic. **(b)** How many grams of oxygen are needed to oxidize 1.00 pounds of this soap?

Solution

(a) The reactants and products are listed in the problem. The $H^+(aq)$ represents the acidic solution:

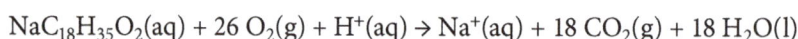

$$NaC_{18}H_{35}O_2(aq) + 26\ O_2(g) + H^+(aq) \rightarrow Na^+(aq) + 18\ CO_2(g) + 18\ H_2O(l)$$

(b) This is a stoichiometric conversion problem like those seen in chapter 3," Stoichiometry—Mass and Mole," and chapter 4," Aqueous Solutions and Their Chemical Reactions." (Moles are the key.)

$$\text{Mass } O_2 = (1.00\text{ lb})\left(\frac{453.59\text{ g}}{\text{lb}}\right)\left(\frac{1\text{ mol } NaC_{18}H_{35}O_2}{306.466\text{ g } NaC_{18}H_{35}O_2}\right)\left(\frac{26\text{ mol } O_2}{1\text{ mol } NaC_{18}H_{35}O_2}\right)\left(\frac{31.998\text{ g } O_2}{1\text{ mol } O_2}\right)$$
$$= 1231.3382 = \mathbf{1.23 \times 10^3\text{ g } O_2}$$

13.8 Applications and Extensions

13.90 (a) If pure water is added to blood plasma, does a hypotonic solution result, or does a hypertonic solution result? **(b)** What will happen to blood cells in the plasma-plus-water mixture?

Solution

(a) Adding pure water to a solution will lower the osmotic pressure to produce a hypotonic solution. **(b)** Hemolysis will occur as water diffuses into the cells, causing the cells to swell and eventually burst (assuming enough water has been added to change the osmotic pressure significantly).

13.94 Dialysis of blood is hemodialysis. The presence of blood cells requires a solution that is isotonic. A typical isotonic solution has the following quantities of solute dissolved in 100.0 mL of water: 0.60 g of sodium chloride, NaCl; 0.040 g of potassium chloride, KCl; 0.20 g of sodium bicarbonate, $NaHCO_3$; and 0.72 g of glucose, $C_6H_{12}O_6$. **(a)** What is the molarity of each of the solutes, assuming the volume of the solution is equal to the volume of the solvent? **(b)** What is the osmotic pressure of this solution at body temperature (37°C)? (Hint: Do not forget that some of the solutes are strong electrolytes.)

Solution

(a) For each solute, it is necessary to convert the mass per 100.0 mL to molarity (moles/L):

$$\left(\frac{0.60\text{ g NaCl}}{100.0\text{ mL}}\right)\left(\frac{\text{m}}{0.001}\right)\left(\frac{1\text{ mol NaCl}}{58.443\text{ g NaCl}}\right) = 0.102664 = \mathbf{0.10\text{ M NaCl}}$$

$$\left(\frac{0.040\text{ g KCl}}{100.0\text{ mL}}\right)\left(\frac{\text{m}}{0.001}\right)\left(\frac{1\text{ mol KCl}}{74.551\text{ g KCl}}\right) = 0.005365 = \mathbf{0.0054\text{ M KCl}}$$

$$\left(\frac{0.20 \text{ g NaHCO}_3}{100.0 \text{ mL}}\right)\left(\frac{\text{m}}{0.001}\right)\left(\frac{1 \text{ mol NaHCO}_3}{84.006 \text{ g NaHCO}_3}\right) = 0.0238078 = \textbf{0.024 M NaHCO}_3$$

$$\left(\frac{0.72 \text{ g C}_6\text{H}_{12}\text{O}_6}{100.0 \text{ mL}}\right)\left(\frac{\text{m}}{0.001}\right)\left(\frac{1 \text{ mol C}_6\text{H}_{12}\text{O}_6}{180.156 \text{ g C}_6\text{H}_{12}\text{O}_6}\right) = 0.039965 = \textbf{0.040 M C}_6\textbf{H}_{12}\textbf{O}_6$$

(b) Three of the solutes are strong electrolytes, and we need to include their van't Hoff factors. The van't Hoff factors for NaCl, KCl, and $NaHCO_3$ are all 2; therefore, each of their concentrations must be multiplied by 2 and the results added to the concentration of the nonelectrolyte glucose to get the total molarity of the solution:

$$\text{Total molarity} = 2 \,(0.102664) + 2 \,(0.005365) + 2 \,(0.0238078) + (0.039965)$$
$$= 0.3036386 = 0.30 \text{ M}$$

It is now possible to enter the appropriate values into one form of the osmotic pressure equation. We do not need to use the van't Hoff factor in this equation, because the van't Hoff factor was already used to determine the total molarity:

$$\text{Osmotic pressure} = \Pi = MRT = \left(\frac{0.3036386 \text{ mol}}{\text{L}}\right)\left(\frac{0.08206 \text{ L}\cdot\text{atm}}{\text{mol}\cdot\text{K}}\right)(310. \text{ K})$$

$$= 7.72414 = \textbf{7.7 atm}$$

Reality Check

The use of the total molarity is acceptable because osmotic pressure is a colligative property.

13.97 While it is less toxic than methyl alcohol, ethylene glycol, CH_2OHCH_2OH, is poisonous. The density of ethylene glycol is 1.1132 g/mL. A dog may die by ingesting 50 mL of ethylene glycol. How many moles of ethylene glycol are in 50.0 mL?

Solution

The is a unit conversion problem:

$$\text{Moles} = (50.0 \text{ mL})\left(\frac{1.1132 \text{ g C}_2\text{H}_6\text{O}_2}{\text{mL}}\right)\left(\frac{1 \text{ mol C}_2\text{H}_6\text{O}_2}{62.068 \text{ g C}_2\text{H}_6\text{O}_2}\right) = 0.896758 = \textbf{0.897 mol C}_2\textbf{H}_6\textbf{O}_2$$

Putting It All Together

13.100 Classify each of the following as a strong electrolyte, a weak electrolyte, or a nonelectrolyte in aqueous solution: **(a)** nitric acid, HNO_3; **(b)** ethanol, C_2H_5OH; **(c)** chlorous acid, $HClO_2$; **(d)** glucose, $C_6H_{12}O_6$; **(e)** ammonia, NH_3

Solution

You may wish to review chapter 4, "Aqueous Solutions and Their Chemical Reactions," where electrolytes were introduced.

(a) nitric acid, HNO_3 **Strong electrolyte** because it is a strong acid.

(b) ethanol, C_2H_5OH **Nonelectrolyte** because it is neither an acid nor base.

(c) chlorous acid, $HClO_2$ **Weak electrolyte** because it is a weak acid.

(d) glucose, $C_6H_{12}O_6$ **Nonelectrolyte** because it is neither an acid nor base.

(e) ammonia, NH_3 **Weak electrolyte** because it is a weak base.

13.102 Two solutions are prepared. The first contains 4.32 g of iodine, I_2, in 250.0 mL of carbon disulfide, CS_2; the second contains 4.32 g of iodine in 250.0 mL of carbon tetrachloride, CCl_4. The density of pure carbon disulfide is 1.263 g/mL, and the density of pure carbon tetrachloride is 1.589 g/mL. Assume that the density of each solution is identical to that of the pure solvent. **(a)** Determine the mass percent of iodine in each solution. **(b)** Determine the mole fraction of iodine in each solution. **(c)** Determine the molality of iodine in each solution. **(d)** Determine the molarity of iodine in each solution. **(e)** Compare the two values in each case, and comment on any similarities and differences.

Solution

Several preliminary calculations are needed because some values have multiple uses.

$$\text{Volume} = (250.0 \text{ mL}) (0.001/m) = 0.2500 \text{ L}$$

Mass of CCl_4 and CS_2

$$(250.0 \text{ mL } CCl_4) \left(\frac{1.589 \text{ g}}{\text{mL}} \right) = 397.25 = 397.2 \text{ g } CCl_4 \times (k/1{,}000)$$
$$= 0.39725 = 0.3972 \text{ kg } CCl_4$$

$$(250.0 \text{ mL } CS_2) \left(\frac{1.263 \text{ g}}{\text{mL}} \right) = 315.75 = 315.8 \text{ g } CS_2 \times (k/1{,}000)$$
$$= 0.31575 = 0.3158 \text{ kg } CS_2$$

Moles of I_2, CCl_4, and CS_2

$$\text{Moles } I_2 = (4.32 \text{ g } I_2) \left(\frac{1 \text{ mol } I_2}{253.808 \text{ g } I_2} \right) = 0.01702074 = 0.0170 \text{ mole } I_2$$

$$\text{Moles } CCl_4 = (397.25 \text{ g } CCl_4) \left(\frac{1 \text{ mol } CCl_4}{153.823 \text{ g } CCl_4} \right) = 2.582513668 = 2.583 \text{ mole } CCl_4$$

$$\text{Moles } CS_2 = (315.75 \text{ g } CS_2) \left(\frac{1 \text{ mol } CS_2}{76.141 \text{ g } CS_2} \right) = 4.146911651 = 4.147 \text{ mole } CS_2$$

We can now use the results of the preliminary calculations to finish the problem (use the unrounded values to minimize rounding errors):

(a) This requires the masses of the components.

CCl_4

$$\frac{4.32 \text{ g } I_2}{(4.32 + 397.25) \text{ g}} \times 100\% = 1.07577573 = \mathbf{1.08\% \ I_2}$$

CS_2

$$\frac{4.32 \text{ g } I_2}{(4.32 + 315.75) \text{ g}} \times 100\% = 1.34970475 = \mathbf{1.35\% \ I_2}$$

(b) This requires the moles of the components.

CCl_4

$$\frac{0.01702074 \text{ mol } I_2}{(0.01702074 + 2.582513668) \text{ mol}} = 0.0065476 = \mathbf{0.00655 \ I_2}$$

CS_2

$$\frac{0.01702074 \text{ mol } I_2}{(0.01702074 + 4.146911651) \text{ mol}} = 0.00408766 = \mathbf{0.00409 \ I_2}$$

(c) This requires the moles of the solute and the kilograms of the solvent.

CCl_4

$$\frac{0.01702074 \text{ mol } I_2}{0.39725 \text{ kg}} = 0.0428464 = \textbf{0.0428 m } I_2$$

CS_2

$$\frac{0.01702074 \text{ mol } I_2}{0.31575 \text{ kg}} = 0.0539057 = \textbf{0.0539 m } I_2$$

(d) This requires the moles of solute and the liters of solution.

CCl_4

$$\frac{0.01702074 \text{ mol } I_2}{0.2500 \text{ L}} = 0.06808296 = \textbf{0.0681 M } I_2$$

CS_2

$$\frac{0.01702074 \text{ mol } I_2}{0.2500 \text{ L}} = 0.06808296 = \textbf{0.0681 M } I_2$$

(e) In each case, compare the two values to see if they differ.

Mass percent: The different density values result in different mass percentages.
Mole fraction: The different molar masses values are the biggest cause of the different values.
Molality: The different molar mass values are the biggest cause of the different values.
Molarity: Neither the density nor the molar mass makes a difference.

13.105 What is the name or the formula of each of the following compounds? **(a)** HOCN;
(b) H_2CrO_4; **(c)** NH_4Cl; **(d)** $CrAsO_4$; **(e)** $CdCl_2$; **(f)** tin(II) oxide; **(g)** thorium(IV) fluoride;
(h) radium oxide; **(i)** krypton difluoride; **(j)** sulfur trioxide

Solution

It may be necessary to review the Nomenclature Resource.

(a) HOCN   **cyanic acid**

(b) H_2CrO_4 **chromic acid**

(c) NH_4Cl **ammonium chloride**

(d) $CrAsO_4$ **chromium(III) arsenate**

(e) $CdCl_2$ **cadmium chloride**

(f) tin(II) oxide   **SnO**

(g) thorium(IV) fluoride   **ThF$_4$**

(h) radium oxide   **RaO**

(i) krypton difluoride   **KrF$_2$**

(j) sulfur trioxide   **SO$_3$**

13.108 What is the name or the formula of each of the following compounds? **(a)** oxalic
acid; **(b)** HCN; **(c)** CuOCN; **(d)** ammonium dichromate; **(e)** UO_2; **(f)** tin(II) thiosulfate;
(g) $Pu(CO_3)_2$; **(h)** chromium(II) phosphate; **(i)** vanadium(IV) bicarbonate; **(j)** N_2O_3

Solution

It may be necessary to review the Nomenclature Resource.

(a) oxalic acid $\qquad$ **$H_2C_2O_4$**

(b) HCN **hydrocyanic acid**

(c) CuOCN **copper(I) cyanate**

(d) ammonium dichromate **$(NH_4)_2Cr_2O_7$**

(e) UO_2 **uranium(IV) oxide**

(f) tin(II) thiosulfate **SnS_2O_3**

(g) $Pu(CO_3)_2$ **plutonium(IV) carbonate**

(h) chromium(II) phosphate **$Cr_3(PO_4)_2$**

(i) vanadium(IV) bicarbonate **$V(HCO_3)_4$**

(j) N_2O_3 **dinitrogen trioxide**

13.111 When a 24.8-g sample of sodium nitrate dissolves in 500.0 g of water in a coffee cup calorimeter, the temperature changes from 25.30°C to 22.51°C. Determine the heat of the solution, in kJ/mol of sodium nitrate, for the dissolution of sodium nitrate in water. Assume that the specific heat of the solution is the same as that of pure water.

Solution

This is a calorimeter conversion problem. The decrease in temperature indicates that the process is endothermic; therefore, the enthalpy change must be positive:

$$\frac{\left(\dfrac{4.184\ J}{g°C}\right)(24.8 + 500.0)g(22.51 - 25.30)°C\left(\dfrac{k}{1,000}\right)}{(24.8\ g\ NaNO_3)\left(\dfrac{1\ mol\ NaNO_3}{84.9947\ g\ NaNO_3}\right)} = 20.99568 = \mathbf{21.0\ kJ/mol}$$

13.114 For very dilute solutions, the molarity and molality are nearly equal. Assuming this is true, what is the freezing point of an aqueous solution of a nonelectrolyte with an osmotic pressure of 6.6 atm at 25°C?

Solution

It is possible to rearrange the osmotic pressure equation ($\Pi = MRT$) to determine the molarity, which, according to the problem, is approximately equal to the molality:

$$M = \frac{\Pi}{RT} = \frac{6.6\ atm}{\left(\dfrac{0.08206\ L\cdot atm}{mol\cdot K}\right)(298\ K)} = 0.2698958 = 0.27\ M \approx 0.27\ m$$

It is now possible to enter the values into the appropriate equation ($\Delta T_f = K_f m$):

$$K_f = 1.858°C/m \qquad \text{(table 13.2)}$$

$$\Delta T = K_f m = (1.858°C/m)(0.2698958\ m) = 0.501466 = 0.50°C$$

The normal freezing point minus the depression gives the freezing point of the solution:

$$T_{freezing} = (0.00 - 0.50)°C = \mathbf{-0.50°C}$$

13.117 Why will water vapor and carbon tetrachloride vapor form a solution, but liquid water and liquid carbon tetrachloride will not?

Solution

In a vapor there are minimal intermolecular forces (ideally zero) to overcome, while in water strong hydrogen bonding must be overcome to form a solution.

13.119 Potassium permanganate, $KMnO_4$, will dissolve in water. At 20°C, 100.0 mL of water will dissolve 6.38 g of potassium permanganate. At 65°C, 100.0 mL of water will dissolve 25 g of potassium permanganate. **(a)** How much potassium permanganate will dissolve in 50.0 mL of water at 65°C? **(b)** If the solution from part (a) cools to 20°C, what type of solution would be present if no potassium permanganate precipitates? **(c)** If the solution from part (a) cools to 20°C, what type of solution would be present if potassium permanganate precipitates?

Solution

(a) This is a conversion:

$$\left(\frac{6.38 \text{ g KMnO}_4}{100.0 \text{ mL}}\right)(50.0 \text{ mL}) = \textbf{3.19 g KMnO}_4$$

(b) Supersaturated

(c) Saturated

13.122 Determine the freezing point of a solution containing 65.0 g of aluminum sulfate in 200.0 g of water.

Solution

The formula is $Al_2(SO_4)_3$ (see the Nomenclature Resource).

It is necessary to determine the molality of the solution:

$$\left(\frac{65.0 \text{ g Al}_2(\text{SO}_4)_3}{200.0 \text{ g H}_2\text{O}}\right)\left(\frac{1 \text{ mol Al}_2(\text{SO}_4)_3}{342.147 \text{ g Al}_2(\text{SO}_4)_3}\right)\left(\frac{1{,}000}{k}\right) = 0.949884 = 0.950 \ m \ \text{Al}_2(\text{SO}_4)_3$$

It is now possible to enter the values into the appropriate equation $(\Delta T_f = iK_f m)$.

Freezing point:

$$K_f = 1.858°C/m \text{ (table 13.2)} \qquad \text{van't Hoff factor} = i = 5 \ (2 \text{ Al}^{3+} + 3 \text{ SO}_4{}^{2-})$$
$$\Delta T = (5) \ (1.858°C/m) \ (0.949884 \ m) = 8.8244 = 8.82°C$$

The normal freezing point minus the depression gives the freezing point of the solution:

$$T = (0.00 - 8.8244)°C = \textbf{–8.82°C}$$

Reality Check

For a solution this concentrated, the van't Hoff factor will probably be less than the predicted 5.